COOKING
FROM THE
GARDEN

COOKING
FROM THE
GARDEN

ROSALIND CREASY

Sierra Club Books
SAN FRANCISCO

Copyright © 1988 by Rosalind Creasy. Photographs copyright © 1988 by Rosalind Creasy and by photographers as credited on page 532.

All rights reserved under International and Pan-American Copyright Conventions. No part of this book may be reproduced in any form or by any electronic or mechanical means, including information storage and retrieval systems, without permission in writing from the publisher.

———

The author gratefully acknowledges permission to reproduce the following copyrighted material:

"John Withee's Baked Beans": *Growing and Cooking Beans* by John E. Withee. Copyright © 1980 by Yankee, Inc. Used by permission of Yankee, Inc. and John Withee.

"Baked Beans in a Flask": *Cooking from an Italian Garden* by Paola Scaravelli and Jon Cohen. Copyright © 1984 by Paola Scaravelli and Jon Cohen. Used by permission of Holt Rinehart & Winston, Inc.

"Broken Arrow Ranch Chili": *The Broken Arrow Ranch Cookbook* by Mike Hughes. Copyright © 1985 by Mike Hughes. Used by permission of University of Texas Press.

"Green Chili with Pork": *The Manhattan Chili Company Southwest-American Cookbook* by Michael McLaughlin. Copyright © 1986 by The Manhattan Chili Company, Inc. Used by permission of Crown Publishers.

"Seafood Chili San Carlos" by Michael McLaughlin and "Chili-Stuffed Monterey Jack Cheese" by Seppi Renggli: first appeared in "Great Chefs' Chili Dishes" by Richard Sax in February 1986 issue of *Bon Appetit*. Copyright © 1986 by Bon Appetit Publishing Corp.

"Tassajara Bread": *The Tassajara Bread Book*, rev. ed., by Edward Espe Brown. Copyright © 1970 by Chief Priest, Zen Center, San Francisco; revision copyright © 1986 by Edward Espe Brown. Used by permission of Shambhala Publications, Inc.

"Stuffed Mirlitons with Shrimp and Crab Butter Cream Sauce" and "Cauliflower Welch" copyright © 1987 by Chef Paul Prudhomme's Louisiana Kitchen. Used by permission of Paul Prudhomme.

"Basic Spaghetti Squash," "Mother's Bread and Butter Pickles," "Creamed Corn," "Green Tomato Pie," "Rhubarb Chard Fritters," and "Stewed Rhubarb": *Lois Burpee's Gardener's Companion and Cookbook.* Copyright © 1983 by Lois Burpee. Used by permission of Harper & Row, Publishers, Inc. and the W. Atlee Burpee Company.

"Braised Peas with Lettuce in the French Style" and "Scallops with Red Celery in a Vinaigrette Sauce": *The Victory Garden Cookbook* by Marian Morash. Copyright © 1982 by Marian Morash and WGBH Educational Foundation. Used by permission of Alfred A. Knopf, Inc.

"Calabacitas Guisadas, Estilo Michoacan" and "Uchepos": *The Cuisines of Mexico,* rev. ed., by Diana Kennedy. Copyright © 1986 by Diana Kennedy. Used by permission of Harper & Row, Publishers, Inc.

"Stir-Fried Pac Choi in Garlic Oil": *Chinese Technique* by Ken Hom and Harvey Steiman. Copyright © 1981 by Ken Hom and Harvey Steiman. Used by permission of Simon & Schuster, Inc.

"Deep-Fried Green Beans": *Ken Hom's Chinese Cookery* by Ken Hom. Text copyright © 1984 by Ken Hom. Used by permission of Harper & Row, Publishers, Inc.

"Mizutaki" and "Tempura": *At Home with Japanese Cooking* by Elizabeth Andoh. Copyright © 1974, 1975, 1980 by Elizabeth Andoh. Used by permission of Alfred A. Knopf, Inc.

"Aubergine (Eggplant) with Yogurt Sauce": *A Taste of India* by Madhur Jaffrey. Copyright © 1986 by Madhur Jaffrey. Used by permission of Atheneum Publishers, a division of Macmillan, Inc.

"Steamed Turkey Breast with Cabbage, Corn, and Peas": *The Four Seasons Spa Cuisine* by Seppi Renggli. Copyright © 1986 by Seppi Renggli, Paul Kovi, and Tom Margittai. Used by permission of Simon & Schuster, Inc.

"Broccoli/Broccoli" and "Eggplant Florentine": *Golden Door Cookbook* by Deborah Szekely and Chef Michael Stroot. Copyright © 1982 by Deborah Szekely. Used by permission of the Golden Door, Inc.

"Garden Squash and Nasturtium Butter Pasta": *Chez Panisse Pasta, Pizza, and Calzone* by Alice Waters, Patricia Curtan, and Martine Labro. Copyright © 1984 by Tango Rose, Inc. Used by permission of Random House, Inc.

Library of Congress Cataloging-in-Publication Data

Creasy, Rosalind.
    Cooking from the garden / Rosalind Creasy.
        p.   cm.
    Bibliography: p.
    Includes index.
    ISBN 0-87156-731-8
    1. Vegetable gardening. 2. Vegetables. 3. Cookery (Vegetables)
4. Gardens—United States. I. Title
SB321.C824 1988
635—dc19   88-3117
                                          CIP

Editor: Linda Gunnarson
Production manager: Susan Ristow
Book design: Paula Schlosser
Jacket design: Paul Gamarello
Front jacket photograph: © 1988 by Philippe-Louis Houze
Composition: Graphic Typesetting Service

Printed and bound by Dai Nippon Printing Company, Ltd., Tokyo, Ja[pan]

10 9 8 7 6 5 4 3 2

PAGE VI: *Heirloom melons, including a 'Hopi' cantaloupe, 'Old Bidwell' muskmelon, and 'Turkey' honeydew.*

For Wendy Krupnick and the many other dedicated stewards of the soil

CONTENTS

ACKNOWLEDGMENTS

A FEW DAYS BEFORE I assembled these acknowledgments, a phrase from an old hymn came to mind: "A grateful heart a garden is." It seemed a fitting way to start thanking the more than 150 people who have "shared my garden" and helped me put together this celebration of the earth's bounty. This book represents a coming together of gardeners and cooks, and in looking back I see that I was completely dependent on the good will and numerous talents of these people. Seeing their heartfelt commitment to our common pursuits expressed in these pages gives me a joyful sense of fulfillment.

The devoted folks involved in the project helped in countless ways. The gardeners each grew a garden, often to my specifications, tirelessly rounding up hard-to-find seeds and plants, drawing a diagram of the garden for me, documenting varieties, and keeping me up-to-date on the garden's progress. The chefs tested recipes and wrote them down in detail, often cooking them more than once so that I could photograph them. But in addition to their professional contributions, these folks also picked me up at airports, drove me to see other gardeners or chefs, fed me, and sometimes even gave me lodging. Theirs was truly a generous effort.

In thanking all these wonderful people, I must start with Wendy Krupnick and Jane Gamble. Without these two women, the book would have had much less heart and would have taken five years to complete instead of three. Wendy, hired at first as full-time gardener, also became chief recipe tester and creator, manuscript reviewer, photographic assistant, and research assistant. Besides putting in twelve-and fourteen-hour days on a nearly routine basis, Wendy contributed the wide knowledge of food she gained while working in many of the West's best restaurants and shared her devotion to and knowledge of horticulture and nutrition. Further, as secretary for the Certified California Organic Farmers, she was able to put me in touch with countless market growers and chefs. You will sense Wendy's spirit and energy throughout the text.

Another talent in evidence belongs to my longtime design partner, fellow gardener, and dear friend, Jane Gamble. Jane updated my basic vegetable growing information and compiled the encyclopedia section of the book. She collected endless data on growing vegetables and herbs and their many varieties, including sources for all we wanted to recommend. Not only was the encyclopedia completed with her usual grace and attention to detail, but as we worked, Jane's constant companionship was vital to my sanity.

Thanking by name the people who helped and acknowledging their specific contributions are complex tasks, not only because so many helped, but also because they often helped in more than one way. To begin, there are those who grew gardens for the book. As you read the garden chapters you'll find out more about these people, and many will appear again and again as authorities on subjects as varied as historical varieties, ethnic cooking techniques, and the preparation of edible flowers. These primary gardeners were Kit Anderson, Jan Blum, Phil Breedon, Georgeanne Brennan and Charlotte Glenn, Emery Tee Bruce Broussard, Sue Bullock, Georgia and Bob Calvert, David Cunningham, Andrea Crawford, Stephen Disparti, Steve Frowine, Sal and Tresa Gilbertie, Mike and Elizabeth Hughes, John Jeavons, Margaret Kinkaid, Carolyn and Paul Kuckein, Debra Lerer, Rose Marie Nichols McGee, Kevin Sands, Carole Saville, Gary Stoner, Vicki Sebastiani, Guy Thomas, Nancy Welch, Molly Wilson, and Jeanne and Dan Will.

Besides the gardeners who grew the featured gardens, there were countless additional garden authorities, most of whom were called upon to speak for hours into my tape recorder. Their areas of expertise ranged from Native American foods to the breeding of modern hybrids. These garden experts included Carl Barnes, Bill Bennett, Peter Chan, Tom Chino, Mahina Drees, Derek Fell, Jonathan Frei, Geri Harrington, Bob Hyland, Rob Johnston, Mary Ann Klein, Robert Kourik, Paul Ledig, Orin Martin, Mas Ogawa, Shepherd and Ellen Ogden, Kaete Reimnitz, Holly Shimizu, Zea Sonnabend, Stefanie Tebbutts, Ruth Troetschler, Perrin Wells, Ken Wesolowski, Kent Whealy, Christie White, Garrison Wilkes, John Withee, Serena Wyatt, and the people at the Philadelphia and San Jose community gardens.

Another group of garden authorities just as crucial to the effort spent hours reviewing the manuscript, answering frantic phone calls, and even sending plants, seeds, and recipes—in short, anything I asked for. These dedicated plant people are Jan Blum, Georgeanne Brennan, Craig Dremann, Charlotte Glenn, and Renee Shepherd.

Numerous chefs, cooking and nutrition authorities, and food historians contributed material ranging from hours of information on tape to comments on the manuscript and a recipe or two. These food authorities are distinguished from many in their profession by their garden savvy. Cooking experts who have shared recipes and information are Elizabeth Andoh, Paul Bertolli, Edward Espe Brown, G. Scott Brown, Joanie Cavagnaro, Lawrence Chu, Emily Cohen, Margaret Creasy, John Downey, Celestino Drago, Kenneth Dunn, Bhadra Fancy, Larry Farmer, Debra Friedman, Doug Gosling, Hansel Hagel, Carol Hancock, Ken Hom, Robin Jeavons, Diana Kennedy, Victoria and Benjamin Lomeli, Sharon Lovejoy, Dean Mager, Kerry Marshall, Thomas J. McCombie, Edmund McIlhenny, Michael McLaughlin, Bruce Naftaly, Paul Prudhomme, Seppi Renggli, Robin Sanders, Norbert Schulz, David Schy, Mark Stech-Novak, Dr. Helene Swenerton, Warren Weber, Jim Westervelt, Ron Zimmerman, and the chefs at Guaymas Restaurant, the Golden Door, Kinokawa, and the Khan Toke Thai House.

Once the recipes or techniques were in hand, they needed to be tested and in some cases prepared for photos. To this end, I had help from many of the gardeners and cooks mentioned above as well as Patty Buck, Sharon Burns, Mimi Frey, Gretchen Gunther, Judith Hand, Glenda Hughes, Gale Kinzie, Maureen and William Phelps, Sharon Redgrave, Dick Sovish, and Diane Weber. Also, the American Institute of Wine and Foods helped me to find and contact numerous cooking authorities.

I must acknowledge the unique contributions of Alice Waters, chef at Chez Panisse in Berkeley, California. Alice contributed not only information but inspiration. It was she who, years ago, broke the restaurateur's dependency on mainstream suppliers to seek out select gardeners and market growers of vegetables and herbs. She even went so far in her quest for the best fresh varieties as to organize her own restaurant gardens.

A special thanks also goes to Jesse Cool, executive chef at Late for the Train Cafe and Flea Street restaurants. Jesse both contributed information and numerous recipes and shared the talents of her staff for an occasional recipe test or food photo.

This book was an editorial tour de force. It demanded hours of much direction and the most dedicated attention to detail. Few authors are privileged to have such a talented supporting staff to work with. On the homefront, to help with the raw manuscript, Alberta Lee and Dayna Breedon supplied hours and hours worth of inspired transcribing and accurate typing. Pallavi Fancy gave needed office support. Material assembled by Maggie Gage for *The Complete Book of Edible Landscaping* was useful in preparing the Part Four Encyclopedia. Later, when my galleys arrived, Larry Breed gave them many hours of careful attention. The folks at Sierra Club Books provided valuable professional and personal support. Publisher Jon Beckmann and former executive editor Diana Landau encouraged the vision and initial concept of the book from the start. As manuscript was delivered, my editor, Linda Gunnarson, worked with me in selecting photographs and framing the text and then assembled and directed the editorial team necessary to bring the project into shape. Freelance writer-copyeditor Suzanne Lipsett breathed life into the manuscript; on numerous occasions I could only wonder how she could work such miracles. Freelancer Mary Anne Stewart contributed her outstanding talents in both copyediting and proofreading as well as boundless garden enthusiasm. Editorial assistant Barbara Fuller gave special attention to the expert profiles that appear throughout the book. And cookbook author and food writer Jeannette Ferrary reviewed all the recipes. The production team was equally dedicated. Production manager Susan Ristow provided consistent attention to quality and detail throughout the production process, with the valuable assistance of her colleague Felicity Luebke. And freelance designer Paula Schlosser skillfully transformed the thousands of words and hundreds of photographs into book form.

Most books have a supporting cast of some sort, but this one—in which the gardens and people actually *became* the book—involved a particularly substantial group. I call these people the enablers. They range from Cynthia Robinson, whom I've never even met, to members of my own family. Cynthia is part of a web of gardeners of which I was unaware until I began working on this book. When I was seeking someone to grow a French garden for me, a friend of mine in California called Cynthia in New Jersey, who in turn called Jeanne and Dan Will. And in another instance, Pat Wellingham-Jones, a friend in the Garden Writers Association of America, helped me locate existing gardens I needed to know about. I called on this network time and again, and it never let me down. Some enablers came through as translators; these included John Dotter, Alice Valenzuela, and Brigitte Magoun. Others—mostly family members—served as drivers as I traveled about the country; my warmest thanks to my daughter Laura, brother-in-law John Creasy, and Nancy and Dick Olds. Friends who took me to gardens and nurseries are Marcy Hawthorne, Jude Lichtenstein, and John and Tina Ward. Brenda Nalls lent me a computer; Robin Diamond, at Callaway Gardens, located photos; Greg Neilson and Carol Klesow of Wine Country Cuisine occasionally provided vegetables for photographs; and Charlotte Walker helped me learn food photography. Thank you, all.

I was the primary photographer for the book, but where I could not be on hand I had help from the photographers listed on the credits page and master photographer David Cavagnaro. For some of the food photos a studio was needed, and I joined forces with Alan and Carol Copeland and Barry Shapiro of Image Point.

My own gardening efforts over the last few years have been bolstered by Wendy Krupnick, of course, and by Paras Fancy, who keeps the garden looking neat; Frank Mac Doran, who makes compost and rototills; Jan Peterson, who has helped during the project; Bif Soper, who started many of the seedlings; and Joe Queirolo, who lends his gentle and sure hand now that Wendy has moved on to other endeavors. Shoring up the project in all sorts of little but critical ways was my husband, Robert, whose constant support has ranged from selecting computers and programs and repairing cameras and tape machines to lending enthusiastic companionship on trips to search out gardens and food. His loving support and sharing makes life rich.

Introduction

THERE IS A CONCEPT I love to contemplate because it is simple, beautiful, and true: that growing, harvesting, preparing, presenting, and eating foods from the garden are all phases of the same activity. Each step is part of the satisfying process of partaking of the earth's bounty. The unbroken arc from garden to table is the subject of this book.

However, meditating on a lovely idea and seeing it into print are, I've learned, two separate things. When I determined to write a book celebrating food from garden to table, I discovered I had taken on nothing less than a major portion of human evolution since the invention of agriculture, with all its diversity and complexity. I wasn't daunted by the hugeness of the project; thinking about gardening and cooking is my greatest pleasure. But it didn't take a genius to see that massive amounts of research would be involved. How was I going to get a grip on the material I needed without spending years in the library? If I was going to write this book, I was going to get my hands in the dirt and work up to my elbows in the

OPPOSITE: *Aïoli monstre is served at the traditional French harvest celebration and features vegetables and garlic mayonnaise. Pictured here are garden fresh 'Dragon Longerie' and filet beans, cucumbers, baby vegetables, roasted peppers, and new potatoes. In the background are 'Rosa Bianco' eggplants, 'Ruby Gold' tomatoes, 'Sweet Mama' squash, 'Violetta' peppers, and 'Hopi Blue' corn.*

Eggplants come in many forms. From left to right are 'Rosa Bianco', 'Listada De Gandia', 'Black Beauty', 'Long White Sword', 'Ronde de Valence' in the front, and a darker 'Rosa Bianco'.

kitchen—*that* was a given from the beginning.

I thought about the problem for a long time. And then I had an idea. I knew I would be interviewing master gardeners, seedspeople, and chefs—why not ask them to participate in the creation of a book I knew they would all have interest in? I could invite the gardeners and seedspeople to grow prototype gardens for the book, demonstrating their particular areas of expertise, and share with me how they cook from them. And I could ask the chefs to contribute recipes using the produce from similar gardens. Once I matched the chefs with the gardens, I would have a *living* library of gardening and cooking wisdom.

Thus was the notion of theme gardening born. It wasn't hard to list the cuisines and growing cultures I wanted to cover: there would be cuisines drawn from American history, such as those from Native American and early colonial times; there would be cuisines from many countries—France, Mexico, Italy, Germany, and the Orient; and there would be specialty cuisines reflecting trends, such as the growing interest in edible flowers and spa foods, now surfacing among passionate gardeners and food lovers. I was ecstatic at solving the problem of tackling my subject but innocent as a babe regarding the amount of work I was undertaking. In the two and a half years since I broached the idea of growing a theme garden with my first contributing gardeners, I have planned and overseen the growing of dozens of gardens throughout the country and gathered recipes and kitchen techniques from countless chefs, all the while growing and cooking in my own trial garden and kitchen the myriad varieties and recipes I was learning about.

And I've traveled. Visiting the theme gardens around the country and interviewing gardeners and chefs face to face became a true odyssey. Though I have been an active gardener and cook for more than half my lifetime and have written about these pursuits for many years, I learned more in this research effort than I ever thought I could know. And it was all great fun. One day I'd be a stone's throw from the Snake River in Idaho standing in a garden and admiring peas with blue pods; the next day I'd be bumping along a ranch road in Texas among the armadillos on my way to savor one of the world's premier pots of chili. Three days later would find me sitting in the office of the creators of Tabasco sauce talking about Cajun food and enthusiastically agreeing to sample some gumbo. Then northward I'd go to a baked bean festival in Maine to speak with the beanmaster there. And I remember the delightful contrast of talking into the night about Indian corn with a member of the Osage nation and then, a few days later, discussing with the chef at The Four Seasons restaurant in New York City the use of fresh herbs in elegant, low-calorie meals. Gardens upon gardens, meals upon meals, for two and a half years. This must be, I often thought, what heaven is like.

I discovered in my travels that a certain frustration I had experienced—in fact, that had partly motivated the writing of the book—was universal among cooks: the limited availability of diverse vegetable and herb varieties. I felt it when I saw my friends working hard to make their own pasta and sauce only to flavor the sauce with tasteless, dried, commercial basil, or when they made a stir-fry with regular cabbage instead of Chinese cabbage. They were creating wonderful meals but stopping short of what were often key ingredients, limiting themselves to the vegetables and herbs available at supermarkets or in neighborhood shops.

The same frustration had plagued me as a gardener. Before I did my research, I simply couldn't find sources of seeds for the many wonderful vegetables I had tasted over the years on my foreign travels. Like thousands of other gardening cooks, I was limited to approximating recipes from other cuisines rather than duplicating authentic ethnic dishes.

This frustration was echoed wherever I went. Chefs who had trained abroad wanted fresh herbs and traditional vegetable varieties to work with. Those who trained in Italy, for instance, wanted to be able to roast radicchio and serve raw purple artichokes for an antipasto. Thai chefs needed fresh coriander root. Some chefs were going so far as to put in their own gardens, while others were creating networks of gardeners. I discovered that a new market for specialty vegetables and herbs had formed and that enthusiastic gardeners were joining forces with restaurateurs by putting in large market gardens to serve them. Farmer's markets were making a comeback, too, as other cooks became aware of the new produce. Small seed companies were springing up to offer specialty and ethnic vegetable seeds. Baby lettuces and carrots, edible flowers, exotic and heirloom vegetable varieties that had been hidden away in private gardens—all were finding a market now. It seemed that both cooking and gardening were poised for a major change.

But there was talk of the need to collect the new

Alice Waters (at right), executive chef of Chez Panisse, and her garden manager, Andrea Crawford, compare notes on the tastes of different nasturtiums. Alice is foremost among restaurateurs interested in the freshest possible salad greens, herbs, and edible flowers and has them grown in her restaurant garden.

information, track down the new sources, and make gardeners' information available to cooks and chefs' knowledge available to gardeners. As most of the world's cuisines, both historically and currently, are heavily dependent on vegetables, there was much for everyone to explore. People wanted to take a closer look at, for example, chili peppers, wild salad greens, and grinding corns. Where could they find the radish varieties used at an authentic German Oktoberfest or the white asparagus the French serve? What varieties of beets were baked in coals in colonial days and how could they be grown? What herbs were used in authentic Oriental and Mexican dishes? What about the hundreds of heirloom vegetables, such as blue potatoes and 'Rattailed' radishes—how were they cooked? And how were fancy herb jellies made? Clearly, somebody had to let the garden genie out of the bottle so we could all feast on the results.

Needless to say, I felt I was on the right track as

Herb jellies are easily made. These are jellies flavored with lavender, basil, and rosemary.

I traveled around and listened to people talk. And my travels not only yielded encouragement and information, they helped me think through and simplify the organization of this book. When I finally came to assemble the information, the result was a three-part structure: Part One covers theme gardens taken from American history and reflecting various growing climates across the country; Part Two covers gardens featuring vegetable and herb varieties from around the world; and Part Three covers gardens that reflect the newest approaches to food now emerging, what might be called the avant-garde in cooking and gardening. Each chapter within these parts is based on gardens grown to a specific theme by participating expert gardeners. To avoid repetition in the text, I have covered specific growing information for most vegetables in the encyclopedia of vegetables that constitutes Part Four.

A word is in order concerning my choice of edibles. I have concentrated on vegetables here, partly because I covered fruits and nuts in great detail in *The Complete Book of Edible Landscaping,* but mostly because vegetables form the foundation of the world's cuisines. Also, you will notice as you read the lists of recommended varieties in each chapter that fewer hybrids are discussed here than is usual in gardening books. I am not against hybrids; in fact, some of my favorite varieties are hybrids, including 'Silver Queen' corn and 'Ambrosia' cantaloupe. But because hybrids are so heavily emphasized in most gardening books and by most major catalog seed companies, and I had limited space, I wanted to stress the often overlooked open-pollinated varieties in the text. Many of the best hybrid varieties that couldn't be left out of any garden book are covered in the Burpee gardens chapter and in the Part Four Encyclopedia.

In addition to exploring all aspects of a particular theme garden, each chapter contains a cooking section, with information on ingredients and cooking techniques characteristic of the cuisine at hand, as well as wonderful recipes—some the generous gifts of my contributing chefs and others from my own test kitchen. The recipes, like the gardens, range from simple to complicated. As a rule, to reflect our new nutritional knowledge, the recipes call for less salt and saturated fat than those in many cookbooks. Few specialized pieces of cooking equipment are needed, but a good sharp knife, blender, food processor, grain grinder for wheat and corn, and salad spinner will facilitate many of the recipes in the book.

The author's trial vegetable garden. The traditional front yard was converted so that hundreds of vegetable varieties recommended by gardening and cooking professionals could be tested. Along the driveway are zucchini and ten varieties of eggplants among the marigolds. The tall trellis supports twelve tomato varieties.

For me, starting to cook begins with the planting of a few vegetables. I see wonderful breakfasts and sensational tarts when I plant Alpine strawberries, and stir-fries when the pea pods and ginger shoots appear. One of my fondest hopes is that this book will inspire not just gardener-cooks like me but also cooks who have never dared to undertake their own planting. Too many people believe that cooking from the garden involves plowing the back forty, but even growing a few basil and tarragon plants or some fancy lettuces among the petunias or some lemon thyme on a windowsill will add immeasurably to your cooking. Try planting some of the vegetables featured in this book, and I hope, as it does for me, the sight of the new plants sprouting in your garden will set your mouth to watering.

PART ONE

TRADITIONAL GARDENS

OVERSEAS TRAVEL IS wonderful, but our own country is equally absorbing in its diversity and richness. As I traveled to gardens and restaurants around the country, I found myself musing on the fun I could have staying on and gardening first here, then there—simply settling down for a few years to experiment with all the plants I was learning about for the first time. Ah, to walk through these woods on a spring day, to eat in that great restaurant again, to learn more from the local gardeners. If only I had all the time in the world!

Despite the leveling effect of the mass media, we gardeners and cooks, like the topography, maintain much of our regional identity. Gardeners in Maine might buy seeds of the latest hybrid tomato variety, ever hopeful of an early harvest, but they also grow the 'Jacob's Cattle' or 'Yellow Eye' beans their families used for generations for their baked beans. Gardeners in Tucson compare notes on chili peppers, Cajun gardeners grow okra varieties their daddies enjoyed, and many Native Americans still grind corns of different colors as their forbears did from time immemorial.

It's true that the majority of us grow such varieties as 'Silver Queen' corn, 'Blue Lake' string beans, and 'Big Boy' tomatoes—tried and tested varieties all. When we buy seeds at a local nursery or from one of the major seed companies, and when we do our produce shopping at the market, we tend to choose from a narrow range of varieties. But the vastly diverse varieties are still there, thank goodness, and they are beginning to surface with increasing frequency across the country.

A collection of Native American corns representing the great range of colors and types of corn that have been bred over the millennia.

Jan Blum, owner of Seeds Blum, in her mandala garden of heirloom kale, broccoli, celery, and onion varieties. Interplanted among the vegetables are 'Lemon Gem' and 'Tangerine Gem' marigolds.

I spent the best part of three years plumbing the depths of this diversity—in one place running my fingers through a sack of 'Bloody Butcher' red corn kernels; in another pulling long, purple radishes out of the ground; and elsewhere getting my chin wet eating a watermelon with yellow stars all over its rind. And when I thought I had seen everything, I came across radishes grown for their pods rather than their roots, navy blue potatoes, and red Brussels sprouts resembling miniature red cabbages.

To a certain point, modern plant breeding has stressed uniformity, and shoppers have fueled this trend by selecting snap beans of all one length, for example, or familiar green cucumbers and round, red radishes. Accounting for that uniformity is outside the scope of this book, but calling attention to the fact that we have not yet lost red-kerneled corn or podding radishes is one of its chief purposes. We are

in a renaissance whose essence involves the rediscovery of our natural wealth. A short five years ago, at a conference on saving heirloom varieties, only a few worried folks, including myself, had gathered together. A similar conference held in 1987 was mobbed, and now a flood of interested gardeners and cooks are out there tracking down varieties they remember from childhood—'Aunt Mary's' sweet corn, for example, or 'Mortgage Lifter' tomatoes. Fancy restaurants are looking for frilly red 'Ragged Jack' kale to line salad plates, and specialty growers are trying to outdo the competition with 'Dragon Longerie' beans and 'Deer Tongue' and 'Tom Thumb' lettuces. Even the gardeners at "living" museums are refining their efforts by replanting their historical vegetable and flower gardens with varieties used by the original residents of their communities.

Still, we are just beginning, and the majority of

old varieties remain to be rediscovered. Just as I would start to feel self-satisfied in my travels, confident that I had finally learned what there was to know, Jan Blum, of Seeds Blum, for instance, would casually mention potato onions, which multiply without being reseeded every year, and serpent garlic. Or Carl Barnes, a corn preservationist in Oklahoma, would enumerate the corn varieties that can be roasted, or tell me how Native Americans tailored their corn selections to the needs of the family cook. And off I'd be on a new adventure, tracking down specifics on these varieties and searching out traditional preparation methods.

Part One, then, conveys the foundations of our vegetable legacy, focusing on the wide range of flavors and many uses of our old, sometimes nearly lost varieties. For instance, in earlier days, specific carrot varieties were grown not only for eating fresh or cooking in soups, but for juicing and storing as well. Corn wasn't simply a fresh vegetable to be enjoyed for a few fleeting weeks; dry and grinding corns were enjoyed throughout the year in a multitude of ways. Part One also looks forward to the direction we are taking with our new hybrids—the sweetest of sweet corns, burpless cucumbers, and disease-free tomatoes. But the foundation of this section of the book is a celebration of our great cultural heritage as expressed in the cook's garden.

Heirloom Gardens

SEEDS ARE A LINK to the past. Immigrants smuggled them into this country in the linings of their suitcases, under the bands of their hats, and in the hems of their dresses. The Germans brought cabbages, the Italians paste tomatoes, and the Mexicans their beloved chilies. According to Kent Whealy, director of the Seed Savers Exchange, from the time of the *Mayflower* to that of the boat people, much of our heritage of heirloom seeds entered the country in just this way.

The home gardens in which these seeds were grown fifty or a hundred years ago were quite different from home gardens today. For one thing, the varieties themselves were notably diverse—for example, there were high-shouldered tomatoes, purple broccoli, and huge, dense beets. Even within varieties, the produce was much less uniform than what we're used to. But an even more fundamental difference related to the seeds themselves: when planting time came, gardeners took seeds not from commercial packages, but from jars in closets where the seeds had been stored from the previous year's harvest. Gardeners in the old days used the seeds of their own open-pollinated plants—varieties capable of reproducing themselves.

OPPOSITE: *Heirloom vegetables 'White Beauty' and 'Pearson' tomatoes, 'Jacob's Cattle' dry beans, 'Sultan's Emerald Crescent' string beans, 'King of the Garden' limas, and 'Calhoun Purple Hull' cow peas, arranged on antique catalogs.*

By the 1930s, commercially marketed seeds of many new varieties were becoming increasingly available to home gardeners. Among these new varieties were many hybrids, some of which proved to be more vigorous and uniform than some of the open-pollinated varieties, and the public accepted them enthusiastically. One of the consequences of using hybrids, however, was that the public could not save the hybrid seeds to plant the next year. To produce a hybrid variety, a breeder crosses two varieties or even two species of plants. But like the mule—a cross between a donkey and a horse—the hybrids cannot reproduce themselves, so the crossing process must be repeated every year by the seed companies.

The increasing use of commercially produced varieties streamlined the home garden, simplifying its planting and standardizing its produce, but in the process old, open-pollinated varieties cultivated for generations were dropped by the hundreds. Some estimate now that thousands of plant varieties were lost forever.

For the last thirty to forty years, American gardeners have favored many of these commercial varieties and many hybrids, but change is in the air. Gardeners are by no means forsaking their favorite hybrids, and no one is denying that the heavy production and uniformity of some hybrids have their place, but many old, open-pollinated plant varieties are gaining new attention. Diversity in all its glory is coming to be valued anew. Against the backdrop of ever-spreading monocultures—huge single-variety crops—the old plant varieties are showing their unusual shapes, colors, and sizes to great advantage. Gardeners and cooks are rediscovering small yellow plum tomatoes, blue cornmeal for tortillas, and rich yellow fingerling potatoes. Restaurants are using 'Ragged Jack' kale to line salad bowls and 'Dragon Langerie' beans—yellow romano beans with maroon lace markings—as additions to appetizer plates.

Collectively these activities are known as the heirloom movement, and the plants grown as a result of it are known as heirloom varieties. In general, an heirloom plant variety is just that—a variety "of special value handed on from one generation to another," as *Webster's* defines the word heirloom. More specifically, most seed people agree that the term applies to any open-pollinated variety more than fifty years old—open-pollinated because the seeds can be saved to reproduce the plant, and fifty years because the number is appropriate for the varieties concerned.

Some of the gardeners growing heirloom varieties today are primarily interested in the taste of the old-timers. The 'Bonny Best' tomato, for example, is renowned for its flavor. Other gardeners are interested in the novelty of the heirlooms and like to amuse the family by serving 'Mortgage Lifter' tomatoes and 'Lazy Wife' beans or to arrive at a Fourth of July picnic with red, white, and blue potato salad made with blue and red heirloom potatoes. Still others appreciate the historical connections—to the 'Mayflower' bean, for instance, or to a lettuce variety brought to this country by a great-great grandmother.

I have been gardening and cooking with unusual varieties for as long as I can remember. Over the years, that especially tasty corn variety, that unusual colored bean, and those vegetables with novelty names seemed to please my soul, and I sought them out to cook with them. But my interest really gained momentum about eight years ago when I attended a conference on seed saving and met numerous other gardeners who were also interested in many of these unusual vegetable varieties. Most of them had a different slant on the subject, however. While many had been drawn to these vegetables and fruits initially by the novelty and taste, they soon became concerned—as I did—about a more global issue: the erosion of the vast gene pool of vegetables that just happened to include most of my unusual varieties.

To stay in existence, plant varieties must be grown and kept growing. We have lost, and continue to lose, thousands of unique varieties, and our irreplaceable gene pool—the bank of varieties that future breeds will draw from—is shrinking alarmingly.

It's critical that we focus on this erosion now and start to rebuild the endangered stocks. The U.S. government and the seed companies are cooperating in saving some varieties in storage facilities, but the bulk of the seed-saving effort rests with the home gardener. Fortunately, reversing the trend does not require sacrifice. Instead, as the gardens and recipes in this chapter attest, it can mean fascination and adventure both in the garden and at the table.

Heirloom gardeners come at their passion from a number of different angles, and the gardens described in this chapter reflect these different emphases. Jan Blum's garden expresses her unending fascination with unusual old vegetables passed down within families, and it's a treasure chest of historical mementoes and

*This harvest from Jan Blum's heirloom garden includes old varieties of broccolis and kales as well as 'All Blue',
'Blue Mechanic', 'Green Mountain', 'All Red', 'Menominee', and 'German Fingerling' potatoes.*

visual treats. The Pliny Freeman garden, part of the outdoor colonial museum at Old Sturbridge Village in Sturbridge, Massachusetts, is a strict historical interpretation of the kitchen garden of Pliny Freeman, a middle-class farmer who lived in post-Revolution days. And Kevin Sands's garden is the expression of a passionate seed saver, deeply involved in the network of individuals and organizations devoted to locating and growing the seeds of old varieties.

You may find yourself drawn to the preservation effort through any of these channels, but it's only fair to mention here what the cooking section of this chapter will reveal—that there are a few caveats. Remember that many heirloom vegetables were selected and maintained to match old-fashioned cooking and storage methods. From a modern standpoint, this often means string beans with strings intact but that have a great beany flavor; peas that are starchy but perfect for soup; and large, heavy "keeper" beets that not only last interminably in the storage cellar but are incomparable roasted in the embers of fires. All in all, you'll find, of course, that part of the great adventure are dishes rich in taste and color as well as living history.

It's true that heirlooms form the focus of this chapter and that they can make an exciting, even absorbing, theme garden on their own. But my research for this book and my own gardening with heirloom varieties have shown me that the venerable old varieties have a place in any garden. Therefore, you will find heirloom varieties cropping up in many chapters of this book. Growing an heirloom garden is a way to focus on these treasures, but the true place of heirloom vegetables is wherever gardens grow. By far, the best way to keep heirlooms going is to keep them growing.

How to Grow an Heirloom Garden

Heirloom varieties are not necessarily rare. You probably already grow a number of them—for example, 'Kentucky Wonder' beans, 'Black Beauty' eggplant, 'Pearson' tomatoes, 'Black-Seeded Simpson' lettuce, and 'Yellow Crookneck' squash are all heirlooms. An heirloom garden filled completely with the more common heirlooms is possible, but my purpose in this chapter is to explore the subject more fully by discussing the uncommon and even unique possibilities of an heirloom garden. To me, there are three reasons to grow an heirloom garden: to have the fun of growing unusual and tasty vegetables; to keep alive the less common varieties; and to learn how to save some of your own seeds.

Choosing and Obtaining Heirlooms

Let's look at how to choose and obtain some of the rarer varieties. The best way to start is to read through the "Recommended Heirloom Vegetables" and garden sections that follow for variety descriptions and then to choose a handful of varieties that appeal to you. Also see "Cooking from the Heirloom Garden" for information on how the varieties are best used. To keep things simple, choose only six to eight varieties to start. Since you are probably planning to save your seeds, you might want to begin with the families whose seeds are easiest to save: the legumes (beans and peas) and the Solanaceae (tomatoes, peppers, and eggplants). I'm assuming you haven't yet grown any of the varieties you choose, and therefore recommend that you treat your heirloom garden as an experimental supplement to your usual one. After all, you won't know starting out how these varieties are going to perform in your particular climate.

With a few exceptions, planning, planting, and maintaining an heirloom garden are the same as with any other modern vegetable garden. However, compared with some of the modern varieties, some heirloom vegetables are more disease prone (for instance, some older types of cucumbers and peas), less productive (some of the colored potatoes particularly), and show less uniformity in the ripening times, shapes, and colors of their produce.

To obtain heirlooms you will probably have to order them by mail. Most local nurseries carry only a limited selection of heirloom vegetable varieties—

perhaps one percent of the heirlooms available—so to obtain seeds of some of the rarer old vegetables, such as 'Cherokee' beans or 'Brandywine' tomatoes, you'll have to contact the seed companies that specialize in heirlooms. These firms are listed under "Sources" at the end of this chapter. If you want to explore heirloom varieties further—perhaps to locate a specific variety you remember as a child, or to track down one of the really rare ones—contact the seed exchanges, which are also listed. Remember, however, that seed exchanges are trading organizations for preserving the seed bank, not commercial seed companies, so you'll have to save your own seeds for trade if you work with any of them.

Saving Seeds

I, for one, never even thought about saving my own seeds when I started vegetable gardening. As far as I was concerned, seeds came in beautiful packages, not from my plants. Recently, though, I have started to learn about seed saving, and I find myself amazed at how simple and satisfying the process is. For example, I merely keep a few 'Dutch White' runner beans each year for next year's crop. I make sure they are completely dry, freeze them for a day to kill any weevil eggs, package them, label them, and put them away. That's all there is to it. Once I went through the process, I felt like a chump for having faithfully sent off to Maine every spring for new packages of seeds of open-pollinated varieties when I could easily have saved my own.

Though the seed-saving process is easy, however, some background is essential. To select and save seeds you're going to have to know some elementary botany, and you'll have to practice some trial and error in applying it. That's why I suggest that you start simply, with only a few heirloom varieties.

Let's begin with a review of the birds-and-bees information people think they know until called upon to explain it. The reproduction of seed plants involves pollination—the transference of pollen, which contains the sperm cells (produced by the male flower part, called the stamen), to the stigma, which contains the ovary, the female organ. Once a plant has been pollinated, seeds form. If the pollen from a flower fertilizes the ovary of the same flower, the process is called self-pollination. To self-pollinate, a flower must have both stamen and stigma, and a flower that does is called a perfect flower. Beans and peas have perfect flowers and are usually self-pollinated. When pollen is transferred, either between flowers on the same plant or between plants, the process is called cross-pollination. Where this occurs, pollen is carried from flower to flower either by an insect or by the wind. Corn, squash, melons, and beets are all cross-pollinated.

In seed saving, the idea is to preserve existing varieties unaltered. To do so, it is necessary to prevent cross-pollination with a different variety in the plant you intend to preserve. Suppose you have a 'Jack-O'-Lantern' pumpkin plant situated next to a zucchini plant. A bee might visit a male flower of the pumpkin plant and then fly over to a female flower on the zucchini plant, thus transferring pollen from one plant to the other—that is, cross-pollinating the zucchini and the pumpkin. If you planted the seed from the cross-pollinated squash the next year, the result would be a cross between the two. Sometimes that cross produces a good offspring (that's one way to get new varieties), but usually you'll just get a weird squash. I remember letting some squash plants mature that had sprouted in the compost pile. I got a cross between a striped summer ball squash and an acorn squash: a striped, tough-skinned, stringy summer squash.

You can see that when you intend to save seeds in order to preserve varieties over the generations, you must always take steps when you plan your garden to prevent cross-pollination. With some plants, such as beans, that have perfect flowers and usually pollinate themselves before they open, cross-pollination is seldom a problem. With others, such as those in the squash and cucumber family, cross-pollination occurs readily, so they must be planted in isolation to ensure that the variety remains pure.

There are a number of ways to isolate plants. First, you can restrict yourself to planting only one variety of each type of vegetable, since pollination does not occur among different genera. Or you can plant potential cross-pollinators far apart from each other (some varieties need only be separated by a hundred feet, while others require half a mile, and this is where your research—and your trials and errors—will come in). For instance, if you and your neighbors grow different varieties of cucumbers or corn within three hundred feet of each other, you won't be able to save the seed, since the pollen from the other varieties will be carried to your plants and might pollinate and change the next generation of

Georgia Calvert grows a miniature heirloom garden in her San Jose, California, front yard. Among her many heirlooms are 'Wren's Egg' and 'Black Valentine' beans (both pictured), 'Belgium White' carrots, 'All Red' potatoes, and 'Chocolate' bell peppers.

your heirloom varieties. A physical barrier might work to isolate your heirlooms, however: rows of tall corn between species of peppers, for example, or an existing building with your potential cross-pollinators planted on either side.

Another fundamental point is one I touched on earlier: saving the seeds of hybrids can be wasted energy, since hybrid plants don't reproduce themselves. In saving seed, then, you'll have to know which are open-pollinated varieties that give viable offspring and which are hybrids. (To prevent confusion, most nurseries label hybrids and F1 hybrids, a form of hybrid, on their seed packets and in their catalogs).

Finally, you have to know the life cycle of the plants you're dealing with. While most of our vegetables are annuals (maturing in one season), many are biennials, which means they take two seasons to reproduce. Some popular biennials are beets, carrots, parsley, and chard. With these you will get no seed in the first growing season.

With these basic botanical concepts under your belt, there are a few more particulars to master for seed saving:

1. You must learn to recognize plant diseases,

Kent Whealy

Kent Whealy is director of the Seed Savers Exchange, an organization devoted to saving endangered open-pollinated varieties of vegetables. More than 600 members of the organization offer heirloom vegetable seeds through Seed Savers publications and help keep alive a gene pool of vegetables as unusual as 'Montezuma Red' beans and 'Afghani Purple' carrots. To do this, Seed Savers operates a preservation farm in Decorah, Iowa, that maintains more than 5000 varieties of heirloom vegetables. Kent, who has a degree in journalism, runs the organization and the gardens and uses his skills as an editor to compile a valuable aid for the gardening public, *The Garden Seed Inventory*. This large book lists and describes nearly 6000 open-pollinated vegetable varieties still sold by 240 companies in the United States and Canada.

To learn about some heirloom varieties and quench my curiosity as to how Seed Savers finds them, I asked Kent to share some of his experiences. He focused on varieties currently offered by seed companies so we all wouldn't be frustrated by hearing about unobtainable seeds.

I first asked Kent about the 'Moon and Stars' watermelon. This intriguing pink-fleshed watermelon is similar to many dark-green ones except that it's covered with many small yellow spots, or "stars," and is usually highlighted by a large yellow spot, or "moon," which is two to four inches across. The plant is a genetic mutation, and foliage is also spotted with yellow.

Kent says members of the Seed Savers Exchange had tried for about five years to find the 'Moon and Stars' watermelon through their network. Then, in 1981, Kent notes, "we were living in Missouri and I did a television spot about the Seed Savers. After it aired, I got a call from Earl Van Doran, who told me he had 'Moon and Stars' and asked if I wanted some seed. I went to his farm, by chance only fifty miles away, and he had a whole field of the melons." For years no one knew where 'Moon and Stars' came from, but Jan Blum, owner of Seeds Blum, which now carries the seed, reports that it is still grown in Russia and seems to have come to America with German immigrants. There is also a yellow-fleshed variety carried by the Southern Exposure Seed Exchange (actually a seed company, not strictly a seed exchange).

Kent talked, too, about the 'Cherokee' bean, also known as the 'Cherokee Trail of Tears'. Not all of our heirloom varieties came from Europe, Africa, or Asia; many are native American. According to Kent, "There was an old fellow, recently deceased, named Dr. John Wyche, a dentist of Cherokee descent from Hugo, Oklahoma. He lived on a mountaintop and had built twenty-two terraced gardens out of stone around his house. He literally hauled all the dirt for his gardens up the mountain. He used to own Cole Brothers Circus, which he overwintered in Hugo, and he enriched his gardens by hauling tons of elephant and lion manure up the mountain, swearing that the odor of the lion manure kept varmints away from his garden. Dr. Wyche's people had traveled over the 'Trail of Tears,' an Indian death march [the forced relocation of the Cherokees from their native lands in the southeastern states to Oklahoma], in 1838. He gave me several varieties of seeds his people had carried over the Trail of Tears; one we call the 'Cherokee' bean or the 'Cherokee Trail of Tears' bean." The 'Cherokee' is a snap bean. The seeds are black, and the pods are very long and purple and grow on vigorous climbing vines. Jan Blum carries the 'Cherokee' in her catalog.

Kent next talked about a tomato called 'Stump of the World'. Out of 510 varieties of tomatoes Kent has grown, he thinks this is one of the best. It's a large, meaty, pink tomato that's incredibly flavorful and has perfect shoulders—round and without flutes. Gardeners in Kent's area, who had always sworn by a large German pink tomato, think 'Stump of the World' is even better. Kent doesn't know where the name comes from; he knows only that the seeds came from the late Ben Quisenberry, who ran a company called Big Tomato Gardens that offered tomato seeds for thirty years. Seeds Blum now carries this tomato.

Kent also mentioned a white corn that he thinks is one of the sweetest of all. "It's so sweet," he says, "you can't dry it for seed on the plant or it will mold. It's called 'Aunt Mary's' sweet corn." According to Kent, a fellow named Berkowitz visited his Aunt Mary in Ohio in the 1930s, became enamored with her corn, and obtained some seeds from her. Two of Berkowitz's friends, W. W. Williams and his father, helped him produce the seeds. Forty years later, Williams gave the seeds to Kent. As Kent says, "When someone like Williams gives me the seeds of something he's kept pure for forty years, I feel it's a gift from the past and I have an obligation to keep it going." Shumway Seed Company carried this variety into the 1970s, and Seeds Blum has now picked it up.

The 'Old-Time Tennessee' muskmelon is another heirloom that Kent likes. He says it grows larger than a basketball and is unusual because, instead of being smooth, the rind has very deep creases. The way it grows is amazing: when the fruit starts to develop, it's very long and creased, like a deflated football; then, as it grows, it balloons and fills out. According to Kent, "It's so very sweet and aromatic you could find it in the dark. People write to me to say they're devotees of the 'Old-Time Tennessee' muskmelon." Fortunately, if you're interested in growing 'Old-Time Tennessee', the Southern Exposure Seed Exchange and Le Marché both carry it now.

Anyone interested in joining Kent and other seed savers can send for a two-page information letter detailing the projects and publications of the Seed Savers Exchange. (Send a stamped, self-addressed envelope to the Seed Savers Exchange, P.O. Box 70, Decorah, IA 52101.) Realize, though, that you are not merely sending for a seed catalog. This is not a commercial enterprise. If you join Seed Savers, you must make a commitment to grow out and save the seeds you obtain, then share them with others. You will, of course, have access to a huge and incredible collection of wonderful vegetables and fruits not commercially available—but that's simply a benefit of what Kent refers to as "saving the sparks of life that feed us all."

---

since some of them, particularly the viral ones, are transmitted by seeds.

2. Always label the seed rows you plant as well as your seed containers, since memory sometimes plays tricks.

3. Never plant all your seeds at once, or the elements might wipe you out.

4. Learn to select the best seeds for the next generation. Select seeds from the healthiest plants and those producing the best vegetables.

5. To maintain a strong gene pool, select seeds from a number of plants, not just one or two (this does not apply to self-pollinating varieties; see "Saving Bean Seeds" below).

6. Get to know the vegetable families, since members of the same family often cross-pollinate.

7. Only mature, ripe seeds will be viable. Learn what such seeds look like for all the vegetables you work with.

Everyone new at seed saving will benefit from reading Robert Johnston, Jr.'s brief how-to pamphlet called *Growing Garden Seeds,* carried by Johnny's Selected Seeds, Foss Hill Road, Albion, ME 04910, $2.50 postpaid. For thorough coverage of the subject, including listings of seed exchanges and sources as well as a rundown on the whole movement, see Carolyn Jabs's book *The Heirloom Gardener.*

Saving Bean Seeds

To give you a model for your seed saving, I have decided to include the method for saving bean seeds. Beans are the easiest vegetable seeds to save. They are mostly self-pollinating, so cross-pollination is not a major concern when you plant them, and you'll be able to grow two or three varieties with few pollination problems. To avoid the minor problems, John Withee, one of this country's most devoted seed savers (he used to plant 250 varieties of beans every summer), suggests planting varieties that are very different next to each other. Then, if any crossing does occur, the seed that results will look different and you'll know your selected variety has been altered. Plant and care for your bean plants as you would ordinarily. When harvest approaches, start choosing the plants that are among the healthiest. With snap beans, let some of the healthy plants mature. It takes about six weeks from the snap bean stage for the bean seed to mature. Let dry bean types mature as you would ordinarily. Beans usually ripen from bottom to top. Pick them as the pods start to crack or the beans will fall out on the ground, where they will probably get wet.

Do not save beans from diseased plants. Diseases borne by bean seeds are anthracnose and bacterial blight. Anthracnose symptoms are small brown spots that enlarge to become sunken black spots. Bacterial blight is characterized by dark-green spots on the pods that slowly become dry and brick red. The most bothersome pest of bean seeds is the weevil.

After you dry your bean seeds thoroughly (see below), pack the seeds in a mason-jar-like container, label them, and freeze them for twenty-four hours to kill any weevils. Then put them in a cool dark place. That's all there is to it.

Storing Seeds

Seeds must be stored carefully to ensure that they germinate in the next season. The greatest enemy of seed viability is moisture, so you must dry the seeds thoroughly before storing them. To dry seeds, lay them out on a screen in a warm, dry room for a few weeks, stirring them every few days. Biting a seed is a good test of its moisture content: if you can't dent it, it's probably dry enough.

Another problem is heat. Seeds must be stored in a cool, dry, dark place, but if properly dry and placed in a sealed container, seeds can also be frozen. They will stay viable for years in a freezer if properly packaged. Freezing also helps protect the seed from insect infestations, not an uncommon problem of seed savers. (Don't freeze beans or peas, though. They need more air than freezing permits.)

The Blum Heirloom Garden

No one could be blasé on the trip to Jan Blum's garden. I drove northward out of Boise, Idaho, gaining altitude as I went. The highway straddles the famous Snake River Canyon, and as I continued northward I hit plateaus where I could see dry grassland and scrub stretching away for miles and miles. The light out there is magical: occasionally the highway will curve to reveal a shadowy gorge with sunlit water glinting or a treed canyon shining. The region looks so untamed I couldn't help wondering how anyone could garden out there. I passed a landmark dam, with its hundred-foot plumes of water spewing skyward, drove up a canyon, traveled for a mile or so, and then turned a corner into a lush garden filled with leafy vegetables and bright flowers. Butterflies and birds flitted about, completing the idyllic picture.

This is the home of Seeds Blum, a mail-order seed company. Now, there are seed companies, and there are seed companies. Some are exceedingly businesslike, with catalogs filled with color photos of uniform beans and tomatoes, but to visit them is to find a suite of offices with nary a plant to be seen. At Jan Blum's seed company the catalog is black and white, but there's plenty of color in the huge vegetable garden, and the office sits in the middle of it all.

Read Jan's catalog and you'll find her passion for open-pollinated varieties of vegetable seeds pouring off the pages. Like many of today's new seed people, Jan is very concerned about the erosion of the gene pool, and much of her dedication is directed toward saving such varieties as the 'Super Italian Paste' tomato and 'Moon and Stars' watermelon for future generations to enjoy. Jan surrounds herself with beautiful gardens filled with heirloom varieties to be tested, both in the garden and in the kitchen. She actively searches for varieties on the brink of extinction and spends hours adding to her catalog the gardening information she turns up. "A great part of my satisfaction," she told me, "comes from people writing to say, for instance, that they haven't seen the 'Moon and Stars' watermelon since the 1930s. Or, 'Oh, my gosh, my grandfather is going to be thrilled when he sees what you carry in your catalog.' Or, 'I've kept thirty varieties of such and such alive for many years. Are you interested in having the seeds?'"

Having worked with Jan for years and experienced her grand enthusiasm for heirlooms, when I needed an heirloom garden for my book, I considered her first as a candidate for growing one. Once approached, Jan and her partner Karla Prabucki jumped into the project full steam ahead. I gave Jan carte blanche to create any style heirloom garden she wished, and when I arrived in the summer to photograph it, it far exceeded my expectations. It was filled to overflowing with unusual, historically rich varieties of vegetables, and it was beautiful.

To begin our chat that day, I asked Jan for her definition of heirloom vegetables. She said she considered any variety that has been around for more than sixty years to be an heirloom but added that she was most interested in noncommercial varieties that have been handed down through families.

Then she went on to explain what she had in mind when she put our garden together. "I had a vast bank to pull from; but I had a small garden area, so I had to be choosy. First, I wanted the garden to be beautiful. Next, I wanted to feature old varieties of common vegetables—for instance, 'Red Lazy Wife' bean. That name implies history! Then I chose old vegetables we don't use today. For instance, I wanted people to say, 'Orach? What the heck is orach?' I also chose German-Russian varieties from the Volga River area of Russia, where my mother's people came from. In the early 1800s, there was a major flow of German people to settle the Volga area. This migration was reflected later in the gardens of immigrant families in this country. Consider the 'Moon and Stars' watermelon, for example. Most of Germany would have been too cold for watermelons, so this was probably originally a Russian variety that the Germans adopted when they farmed the Volga region. Watermelons became integrated into German cuisine, and watermelon pickles are now a tradition in German-American communities."

Other German varieties Jan included in her garden were the 'Hungarian Blue-Seeded' poppy—a colorful rose-colored, bread-seed poppy good for pastries—and 'Ragged Jack' kale, also known as 'Russian Red' kale. The latter is one of Jan's favorite vegetables, as it is both tasty and beautiful, with its scalloped oaklike leaves and purple-colored veins. It is also the best raw kale for salads and in its immature stage has become very popular with restaurateurs on the West Coast.

Red orach is a German vegetable so beautiful that Jan used it as a background for the lettuce and serpent onions. "The red color of the foliage is wonderful," she said, "and this orach is the very first thing up in the spring. Like spinach, you can steam and cook it as a green, or you can use its red leaves

Jan Blum's frontyard heirloom garden near Boise, Idaho. In the back left bed are serpent garlic, red orach, and 'Blue Podded' peas underplanted with 'Salad Bowl' lettuce. In front of these heirlooms is a bean teepee for 'Lazy Wife' beans. In the foreground are bread-seed poppies, 'Ragged Jack' kale, sea kale, and 'Salad Bowl' lettuce. The back right bed contains carrots, sorrel, 'Giant' chives, and 'Moon and Stars' watermelon. In the front right bed are chives and red dianthus.

raw in salads. But, unlike spinach, you can cut it back all summer. Be warned, though. Like beets, orach will turn other ingredients red."

Jan also included other unusual vegetables. 'Hamburg Rooted' parsley has strong parsley-flavored leaves and an edible white tap root about six inches long. The 'Rattailed' radish, which differs from most radishes in that its roots are inedible, is prized for its foot-long seed pods, which can be pickled, used raw in salads (sparingly), or cut up like green beans in stir-fries.

Besides the German and German-Russian vegetable varieties, Jan couldn't resist including some of her personal favorites in the garden. For instance, she planted 'Blue Podded' peas, which have purple pods and flowers. They are tasty and sweet and the plants look lovely in the back of the flower bed. And she included beetberries. These berries have a bland flavor but are fun to use because of their red color and seedy, strawberrylike texture. Kids especially enjoy this very old shade-loving garden novelty.

One vegetable Jan couldn't resist adding was 'Red Lazy Wife' pole bean, a red-seeded variety of 'Lazy Wife' that produces large, lush vines. The name supposedly refers to the fact that the beans are relatively stringless. Another variety was a pumpkin—'Rouge Vif D'Etampes'. Originally from France, this is a squat, cheese-type pumpkin, twelve to eighteen inches wide and eight inches tall. It is a deep reddish-orange, deeply fluted, and to Jan looks like the pumpkin for Cinderella's carriage.

During my visit, Jan pointed out that many plants, including carrots, some lettuce plants, and three different kinds of chives, were going to seed. As she said, "In the era this garden represents, there were, of course, few seed companies or produce markets. People were dependent upon the garden, and at any given time during the growing season there would be seedlings filling in, produce ready for harvesting, and seed heads forming for next year's seeds. These seed heads are a bonus that most modern gardeners are unfamiliar with. In addition to producing seeds, the heads can be used in all their different stages. Fresh carrot blossoms are long-lived, white, and lacy—excellent for flower arrangements. Lavender chive blossoms look beautiful both in flower arrangements and salads. The spikes of beetberries are good in flower arrangements, too; when used fresh, the berries stay intact." She noted that other seed heads for arrangements include those of orach (both fresh and dried), pop-

pies, elephant garlic, and leeks. "Sometimes," Jan concluded, "our modern gardens can seem sterile and one-dimensional in comparison."

Jan mentioned, too, that it is not just heirloom vegetable varieties that are endangered, but old, open-pollinated flower varieties as well. Feeling, as I do, that vegetables and flowers belong together, Jan therefore had completed the vegetable-garden design with heirloom varieties of flowers. Old varieties of red dianthus surrounded the ruby chard, and the borage and bergamot (or bee balm) were included, too, because their flowers are edible as well as beautiful. While I was there, the butterflies' favorite, 'Clary' sage, was in full bloom, its soft pink flow in evidence all over the garden. Hollyhocks were in bloom—the graceful single white ones called 'Tomb of Jesus'— as was another old-timer, 'Love Lies Bleeding' amaranth, with its long, pink-chenille tassels. The flowers softened the look of the vegetable beds and to the untrained eye made the garden appear to be a lovely frontyard cottage garden.

What a treat it was to experience this rich garden. I took my time photographing, and my visit with

The ingredients of an heirloom stir-fry from Jan Blum's garden: 'Blue Podded' peas, 'Giant' chives, beet-berries (in the bowl), carrots, serpent garlic, 'Ragged Jack' kale, and green orach.

Jan stretched out to a delicious five days—delicious largely because we ate primarily from the garden. The heirloom stir-fry and succulent beerocks Jan prepared were particularly enjoyable, I thought. I left with the gentle satisfaction that the many old heirlooms Jan had chosen were in very good hands indeed.

The Pliny Freeman Garden

I went to Old Sturbridge Village, an outdoor museum of living history interpreting life in New England during the fifty years after the Revolution, on a classic Massachusetts autumn day. By happy accident, I met Christie White, the Training Interpreter for Horticulture at the village, as she was dodging the mud puddles, clad in her brogans and bonnet. I was just leaving the cider mill in Old Sturbridge Village and someone pointed her out as the right person to talk with, the one who oversaw the vegetable gardens and brought the colonial experience to visitors. I introduced myself, and within seconds we were comparing notes on Indian flint corn and old 'Case Knife' beans. It was soon obvious to me that Christie was well on her way to fulfilling her professional goal: to see that the vegetable gardens of the village were filled with the same varieties that were grown in the 1830s. Thus, the gardens would be as true to the spirit of this New England village as the saltbox houses already were.

Christie's vast experience with heirlooms made her the obvious choice as my prime resource for information on heirloom gardening in a historical context. When I interviewed her at Old Sturbridge Village, I found her perspective on these vegetables and their growers to be quite different from that of most heirloom gardeners I've known. Other gardeners grow heirlooms for their taste or to preserve endangered seeds, but Christie's main interest is the larger historical settings of the heirlooms. Christie is also fascinated by the lives of the gardeners who had once tilled the soil around the village's homes. The extent of her absorption didn't really become clear, though, until I began transcribing my notes and noticed her consistent, eerie use of present-tense verbs to refer to things that had happened 150 years ago.

Christie led me to a garden that once belonged to a middle-class farmer by the name of Pliny Freeman. As was typical of the times, Mr. Freeman had a kitchen garden adjacent to his house in addition to the farm that provided grain, meat, and cider for the family. The kitchen garden, which covers about a quarter of an acre, would have been tended by his wife and children.

The soil in the Freeman garden is sandy and slightly acidic. Christie has it maintained as closely as possible to the way it was cared for by the Freeman family. It is dressed with manure and wood ashes. The crops are rotated annually, and the varieties of vegetables grown, except for the cucumbers, are relatively carefree, thus making them a good choice for modern New England gardeners. Christie obtained most of the seeds for the Freeman garden from DeGiorgi Company and Wyatt-Quarles.

Here's what Christie explained to me about gardening as an exercise in history: "When we plan the gardens at the village, we allot certain portions of the garden based on what we think the people emphasized in their diet, so that much of the garden space is given over to vegetables that store well—carrots, beets, and turnips, for instance. There is a generous planting of beans and peas, too, because they were traditional in the diet of the time. We have receipts [recipes] for them, primarily for winter use. In contrast, less space is given to lettuce, for example. A farmer like Mr. Freeman grew only one type of lettuce—cos, a romaine type—and a mustard, but he supplemented these greens with easily gathered wild dandelions. As was customary, wild greens supplemented the few greens people grew in their gardens. Summer squash is grown at the Freeman house, and we don't preserve that in any way; but we might have three hills of summer squash to seven or eight hills of winter squash of various types, and pumpkins are grown right in with the field corn for winter vegetable use.

"In the Freeman garden, some vegetables interest our visitors because they're unfamiliar. In particular, we grow a cushaw, a good winter-keeping squash, actually closely related to the pumpkin. It's a very large, dramatic, gourd-shaped squash that's pale green in color with darker green stripes. It has orange flesh that is very like pumpkin in flavor.

"The beets and carrots look like modern ones, but what fall visitors often notice is that the 'Early Blood-Red Turnip Beet' and the 'Long Orange' carrot are generally much bigger and much more variable in size and shape than supermarket varieties. These large beet varieties grow to four or five inches across without becoming woody or unpleasant and

The Pliny Freeman garden at Old Sturbridge Village in Sturbridge, Massachusetts.

dry, because they were beets not only designed to be eaten fresh, but also to be stored in the root cellar. The root vegetables really have to attain a certain minimum size before they'll store well. Small, very thin carrots and tiny beets tend to shrivel and wither in storage.

"We grow cabbages with storage in mind. 'Late Flat Dutch' and 'Drum Head' cabbage both form very firm, tight heads. We store them by hanging them upside down in a root cellar or we bury them in an outside pit, or grave, as it was sometimes called.

"We also grow peas in the Freeman garden. Peas are an example of a vegetable that has been modified so much in recent years that it's very hard to obtain authentic varieties dating back as far as the 1830s. We did obtain an old variety called 'Early Alaska', but for our tall-growing peas, until recently we have had to grow a variety called 'Tall Telephone'.

Obviously, with a name like 'Telephone', this pea doesn't go back to 1830, but it does resemble a variety that was grown at the time. 'Tall Telephone' requires staking on pea brush—dead prunings of shrubs or trees—which was the traditional way, and is still a very fine way, to stake and support peas.

"We also grow parsnips. I was raised on parsnips, and I'm always surprised by people who are unfamiliar with them. Most of the children who visit us have never even heard of them. But parsnips were very common in the 1830s. They are still enjoyed by the English and are prepared in a number of different ways. They store so well that we can leave them, as many people did, in garden rows over the winter and dig them up in March for a very sweet, delicious vegetable.

"Our bean, which we grow primarily for use as a shell bean, is the 'True Cranberry'. The shelled bean is as red as a cranberry. People visiting us aren't familiar with the traditional practice of leaving pole beans on the vine to mature in the pod for threshing, shelling out, and use as a dry bean. Accustomed only to eating beans fresh, they're often critical of our pole beans when they see them overmature. It's very common to hear a visitor comment, 'You should have picked your beans two weeks ago.' Then we have to explain that people in the 1830s, if they were growing a bean primarily for storage, would pick some of those beans in the very young, tender stage for immediate cooking, but would leave most of the crop in the garden to mature for threshing so they could have beans over the winter.

"In addition to the vegetables, there are a few culinary herbs growing in the Freeman garden: horseradish, sage, basil, parsley, marjoram, chives, mint, dill, and summer savory. Some were eaten fresh and others were dried. Unusual for today's garden are the hops that were grown to make a yeast culture.

"Many of our visitors remark on how their own gardens differ from those generally grown in the last century. The modern garden is designed for fresh eating in the summer, and if the time, space, and surplus vegetables are available, the gardener will put aside some things for winter. In the nineteenth century, the family garden was grown primarily for a year-round supply of vegetables; the fresh vegetables and greens of the summer months were a bonus to enjoy."

You can visit Old Sturbridge Village and see the Freeman garden and the other historical vegetable, flower, and herb gardens there. They are planted and interpreted to the public every year. Christie is doing more behind-the-scenes work these days, but with a little luck, you might run into her. For my part, I'd visited Old Sturbridge Village many times before, but I came away this time with a valuable new perspective on the heirloom vegetables I had long enjoyed. I felt as if an important piece of a fascinating puzzle had slipped smoothly into place.

The Sands Heirloom Garden

In talking with Kevin Sands, whose garden in Decorah, Iowa, emphasizes the seed-saving aspect of heirloom gardening, I couldn't help thinking about the many ways in which gardening can enrich your life. A few years before our conversation, Kevin, already a dedicated gardener, read in a national gardening magazine about Kent Whealy and the Seed Savers Exchange in Decorah. Realizing that they were practically neighbors, he went to visit Kent's preservation garden—where Kent preserves as many thousands of varieties of open-pollinated heirloom vegetables as possible—and now Kevin's garden is filled with heirloom varieties too. "Growing my garden was always rewarding," he told me, "but locating and growing heirloom vegetables gave it one more dimension. Now I delight in visiting Kent's garden and comparing tomatoes, or poring over the Seed Savers Exchange yearbook and picking out my vegetables variety by variety. When I find one that sounds like it would do well in my area, I explore further. For instance, if I can find an old tomato variety like 'Brandywine'—for years the choice of a tomato collector I've heard about—that makes it interesting. A pole bean like black-seeded 'Kentucky Wonder', famous a hundred years ago in the Cincinnati area, adds another dimension, and the beans even seem to taste better."

When I asked Kevin, a family-practice doctor, how he started gardening, he chuckled and answered, "Well, I used to dread gardening because I remembered having to pick beans when I was little, so I avoided it for twenty years. But seven or eight years ago I started with a few tomato plants and such, and currently I have twenty raised beds full of vegetables."

Now Kevin's passion for heirloom vegetables permeates his life. Last year, one antique variety of miniature pumpkin, responding to his wonderful loamy soil, produced a large harvest of little fluted pumpkins. Inspired by the bounty, Kevin made his daughter a stand in the front yard to sell them, and swarms of neighborhood children soon appeared. Neighboring gardeners, also inspired, ask for seeds whenever they see some of his vegetables, and at potluck suppers he gains new adherents to seed preservation when he brings his unusual 'Moon and Stars' watermelon, covered with a yellow "moon" and a sprinkling of "stars" (also grown by Jan Blum, as noted in "The Blum Heirloom Garden," earlier). "The melon's certainly a conversation stopper," he says, "but even more, once people taste it, they become converts."

I couldn't help feeling envious of Kevin when he explained how he chooses the vegetables he grows

Kevin Sands's garden in Decorah, Iowa. Heirlooms include, in the foreground, 'Early Jersey Wakefield' cabbages and 'De Cicco' broccoli. In the back beds are 'Large Greasy Lake' beans, herbs, and 'Howling Mob' corn.

from season to season. Can you imagine being able to walk, as Kevin does, through Kent Whealy's Seed Savers garden, with its thousands of varieties of vegetables, to see what grows well in your area and what looks and tastes good? Think of taking home a selection of onions or peppers to cook and test, or, if you're a historian, selecting from varieties that were carried westward on Conestoga wagons or that even came over on the *Mayflower*. Said Kevin, "We have great spring growing conditions here in Iowa, so I start early and go over to taste lettuces, carrots, and peas in their prime. Then, one day in the summer, I'll go over again to sample tomatoes and peppers, and again to check out a few melons that are at their peak. Kent is generous with his information and, of course, with seeds too."

I asked Kevin to tell me about the varieties he settled on for his summer garden. He started with the 'Gnuttle' bean he had gotten from Don Zubler, a member of the Seed Savers Exchange from Kansas. "Along with the beans," Kevin said, "Don sent a letter detailing their entire history. They are considered to be an Amish variety, he said, and he thought they were brought West in pioneer times. 'Gnuttle' is a cut-short bean, which means that the beans inside the pod are jammed so close together that they become oblong. The pods have small strings on them, but pulling them off is easy to do while you're picking the beans. These are delightful beans that taste very good. Don's health is failing and he doesn't feel that he's going to garden any longer, so my growing the 'Gnuttle' means a lot to him. His mother grew it, and her ancestors before her, and that simply makes it very important that I keep it going. I guess, too, that the bean represents a little piece of immortality for him."

Kevin went on to talk about a type of lettuce called 'Mescher' bibb that he had just grown out for the first time. This variety, another heirloom with a silken thread to the past, has a heart that's about eight inches across. The lettuce is hardy and tasty. Kevin had obtained the seeds from the Seed Savers Exchange, which in turn had received them from Mrs. Mescher, an eighty-six-year-old retired schoolteacher. She had grown 'Mescher' and saved seed from it in her garden since 1909. And Mrs. Mescher had obtained the seed from a neighbor, Granny Wallace, who had received it from her grandmother in 1849. Grandma, in turn, had kept it from the late 1700s.

Other vegetables Kevin was growing for the first time included an Oriental fluted pumpkin he obtained from a woman from Laos. This pumpkin was particularly valuable because its woody stem seemed resistant to squash borers. Another was a yellow German fingerling potato from a seed saver in Rochester, Minnesota. "Rochester is only a little bit north of here," said Kevin. "I usually try to trade seeds with people who live fairly close; that way the vegetables most often do well, because they come from the same climate."

There were other heirlooms in Kevin's garden: 'Amish' beet, 'Bronze Arrowhead' lettuce, 'De Cicco' broccoli, 'Dominant' cauliflower, 'Early Jersey Wakefield' cabbages, 'Howling Mob' corn, and 'Wren's Egg', 'Mayflower', and 'Large Greasy Lake' beans. Kevin had obtained many of these seeds through the Seed Savers Exchange and was planning on trading seeds from the harvest to other members. But many of the unusual varieties he has grown are available to the gardening public through specialty seed companies. Two seed companies that carry most of the varieties Kevin has grown are Seeds Blum and Southern Exposure Seed Exchange.

Kevin is always giving thought to next year's garden and, when I spoke with him, had recently visited Kent and decided on two more varieties: a tasty yellow plum tomato and a 'Cream of Saskatchewan' watermelon (called cream because its flesh is nearly white). Kevin had also chosen 'Aunt Mary's' sweet corn from the many varieties Kent had grown that year.

"But I'm trying to hold myself back and to go rather slowly," he told me. "It would be easy to write to a hundred different people in the Seed Savers Exchange and get a hundred different varieties, but I could easily get lost in trying to save the seeds. Each vegetable requires different techniques, and I'm just learning. This year, for example, I waited too long for my lettuce seeds to ripen, so I didn't really get good seeds. Fortunately I hadn't planted all the seeds of any of my varieties, including the lettuce, so I'll be able to plant it again next spring, and then I'll know when to go after the seeds. This past year, I learned how to keep my corn from cross-pollinating, and how to keep the squashes isolated."

Growing the garden and enjoying the harvest obviously give Kevin delight, but tracking down interesting old varieties and keeping them going seem even more rewarding to him. I can just see him in the winter, with the temperature at ten below zero, planning next year's garden and perusing the Seed Savers Exchange yearbook. He sums up his increasing involvement when he says, "All in all, picking a tomato from a big-name catalog just doesn't suit me much any more."

Recommended Heirloom Vegetables

In this section I cover heirloom varieties not covered elsewhere in the book that have features that make them special. The numbers in parentheses following variety names correspond to the numbers of the seed companies in "Sources" where the varieties are available. For varieties carried by most of the sources, no number is given. Regarding cooking, most of these vegetables are prepared in a way similar to cooking methods for modern vegetables, but there are a few exceptions covered in the cooking section of this chapter. This list represents only the beginning of an adventure in heirloom vegetables. For information about open-pollinated varieties, most of which are heirlooms, obtain a copy of *The Garden Seed Inventory*, edited by Kent Whealy; it details nearly 6000 varieties and their sources.

BEANS　The 'Kentucky Wonder' (also called 'Old Homestead') pole bean has been one of the most popular varieties since the mid-1800s. It is still one of the tastiest and prolific bean varieties available. The plants are rust resistant. A historical note: the 'Case Knife' (4) pole bean is one of the oldest commercial varieties of string beans grown in the United States. 'Stringless Black Valentine' (3, 5, 8, 9) is a bush string bean that withstands cooler spring temperatures than most bean varieties. 'Tongue of Fire' (1, 4) and 'Wren's Egg' (3, 8) are superior horticultural-type beans, excellent for shelling. 'King of the Garden' and 'Christmas' are large-seeded pole limas with a great nutty taste. For heirloom dry bean varieties, see the "Baked Bean Gardens" and "Native American Gardens" chapters. See the "Italian Gardens" chapter for Italian varieties and the "French Gardens" chapter for French varieties.

BEETS　'Winter Keeper' (1, 10) is a large-rooted variety. It stores well in the root cellar and is wonderful for roasting in the coals. 'Crosby Egyptian' is the early beet of choice. It has a rather flattened shape

Tomatoes come in a tremendous range of colors and shapes. These heirloom tomatoes were harvested from the Seed Savers garden run by Kent Whealy in Decorah, Iowa.

and can be planted and harvested earlier than most other varieties.

BROCCOLI   The older varieties are not as uniform as modern ones, and instead of producing picture-perfect heads all in a few weeks, they put out small heads over a few months. This irregular maturing is what Jan Blum, owner of Seeds Blum, calls gentle diversity. Good varieties are 'De Cicco' (4), a green broccoli, and 'Purple Sprouting' (1, 2, 10), a purple heading type. Both are sprouting types that produce one medium-size head and many small offshoots with heads only a few inches across.

CABBAGES   'Early Jersey Wakefield' is a very popular conical-shaped variety from the early 1800s. It is resistant to the disease called yellows. 'Early Flat Dutch' (3, 5, 9), also called 'Stein's Drumhead', is a foot across, flat on top, and 10 to 12 pounds at maturity. Its dense, fine flesh is terrific for sauerkraut, and the plant tolerates heat fairly well.

CARROTS   'White Belgium' (8), an old variety that is completely white, inside and out, can become too strong-flavored in warm weather, but it's tasty in cool weather. 'Oxheart' (3, 8) is a dense-textured, short, stubby carrot with good flavor. It can grow to a pound in weight and stores well in a root cellar.

CORN   For some old-fashioned eating, try 'Aunt Mary's' (8) and 'Shoe Peg', also called 'Country Gentleman'. The taste of these corns is not just sweet but "corny" as well. The kernels on 'Shoe Peg' grow every which way on the cob and are long, thin, and a little crunchy. The plant is resistant to Stewart's wilt. For great popcorn, try 'Strawberry', a beautiful miniature ear. See the "Native American Gardens" chapter for flour and hominy corn varieties.

LETTUCE   'Oakleaf' is a noble lettuce that gives tender, oak-leaf-shaped leaves throughout the spring and again in fall. 'Tom Thumb' (3, 6, 8, 9) was a popular Victorian restaurant variety. It produces very small tender bibb-type heads. 'Bronze Arrowhead' (8) is like a red 'Oakleaf', vigorous and good for fall gardens.

MELONS   'Jenny Lind' (6, 8) is a flavorful small melon, which, according to Pinetree Garden Seeds, produces fairly sweet, turbaned melons under less than ideal melon-growing conditions. 'Moon and Stars' (8, 9) is a unique watermelon discussed earlier in this chapter.

ONIONS   Using multiplier onions is a wonderful way to grow onions. Try 'Yellow Potato Onion' (8, 9), the most common and largest form, which is also quite drought tolerant. 'Red Potato Onion' (9) is a red-brown multiplier onion that has purplish leaves when young. (See the Part Four Encyclopedia for more information on potato onions.)

ORACH   This is a midsummer spinach substitute. For colorful salad greens, try 'Red Orach' (1, 8).

PEPPERS   Try 'Permagreen' (8), a dark-green to almost black sweet pepper. 'Sweet Bullnose' (1) is one of the earliest green bell peppers. 'Hungarian Paprika' (9) is an authentic old Hungarian paprika variety good for drying and grinding. All three peppers have excellent flavor.

POTATOES   Some of the old potato varieties you might want to try are 'Yellow Finn' (8) and 'Bintje' (8)—both waxy, yellow, rich-fleshed varieties and 'All Blue' (8) for the novelty of blue-fleshed potatoes.

PUMPKINS   'Rouge Vif D'Etampes' (8) is fluted, squat, and red-orange. This medium-size pumpkin is a good producer and a tasty variety. 'Connecticut Field' (3) has been the standard Jack-O'-Lantern variety since the 1700s.

TOMATOES   Some of the old varieties of tomatoes still have the great flavor you might remember from years ago. Try 'Oxheart' (5, 8), a late, very large, tasty tomato. 'Brandywine' (5, 8, 9), an old Amish variety, has potatolike foliage. 'Mortgage Lifter' (5, 9) is a very large, red-pink variety from West Virginia. For a great paste tomato, try 'Super Italian Paste' (8). 'Bonny Best' is another of the old-timers known for good flavor; as with most of the heirloom tomatoes, its fruits are variable in size and shape. For the largest selection of old tomato varieties, see the Long Island Seed and Plant catalog. For some unusual-colored heirloom tomatoes, see the "Rainbow Gardens" chapter.

TURNIPS   For a turnip with that old-time flavor and good keeping quality, try 'Purple Top White Globe'. For a yellow one, try 'Golden Ball' (1, 3).

Poppy seeds are a long-time favorite ingredient in the breads and pastries of Middle Europe. The bread-seed poppies make beautiful additions to a flower border as they will bloom most of the summer; their decorative seed heads are handsome in dried arrangements; and the seeds themselves are tasty on breads, bagels, and pastries. These poppies and seeds come from Jan Blum's garden.

Cooking from the Heirloom Garden

With a few exceptions, most heirloom varieties of corn, tomatoes, beans, etc., can be cooked in the same ways modern varieties are. But the exceptions are worth noting—for example, some old varieties of snap beans need stringing, and some peas are intended for drying and soup making, not for eating fresh. Many of the old ways of cooking these vegetables can enrich your table fare, but you will need some guidance.

To give you an idea of how our ancestors prepared these old vegetables and to gather some of their recipes, I contacted Debra Friedman, Lead Cooking Interpreter at Old Sturbridge Village in Sturbridge, Massachusetts. (See the profile of Debra for an overview of how early Americans—from the 1780s through the 1830s—prepared vegetables, and see the old-time recipes she collected, presented later in this chapter.) What follows is a list of some basic vegetables and ways to prepare them, as well as some historical notes on them from Debra. You might be appalled, as I was, at how long most vegetables were cooked in the old days, and you will probably choose not to follow this aspect of colonial cooking.

BEANS   Most of the old varieties of green beans have a string down the side (hence the name string beans) that must be removed. This is easiest to do during picking. Simply break the bean pod off right under the attachment and pull down, leaving the cap and string on the vine.

Debra reports, "A lot of the old-time recipes for baked or boiled beans were very bland. Cooks then might have boiled the beans and added some butter or parsley, or baked them with pepper and salt pork with an occasional onion thrown in. But the type of baked beans with molasses, mustard, or catsup that everybody is so fond of today was yet to appear. Most of the baked beans then were a very hardy side dish served at breakfast or dinner. Green beans were eaten for only a short period, when a few of the dry beans were picked in the immature stage."

BEETS   Most of the old varieties of beets are large, dense, "keeper" types, meant to be preserved in the root cellar or pickled. These beets take a little longer to cook but are still the best for borscht, pickling, or baking. Debra recounts, "Back then, the tops were used as well as the roots. It was suggested that the tops, or greens, could be boiled for about twenty minutes, and the roots an hour and a half to three hours—clearly overcooked by our standards. Also, the beets themselves, with their fairly tough skins, could be roasted as potatoes might be—whole in the embers of the fire. This is certainly one of the all-time best ways to cook beets."

CABBAGES   The old varieties of cabbages are usually dense and rot resistant, selected to be preserved in the root cellar. This dense, fine grain makes them perfect for pickling and, of course, for making sauerkraut. See the "German Gardens" chapter for sauerkraut recipes.

Debra suggests, "Cooking advice of the time suggested that you cut the cabbage head in wedges and boil it an hour to an hour and a half—this seems a travesty to us. Quite often, the boiled wedges would be served as part of a boiled dinner. This was a very easy way of preparing dinner without having to check it periodically. Another favorite way to serve cabbage was as coleslaw or hot slaw." (See the recipes that follow for versions of these suggestions.)

CARROTS   Many of the old carrot varieties are meant for storing and are very dense and large. Enjoy them baked, steamed, or in soups and juices. Debra reports, "It was suggested that you boil young spring carrots (the thinnings) for an hour and older carrots for one to two and a half hours. This is, of course, terribly overcooked by modern standards. People were very fond of cooked carrots cold as well. In fact, people of this period probably did not eat carrots raw."

CUCUMBERS   Old cucumber varieties are not the best vegetables to grow today, since the plants are quite disease prone. Try using old cooking methods on modern cucumbers instead.

Says Debra, "Cucumbers in this era were generally served pickled, stewed with a gravy, or fried. In fact, fried cucumbers were a popular breakfast dish."

LETTUCE   Heirloom lettuce varieties are very similar to today's lettuces and are often identical. Colonists did eat lettuce raw, but most often they cooked it. Debra reports, "Lettuce was often boiled and then put into the drippings underneath meat, almost to

OPPOSITE: *For a look at our cooking heritage, visit Colonial Williamsburg in Virginia.*

Debra Friedman

After Christie White and I talked about the heirloom vegetables grown at Old Sturbridge Village, she introduced me to Debra Friedman, Lead Cooking Interpreter at the village. We found Debra serving a huge platter of roast pork, applesauce, mashed potatoes, carrots, gravy, fresh baked rolls, and Indian pudding at one of the historic houses. The recipients of the food were a few lucky interpreters, all in costume, demonstrating how residents ate in the 1830s. Imagine being hungry and watching such a feast! It was all I could do to resist snitching a freshly baked roll from the tray, but visitors to Old Sturbridge Village are not allowed to eat food prepared in the houses because of health regulations.

Months later I visited the village again to talk to Debra about what early Americans ate. Considering our heritage, it's no wonder Americans have given vegetables so little attention all these years. It would be appalling if we boiled young carrots or cabbage wedges for an hour to an hour and a half as our ancestors did.

Debra pointed out ways in which modern gardeners and cooks could learn from the old ways of cooking from the garden, however. For example, our ancestors grew their own parsnips and kept them in the ground during the winter for spring eating. "You can't beat the flavor—certainly not from the grocery store," Debra says. "You'll never get sweetness like that. And modern cooks could also enjoy some of the old recipes that call for using vegetables in different ways. Mashing turnips and potatoes together is wonderful—and so is baking beets or roasting vegetables with meat. Also, some of the old varieties hold up better in soups or stews. Today we get exotic and overlook some of these wonderful old vegetables. Sometime when you're really busy and want to fix vegetables quickly and with little preparation, try some of the old cooking methods, such as boiling a dinner or baking vegetables."

We can also learn from the way our ancestors arranged meals, particularly their manner of carrying over dishes from one meal to the next. Coleslaw, applesauce, and onion soup made for a meal one day would all be spread out the next day, even if there weren't enough of any one thing to go around. "If you had cold carrots and beef for supper one afternoon, they would be fried for breakfast or used in pies or puddings the next morning," says Debra. "Vegetables weren't considered just side dishes or eaten only for dinner, either. Though the cooking style was a lot simpler then, the diversity in each meal was rich. This meant eating a variety of foods at one meal, rather than our present-day 'nuclear' meal of just a meat, a starch, and a vegetable."

Debra continued to explain that the major meal of the day in the 1830s was served any time between noon and two, depending on the family. It consisted of boiled meat—most often beef, pork, or chicken—and three or four different boiled vegetables. The vegetables were usually mounded around the meat and served on one big pewter platter, or "charger." This platter was often the centerpiece of the meal and was surrounded by numerous other dishes: puddings, vegetable pies, breads, cheeses, and pickles. Tea, or supper, was served between five and six in the evening and often consisted of leftovers from the earlier meal.

Desserts were often fruit—either stewed or fresh—and different kinds of cakes, gelatins, and custards. Pies and puddings were entree items. In fact, pie for breakfast was very common. So was pudding for breakfast or for tea in the evening. A bowl of Indian pudding, made with cornmeal, might be the main course for the evening meal rather than a dessert, as it might be today.

Use of vegetables in early American times is not well documented because most recipe books say only how to boil them and for how long. Certainly our ancestors did not cook vegetables in many of the fancy ways that we do today. Most often vegetables were boiled, usually until they were at least fork tender, and often they were mashed. Butter—lots of butter—or occasionally lard, cream, salt, pepper, or vinegar were used as seasonings. Vegetables were also commonly roasted in meat drippings in the pan or in fire coals. Beets, carrots, turnips, potatoes, and even lettuce were cooked this way.

"Most vegetables were cooked in this era," Debra says. "Not many people ate them raw. We don't find recipes for raw vegetables, so we don't know if our ancestors ever just went out and ate a carrot or some celery from the garden. They would serve radishes raw, but not many other vegetables." Furthermore, fresh vegetables were eaten for only a few weeks during the summer; vegetables were dried or stored for the rest of the year.

"You also don't find much about what herbs our ancestors cooked with, but that's not to say they didn't use any," Debra says. "A lot of recipes say 'season to taste,' or occasionally, 'add sweet herbs,' though they don't usually say what herbs or how much to add. We know they did incorporate herbs in some dishes, particularly in different kinds of beans. Recipes say to boil beans with parsley or summer savory. But obviously not many herbs were used. I think it would depend on the cook. Instead, to add flavor to dishes, they served spices and condiments

as side dishes, or made sauces of different kinds of herbs and put them on the meat or vegetables. For instance, they use mint sauces and sage in the stuffing. They used vinegars and cucumbers—they made cucumbers into a sauce for fish.

"In early America, most vegetables were boiled, and the cooking water was generally discarded. In fact, recipes often said to use enough water to remove any bad taste and to drain the vegetables well. Vegetables like summer squash were boiled for forty-five minutes. By today's standards this would be overcooked, but our ancestors weren't aware that they were boiling the nutrition out of the vegetables.

"In fact, glorifying vegetables wasn't part of the traditional English diet they inherited. That diet consisted more of meat and starch than of vegetables, and primary sources of information emphasized vegetables much less. Old diaries and journals tell all about the different meats, desserts, and breads, but they say little about vegetables. So, in the nineteenth century, you find the same old vegetables served over and over again, with few of the varieties we have today. Stressing fresh vegetables in the diet is a very, very new idea."

Talking with Debra certainly made me aware that, like central heating and running water, vegetables fresh from the garden are a luxury of the twentieth century that I certainly wouldn't want to give up.

---

stew it. Quite often in the spring, it was stewed up together with fresh green peas."

PEAS   Many very old varieties of peas are soup peas. They are good for drying and contain less sugar than modern varieties. Debra reports, "They suggested that fresh peas be boiled a minimum of thirty minutes and older peas be boiled sixty to ninety minutes for pea soup."

RADISHES   Since radishes were an early and abundant spring crop, they were eaten raw two or three times a day. They would be soaked in salt water and sliced. The young, tender radish greens were used, too, either cooked or raw.

SQUASHES   Most old varieties of summer squash are quite similar to today's and can be used in the same ways. Debra reports, "It was suggested that summer

squash be boiled at least three-quarters of an hour. Quite often it was mashed with butter. Summer squash with a dark yellow rind was favored because it stood up to lengthy boiling."

Old winter squashes are quite similar to modern ones and are used as modern ones are. Debra notes, "Winter squashes and pumpkins were put into pies and puddings, which, of course, were side dishes for meals—they had not yet become desserts. Not until the twentieth century were pies and puddings accepted as dessert items. So you would find a squash pie or squash pudding served in addition to other vegetables, other starches, and meats."

TURNIPS   Large old varieties of turnips were used like beets, as keepers for winter eating. They are great for boiling and preparing with other root vegetables. Some of the modern varieties are small summer types, better for quick cooking or eating raw in salads as "baby" turnips. Says Debra, "Quite often, the roots were mashed. You don't find as many references to serving turnips whole or in chunks as you might find today. And, quite often, cooks of the time added cream and butter, or sometimes fat, to turnips, or even mixed mashed turnips with mashed potatoes to make what they called turnip sauce."

Following are recipes gathered by Debra Friedman from old American cookbooks to give us some idea of how our ancestors cooked. These are followed by some modern adaptations of traditional heirloom recipes. In keeping with the notion that heirloom varieties belong in the mainstream, and even on the leading edge, of modern international cooking, modern recipes incorporating some of the more unusual and colorful heirloom varieties are scattered throughout this book in the cooking sections of other chapters.

STEWED CUCUMBERS

"Peel and cut cucumbers in quarters, take out the seeds, and lay them on a cloth to drain off the water: when they are dry, flour and fry them in fresh butter; let the butter be quite hot before you put in the cucumbers; fry them till they are brown, then take them out with an egg slice spatula, and lay them on a sieve to drain the fat from them (some cooks fry sliced onions, or some small button onions, with them till they are a delicate light-brown colour, drain them from the fat, and then put them into a stew-pan with as much gravy as will cover them); stew slowly till they are tender; take out the cucumbers with a slice, thicken the gravy with flour and butter, give it a boil up, season it with pepper and salt, and put in the cucumbers; as soon as they are warm, they are ready.

"The above, rubbed through a tamis, or fine sieve, will be entitled to be called a 'cucumber sauce.'"

William Kitchiner, *The Cook's Oracle*, 1823.

Note how our language has changed since 1823. An egg slice spatula is a slotted spoon, and gravy in this context refers to stock or broth. When I cooked this recipe I found the additional butter and flour to be unnecessary for thickening this "gravy." Instead, I removed the cooked cucumbers from the pan, added some chopped lemon thyme (dill with a few drops of lemon juice would do just as well), and reduced the sauce by simmering until thickened. Very tasty.

CARROT PIE

"A very good pie may be made of carrots in the same way you make pumpkin pies. Stew and strain it through a coarse sieve. Take 2 quarts of scalded milk and eight eggs. Stir carrots into it; sweeten it with sugar or molasses. Salt it, and season with ginger, cinnamon, or to your taste. Bake with a bottom crust."

E. A. Howland, *New England Economical Housekeeper*, 1845.

As far back as colonial days, such a pie was frequently made with any type of winter squash and served either as a side dish with the rest of the meal or on its own for breakfast (my favorite). You can vary the amount of sweetener to taste, and you can also bake the pie without the crust as a custard.

This old-fashioned recipe is rather vague, so see the following contemporary pie recipe in which cooked and mashed or sieved carrots can be featured.

PUMPKIN, SQUASH, OR CARROT PIE

SERVES 6 TO 8.

1¾ cups pumpkin (see below), squash, or
    carrot puree
½ cup honey or ¾ cup white or brown sugar
1 cup milk, cream, or evaporated milk (use 1½
    cups if not using honey)
1 teaspoon cinnamon
½ teaspoon ginger
¼ teaspoon nutmeg
⅛ teaspoon allspice or cloves
3 eggs
Unbaked 9-inch pie shell

Preheat oven to 425°.

Place all ingredients in a blender and blend. (You may have to do this in 2 batches, depending on capacity of blender. If so, mix batches before pouring into pie shell.) Pour into pie shell. Bake at 425° for 15 minutes, then reduce temperature to 350° and bake 45 minutes longer or until set. Let cool at least 30 minutes before serving.

To make your own pumpkin puree: Preheat oven to 350°. For best results, use a "sugar" pumpkin or another variety bred for eating, not a Jack-O'-Lantern type. Cut in half, remove seeds and strings (save seeds for toasting), and place cut side down on a cookie sheet. Bake until very soft, 1 hour or longer.

Let cool, remove skin and any coarse fibers, and puree flesh in a blender, food processor, or food mill. One small to medium pumpkin makes about 1 quart of puree.

COLD SLAW

"Select the hardest, firmest head of cabbage. Cut it in two, and shave it as fine as possible. A cabbage cutter is the best. It must be done evenly and nicely. Lay it in a nice deep dish. Melt together vinegar, a small piece of butter, pepper, a little salt. Let it scald and pour over it."

L. G. Abell, *The Skillful Housewife's Book,* 1846.

HOT SLAW

"This is made in the same manner [as cold slaw], except it is laid in a sauce pan with the dressing, and just scalded, but not boiled. Send it to the table hot."

L. G. Abell, *The Skilled Housewife's Book,* 1846.

For a modern version of hot slaw, try the following:

SERVES 6 TO 8.

1 medium head cabbage, finely shredded
¼ cup each butter and cider vinegar
½ teaspoon pepper

Put all ingredients in a large frying pan or wok on medium heat. Cover and cook about 5 minutes, stirring frequently.

Variation: Add 1 tablespoon finely chopped tarragon, dill, or other garden herbs and ¼ to ½ cup finely chopped or shredded carrots, green beans, and/or peas, 1 teaspoon mustard seed, and 1 teaspoon sugar or ¼ cup apple juice. Then cook as above.

RADISH PODS

"Gather them in sprigs or bunches, young and tender and letting them stand in salt and water three days; then pickle like cucumbers."

L. G. Abell, *The Skillful Housewife's Book,* 1846.

FRICASSEE OF PARSNIPS

"Boil in milk till they are soft, then cut them lengthways into bits two or three inches long; and simmer

in a white sauce, made of two spoonsful of broth, a bit of mace, half a cupful of cream, a bit of butter and some flour, pepper and salt."

Silas Andrus, *The Experienced American Housekeeper,* 1829.

TURNIP PUREE

John Downey, chef and owner of Downey's in Santa Barbara, California, offers this way of preparing a vegetable that he believes deserves much more credit than it usually receives. Delicious!

SERVES 6.

¼ cup butter
2 tablespoons water
5 pounds turnips, well peeled and sliced
Salt and white pepper to taste
1 cup heavy cream

Place butter with 2 tablespoons water in a thick-bottomed pot with a tight-fitting lid. Add turnips and a little salt and white pepper. Cook over lowest heat, stirring occasionally, for 1 to 1½ hours, until the turnips become very mushy. Remove lid and allow water to evaporate, but be careful not to burn. When fairly dry, remove from heat and cool. Pass through a food mill or meat grinder. (A food processor is okay, but may leave lumps.) If juicy, drain puree in a conical strainer, saving the juice. Combine juice with cream in a saucepan and reduce over medium heat until thick. Add turnip puree to cream and warm through; check seasoning and serve.

ROAST PARSNIPS

John Downey provides this recipe as well, noting that the dish is an old holiday favorite in England, popular with roast turkey but good with roast pork or beef too.

SERVES 6.

6 medium parsnips
4 tablespoons meat drippings (turkey, pork, or
*   beef) or butter*

Preheat oven to 400.

Peel parsnips and cut into pieces approximately 3 by ¾ inches. Blanch these in a pot of boiling water for 1 minute. Drain well and spread out to cool and dry. Heat an ovenproof skillet, add fat, let get very hot, then add parsnips and sauté for a few minutes over high heat. Place in oven to finish cooking—about 30 minutes. Drain and serve. Alternately, roast parsnips right in the meat pan after blanching. They will be tastier but will hold more fat.

BEEROCKS

Many of our "heirloom" recipes came from English kitchens, but our early American heritage draws from other nationalities as well. This old family recipe from Jan Blum's Grandma Bender originated in Germany. These days, Jan uses a vegetarian filling instead of meat. As you may notice, beerocks are very similar to Russian piroshkis.

SERVES 16 AS SIDE DISH OR 8 AS MAIN COURSE.

1 pound ground beef
2 large onions, chopped
¼ cup oil
1 large head cabbage, loosely shredded

A few leaves of kale or other leafy green
  (optional)
Salt and pepper to taste
Bread or pizza dough, using about 8 cups
  flour and raised once (or substitute frozen
  bread dough or 2 packages hot roll mix,
  raised once)

Preheat oven to 450°.

In a large skillet, brown meat and onions in oil. Add cabbage (and other greens if using), salt, and pepper and steam (with lid on) until crisp-tender. Skillet will be very full at the beginning but cabbage will shrink during cooking. Do not overcook. Remove lid as soon as cabbage is wilted or mixture will become too "juicy."

After dough has risen, roll out as thinly as possible on a floured board to make a rectangle and cut into 8-inch squares. Spoon filling into centers of squares, being careful not to get any oil on dough edges. Join 4 corners of each square in center and pinch each seam closed to make an envelope. Place

Making beerocks with cabbage, 'Ragged Jack' kale, potatoes, poppy seeds, and potato onions.

beerocks on an oiled cookie sheet; then turn seam side down to oil both sides. Bake about 15 to 20 minutes until nicely browned. Serve immediately. Good with mustard.

NEW ENGLAND BOILED DINNER

This is one of my favorite cold-winter-night dinners. I have enjoyed it since I was a child. And it's wonderful, too, cooked up in hash the next day.

SERVES 8 TO 10.

> *3 to 4 pounds corned beef*
> *2 tablespoons pickling spice in cheesecloth bag*
> OR *6 whole cloves, 4 whole allspice, ½*
> *teaspoon peppercorns, 1 tablespoon*
> *mustard seeds, and 2 bay leaves in*
> *cheesecloth bag*
> *5 to 6 medium potatoes, quartered*
> *5 to 6 medium carrots, cut in chunks*
> *2 large onions, thickly sliced*
> *4 turnips and/or 4 golden beets, peeled and*
> *quartered (optional)*
> *1 medium head cabbage, cut in 6 or 8 wedges*

Glaze

> *¼ teaspoon ginger or cloves*
> *⅓ cup Dijon mustard*
> *2 tablespoons brown sugar*
> *2 tablespoons oil*

Preheat oven to 350°.

Put meat in a large kettle or Dutch oven and add water to cover. Boil for ½ hour; pour off water and discard. Add fresh boiling water to cover meat, add spices, and simmer 1 hour per pound of meat (minus first ½ hour) or until fork tender. Remove meat to an 8-inch cake pan, fat side up. Add potatoes, carrots, and onions (and optional vegetables, if desired) to kettle, cover, and boil for 15 minutes. Place cabbage on top of other vegetables and cook 10 minutes longer or until tender. While vegetables are cooking, make glaze by mixing spices with mustard and brown sugar. Slowly beat in oil. Paint meat with glaze and bake for 15 to 20 minutes. Place meat on a large serving platter and surround with vegetables. (Discard cooking water and spices.) Cut meat across grain. If desired, serve with horseradish and/ or pickles.

RED-FLANNEL HASH

This hash is a New England tradition. Leftover corned beef like that above was often served as hash the next day.

SERVES 4.

> *2 to 4 tablespoons oil*
> *1 cup chopped corned beef*
> *2 cups diced boiled potatoes*
> *2 large beets, cooked and chopped*
> *Salt and pepper to taste*

In a large frying pan, heat oil over medium heat. Combine beef, potatoes, and beets, and spread mixture in pan. Cook slowly until a nice brown crust forms on the bottom. Turn out onto a plate and serve with fried eggs for breakfast or with a salad for supper.

BRUSSELS SPROUTS WITH CREAM AND NUTS

Brussels sprouts were one of the many vegetables that Thomas Jefferson introduced to America, and they quickly gained popularity. Be careful not to overcook them; they are wonderful combined with whatever kind of nuts grow in your area.

SERVES 6.

> *½ to 1 cup walnuts, hazelnuts, or roasted and*
> *peeled chestnuts*
> *1½ pounds (about 6 cups) Brussels sprouts*
> *2 tablespoons butter*
> *¾ cup heavy cream (or substitute light cream)*
> *Salt, pepper, and nutmeg to taste*

If using walnuts or hazelnuts, first roast in a medium oven until fragrant but not brown. Rub skins off hazelnuts. Chop nuts coarsely. Wash sprouts thoroughly and cut a small X in the bottom of each for even cooking. Bring about 3 cups water to a boil, add sprouts, and cook 5 to 10 minutes, until barely tender. In medium skillet, sauté drained sprouts in butter for about 3 minutes. Add cream, nuts, and seasoning, and simmer, stirring, for 3 minutes.

BAKED BEETS

In days of old, the large keeper beets, which were a winter staple, were slowly roasted over coals, a process that intensified their flavor and natural sweetness. Baking is still the best cooking technique for beets. If you've never tried it and you're a beet lover, you'll be pleased with the results.

Preheat oven to 300°. Scrub and trim fresh beets but leave whole. Place in a casserole or baking dish and cover tightly. Bake for 1 hour or more, depending on size of beets, until just tender. Peel, if desired, and slice. Serve hot.

Sources

Seed Companies

The seed companies listed below carry many heirloom and open-pollinated vegetable varieties. Most also offer seed exchanges, as does *National Gardening Magazine*, 180 Flynn Avenue, Burlington, VT 05401. Many other seed companies carry numerous heirlooms, but because heirlooms are not their specialty, you must search for them in the catalogs. Among these companies are Burpee, DeGiorgi, Henry Field's, Gurney, Harris, Hastings, J. L. Hudson, Park, Stokes, and Wyatt-Quarles. Also see the "Baked Bean Gardens," "Chili Gardens," "Oriental Gardens," "French Gardens," and "Italian Gardens" chapters for more heirloom varieties.

1. Abundant Life Seed Foundation
   P.O. Box 772
   Port Townsend, WA 98368
   This is a nursery devoted to saving heirloom seeds. Membership $6.00 to $10.00, depending on ability to pay.

2. Bountiful Gardens
   Ecology Action
   5798 Ridgewood Road
   Willits, CA 95490
   This firm carries quite a few organically grown open-pollinated vegetable varieties. Many are European varieties. Catalog: $1.00.

3. Good Seed
   P.O. Box 702
   Tonasket, WA 98855
   Good Seed offers a nice selection of heirloom beans, corn, tomatoes, and other vegetables. It also provides the dates of many of the variety introductions. The company is willing to swap with customers for varieties it doesn't have.

4. Johnny's Selected Seeds
   Foss Hill Road
   Albion, ME 04910
   Johnny's sells seeds of many open-pollinated vegetables, particularly those that do well in northern climates.

5. Long Island Seed and Plant
   P.O. Box 1285
   Riverhead, NY 11901
   This organization carries only open-pollinated varieties and is devoted to genetic diversity. It carries nearly 100 varieties of tomatoes.

6. Pinetree Garden Seeds
   New Gloucester, ME 04260
   This seed company is interested in offering inexpensive seeds to the public. It carries a number of open-pollinated varieties.

7. Redwood City Seed Company
   P.O. Box 361
   Redwood City, CA 94064
   This firm carries a very large selection of open-pollinated heirloom vegetables and the seeds of many fruit trees. It also produces a brochure that gives information on heirloom seeds. Catalog: $1.00.

8. Seeds Blum
   Idaho City Stage
   Boise, ID 83706
   Jan Blum raises her own seed for many of the old varieties being dropped by larger seed companies. She also runs a seed exchange. Catalog: $2.00.

9. Southern Exposure Seed Exchange
   P.O. Box 158
   North Garden, VA 22959
   This nursery carries seeds for the mid-Atlantic region and includes many heirlooms in its offerings. Catalog: $3.00.

10. Territorial Seed Company
    P.O. Box 27
    Lorane, OR 97451
    This seed company specializes in seeds for the Northwest. It carries many open-pollinated seed varieties.

Seed Exchanges

A saved seed should be a shared seed. Help spread the wealth by joining a seed exchange. And help spread the word—the more people who save and trade their seeds, the more varieties we will all have to grow and enjoy.

Native Seeds Search
3950 West New York Drive
Tucson, AZ 85745

This organization is devoted to seeking out and perpetuating seeds of native southwestern crop plants and their wild relatives. The ten-dollar yearly membership includes a newsletter. A price list is available to nonmembers for one dollar.

Seed Savers Exchange
Kent Whealy, Director
P.O. Box 70
Decorah, IA 52101

This is the place to start if you are interested in seed saving. Join Kent and hundreds of others in this organization; membership is twelve dollars in the United States and sixteen dollars in Canada. Membership brings you a directory of names of other seed savers and what they want to trade plus information on seed saving. The directory is probably the most exciting seed catalog you will ever see. However, don't order seeds unless you are dedicated to growing and preserving these heirlooms. To receive a two-page information letter detailing the projects and publications of the Seed Savers Exchange, send a stamped, self-addressed envelope to the above address.

Demonstration Gardens

Many historic gardens grow heirloom vegetables and are interesting to visit. In addition to those named below, a list of others is available from the Association of Living Historical Farms and Museums, % The Smithsonian, Washington, D.C. 20560.

Genesee Country Museum
P.O. Box 1819
Rochester, NY 14603

This demonstration garden is one of the most active and helps gardeners new to heirloom gardening.

Monticello
Box 316
Charlottesville, VA 22902

Researchers are working hard at reinstituting the vegetable garden at Monticello to reflect the era as well as the genius of one of our nation's most inspired gardeners, Thomas Jefferson. Visitors are welcome to the garden.

Books

Bubel, Nancy. *The New Seed Starter's Handbook.* Emmaus, Pa.: Rodale Press, 1988.

This book contains basic information on how to start most plants from seed as well as valuable botanical information on how to select and save your own seed. The book is a must for seed savers.

Jabs, Carolyn. *The Heirloom Gardener.* San Francisco: Sierra Club Books, 1984.

This is the definitive book on heirloom gardening. It covers the history of seed saving and gives sources of seed as well as information on how to save your own seeds.

Jeavons, John, and Robin Leler. *The Seed Finder.* Berkeley: Ten Speed Press, 1983.

This detailed guide tells where to find many of the old-time varieties.

Mooney, Pat Roy. *Seeds of the Earth.* Ottawa: Inter Pares, 1979.

This book takes a global view on the shrinking gene pool of edible plants. Mooney examines the corporate ownership of seeds and asks whether they should be a private or public resource.

The Second Graham Center. *Seed and Nursery Directory.* Pittsboro, N.C.: The Second Graham Center, n.d.

A valuable catalog of seed companies that carry open-pollinated varieties of seed. Catalog: $2.00, % Rural Advancement Fund, P.O. Box 1029, Pittsboro, N.C.

Vilmorin-Andrieux, M. M. *The Vegetable Garden.* Berkeley: Ten Speed Press, 1981.

This is a marvelous reprint of a classic first published in 1885. It contains descriptions of and growing instructions for hundreds of old varieties. I counted fifty-five pages on peas alone.

Whealy, Kent, editor. *The Garden Seed Inventory.* Decorah, Iowa: Kent Whealy, 1986.

This book is a must for all gardeners interested in seed saving. It is actually a computer inventory of all the known, nonhybrid vegetable seeds now being offered by seed companies. Vegetable variety names and all the known sources of seed are included.

Baked Bean Gardens

I HAD NEVER EATEN bean-hole beans before, but there I was in southwestern Maine driving with relatives to South Paris, home of the Oxford County Bean-Hole Bean Festival. As we drove along we passed yard after yard populated with iron deer, gnomes, bird baths, and even an occasional flamingo. This part of Maine must be the lawn-ornament capital of the world, I thought. When I commented on the great array, my brother-in-law suggested I keep an eye out for a local phenomenon: "fat fannies." Well, that got my attention, and sure enough, I soon saw one. A fat fanny is a two-dimensional plywood lawn ornament that looks like a portly woman leaning over in her garden and seen from behind. These colorful figures have painted-on calico bloomers and Raggedy Ann socks and shoes. As we approached the festival, our sightings of these cheerful decorations became increasingly frequent.

As you might have guessed, bean-hole beans are baked beans cooked in a hole in the ground, with heat supplied by heated stones or bricks. The pot of beans is placed in the hole

OPPOSITE: *A harvest of heirloom bean varieties from Jan Blum's collection. Many are excellent for baking. Starting clockwise from top right are 'Adventist' (yellow), 'Vermont Cranberry', 'Squaw' (brown and white), 'Basque' (maroon and white), 'Rattlesnake' (gray with black streaks), 'Black Beauty', and 'Hillary's Snap' (round and pink with streaks).*

and covered with sand, and the beans are left to cook very slowly. The long, slow cooking process and the slightly smoky taste make the beans a real treat. I had heard about bean-hole beans years ago from bean collector John Withee, well known in garden circles as "Mr. Bean," and now I was anxious to try them for myself.

We arrived at the fairgrounds early, before the crowds. I had an appointment to talk with the bean-master, Larry Farmer, and before the bean pots were taken out of the ground, he shared a little bean-hole lore with me.

Bean-hole beans are a holdover from New England logging days. Years ago, for a few months each spring, crews of woodsmen used to float logs down the rivers to sawmills. A front crew would go along to free any jams that occurred, and a rear crew would follow, often days behind, to refloat grounded logs. A cookee (helper cook) would be sent ahead of the whole operation to make a bean hole onshore and prepare the beans. The crews would dig up and eat the beans whenever they arrived.

Beanmaster Larry Farmer scoops up the first sample of baked beans at the annual Oxford County Bean-Hole Bean Festival in Maine.

To celebrate this tradition and to enjoy a great batch of beans, the citizens of Oxford County hold a bean-hole festival every year on the last Saturday in July. On the Wednesday before the festival, the beanmaster assembles his crew to dig the approximately eighteen bean holes. Next, the antique kettles of all different sizes are scoured, and a half-ton of pea and red kidney beans are washed and left to soak in the kettles overnight. The next day, the two-foot-deep holes are lined with bricks and filled with firewood. The fires are ignited and, in order to make the bricks hot enough, left to burn all night.

Early Friday, the crew assembles to precook the beans. They suspend the bean pots on a scaffold over the bean holes and boil the beans until tender. They mix molasses, brown sugar, dry mustard, salt, and pepper with the beans and put slabs of lean salt pork on top. Then the pots are lowered into the holes, covered with sand, and left to bake for twenty-four hours.

Larry showed me the bean-hole area, and as we walked around it I could feel the warmth of the sand through the bottoms of my shoes. Larry told me that 850 pounds of beans were cooking—400 pounds of red kidney beans and 450 pounds of pea beans—and that about three thousand people were expected that day. It was still too early for the feast, so we left and explored the rest of the festival. One of our party was a visitor from Germany, and it was interesting to see this display of America—the dunking booth, the truck and tractor pulls, the country and western band, the craft booths, and of course, the fat fannies—through her eyes.

A few hours later the sand was cleared away, the tops were taken off the bean pots, and, as we watched anxiously, the beanmaster tested the beans from the first two bean pots—one of each kind. He proclaimed them ready and the crowd started to line up. Once our plates were heaped with beans, barbecued hot dogs, sauerkraut, and pickles, we all settled down to enjoy a great meal. Seldom does the humble bean receive such honor.

How to Grow Dry Beans

Why grow your own dry beans when they are readily available and incredibly cheap at the grocery store? And why prepare homemade baked beans when all you need to do is open a can and have a meal? Well, frankly, calling canned baked beans true baked beans is like calling canned spaghetti true spaghetti. In both cases, a highly complex dish has been reduced to boring simplicity. Dry beans are actually a noble food and in my opinion would receive more respect if only they were more expensive.

Dry beans that are baked and canned commercially usually taste like sweet mush. The bean taste is overwhelmed by sugar, and the canning process plus the bean variety used causes the beans nearly to disintegrate. Eating home-grown varieties of dry beans baked with care is a completely different experience. Their flavors can be earthy, meaty, even nutlike. Their textures can be creamy, fluffy, soft and moist, or potatolike. And the beans don't all turn to mush when cooked.

The average grocery store carries only three or four dry bean varieties, so if you want to experience the full range of dry bean tastes and textures in your home-cooked baked beans, you will have to grow your own. In reality, there are literally hundreds of varieties of dry beans, but finding more than a few dozen kinds to grow would be a challenge. If you are inspired to explore the range of dry beans, plan a baked bean garden and order some of the more unusual varieties from the seed companies listed in "Sources" at the end of this chapter. Then, if you become as enamored with beans as I am, join the Seed Savers Exchange and trade varieties with them. Bean seeds are some of the easiest to save, and many treasured heirloom varieties have been preserved over the years. The Seed Savers Exchange catalog lists nearly 150 heirloom dry beans, with names such as 'Mortgage Lifter', 'Wren's Egg', 'Montezuma', 'Squaw Yellow', 'White Marrowfat', 'Old Cornfield', and the famous 'Lazy Wife', named for its ease of shelling. See the "Heirloom Gardens" chapter for more information on the Seed Savers Exchange and saving your own bean seeds.

In this country, baked beans are most closely associated with the New England states. The colonists were introduced to beans by native Americans. Beans quickly became a staple, and the bean pot filled with beans, bacon, and a little molasses is still part of a Saturday-night ritual in many families. Some of the old New England varieties, such as 'Yellow Eye', 'Jacob's Cattle', 'Soldier', 'Red Kidney', and 'Vermont Cranberry', remain popular with gardeners and local cooks and are carried in local specialty stores and listed in a number of seed catalogs.

New England–style baked beans is only one baked bean dish among many. There are other baked bean recipes and other types of dry beans that can be baked. Varieties of beans and methods of cooking them come from other parts of the country and from other cultures as well. Like potatoes and rice, beans absorb flavors very well and can be spiced with chilies, garlic, onions, sage, savory, and cumin, or combined with all types of meats. Because they are such a nutritious and versatile food, over the centuries varieties of beans have been adapted to many different cuisines. Thus, we find dry bean varieties such as lima and white pea beans, French horticultural and flageolet beans, Swedish brown beans, South American pinto and black beans, and Italian cannellini and borlotto beans—all of which can be baked.

The dry beans discussed in this chapter are all species of *Phaseolus,* also known as the common bean. They are usually categorized in two ways—by their growth habit and by the stage at which they are eaten. Generally, dry beans are produced on short, bushy plants about two feet high and are referred to as bush or dwarf beans. Other varieties grow on long vines six, eight, even twelve feet high, and are referred to as pole beans. Some bean varieties are best described as semitrailing, or dwarf-trailing, as their vines are usually three or four feet long and seem to sprawl over each other.

Common beans are further categorized by the stage at which they are the most flavorful and have the best texture for eating. If the pod is eaten in its immature stage, then the bean is called a snap, string, or green bean. If the pod is tough or stringy and the bean seed is removed from the pod when mature and eaten fresh, the bean is called a shelling or shelly bean; the French horticultural beans are the best known in this category. If the pod is tough and the bean seed is tastiest when eaten in its dry state, the bean is called a dry bean. However, most varieties of beans can be eaten in more than one state. Snap beans can be eaten in their fresh-pod, shelled-bean, and dry stages, and most shelly beans and dry bean varieties can be eaten in both the shelling and dry stage. Some exceptions are 'Black Valentine', 'Bonus Small White', 'Dwarf Horticultural', and some varieties of flageolet—all can be eaten as snap beans as well as shelly and dry. Snap beans are fine to eat in their dry state, but most varieties tend to get mushy more readily than the other types when baked.

Dry beans are certainly among the easiest vegetables to care for in the garden, and they are grown for the most part in the same way snap beans are grown. But dry beans take less effort, because they do not require the tedious, constant harvesting of snap beans. Dry beans are harvested all at once, at the end of the season. In fact, a baked bean garden makes a rewarding first garden and a good choice for gardeners with limited time.

To grow a baked bean garden, start planning early in the spring. Few local nurseries carry a good selection of seeds, so you will need time to place a mail order. Before you order your seeds, determine what kinds of dishes you want to make with the beans and choose the appropriate varieties. Then decide whether you are going to plant bush or pole beans. While most varieties of dry beans are only available as bush or dwarf plants, some dry beans, such as limas and horticultural beans, come in both bush and pole varieties. And many varieties of dry beans—particularly the pinto beans, 'Pink Half Runner', and 'Black Turtle'—are semitrailing and will readily climb, given support. You can plan a garden around the bush or pole forms. Bush varieties take less room in the garden and produce in a shorter season, but pole types usually yield more per foot of growing space.

Because bean seeds rot readily in cold soil, once you have obtained your seeds, plant them only when the weather and soil have completely warmed up. See Part Four, "An Encyclopedia of Superior Vegetables," for complete cultural information on planting and growing beans.

Toward the end of the growing season you will probably notice that the different varieties of beans are maturing at slightly different rates; first one variety ripens and then another. This might stagger your harvest somewhat, but if the weather is dry and you keep an eye on them, and the beans aren't falling out of their shells, you can wait until all the varieties are ripe before you harvest. There are a number of harvesting and drying methods. One time-honored way is to harvest whole plants before the pods are completely dry and drape them over a crude drying frame out in the garden to prevent the pods from rotting on the ground. Alternatively, you can put the plants on a dry surface in a dry garage or sun porch. Both these methods work well in rainy climates or very short seasons. In a dry climate, you can let the pods dry completely in the garden and harvest the whole plant or pick the pods individually. Keep an eye on

the drying plants, though, because in some of the varieties the pods tend to curl open when dry, which means you could lose your crop on the ground. If you like, store the uprooted dried plants temporarily in a burlap sack or old pillow case and put them in a dry garage or attic.

Once the pods are harvested and dried, you must thresh the beans—that is, separate the seeds from the pods. There are a number of threshing techniques, but in all cases beans and pods must be completely dry before you thresh them. For a small batch, just shell the beans out by hand, but for any sizable harvest this will be much too tedious. Another way is to lay the pods on a tarp or sheet and strike them with a flail (a piece of wood or leather that swivels on a handle) or a big stick. But be careful. Your blows must be cushioned when you flail, because hitting the beans when they are directly on the floor will break them. To avoid this, make sure you keep a layer of the chaff on the bottom of the pile to absorb the blows.

Another method for threshing, and the one that works best for me, comes from John Withee. He suggests you take a burlap bag or an old pillow case, cut a six-inch hole in the bottom corner, and tie the hole closed with a string. Put the whole dried plants in the bag and then hang the bag on a branch or shed door and beat on it with a stick or two. This loosens the beans from the pods and they fall to the bottom of the bag. When it feels as if most of the beans are free from the pods, hold a pan under the hole, untie the string, and let the beans fall into the pan. Take out the chaff, refill the bag with plants, and repeat the process until all the beans are threshed.

Once threshed, your beans must be winnowed. One method is to pour the beans and chaff from one container to another while the wind is blowing (see the "Grain Gardens" chapter for other methods). This removes the lightweight materials, but you still have to examine the beans carefully and remove small stones and any bean beetles—if you've had an infestation—by hand.

The final step is preserving the bean harvest. Two threats to beans are moisture, which will cause them to mildew and rot, and insects. Control the rotting problem by making sure the beans are completely dry when you store them and then by storing them in a dry place. As for insects, John Withee says any container that keeps out bugs will do, but glass jars have the advantage of what he calls see-through and keep-out. See-through is helpful because bean weevils can turn a jar of beans into bean dust. These tiny insects lay eggs in the beans while they are out in the garden, and the eggs can hatch in your bean jars. Glass jars allow you to see easily if you have a weevil problem, and sealing them prevents weevils from escaping and finding a new batch of beans to feast on. If you think you might have weevils, put the jars in the freezer for three or four days to help kill the eggs before you put the jars away in the closet. Stored in ideal conditions, dry beans can keep for years, but they are best used by the next season's harvest. With age they get harder and tougher and require longer cooking, and they lose some of their fresh taste.

The Vermont Bean Seed Company Garden

For years I have ordered bean seeds from the Vermont Bean Seed Company—everything from 'Dutch White' and scarlet runners to 'Christmas' limas, 'Romano' beans, and 'Cranberry' pole beans, to name a few. Since the company specializes in beans, it seemed the most obvious choice when I was looking for someone to grow a demonstration baked bean garden. Sure enough, when I called owner Guy Thomas, he said he would be delighted to grow one for me.

I visited Guy, and we planned a plot for the next summer. He decided the best place for it would be in his own front yard. I wanted a typical New England setting for my garden, and he certainly had one. The garden was to be planted in front of a large, classic, Vermont-style barn. We planned for the garden to be about twelve feet square and to contain eight varieties of beans good for baking, including 'Jacob's Cattle', 'Pink', 'Yellow Eye', 'Red Kidney', 'Swedish Brown', 'Soldier', 'Black Turtle', and, Guy's favorite, 'Vermont Cranberry' beans. They were all bush varieties and were planted in single rows a little more than a foot apart.

We kept in touch throughout the summer, and I continually heard about how bad the weather and insects were. So I was surprised, at the end of the season, to hear Guy say that though the baked bean garden hadn't looked too attractive, in spite of everything he'd still had a decent harvest. And while the garden had been under siege most of the summer, it

had been incredibly easy to grow. Guy planted the seeds in early June, kept the garden watered—which was no problem that year since the weather was actually too wet—and pulled a few weeds. The beans mostly took care of themselves until harvest time. The plants started to die back and turn brown, and after a frost in mid-September, he brought the pods inside for further drying. They were then threshed and stored in jars.

During the growing season the garden had been severely infested with Japanese beetles, but while the

Guy Thomas's bean garden in Vermont is filled with varieties well suited for New England–style baked beans, including 'Vermont Cranberry', 'Jacob's Cattle', 'Soldier', 'Yellow Eye', 'Red Kidney', 'Swedish Brown', 'Pink', and 'Black Turtle' beans.

foliage was disfigured, Guy didn't see much effect on the harvest. Guy doesn't like to spray with insecticides, so he used pheromone traps and said they worked quite well in keeping the beetles under control. The only thing he would have changed was the layout of the garden: the rows were too close together to permit easy weeding, and the plants became tangled together.

Guy and I agreed that a bean garden is one of the easiest gardens for a beginner. As he said, "After very little attention and with a small garden space, I ended up with superior varieties of beans that will be cooked up with maple syrup and bacon, or with onions and chilies, for great eating all winter long."

The Creasy Baked Bean Garden

When I started my research on baked beans I first focused on New England baking varieties. I had grown up on them in Boston, and it hadn't occurred to me that there were any other kinds. After I was well into my research and had arranged for the baked bean garden to be grown in Vermont, I came upon a fascinating recipe for Italian-style baked beans made with olive oil, garlic, and sage. Of course! How obvious! Beans are such a nutritious staple and are so easy to grow and prepare that there had to be numerous ways that different cultures made use of

Wendy Krupnick sets out kale plants in the Creasy garden, with dry bean plants in a row behind her. The row includes beans that are delicious for baking: from left to right, cannellini, 'Santa Maria Pinquito', 'Coco Nain Blanc', and 'Jacob's Cattle' beans.

them. I soon learned that baked beans are used in cassoulet, one of France's most famous dishes, and in baked 'Santa Maria Pinquito' beans, a well-known Mexican dish. With that in mind, I decided to plant my own baked bean garden where I could try out more than just New England–type beans. I discovered that French horticultural beans were traditionally used in cassoulet, cannellini beans were the ones most often used in Italy for baking, and 'Santa Maria Pinquito' were traditional for Mexican-style baked beans, so I included all those types in my international baked bean garden. I then added a fourth type of bean—the New England variety 'Jacob's Cattle'. Exotic beans notwithstanding, to my mind no baked bean garden would be complete without a traditional American variety.

The first step in creating my garden was, of course, to obtain the seeds. I contacted Jan Blum, owner of Seeds Blum, for the 'Jacob's Cattle' beans. David Cavagnaro, who told me about 'Santa Maria Pinquito' beans, sent me some of his seeds, and I ordered seeds of the French 'Coco Nain Blanc' from Le Marché. I then called around to locate cannellini beans, but to no avail. It was too late in the season to order them from Italy, but I was fortunate to find some in a grocery store in San Francisco's Italian district.

I planned a bean area in my frontyard garden. The beans would replace the wheat in the long bed that runs parallel to my front walk. I had some thoughts about how the plot would look when all the plants turned brown, but decided a few weeks of brown foliage wasn't worth worrying about. I enlarged the bed a little to give the beans more room to spread and ended up with a bed that was twenty-six feet long and four feet wide. As far as I knew, all the bean varieties I had selected were bush types, not pole beans. But I was taking a chance with the commercially produced cannellini beans, since they were sold for cooking and were not labeled as to their garden use.

In the middle of June, my assistant Wendy and I turned the bed over, worked in some compost, and planted the four varieties of dry beans in four sections about six feet long by four feet wide. We arranged all the sections in double rows and, after the planting, put drip irrigation lines in place. The beans came up readily, were given a light weeding, and in a few weeks covered the beds. Maintenance for the rest of the season was minimal. We irrigated the plants every week and did little fertilizing, as the soil is fertile.

Philip Breedon grew a bean garden in Beverly, Massachusetts, under John Withee's guidance and found that John's bag method of threshing works well. Philip cut a small hole in the bottom of a feed bag, tied the hole shut, put his dry bean plants in the bag, and hung the bag on a shed door. After beating the bag with a stick to loosen the beans, he carefully opened the bag at the bottom, and the beans slid right out into a bowl.

Though we had a few cucumber beetles and some spider mites, the plants were remarkably trouble free. There was only one minor concern: the plants outgrew their beds and spilled over the walk. The 'Santa Maria Pinquito' beans spread even farther than the others by a few feet and could be best described as semitrailing.

We harvested the cannellini, 'Jacob's Cattle', and 'Coco Nain Blanc' beans starting in mid-September, about 100 days after planting. Three weeks later, the 'Santa Maria Pinquito' beans were ready and harvested. To thresh the beans, we shelled some by hand; then we decided to try John Withee's method and

I first met John Withee at a seed-saving conference in 1981. He had brought with him a partitioned box containing more than 400 varieties of heirloom beans, and he engaged even the most blasé gardener among us as he expounded in his wonderful Maine accent on the vast range of beans that have been gathered throughout the world. I left the conference inspired to try beans with names such as 'Jacob's Cattle', 'Black Valentine', and 'Vermont Cranberry' and to start saving my own bean seeds. When I decided to include a chapter on bean gardens in this book, John Withee was my obvious choice for an expert on the subject.

John Withee

John grew up in Maine, where he spent his teen years as a market gardener. As an adult, he became a medical photographer and moved to Massachusetts. Always an avid gardener, his attempts over the years to locate an old variety of beans he had enjoyed as a child sparked a lifelong interest. After retirement, growing and preserving old bean varieties became his consuming passion.

John and I met to discuss beans in a historic New England inn. As we delved into the subject, I looked around the dining room. Who would guess that the liveliest discussion there was about beans? First I asked John what he feels constitutes a good pot of baked beans. "The best baked beans I ever had," he said, "were baked by my wife's father, Charlie, in an old iron wood stove. Charlie was born in 1880 and, like myself, grew up on a farm. And on a farm, beans were a staple. You had baked beans every way you could fix them. I remember when my father bartered for a barrel of 'Yellow Eye' beans when I was a youngster. The barrel was a big wooden one something like a flour barrel, and we ate from it all winter long. It was a primary source of food. But try as I may, I haven't duplicated the flavor that Charlie squeezed out of his beans.

"Charlie started with good beans—'Jacob's Cattle'," John says. "He never used salt pork; instead, he used slab bacon smoked by a local butcher. When you try to substitute slab bacon these days, you get the same fake bacon everywhere. It isn't really smoked—it has some painted-on substance. That smoky slab bacon Charlie used was just enough to turn his beans to a little bit of an advantage. And his beans were far less sweet than any canned beans you buy today. To come close to duplicating Charlie's beans, you need to take the average baked bean recipe and cut the sugar ingredients in half. This gives you the flavor of the beans—not just the sweetener."

I asked John for some guidelines for making great baked beans. First, he stressed, you have to control the salt. It's hard to determine how much salt to add until the salt pork, which most people use, has been cooked. Since you can't take away salt once you've added it, John recommends that you wait until the beans are nearly done cooking, then taste and salt if necessary.

Another thing to know when baking beans, John says, is the hardness of your drinking water. In some areas, hard water causes hard beans; very hard water can ruin a whole batch. If your household water leaves heavy mineral deposits in your tea kettle, and if the dry beans you serve are sometimes quite hard, even when cooked, John suggests you get soft water to cook your beans in. Bottled distilled water is probably the best solution; avoid artificially softened water.

John has strong opinions about how he likes his baked beans to taste. "I don't use onions, period. I want to taste the beans, not the onion," he says. Bean connoisseurs differ widely regarding salt pork, and John takes a stand here, too: "I have eaten excellent beans baked up in Maine by people older than I am, but they use what I consider excessive amounts of pork. They put a big slab at the bottom of the pot and another on the top. I think one piece is enough."

Next I asked John how he makes his favorite

batch of beans (see his recipe). "I take one pound of 'Yellow Eye' or 'Jacob's Cattle' beans—about enough to fill a bean pot," he says, "and I cover them with water and soak them overnight. In the morning, I cover the pot and put the beans on the stove to simmer until the seed coats crack when I blow on them; that's how the old-timers tested beans. You take a spoonful of beans and blow on them, and if they're properly precooked, the skins crack and split away from the beans. I suppose you could also time them by hours.

"Once the beans are properly precooked, I drain them, keeping the liquid, and put them in a bean pot. Although recipes often say to discard the cooking water, you'll be throwing away some of the vitamins if you do. I mix about a quarter cup of the cooking water with about a quarter cup of molasses, maybe a tablespoon or two of powdered mustard, and, as a final touch, a shake or two of ginger. Too much ginger will ruin the pot. Then I pour the molasses mixture and some more of the cooking water into the bean pot until the beans are covered. I also like about a quarter of a pound of smoked bacon with the beans, so I put that in. I smoke my own salt pork, in effect making my own bacon. To do this, buy salt pork, wash off the salt, let the meat dry, and hang it to smoke. I don't cook it; I just smoke it for a couple

of days. [See the "Herb Gardens" chapter for information on smoking meats.] I continue adding extra water a little bit at a time so that the beans remain covered with liquid as they are baking in a covered pot.

"We all have our own ideas about what makes a good mess of beans," John says, "but I laugh when I hear people say to remove the cover for the last hour to brown the top. If you remove the lid, maybe ten or fifteen beans will get brown, and that won't change the rest of the pot a dang bit. Besides, who wants a bunch of hard, dry beans on top?"

Cassoulet, chili, baked beans: like all great dishes, these inspire a lot of passion and some dispute. Devotees may differ on one fine point or another—for example, whether 'Jacob's Cattle' or 'Yellow Eye' beans are best, or whether you uncover the beans at the end—but, basically, the passion rises from years of refinement and appreciation. If you look past the uproar, you find only the fine points are in dispute, not most of the basics, and following some general guidelines can make for wonderful eating. Making baked beans with 'Jacob's Cattle' beans and using John's methods certainly made my beans terrific. Who would think that meaty, beany baked beans could taste so good?

I must confess, though, I still use onions.

found it much faster. See "How to Grow Dry Beans," earlier in this chapter, for information on that method.

After the beans were threshed, we were so anxious to try some that we forgot to weigh the harvest until after we had cooked a few batches, but we estimated the yield to be about seven pounds of dry beans for the approximately 100 square feet of beds. That was enough to make at least two recipes of baked beans of each variety. We thoroughly enjoyed trying the different types of dry beans and testing the recipes using them. The French beans were delicious. The Italian-style baked beans were creamy and rich; the Mexican beans held their shape and had a rich, beany flavor; and the 'Jacob's Cattle' were their usual wonderful selves. There was no question that growing our own beans had been worthwhile—the gain in flavor far outweighed the minimal effort the baked bean garden required.

Recommended Beans for Baking

Hundreds of varieties of beans exist for drying and baking. Our ancestors relied on them for generations, and most of the varieties listed here are actually heirlooms. Some, but by no means all, varieties of dry beans most prized for baking are discussed in this section. The numbers in parentheses next to most variety names correspond to the seed companies listed in "Sources" at the end of this chapter. No numbers are given for varieties available from most of the sources.

Seed catalogs and garden books do not always make clear whether their growing times refer to the snap, shelling, or dry stage. Therefore, the number of days to maturity noted for varieties listed below can only be considered approximate.

'COCO NAIN BLANC'   This variety is one of several French white beans that are traditionally used in cassoulet. The bean is about the size of a kidney bean but rounder.

How to grow: 'Coco Nain Blanc' beans grow on short, bushy plants. They are vigorous and high-yielding and mature in about 70 to 80 days. (3)

How to prepare: These beans can be enjoyed in their shelling and dry stages, for soups and for baking, particularly for cassoulet.

'GREAT NORTHERN WHITE' (also called pea bean)   This dependable, oval, white bean has been around for years and is often available in grocery stores. It's larger than the 'Navy' bean with which it is often compared.

How to grow: This bean is easily grown and is very prolific. It produces shelly beans in 65 days and dried beans in 85 to 95 days. Plants are bush. (6, 7)

How to prepare: This white bean is good in soups, has excellent flavor, and is preferred by many over the 'Navy' bean for baking. It's a favorite in the Midwest.

ITALIAN   One type of Italian dry bean good for baking is cannellini. Cannellini beans are meaty and look like small, white kidney beans. The term cannellini refers to a class, not a variety, of beans, and a few varieties are available from Italian seed companies. A bush variety available from Fratelli Ingegnoli is 'Cannellone bianco'. Cannellini beans of unspecified varieties are available from Italian grocery stores in some communities.

Another type of Italian dry beans—borlotto—can also be used for baking. Borlotto bean varieties come in both bush and pole types. The pods of most varieties are striped with red, and the white beans within are larger than cannellini beans. I have had only limited experience with borlotto beans but assume they are easy to grow, as they are grown commercially in Italy. See the "Italian Gardens" chapter for information about how to order both these types of beans from Italian seed companies.

How to grow: In my limited experience, cannellini are easily grown bush beans. The variety I bought at an Italian grocery store took approximately 100 days to produce dry beans.

How to prepare: Both cannellini and borlotto beans are great for shelly and baked bean recipes. They are creamy in consistency and have a mellow bean flavor.

'JACOB'S CATTLE'   Also known as the 'Trout' bean, this is one of the most beautiful and tasty of the heirloom baked bean varieties. It's an old Vermont and Maine favorite. The seeds are white with deep maroon splotches; in fact, in coloring they resemble Appaloosa horses.

How to grow: The plant is a bush type that grows to two feet tall and is not a heavy producer. It matures in 85 to 95 days.

How to prepare: This bean is superb for shelling and eating fresh or for use dry. When baked it keeps its shape and is very meaty. Great bean flavor—my favorite!

LIMA   There are many varieties of lima beans; the two that John Withee recommends for dry limas are the pole varieties 'King of the Garden', which produces in about 100 to 110 days (6, 7), and 'Christmas' (6, 7), which produces in about 100 to 110 days. For a bush lima that is good dry, try 'Dixie Speckled Butterpea' (7). It produces in about 90 days.

How to grow: Lima beans need a warmer soil in the spring than most beans. Cold soil causes the

Italian-style baked beans can be made from cannellini beans seasoned with garlic, olive oil, and sage. The dish is served with Italian bread and red wine.

seeds to rot. Lima beans also need a fairly long, warm summer to perform well. The two pole varieties are vigorous growers and need strong support.

How to prepare: Dry lima beans have a rich, buttery flavor and are quite different in taste from other beans. When prepared for baking they are generally not precooked as long as other common dry beans or they get mushy.

'RED KIDNEY'   This dark-maroon kidney-shaped bean is a great rich-tasting baking bean.

How to grow: This large bean takes a little longer to mature than some other bush beans—95 to 112 days—but is worth the wait.

How to prepare: Another old-timer, this popular bean is one of the best varieties of dry beans for all types of uses, from New England baked beans to Texas chili. The large, red, kidney-shaped beans have a hearty, sweet, classic "beany" flavor.

'RED MEXICAN'   This bean is dark red and fairly small.

How to grow: The plant is an average-size bush type and grows to a little more than a foot high. It produces in about 85 days. (1, 7)

How to prepare: The 'Red Mexican' is a great, flavorful baking bean. It holds its shape well with long hours of cooking.

'SANTA MARIA PINQUITO'   These buff-pink beans are very small, between a quarter and third of an inch long, and kind of square-shaped. Their ends seem to get flattened by being crammed up against each other in the pod.

How to grow: These beans grow on vigorous semitrailing vines that take a longer-than-average season to mature, about 120 days. (4, 5)

How to prepare: In California, these beans have been valued for their great flavor since the days of the early Spaniards. They are low in starch and stay intact when cooked. They are great for baked beans (see the recipe in the cooking section) and refried beans.

'SOLDIER'   The slender, kidney-shaped, white seed is marked with a characteristic "soldier" in yellow-brown on the eye. The rich and meaty 'Soldier' bean is a well-known New England heirloom, passed from generation to generation.

How to grow: This hardy bush variety is very easy to grow in cool climates and reaches a height of eighteen inches. It does well in drought and matures in about 85 days. (3, 5, 6, 7)

How to prepare: The 'Soldier' is used as a dry bean for baking.

'SWEDISH BROWN'   These beans are plump, oval, and brown and have a dark eye rim. They are usually hard to find.

How to grow: These are very hardy bush beans that will grow anywhere. They are especially well adapted to northern climates and are popular in Scandinavian-settled areas in the United States. The beans reach maturity in 85 days. (1, 7)

How to prepare: The 'Swedish Brown' is best used as a dry baking bean.

'VERMONT CRANBERRY'   This bean is round and deep maroon and has fine flavor. It really looks just like a cranberry.

How to grow: This variety does well in all climates. There is a climbing variety (7) and a bush variety (5, 7). Both produce shelling beans in about 60 days or dry beans in 90 days.

How to prepare: For a shelling bean, both climbing and bush varieties are great in soups or served steamed with butter. They are also high-quality, meaty, baking beans.

'YELLOW EYE'   This oval, white bean with its yellow eye is an outstanding baking bean and a household garden tradition in New England.

How to grow: This very prolific bush bean reaches eighteen inches in height. It is hardy and starts well under adverse conditions. It is disease resistant and reliable and matures in about 85 days. (2, 5, 6, 7)

How to prepare: The 'Yellow Eye' is an excellent soup bean and baking bean. It takes less time to cook than other dry beans.

Cooking from the Baked Bean Garden

For eons, human beings have respected the life-giving bean. In fact, many cultures have depended upon it for basic nutrition. Dry beans, in particular, are almost one-quarter protein, are full of iron and B vitamins, and contain substantial amounts of zinc, magnesium, and copper. The protein, however, is incomplete in a few basic amino acids, so beans must be combined with grains, seeds, dairy products, or meat to complete the protein. In recent years, dry beans

have been analyzed by health professionals and found to be even more valuable than generally believed. The properties of dry beans offer welcome solutions to some of today's health problems. Unlike much of the food we eat, dry beans are high in fiber, potassium, and complex carbohydrates and very low in fats and sodium. While not low in calories—for example, there are 127 calories in half a cup of cooked kidney beans—beans can nevertheless be valuable for the dieter, since they are filling and their complex carbohydrates are slow to break down, which helps stabilize blood-sugar levels. For the latter reason, dry beans are recommended for certain kinds of diabetics by the American Diabetes Association.

Most traditional American recipes for dry beans are quite high in salt and saturated fats. If you must control these in your diet, try cooking your baked beans Italian style (see recipe). Made with olive oil, not pork, the dish is low in sodium and saturated fats. You'll also find that recipes using pork take less pork when made with ingredients from your baked bean garden, because the beans themselves are more flavorful and you can use fresh herbs and tomatoes for extra good eating.

There is one more aspect of dry beans to be discussed: flatulence. The gas in beans comes from fiber and from sugars called alpha-galactosides. Dry beans arrive in the intestines mostly undigested and are worked on by bacteria that break them down. In the process the bacteria produce carbon dioxide, hydrogen, and other gases. Some people have little problem with flatulence and eat beans without worry, but others avoid them because of the problem. In the past, some cooks have simmered beans with a little baking soda in the belief that this cuts down on gas, and you'll find some traditional recipes with this addition. However, the baking soda destroys valuable nutrients and its effectiveness is questionable. Another suggested remedy is to soak the beans overnight and throw out the soaking water rather than using it for cooking. This eliminates some of the dissolved sugars. Unfortunately, while this technique does help the gas problem somewhat, some of the nutritional value is poured off in the process. One bean variety, 'Jacob's Cattle Gasless', is reputed to produce much less gas. It's available from Seeds Blum.

OPPOSITE: *Baked beans and brown bread are a wonderful New England tradition. Cooking brown bread in a plum-pudding mold makes the meal more festive.*

Homemade Baked Beans

Dry beans are a marvelous vehicle for flavors of all sorts, and their meaty, rich flavors combine well with most herbs and spices. In this country the most popular way to fix them is with molasses, a little salt pork, and usually a bit of mustard. Other cultures add an array of herbs, meats, and even oils to their dry beans. Much of the preparation of dry beans is similar, no matter what type of baked beans you are making, but small differences in techniques crop up in the recipes that follow in keeping with the cooks' individual preferences.

The first steps in preparing dry beans are always the same, however: the beans must be sorted, cleaned, and then reconstituted. The night before cooking your beans, measure out the dry beans—one cup equals approximately two to three cups cooked, and a standard bean pot holds two cups of dry beans, or one pound. Examine the beans and remove those that are shriveled and damaged. In both store-bought and home-grown dry beans, look carefully for small stones. Wash the beans in a large saucepan, cover them with water, and remove any beans that float to the top. Drain the beans, add three to four cups of water for each cup of beans, and let them soak overnight.

The next morning, simmer the beans in a covered saucepan until tender. Most varieties will take about two hours to cook. Presoaked dry limas will cook in less time—often half an hour is enough—but some of the navy beans and beans more than a year old can take up to three hours. This is where John Withee's "blow method" of determining doneness is helpful (see profile). If you were not able to presoak the beans the night before, boil them slowly for an hour, turn off the stove and let them sit for an hour, and then simmer them until tender as above. Or follow Diana Kennedy's directions, which are, with no presoaking, boil the beans very slowly in a covered pan for two to two and one-half hours until they are soft. Make sure the beans stay covered with water while they are cooking. Diana recommends that, if more water is needed, you add boiling water, not cold water.

Once your beans are tender, drain them and reserve the liquid. Preheat the oven. To the beans add the flavorings, oils, and vegetables, if any, and put the bean mixture in a traditional two-quart bean pot or other heavy casserole. Place the salt pork, if called for, half on the bottom of the pot and half on top of the beans; then pour the bean liquid over the beans until it just covers them. Cover the pot and bake in the oven at the designated temperature, usually for the better part of a day. Check the beans every two hours or so to make sure there is enough water, adding some if the level goes down much. You have a lot of latitude as to cooking time depending on the recipe and type of bean used. Serve your New England–style baked beans with cider or beer, coleslaw, and brown bread or cornbread.

Bean-Hole Beans

You cook bean-hole, or campfire, beans as you would any food cooked in retained heat. As with a clambake, for example, you dig a hole and put in some heat-retaining rocks. Then you build a fire in the hole, let it burn for two or three hours till the rocks are hot, remove the coals, add the food, put the coals back in, fill the hole with dirt to exclude all oxygen, and let the food cook at a slow rate. You can turn the digging-up into a fine ceremony, so bean-hole beans, especially those made with extra-tasty homegrown beans, are great for a party.

As a first step, choose a pot that suits the purpose. It should have a lid that hangs over the edge rather than one that sits in the top of the pot; otherwise, dirt will get inside. And it's best if the pot has a bail or chain or some other device that goes around the pot for lifting it out of the hole.

Plan to start bean-hole beans the evening before your party. Or you can delay the start until morning—there's a chance that the beans won't be fully cooked by evening and will need to be finished in your oven. In any case, you must prepare the bean hole and start soaking the beans the day before. You can dig the hole in any kind of dry soil (never wet), but dry sandy soil is the easiest to handle. Make the hole eighteen inches to two feet deep. When you dig the hole, pile the soil nearby to use later. Be sure to make the hole wide enough to contain the pot, some air space, and the heat-retaining rocks. By the way, any heat-retaining objects, such as bricks or tiles, will work. According to John Withee, the loggers up in the Maine woods even used to throw a piece or two of logging chain into the bottom of the hole.

Put a few good-size rocks or bricks in to cover the bottom of the hole and then arrange some around the inside so that they will surround the pot. Leave

about an extra two inches of air space so the rocks won't touch the pot.

Make a sizable fire of scrap wood, charcoal, or anything else that will heat up the rocks well, and keep it burning for about three hours. If, as John Withee recommends, you start the fire only twelve hours before the bean feast, make sure the fire is large and hot. At the same time you start the fire, begin precooking the beans. Once the rocks are very hot, and you have two or three quarts of glowing coals, combine all the other ingredients (see recipe) with the precooked beans in a pot. Take a shovel and dig out most of the coals from the bean hole, leaving a few on the bottom. Cover the pot, lower it into the hole, and then place the remaining coals around the pot. Cover the coals with soaked batches of newspaper, ten pages or so thick, or a wet burlap bag. This keeps the charcoal dirt-free, which means it will stay hotter and also cleaner for digging out later. Cover the newspaper or burlap with all the fill from the hole and tamp it down well. Any air holes might cause the beans to burn. If rain threatens, throw a plastic tarp over the top of the pile to keep it from cooling off too fast.

To serve the beans, remove the soil, heave the pot up, and bring it inside. Clean the top off well before you remove it and then test the beans for doneness and seasonings. Finally, serve the beans and let the festivities begin!

JOHN WITHEE'S BAKED BEANS

This recipe is from *Growing and Cooking Beans*, by John Withee. For more detailed information, see the profile of John in this section.

SERVES 6 TO 8.

> 1 pound dry 'Jacob's Cattle', 'Yellow Eye', or 'Soldier' beans
> 1 teaspoon salt
> 2 tablespoons dry mustard
> ½ teaspoon powdered ginger
> 4 tablespoons blackstrap molasses
> ¼ to ⅓ pound smoked bacon, cut in pieces

Soak beans overnight in a saucepan. Bring to boil in same water—adding more water, if necessary, to cover—and simmer, covered, 1½ to 2 hours until tender. Reserve cooking water. Set oven at 250°. Season beans with salt, mustard, ginger, and molasses. Put in a bean pot with half the bacon pieces on the bottom and half on top. Cover and bake for 10 hours. Check water level occasionally, adding reserved cooking water or fresh water if level recedes.

HOME-GROWN BAKED BEANS

The following adaptation of traditional baked beans is very similar to John Withee's recipe, but I like the addition of onion and herbs and found 6 hours of baking time sufficient.

SERVES 6 TO 8.

1 pound dry 'Jacob's Cattle' beans
2 tablespoons dry mustard
½ teaspoon powdered ginger
4 tablespoons molasses or maple syrup
¼ pound thick sliced bacon, diced
1 medium onion, diced
¼ cup chopped parsley and/or celery leaves (optional)
2 teaspoons minced fresh thyme or rosemary (optional)

Soak beans overnight in a saucepan. Add more water if necessary to cover at least 1 inch. Cover and simmer 1 to 2 hours until tender. Stir in remaining ingredients, place in bean pot, cover, and bake at 275° for 6 to 7 hours. Uncover for the last 2 hours of baking; add additional water if necessary to keep moist but not soupy. Serve with brown bread (see recipe) or cornbread (see recipe in "Native American Gardens" chapter), garden green salad, and cider or beer.

BOSTON BAKED BEANS

This recipe comes from the venerable old Durgin-Park restaurant in Boston.

SERVES 10.

2 pounds dry beans (California pea beans preferred or York State beans)
1 teaspoon baking soda
1 pound salt pork, cut into 1-inch cubes

1 medium onion
8 tablespoons sugar
⅔ cup molasses
2 teaspoons dry mustard
4 teaspoons salt
½ teaspoon pepper
Hot water

Soak beans overnight in a saucepan. In the morning, add more water, if necessary, to cover and parboil beans for 10 minutes with 1 teaspoon baking soda. Then run cold water through beans in a colander or strainer. Spread half of cubed pork on bottom of bean pot with whole onion. Put beans in pot. Cover with rest of pork. Mix other ingredients with hot water. Pour over beans. Add enough water to make level with beans. Bake in 300° oven for 6 hours. Add water while cooking to keep beans moist.

BEAN-HOLE BEANS

See the text for more information about this traditional method of baking beans, which is still used for feasts in New England today. We have gauged the quantity to feed a moderate-size crowd.

SERVES 20 TO 25.

4 pounds dry beans
1 pound salt pork, cubed
2 tablespoons dry mustard
1½ tablespoons salt
1 teaspoon pepper
¾ cup molasses

Soak beans overnight. Add more water if necessary and simmer, covered, 1 to 2 hours until tender. Oil the bottom of a 2- to 3-gallon iron kettle with a lid. Add cooked beans, cooking liquid, and all other ingredients, leaving about half the pork on top of beans. Liquid should be level with top of beans; if not, add more water as needed. Cover with aluminum foil and then lid. Lower into prepared bean hole, bury, and leave for the day or up to 24 hours.

STEAMED BROWN BREAD

This tasty whole-grain bread is the customary accompaniment to baked beans in New England and the perfect complement to a hearty winter meal. It is surprisingly easy to make and keeps well refrigerated or frozen, although it usually vanishes quickly. It is excellent toasted and spread with ricotta or cream cheese for breakfast.

SERVES ABOUT 10.

> 2 cups buttermilk
> ½ cup molasses
> 1 cup cornmeal
> 1 cup rye flour
> 1 cup whole-wheat flour
> 2 teaspoons baking soda
> ½ teaspoon salt
> ¾ cup raisins

Mix buttermilk and molasses in a bowl; then add remaining ingredients and stir well. Pour into a buttered 1-quart pudding mold or 2 1-pound coffee cans, buttered. Containers should be ¾ full. Butter inside of pudding lid or aluminum foil if using cans (tie on foil to make a tight seal). Place in a large kettle on a rack or trivet and add 1 inch of boiling water. Cover kettle and keep at a simmer on low heat for 3 hours. Check occasionally and add boiling water if necessary. Remove mold from kettle and set on a cooling rack. Remove lid and cool for about 20 minutes before turning out.

PENNSYLVANIA DUTCH LIMA BEAN CASSEROLE

This recipe is based on one contributed by the Vermont Bean Seed Company and was originated by Ruth Loft. The casserole is delicious served at Easter with baked ham and sweet-and-sour red cabbage.

SERVES 8.

> 1 pound dry lima beans
> 2 teaspoons salt
> ⅓ cup butter
> ½ cup brown sugar
> 1 tablespoon dry mustard
> 1 tablespoon molasses
> 1 cup sour cream

Wash beans, soak overnight, and drain. Add water to cover beans and 1 teaspoon salt; then simmer 40 minutes or more until tender. Drain. Rinse in hot water and place in medium casserole. Add butter to hot beans. Mix sugar, mustard, and remaining 2 tea-

spoons salt in small bowl and sprinkle over beans. Stir in molasses. Pour sour cream on beans and mix all quickly. Bake at 350° for 1 hour, uncovered.

BAKED 'SANTA MARIA PINQUITO' BEANS

David Cavagnaro, well-known photographer and demon gardener, tells us that 'Santa Maria Pinquito' beans were brought into California from Mexico by Mexican farm workers. The beans are not readily available commercially, so to have a suitable supply, try growing them yourself. These small beans are excellent for baking and for refried beans.

SERVES 12 TO 14.

> 2 pounds dry 'Santa Maria Pinquito' beans or pinto beans
> 1 California bay leaf or sweet bay leaf
> ¼ pound salt pork or bacon, cubed
> 1 bell pepper, chopped
> 1 onion, chopped
> 3 cloves garlic, chopped
> 1 to 2 teaspoons cumin (optional)
> ½ teaspoon freshly ground pepper
> 2 cups homemade salsa, OR 2 cups homemade tomato sauce plus fresh or dried chilies to taste, OR 4 ripe tomatoes and 1 or 2 hot peppers, chopped
> Fresh cilantro

Soak beans in plenty of water for about 12 hours. Simmer, covered, for 1 to 2 hours until tender. Drain about half the liquid and reserve. Add remaining ingredients except cilantro and pour into a baking pot, casserole, or heavy kettle. If liquid does not cover beans, add some of the reserved cooking liquid. Cover and bake at 275° for 6 hours. Uncover for about the last 2 hours and check liquid level occasionally. Garnish with fresh cilantro. Serve with garlic bread, tortillas or cornbread, and a green salad.

CASSOULET OF DUCK, PORK, AND LAMB

Cassoulet is one of France's most famous country-style dishes. It is very rich and is generally served with only a light salad and some good bread, followed, perhaps, by a piece of fresh fruit. Tom McCombie, chef and owner of Chez T.J.'s in Mountain View, California, contributed this recipe. While he was in France, he went to Carcassonne, considered the home of this famous dish, in order to sample many different kinds of cassoulet. He then developed his own recipe.

SERVES 10 TO 12.

Pork, Lamb, and Duck

> 2-pound pork roast, such as a loin cut or pork
>   butt
> 2-pound lamb roast, such as a leg or shoulder
>   cut
> 3 pounds lamb bones and/or pork bones
> 2 4½-pound ducks
> Salt and black pepper

Lay pork, lamb, and bones on a large baking sheet. Rub them generously with salt and pepper. Roast meats in a 375° oven until a meat thermometer inserted into lamb or pork reads 165°. Remove meats from oven and allow to cool. Scrape any cooking juices from baking sheet and add to bean cooking liquid (see below). Bake ducks on a separate sheet in oven while cooking lamb and pork; they will be done cooking when other meats are. Drain off duck fat and reserve for later. Scrape cooking juices and save for bean cooking liquid (see below). When meats are cool, cut lamb and pork into 1½-inch chunks. Quarter the duck, trimming off excess fat and bones (but do not debone).

Beans

> 1 pound salt pork with rind removed
> Rind from above
> 2 pounds dry 'Coco Nain Blanc' or 'Great
>   Northern White' beans
> 2 gallons cold water
> 1 yellow onion, sliced
> Cooking juices from above
> Bones from above
> 3 cloves minced garlic
> ¼ cup tomato paste
> 1 bay leaf
> 1 teaspoon whole thyme leaves
> 1 teaspoon ground white pepper

Cut salt pork into ½-inch cubes. Blanch salt pork and rind in 1 quart boiling water for 5 minutes. Drain and discard water. Wash beans and cover with 2 gallons water. Add salt pork, onion, reserved cooking juices, bones, garlic, tomato paste, bay leaf, thyme leaves, and pepper. Slowly bring beans to a simmer. Carefully remove any scum that appears on the surface. Cook beans for 1½ hours until tender. Check seasoning periodically and add more water if necessary to keep beans in a broth. When done, allow beans to cool in cooking liquid.

Sausages

> 1 pound ground pork with at least 33 percent
>   fat content
> 2 teaspoons salt
> ⅛ teaspoon ground black pepper
> ⅛ teaspoon ground allspice
> Large pinch of ground cloves
> 1 clove minced garlic
> ½ cup cognac

Mix together all ingredients. Form mixture into 2-inch patties 1-inch thick. In a large sauté pan, brown patties on both sides. Set sausages aside with pork, lamb, and duck.

Assembling Cassoulet

> Cooked beans in their cooking liquid
> Cubed pork
> Cubed lamb
> Quartered duck
> Browned sausages
> 2 cups dry white bread crumbs
> ½ cup reserved cooking fat

In a large, deep baking dish, spoon a layer of beans onto the bottom. Next add a layer of assorted meats. Add another layer of beans and another layer of meats. Continue layering in this way until all beans and meat are used. Add as much cooking liquid from beans as necessary to fill the dish. Top cassoulet with bread crumbs and drizzle with cooking fat. Bring cassoulet to a simmer on top of stove. Bake cassoulet, uncovered, in 350° oven for 30 minutes. Using back of spoon, push down the skin that forms on top into the liquid beneath. After another 30 minutes, repeat. If cassoulet seems dry, add a little more bean liquid. Leave crust that forms during the last 30 minutes of baking.

FAGIOLI AL FIASCO (BAKED BEANS IN A FLASK)

This recipe is from *Cooking from an Italian Garden,* by Paola Scaravelli and Jon Cohen. To quote Paola, "When I was a child bread was baked once a week at the villa. Since the brick oven was large, it took time and lots of wood to heat it, so that it was practical to bake other foods at the same time. One of the real treats was beans baked in a flask, *fagioli al fiasco.* Beans were placed in a large chianti flask from which the straw wrapping had been removed, and water, oil, garlic, and sage were added. Fresh sage leaves were placed on top of the beans in the neck of the flask to seal in some of the vapors. The flask was deposited in the oven on the smoldering embers and left for a few hours. When retrieved, the water was absorbed, the beans cooked, and the flask intact. We would eat the beans cold with lemon juice, olive oil, salt, and pepper. Beans cooked in this simple manner were light, tender, and richly flavored. We have found that exactly the same results can be achieved in any modern kitchen.

"It is important to cover the beans only partially. Vapor must be allowed to escape during cooking, otherwise there's danger of the jar or bottle exploding."

My assistant Wendy and I have tried cooking cannellini beans this way and they are superb. We couldn't figure out how Paola got the beans out of the chianti bottle, so we cooked them in a mason jar, as she suggests in her book.

SERVES 6 TO 8.

> *2 cups dry white kidney beans or cannellini*
> *   beans*
> *1 tablespoon flour*
> *3 sage leaves*
> *2 garlic cloves, roughly chopped*
> *1 tablespoon olive oil*
> *Hot water*
> *Salt and freshly ground pepper to taste*
> *1 lemon, cut in wedges*
> *Olive oil for serving with beans*

Soak beans for 8 hours or overnight in 5 cups of water with 1 tablespoon flour. When ready to cook, preheat oven to 325°. Drain and rinse beans, combine with sage and garlic, and pour into a 1-quart mason jar. Add olive oil and enough hot water to reach approximately ¾ inch above top of beans. Place jar in rear of oven, partially cover top of jar with aluminum foil, and bake until beans are tender, about 2 hours. Beans should cook at a slow simmer. Adjust oven temperature if necessary. Transfer beans to a terra-cotta bowl, season with salt and pepper, and serve warm or at room temperature with lemon wedges. Provide olive oil at the table for those who want to add it.

Sources

Seed Companies

1. Good Seed
   P.O. Box 702
   Tonasket, WA 98855
   This company specializes in open-pollinated varieties of vegetables and carries a number of unusual varieties of dry beans.

2. Johnny's Selected Seeds
   Foss Hill Road
   Albion, ME 04910
   Johnny's carries many varieties of beans, including the three most popular for New England–style baked beans: 'Soldier', 'Jacob's Cattle', and 'Yellow Eye'.

3. Le Marché
   Seeds International
   P.O. Box 190
   Dixon, CA 95620
   Le Marché offers a number of heirloom American-style dry beans as well as French ones. The firm also carries a large selection of imported snap bean varieties. Catalog: $2.00.

4. Nichols Garden Nursery
   1190 North Pacific Highway
   Albany, OR 97321
   This nursery carries 'Santa Maria Pinquito' and 'Dark Red Kidney' beans.

5. Redwood City Seed Company
   P.O. Box 361
   Redwood City, CA 94064
   Redwood City Seed Company offers many of the best varieties of beans for baking. Catalog: $1.00.

6. Seeds Blum
   Idaho City Stage
   Boise, ID 83706
   Seeds Blum carries most of the old heirloom varieties of beans, many of which are great for baking. Catalog: $2.00.
7. The Vermont Bean Seed Company
   Garden Lane
   Bomoseen, VT 05732
   True to its name, this company carries many varieties of beans good for baking.

Festival

Bean-Hole Bean Festival
Oxford County Fairgrounds
State Route 26
South Paris, ME 04281
This is an annual event held the last Saturday afternoon in July. Genuine bean-hole beans are served with music, great hospitality, and hot dogs, brown bread, sauerkraut, and a beverage.

Books

The following three books are all out of print. Look for them in libraries and used-book stores.

Dragonwagon, Crescent. *The Bean Book*. New York: Workman Publishing Company, 1972.
This little book contains many different recipes for dry beans, including a few for baking them.

Turvey, Valerie. *Bean Feast*. San Francisco: 101 Productions, 1979.
This compendium of international bean recipes contains a few baked bean recipes plus lots of other great recipes for dry beans.

Withee, John E. *Growing and Cooking Beans*. Dublin, N.H.: Yankee, Inc., 1980.
The definitive book on growing and cooking beans. John covers dry beans and how to bake them in great detail.

Native American Gardens

WHEN I WROTE TO BILL BENNETT to ask whether it was time to come photograph his corn-planting ceremony at the Plimouth Plantation's Wampanoag Indian garden, this was his reply: "As I write this, a pair of Canada geese are swimming out in the pond behind the house. The red maple is getting ready to bloom—but the oaks and the dogwood are still holding back. They are the traditional harbingers of planting time round here. The whip-poor-will and the catbird are not heard from either. They are both primarily insect-eaters and their calls (the catbird often imitates the whip-poor-will) are a sound heard when it's warm enough in the evening for insects to be about. When all those things happen, it's time to plant the corn!"

Most gardeners with whom I correspond would have replied with a calendar date, not a reading of their natural environment. Today most gardeners determine planting dates by consulting a book or local nursery. But, traditionally, Native American gardeners have used a different system. Their knowledge has come from observing the natural world and from working on an intuitive level.

When I planned this book I wanted to include a Native

OPPOSITE: *'Hopi Blue' corn is the most famous of the colored corn varieties. It is easy to grind and makes flavorful cornbreads and tortillas.*

American garden, and my reasoning reflected one of life's many contradictions. True, I write garden books, but it is still my conviction that gardening is an intuitive process that is often best learned by observing and interacting with the natural world rather than by simply reading a book. Bill Bennett's letter thrilled me in its evocation of the garden as the co-creation of gardener and land.

The Native Americans of past generations were fabulous gardeners. In fact, according to Bill—who is operations manager of the Wampanoag Indian Program at the Plimouth Plantation in Plymouth, Massachusetts—after the Pilgrims landed, the Native American women were producing five times as much food per acre as the British colonists were. I had always had respect for the native gardeners, but now I wanted to explore their methods in depth.

My other motive was to research and document the native origins of many of our modern food crops and learn about the old varieties. When I began work on this book, I was struck by how many references were made to native foods. I had been under the impression that most of our basic vegetables came from Europe. Not so—most are New World, including beans, snap and dry; squash, summer and winter; peppers, sweet and hot; and, of course, corn.

Finally, as a gardener and cook, I had been exploring alternative corns—the grinding corns. I call them alternative because when you pick up a garden book and look up corn, 99 percent of the information concerns sweet corn eaten fresh from the garden. Like the dry beans discussed in the "Baked Bean Gardens" chapter, this is an example of how we gardeners have limited our scope. Fresh sweet corn is available to us for only a few weeks of the year, and while it is certainly one of the most delicious garden vegetables, grinding fresh-roasted corn kernels to use in dishes such as cornbread and Indian pudding throughout the year makes a very flavorful addition to your table fare.

Native American cultures are very diverse, and their geographical locations range from the high mesas of the Southwest to the swamps of the South, the northern woodlands of New England, and the Northwest. Historically, many were hunting-gathering societies. Others were agrarian. For this chapter, I have concentrated on the agrarian tribes and those of their foods and garden practices we might benefit from. Cultivated food crops, however, were only a part of Native American cuisine. I encourage you to become acquainted with the wild plants native to your area to supplement your native food crops and to use as seasonings. You'll find much support and information available if you embark on such an adventure, for there are organizations and informed people throughout the country who are willing to share their knowledge.

To name just a few sources, and at the same time give you a feeling for their commitment to Native American culture, I want to talk about some of the people who helped me assemble the information in this chapter. First are the aforementioned Bill Bennett and the Wampanoag Program at Plimouth Plantation, whose demonstration garden is described in detail later in this chapter. Next is the National Colonial Farm in Accokeek, Maryland, which maintains a garden that is an authentic reproduction of an early colonial garden. When I talked to staff horticulturist Mary Ann Klein, she made me very aware of how dependent the early European settlers were on local tribes for food and cooking methods, and of why, consequently, many of our modern dishes are based on the table fare of these indigenous cultures. Both the National Colonial Farm and Plimouth Plantation are open to the public.

Carl Barnes, a corn collector from Turpin, Oklahoma, was another valuable source. Carl is dedicated to maintaining the diversity of corn varieties and has formed an organization called CORNS. Its members are dedicated gardeners who grow many of the old corn varieties and save the seeds. Carl was able to help me sort out some of the Native American varieties and their uses.

Mahina Drees of Tucson, Arizona, also helped immensely. Mahina is one of the founders of Native Seeds Search, an organization dedicated to saving the food plants of the Native Americans of the Southwest. She and other members of the organization seek out ancient varieties and redistribute the seeds to Native Americans who had replaced the old varieties with hybrids that weren't successful, as well as to other gardeners interested in plants acclimatized to desert conditions. Native Seeds Search maintains a demonstration garden at the Tucson Botanical Garden, offers classes, and maintains a growers' network dedicated to keeping these valuable plants alive.

In putting together this material, I concentrated on the food crops themselves and could only hint at some of the related philosophical and religious underpinnings of the Native American cultures. If

The author's southwestern Native American garden, planted with hot peppers, bush beans, amaranth, and sunflowers.

you find yourself involved in growing a Native American garden, however, you will surely want to explore these areas further—in fact, you will hardly be able to help it, so pervasive are the world views that knit all aspects of life into cohesive wholes within Native American societies.

How to Grow a Native American Garden

Years ago, my business partner, Jane Gamble, and I had a huge vegetable garden together. One spring day we decided to plant our corn and beans together as the Native Americans had. Well, sir, what a tangled mess resulted. We ended up with bean vines that strangled, distorted, and bent to the ground the usu-

ally vigorous corn. Obviously, those earlier gardeners knew something we didn't!

In most ways the Native American garden doesn't differ much from any others. The corn, beans, and squash, for instance, are planted and maintained as are their modern cousins. However, there is a specific technique of hilling you might want to try, as well as a crop you might not have grown—namely, grinding corn.

The mistake we made when we planted our corn and beans was to plant 'Silver Queen' corn and 'Kentucky Wonder' snap beans in the same hill and at the same time. What the Native Americans knew was this: in all but the coldest climates, to prevent mayhem, you must plant the beans after the corn is a finger-length high and use only varieties of beans that are not rampant growers. Simple knowledge, but vital.

The specifics are as follows: Plant four to six corn seeds to a hill. Two or three weeks later, when the corn plants are up and starting to whorl, thin them to the four healthiest and plant two or three bean seeds on the north side of the hill. The variety of corn is not crucial as long as you avoid dwarf types. You can experiment with the bean variety, too, but basically it should have rather short vines. If in doubt, the safest variety to use is 'Genuine Cornfield' beans. See "Recommended Native American Vegetables" for information on where to get them.

Next, let's look at grinding corns. They are grown basically the same way sweet corn is (see Part Four, "An Encyclopedia of Superior Vegetables"), but you leave the ears on the cob and allow them to mature and dry on the stalk in the field. If the weather is unusually wet, or if you have problems with birds and other pests, bring the ears into a dry garage or attic. When they are completely dry—which can take weeks or, more often, months—you can husk and store them in a dry place or remove the kernels and store them in jars or cans in a dry closet. See the section on storing beans in the "Heirloom Gardens" chapter for information on storing seeds. If you have only a few ears to shell, remove the kernels by rubbing two ears together. For large harvests this can get tedious, so you might want to try an inexpensive little gadget, the corn sheller, available from Henry Field's (see "Sources" at the end of this chapter).

The kernels of grinding corns contain more starch than those of fresh-eating corns, so you must isolate them from your hybrid sweet corn. Otherwise, cross-pollination could result in some very starchy corn on the cob. This is not a serious problem with most varieties but it can be annoying and, in the case of the supersweet varieties, unpalatable.

This brings up another pollination problem. Since many of the Native American vegetable varieties are rare, you will probably want to save your seeds from year to year. Saving bean seeds is simple, but corn and squash plants must be carefully isolated to prevent cross-pollination from other varieties. See the "Heirloom Gardens" chapter for more information.

To grow a Native American garden, then, use the above information, look over the following gardens and the "Recommended Native American Vegetables" section, and then consult Part Four, "An Encyclopedia of Superior Vegetables," for specific growing information on the basic vegetables.

The Plimouth Plantation Garden

"Toward the end of March, the Canadian geese starting to move north again was the signal for the Wampanoag tribe to move to summer quarters in the rich bottom land near the Eel River." This was how Bill Bennett began his explanation of the Wampanoag garden at Plimouth Plantation, a living-history museum of seventeenth-century Plymouth, in Massachusetts. As operations manager for the Wampanoag Indian Program at the museum, Bill was discussing how the Wampanoags maintained their food crops.

As Bill explained, "With all the Eastern Algonquian clans, of which the Wampanoag are one, it was the female who was the farmer. It was her job to raise the "Three Sisters of Life"—the corn, beans, and squash. The woman was the farmer because she was considered a life giver, and she and the earth, another life giver, worked their magic together. The men would burn the trash and break up the earth, but once the planting had begun, men were not allowed in the garden. In my tribe, the Osage, the men had to remain silent when they were doing their work so that there would be no male voices heard in the female's magic.

"Growing primarily these three crops, the Wampanoag woman was able to produce about two hundred English bushels of food per acre. In contrast, the English, who considered themselves on the leading edge of an agricultural revolution, were only producing a fifth as much food per acre—about forty bushels. Writers from Europe consistently noted that not only the Wampanoag, but all the tribes from Virginia to southern Maine, were extremely productive. The females produced about 70 percent of the tribes' total food from the garden, and they foraged another 10 percent. The men obtained the remaining 20 percent. But that's not to say that the women did 80 percent of the work. It was actually a pretty even division of labor; it just took more time to get the fish and clams and to hunt for game.

"Looking at the demonstration garden here at Plimouth, we can see how all that food was produced. The Native American garden, with the hills interplanted with corn, beans, and squash, represented a marvelous evolution of symbiotic plantings. The beans provided the nitrogen for the corn, the corn plants provided poles for the beans, and the spines on the pumpkins and squash provided protection for the others. They saw this symbiotic triangle, which we look upon today as technology, as *manitou,* or magic. That's why the crops were called the "Three Sisters of Life." The Wampanoag knew that when these three plants grew together, things would turn out okay."

Planting in hills was also significant, Bill pointed out, particularly at the Wampanoag garden's latitude, which is forty-two degrees north. In this cold climate, using the angled side of the hill was a necessary way of absorbing the sun's energy.

"Once the field had been cleared and the soil prepared, it was time to make the corn hills. The herring usually run around the end of April, and once the Wampanoag caught them, they would spread the fish around the field and then mound the corn hills over them, one herring per hill. In this part of the country, the hills were two feet in diameter and six inches high and ranged from two and a half to three feet apart. In dry parts of the country, the hills would be five or more feet apart, to allow the corn's roots to stretch out and get all the available water.

"After the hills were made, the Wampanoag would wait to plant until the dogwood blossoms changed from beige to white, or the wild plum started to bloom. Lacking both of those, they would watch for the opening of the buds on the oak trees. These natural phenomena would occur because the soil had achieved a certain temperature, and that exact temperature would cause the corn to germinate quickly, without rotting or sitting there too long as a target for the crows and sea gulls."

Because of the northerly latitude, the Wampanoag planted the beans at the same time as the corn. In warmer climates a tribe would wait a few weeks to plant the beans so that the latter would not overgrow the corn. 'Pinto', 'Red Kidney', and 'Soldier' beans are planted at the Wampanoag garden. Bill told me that those are the closest equivalents he could find to the varieties planted years ago. Though usually described as bush beans, the ones Bill has grown produce short climbing vines. The varieties of corn planted are 'Northern Flint' and 'Mandan Maid', both flint corns raised for grinding and good storage capabilities.

A few weeks after putting in the corn, the Wampanoag planted squash and pumpkins on the sides of the hills. The squash and pumpkins were raised as food, of course, but planting this way allowed them to trail out through the garden and shade the earth, keeping weeds out and moisture in. Until the squash reached this point it was necessary for the Wampanoag women to pull the soil up around the corn hills with a hoe, an effective process we call dry mulching today. The spiny vines also helped keep out raccoons and even animals as large as deer. As Bill said, "They just don't like to walk through those pumpkin vines. Step on one barefoot and you'll understand.

"Once the squash filled in, the Wampanoag women harvested and controlled the pests, perhaps hand picking insects. To control the major predators, the Wampanoag built corn watches (crude wooden platforms) in strategic areas around the garden. During the day, boys of thirteen or younger would sit on the platforms with piles of stones; when a predator approached, they would throw stones to scare it away. After sunset the men would patrol the fields, perhaps urinating in them to discourage the animals. The dogs that accompanied them would mark the fields, too, and this was a fairly effective countermeasure against the raccoon, the prevalent night predator."

Bill went on to say that the midsummer ripening of the corn was one of the major holidays of the year, and that historically the camp remained set up until the last of the corn ripened and the Canada geese started to fly away. If you want to visit the demonstration garden and attend the interpretive programs, it is open 9:00 A.M. to 5:00 P.M. from May 1 until October 31.

The Bullock Native American Garden

When I stepped off the ferry onto Long Island, it was like coming home. This was my parents' birthplace, and I had spent my childhood summers here on the beaches and in the woods. I was on my way to East Hampton, accompanied by my sister and her husband, to see Sue Bullock's Native American garden. As we drove along the island, the memories came flooding back. We passed the landmark Big Duck, a building in the shape of a duck, and came to the

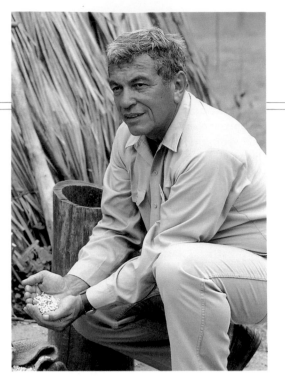

Bill Bennett

Bill Bennett, operations manager for the Plimouth Plantation's Wampanoag Indian Program, is a member of the Osage nation. He grew up in New England and taught marketing at the college level until 1978. While teaching, Bill's interest in natural history grew, leading him to embark on a new career pursuing his passionate interest in the natural world. Today, at Plimouth, Bill delights in interpreting the natural and cultural world of the Wampanoag for the public.

During the few days I spent immersed in Bill's world, I was repeatedly impressed by his enthusiasm. Many times each day he picked sumac berries for visitors to taste, marveling at the lemony flavor, and answered countless questions about the corn watches and corn hills. As we walked through the woods, Bill uncovered Indian pipe growing in the pine needles, his love for the natural world in full bloom.

As we discussed the Wampanoag garden, our conversation naturally turned to the philosophical aspects of the Wampanoag culture. "Native Americans' attitudes about crops were highly religious," Bill notes. "Most of their ceremonial life revolved around the garden. For instance, their new year started with the corn planting, and a twelve-month cycle was measured from that time. And a special holiday feast was held in mid-August, when the corn was ripe and could be eaten in its milk stage.

"To more fully appreciate the Wampanoags' religious views," Bill says, "it helps to understand the concept of *manitou,* an Algonquian word that means spiritual energy or supernatural force—something like electricity. It's the power in the earth and in the spirits of plants and animals. To maintain *manitou,* the Wampanoag acknowledge it through ceremonies and by honoring taboos. For instance, corn stalks are always returned to the soil, never discarded. Corn planting follows specific rituals: seeds are always planted on the south (sun side) of the hill first and planted on the south (sun side) of the hill first and with the correct hand, right or left depending on the tribe. And men are not permitted in a garden at planting time. Conversely, *manitou* can be lost if its power is grounded in some way—for example, if the body of an animal is desecrated, or if any of the rituals or taboos are ignored."

Bill also talked at length about corn, one of the most common Native American crops. "The Wampanoag believe that corn and other vegetables were originally brought to them by the Crow," he said. "The Crow came to show the Wampanoag how to grow food and arrived with a corn kernel in his beak, a bean seed in one ear, and a squash seed in the other. In contrast, archeologists say that corn originated more than five thousand years ago in Central America. They theorize that a highland grass, teosinte, became hybridized and produced a cob close in size to a little finger. It had three rows of grain, and from this the tribes ultimately bred corn similar to the eight-row variety we eat today. When you think about the development of corn, you become aware of a symbiotic relationship between it and man. Once the cob filled out, the corn could no longer grow wild. Can you imagine a cob—maybe six inches long and with eighty-five kernels on it—falling to the ground and new corn sprouting from each of those kernels? With all that competition and shading, the plants could never grow to full height, get pollinated, and produce more corn. Once it had been domesticated, corn needed man to plant it—and, of course, man came to rely on corn.

"The next question is, How did corn from Central America reach New England? Evidence shows it was traded from tribe to tribe in the Yucatán Peninsula, and through the centuries it spread north. Over time, different tribes adapted the corn, selecting the species most suitable for their individual storage or cooking needs.

"The technology of planting and care developed with the species: when to plant, precisely how far apart to set the seeds, how much water to give the plants, and what other plants could be grown with the corn. All this information had to be transmitted from one tribe to another, and because no written language existed, the procedure was ritualized, the knowledge about proper care effectively passing from one generation to the next with little deviation. For this reason, my tribe, the Osage in Oklahoma, practices rituals similar to those of the Algonquians in New England."

Bill notes that while most of us think of garden vegetables in terms of the food they produce, Native Americans used portions of corn and other vegetables for tools, medicines, and cosmetics. For instance, corn husks were twisted to make baskets and woven moccasins. Cobs were boiled in water to make a medicinal wash for poison ivy. Raw smut fungus from corn was given to women to induce labor and help with delivery and was used to treat heart problems.

The insides of pumpkins—the flesh attached to the seeds—were sun dried and reduced to powder for highlighting women's cheekbones.

At the end of our conversation, Bill emphasized that he's learned most of what he knows about Wampanoag gardens as most modern Native Americans have: through research and observation. Learning about the ways of his Native American ancestors has also enabled him to look at nature more closely and with a new awareness.

For further information about local Native Americans, Bill recommends contacting your state archeological office. For a broader view, contact the Smithsonian Institution, the Bureau of Indian Affairs through the United States Department of the Interior, or the Library of Congress—all in Washington, D.C. Another good source is the American Indian Archeological Institute, P.O. Box 260, Route 199, Washington, CT 06793.

---

teepee at the Shinnecock Reservation's Indian Trading Post, where we hoped to find Alice Bun, a Shinnecock and our father's longtime friend. Sure enough, there she was—well over eighty and still beautiful. We chatted about old times, and when I told Alice about my project, she was intrigued and recommended some books on Native American cooking.

After we left Alice, we headed toward Sue Bullock's in East Hampton. I had met Sue at a lecture I had given in New York City. When I announced that I was looking for growers for my theme gardens, she volunteered to grow a Native American garden. The idea excited her, since it linked her interests in Native American cultures and gardening. Sue and I planned the garden long distance. I had her contact Mary Ann Klein, staff horticulturist at the National Colonial Farm in Accokeek, Maryland, who helped her choose appropriate crops and sent her most of the seeds.

The plants in Sue's beautiful garden were so healthy I asked her about her soil and climate. "The soil is fantastic here," she responded. "This used to be farmland and just about anything grows well, even though we're right on the ocean. The drainage is excellent and, except for adding compost to make sure the nutrients get back into the soil, we really have no problems at all. The corn is incredibly high and healthy, and my hollyhocks are probably eight or nine feet tall. I water everything with soaker hoses and try to grow everything organically. My main pest problem is slugs. One of my early-morning spring activities is to collect them all. Still, killing creatures is becoming a problem philosophically. My only other insect pests are Japanese beetles and squash borers. I hand pick the beetles and feed them to the chickens. I spot squash borers when vines start to wilt; I just slit a stalk with my fingernail until I find the pest. Then I pull it out and kill it. For some reason I kill squash borers without remorse."

Sue planted 'Virginia Gourdseed', which grew beautifully, and 'Hopi Blue' corn. The 'Hopi Blue' was from my garden, and our planting was experimental, since some of the types of Hopi corn don't do well in eastern gardens. Sure enough, the 'Hopi Blue' didn't attain any real size. Sue also grew two kinds of pumpkins, 'New England Sugar' and 'Connecticut Field', and for beans she grew 'Genuine Cornfield', 'Purple Pod', 'Case Knife' brown-seeded pole beans, and 'Sieva' limas. She also grew 'Mammoth' sunflowers and sage.

Sue ate little from the garden. For one thing, raccoons moved in on the corn. Further, since the garden was small and produced only a modest harvest of seeds for all the varieties, those were needed for the next year's garden. But what little she cooked,

Sue Bullock enjoyed growing a Native American garden on Long Island. Her garden includes 'Virginia Gourdseed' corn, pumpkins, and beans.

she really enjoyed. She was pleasantly surprised at how tasty all the beans were and described the varieties as having lots of delicious bean taste and no strings. The 'Purple Pod' beans were dark purple when raw and green when cooked, and almost identical to the 'Royalty' beans with which she was familiar. Sue said the 'Sieva' limas were outstanding in flavor but bore a very small crop, so next year she would plant many more than the nine plants she had this year. All in all, she thought the beans superior.

Sue cooked and enjoyed the few ears of 'Virginia Gourdseed' corn. She described them as tasting like the corn she ate as a child, with a flavor somehow less refined than that of modern corns. The corn wasn't as tender or sweet as the corns she had grown

used to but had more true corn taste—a pleasant change, she said. Sue saved some seeds for next year and is anxious to try them again.

Philosophically, Sue feels a kinship with Native American gardeners and their relationship to the earth and its creatures. "I really believe that the earth is a living being," she told me, "and is allowing us to live on her and that we owe her respect and gratitude for nurturing us. When the Hopis plant their corn, they pray and bless it as they put the kernels into the ground. I try to do the same, and when I harvest something I thank the plant. I appreciate what it's produced. I believe that all creation is interrelated, and if a person feels that way his or her garden will respond accordingly."

Recommended Native American Vegetables

This section lists some of the most outstanding varieties of Native American vegetables, though the emphasis is definitely on corn. For historical reasons and for their uniqueness, I chose vegetable varieties grown by Native Americans at least a hundred years ago, or varieties that closely approximate them. Next to most variety names you'll find numbers in parentheses corresponding to the seed companies listed in "Sources" at the end of this chapter. No numbers are given for varieties carried by most of the companies listed. One seed company in particular specializes in Native American varieties: Native Seeds Search. For detailed growing information on all the vegetables, see Part Four, "An Encyclopedia of Superior Vegetables," and for detailed cooking information, see the "Cooking from the Native American Garden" section that follows.

BEANS Beans were a most important crop for the Native Americans. Many varieties are covered in the "Baked Bean Gardens" chapter, but following are other types to try.

Common beans (Phaseolus vulgaris): These are the beans we are most familiar with. Close relatives of our modern snap and dry beans, they are cooked in many of the same ways. For authentic varieties to eat as snap beans, try the following pole varieties: 'Cherokee' (8), 'Genuine Cornfield' (3, 8, 9), and 'Hopi String Bean' (5).

For dry beans, try some of the modern bush varieties that research indicates are probably closely related to the originals grown by Native Americans, such as 'Red Kidney', 'Jacob's Cattle' (2, 5, 7, 8), and 'Pinto'. Native Seeds Search carries numerous authentic Native American beans, including "eye of the goat" and Tarahumara varieties.

Scarlet runner beans (P. coccineus): Usually considered European but actually native to the Americas, the plants have ten-foot red-flowered vines and bear long green pods. The seeds are red with black markings. Many strains and varieties of scarlet runners are available from most seed companies. Also try varieties from Native Seeds Search (5) obtained from native peoples of the Southwest, but since these bear late in the season, they are best suited to southern latitudes.

Tepary (P. acutifolius): Another Native American bean, the tepary (6, 7) is a small, flavorful bean that can be brown, greenish, white, black, or red-brown with mottling. The different colors have ceremonial significance with some western tribes, though many tribes consider the white ones best for eating. Teparies still grow wild in some areas of the Southwest.

The bushy tepary plants are extremely vigorous and are acclimatized to the desert, since they are highly tolerant of drought, intense heat, and alkalinity. They grow poorly in humid areas of the country. Tepary plants can carry common bean-mosaic virus and should not be grown in gardens where bean seeds are being saved. Though Native Seeds Search carries six varieties of teparies, most seed companies sell these beans under the generic name tepary, with no variety designation.

Lima beans (P. lunatus): Lima beans—large, green, very flavorful and meaty shelling beans—are also native to this hemisphere. Varieties to try are 'Bandy' (or 'Hopi') lima (1) and the 'Sieva' varieties, sometimes called baby limas (3, 4, 7). Native Seeds Search (5) carries four varieties of limas from the Native American tribes of the Southwest.

CORN, MAIZE, or INDIAN CORN *Zea Mays* What pleasure awaits those who go beyond seeing corn as only corn on the cob, and past tasting corn only for its sweetness. There are many more aspects of corn to explore: fresh corn roasted over coals, flavor-packed roasted dry kernels in soups and stews, and a great variety of corns of myriad colors for grinding, to name just a few.

I have a vivid memory of being given my first ear of 'Hopi Blue' corn ten years ago. It was lovingly put in my hand, and the giver looked me in the eye saying, "This corn represents life—share it with others and do not profit from it." This fleeting ceremony made a lasting impression on me; it was so different from how I usually obtain my seeds.

To the Native American, corn, often called Sacred Mother and considered a gift from the gods, has always represented much more than nutrition and has traditionally been steeped in ceremony. Among different tribes corn might symbolize fertility, renewal, or power, and sometimes kernels of different colors represent different families or tribes. From antiquity onward, the midsummer ripening of the new crop has been a time of celebration.

There are many variations of *Zea Mays*. Botanists differentiate among them by whether, for instance, the seeds are wrinkled or smooth, or whether the kernel is hard or only half hard throughout. Most gardeners and cooks are more interested in more practical distinctions: how and where varieties can be grown and how they can be used in the kitchen. Thus, the layman's categories of corn are sweet, pop, and grinding, names that relate to the varieties' major use. But these categories, while useful, have limitations, since almost all types of corn can be eaten in their immature or "milk" stage as corn on the cob, and all but the sweetest corns can be ground for meal. Things get complicated in the case of popcorn, which forms its own category in modern terms but whose varieties were used by Native Americans primarily as grinding corn—and, of course, can still be used so today. Therefore, we need to expand and clarify these three categories to get a broad, practical grasp on corn.

Let's start by considering the makeup of a corn kernel. Like the wheat berry, the corn kernel has an embryo and an endosperm, the nutritive tissue that surrounds the embryo. As the kernel matures, the endosperm's sugars slowly turn into starch. In our modern sweet corns, breeders have selected a gene in the corn that impedes the conversion of sugars to starch so that the kernel remains sweet for a long time. But the corn varieties that are more versatile in the kitchen and that were much more widely used by Native Americans are high in starch, not sugars. For our purposes here, I refer to these more traditional though less well known corns as grinding corns. For more information on corn varieties for eating fresh on the cob, see the Part Four Encyclopedia.

Grinding corns are distinguished by the kind of starch they contain—soft or hard—and by the proportion of starch in the kernel. Corns whose kernels contain primarily hard starch are popcorns (in this context treated as grinding corns) and flint corns. In these corns, the kernels are primarily, but not always, smooth, translucent, and hard. Most are difficult to grind by hand for meal, but are valuable because they grow well in northern climates and in high altitudes. Both popcorns and flint corns store very well. In another type of grinding corn, dent corn, there is hard starch on the sides of the kernels and soft starch on the top, which "dents" when the kernel dries. Dent is easier to grind than flint and grows particularly well in the South and Midwest, but many dent varieties have been adapted to other areas of the country.

Flour corns, many of which are called soft corns, are varieties of grinding corns that contain mostly soft starch. They are not only the easiest to grind by hand, they make the best corn flour, which is finer than cornmeal. The flour corns are grown primarily in the West and Southwest, but some have been adapted to other areas.

One final kind of grinding corn can be called combination corn—corn with more than one type of kernel to an ear. Perhaps more than any other, combination corn symbolizes the Native American's intimacy with the workings of nature, for, as detailed below, it reflects a sure and sophisticated approach to selective breeding.

The following list further clarifies our use-oriented categories while acknowledging frequent crossovers and muddying of boundaries. It's worth mentioning that once I plunged into the world of corn from the Native American perspective, the subtle distinctions suggested the Eskimos and their myriad words for snow. The problem was compounded by the ways our uses of the same corns have changed in many cases, and in the scarcity or disappearance of some varieties altogether. In this list I have given authentic varieties wherever possible, but I substituted modern equivalents for those no longer available. In choosing some of the varieties, I had much help from Carl Barnes, who helped me sort through the varieties and recommend the best ones for different parts of the country. The seed companies in the "Sources" section carry many varieties of Native American corns; other nurseries that have a selection are Le Marché, Tater Mater Seeds, and Nichols Garden Nursery. If you become particularly interested in the more unusual corn varieties, contact Carl Barnes, Route 1, Box 32, Turpin, OK 73950; Carl has small amounts for sale. Send a stamped, self-addressed envelope to obtain a catalog.

Combination corns: Take a look at an ear of the so-called ornamental Indian corn sometimes sold for fall decoration. You'll see a mixture of red, yellow, blue, magenta, and white kernels, and maybe even some striped ones, all on a single ear. Most of us hang this kind of corn on a door or in the kitchen and then throw it away. Doing this is a silent admission that the subtleties therein are far beyond us. Because it's called ornamental, we don't even con-

A selection of edibles similar to those that sustained the colonists. The vegetables were grown at the National Colonial Farm in Accokeek, Maryland, and include 'Virginia Gourdseed' corn, dried crookneck squash, and dried string beans commonly served in a dish called leather britches beans.

sider this corn edible. But according to Carl Barnes, corn is corn, and the so-called ornamental corn is just as edible as the rest. Some types of Indian corn are combination corns—corn whose ears contain more than one type of kernel.

The combination corns symbolize the very basic contrast between Native American and most commercial plant breeders with respect to plant-breeding philosophy. Carl Barnes sums up this difference: "The Native Americans bred for diversity, not uniformity." He told me about going through a cornfield on the Santo Domingo reservation and being shown ears that contained both dent and flint kernels of different types, sizes, and colors. The grower had selected for different proportions of dent and flint on the ears to suit the tastes and cooking practices of the household. Not only was this diversity good for the kitchen,

but it provided a safety net for the tribe, since it meant that a genetic mix was maintained in case of adversity. Unfortunately, our modern corn supply has no such safety net. We breed for uniformity, and according to some social scientists and critics, after years of inbreeding, most of our corn varieties are now much too closely related.

By choosing to grow some sophisticated combination corns, you can do some selective breeding of your own. Once you get going, you'll be able to select the types of kernels and the proportion you want in your own strain. Order some of the Tarahumara flour/flint combination varieties from Native Seeds Search; try 'Mexican June' (3), a blue-and-white corn; or plant some of the so-called Indian or ornamental corns (2, 3, 8), though there is no guarantee that the latter will be combination corns, since some are and some aren't. The great majority of the ornamental corns are flint types, so classified because of their desirable smooth and shiny decorative kernels. Another characteristic of ornamental corn is that its kernels stay tightly on the cob.

Combination corns that are sometimes included under the flint corns (see below), probably because they do well in northern gardens and have therefore lost their indigenous associations, are the 'Mandan' corns from the tribes of North Dakota. The 'Mandan' corns are softer than most flints and are easier to grind. There is a five-colored 'Mandan Bride' (1, 2) and a purple-black variety called 'Mandan Black' (1).

Dent corns (Z. M. var. indentata): Dent corns are some of the most versatile and widely grown varieties of corn, and are often called field corn (see the "Field corns" entry below). Some authorities estimate that 80 percent of the corn grown in this country is dent. Dents can be used for eating fresh, roasting, grinding, and making hominy (discussed below). Dent corns do particularly well in the Midwest and Southeast. 'Virginia Gourdseed' (9) is a very old variety that is well adapted to the Southeast. For the Midwest and Southeast, try 'Trucker's Delight' (4), a sweet white corn good for hominy, roasting, and eating fresh. 'Hickory King White' (3, 8, 9) is a dent corn with white kernels; it's considered one of the best for hominy since the skin of the kernel separates off easily. 'Reid's Yellow Dent' (3, 4, 9) is a versatile yellow corn used for hominy, grits, tortillas, and meal. My favorite dent corn is called 'Bloody Butcher' (8). Of unknown background though certainly related to some of the Native American varieties, 'Bloody Butcher' has deep-red kernels that, when ground, make a tasty, red-flecked cornbread.

Flint corns (Z. M. var. indurata): This corn is called flint because the starch is so hard. Grind this corn in a grain mill. (For information on grinders, see the "Grain Gardens" chapter, or take your corn to a local miller.) Flint corns are great ground into meal for Indian pudding, cornbread, soups, and stews. Varieties to grow are 'Longfellow' (2), an eight-row flint with orange kernels that makes a sweet cornbread, and 'Vermont Yellow Flint' (1); both are good for northern gardens. 'Tarahumara Flint' (5) and 'Hopi Blue Flint' (1, 5, 8) are ancient varieties grown in the higher elevations of the Southwest.

Flour corns (Z. M. var. amylacea): The so-called flour corns are made up primarily of soft starches and grind more easily than the flint and dent corns. They are used in tortillas, piki bread (a traditional Hopi bread), and soups and stews. Flour corns come in many colors and are best grown in the Southwest and West, though many varieties will grow as far north as Canada. Some of these varieties are becoming well known in gourmet circles, and as appreciation for them grows, they are coming to be sold at premium prices for blue-corn tortillas and chips.

One of the best-known flour corns is 'Hopi Blue' (4, 5, 7). Many strains of it are available from seed companies, and the colors range from almost black to purple. The plants are quite drought tolerant and vigorous. Not all the Hopi blue corns are flour corns; some are flints. Other flour corn varieties that make blue cornmeal are 'Blue Corn' (6), 'Sandia Pueblo Black' (7), and 'Navajo Blue' (5). White flour varieties are 'White Posole' (6) and 'Navajo Hominy' (5), two white corns favored for posole, a southwestern version of hominy.

Field corns: Occasionally you will see references in cookbooks to field corn. Field corn is a term generally used for a local feed or grinding corn and is usually a dent corn, though it can be a flint or even a combination of flint and dent. Most field corn will make good cornmeal.

Popcorns (Z. M. var. everta): The popcorns are the hardest types of corn. A hard starch forms the outer shell; the inside consists of a small amount of soft starch. When heated in the fire, the soft starch starts to expand and steam, pressure builds up, the unyielding hard starch suddenly explodes—and *voilà,* popcorn! Whereas contemporary Americans grow popcorn almost exclusively for popping, the Native Americans grew popcorn for grinding, though they popped it, too. If you're drawn to the idea of restoring old ways, an interesting variety to try is 'Indian Popping' (6) corn. The cob is four inches long and the kernels are red and yellow.

Sweet corns (Z. M. var. saccharata): Native Americans ate most corns in their immature state as corn on the cob. The Native American varieties are certainly not as sweet or tender as our modern ones, which have been bred for high sugar content and refinement, but some argue that they have more "corn" taste.

No matter what the corn type, when you want to eat corn fresh off the cob you'll need to find out by trial and error when it is ripe. Peel back a husk and puncture a kernel with your thumbnail to determine whether it is tender and if the juice is "milky" and white. If it is, bite off a few kernels to test the taste. Unless or until you become familiar with particular varieties, kernel color will be no indicator of readiness, since some of the colored varieties have white kernels in the sweet, or "milk," stage, while others have colored kernels.

The following varieties are particularly flavorful. 'Black Aztec' (1, 7) for sweet, fresh eating, or dried to make a blue-green cornmeal, and 'Hopi Bantam' (5), a white corn acclimatized to the low desert.

JERUSALEM ARTICHOKES *Helianthus tuberosus* Native Americans dug and used Jerusalem artichokes, sometimes called sunchokes, for centuries. These easily grown tubers have a crunchy texture and a mild herbal flavor. Taste some to be sure you like them before you plant, though, because they are hard to get rid of. They are herbaceous perennials that grow to around six feet tall. In spring, plant tubers six inches deep in good garden soil. Choice varieties that are not knobby and are easily peeled are 'Fuseau' (8) and 'Smooth Garnet' (8). Jerusalem artichokes need only the most rudimentary care during the growing season. Dig up tubers after the plants have died down in the fall and the frosts have arrived, or mulch heavily and leave them in the ground and dig them up as you need them. To prepare them, wash them well, cut them up, and add raw to salads; or try them boiled in soups, fried, or wrapped in foil and roasted.

PEPPERS Native American tribes bordering Mexico used chili peppers of varying hotness. See the "Chili Gardens" and "Mexican Gardens" chapters for detailed information on varieties and how and where to grow them and for cooking information.

SQUASH *Cucurbita Pepo; C. moschata; C. maxima; C. mixta* Both summer and winter squash and pumpkins were widely grown by Native Americans. For winter types, select from 'Green Striped Cushaw' (7, 8, 9), a whitish-green squash with green stripes and a moist yellow flesh good for pies. Some southwestern varieties are 'Santo Domingo' (6), a large yellow-and-green-striped squash with sweet flesh; 'Tarahumara' (6), a long or round striped squash; and 'Hopi Cushaw' (5), similar to 'Tarahumara'. Squash similar to Native American varieties are our modern scalloped, acorn, and hubbard types. By the way, Native Americans ate winter squash in their

All squash blossoms are not only edible but are delicious stuffed or used in soups and fritters.

immature stage as we do summer squash. For pumpkin varieties similar to those grown by Native Americans, choose from 'Small Sugar' (1, 8, 9) and 'Connecticut Field' (8, 9).

For summer squash, the most common variety and a very old one is 'Yellow Crookneck'. In addition, select from those carried by Native Seeds Search; the squash carried by the company has been gathered from the tribes of the Southwest.

Cooking from the Native American Garden

This section on cooking from the Native American garden has corn as its primary focus, though other vegetables are represented as well. And though domesticated foods take precedence here, much of what the Native Americans ate was wild. For example, besides containing much flint corn, the diet of the northeastern tribes also included wild blueberries, chestnuts, mint, fiddlehead ferns, seafood, and game. In contrast, the southwestern tribes relied heavily on the soft flour corns, augmenting them with tepary beans, wild chili peppers, yuccas, pine nuts, mesquite beans, and game animals.

I can only hope to whet your interest in Native American cooking in this brief overview. For more information on this vast and fascinating subject, consult the books listed in "Sources."

Until the Europeans arrived, the Native Americans had no metal cooking containers; they boiled liquids in pottery, but only in a limited way. Therefore, some of the ancient cooking methods—cooking in embers, for instance—differ markedly from the techniques most Native Americans use today. On the other hand, cooking in the ground as you would for a clambake, barbecuing, and popping corn are ancient methods Native Americans still enjoy, and these techniques have become part of our national cuisine. Likewise, ancient native dishes such as clam chowder, cornbread, chili, and succotash have been absorbed into our modern food culture, though they have been modified over the years. Consider cornbread, for instance, whose evolution reflects the nation's changing tastes. Corn flour has no gluten and does not rise in dough like wheat flour, so many of the old corn dishes are heavy by modern standards. Native Americans made cornmeal into unleavened cakes and roasted them in embers; but the colonists brought yeast and wheat for baking, so cornbread became a yeasted bread. When baking soda was invented in the mid-1830s, it came to be used in cornbread to speed up and facilitate its preparation. Thus, the cornbread made from a modern recipe has come quite a long way from the ancient unleavened cornmeal journey cake.

You'll find both old recipes and modern adaptations of old concepts in the recipe section of this chapter. But first you'll need some basic information about the produce in a typical Native American garden—how various foodstuffs were treated and the roles they characteristically played in the diet of our native peoples.

Beans

Beans were second in importance only to corn, and there were almost as many ways of preparing them as for corn. Also, beans and corn form a complete protein when combined, so the two were often used together. Though many varieties of beans were available, they were all cooked in similar ways: boiled or fried. While eaten fresh for a short time of the year, even the green snap beans were dried whole and reconstituted. Fresh shelling beans were eaten boiled or in soups or stews, but most of the beans grown were dried for storage and later soaked in water for use. When using beans in these ways, note that most dried-bean varieties generally take about the same amount of time to cook, but, as Mahina Drees of Native Seeds Search notes, tepary beans are an exception, and take quite a bit longer. See the "Baked Bean Gardens" chapter for more information on preparing beans.

Corn

As corn was their staple food, most tribes learned to use it in myriad ways, including many we still enjoy, such as corn on the cob, succotash, tortillas, popcorn, hominy, and cornbread.

In some forms corn is not easily digestible, so some native techniques were aimed at making it more so. One way was to parch the corn by heating it in hot sand or, when such implements appeared, in a cast-iron pot until it was brown and the starches had softened. Another way, still used today, was to remove the outer skin with lye, lime, or ashes, thus making hominy (covered in detail below). Grinding by hand with a mortar and pestle was the most common way to prepare corn, and you certainly have the option

OPPOSITE: *A candle-lit dinner featuring Native American foods, including game hen with wild rice stuffing, acorn squash filled with filbert butter and maple syrup, roasted Jerusalem artichokes, and cornbread with currants. The flowers are from a southwestern native plant, the yucca.*

to grind your corn this way, though few of us are so inspired. For winnowing and grinding methods, see the "Grain Gardens" chapter. I have used a meat grinder for my corn, putting my 'Hopi Blue' through a few times, but it's a tedious business and the resulting meal is quite coarse. I finally purchased a grain-grinding attachment for my Kitchen Aid mixer and it works beautifully.

Following is a list of the basic ways Native Americans prepared corn.

Popping: Not all corns will pop, only those with a hard outside shell that are designated as popcorn. Native Americans used to throw popcorn in the coals, removing it when it popped, or they would grind the unpopped or popped kernels into meal and then use it as they would any other cornmeal.

Fresh: All the agrarian tribes enjoyed fresh corn on the cob, and they often had particularly sweet varieties that they used for this purpose. They also scraped the fresh kernels off the cob and used them in soups, fritters, chowders, and succotash.

Succotash, a nutritious combination of beans and corn, was enjoyed in either the fresh summer stage or reconstituted from dried beans and corn in winter. This was one of the first dishes the colonists adopted from the Indians. It became the custom in Plymouth to serve a winter-style succotash on Forefathers' Day, December 22, to celebrate the anniversary of the Pilgrims' landing. This dish consisted of dried beans, hominied corn, fowl, and corned beef. Succotash has infinite variations. Additions include meats, squash, peppers, and onions. Fresh or dried seasonings and even sweetening can be used. There are no rules for this dish; its popularity is due precisely to the good combination of flavors it can afford.

Perhaps the most favored way of preparing green corn was to bake it directly in the fire: one brushed aside the ashes, laid the unhusked ears on the hot stones or on the ground, covered them with ashes, and built a new fire over them. When the fire died down, the ears were removed and eaten; they had excellent flavor and supposedly never got scorched. As a guarantee against scorching, a few modern authorities recommend soaking the corn ears in water before roasting them. Native cooks sometimes roasted the corn until the ears were completely dried and parched, and then shelled and stored the kernels for future use boiled whole or ground.

Dried: Stews, the main dish of many tribes, often contained whole kernels of dried corn. All types of corn were used in stews, but whichever was used was usually parched or made into hominy before being boiled with meats, beans, squash, or other vegetables, and a wide array of wild seasonings. If the corn was used without being parched or made into hominy, it was soaked in water for a day or two and then cooked for several hours. But by today's standards the skins can still be quite tough.

Meal ground from whole dried corn kernels is the form of dried corn we are most familiar with today. Many of the corn varieties grown for cornmeal have a high content of soft starch, which grinds easily and can be cooked or baked simply to make a digestible food. The hard-starch corns were often parched or hominied and ground to make them easier to cook with and digest. Native Americans parched corn in coals, but you can do it by putting whole kernels of nearly any grinding corn in a cast-iron skillet and cooking them over low heat to brown them evenly, stirring often to avoid burning the kernels. The perfume will fill your kitchen. Once the corn is browned, grind it as you would normally. Parched corn has a particularly nutty taste, and I highly recommend you try it. As far as I can tell, all the grinding corns can be parched. I tried parching some 'Hopi Blue', a flour corn, and was delighted with the results; it tasted the way popcorn smells. Historically, the parched meal was taken on hunting trips and eaten raw in small quantities, mixed with water and drunk, or cooked into stews. This meal was used to make journey cakes, which gave the name to our contemporary johnny cakes. Today, we can reconstitute parched dent corn in stews and use parched dent, flour, or flint corn for a wonderfully flavorful cornmeal.

Cornmeal today, unparched and usually made from dent corns, is widely used for cornbread, muffins, spoon breads, Indian pudding, cereals, and pancakes. Flour-corn cornmeal can also be used to make delicious tortillas. However, the texture will not be as smooth as that of common tortillas, which are usually made from masa harina, a hominy meal, and the flavor will be distinctively "corny."

Hominy: Hominy, an Algonquin word, refers to the process of removing the tough outer hull of the corn kernels by soaking them in an alkaline solution. Originally, ashes and lime were used in this process, and according to Harold McGee, author of *On Food and Cooking*, modern research has shown this to be a remarkable way of improving the nutritional value of the corn. The alkaline substance not only softened the outer hull, but more importantly, though nutrients were lost, it corrected the amino acid imbalance in corn protein and made the protein more usable by the body.

Hominying goes back to the Aztec and Mayan civilizations, and over the centuries lye, ashes, burned shells, and naturally occurring lime and soda all have been used. The hulled corn was added whole to stews or dried and then cooked whole or ground. Today few cooks bother to hominy their own corn but buy it canned instead. I have found a big difference in the flavor of freshly made whole hominy, though; it is much "cornier" than modern-day canned hominy and worth the effort.

Especially in the southern United States, hominy is still commonly served in a number of ways, either whole or as "grits" (the broken kernels). Posole is the term used for hominy in the Southwest, though it also refers to a dish made with hominy and various other ingredients, such as pork and chilies.

Tortillas are one of the most familiar foods made today from corn treated in this way. The meal made from pounded or finely ground hominy (masa harina) is called masa. It is mixed with enough water to make a dough that can be flattened into very thin patties, which are heated on a griddle, or *comal* Tamales are also made from masa harina.

A great number of techniques for making hominy are in common use; the choice depends on the type of corn, which alkaline substance is used, the age of the corn, and the intended purpose. In *The Cuisines of Mexico*, Diana Kennedy describes the process in detail; *Joy of Cooking* gives a method, too. Ultimately, you will need to experiment with your own corn to determine the best technique to suit your needs. (*Note:* Never use aluminum utensils when working with lime.) Here are some basic proportions: for 4 cups corn kernels, use 8 cups water and 1/2 cup lime (we obtained our lime, called *cal,* from a Mexican restaurant that makes its own tortillas) or 1 cup cooking ash, discussed below. If you use a rocky, unpowdered lime, first dissolve it in a separate container of water and then pour the liquid off into the corn. Soak the corn kernels in the water overnight; then add the lime or ashes, bring to a boil, and simmer covered for 1 to 2 hours. Let stand several hours to overnight, and then wash several times in fresh, clean water, rubbing the hulls loose and rinsing them away.

Generally, dent corns with large and uniform kernels are preferable for making hominy. See the varieties of corn particularly suited to this process in the "Recommended Native American Vegetables" section earlier in this chapter.

Corn smut: This fungus disease of corn was a delicacy to the Aztecs and is still used by many Native American tribes, particularly those of the Southwest. Modern epicures, especially those interested in Mexican cuisine, have honored it, as they do another fungus—the mushroom. Corn smut is known by the name *huitlacoche,* and, according to Gary Nabhan of Native Seeds Search, it has a slight corn taste. Diana Kennedy describes its taste as inky and mushroomy.

The kernels of the affected corn become deformed and covered with a sooty, gray-black mold. If you are interested in trying this ancient treat, you must first have smut in your cornfield—a mixed blessing, obviously. The disease is most apt to appear in warm, rainy weather. If you locate any deformed ears, remove them and cut into the discolored swellings. If the inside is still firm and light colored, cut the smuts off and fry them in butter as you would mushrooms. Or use Diana Kennedy's recipe for quesadillas. However, if the insides are mushy or powdery, you are too late, and you'll need to dispose of the affected ear to prevent the disease from spreading.

Culinary Ashes

Many Native American tribes used to incorporate ashes from different woods into their cornbreads, and some continue this practice today. The Hopis used chamisa ash, which enhances the blue color of blue cornmeal and has a special religious significance. The ashes add nutritionally valuable minerals and may act as something of a leavening agent, since they are alkaline, like soda. Other tribes used juniper or hickory ashes.

If you want to try using ashes in your corn dishes, Mary Ann Klein, staff horticulturist at the National Colonial Farm in Accokeek, Maryland, recommends that you use a hardwood such as hickory. After burning the wood, look for the pearl ashes—the light-gray ashes on top—and make sure they are clean, not gritty. I asked Mary Ann if you could taste the ashes in the cornbread and she said yes. I then asked her if she liked it and she replied, "I prefer baking soda."

Seeds

Seeds, particularly those of pumpkins and sunflowers, were often used like nuts, but they are higher in protein and lower in fat. Today, while most of us appreciate the tasty flavor of sunflower and pumpkin seeds, we relegate them to the bird feeder or compost pile rather than take on the tedious task of hulling. Luckily for us, there are "naked-seeded" varieties of pumpkins available that serve very well and are multipurpose. 'Trick or Treat' (4) and 'Naked Seeded' (6) are worth trying. No efficient method has yet been found for hulling sunflowers, though some gardeners have reported that they can crush sunflower seeds with a rolling pin and float the hulls off with water. You can enhance the flavor of hulled seeds by roasting, which can be done in a dry skillet or in the oven. Take care that the heat is low to medium and that the seeds roast only to the point of becoming fragrant or slightly browned so that you will not burn the delicate oils. Then grind the seeds to a meal or to "butter" in a grinder or blender and use in breads, cakes, patties, or combined with squash.

Squash

Fresh and dried squash were boiled, baked, fried, or put in stews. Often Native Americans dried them by cutting them into spirals or thin slices and hanging these to dry, or, with the hard types, by storing them whole. Native cooks seasoned squash with nut or seed butters, meats, fat, or maple syrup. The colonists used butter plus spices such as cinnamon and nutmeg. Squash blossoms, too, were used often in cooking (see also the "Mexican Gardens" chapter).

As you can see from this overview of Native American cooking, there is much more to explore. For example, I became very intrigued with ghost bread. The Seneca Indians enjoyed this fried bread at a feast given the tenth day after a member of the tribe had died. After the feast, some of the bread was left out overnight, and if it was found disturbed the next morning, this was seen as a sign that the ghost of the departed was displeased with how his or her earthly belongings had been divided.

And I am still trying to learn which of the wild herbs were used, and more about how piki bread is made, but most of all I want to continue to learn more ways of using corn. What little new knowledge I have attained has enriched my table considerably. The following recipes can serve as gentle paths into the world of Native American cooking.

FRESH CORN PUDDING

The simplest corn pudding is just fresh corn scraped off the cob (it should be mature sweet corn—milky but not starchy), put into a buttered baking dish or pan (with a little cream or butter if you like), and baked or simmered about an hour until thick like pudding. You can add diced squash and peppers or sweeten to taste before cooking. Serve the delicious pudding in the following recipe as a side dish, breakfast dish, or dessert.

SERVES 4.

> 2 tablespoons butter
> 2 tablespoons flour
> 1 cup milk
> 6 ears sweet corn, scraped (about 2 cups)
> 3 eggs, separated
> ½ teaspoon salt
> 1 to 3 teaspoons sugar, or ¼ cup minced sweet
>   pepper and a little hot pepper—fresh,
>   dried, or bottled

Preheat oven to 350°.
    Melt butter in a saucepan, add flour, and gradually add milk, stirring constantly over medium heat until thickened. Remove from heat; stir in corn, beaten egg yolks, salt, and any other seasoning ingredients. Beat egg whites until peaks form and fold into corn mixture. Pour into a buttered baking dish and bake for about 30 minutes.

SUCCOTASH

In this modern version of "summer succotash" meat is optional so that the rich flavors of the fresh vegetables can become the stars.

SERVES 4 TO 6.

> 3 tablespoons butter or 2 strips bacon (see
>   variation below)
> ½ onion, chopped
> ½ sweet pepper (green, red, or yellow)
> 2 cups fresh corn kernels (scrape rather than
>   cut the corn if a creamy dish is desired)

Succotash is certainly one of the richest and most satisfying Native American dishes. This summer version is made with fresh giant limas, fresh corn, and red peppers.

2 cups fresh shelling beans (many prefer limas)
1 cup water
Salt and pepper to taste
Optional: fresh hot pepper to taste, minced; 1/4 cup milk or cream; 1 teaspoon sugar; 2 tablespoons minced parsley as garnish

Melt butter in a saucepan and sauté onion (and hot pepper, if using) a few minutes to soften. Add sweet pepper and cook a few minutes longer. Add corn, beans, and 1 cup water (and optional hot pepper and/or sugar); cover and simmer about 15 minutes (large limas will need more time). Season and add milk or cream, if desired. Heat through, garnish with parsley, and serve.

Variation: Omit butter from recipe and cook bacon in a skillet until crisp. Remove bacon and sauté onion and pepper in bacon fat. Put sautéed onion and pepper in a saucepan with corn, beans, water, and optional hot pepper, omitting sugar, and cook as above. Serve garnished with crumbled cooked bacon.

LEATHER BRITCHES BEANS

Native Americans preserved green beans for winter use by stringing them on heavy thread to dry for a couple of weeks. The dried beans can be prepared for eating as described below. Remember that our modern "stringless" varieties of snap beans are a new development. In the old days one ate fresh or reconstituted cooked beans whole by holding onto the end of the bean with the fingers and drawing it out across the teeth to separate the meaty part from the string.

SERVES 6 TO 8.

1 pound dried string beans
1/4 pound cubed ham, bacon, or salt pork (or other game meat)
Salt and pepper to taste
1 small onion, diced (optional)

Wash dried beans, and soak them in 2 quarts water for about an hour. In a pan or skillet, sauté meat for a few minutes (add some oil with lean meat, and add onion, if desired). Add beans and water, season, and simmer, covered, for 2 to 3 hours or until beans are tender. Check occasionally and add more water if necessary. Before serving, add salt and pepper to taste. Serve with cornbread to soak up the juice.

NATIVE SQUASH STEW

It is very difficult to give a recipe for a Native American stew, since the idea is to prepare a hearty dish out of whatever ingredients are available seasonally. Whether you use fresh or dried vegetables will depend on your garden and the time of year. Most of us today have access to domesticated meat only; as you'll see, the recipe that follows from Mahina Drees uses turkey. Mahina and fellow Native Seeds Search founder Gary Nabhan have modified this recipe to their liking.

SERVES 8 TO 10.

1 pound raw turkey meat, ground
1 large onion, chopped
1 or 2 tablespoons oil
Water to cover
4 cups peeled and cubed winter squash
6 fresh mild green chilies, peeled and chopped, OR 1 small can of chopped mild chilies
1 or 2 cloves garlic, chopped
Salt and pepper to taste
2 peeled tomatoes, chopped (optional)

In a large cast-iron stew pot or skillet, brown turkey meat in oil with onions. Barely cover with water, add remaining ingredients, and simmer, covered, over low heat for 30 to 45 minutes or until squash is tender.

JOHNNY CAKES (HOE CAKES, CORN PONE)

As griddle cakes became one of the evolutionary paths of cornbreads, several names and techniques passed into and out of use. There seems to be very little consistency as to which names match which proportion of ingredients or even which ingredients are included. The liquid may be water, milk, stock, or a combination of these; there may be baking powder or soda or none; sweetener may or may not be used. And when wheat flour, eggs, and leavening are used, the result is cornmeal pancakes, still delicious but a far cry from the original journey cakes, which had to be tough traveling fare. This version is remarkably light and tasty considering its simplicity.

SERVES 3 TO 4.

> 1 cup cornmeal
> 1½ cups boiling water
> ¼ teaspoon salt
> 1 tablespoon butter
> 1 tablespoon molasses or maple syrup
> ½ cup milk

Put cornmeal into a saucepan on low heat and slowly add boiling water, stirring constantly. Cook and stir

Blue cornbread is made from 'Hopi Blue' corn. The home-grown meal is a tasty change from the usual yellow-corn varieties. The flowers are Mexican zinnias.

until very thick, about 5 minutes. Add remaining ingredients, beating in milk slowly to make a batter that can be dropped by the spoonful. Drop onto a greased griddle or nonstick pan at a medium temperature to cook until brown, abut 10 minutes on each side. Serve hot as a side dish or with butter and maple syrup for breakfast.

BASIC CORNBREAD

The variations in cornbread are infinite, which is one reason for its popularity as a staple food. It may be cooked on a griddle, in a skillet, or in the oven. The cornmeal may be yellow, blue, white, or red; may be ground coarse or fine; and may include wheat flour for a lighter bread. Sometimes the bread is sweetened, and sometimes it is seasoned with minced vegetables, herbs, peppers, and cheese. One thing that is constant is the delicious flavor and satisfying nature of the cornbread—especially when made with home-grown, home-ground cornmeal. The recipe below is a modern version with some suggested additions. For the wonderful novelty of it, I like to use blue cornmeal with some minced red and green peppers.

MAKES 1 LOAF OR 12 MUFFINS.

> 1½ cups cornmeal
> ½ cup whole-wheat pastry flour or
>   unbleached white flour
> 2½ teaspoons baking powder
> ½ teaspoon salt
> 1 egg
> ¼ cup vegetable oil
> ⅛ to ¼ cup brown sugar, honey, or maple
>   syrup
> 1 cup milk
> Optional: up to 1 cup of minced, briefly
>   sautéed vegetables, such as sweet and/or
>   hot peppers, and onion; about ¼ cup
>   minced fresh herbs, such as basil,
>   oregano, parsley, or cilantro; 1 teaspoon
>   chili powder or cumin; ¼ cup grated
>   sharp cheese; up to 1 cup fresh berries; or
>   ½ cup cooked and drained beans
> 1 standard loaf pan, 8-inch-square baking pan,
>   or muffin tin

Preheat oven to 400°.

Sift together dry ingredients. In a bowl, beat egg

and add oil, sweetener, and milk. Stir in dry ingredients and any additions and mix briefly. Pour into a greased standard loaf pan, 8-inch-square baking pan, or muffin tin, and bake for about 30 minutes (20 minutes for muffins).

BAKED WINTER SQUASH WITH MAPLE NUT OR SEED BUTTER

A nut or seed butter is a wonderful complement to squash. The rich flavors seem meant for each other. You can make your own nut or seed butter (see instructions under "Seeds" earlier in this section) or try some of the many types that are available in natural foods and specialty stores.

Basic baking directions are given below; the time will vary, and the number of people served will depend on the size and variety of the squash. The cooked squash can be seasoned or stuffed however you like.

SERVES 4 AS SIDE DISH.

> 2 acorn or other small squash (about 1¼
> pounds each) or 1 medium squash (about
> 2½ pounds)
> 3 tablespoons each dairy butter, nut or seed
> butter, and maple syrup

Place squash on a baking pan and bake at 350° for ¾ to 1½ hours until soft. You may want to turn the squash a couple of times to ensure even cooking. Cut in half and remove seeds (save to wash and toast for snacks, if you like) and strings; if using 1 squash, cut again to make 4 servings. Put back on baking pan cut sides up. In a small saucepan, melt dairy butter, add nut or seed butter and syrup, and stir to mix. Spoon moisture into squash cavities and coat surfaces. Return to oven for about 10 minutes to heat through before serving.

INDIAN PUDDING

Dried-corn Indian pudding used to be made from parched cornmeal cooked in boiling water—sometimes with pumpkin flesh, nut meats, fat, or maple syrup—until it reached a firm but soft, puddinglike consistency. Steamed puddings were made with the same basic ingredients, although wheat flour was added when it became available, to help glue the mixture together. The ingredients were steamed in a large kettle of boiling water for several hours or, to make enough for feasts, baked in a pit overnight.

Spoon breads, made with less milk and beaten egg whites, are a delicious variation on the puddings. With the addition of onions, peppers, herbs, and/or cheese (and with the sweetener left out), a spoon bread makes a substantial main dish.

The Indian pudding below makes a wonderful dessert or breakfast.

SERVES 6.

> 1 cup cornmeal
> 4 cups milk, scalded (3 cups if using apples)
> ½ teaspoon each salt, ginger, and cinnamon
> ¼ teaspoon nutmeg
> 2 tablespoons butter
> ½ cup molasses
> 1 egg, beaten
> 1 cup cold milk
> Optional: ½ cup raisins; or add 2 cups thinly
> sliced apples and decrease hot milk by 1
> cup

Preheat oven to 290°.

In a double boiler over boiling water, or in a pan over low heat, slowly add cornmeal to scalded milk, stirring constantly until it thickens and starts to bubble. Remove from heat, beat in spices, butter, molasses, and any optional ingredients and let cool slightly. Beat in egg and pour into a buttered baking dish. Carefully pour the cold milk over the top and place in oven. Bake 3 hours; then let cool thoroughly. Serve with cream, ice cream, or yogurt, if desired.

Sources

Seed Companies
1. Abundant Life Seed Foundation
   P.O. Box 772
   Port Townsend, WA 98368
   This organization is interested in preserving open-pollinated varieties of vegetables, including many Native American varieties. The membership fee covers the catalog and newsletters. Membership: $6.00 to 10.00; sliding scale based on ability to pay.

2. Johnny's Selected Seeds
   Foss Hill Road
   Albion, ME 04910

   Johnny's carries seeds for some of the Indian crops that do well in northern climates.

3. Hastings
   434 Marietta Street NW
   P.O. Box 4274
   Atlanta, GA 30302

   This company, a southern specialist, offers seeds of some of the varieties of roasting and grinding corns that grow well in the South.

4. Henry Field's Seed & Nursery Company
   Shenandoah, IA 51602

   This seed company carries many varieties of grinding and hominy corns, as well as utensils to help you shell the corn. It also carries 'Cornfield' beans and 'Connecticut Field' pumpkins.

5. Native Seeds Search
   3950 West New York Drive
   Tucson, AZ 85745

   This organization offers the largest selection of Native American varieties in the United States but emphasizes the Southwest. It maintains a Native American demonstration garden at the Tucson Botanical Gardens (2150 North Alvernon Way, Tucson, AZ 85745) and publishes a newsletter and catalog for members. Membership: $10.00. Price list for nonmembers: $1.00.

6. Plants of the Southwest
   1812 Second Street
   Santa Fe, NM 87501

   This nursery specializes in seeds of plants that grow well in the Southwest, including many Native American varieties. Catalog: $1.00.

7. Redwood City Seed Company
   P.O. Box 361
   Redwood City, CA 94064

   This nursery carries many Native American varieties of corn, beans, squash, and seeds of wild native species. Catalog: $1.00.

8. Seeds Blum
   Idaho City Stage
   Boise, ID 83706

   Seeds Blum offers seeds of many Native American varieties of vegetables. Catalog: $2.00.

9. Southern Exposure Seed Exchange
   P.O. Box 158
   North Garden, VA 22959

   This company carries a good selection of Indian corns, a Hopi sunflower, and some heirloom squash. Catalog: $3.00.

Festivals

Indian Foods Dinner
Jimersontown Presbyterian Church
150 Broad Street
Salamanca, NY 14779

The Seneca Indians put on a classic Indian meal on the second and third Saturdays in November. They serve hulled corn soup and parched corn mush made from their own corn, along with venison and deep-fried ghost bread, a traditional Seneca biscuit. Reservations must be made in advance by writing to the above address.

The Feast of San Esteban
Pueblo of Acoma Tourism
P.O. Box 309
Pueblo of Acoma, NM 87034

A southwestern Indian festival is held at the pueblo every September 2. The festival includes traditional dancing as well as feasting. The food offered includes fry bread, tamales, green chili stew, and pumpkin cookies.

Usquepaugh's Johnnycake Festival
Kenyon Corn Meal Company
Usquepaugh, RI 02892

This festival is generally held on the fourth or last weekend in October. You can spend a day feasting on clam chowder and johnny cakes made the old-fashioned way.

Demonstration Gardens

The National Colonial Farm
Accokeek Foundation
Piscataway Park
3400 Bryan Point Road
Accokeek, MD 20607

This wonderful farm is across the Potomac River from Mt. Vernon. On the grounds are a recreated barn, smokehouse, tobacco barn, farmhouse, and stable. In the gardens are crops of corn, tobacco, and beans, and there's a separate herb garden. All the varieties planted were grown in the colonial era. The farm usually has a summer corn festival that is open to the public.

Plimouth Plantation
P.O. Box 1620
Plymouth, MA 02360

This fascinating village is a recreation of the Pilgrims' first settlement and a Native American summer settlement with a garden. Numerous lectures and demonstrations of Native American garden techniques and foods are presented.

Books

The following books may be difficult to locate. Some are available from the Plimouth Plantation (see above).

Anderson, Jean, and Yeffe Kimball. *The Art of American Indian Cooking*. New York: Simon & Schuster, 1986.

This book contains a large sampling of Native American recipes, including piñon soup, adobe bread, pumpkin soup, and salmon chowder, as well as many less authentic recipes. It is available for a fee from Native Seeds Search.

Humphrey, Richard V. *Corn: The American Grain*. Kingston, Mass.: Teaparty Books, 1985.

This booklet is the second in a series on antique eating. It contains fascinating information about America's most important native food: corn.

Kavasch, Barrie. *Native Harvests*. New York: Vintage Books, 1979.

Probably the most complete work on Native American cooking, this book covers the cooking of most of the eastern tribes and some of the western ones. It contains recipes for nut butters, wild edibles, mushrooms, and wild game.

Kavena, Juanita Tiger. *Hopi Cookery*. Tucson: University of Arizona Press, 1980.

This cookbook is packed full of Hopi recipes. You'll find out how to make Hopi finger bread, piki bread, baked prairie dog, and venison hash and how to use culinary ashes.

Niethammer, Carolyn. *American Indian Food and Lore*. New York: Collier Books, 1974.

This comprehensive study of Native American foods contains 150 recipes. It is available from Native Seeds Search.

Parker, A. C. *Iroquois Uses of Maize and Other Food Plants*. In *Parker on the Iroquois*, edited by William N. Fenton. Syracuse: Syracuse University Press, 1968.

This is a new edition of a book originally published in 1910. Detailed information is given on Iroquois cooking and customs involving corn.

Chili Gardens

A S I APPROACHED THE FAIRGROUNDS, I asked myself how I was possibly going to eat all that chili and not burn up. This was my first chili cook-off, and I was a judge. How much chili does a judge eat? Do the folks make it really hot? I like spicy food, but I don't have a mouth made of asbestos like some people I know. I had been to wine and produce tastings, but never a chili tasting. How could I possibly clear my mouth from one bite to the next?

I was early for the judging because I wanted to talk with the entrants about what they put in their chilis. As I entered the cook-off area, I was surprised at the festival atmosphere. The lawn was surrounded by dozens of carnival-type booths, all decked out. A couple of middle-aged ladies were cooking away in a booth labeled "The Hot Flashes." On the sign for another booth was a giant can of Hormel chili with the international "prohibited" symbol across it—the "Hormel Busters," of course. There were the "Heart Burners," "Chili's Angels," "Rattlesnake Rick's," "Earthquake Chili," and even a group dressed in camouflage garb proclaiming their chili

OPPOSITE: *Chili peppers harvested at the National Arboretum in Washington, D.C. Starting clockwise from top right are 'Tabasco' (narrow red), 'Red Cherry' (round red), 'Aurora' (blunt purple), 'Mexican Improved' (serrano type, green), 'Caloro #61' (large yellow), and 'Fiesta' (long orange).*

Contestants at a chili cook-off put together a batch of "Rambo Red" chili.

"Rambo Red." Hundreds of visitors were wandering around getting pointers, tasting the chilis, and buying drinks and mouth-watering bowls of chili. What fun!

When it came time to judge the chili, I joined twenty or so other judges in a hall. There the officials explained the procedure. Cups of chili were laid out on a long table with only a number to identify each one. Between all the cups were trays of soda crackers and cut-up pieces of celery. (So *that's* how you clear your palate, I thought.) There were also a few bowls of sour cream, used to put out the fire if a chili was too hot. And, of course, there was beer. For guidelines we were told to first ask ourselves if we would want to eat a whole bowl of this chili. We were to look for depth of flavor—a lasting one—and a chili that wasn't too salty and certainly not sweet. We were to seek a traditional taste. And, above all, we were not to talk or make faces. The only communication allowed was to warn our fellow judges if we ran across a "killer chili"—in other words, one that was too hot.

It would be nice to say I had such a sophisticated palate that I picked all three winners, but in fact I liked only one of the winning chilis. It amazed me that most of the chilis were fairly mild, that they varied greatly, but that the winners were quite similar and, furthermore, very salty. The winning chilis

were dark red-brown, full of flavor, and smooth in texture. (See the profile of Carol Hancock in this chapter for information on what makes championship chili and how to enter a cook-off.)

How did this Yankee, who grew up never eating anything spicier than a gingersnap, wind up as a chili judge? Like many other Americans, for years I had ignored chili and chili peppers of all types. But as my tastes changed and I was exposed to more and more hot Mexican and Oriental dishes, I, like many others, gradually started to enjoy spicy foods. I even began making chili using a commercial chili powder. The result was good, but when my husband brought back separate chili spices from Texas and I started making chili with fresh ground cumin and selected ground chilies, what a revelation! Chili peppers weren't simply hot; they actually had complex and varying flavors. This appreciation of fresh ground chilies led naturally to the next step: growing and cooking with fresh green and red chilies of all different varieties. A whole new world had been opened up.

Before we proceed further, just what is chili? When they hear the word chili, most people immediately think of the cooked dish made with meat, spices, and chili peppers (though many a Texan would call that chili con carne). But the term chili is also commonly used to refer to hot peppers. Some use chili to refer to any member of the *Capsicum* genus, hot or sweet. Other folks call all hot peppers chilies. Many westerners use the word chili to refer only to the hot pepper varieties used in Southwestern and Mexican cuisine, not Italian or Oriental hot peppers. For my purposes I have chosen to use the term chili peppers as a blanket term covering all hot peppers; the word chili I reserve exclusively for the dish.

The cooked dish, chili, is truly native to the Americas. Its roots trace back to the Aztecs, who, historians note, made stews with meat and chili peppers. Through the ages, the practice of combining these peppers with meat migrated northward until it was adopted by different tribes of native Americans, some of whom pounded the meat and dried it with chili peppers to make a trail jerky, and others of whom made a green chili stew. The meat-and-chili-pepper jerky, which was usually reconstituted into a cooked dish, was eventually adopted by trail drivers, who spread this hearty meal throughout the Southwest as they drove their cattle to market. Thus was the passion for the dish most Americans call chili dispersed.

Though there is much heated debate as to whether chili should be made with beans, tomatoes, or other vegetables, everyone agrees that one ingredient is essential: chili peppers. You can't make chili without them, and therefore they receive the most attention in this chapter. Gardeners in mild climates have the delicious advantage of being able to experiment with hundreds of chili pepper varieties. A somewhat more limited but still large array of varieties does well in northern climates. In both climates chili lovers can give themselves a real treat by growing their own chili peppers.

How to Grow Chili Peppers

Chili peppers are members of the *Capsicum* genus. Their hotness comes primarily from capsaicin, a pungent and irritating phenol. This chemical is located in the chili pepper's placental tissue, which is found in the light-colored veins on the walls of the pepper and around the seeds. With a few notable exceptions, most garden chili peppers and sweet peppers fall into the same species, *Capsicum annuum*, but the sweet peppers have had the hotness bred out of them. Until recently, the average American gardener has ignored chili peppers, so our plant breeders and seed people have not given them much attention. Consequently, these fiery cousins are usually less domesticated versions of the sweet bell pepper. In fact, chili peppers still grow wild in many areas of the Southwest and Mexico and are harvested by the native Americans there.

Because of their "wildness," most chili peppers differ from bell peppers in a few growing characteristics—namely, pollination methods, ripening times, and disease resistance. Before proceeding further with specifics on growing chili peppers, you might want to refresh your memory on basic pepper culture. Information on planting, fertilizing, and pest problems is covered under "Peppers" in Part Four, "An Encyclopedia of Superior Vegetables."

Chili peppers are perennial plants usually grown as warm-weather annuals. The less domesticated ones are often slow to germinate and grow slowly. (Some, if given much sunlight, make wonderful house plants.) The plants are generally taller, more open, and rangier than bell pepper plants. Some varieties hold their fruits on top of the leaves in a decorative way, but most of the plants produce fruits that hang down.

Certainly among the most beautiful vegetables, chili pepper fruits can be large or small and round, blocky, conical, or elongated. Unripe, they can be green, black, yellow, orange, white, or purple. They ripen through a range of colors including orange, or even brown, but most become red. (The chapter-opening photograph illustrates the color range of chili peppers; these were harvested from the chili garden at the National Arboretum in Washington, D.C.) Chili peppers range in hotness from mild to fiery hot.

Chili peppers, like tomatoes, evolved in the tropics and semitropics. Consequently, most varieties are quite easy to grow in most of the southern parts of the mainland United States and in Hawaii. They are grown the same way as bell peppers. However, the lack of standardization and of specific growing information for the more unusual varieties can be frustrating.

Over the years I have grown and enjoyed many types of chili peppers but have never methodically studied them. So to obtain further information, I contacted several people knowledgeable about growing chili peppers on both the East and West Coast. For some overall information, I started with Craig Dremann, owner of the Redwood City Seed Company, in Redwood City, California. Craig has grown out plants of more than twenty varieties of the chili peppers he carries in his catalog and has studied hundreds of plants throughout their life cycle. He has experimented with germination methods, grown out some of the wild varieties, noted ripening times, and sorted out the pertinent botanical information. Craig has collected his observations in a pamphlet entitled *Chili Peppers in California*, a valuable aid if you become interested in experimenting with different varieties (whether you live in California or not).

Pollination

Generally, the literature on chili peppers describes pollination as being accomplished by the wind, but Craig's evidence shows that in his plot chili peppers seem to be pollinated by insects. Curious as to why his plants had low yields at times, Craig suspected pollination problems and started to note which insects visited the chili plot and how often. Eventually he concluded that the plants' small, drooping flowers were hard for honeybees and bumblebees to hang on to, and that a few types of small, wild, solitary bees were mostly responsible for pollinating his pepper plants. He also concluded that these miniature bees might not always be present in all parts of the country. So he suggests that wherever you live, if your pepper plants are dropping flowers and not setting fruits, if your plants are healthy, and if the weather has not been too cold or too hot, lack of pollination may be your problem. If you suspect it is, try hand-pollinating some of the flowers with a small camel's hair brush: pick up some of the pollen with the brush and transfer it to the stigma. Craig has obtained nearly 100 percent fruit set after hand-pollinating his chilies. If you are unsure of the anatomy of your pepper's flower, take one or two to a nursery and have the pollinating procedure explained to you.

Hotness

Whenever I talk with gardeners and chefs about chili peppers, the conversation always turns to the peppers' hotness. And the question always arises as to what makes the same chili pepper variety fiery hot one time but milder another. I have planted the same variety one year to have it come up mild, while the next year it came up quite hot. In discussing this inconsistency with seed people, I learned that there can be different reasons for the variation. Most agreed that the main reason was climatic differences. A somewhat mild chili pepper, for example, might get hotter than usual if it is grown under the stress of hot and dry conditions. A large difference, however, would be very unusual. A 'Jalapeño' might be milder one year than another, or milder in a wet climate than a dry, but it will still be quite hot, and a mild chili such as an 'Ancho' will never be extremely hot.

Another factor affecting the hotness of chili peppers involves different strains, or subtypes, of the same variety. For instance, Johnny's Selected Seeds in Maine might offer 'Jalapeño' peppers in its catalog, and Horticultural Enterprises in Texas might carry 'Jalapeño' too, but the seeds could be of different strains and the fruits could be a little different. Though both are called 'Jalapeño', the one from Johnny's might be milder than the one from Horticultural. (See the introduction to Part Four, "An Encyclopedia of Superior Vegetables," for a discussion of variety strains.)

Putting aside these minor variations, what everyone wants to know is, Which variety is the hottest? When I discussed this question with Craig, he said the hotness of chili peppers had particularly interested him and he had actually tested the varieties in his catalog and rated their hotness. He used a variation on the Scoville Organoleptic Test that has been in use since 1912.

Craig feels that there is controversy over which chili pepper variety is the hottest because the really hot ones are so hot your mouth can't measure the difference. Therefore, to test them, he found, you must dilute them until you can just barely detect the heat. Then you measure how many ounces of the diluting liquid it took to do that. For example, if one ounce of a certain chili pepper produces a barely detectable hotness in 1000 ounces of tomato sauce, then on Craig's hotness scale this pepper would measure 1000. For your frame of reference, a red-ripe 'Jalapeño' measures 1000 on Craig's scale. He found that the chili peppers in his catalog range from a mild one, such as 'Ancho', which measured 250 on the scale, to the 'Tepin' (a very small pepper popular in Mexico), which rated 31,000. Now you can really appreciate how very hot the 'Tepin' is, because one ounce of that pepper would produce a detectable hotness in 31,000 ounces, or about 240 gallons, of tomato sauce. If you're interested in the hotness scale and the rating of other peppers, consult Craig's pamphlet.

Very hot chili peppers such as the 'Tepin' can actually burn you. Craig recommends that if you're going to eat a chili pepper you've never had before, taste it very, very carefully. When he tries a new pepper he bites into it very slightly with his teeth, and then gingerly tastes the top of his teeth to see what is happening. He then proceeds gradually to bite through the skin and then finally into the chili pepper itself. He avoids using his tongue and lips until he knows the pepper is sufficiently mild.

Growing Chili Peppers in the North

As a rule, northern gardeners will have more difficulty growing chili peppers than gardeners in southern latitudes. For one thing, the shorter growing season means many of the slower varieties might not fully ripen. Also, some of the chili peppers will not get as fiery in northern gardens. To find out about the problems a northern gardener might have growing chili peppers and how to overcome them, I contacted Rob Johnston, Jr., owner of Johnny's Selected Seeds in Albion, Maine, and Roger Klein, Extension Vegetable Crops Specialist at Cornell University in Ithaca, New York. Rob pointed out that trying to

Community gardeners from Mi Tierra Community Garden in San Jose, California, display their harvest of chili peppers. In the background is a chayote vine and at their feet are tomatillo plants.

grow native southwestern plants in a northern garden has its limitations. If you transplant chili peppers from the Southwest to the Northeast, you get cooler weather and much more humidity. The summertime humidity can cause disease problems, and the more unusual varieties of chili peppers can be quite susceptible, since they have had little breeding for resistance. To avoid disease problems, do not plant chili peppers where plants from the same family—such as tomatoes and eggplants—were grown in the past year or two. In addition, keep down populations of aphids and other sucking insects that sometimes spread virus diseases.

Because chili peppers evolved mostly in southern latitudes, some species and varieties are triggered to flower only when the days get shorter. But in northern latitudes, cold weather will follow the short days of fall so closely that the fruit of your peppers will have no time to develop. Says Rob Johnson, "If I grow short-day chili varieties in Maine, I'll just get big plants with no flowers. But some of the varieties are day-length neutral, which means, all other things being equal, they'll flower and mature just as fast in a long day as they will in a short day. For instance, my 'Early Jalapeño' peppers are day-neutral. You have to specify which 'Jalapeño' you need, however, because there are many 'Jalapeño' strains on the market. On the other hand, 'Hungarian Wax' has adapted here extra well. I imagine it's very productive anywhere, and it has really good culinary qualities. In contrast, 'Thai Hot' tends to be more short-day. You get a big plant about three feet tall, and it might set only a few fruits at the bottom." To ensure success, most of my authorities agreed, northerners should probably start chili pepper experiments with varieties of *Capsicum annuum* such as 'Serrano', 'Jalapeño', and 'Hungarian Wax', since they are mainly day-length neutral. Then they can go on to other species of *Capsicum*, such as *C. frutescens* and *C. chinense*, and their varieties—for example, 'Tabasco' and 'Habanero'—since they are more difficult to grow. In addition, you might want to experiment with growing some indoors in the winter. See the information on growing plants indoors in the "Culinary Herb Gardens" chapter.

Roger Klein grew a variety trial garden for chili peppers in Ithaca, New York. Various peppers from this garden have been evaluated and the results presented in a paper, *Hot Peppers—Summary of Data and Information—1984 Variety Trial and Taste Evaluation*. For the trials, Roger grew twelve pepper varieties, and a panel of ten hot-pepper connoisseurs evaluated them for eating qualities. To compare the peppers, the experts took only strips from the pepper wall, avoiding the seeds and placental tissue that would have made the peppers hotter. The chili peppers were evaluated for heat, flavor, and texture on a scale of one to nine, with nine being excellent and one being poor.

The twelve chili peppers evaluated were 'Anaheim', 'Key Largo', and 'Jalapeño' from Harris Seeds; 'Hades Hot' and 'Pimento' from Stokes Seeds; 'Large Red Cherry' from Johnny's Selected Seeds; 'Long Cayenne' and 'Zippy' from the W. Atlee Burpee Company; 'Red Chili' from Fredonia Seeds; and 'Serrano', 'Hungarian Yellow Wax', and 'Floral Gem' from the Ferry-Morse Seed Company.

The varieties with the most intense heat were 'Red Chili' (8.3), 'Serrano' (7.6), 'Long Cayenne' (7.2), and 'Hades Hot' (6.8). 'Key Largo', 'Pimento', and 'Zippy' were very mild, with rankings from 1 to 1.6. Those that were considered the most flavorful were 'Large Red Cherry' (7.3), 'Floral Gem' (6.9), and 'Jalapeño' (6.9). Others that ranked favorably were 'Hungarian Yellow Wax' (6.6), 'Anaheim' (6.6), and 'Serrano' (6.0). The preferred crisp peppers were 'Large Red Cherry' (6.5), 'Anaheim' (6.3), and 'Jalapeño' (6.1), but 'Hungarian Yellow Wax' (5.6) and 'Floral Gem' (4.8) were rated acceptable. 'Hades Hot' and 'Long Cayenne' (both 2.4) were evaluated as too soft.

This study proved to my satisfaction that some chili pepper varieties perform well in northern climates and are well worth growing there. Still, owing to variations in different strains of chili peppers within one variety, you will come closest to matching the results of this trial if you order seeds for the varieties tested from the supplier noted for each one.

There are thousands of chili peppers to explore, a great many of which are carried by the seed sources listed at the end of this chapter. Most of my chili experts recommend that you start with some of the more familiar varieties and limit your chili patch to four or five new varieties each year. Watch to see which ones of these grow best in your climate and have the best flavor. Eventually you will select a good number of productive and tasty varieties for your garden. And through the years you will find your pot of chili getting richer and richer.

The Hughes Chili Garden

As I drove my rental car from San Antonio to Ingram, Texas, I was struck by the beauty of the countryside. My previous experiences in Texas had been in the dusty border towns. But as I started into the hill country, with the soft gray-greens of the junipers and sages offset by the creamy yellows of the soil and sandstone, I had the feeling that nature had been kinder here. Fields of yellow and mahogany Mexican hats waved in the wind, and as a wildflower fan, here and there I was pleased to glimpse clusters of columbine or bobbing heads of black-eyed Susans. No wonder Lady Bird Johnson, with her ranch not too far away, had become so involved with wildflowers; this had to be their intergalactic headquarters.

I was on my way to Mike Hughes's Broken Arrow Ranch. I had met Mike and his wife, Elizabeth, at a cuisine seminar in San Francisco, where they were promoting their wild game business. During the 1930s exotic axis, fallow, and Sitka deer had been let loose in the hill country of Texas and now had overpopulated to the point that they were crowding out native animals. The authorities estimate that more than 160,000 of these exotic animals now roam the backcountry of Texas. Mike had formed a company to harvest the animals and to sell the venison to restaurants all over the United States. As we talked at the seminar, he mentioned his recently published book on ranch cooking and his venison chili. The chili sounded so good it piqued my interest, even though I had just finished a plate of smoked duck with endive. As we chatted, I asked Mike if he liked to garden and how he felt about growing chilies. As he was enthusiastic about both, I asked him if he would grow a garden for me specifically for this book. He welcomed the idea, adding that his assistant, Perrin Wells, knew a lot about chili growing. They would be a great team.

As I bounced out the dirt road to Mike's ranch and wound through the trees and clearings, a wild turkey scurried down the road ahead of me. Next I startled a family of axis deer. How different this reality was from my world of asphalt and lawns. And when I approached the chili garden, Perrin went to his car, pulled out his shortwave radio, and called Mike to join us. (Only in Texas, I chuckled to myself, with such large properties, would you have to radio to the house from the garden.)

The chili garden sat in a field of Mexican hats just past their peak. As we entered the garden we passed a raccoon trap. This garden had been plagued by one disaster after another. In fact, until the week before, I hadn't been sure there would be a chili garden to visit. Late spring rains had been gully washers that produced local flooding, immediately followed by searing drought. Then the raccoons moved in on the corn. But here we were, and through loving care the garden had mostly recovered. Mike began the tour with the chili collection—the 'Jalapeño TAM', 'Serrano', and 'Anaheim' chilies—and went on to show me the bell pepper varieties—'Gypsy', 'Golden Summer', 'Burpee's Early Pimento', 'Sweet Banana', and 'California Wonder'. Around the peppers were 'Burpee's VF Hybrid' and 'Celebrity' tomatoes, pinto beans, cucumbers, elephant garlic, and what was left of the yellow dent corn after the raccoons had feasted.

In Texas, vegetable gardens are started early in

Mike and Elizabeth Hughes harvest chilies and tomatoes from their chili garden in Ingram, Texas.

the year, so Mike had planted the garden in early March. Tomatoes, peppers, squashes, and beans need to be in and producing well before the weather gets too hot. In July and August the plants get rangy and withered looking and because of the high temperature will not set fruit. Mike then takes his tomatoes out, but because the peppers are a little more tolerant, he cuts them back to encourage regrowth. Actually, soon after I left, a big old bull knocked the fence over and ate the garden down to a nubbin, but the peppers recovered to produce a healthy fall crop. After the bull incident, Mike put up a stronger fence and planted his usual fall garden of beans, cucumbers, and squash.

Given that the seasonal planting of gardens in Texas is different from that in much of the country, I asked Mike what other aspects of Texas gardening were like. He filled me in on caliche (a condition in dry regions where crusted calcium carbonate forms on certain soils, preventing roots and water from penetrating) and alkaline soil. The soil in Mike's garden is loamy sand, though the sand is limestone, not silica. Mike has to improve the drainage by digging the soil well and adds ferrous sulfate to acidify the soil. He also adds organic matter and, because the soil is deficient in nitrogen, a nitrogen fertilizer.

In preparation for the cookout that evening, when the day cooled we went back to the garden to harvest fresh chilies for the cornbread, as well as tomatoes, sweet peppers, and cucumbers for the salad. Texas-style venison chili, cornbread with fresh 'Jalapeño' peppers, and tomatoes from the garden—what a feast!

The next morning, as I left the ranch house for the car, an armadillo hopped across the path (I didn't know armadillos hop), and a bright-red cardinal whistled past me. Still remembering the taste of Mike's chili from the night before, I was taking a small part of Texas with me.

I met Perrin Wells at Mike Hughes's ranch in Ingram, Texas, while visiting Mike's chili garden. Perrin was born and raised in Texas and received his horticulture degree from Texas A & M. He spent four years as a gardener for Disney World and is now general manager of Mike's Texas Wild Game Company in Ingram.

To begin, I asked Perrin for his definition of chili. He said, "To me, all chilies are peppers, and all peppers are chilies. Some chilies are hot and good for making powder used in a dish called *chile con carne*, not chili."

Perrin Wells

popular among Texans. 'Anaheim' chilies, which have a nice mild chili taste, are among the most common chilies in Texas. They're generally grown to maturity, but before they turn color they're roasted under a broiler and peeled. Perrin likes to make grilled cheese sandwiches filled with 'Anaheim' chilies. And "probably the most flavorful green chili of all," says Perrin, "is the 'Poblano'. It's a green chili about the size of a bell pepper but more heart shaped and coming to a point at the base of the fruit rather than having a bulldog nose like a bell pepper. It gets a dark

According to Perrin, a number of chili peppers grow in Texas; among the most popular are 'Jalapeño', 'Serrano', 'Poblano', 'Anaheim', and one of the hottest, 'Pequin'. Although usually eaten cooked or pickled, the 'Jalapeño' is sometimes served raw. Perrin says the 'Jalapeño' can be a good bit hotter than most people like, however, and can produce more gastric disturbance than some other chili peppers: "It can burn you coming and going." He adds that a milder form of 'Jalapeño' developed by Texas A & M, the 'TAM', is popular in parts of Texas, but it still has the potential to get hot when grown with too little water.

In Perrin's experience many Texans and southwesterners actually favor the 'Serrano' chili, which they say is more flavorful than the 'Jalapeño'. Some Mexican-Americans in Texas enjoy 'Serrano' chilies dipped in a little dry salt; they say the salt quells some of the heat. Perrin favors the 'Pequin', a pepper about the size of a little green English pea. The 'Pequin' is particularly hot, and Perrin says it gets hottest in the summer after an extended drought.

According to Perrin, other chili peppers are also

green-black skin and isn't as fleshy as a bell pepper. When mature, it can be roasted and peeled and is excellent sliced into strips for recipes. It can be hot, depending on weather conditions. In Texas, 'Poblano' peppers are commonly used for a dish called chiles rellenos, or stuffed chili peppers. When the 'Poblano' is dried, it looks a little like a prune and turns a dark red-brown color. It makes an excellent chili powder because it's so flavorful, but it's not as readily available as other commercial chili powders."

Before I left Ingram, I visited Perrin's garden and was impressed with the health and productivity of all his chili peppers. His plants were two to three feet tall and covered with chilies. Around the plants was a deep mulch of grass clippings completely covering the soil. Perrin had a large harvest and was soon going to pick the fruits and then cut the plants way back to stimulate the plants to produce another harvest in the fall. Just before I was ready to leave, he handed me one of his so-called milder peppers and suggested that I try it. I can't believe I actually did. I guess to a Texan it was mild, but for me it was a scorcher!

Recommended Chili Peppers

Following is an overview of some recommended types of chili peppers you can grow in your garden. The numbers in parentheses after the pepper names refer to the seed companies listed at the end of this chapter. When there is no number following a name, the pepper is readily available from most of the sources listed. Horticultural Enterprises, the Redwood City Seed Company, and Pepper Gal carry almost all the chili pepper varieties on the list.

Be aware that there is much confusion concerning pepper names. This is due partly to the fact that some peppers have one name in their fresh state and another when dried. Furthermore, sometimes a name is dependent on where a pepper is grown and other times on how it is prepared. For information on how to grow peppers, see Part Four, "An Encyclopedia of Superior Vegetables."

Following the chili pepper listings is a brief listing of other chili ingredients you might consider growing in your garden. These vegetables and herbs are commonly used in preparing delicious homemade chilis.

ANCHO (also called poblano, pasilla, and mulato) There is more confusion about the category of chili peppers known as anchos than with any other. Ancho peppers are among the many that are covered by the name poblano when they are green. In Mexico, this same pepper, when dried, is referred to as an ancho, though most American growers and seed suppliers use the term ancho for the fresh green pods as well as the dried ones. These generally wedge-shaped peppers are three to five inches long and two to four inches wide at the shoulders, though there is some variability in size and shape. When immature the fruits are dark green, almost black, but with maturity they turn red.

How to prepare: When anchos are in the green stage the skin is usually roasted and peeled before using. Once peeled, the mild ones can be stuffed with cheese or meat, and both the mild and hot ones cut up and used in vegetable dishes, casseroles, sauces, or chili. In their dried form, anchos are soaked and ground to make a paste used in sauces. Ancho peppers range from mild to hot, and Carolyn Dille and Susan Belsinger, in their excellent book *New Southwestern Cooking,* describe them as having almost an apple flavor. In my own experience, and in talking to other chili mavens, ancho (or poblano) peppers are among the most choice and flavorful of the chilies.

BANANA According to Jean Andrews in her book on peppers, the banana pepper was probably introduced into the United States from Hungary. It is now one of the most widely grown types of hot pepper in the home garden. Banana peppers include sweet varieties as well as the 'Hungarian Wax' type, which are hot. 'Early Sweet Banana', 'Sweet Banana', and 'Sweet Hungarian', as well as the spicy 'Hungarian Yellow Wax', are cultivars of the banana pepper type. These peppers range from two to six inches long.

How to prepare: While generally eaten in their yellow stage, banana peppers turn red when fully ripe. All of the banana-type peppers can be used in the yellow stage for pickles. The sweet ones are good in salads, omelettes, and sauces.

BIRD (also called pequin and petine) The 'Pequin' (5, 6) and 'Tepin' (4, 6) peppers are tiny, about the size of a pea, as are all bird peppers. They are fiery hot chilies and are usually consumed green, but they turn red if allowed to ripen. Both grow wild in areas of Mexico and along the Mexican-American border. Despite their size, they pack a real wallop and are only used when a very hot pepper is desired. These peppers need a long, hot growing season. Start them indoors early in the spring and set them outside when the weather warms up. If you live in a short-summer area or want to grow them in winter as houseplants, you may bring them inside in the fall. For detailed information on bringing plants inside for the winter, see the profile of Rose Marie Nichols McGee in the "Culinary Herb Gardens" chapter.

How to prepare: These peppers are usually added to dishes for a very hot result. Sometimes they are combined with a mild but very flavorful chili pepper. By adding bird peppers such as the 'Tepin', you can have both the flavorful and hot tastes in the same dish.

CAYENNE This category of peppers is the primary one used in Creole and Cajun cooking and is also familiar to us when we buy it in its ground form as cayenne pepper. Cayennes are among the hottest types of peppers commonly grown in the home garden. A few of the cultivars of cayenne peppers are 'Long Cayenne' (4, 7) and 'Red Chili' (4, 6). These peppers are usually three to four inches long and quite narrow, though some varieties are somewhat wedge-shaped. The peppers are medium green but turn red when ripe.

How to prepare: Cayennes are used to provide hotness without much of the pepper-flavor overtones. The fresh or dried peppers can be used in chili and to give gumbos and Creole dishes their special spiciness. See more about cayenne peppers in the "Cajun Gardens" chapter.

'DE ARBOL'   Mexican people consider the 'De Arbol' (4, 6) one of the best of the very hot peppers. Craig Dremann found it to have the same hotness rating as 'Cayenne' in his testing. The fruits are about two and a half inches long and less than half an inch wide. They are light green when immature and red when ripe. These peppers can also be grown as houseplants; see "Bird" peppers, above.

How to prepare: 'De Arbol' can be substituted when you want the hotness of a cayenne but would enjoy some of the subtle overtones that a cayenne can't give. It's analogous to using brandy instead of distilled alcohol. 'De Arbol' is used with meats, in chilis, in salsas—whenever you need a very hot pepper.

JALAPEÑO (called *chile gordo* in Mexico) Jalapeños are probably the best known of the hot peppers. These medium-hot to hot peppers originated in Mexico and are still widely used there today. They are usually sold in seed catalogs under the name 'Jalapeño', though there is an 'Early Jalapeño' (2) for short seasons, and a much milder form bred at Texas A & M, the 'Jalapeño TAM' (3, 4). The jalapeño is a good example of a chili pepper that has many strains or subtypes. Often where you procure your seeds will make quite a difference. In Mexico there are numerous chili peppers of the jalapeño type, and many Mexicans seem to prefer their strains, saying theirs are more flavorful than the ones grown in the United States. The jalapeños as a group are quite similar in shape and size, all being fairly thick-walled and ranging from one and a half to three inches long and about an inch across. The immature pods are dark green, ripening to red, and are quite hot.

How to prepare: Jalapeño-type peppers are popular in many different dishes. They are used fresh or pickled in salsas or in meat and vegetable dishes. They are good for appetizers and can be sliced and put on nachos, in salads, or even on pizzas. The chopped, pickled types are great in sandwiches or dips. Because the fruits are fleshy, they don't dry very

well unless they are smoked. Smoked jalapeños are called *chipotles;* when preserved in a tomato sauce, they are called *chipotles en adobo.* Both are sometimes available in Mexican markets.

LONG GREEN   The long greens are a group of chili peppers that includes Californian and New Mexican types. Well-known cultivars are 'Anaheim' (1, 4, 6), 'Colorado' (1), 'New Mexico' (3, 4, 6), and 'New Mexico #6' (5). The fruits are long and narrow, generally reaching six to seven inches in length and one to one and a half inches in width. One variety, 'Numex Big Jim' (1, 4, 5), is quite a bit longer. When immature, long greens are light green, but when mature, they are crimson. In their red-ripe state they are strung and dried in the sun to make what is called a ristra.

How to prepare: Long green chili peppers are often roasted in the green state and used fresh; they can also be frozen for later use. Dried, they are used in the preparation of chili powder. Their pungency varies from mild to hot, depending on the cultivar and the growing conditions. These chilies are well known to consumers as those sold under the Ortega label.

PEPPERONCINI   See the "Italian Gardens" chapter.

SERRANO   Serrano peppers are probably the most popular of the fresh chili peppers used in Mexico and the American Southwest. They are an inch or so long and a little more than half an inch wide. They are green when immature, ripening to red. The plants have gray-green leaves and are striking when covered with ripe fruit.

How to prepare: Serrano peppers are quite hot and are used fresh in salsas or in guacamole and chili. Fairly thin-walled, they can be dried and ground up for use in chili powder. In Texas, cooks using fresh peppers choose 'Serrano' when they want a dish to be quite hot; for a milder dish—perhaps to serve a visitor to Texas—they generally choose the 'Jalapeño'.

In addition to chili peppers, the following vegetables and herbs can be used in homemade chili and make fine additions to your chili garden.

CORN   Any sweet corn variety is good when used fresh in garden chili. Corn is also used in a well-known variation of chili called tamale pie. When it comes to making the cornbread to accompany your chili, see the "Native American Gardens" chapter for information on all types of dry corn and how to

Carol Hancock, winner of the 1985 International Chili Society World Championship Cook-off, was a novice chili cook until she entered her first cook-off six years and thirty-five cook-offs ago. A Californian originally from Oklahoma, she now produces her own chili commercially as well as being a chili judge.

I consulted Carol for an expert's opinion on what makes good chili before I experimented with variations using ingredients from the garden. To give me a better idea about championship chili, Carol arranged for me to judge a cook-off. I became so intrigued with the cook-off that I asked her to share her knowledge about cook-offs and about what makes good chili.

To understand what makes award-winning chili, Carol tells me, "you have to understand that cook-off chili is not as pleasing to eat as your home-style chili. Cook-off chili has to hit the judges immediately. It has to have everything—the heat, the spices, and the texture of the meat—all in one bite. If you sat down at home and ate a bowl of cook-off chili, it would probably be so powerful you'd end up with indigestion."

Most prize-winning competition chili "is a combination of meat and spices—period," Carol continues. "No beans, no corn, no cauliflower or carrots, no big globs of tomatoes, not even chopped onions on top—just meat and spices. Competition chili that has been winning cook-offs over the years is usually what is best known as Texas chili. To further qualify, award-winning chili is made with high-quality meat free of fat or gristle. The chili must have a pleasing consistency—not so thick that you can eat it with a fork, but not so runny that you can slurp it through a straw—and it shouldn't be too spicy and hot to eat. It should have a nice red-brown color and be filled with flavor." To get a better idea of what championship chili is like, see Carol's recipe in this section.

Carol Hancock

If you'd like to enter a cook-off, contact your newspaper's food editor to find a nearby cook-off, or join the organization listed below. On the day of the cook-off, show up with your team of helpers (if you want one), a recipe, a stove, and all of your chili ingredients. According to Carol, "Most cook-off chairmen will provide you with a table and two chairs. Sometimes they provide a booth, too, to shade you from the sun or rain. When it rains, I've seen determined chili cooks sit inside their steamy cars and chop onions on a cutting board.

"You cannot pre-prepare any ingredients, though you can use canned tomatoes, canned peppers, beef broth, and canned beverages. Some people put beer or wine in their chili," Carol says. "You can't come with the meat already marinated or with any ingredients that have already been combined, either. During a cook-off, you get from eleven o'clock in the morning until noon to prepare your ingredients—for example, to chop onions and cut meat. From noon until three o'clock you actually cook. At three o'clock, you fill a large Styrofoam cup to within an inch of the top with your chili—it can have no garnishes, no sour cream, no cheese, no beans, just chili—and take it to the judges' table. Then you sit back and wait. Suspense—will they think it's great or not?"

Consider joining the International Chili Society, Box 2966, Newport Beach, CA 92663. The Society's membership fee is fifteen dollars a year, which allows you to participate in any sanctioned chili cook-off and includes a quarterly newsletter giving locations for all chili cook-offs throughout the country.

Entering a chili cook-off is a great experience, and according to Carol, someone with a new recipe has as much chance of winning as someone who finds his or her great-grandmother's recipe in the attic. But whether or not you win, the festivities and great eating make for an unusual and fun-filled experience.

grind it. See the Part Four Encyclopedia for sources of and information on growing corn.

GARLIC See "Onions" in the Part Four Encyclopedia for a discussion of garlic.

HERBS See the "Mexican Gardens" chapter for herbs used in chili.

ONION The strong-flavored yellow or brown onions are usually best for chili.

PEPPER, BELL Sweet bell peppers are often used in chili. Any variety seems to do well, though the thick-walled, red-ripe ones seem the most flavorful.

TOMATO When chili cooks use tomatoes, they often prefer to use the meatier plum tomatoes rather than standard ones so that the chili won't get too thin. See the "Italian Gardens" chapter for information on and sources of plum tomatoes. If you don't have fresh tomatoes, substitute canned ones and drain them well. See the Part Four Encyclopedia for information on growing tomatoes.

Cooking from the Chili Garden

People get hot under the collar when they talk about what makes good chili. Discussions go round and round on which type of chili powder is best, or whether the 'Serrano' or 'Poblano' is the tastiest chili pepper. But the emotional fever really starts to rise when you get to the more basic questions. If you add beans or tomatoes, can you still call it chili? Purists cringe at the thought. Should the meat be cubed or ground? Some chili cooks say ground meat becomes mush. Or, heaven forbid, can you leave out the meat and still call it chili? That heresy can make a chili purist see red.

Opinions about what makes good chili seem to be regional. Chili cooks in Texas swear by a trailside-style chili made with meat, garlic, and powdered chili peppers. Yet there are chili cooks in Cincinnati who, declaring they come from the chili capital of the world, rave about chili made with meat, chili powder, cinnamon, ginger, and tomatoes. And according to Michael McLaughlin, chef of the Manhattan Chili Company restaurant in New York, Californians like a chili with everything under the sun in it—what he calls Technicolor chili.

Obviously, my goal is to make chili from the garden. And garden chili, by definition, must deviate from pure Texas-style chili. So for me the question became, How far can I veer from a purist's vision and still call the dish chili? To answer that, I first needed a solid grounding in what professional chili chefs say makes a good "bowl of red." And to that end I interviewed Carol Hancock, who is a World Championship Chili Cook-off winner, and learned about championship Texas-style chili. I then contacted Michael McLaughlin and discussed his views on varying chili ingredients. Michael offered a few guidelines for creating a personal chili style, including how to use many different types of vegetables and fresh herbs. Finally I talked with Dean Mager, a chili cook-off enthusiast who likes to create his chili from the garden.

As we review the following chili ingredients and see how a pot of chili comes together, you'll probably find the accompanying personal views of chili chefs Carol Hancock and Michael McLaughlin of interest.

Meat

Meat is a component of most chili. While beef is the most traditional, pork, lamb, chicken, rabbit, buffalo, any kind of venison, and even rattlesnake are all used. A few guidelines for using meat in chili are as follows. When making a long-simmered chili, such as Texas-style, avoid very lean cuts of meat, as they will not hold up well. When using beef, choose well-marbled bottom round or chuck; if using pork, choose a shoulder cut. Meat for chili is usually cut into very small cubes averaging a quarter to a half inch in size. As an alternative, you can use a very coarsely ground meat, described by butchers in some parts of the country as "chili grind." Regular-grind hamburger usually becomes too mushy. Most chili chefs recommend that you not brown the meat, because this seals the outside and prevents the meat from absorbing the flavorings as well. For less traditional types of chili, such as black bean and chicken chili, veal chili, or seafood types, the meat or seafood is added toward the end so that it will not become stringy or overcooked.

OPPOSITE: *There are as many kinds of chilis as there are chili cooks. Pictured here are Carol Hancock's championship Texas-style chili and our garden chili.*

V.O.M.
CHILI
COOK OFF
1986

Tomatoes

Do tomatoes belong in your chili? Opinions vary widely. Some experts forbid them; some say only in the form of tomato sauce, while others say chopped fine, and still others recommend whole chunks. In any case, the tomatoes should not be watery, and plum (paste) tomatoes, either fresh or canned, seem best. Fresh tomatoes should be peeled and seeded or strained. Leaving many seeds in the chili offends most palates.

Beans

Even the most carnivorous chili lover has no argument with beans as an accompaniment to chili. The debate centers around this question: Should beans be added to the chili or served alongside? In either case, dry 'Red Mexican', 'Pinto', or 'Red Kidney' beans hold up well with a strong-flavored chili. But some of this country's best chefs swear by black beans too (see the recipe for black bean and chicken chili). Vegetarians usually add dry beans such as kidney or pinto types to their chili to provide protein and give body to a meatless chili. And, of course, all types of shelled beans can be added to vegetable-style chilis.

Before adding dry beans to chili, you must look them over, sorting out spoiled ones and small pebbles, and soak them overnight in enough water to cover. The next day, cook the beans until tender and add them to the chili before cooking it. (See the "Baked Bean Gardens" chapter for detailed information on how to cook dry beans.) If you're going to serve dry beans alongside your chili, then cook the beans as noted above and serve in a separate bowl.

Chili Peppers

When we talk about flavorings for chili, the star of the show is the chili pepper in all its forms. For me, exploring the flavors of all the chili peppers is a little like studying wines. The many subtle differences in the types and varieties of chili peppers seem endless. South Americans have been cooking with them for thousands of years and have developed a vast array of uses based on their nuances. Most cooks in this country, including myself, have a working knowledge of only a small handful of chili pepper varieties. The excitement of the chili garden, for me, has been

in educating my palate to the many available flavors of and uses for chilies.

Chili peppers are used almost universally in making chili. We first think of their hotness, of course, but what would a bowl of chili taste like if all it contained was hot-tasting meat? To me, while the heat is exciting, the sometimes earthy, sometimes nutty, and even chocolatelike overtones of chili peppers are what make a bowl of chili so rich and satisfying.

Chili peppers can be used in both their dried and fresh form. Each contributes its own flavor. Even the way the chili pepper is prepared can make a difference. 'Jalapeño' chilies are smoked when they are dried, and this produces a distinctive flavor. Fresh green chilies are often roasted over coals to remove the skins, a process that sweetens the peppers and adds still another flavor. Once you start experimenting with the many types available, you'll see how combining a number of chili peppers gives even more dimension. Most often, one or two types of mild chili peppers are chosen for their flavors and another one is added for its hotness.

Most of us start making chili with a commercial chili powder. This is certainly the easiest way to make chili and, for beginners, doubtless the best way to start. These chili powders are a blend, just as curry is, and they usually contain ground mild chili peppers, hot chili peppers, paprika, oregano, cumin, garlic, and salt. The mild chilies, including paprika, provide the chili pepper taste, the hot ones provide the heat, and the other herbs broaden the spectrum of flavors. Brands differ slightly in the proportions and kinds of herbs and chili peppers used, and you'll probably find you like some better than others. If you want to try a range of commercial chili powders, try some of those recommended in the recipes that follow and those offered by the suppliers listed in the "Sources" section. If you want to experiment further and fully incorporate the advantages of a garden, see the following sections, which cover the use of home-grown chili peppers, both dried and fresh. Let's start with the dried chili peppers first.

Dried chili peppers: The chili peppers most commonly dried are the poblanos (called anchos in their dried form); the 'Cayenne', 'Pequin', 'Tepin', and 'Thai' varieties; and the 'California and New Mexico' types. Peppers must be fully ripe before they are dried or they will rot. Thick-walled peppers such as 'Red

Ristras made of long, red chilies hang to dry on a Santa Fe home.

Cherry' and 'Jalapeño' are likely to rot even when ripe; they may be preserved by pickling and are then referred to as *escabeche*.

For eons people in hot, dry climates have strung chili peppers on ristras. Making a ristra is very simple. For small peppers, all you need is a large needle and fairly strong string; simply string the chili peppers one by one, inserting the needle through the peppers or their stems. Large chili peppers are usually tied by the stems along the string. If you live outside the arid West, heed Craig Dremann's advice: leave at least an inch between peppers for air circulation or else they might rot. In arid climates, once the peppers are strung, hang them in the sun to dry. In humid climates (with more than 30 percent humidity), dry ristras inside a sunny room. While it is traditional to string the California and New Mexico types, the others listed above plus any thin-walled chili pepper can be dried this way.

An alternative to making a ristra is to cut the ripe chili peppers lengthwise in strips and put them on a rack in a food dryer or a gas oven with only the pilot light on. Alternatively, lay the strips outside on a warm, sunny porch. Turn the peppers once in a while to make sure they dry evenly. Depending on the process you use, dry them for a few days to a week until they become leathery, not brittle. Once leathery, put them in glass jars with tight-sealing lids. If you suspect you might have insect problems, store the dried chilies in a freezer.

Once you've dried your chili peppers, how do you use them? There are a number of ways. You can grind them into a powder, make them into a paste, or, as is often done in Oriental cooking, incorporate them into the oil you use in the dish you are making.

The most common way to use the hot, dried chili peppers is to toast and then grind them. Toasting brings out more of the flavor. To do this, either break

After I had eaten many bowls of Texas-style chili, I wanted to try to make more of a garden-type chili. But the question was, How far afield could I get from the basics? I had found many unusual chili recipes in food magazines—particularly those from Michael McLaughlin—so I decided to contact him for some guidelines. Michael certainly has chili credentials: he is chef and part owner of the Manhattan Chili Company, a popular New York restaurant, and co-author of *The Silver Palate Cookbook.*

Michael McLaughlin

When I called Michael, he had just finished writing his book on chili and its accompaniments, *The Manhattan Chili Company Southwest American Cookbook,* and was anxious to talk about his favorite subject. "Of course," he says, "some people might think I'm a chili heretic, but we do have a lot of fun with it." Michael serves ten different chilis at the restaurant and has included recipes for these in his book. He serves Texas-style chili, but he also serves chilis with fresh herbs and vegetables, and as a gardener those interest me the most. Other variations he offers include seafood chili, chili with beans, green chili, and even meatless chili.

When talking with Michael, the first question I asked was, What's chili? His answer: "Chili, a hundred years or so ago, was a primitive Texas trail-drive dish. But now, for me, chili is, within limits, a springboard for whatever imaginative things you want to do with the basic dish as long as you still acknowledge its origins." While Michael can't see putting blueberries or smoked fish in chili, he thinks there's a lot more latitude than most people believe. "I know a lot of fairly serious chili cooks who put, for example, red wine in chili," he says. "But in a review of our restaurant, one writer said that's just where she drew her personal line. To her, there was no such thing as chili with wine in it. Yet, to me, wine is not particularly radical. Needless to say, our vegetarian and seafood chilis were completely unacceptable to her,

and she chose not to even taste or review them. So, you see, where you draw the line is really personal. I, myself, pay attention to historical and regional differences."

Michael went on to say he doesn't think he's doing anything so radical in his chilis that someone somewhere else in the country isn't doing also. For instance, Texas and Mexico have long seacoasts, so he's sure some people in those places must make seafood chili. And meatless chili, he believes, is an idea that can't be ignored. Then there are all the nontraditional meats that have been used for years—lamb, venison, and buffalo, for example—Michael feels free to use all kinds of meat. As he says, "Some people make radical changes and others make only small ones—such as using olive oil instead of bacon fat—small personal adjustments that the chili cook is expected to make. I expect people to make those adjustments to my recipes, too, because chili is a very personal dish."

I asked Michael to comment on making chili from the garden, and while he said he's never had that pleasure, he has certainly used fresh ingredients. To begin with, Michael explains, "there is much more to chili peppers than heat. Their flavor is very important, too. I would sooner use twice as many pods of a good-flavored mild chili like a 'Poblano' than half as many hot but flavorless pods.

"You also must realize," says Michael, "that fresh chilies aren't necessarily a part of the chili tradition, which uses primarily chili powder and ground dried chilies. There is, however, a traditional green chili with pork, *chile verde,* made with fresh 'Poblano' and 'Jalapeño' chilies. The 'Poblano' gives it a great pepper flavor, and the 'Jalapeño' gives it the heat. In my book, that recipe calls for fresh green chilies, but at the restaurant I can't use the fresh 'Poblano' because of the time required to roast that many fresh peppers. When I used 'Poblano' peppers to test the recipe for the book, the chili was just extraordinary, about the best I've ever made. And once, while doing a chili workshop in Minneapolis, I needed some fresh chilies, and someone finally found me some hot banana peppers at a roadside stand. They were delicious—extremely hot—and fun to cook with. But I wouldn't see those in a market in New York, I'm sure. If you're interested in a variety of fresh peppers and in experimenting and comparing them, I think you almost have to grow your own. I know people who do, and they have great fun with the seasonal variation in flavor and heat and with the different varieties."

Michael and I also discussed other components of garden chili besides peppers, such as herbs and other vegetables. When using an herb in its fresh state rather than dried, Michael notes, you must use much more of the herb. If you want to add oregano to your chili, he recommends using Mexican oregano (see the "Mexican Gardens" chapter) rather than the usual garden variety because the flavor is much better. When using fresh tomatoes, Michael suggests that you choose plum tomatoes because they have more flesh and are less juicy than regular tomatoes. He prefers to chop the tomatoes very finely so that no large chunks float in the chili.

Talking with Michael was valuable because of the practical advice he gave me, but most important was his idea that each person can develop his or her own personal chili style and draw his or her own line as to what constitutes chili. If Michael's information has inspired you to make your own garden chili, you might try starting with two of his recipes included in this section.

---

up the dried peppers and remove the seeds and stem, or leave them whole. (If you leave in the seeds, your powder will be a lot hotter.) In an ungreased heavy frying pan or a *comal* (Mexican griddle), toast the chilies over medium heat for thirty seconds to a minute. Watch carefully and turn constantly. When you just start to smell the peppers, remove them from the pan. Be careful not to burn them or they will get quite bitter.

To grind dried chili peppers, break up the pieces and run them through a spice mill or clean coffee grinder. Sift the powder if there are fairly large pieces left. Store in glass jars in a dark, cool place.

To make your own chili powder blend, dry some oregano, roast and grind some cumin if you want to include it, and then choose from your varieties of dried chili peppers. Generally, for a flavorful chili, choose at least one mild chili pepper, such as an ancho or a New Mexico or California variety, and then combine it with a smaller amount of a very hot chili pepper, such as a 'Cayenne', a 'Jalapeño', a 'Serrano', or a tiny bird pepper or two. Toast and grind the chili peppers and combine them with the other spices, or keep the powders separate and decide which chili peppers give you the taste you like as you add them. Some chili enthusiasts put dried garlic and onion in their chili powder; I prefer to add these ingredients fresh.

You can use chili paste in place of powdered chilies in your recipes. If you choose the paste, you won't need a spice mill or coffee grinder to prepare the chilies.

To make a chili paste, stem the chilies, break them into pieces, and pour boiling water over them. Let them sit for a few hours; then drain them, reserving the liquid, and puree them in a food processor. Strain the mix to remove any whole seeds and hard pieces. Stir in some of the liquid until the consistency is to your liking. Michael McLaughlin gives detailed instructions in his chili cookbook (see "Sources") for making chili paste and determining the proportions of chili peppers. He also suggests that you mix in some *adobo* (tomato sauce) from canned *chipotles*. Keep the paste in a jar and refrigerate or freeze.

To incorporate dried chili peppers into the oil to be used during cooking, break up the chilies into fairly small pieces and fry them in oil. Fry the pieces until you smell the peppers and then remove them from the oil with a slotted spoon. Pour the now spicy oil out of the pan and add it back gradually to the cooking pan and its contents, testing for hotness as you go. This method is often utilized with Chinese stir-fry dishes.

If you have no garden chili peppers to dry but want to make your own chili powder blend, visit your nearest Mexican market or order dried peppers from the sources listed at the end of the chapter. Because of the confusion in the nomenclature of chili peppers, you might find that the names on packages of chili peppers at a Mexican market differ from those used here. There are numerous reasons for this. First, many peppers have different names in Mexico. Also, Mexicans often have one name for a fresh chili pepper and another for that same pepper in its dried state. In addition, peppers are sometimes mislabeled, and finally, certain kinds of chili peppers, such as *quajillo* peppers, are usually unavailable in the United States in any form. Look for the pepper names we've been using in this section, as well as *mulato* and *pasilla* for fairly mild ones, and *chipotle, quajillo,* and *serranito* for very hot ones. See "Recommended Chili Peppers" to cross-reference the fresh and dried chili pepper names. When choosing chili peppers at a market, look for ones that appear fairly fresh. Unless you are getting *chipotles,* which are smoked, the package contents should not look dusty.

Fresh chili peppers: It's a real treat to pick your chili peppers fresh from the garden and use them in your chili. Many varieties are superb and most are traditionally harvested green. Among them are poblano, one of the most choice and flavorful; 'Jalapeño', which gives heat and some chili flavor; 'Serrano', for a rich chili flavor and lots of heat; and 'Cayenne', 'Tepin', and 'Pequin', used expressly to give a fiery hotness to chili.

The majority of fresh green chili peppers have fairly tough skin, and most people prefer to roast and peel them. Roasting blisters the skin so that it can be removed more readily and gives the peppers more flavor in the process. To roast a chili, or even a sweet bell pepper, put the pepper directly in a gas flame or over the burner of the stove. Keep the pepper in the flame until it starts to blister and blacken. Turn it from side to side to roast it as evenly as possible. When the pepper has blistered quite a bit and the skin has loosened, put it in a brown paper bag and close the bag for a few minutes. Then, using rubber gloves, remove the pepper from the bag and skin it, using the back of a knife or your fingers. Some folks swear that placing the pepper under running water helps remove the skin, but others say that doing that steals some of the flavor. Whichever method you use, you'll find the job somewhat time-consuming and you will probably not get all the skin off.

If you are skinning more than two or three peppers, try putting them under a broiler or over a charcoal grill. After the chilies are peeled, you can use them immediately or freeze them, though the quality will deteriorate after a few months in a freezer. Roasted and minced, fresh chili peppers are a fantastic addition to your chili, and well worth the extra effort.

Controlling the heat: If you find that your peppers are too hot for your taste, slice them open and remove and discard the seeds and veins, since that is where most of the hotness resides. Another hint is to add the hottest peppers last when incorporating your flavorings. Put in half the amount called for and taste as you go along. While commercial chili peppers can vary in hotness quite a bit, garden chili peppers seem to vary even more. You can always make your chili hotter with powdered 'Cayenne' or 'Serrano' peppers, but it's much more difficult to cool it down. An extra word of caution: remember to use gloves when working with chili peppers, as you can burn your hands or get a surprise two hours later when you scratch yourself and find you have chilies under your fingernails. And, of course, be extra careful not to rub your eyes or face while you are working with chilies.

Other Flavorings

Only the fanatic enjoys a chili made with just meat and chili powder. Having only two flavors makes chili rather flat. The most popular additions are onions and garlic. Pungent yellow onions and fresh minced garlic both add to the aroma and help round out the flavor.

In addition to onions and garlic, a number of herbs and spices are also often added to chili to give it more interest. Cumin and oregano are so standard that over the years they have been routinely added to most brands of commercial chili powder.

While commercial chili powders have their place, if you want to make a quantum leap in the richness of your chili, start roasting and combining your own fresh herbs and spices. I can't get over how much difference freshly roasted cumin made to my chili. It was like taking earmuffs off in the middle of a concert. There was so much more richness to the flavor.

Putting the Chili Together

With the exception of lean-meat or vegetarian chili, most chilis are assembled in a similar order. Choose a large, heavy kettle—some Texans insist that it be iron or the chili won't taste quite right. The iron kettle is fine if you're making Texas-style chili, but if you're going to use tomatoes, wine, or other acidic ingredients in your chili, they will react with iron. This is also true of aluminum pans, so use enamel or stainless steel. Gently cook the onions and garlic, if you're using them, in a little oil until they are tender and translucent. Then remove them from the pan, add the meat, and cook. Stir the meat until it is no longer pink, but has not yet browned. If you're using ground meat, make sure it is well crumbled. Then put the onions and garlic back in the pan and add the chili powder and spices. Cook and stir for a few minutes and then add any liquid and tomatoes if they are called for. Simmer for one to two hours until the meat is tender and the consistency is what you prefer. Some folks cook down their chili to thicken it; others prefer to add a little cornmeal at the end. Cornmeal not only thickens the chili, but it also binds the extra grease that usually appears on the surface.

Garden Chili

Garden chili differs somewhat from most kinds of Texas chili, so when I was researching chili at the cook-off, I walked around looking for contestants who were using primarily fresh ingredients. When I got to Dean Mager's booth and asked him about his fresh vegetables, he commented that he used them because he liked a variety of flavors, not the uniformity of a Texas-style chili, which he thought was boring.

I then asked Dean what it was like to make cook-off chili with garden vegetables and herbs. He said that it was a lot of fun, but he and his chili partner found it harder to compete, since keeping the chili consistent from contest to contest was almost impossible. For example, how hot were the chili peppers this time? How juicy were the vegetables? How sweet or acidic were the tomatoes? Was the cilantro or onion flavor stronger than usual? Dean continues to make his garden chili, however, because he prefers its many flavors.

For home-style garden chili, you're going to have some of the same experiences as Dean had. Making garden chili can be an exciting challenge or a frustrating experience. As always when you're cooking from the garden, you have one more level of complexity to contend with. What is the garden producing today? Are the chili peppers stronger? Has the

cilantro bolted? Will the new variety of tomatoes you're trying be watery or extra sweet? Are the bell peppers as sensational as they were last year? All in all, though, the potential is unlimited. Your best pot of chili, the one you'll always remember, is just waiting to be made, and its most subtle nuances are forming in your garden.

There are as many variations of chili as there are chili cooks. The following recipes range from pure Texas-style chili to Vicki Sebastiani's recipe, which contains no chili peppers and is filled with tomatoes. Vicki calls her recipe Italian chili, but is it chili to you? You'll see that there's a wide-ranging passion for the dish called chili, and to me the garden provides us with a chance to explore new variations on a traditional theme.

GARDEN CHILI

Making this chili, full of lively fresh flavors and colors, is a festive way to celebrate the late-summer harvest. Be creative and flexible and use what vegetables and herbs your garden offers. You might want to try a vegetarian version (see note below).

SERVES 8 TO 10.

> *½ pound dry beans (recommended: pinto, kidney, or red Mexican; about 1¼ cups) or 2 to 3 cups fresh shelled beans (omit precooking)*
> *¼ cup olive oil*
> *2 onions, chopped*
> *1 pound chuck roast or steak, cut into ½-inch cubes*
> *4 cloves garlic, minced*
> *1 or 2 chili peppers, minced*
> *3 tablespoons chili powder*
> *2 teaspoons cumin*
> *2 quarts chopped tomatoes (about 8 medium)*
> *1 or 2 sweet peppers, diced*
> *2 small or 1 larger summer squash (recommended: 1 each yellow and green zucchini), diced*
> *¾ cup fresh corn kernels (from 1 ear)*
> *1½ tablespoons minced fresh oregano*
> *¼ cup minced fresh basil and/or parsley (optional)*

Cover dry beans generously with water and soak

overnight. Before cooking, add more water if needed to cover beans and simmer 1½ to 2½ hours until just tender. In a large kettle, sauté onions in olive oil until soft. Add meat, garlic, chili peppers, chili powder, and cumin and sauté about 4 minutes. Add tomatoes, cover kettle, and simmer about 1 hour, stirring occasionally. Add remaining vegetables and herbs (and fresh shelled beans, if used) and simmer ½ hour longer. Serve with cornbread and a green salad.

Note: For a vegetarian version, omit meat and double the quantity of beans and garlic.

SHOTGUN WILLIE CHILI

This recipe for classic Texas-style chili won Carol Hancock first place in the 1985 International Chili Society Championship Cook-off.

SERVES 12 TO 16.

> 2 to 3 tablespoons cooking oil
> 6 pounds prime beef, cubed or coarsely
>   ground
> 4 medium onions, finely diced
> Black pepper
> 1 cup water
> 1½ tablespoons oregano leaves
> 1 can (15 ounces) tomato sauce or 2 cups
>   homemade tomato sauce
> 1½ cups pepper paste (from New Mexico or
>   pasilla peppers; see technique for making
>   paste in text)
> 4 cups beef broth
> 2 tablespoons vinegar
> 1 teaspoon Tabasco sauce
> 16 tablespoons (1 cup) Reno Reds Chili
>   Seasoning (can be ordered from Stewart's
>   Chili Company, Box 574, San Carlos, CA
>   94070) or any high-quality chili powder
> 2 tablespoons ground cumin
> 1 teaspoon cayenne pepper
> 1 tablespoon monosodium glutamate
> ½ teaspoon sugar
> 14 cloves garlic, crushed
> Salt to taste

Heat oil in a frying pan over medium heat. Brown a small batch of beef at a time in the hot oil, adding onions and black pepper to each batch. As each batch browns, remove from pan and place in a large cooking pot. Bring oregano leaves to a boil in 1 cup water

and steep like tea. Strain and add strained liquid to meat mixture. Add remaining ingredients, blending well. Cover pot and simmer 2 hours, stirring occasionally.

BLACK BEAN AND CHICKEN CHILI

This recipe was contributed by Jesse Cool, owner and chef at Flea Street Cafe and Late for the Train restaurant in Menlo Park, California. This Mexican-inspired chili is filled with rich flavors.

SERVES 8.

> 2 cups dry black beans
> 2 pounds meaty chicken (breasts and/or
>   thighs)
> 3 cups water
> Salt and pepper to taste
> ¼ cup olive oil
> 1 large onion, chopped
> ½ cup chopped celery
> ¼ cup minced garlic
> 3 tablespoons chili powder
> 2 tablespoons cumin
> 3 tablespoons butter
> ½ cup currants or raisins
> ½ cup chopped carrots
> 1½ ounces bittersweet chocolate
> Pinch of cinnamon
> Cayenne pepper OR 1 or 2 fresh hot peppers,
>   to taste

Cover dry beans generously with water and soak overnight. Add more water if necessary and a little salt. Bring to a boil and simmer until tender but not mushy.

Put chicken in a pot with 3 cups water, salt, and pepper. Cover and simmer until chicken is done, about 30 minutes. Remove chicken from broth and reserve broth. Debone chicken and cut into bite-size pieces.

Sauté onion, celery, garlic, and hot pepper (if using) in olive oil until tender. Add chili powder, cumin, and butter and sauté for 1 more minute. Add currants or raisins, carrots, 2 cups of reserved chicken broth, chocolate, and cinnamon, along with beans (in their cooking water) and cayenne (if using). Add more broth if necessary. Let cook, covered, on low heat about 45 minutes. Add chicken, taste for seasoning, and simmer about 30 minutes longer.

Serve for dinner with rice, sour cream, fresh cilantro, and grated cheddar cheese, along with a big green salad with a salsalike dressing. This chili is even better the next day and can be used in omelettes with cheddar cheese, in burritos, or even on corn chips with guacamole as an appetizer.

ITALIAN CHILI

A particular favorite of Sam and Vicki Sebastiani is Vicki's Italian version of California chili. It's especially good with crisp green salad and crusty French bread. This is an example of a chili that doesn't even have chili peppers in it—is it really a chili? It certainly lends itself to chilies; so if you prefer, Vicki recommends adding a few pepperoncini peppers and serving it with a glass of zinfandel.

SERVES 8.

> *3 large onions, peeled*
> *2 green peppers, cut into large chunks*
> *4 cloves garlic, minced*
> *⅓ cup olive oil*
> *1½ pounds Italian sausage*
> *2 28-ounce cans Italian whole tomatoes, drained, or about 10 medium tomatoes, peeled*
> *2 15-ounce cans kidney beans, drained, or about 3½ cups cooked beans*
> *1 15-ounce can tomato sauce or 2 cups homemade tomato sauce*
> *2 cups red wine*
> *2 tablespoons EACH freshly chopped oregano and basil OR 2 teaspoons EACH dried oregano and basil*
> *1 teaspoon salt*
> *½ teaspoon freshly ground pepper*
> *1½ cups freshly grated Parmesan cheese*

Halve onions and slice thinly. In a large skillet over medium-high heat, sauté onions with peppers and garlic in olive oil until light brown. Transfer to a large kettle and set aside. Sauté whole Italian sausages, in skins, until very lightly browned, about 2 to 3 minutes. Remove from skillet and slice into ¼-inch pieces, removing skins if desired. Add sausage to kettle. Stir in tomatoes, kidney beans, tomato sauce, wine, herbs, salt, and pepper. Simmer for 1 to 2 hours until thickened. Stir in Parmesan cheese just prior to serving.

Italian-style chili features tomatoes and herbs and makes a great picnic meal.

GREEN CHILI WITH PORK

This chili is from Michael McLaughlin, chef of the Manhattan Chili Company restaurant and author of *The Manhattan Chili Company Southwest American Cookbook*. Michael says in his book, "This is the 'other' chili, the southwestern green chili rarely found east of Colorado. Of all the chili pilgrims who show up weary but hopeful on our doorstep, those who seek Green Chili seem to have traveled farther and longer than the others. The trip is worth it: Who says chili has to be red?"

SERVES 6 TO 8.

> ¼ cup olive oil
> 2 large yellow onions, peeled and coarsely chopped
> 8 medium garlic cloves, peeled and minced
> 8 fresh jalapeños, stemmed and minced
> 3 carrots, peeled and sliced crosswise into ½-inch pieces
> 1½ tablespoons dried (preferably Mexican) oregano or 3 tablespoons minced fresh oregano
> 2½ to 3 pounds boneless pork shoulder, cut into ½-inch cubes
> 5 cups chicken stock or canned chicken broth
> 1 teaspoon salt
> 1 can (28 ounces) Italian plum tomatoes, crushed and well drained, or about 5 medium tomatoes, peeled, crushed, and drained
> 1 potato (about 8 ounces), peeled and grated
> 12 large fresh poblano chilies (about 1½ pounds total weight), roasted and peeled, or 1 can (27 ounces) whole roasted mild green chilies, drained

In a 4½- to 5-quart heavy, flameproof casserole or Dutch oven, warm the oil over medium heat. Add onions, garlic, jalapeños, and carrots, and cook, stirring once or twice, for 10 minutes. Stir in oregano and pork cubes and cook, stirring occasionally, until pork has lost all pink color, about 20 minutes.

Stir in chicken stock, salt, tomatoes, and grated potato. Bring to a boil, lower the heat, partially cover, and cook, stirring occasionally, for 1½ hours.

Cut chilies into ½-inch strips. Add them to chili and cook, stirring often, for another 30 to 45 minutes, or until pork is tender and chili thickened to your liking. Taste, correct the seasoning, and simmer for another 5 minutes.

SEAFOOD CHILI SAN CARLOS

This recipe also comes from Michael McLaughlin's book. About this dish, he comments, "Nothing could be further from chili's landlocked traditions than this briny seafood stew. Nonetheless, the flavor is unmistakably that of chili, and the roll-your-sleeves-up-and-dig-in heartiness is totally authentic. As with any of the world's bouillabaisse-like stews, using readily available fresh seafood takes precedence over fidelity to the recipe. Since the chili base must be made at least 24 hours in advance, this is perfect party fare."

SERVES 8.

> ¼ cup olive oil
> 1 large yellow onion, peeled and coarsely chopped
> 2 leeks (white part only), well cleaned and chopped
> 1 large celery stalk, chopped
> 8 medium garlic cloves, peeled and minced
> 2 tablespoons dried oregano (preferably Mexican)
> 4½ teaspoons ground cumin, from toasted seeds
> 1 35-ounce can Italian plum tomatoes, with their juice, or about 7 medium tomatoes
> 2 cups homemade fish stock or bottled clam juice
> 2 cups dry red wine
> ½ cup chili paste (see technique for making chili paste in text)
> 1 tablespoon salt
> 1 teaspoon cayenne pepper, or to taste
> 2 medium red bell peppers, stemmed, cored, and diced into ½-inch pieces
> 2 medium green bell peppers, stemmed, cored, and diced into ½-inch pieces
> 12 littleneck clams, scrubbed
> 12 mussels, scrubbed and debearded
> 1½ pounds scrod or other lean white fish filets, cut into 1-inch pieces
> 12 large shrimp, shelled and deveined but with tails left on
> ¾ pound bay scallops
> ½ cup minced fresh cilantro

Heat oil in a 4½- to 5-quart heavy, flameproof casserole or Dutch oven. Add onion, leeks, and celery, cover, and cook, stirring once or twice, for 20 minutes or until vegetables are very tender. Add garlic, oregano, and cumin, cover, and cook for 10 minutes, stirring occasionally.

Add tomatoes (breaking them up with your fingers), their juice, fish stock, red wine, chili paste, salt, and cayenne pepper. Bring to a boil, skimming any scum that forms. Lower the heat, cover, and simmer, skimming and stirring occasionally, for 1 hour.

Stir in red and green bell peppers and simmer, uncovered, for another 20 minutes. Cool to room temperature, cover, and refrigerate overnight.

Bring chili base slowly to a boil, stirring often. Lower the heat so chili simmers briskly. Add clams and mussels, cover, and cook for 10 minutes, removing shellfish as they open and arranging them in chili bowls. After 10 minutes, discard any that have not opened.

Stir in scrod and shrimp, cover, and simmer 1 minute. Add scallops, cover, and simmer until shrimp and scallops are just opaque and scrod is just beginning to flake, about 4 minutes.

Ladle chili over shellfish in bowls, distributing shrimp evenly. Sprinkle each serving with cilantro.

CHILI-STUFFED MONTEREY JACK CHEESE

This recipe from Seppi Renggli, chef of the Four Seasons restaurant in New York City, first appeared in "Great Chefs' Chili Dishes" by Richard Sax in the February 1986 issue of *Bon Appétit*. Richard says, "This unusual chili is a striking presentation: molded cheese packed with a savory stuffing. Whether it's a true chili is a good question—but there's no question that it makes mighty good eating."

SERVES 8.

> 2 tablespoons olive oil
> 1 large onion, coarsely chopped
> 2 medium garlic cloves, minced
> 1¼ pounds ground round
> 1 teaspoon salt
> ½ teaspoon ground hot chilies or cayenne
>   pepper
> ¼ teaspoon ground cumin
> ½ cup dry white wine
> 1 cup chicken stock
> 1 cup cooked rice
> ½ cup diced red bell pepper
> ½ cup diced green bell pepper
> ½ cup raisins
> ½ cup sliced almonds, toasted

> 1 jalapeño chili, seeded and deveined, finely
>   chopped
> 1 tablespoon cornstarch
> 2 tablespoons water
> 1¼ pounds Monterey Jack cheese, cut into ⅛-
>   to ¼-inch-thick slices
> 1 tablespoon dry bread crumbs
> Boiled new potatoes or warm flour tortillas

Heat oil in large, heavy skillet over medium heat. Add onion and garlic and cook until translucent, stirring occasionally, about 8 minutes. Increase heat to medium-high and add ground round. Cook until brown, breaking up meat with large spoon, 6 to 8 minutes. Add salt, ground chilies, and cumin. Stir 2 minutes. Pour off excess fat. Add wine to skillet and bring to boil, scraping up browned bits. Add stock and bring to boil. Reduce heat, cover, and simmer 30 minutes.

Mix rice, bell peppers, raisins, almonds, and jalapeño chilies into meat. Increase heat to medium-high and stir until most of liquid is absorbed, about 7 minutes. Reduce heat to medium-low. Dissolve cornstarch in water; add to meat and rice mixture. Stir until sauce thickens slightly, about 2 minutes. Adjust seasoning. Cool to room temperature. (Recipe can be prepared 1 day ahead; in that case, chill.)

Position rack in center of oven and preheat to 350°. Generously butter 9 x 2-inch round cake pan. Line bottom with parchment; butter paper. Cover bottom of pan with cheese slices, cutting to fit and overlapping by ¼ inch. Cover sides of pan with cheese, overlapping slices generously. Gently pack chili into pan. Cover with remaining cheese. Sprinkle with bread crumbs. Place pan in roasting pan. Add enough simmering water to roasting pan to come halfway up sides of cake pan. Bake for 45 minutes.

Cool chili on rack 30 minutes. Run small knife between cheese and sides of pan. Invert chili onto heated platter. Serve with potatoes or tortillas.

BROKEN ARROW RANCH CHILI

This recipe for Texas-style chili comes from *The Broken Arrow Ranch Cookbook* by Mike Hughes. Mike and his wife, Elizabeth, made this chili for me at their ranch using venison, which gave it a richer taste than most chilis. To do the recipe justice, be sure to use cubed meat or coarsely ground, not regular ground, beef.

SERVES 8 TO 10.

2 tablespoons cooking oil
3 pounds lean chuck or venison, coarsely
*   ground or cut into ½-inch cubes*
1 12-ounce can beer (or more as needed)
1 large onion, chopped
3 cloves garlic, finely chopped
1 jalapeño pepper, finely chopped
5 tablespoons chili powder
4 teaspoons ground cumin seed
1 tablespoon paprika
1 teaspoon salt
¼ teaspoon black pepper

Use a large, heavy, cast-iron or aluminum pot with a tight-fitting lid. Heat oil and brown meat in oil. Add ½ can beer and cook browned meat, covered, over low heat for about 1 hour. Stir occasionally to prevent sticking. Drain juices into a skillet and sauté onion, garlic, and jalapeño in juices. Pour this mixture back into the pot with the meat and add remaining ingredients. Cook covered over low heat about 1½ to 2 hours, adding more beer if needed. The fun of cooking chili is making your own adjustments. Add chili powder, cumin, and salt to taste.

Sources

See also 'Sources" in the "Mexican Gardens" chapter.

Seed Companies

1. Horticultural Enterprises
   P.O. Box 810082
   Dallas, TX 75381
   Specializing in peppers, this seed company carries thirty varieties of sweet and hot peppers, plus seeds of chia, epazote, and cilantro. The catalog gives a limited description of the pepper varieties.

2. Johnny's Selected Seeds
   Foss Hill Road
   Albion, ME 04910
   This seed company places an emphasis on northern gardens. Among its offerings are a few varieties of chilies for northern climates and a

variety of cilantro that is slower to bolt than most.

3. Le Marché
   Seeds International
   P.O. Box 190
   Dixon, CA 95620
   Le Marché carries many types of hot peppers, including 'Ancho', 'New Mexico', 'Jalapeño TAM', 'Thai Hot', and 'Culinar Paprika'. Catalog: $2.00.

4. Pepper Gal
   10536 119th Avenue N
   Largo, FL 33543
   This nursery lists about fifty varieties of hot peppers. There is no description of the varieties in the catalog.

5. Plants of the Southwest
   1812 Second Street
   Santa Fe, NM 87501
   This company carries seeds of plants adapted to the Southwest, including eight varieties of chili peppers. Catalog: $1.00.

6. Redwood City Seed Company
   P.O. Box 361
   Redwood City, CA 94064
   Redwood City Seed Company carries many varieties of chili peppers, including many of the unusual ones. The catalog provides a good description of the varieties, including their rating on the company's hotness scale. Catalog: $1.00.

7. Stokes Seeds, Inc.
   P.O. Box 548
   Buffalo, NY 14240
   Stokes carries ten varieties of chili peppers, with a good selection for northern gardeners.

Mail-Order Sources of Ingredients

Casa Moneo
210 West Fourteenth Street
New York, NY 10011
   This firm carries just about every dried pepper or spice for chili that you could want.

Santa Cruz Chili and Spice Company
P.O. Box 177
Tumacacori, AZ 65640
   This company is a source for chili powders, pastes, and salsas.

Books

See also "Sources" in the "Mexican Gardens" chapter.

Andrews, Jean. *Peppers, the Domesticated Capsicums*. Austin, Tex.: University of Texas Press, 1984.
> *Peppers* is the most complete and beautiful book on the subject. It contains detailed botanical and historical information on pepper varieties.

Brennan, Georgeanne, and Charlotte Glenn. *Hot and Chili*. Berkeley: Aris Books, 1986.
> This book is a five-part instructional manual for cooking with chilies. Recipes for using chilies are included.

Eckhardt, Linda West. *The Only Texas Cookbook*. New York: Bantam Books, 1986.
> One of the Hugheses' favorite Texas cookbooks, it contains a few chili recipes, including Seven Pepper Chili and a traditional Texas-style chili called Road Meat Chili.

Hughes, Mike. *The Broken Arrow Ranch Cookbook*. Austin, Tex.: University of Texas Press, 1985.
> Mike's book covers many southwestern recipes and contains a number of basic chili recipes, particularly those made with wild game.

McLaughlin, Michael. *The Manhattan Chili Company Southwest American Cookbook*. New York: Crown Publishers, 1986.
> This is the best book available on how to make all different kinds of chili. It contains ten recipes for making chili, as well as detailed instructions for peeling chili peppers and making chili paste. The book also contains recipes for chili accompaniments, from appetizers to desserts.

Grain
Gardens

WHEAT, GODDESS OF THE EARTH. The hair on the back of my neck stood on end as we prepared to harvest my first crop. Friends helped gather the tools, lending a sense of ritual. Did we feel a tie to our ancestors on some cellular level? Were we moved by the poetry of producing the staff of life from the ground up? By the historical and biblical associations of harvesting wheat? Whatever the reason, there was definitely something primordial about gathering the stalks.

Later, reflecting on the deeply satisfying harvest, I began to wonder why so few gardeners grow wheat and why I had never planted it before. I had always assumed that growing wheat—or any grain, for that matter—was too big a production for my small yard. In my ignorance, I had believed a McCormick reaper and a quarter section of rolling prairie were necessary to do the project justice. And even with sufficient land to produce grain by the bushelful, I had wondered, how would one manage without a miller down the street? To my mind, processing a wheat harvest suggested the kind of work involved in canning an acre of tomatoes—that is, a full season's labor. With wheat, we didn't seem to have the option of growing just a little for pleasure and fresh eating.

OPPOSITE: *Hard spring wheat grown at the Common Ground Minifarm in Willits, California, and Gary Stoner's whole-wheat bread made from the just-ground wheat.*

When I reviewed my literature on grain growing, I saw why I—and others too—had been intimidated. Writers on the subject of grains tend to speak in terms of bushels per acre and to focus on what kind of scythe to buy, on lodging and weed problems, and on how much wheat a family of four needs for a year. No wonder few gardeners grow grains!

Well, I have now grown and harvested wheat and have had the pleasure of living for a while with about ten pounds of the berries in large glass jars on my kitchen counter. (I put them in a cupboard after a few days, but at first it was fun just to look at the berries and marvel at what I'd done.) My grain plot measured just three feet by twenty-two feet, it required little care, and three rank amateurs were able to cut, thresh, and winnow the harvest with nothing more sophisticated than a pair of garden shears and an old vacuum cleaner. I figure my wheat patch yielded enough grain to make about fifteen to twenty loaves of the world's best bread, with a little left over to use in cereal and wheat-berry jambalaya. I am now experimenting with ways to cook wheat berries whole and with simple methods of turning them into flour.

My wheat odyssey began three years ago, when I started planning this book and decided I wanted it to contain a grain garden. In exploring the possibilities, I contacted John Jeavons, author of *How to Grow More Vegetables.* I knew he had grown a lot of wheat and that his chief interest was maximum production in a minimum amount of space. If anyone could help me figure out how to grow a small-scale suburban grain garden, it was John. He was very encouraging. He figured that a person using his methods could grow enough wheat for twenty loaves of bread in a 100-square-foot bed. He also suggested other grains to try: rye and a high-protein grain the Aztecs had grown called amaranth. John offered to grow a prototype grain garden for me at his minifarm to give me a chance to evaluate the process.

The information in this chapter on the maximum production of grains in small areas comes from John and his apprentice, Gary Stoner. For readers who are mainly interested in growing just a little to get their feet wet, I have described my experiences with a very small suburban frontyard wheat garden. Those who want to put in a large grain garden will find most of the necessary information in the following pages, but on some of the finer points they may want to consult the source books listed at the end of the chapter. Gardeners planning grain gardens of any dimension will need some basic grain-growing information.

How to Grow Grains

Most cereal grains are members of the grass family. The most familiar are wheat, rye, barley, corn, oats, and rice. Sorghum and millet are less well known. Other cereal grains we sometimes use that are not in the grass family are amaranth and buckwheat. The information that follows is an overview of grain growing, but it pertains particularly to wheat and rye since these grains are the most popular and can be put to the most uses by the home gardener and cook. See "Recommended Grains" later in this chapter for information on individual grains and the "Native American Gardens" chapter for information on grain corn. Small-scale grain growing is discussed in the sections that follow on the minifarm and suburban grain gardens.

Climate

One way to categorize cereal grains is by the season in which they are grown. Winter wheat, winter rye, and winter barley, for example, are planted in the fall, grow a small amount over the winter, and finish their growth in late spring or midsummer. The winter grains usually have large yields and can be very useful for home gardeners, because they can often be harvested early enough to allow a crop of summer legumes—bush beans, soybeans, or limas, for example—to be grown in the same plot.

Spring barley and rye are grown when winter weather is too cold to permit the growing of winter grains. Spring wheat should be the choice of gardeners who live in areas of the country too cold for winter wheat. Another reason to choose spring wheat is that its protein content is somewhat higher than that of winter wheat. Spring wheat is planted in early spring and harvested in mid- to late summer.

At least one of the grain crops, and usually more, will grow in most parts of the continent, from the Arctic Circle south to Georgia, and in all parts of the West except the most arid deserts. Rye does not grow well in hot weather, but some rye varieties withstand cold to −40 degrees Fahrenheit and are therefore usable in the northern tier of the United States and in Canada. Winter wheat can be grown where the average winter low temperature does not drop below 20 degrees.

All the cereal grains require full sun and prefer well-drained, fairly fertile loam, though rye is less fussy. The grains produce best when they have a relatively long cool season in which to grow. Fall-planted grains germinate, produce a good root system and a modest amount of leaf growth, and then go dormant during the winter. When the weather warms up in spring, they start to grow quickly. Spring wheats are planted as early as possible in the spring—as soon as the ground can be worked or around the date of the last expected frost. They do best where there is a long, cool spring.

Planting

If you are interested in growing more wheat than the ten- to twenty-pound harvest described in the gardens that follow, here are some rough figures to help you determine how much space you will need. A bushel (about sixty pounds) of wheat can be harvested from an area of 1300 to 1400 square feet with average soil. For the typical family of four, this bushel will supply enough flour for cakes, pancakes, and some yeast and quick breads for a year, but will not be enough for making the majority of the family's daily bread.

Order seeds from the seed companies listed at the end of this chapter under "Sources" or buy them from local feed or natural food stores. For rye seeds, make sure to order those labeled cereal or grain rye or you could wind up with one of the more commonly available grass varieties.

In the East and Midwest, plant winter wheat after the Hessian fly is no longer a problem—in mid-September in Michigan but as late as the end of October in Georgia. Ask a local university agricultural extension agent (a good source of basic regional planting information in general) for the exact date for your area. In the West, for the cold-winter areas plant winter wheat when the average daytime temperature is around 60 degrees Fahrenheit, and in mild-winter areas plant when it's around 50.

Plant grains in much the same way you would plant lawn grass. Turn the ground over and work in

Hard spring wheat growing in the author's northern California grain garden catches the rays of early-morning light, inspiring visions of homemade bread later in the season.

manure and fertilizer if necessary. Then rake the surface smooth and broadcast the seeds as evenly as possible. Use approximately four to six pounds of seeds to cover 1000 square feet (less where the soil is rich or the winters mild or arid). Rake the seed bed over so the soil covers the seeds. In small areas where birds might be a problem, cover the seeded area with netting.

Fertilizing

Fertilizers with too much nitrogen or soils lacking potassium cause lodging, a common problem in cereal grains. This is a condition in which the heads get too heavy and the stalks fall over, making the grain difficult to harvest and, in severe cases, causing the vegetation underneath to rot. To prevent lodging, supplement the soil annually with compost or manure (not high-nitrogen fertilizers) and some form of potassium and phosphorus. In addition, you might rotate grain crops with legumes, such as beans, peas, or clover. Such a rotation will provide the soil with the right amount of nitrogen. If rotation is not feasible, treat your soil with a moderate amount of blood or cottonseed meal and manure.

Pests and Diseases

Weeds are the biggest problem with large fields of grain, because weeds compete with grains. Also, weed seeds and leaves inevitably find their way into the harvested grain. The best solution is to rotate grains into a weed-free vegetable garden, but if this is not possible and you only have weedy soil to work with, there are a number of alternatives. The summer before you plant your grain garden, plant the weedy field a few times with green manure crops (crops that enrich and provide the organic matter most soils need), such as clover or buckwheat. Grow each crop out for a few months and till it under; then replant. Do this a couple of times until most of the weeds have been germinated and tilled under. Or sterilize the soil by soil solarization (see Appendix B, "Pests and Diseases") or plant the grain in narrow rows so you can get between the rows to weed without knocking over the plants.

As far as insect pests and diseases are concerned, small-scale wheat and rye growers don't have much to worry about. Green aphids and Hessian flies bother these crops occasionally, but the aphids are seldom a serious problem and you can avoid the flies by watching planting dates. Diseases are rarely a concern for the home grower.

Harvesting

Spring-planted varieties ripen in summer. Harvesting of winter-planted grains in southern sections of the country begins in late May or early June. The farther north you go, however, the later the grains ripen—sometimes they aren't ready for harvest until the first of August.

Most plants of the cereal grains turn yellow when ripe, although some varieties turn brown or almost red. Two other indications of ripeness are the bending or drooping of the seed heads and a sudden interest on the part of the birds. In very dry weather, if you are harvesting a small area by hand, you can let the wheat get very ripe. Commercial operations do not have this option, because the rough machine treatment knocks the grains loose.

Before you actually start cutting, look over your crop carefully to select next year's seed grains. For the criteria to use in making your selection, see John Jeavons's comments in the profile of Jeavons in this chapter. Store these seeds in clearly marked jars in a cool place separate from the rest of your harvest.

Scythes are usually used to harvest large plots of grains. The scythe is a long-handled, curved-blade tool that cuts off the stalks at the base. Farm-supply stores carry scythes, and sometimes you can find a used one by advertising locally. A grain cradle, a tool with long wooden fingers that catch and direct the stalks of wheat or rye, is very useful if you have much of a harvest.

A 1000-square-foot area can be harvested manageably with a sickle, a short-handled cutting tool. To use the sickle, hold a handful of stalks in one hand and cut off the plants at the base with the blade. Make sure to lay down all the cut plants in the same direction to facilitate the gathering of the grain.

Processing

If you live in a humid or rainy climate, you might need to dry the harvested grain heads before threshing and storing them. In this case, for a large harvest, use twine to tie stalks in bundles small enough to be carried easily; then stack the bundles in the field in traditional shocks. A shock is a stack of half a dozen bundles arranged grain end up and leaning against each other. Cover the shocks with bird netting, and if rain is expected, cover them temporarily with a tarp too. To dry a small harvest, put the shocks in a dry garage. Remove the dried bundles in ten days to two weeks.

Let's take a moment to look closely at a harvested wheat head in order to determine what needs to be done next. The wheat seeds, known as berries, must be separated from the inedible parts of the plant in a process called threshing. The extraneous matter, termed chaff, includes the hull, which is the casing that holds the wheat berry in the head. The freed wheat berry consists of three parts: the outer coating, called the bran and well known as a source of fiber or roughage; the embryo, or wheat germ, a powerful source of nutrition; and the endosperm, which contains most of the grain's food energy in the form of starch. Refined white flour consists of the endosperm only. The flour you'll make from your wheat berries will be—*voilà!*—whole-wheat flour and will consist of the bran and germ as well as the endosperm.

There are several different methods of threshing the grain. To thresh large amounts of grain, you'll probably want to buy some equipment for that purpose, such as a bicycle-powered threshing machine or an old-fashioned flail (a simple hand tool consisting of a handle and a freely swinging piece of wood or leather used to beat the grain heads). See a book on large-scale grain growing for types of threshing aids and techniques and see the "Sources" section at the end of this chapter for places that carry some of these tools.

Winnowing the grain—removing the actual grain from the chaff—is best done on a windy day. If there's no wind to help, use a fan. The object is to blow, or winnow, the hulls and straw out of the grain.

Put a pound or so of grain in a bucket and transfer the grain into another bucket from a height of three feet or so. Pour the grain back and forth a number of times. Not all the extraneous matter will be removed, but the longer you work, the cleaner the grain will get. If the chaff bothers you, just before using the grain wash it, and the little pieces of chaff will float to the top, where you can skim them off. Most people don't bother with washing the grain, though, and treat the chaff as a harmless part of the grain's roughage. Do look through your grain carefully for small stones or dirt, however, and remove them by hand. And be warned: if you wash the grain, make sure to dry it before grinding or it will gum up the mill.

Put the grain in an airtight container and store it in a cool, dry place. It will keep for years; but the older it gets, the less fresh it will taste. As a precaution against insect infestation, before storing, heat the grain to 140 degrees Fahrenheit for thirty minutes to kill any insect eggs that might be in it. (Remember not to do this to next year's seed grain or you will kill it.) Alternatively, freeze the grain. In either case, grind the grain as you need it. Or grind it all at one time and freeze the flour.

The Common Ground Minifarm Grain Garden

When John Jeavons and I conceived of growing a demonstration grain garden, our primary goal was to show that a small plot of ground could produce a respectable enough amount of wheat to make the effort worthwhile—enough to allow a bread-making maven to enjoy a few dozen loaves from the ground up. With this goal in mind, John and his apprentice, Gary Stoner, planned a garden to my specifications that, in fact, included not just wheat, but rye as well, another grain well suited for home gardens. The garden contained two different types of Utah hard spring wheat—two plots of H. R. S. '907R' and one of H. R. S. 'Moon Grow'—and a small plot of 'Hungarian' cereal rye.

The Common Ground Minifarm is a demonstration farm in Willits, in northern California. The object of the farm is to demonstrate biointensive techniques for growing food in a simple, sustainable, and ecologically sound way using a minimum of resources. The winter temperatures at the farm are in the teens and low twenties, and summer temperatures often reach the hundreds. The native soil is sandy loam of very low fertility; in fact, before the farm proved differently, the locals considered it good only for grazing. But John and the staff double-dug the beds and added copious amounts of organic material and fertilizers. These preparations were in keeping with John's conviction that good soil is the key to a productive garden, and his data certainly support this belief. In the first year, the grain production on the minifarm's 175-square-foot plot was 75 percent of the national average. Today their three-year-old beds produce close to three times the national average.

If your soil is the ordinary garden variety, you will have to plant more square feet or improve your soil in order to match the minifarm's production. For more information on John's soil-preparation methods, see his book *How to Grow More Vegetables*.

With the plot for our grain garden prepared, Gary sowed the grain in flats in March to get an early start on the season. Two weeks later he selected

John Jeavons, author of *How to Grow More Vegetables,* has been involved with the Biodynamic/French Intensive Method of gardening since the early 1970s. John has helped run Ecology Action in Palo Alto, California, and has now moved part of the organization north to Willits, California, where he runs an apprentice program, a demonstration garden, and a seed company. John has been growing and experimenting with grains since 1973, and I asked him to share some of his thoughts on the subject.

John is so enthusiastic about grains that he feels even a plot five feet by five feet is worth planting. He suggests that you try it just to see your own golden waves of grain swaying in the breeze. He also feels learning about grains and sharing the experience with children is valuable.

"While you usually think in terms of the harvest for the kitchen, growing wheat in your garden has other benefits," John says. "For one thing, wheat and other grains greatly benefit the soil. The roots of a wheat plant might extend into the soil to a depth of four to six feet and to a width of four feet. This massive root system fiberizes the soil and helps break up large clods. It's great for crop rotation."

John says you can realize even further soil benefits if you harvest some of the green growth for the compost pile during the growing season. To do this, cut the plants back to six to eight inches early in the season—if they're growing vigorously—before they've sent up stalks. If the wheat continues to grow vigorously, you can sometimes repeat this procedure two or three more times. (Some people even let their chickens graze the wheat at this stage.) This cutting back can also prevent lodging (falling over of the stalks) during spring storms, and some documentation indicates that it might actually increase yields slightly.

John recommends that, if you decide to grow wheat when choosing your grains, you consider planting another fifteen percent of your harvest in rye. You can then combine rye flour with wheat for better nutrition. Studies show that the phytates in wheat tie up iron, and that rye in small amounts helps to buffer this effect while having little effect on the consistency or taste of the bread.

John points out one last consideration: "If you're growing open-pollinated—not hybrid—varieties, remember to save some seeds from your best plants for next year. Analyze your seed choices with three qualities in mind. First, determine whether you want plants with long or short stalks. Long stalks are easier to harvest because you don't have to lean over to do so, but short stalks don't lodge as readily and would be your choice if you've had problems with that in the past. Next, look for the heads that have the most and the heaviest grains. The selection is an art: it's hard to get all three qualities—correct stalk length, high-quantity grains, and heavy grains—all in one plant. After a few years of seed selection, however, you'll find the grain that grows and produces best in your garden. With good selection, you can sometimes double your yield in three or four years."

John's observations through many seasons suggest to him the most obvious reason to grow your own grains: "Freshly harvested wheat is different from what you buy in the store. When you open your jar of wheat berries in the first few months after harvest, they're alive; they smell so fresh. It smells like wheat with a molasses overtone. And isn't fresh, wholesome wheat what it's all about?"

John Jeavons

the most vigorous seedlings and planted them in the beds five inches apart. (Remember, the goal of the research at the minifarm is always peak production in a small area.) The beds were quite weed free, but with such a strong start the wheat could have crowded out almost anything. Gary easily pulled the few weeds that did appear, since the grains were planted in beds, which are easier to maintain than a solid field.

To fertilize the beds, Gary added compost at the rate of six cubic feet per 100-square-foot bed, eight pounds of cottonseed meal, five pounds of bone meal, five pounds of green sand (an iron potassium silicate and a good source of potash), and one pound of kelp meal. These were broadcast across the top of the bed and forked in lightly to a depth of two to three inches.

In dry weather they watered the grains lightly every day, as is the practice at the minifarm for all crops. Gary recommends that "if you don't want to use this method, at least make sure the grains get adequate moisture at the beginning when they first

get established and again just as they begin to head up."

In early May, Gary and John started to judge the ripeness of the wheat by watching its color (it must turn golden) and by checking a few of the wheat berries. Wheat goes through three stages. In the early stage, called the milk stage, the berries are soft and have a kind of milky texture. Then they progress to a soft-dough stage, when they are chewy and you can dent them with your fingernail or teeth. In the hard-dough stage you can't dent the grain at all. At that stage the berries are ready for storage, and that's when the wheat is harvested at the minifarm.

When I arrived at the minifarm to join John and Gary, the crop was ready to be harvested. Wheat is usually harvested at ground level with the heads left on the straw. But because the minifarm's staff keeps careful records of organic matter produced as well as grain yields, they clip the grain heads off at the top with sheep or pruning shears and then go back

Gary Stoner weeds amaranth, with the Common Ground Minifarm wheat garden in the background.

and clip the straw off at the bottom. They keep the two separate for measurement.

The total harvest from the minifarm's 175-square-foot trial plot was eleven pounds—seven pounds from the two plots of H. R. S. '907R' spring wheat equaling 125 square feet, almost two and a half pounds of H. R. S. 'Moon Grow' from twenty-five square feet, and a pound and a half of 'Hungarian' cereal rye berries from a twenty-five-square-foot plot.

At the minifarm they use a hand mill to grind the grain for flour. Because hand grinding grains in large quantities is tedious, they have a bicycle attachment to power the mill.

Most of the wheat heads are stored in burlap sacks and threshed later. But as Gary says, "After the harvest we're usually so anxious to enjoy some when it's at its freshest and most aromatic, we thresh some right away. We throw a threshing party and get out a clean old sheet and put on clean tennis shoes. Then we lay the wheat heads out on the sheet a few handfuls at a time and dance on it, scuffing our way around the sheet. The kids love it and come running to join us. We scuff until the chaff breaks away from the berries, and then gather everything up in the middle of the sheet and pour it into a large bowl. When the wind is blowing, we winnow it by transferring the material from one bowl to another. The chaff blows away as the wheat pours from one bowl to the next. We then store the berries in a clean glass jar. When we use the wheat through the year, we try to grind the flour on the same day we use it.

"Flour is our favorite way to use wheat, but we also use the whole berries. We sprout all the grains and put them in salads, and of course we bake with them. We also crack wheat and use it in tabouli and other bulgur dishes. But, of course, what we enjoy most is our own whole-wheat bread. I love to work with the fresh wheat flour. One of my all-time favorite bread cookbooks is *The Tassajara Bread Book* by Edward Espe Brown. For other ways to use grains, we use both Mollie Katzen's *The Enchanted Broccoli Forest* and Ellen Ewald's *Recipes for a Small Planet*."

The grain garden had obviously done very well. John had been growing grains for years, but this was Gary's first try, and his comments reveal his surprise at how easy it had been to grow grain successfully. "Once the bed was prepared and the grains were planted and coming up," he said, "they didn't need any staking and tying or pruning or extra feeding—in fact, they needed no constant harvesting and

attention at all. The grains pretty much took care of themselves. This is certainly a contrast with the other plants I'm used to caring for, like beans, lettuce, and broccoli."

To conclude, Gary said, "All in all, growing grain has been a very satisfying experience. It feeds you, of course, but in addition it's beautiful to watch as it grows."

The Suburban Grain Garden

I came home from the harvest session at the Common Ground Minifarm dying to grow wheat in my own garden in the fall. Not only did I want to enjoy my own harvest, but I wanted to see if I could further simplify the minifarm's garden methods for even the most casual gardener.

The front yard contains the only sunny spot in my garden in the winter. Consequently, the grain garden I was planning had to look beautiful. After all, being the neighborhood garden designer, I had a reputation to keep up. In addition, I wanted to show the world how beautiful a grain garden could be. With a little luck, I would wow the neighbors and confound the joggers with my wheat garden.

Wheat has plenty of potential as an unusual and beautiful garden crop. Grains, as they grow, can form a solid green background that highlights other plants. In fact, they offer nearly the uniformity and shape of a small hedge. I was planning a giant flower border down the front walk, and I visualized the wheat as an unorthodox backdrop. I would plant the wheat where trellised tomatoes had grown all summer. The bed was three feet wide and twenty-two feet long—sixty-six square feet in all.

As it turned out, the wheat, not my flower border, was the star of the garden. At least once a week, when I looked out the window I would see a couple of bicyclists or a panting jogger standing and enjoying the view. Some would have quizzical looks on their faces—What was she up to now? If I happened to be outside, I'd tell them I was growing wheat, and the smiles would be instantaneous. "How wonderful!" they would say, as if something were right with the world.

But I'm getting ahead of myself. After I decided where my wheat was going to grow, I ordered spring wheat seed from Bountiful Gardens. One packet was enough. Even though I was going to grow it in winter, John recommended spring wheat, because it contains more protein than the winter varieties. His research had shown a lot of latitude in the climate requirements of most grains and had indicated that spring wheat would work out well.

Wendy Krupnick, my assistant, turned over the tomato bed in mid-November and spread and lightly worked in two or three inches of well-aged manure. The soil in the bed is of slightly alkaline clay to which a good amount of organic matter had been added over the previous year. It's good soil, but not super. Instead of planting the wheat from flats, as Gary and John had done, we decided to broadcast the seeds over the bed and rake them in. We watered the bed, and within a short time the wheat was up. Since it was the rainy season, we didn't have to water again until late April. Beginning then, we watered once a week until late May, when the grain started to turn golden. The only other care we gave the wheat was a little thinning when the grain was about a month old—too many seeds had sprouted. Also, we had to pull weeds for an hour or so.

My only real concern for the wheat arose during a few hard winter storms. By late February the wheat was knee-high and lush. As a precaution against lodging in a storm, John had recommended that we cut the grain back if it got that high during the rainy season, but we had not done so because I wanted to see how carefree it could be. Sure enough, one morning after a stormy night I went out and found half the wheat had fallen over. It righted itself, but only to be knocked over again in the next storm. Again it righted itself. At that point, as an experiment, we cut some of it back to six inches high. The cut wheat didn't fall over again as the rest did. (In subsequent years I have had uncut wheat fall over and stay lodged. I therefore recommend you either cut it back mid-season or support the wheat by putting stakes and string around the bed.)

In the first week of June, my friends Maureen and William Phelps came over to help me harvest the wheat. We had a whole Saturday afternoon, so we decided to try a few different methods to determine which was the easiest. Of the various ways we tried, here's the method we agreed was best for harvesting a small plot of wheat. Assemble two old bed sheets; a pair of old scissors, hedge clippers, or trimmers; a basket for the few heads of green wheat you might

The author's grain garden in the spring, with wheat serving as a backdrop for a blaze of ranunculus and calendulas. While the flowers were showy, it was the wheat that made joggers pause to enjoy the garden.

have; mason jars in which to store the wheat berries; two large metal bowls (or, if possible, something as large and lightweight as a canner), and a cannister vacuum cleaner (you'll see!). You'll also need a hard surface, such as a driveway—on which to stomp the wheat—and clean tennis shoes.

We began by spreading a sheet next to the wheat. We tried different implements to cut it with and agreed

Maureen and William thresh the wheat on the driveway using the "tennis shoe twist."

the scissors and trimming shears seemed to work the best. We kept a wheelbarrow handy for taking the stalks to the compost.

The first cutting method we tried was to grab handfuls of heads at a time and cut them off with scissors, leaving the stubble standing. We piled up the heads on the sheet. When we had completed the first quarter of the bed, we moved the sheet to the driveway and performed the "tennis shoe twist" on the heads of wheat. This twisting motion was our threshing technique—it removed the wheat berries from the shafts. When the heads seemed to be disintegrated, we lifted the corners of the sheet and gathered the wheat and chaff into the middle. We then reached in and removed the largest pieces of the chaff by hand and poured everything else into a large metal container.

We attempted to winnow the grain by pouring it from one container to another, hoping the wind would pick up the chaff and blow it away, as all the books assure readers it will. But we didn't have much wind, and it soon became clear that this method was not going to work. At that point, William suggested we use a cannister vacuum cleaner in reverse to simulate wind. This worked like a charm. Maureen was able to remove 90 percent of the chaff in the first batch in thirty seconds. We soon developed a swirling technique for moving the vacuum cleaner nozzle; we found it was important not to hold it too close to

the wheat berries or it would blow them out of the container. I think even a brisk wind would be runner-up to William's vacuum method.

When this batch was done and in jars, we went back and cut the stubble off at ground level with the hedge clippers and took it to the compost pile. Then we started on the next quadrant.

An alternative cutting method we tried involved grasping the stalks in one hand and cutting them off at ground level with the other, and then inverting them over the sheet and cutting the heads off with scissors. This seemed a workable method. We also tried gathering up a handful of sheaves with the heads still on and beating it on the sheet to remove the berries. This was not successful at all—it had wheat berries flying all over the driveway.

We estimated that harvesting the sixty-six square feet of wheat had taken about three hours—about ten minutes to set everything up, twenty minutes to harvest, and another two and a half hours to separate the wheat from the chaff and clean up. Also, a good portion of the total was taken up with posing for pictures, so we figured we could probably have done the whole job in two hours, start to finish.

We all concluded that it's a snap to harvest a small bed of wheat and a lot of fun besides. The only real work is the threshing and cleaning up. For our virtually carefree crop and three hours of work, we ended up with a little more than ten pounds of fresh, organically grown wheat berries. Notice that we aced out the minifarm wheat production. Eat your heart out, John Jeavons!

Recommended Grains

There are seven types of grain to consider for the home garden. All are fairly easy to grow, but some are much easier to prepare for the table than others and should be given priority. The numbers in parentheses following the grain descriptions correspond to those of the seed companies listed in the "Sources" section, thus indicating where the grains are available.

BARLEY *Hordeum vulgare* There are two types of barley—winter and spring. Barley has the widest climate range of the common grains: some varieties are tolerant of very cold winters and some of quite warm summers. Consult your local university agricultural extension agent for recommended varieties. The barley bred for human consumption is called six-row barley.

How to grow: Barley is grown and harvested in ways similar to those for wheat, but barley is much harder to prepare for the table. The hull of wheat separates easily from the grain, but barley's hull does not. Commercial processors run barley through large abrasive disks in a procedure called pearling, which removes the hull and germ—and most of the nutrition. The home gardener can run a small amount of barley through a blender to remove the hulls and then winnow it with an electric fan to remove the chaff.

How to prepare: Though barley is rather bland, it is good in soup, cereal, and pilaf. Barley flour, made from grinding the winnowed grain, has no gluten, and is used only in small amounts in bread. (1)

BUCKWHEAT *Fagopyrum esculentum* Buckwheat is known for its nutty flavor and has been a favorite grain for pancakes for generations.

How to grow: Buckwheat is an annual flowering plant that is very easy to grow. It is sown in place, a half a pound per thousand square feet, at least three months before the first fall frost. It produces best if it flowers in cool weather, though when it is planted for a green manure crop it is often planted in spring. Buckwheat will grow in poor soil, but it produces more on better soil. It is a very vigorous grower, will crowd out most weeds, and is seldom bothered by pests. Most people use only a small amount of this strong-flavored grain in a year, primarily for pancakes, so a few hundred square feet is usually enough for the average family. The seeds in a buckwheat plant do not mature all at once, so you need to decide when the majority are ripe and harvest the heads then. Let the stalks dry in the field and then thresh by hitting the stems against the insides of a clean garbage can. Winnow to remove chaff as you would for wheat. Removing the hulls requires a different procedure. Buckwheat hulls usually separate from the small seeds after the grain has gone through a grain mill. To sift out the hulls, force the flour through a fine sieve. The hulls have the strongest flavor, so the more you remove, the milder the flour will become.

How to prepare: Use buckwheat flour in your favorite pancake recipe, and see *Whole Grains* by Sara Pitzer for a number of other recipes using cracked buckwheat, or groats. (1, 2)

CORN *Zea Mays* See the "Native American Gar-

dens" chapter for information on grain corn and the Part Four Encyclopedia for information on how to grow corn.

GRAIN AMARANTH *Amaranthus hypochondriacus* Amaranth was a staple of the Aztecs, though it is unusual for a grain, as it is not a member of the grass family. Some amaranths are grown for their leaves, which are eaten like spinach; other types produce an edible grain. Grain amaranth is an easily grown annual plant that can reach seven or eight feet in height. It has large red and yellow plumes and is very dramatic in the garden. The plumes bear small seeds that can be easily winnowed, and these can be ground for flour for use in breads or even popped like corn. The flavor of amaranth grain is quite mild and nutty, and amaranth is higher in protein than all other grains. In addition, the amino acids in amaranth are complementary to those in whole wheat and corn, and in combination with those of either, they form a protein as complete as that in meat. Amaranth flour contains no gluten, a protein present primarily in wheat that becomes elastic when moistened and stretched; therefore amaranth must be combined with wheat flour to make risen breads. When amaranth plants are young, you can eat their tender leaves as you would eat spinach leaves. They are as nutritious as spinach leaves but lack their strong flavor. See the recipe for amaranth bread in the cooking section.

How to grow: Start seedlings of grain amaranth after all danger of frost has passed. Plant in full sun and in rich, well-drained soil and keep fairly moist. Generally, seeds will grow with great enthusiasm. Harvest the heads when the seeds start to drop and dry them for a few days. Thresh as you would other grains. The object is to knock the shiny seeds loose from the heads; they will separate quite easily. Winnow to remove the chaff and use whole in cereals and breads or grind into a flour.

How to prepare: See the booklet called *Amaranth Round-up* recommended under "Sources" for more information on this wonderful food. (1, 2, 3)

OATS *Avena sativa* Oats are recognizable to most people because of their use in cereals and cookies. They are one of the tastier grains and one of the highest in protein content.

How to grow: There are spring and winter types of oats, but the winter oats have a limited range since they are hardy to only 10 degrees Fahrenheit. Generally, oats are grown and harvested in ways similar to those for wheat, though oats are a little less demanding and the plants are much taller. The problem for home gardeners is usually the same as that with barley: removing the hulls of the oats is very difficult. Commercially, oats are rolled through large rollers or are steel cut. One new variety, 'Freedom Hulless', is reputed to be hulless. (2)

How to prepare: Rolled oats are famous as cereal and can be used in granola and, sparingly, in breads and muffins. Oat flour contains no gluten. (1, 2)

RYE   *Secale cereale*   Rye has a semi-sour taste and has been used in European cooking for generations. It's at its best when combined with caraway seeds in wonderful German bread.

How to grow: Rye is the most foolproof of all the grains to grow—it's a great choice for beginners. Follow the basic directions for growing and harvesting wheat, but be aware that there is more latitude in the soil preparation and climate restrictions. One word of caution about rye: it is vulnerable to the disease known as ergot fungus. This fungus is a nerve poison to humans and animals. If small, black, grain-size growths form on the heads as the rye is developing, destroy the rye.

How to prepare: For cooking, use rye berries whole as you would wheat berries. Rye flour contains almost no gluten, so it can only be used in small amounts in risen bread. But rye makes marvelous crackers. (1, 2)

WHEAT   *Triticum aestivum*   Wheat is truly the staff of life, the most commonly grown grain in this country.

How to grow: Wheat has the most demanding cultural requirements of all the grains. See the information earlier in this chapter concerning climate restrictions. Wheat will not grow well in very acid soil; it prefers a pH of 6.4. Usually, a local nursery or university agricultural extension agent can tell you if your soil is too acidic and, if so, how to rectify it. Drainage for wheat must be excellent. Do not plant wheat where there is standing water in the winter or spring.

How to prepare: The many types of wheat are used in diverse ways in cooking. Hard winter wheat, the most common of all the wheats, is high in gluten and used primarily for bread. Soft red winter wheat is used for pastry and crackers, and soft spring wheat, though lower in gluten than some others, makes a tasty bread. Hard spring wheat is used primarily for

bread, and durum wheat, also a spring wheat and best known for its very high gluten content, is refined and used for pasta and semolina. Enjoy the rich, nutty taste of whole wheat in breads, cookies, and pancakes. You'll need to modify some of your white-flour recipes to use your whole-wheat flour, because the germ and bran give the latter distinctive properties. Pastry made with whole-wheat flour is harder to roll out, the bran in whole-wheat pasta absorbs liquid and makes the proportions different in the recipe, and whole-wheat flour makes a denser bread. Use wheat berries whole in the many ways you would use rice; also, see the recipes in the cooking section. For more information on wheat, see the books listed under "Sources." (1, 2, 3)

Cooking from the Grain Garden

As mentioned earlier, grains such as barley and oats, while wonderful to eat, are difficult for home growers to thresh. Fortunately, we are left with the most versatile and popular grains: wheat and, to a lesser degree, rye. Wheat and rye can be used in many forms: whole; sprouted; cracked, which means the grain has been ground into a very coarse meal; and ground completely into flour. The whole grains are used like rice; the sprouted grains are used in entrees and salads. In all cases, home-grown grain is healthful, for it retains its outer coating, called the bran and famous for its fiber, and the embryo, or germ, which is rich in nutritional content. Wheat and rye are interchangeable in recipes calling for whole or cracked berries, though rye takes less time to cook. As flour, however, they are quite different, as rye has much less gluten.

Whole Wheat and Rye Berries

After planting my wheat garden, I happened to attend a national cuisine conference. What a privilege it was to enjoy food prepared by some of the country's best

OPPOSITE: *Two loaves of whole-wheat bread made by Edward Brown using the sponge method. One is a standard whole-wheat loaf, and the other, a round loaf of whole-wheat sourdough bread, has a crunchy crust.*

When we think about wheat, bread is what comes to mind—warm, fragrant, comforting bread. As often as I've made bread, each new time is as pleasurable as the first: the smell of it cooking, handing a slice to one of my children, and, of course, eating it. The look in John Jeavons's eyes (see the photo of John in this chapter) when we handed him the loaf Gary Stoner had just taken from the oven also illustrates the human experience of receiving this warm token of someone's love.

I wanted to convey this feeling of pleasure to others who have never made their own bread; so I went to Edward Espe Brown, author of *The Tassajara Bread Book*, to get his thoughts. His 1970 book on bread making was the first on the subject to influence me.

Before writing his book, Edward had baked bread for years for the Zen Buddhist monastery in the mountains above the Carmel Valley of California. Visitors there would often find their way down to the kitchen to ask how he made such wonderful bread, and he would invite them to come back at five in the morning so he could show them. When Edward had first arrived at the monastery, the original cooks had taught him to make bread by the sponge method. This involves mixing the water for the bread with yeast, sweetening it, adding about half the flour, and letting it rise. To this dough are added oil, salt, and the rest of the flour. Edward finds this an easy way to make bread because the bread is like a sponge when it rises—the dough gets a lot of air in it and becomes soft and workable. In fact, he says it's so easy that he kneaded forty-five loaves in less than three hours a few days before my visit.

Edward Espe Brown

Not only can bread making be easy, it can also be faster than many people realize. Edward notes that a friend of his puts her dough in her car while she goes out to run errands with her children. When the time comes, she punches down the bread. Depending on where you live and the season, Edward says, "the car is usually nice and warm—a good place for bread to rise."

As we talked during my visit, the smell of bread perfumed the air. Edward told me he finds the process as well as the product of bread making fulfilling. "It's very sustaining," he says. "My grandmother's life was difficult, but through it all she baked her bread. It was something she could do all her life. A real grounding.

"Making bread is special, a simple activity that has the capacity for renewal," he continues. "It's an honest to goodness way to give and receive love. It means so much more than going to the store and getting a card. It's almost spiritual: spiritual not as supernatural, but as something down to earth and, in a way, very ordinary—but at the same time nourishing and satisfying. There's something about working the dough, too—it's very nice to work with, to have something so pliable in your hands as you rhythmically move your whole body. With the dough in your hands, you become bread making itself.

"We don't mature by driving the freeway, or watching television, or opening up TV dinners," Edward says. "We grow older, but we don't mature. Cooking seems to touch people, to involve them—especially the process of bread making, working with the living dough. Bread making connects you with the world."

chefs. Dinner was served on a ship floating in San Francisco Bay, and to my surprise, wheat-berry jambalaya was on the menu. Ken Dunn, executive chef at the Mayfair House in Coconut Grove, Florida, had created this dish. Though I would never have thought to make jambalaya with wheat berries (it is traditionally made with rice), it was excellent. Everyone was as enamored with the wheat berries as I was.

Once home, I started to look into other ways to serve whole wheat berries. The major problem seems to be getting them tender enough; if they are not cooked sufficiently, their chewiness can be a bit distracting. Whole wheat will always be a little chewier than rice, but, with a little more liquid and a longer cooking time, it can be substituted in any rice recipe. The wheat flavor is great in pilaf, rice pudding, or any other rice entrees. Whole rye berries can be used in similar ways, but their cooking time is fifteen to twenty minutes shorter than that for wheat, and their flavor is more pronounced.

BASIC WHEAT BERRIES

SERVES 3.

> *1 cup wheat berries*
> *2½ cups water*

Combine in a saucepan. Cover, bring to a boil, lower heat to lowest setting, and cook 1 to 1½ hours, until water is gone and grains are soft. Check to prevent burning; you might have to add more water. For even more flavor, try cooking the berries in stock or vegetable juices. Add fresh herbs and other flavorings, such as onion, tomatoes, and garlic, and serve as a side dish or try them in the following recipes.

HEARTLAND JAMBALAYA

This recipe comes from Ken Dunn, executive chef at the Mayfair House in Coconut Grove, Florida.

SERVES 4.

> *3 cups hard red Kansas wheat berries or other whole wheat berries*
> *2 to 3 quarts chicken stock*
> *2 smoked pork hocks*
> *1½ cups julienne of bacon, cooked crisp*

> *2 tablespoons fresh shallots, chopped*
> *1½ teaspoons fresh minced garlic*
> *¼ cup each finely chopped fresh basil, sage, and marjoram*
> *1½ cups diced red or green peppers*
> *2 tablespoons chopped fresh yellow chili peppers*
> *1 tablespoon finely julienned ancho chilies (or other fresh mild chilies)*
> *1¼ cups bratwurst, bias sliced*
> *12 medium shrimp, peeled and deveined*
> *½ cup ham, cut into ⅛ × 2-inch pieces*
> *Salt and pepper to taste*
> *¾ cup canned yellow hominy, sautéed crisp*
> *12 ears fresh baby corn, shucked (optional)*
> *4 fresh nasturtium flowers with leaves (optional)*

Soak wheat berries in water overnight to soften. Place drained berries into heavy-bottom saucepan with chicken stock and pork hocks. Place over medium heat. Bring to simmer. Continue simmering until berries are tender (about 1 to 1½ hours). Start with 8 cups stock, adding stock to keep contents covered until grains are tender. Drain excess stock, reserving for later use. Remove hocks and discard.

In sauté pan, cook bacon until crisp. Remove from pan. Reserve only enough fat to sauté shallots and garlic. Add shallots and garlic. Sauté lightly. Add herbs and all peppers. Sauté lightly.

Add shallot mixture to wheat-berry mixture, along with one-quarter of remaining stock and bratwurst, shrimp, and ham, simmering until shrimp are opaque. Season with salt and pepper. In a separate pan, poach corn in chicken stock until just tender.

To assemble: Place wheat and vegetable mixture into a soup bowl; make a small indentation on top. Stand corn on end in indentation. Sprinkle hominy on top; place flowers in center of corn. Serve immediately.

OVERNIGHT WHEAT-BERRY CEREAL

SERVES 4 TO 6.

Place 1½ cups wheat berries and 3½ cups water in a medium saucepan with a tight-fitting lid. Cover pan and simmer at lowest setting for 1½ hours. Turn off heat and let pan sit overnight. In the morning, stir and check for moisture; unless there is still water at bottom of pan, add ¼ to ½ cup milk, water, or apple juice, and simmer ½ hour longer.

Crockpot method: Allow 10 to 12 hours or more for the wheat to cook through. Place 1½ cups wheat berries and 3 cups water in crockpot. Cover and set to high for 2 hours. Turn to low and leave for 8 to 10 hours.

Variations: Use a mixture of home-grown grains, such as rye, millet, oats, or amaranth. Cook ¼ cup finely chopped dried fruit or raisins with the grains. Use apple juice for part of the cooking water and add ½ teaspoon cinnamon. Add 1 teaspoon vanilla.

Serving suggestions: Serve with milk, yogurt, or cottage cheese. Add fresh or home-canned fruit and/or chopped nuts or sunflower seeds. Top with maple syrup or honey. Good cold as well as hot.

Note: Whole wheat berries make a chewy cereal. If a finer-textured porridge is desired, crack wheat in a grinder or blender, or make bulgur, as directed below, and then follow the directions for wheat-berry cereal but reduce cooking time.

WHEAT-BERRY MUFFINS

MAKES 12 MUFFINS.

> *1 large or extra-large egg*
> *1 cup milk*
> *1 teaspoon vanilla*
> *2 to 4 tablespoons sugar, brown sugar, honey,*
> *   or molasses*
> *¼ cup oil or melted butter*
> *1½ cups leftover wheat-berry cereal or cooked*
> *   wheat berries*
> *1 tablespoon baking powder, sifted into*
> *1½ cups whole-wheat pastry flour*
> *Optional: ¼ cup dried fruit or raisins, finely*
> *   chopped; 1 tablespoon grated orange*
> *   rind; 1 teaspoon cinnamon and/or ½*
> *   teaspoon ginger or nutmeg, and/or ¼*
> *   teaspoon allspice or cardamom*

Preheat oven to 400°.

In a large bowl, beat egg. Add milk, vanilla, sweetener, and oil. Stir in wheat berries, baking powder and flour, and any other additions. Stir briefly; then spoon into greased or paper-lined muffin tins. Bake for about 30 minutes.

WHEAT-BERRY CUSTARD

This recipe will remind you of rice pudding.

SERVES 6.

> *3 eggs*
> *1 cup cooked wheat berries*
> *1½ cups milk*
> *2 tablespoons honey or maple syrup*
> *⅓ cup raisins, chopped dates, or other*
> *   chopped dried fruit*
> *1 teaspoon vanilla*
> *¼ teaspoon freshly grated nutmeg*

Preheat oven to 300°.

Beat eggs, add remaining ingredients, and beat well. Pour into a buttered heavy baking dish or casserole. Place baking dish in a pan; pour boiling water into pan to reach halfway up sides of dish. Bake for about 1½ hours or until set. Serve warm or cold for dessert, breakfast, or snack. Excellent topped with fresh fruit.

Sprouted Wheat

Most of us are familiar with alfalfa and mung bean sprouts, but wheat seeds, or berries, can be sprouted as well, as long as they haven't been heat treated for insect control. They are worth the few days of advance planning necessary, because, as the starch in the grain is transformed into sugars, a unique, delicious, and versatile product is made. You can put sprouted wheat berries in breads or cook and use them in casseroles or salads. They take less cooking time than raw wheat berries. At different stages of sprouting they are used in different ways. I highly recommend *Laurel's Kitchen Bread Book* for its excellent information about sprouting grains, making and using malt, and making a wonderfully moist and naturally sweet bread out of nothing but sprouted wheat. This book also contains recipes for crackers and yeasted whole-wheat bread using sprouted wheat. What follows are simplified directions for sprouting wheat.

To sprout wheat, on the first evening, place the berries in a bowl with at least double the volume of water and let sit overnight. Drain and let sit at room temperature, rinsing and draining twice a day for two or three days, or until the sprouts are just showing. At this stage the sprouts are ready for use in sprout bread. To use in entrees, salads, and the recipe for wheat patties that follows, let the sprouts grow for another day or two, but do not let them get longer than a quarter inch. If the sprouts are ready before you are, refrigerate them. I cook them before using them in a salad, since they're too chewy for my taste when raw. To figure out how much sprouts to use in a recipe, note that the volume of the wheat approximately doubles when sprouted.

SPROUTED-WHEAT PATTIES

MAKES 8 PATTIES.

2 cups sprouted wheat
1 onion, quartered
2 cloves garlic
⅛ to ½ cup fresh herbs, depending on flavor
*   and strength you prefer*
1 egg
⅓ cup milk
1 small carrot, grated
1 cup dry bread crumbs
½ cup ground nuts, lightly toasted

Preheat oven to 450°.

Put all ingredients except bread crumbs and nuts in an electric blender and blend until smooth. Pour into a bowl and stir in bread crumbs and nuts. Spoon onto greased cookie sheet and flatten to form patties about ½ inch thick and 3 inches in diameter. Bake for about 15 minutes or until bottoms are golden brown. Turn and bake about 10 minutes longer. Add a slice of jack or Swiss cheese for the last minute and serve with fresh tomato slices from the garden.

Cracked Wheat

The most common way to use cracked grains is to make delicious hot cereal. The grain is cracked to reduce cooking time and to give a smooth texture to the porridge. To prepare wheat for a cooked cereal, first roast it in a 200-degree oven for about forty minutes, stirring it around a few times. Let it cool and then put it in a blender or grain mill. Grind it, a cup at a time, to a coarse meal. Store in an airtight container. For three servings of cereal, put half a cup of meal, two cups of water, and a dash of salt into a saucepan and simmer for about half an hour. Watch carefully toward the end of the cooking time to pre-

vent the cereal from sticking; add a little more water if necessary. Don't stir very much or the gluten will develop and the cereal will be gummy. Serve with milk, brown sugar, and butter, or your favorite cereal embellishments.

A variation on cracked wheat is the bulgur wheat used in tabouli. To make bulgur, boil the wheat berries for about half an hour and then drain them. Place them on a cookie sheet in a 200-degree oven for about an hour until they are completely dry, turning occasionally. Grind to the desired coarseness.

TABOULI

SERVES 6 TO 8.

1 cup bulgur
1 cup boiling water
2 to 3 medium tomatoes, finely chopped
1 cup minced fresh parsley
¼ to ½ cup minced fresh mint
½ cup minced onion or green onions
⅓ cup lemon juice
⅓ cup olive oil
Freshly ground black pepper to taste
1 teaspoon salt (optional)

Tabouli is a wonderful Middle Eastern dish made with bulgur wheat and flavored with lemon and fresh mint.

Optional: 1 clove garlic, pressed; 1 cucumber,
finely chopped; 1 sweet pepper, chopped;
¼ to ½ cup grated carrots; ½ cup cooked
garbanzo or other beans; ¼ cup
sunflower seeds

In a large bowl, pour boiling water over bulgur, cover, and let sit 1 hour, tossing gently after about 20 minutes. Add all other ingredients and mix well but gently. Cover and refrigerate for at least 3 hours. Stir before serving and taste for seasoning. Garnish with slices of any of the vegetables, sprigs of mint or parsley, and/or black olives, or feta cheese. Serve on lettuce leaves; inner romaine leaves make great dippers for scooping up the salad.

Whole-Wheat Breads

Once you've grown and harvested wheat or rye, you must grind it into flour if you plan to make bread or pastries. If you've grown bushels of grain, you'll need to purchase a professional-size electric mill or take the grain to a miller, but if you have only a few pounds, neither option is practical. How do you scale down the usual methods of grinding grain? That was the question that arose after my small grain harvest. The day my wheat was harvested, my friend William Phelps was inspired to go home and experiment with making flour. He tried his Cuisinart, but it was too noisy, took too long (fifteen minutes), and didn't grind finely enough. Then he tried his coffee grinder. The flour was good but a blade was nicked in the process, and he decided grain grinding was too hard on the machine. I tried my blender but had the same problems William had with the Cuisinart. So much for an easy solution. At that point, I decided to purchase a mill and contacted the Whole Earth Access store (see "Sources"). The store carried small, hand-powered Corona grain mills ranging in price from forty to sixty dollars. I was told that customers also had had success with the grain-mill attachment to the Kitchen Aid mixer. At $105 this was more expensive, but since I had the mixer, I ordered the mill. It works very well, though the flour is a little coarser than normal. Currently, I'm experimenting with putting the flour through more than once to make a finer product. The answer to grinding your grain seems to be a grain mill, either borrowed or bought. One reminder before grinding grain: clean the wheat berries well to wash out any small stones.

For aficionados, bread is the most satisfying and fitting end to the process of growing wheat. For years this country's most common recipes for bread called exclusively for all-purpose white flour. You could find an occasional recipe for whole-wheat bread, but it would call for a mixture: half whole-wheat flour and half all-purpose white flour. The idea was to assure light loaves. All-purpose white flour is higher in gluten than whole wheat and contains less bran, which inhibits the rising process somewhat.

However, tastes have changed, and many people now feel they want more substance and wheat taste to their bread. Many recipes in newer cookbooks reflect this change. One of the recipes below was perfected by William using a food processor. However, if you're making bread for the first time, try the basic yeasted bread recipe in *The Tassajara Bread Book* or the meticulous, step-by-step directions given in *Laurel's Kitchen Bread Book* (see "Sources"). The former gently walks you through the sponge method of bread making, and the latter takes you every step of the way from grinding the grain through all the variations you could ever want.

TASSAJARA BREAD

This recipe is an adaptation of the shortened version (for experienced bakers) from *The Tassajara Bread Book,* revised edition, by Edward Espe Brown (Boston: Shambhala Publications, 1986).

MAKES 2 LOAVES.

> *1½ tablespoons dry yeast (2 packages)*
> *3 cups lukewarm water (85 to 105°F)*
> *¼ cup sweetening (honey, molasses, or brown*
>   *sugar)*
> *1 cup dry milk (optional)*
> *7 cups whole-wheat flour (substitute 1 or*
>   *more cups unbleached white flour if*
>   *desired)*
> *4 teaspoons salt*
> *⅓ cup oil (or butter or margarine)*
> *1 cup whole-wheat flour for kneading*
> *2 standard loaf pans*

Preheat oven to 350°.

In a bowl, dissolve yeast in water and stir in sweetening and dry milk. Stir in 4 cups whole-wheat flour to form a thick batter. Beat well with a spoon (about 100 strokes) and let dough rise for 45 minutes.

Fold in salt and oil; then fold in additional 3 cups flour until dough comes away from sides of bowl. Knead dough on a floured board for about 10 minutes, until dough is smooth, using more flour (about 1 cup) as needed to keep dough from sticking to board. Let dough rise 50 to 60 minutes until it has doubled in size and then punch down. Let rise for 40 to 50 minutes until double in size again.

Shape dough into loaves and place in pans. Let loaves rise for 20 to 25 minutes and brush tops with a beaten egg. Bake for 1 hour or until golden brown. Remove loaves from pans and let cool.

WILLIAM'S FOOD-PROCESSOR WHOLE-WHEAT BREAD

Many people comment that when you use a food processor to make bread, the process goes too quickly and you can't tell when it's right. William Phelps found that you can tell; it just takes a little practice. He learned that the amount of liquid you need to add varies quite a bit depending on the kind of flour you're using. The following recipe calls for 2 cups of water, but when he made it using freshly ground flour from recently harvested wheat, he found he either had to reduce the water to 1¾ cups or add about half a cup more flour. Too much liquid increases the load on the machine greatly, slowing down and even overheating the food processor. William suggests that you always have extra flour handy and ready to add if this happens. With too much liquid, the dough becomes stiff, and the bread turns out hard and dry. When the proportion of flour to liquid is correct, the dough forms a ball and comes right out of the machine with almost no effort. The dough rises wonderfully, and the bread is moist.

Note: Not all food processors can be used to make bread dough. Be sure that yours can before trying this recipe.

MAKES 2 LOAVES.

1 package dry yeast
½ teaspoon sugar
¼ cup warm water (105 to 110°F)
3 tablespoons molasses or honey
2 cups cold water
4 cups whole-wheat flour
2¼ cups unbleached white flour
3 tablespoons butter
2 teaspoons salt
2 standard loaf pans

Preheat oven to 350°.

Dissolve yeast and sugar in ¼ cup warm water to activate yeast (the mixture should begin foaming within minutes). In a container good for pouring into processor's feed tube, dissolve molasses or honey in 2 cups water. Install dough blade in machine. Add flour, butter, and salt. Process to combine—about 20 seconds. With machine still running, pour in yeast mixture. Then pour water and molasses mixture through the feed tube in a steady stream. (Do not pour too quickly or flour will not absorb liquid. If this happens, stop machine and stir by hand to combine; then resume processing.) After all liquid has been added, continue processing until dough begins to form a ball; let machine run for about 60 to 90 seconds until dough becomes smooth and barely sticky and cleans the sides of the bowl. Do not overprocess.

Turn dough out onto a lightly floured board and shape into a smooth ball. Place in a greased bowl, turning to coat dough. Cover bowl with a damp towel and put in a warm place to rise until dough has doubled in size (about 1 to 1½ hours). Test dough by inserting your index finger about an inch; if the hole remains and does not close up, dough is ready. Working in the bowl, gently punch down dough and shape into a ball again. Cover with the damp towel and place bowl in a warm place for a second rising of about 45 minutes to an hour. Use the finger test to tell when dough is ready. Turn dough out onto the floured board. Gently deflate and divide it in two; fold the halves and shape into balls. Let dough rest for 8 to 10 minutes. Grease and flour loaf pans (William usually uses cornmeal to flour the pans). Shape dough into loaves, put in pans, and let rise for the third time (this is called "proofing") until the finger test shows it's ready (about 45 minutes). Bake for about 45 minutes.

Rye Breads

Breads made with a combination of whole-wheat and rye flours are more nutritious than those made with straight whole wheat. The reason is that the rye has a buffering effect on the chemical in wheat that ties up iron. Here is a very tasty bread using rye flour.

MINIFARM RAISIN RYE BREAD

This is a recipe for a hearty bread, full of flavor, from Robin Jeavons, John's wife. I enjoyed it toasted and spread with ricotta cheese and fresh plum jam. You can bake this bread in a conventional oven or, as Robin does, in a solar oven. If you're going to use a solar oven, start the process at 8:00 A.M. for bread ready to eat around 2:30 P.M.

MAKES 2 LOAVES.

> *1 cup raisins*
> *2¼ cups hot water*
> *⅓ cup molasses*
> *2 tablespoons margarine or butter (optional)*
> *1 tablespoon caraway seeds (This makes it pumpernickel. A delicious variation is 1 tablespoon grated orange peel instead of caraway seeds.)*
> *1 package dry yeast*
> *3 cups rye flour*
> *3 to 4½ cups whole-wheat flour*
> *2 standard loaf pans*

Preheat oven to 375°.

Soak 1 cup raisins in enough boiling water to cover for about 10 minutes. Drain, reserving raisin water.

In a large bowl, stir together raisin water plus enough hot water to make 2¼ cups; also stir in molasses, margarine or butter, caraway seeds, and raisins. When liquid has cooled to the right temperature (warm, about 102 to 104°F), add yeast and stir to dissolve.

Add 2 cups flour and stir in thoroughly; then add 2 more cups and stir vigorously. This is the start of the kneading process. Add 1 or 2 additional cups flour or enough to make a moderately stiff dough. For the last cup or so, dump dough on a floured board and knead flour in gradually. Knead about 15 to 20 minutes. Place dough in an oiled bowl, cover with a damp towel, and let rise in a warm place for about 1½ hours.

Push air out gently, pull dough apart into two equal pieces, and shape the halves for loaf pans or into any other shape desired. This is a good dough for kids to work into braids, bubble loaves, frogs, bagel shapes, and so on. It even makes good pizza dough (without the raisins).

Let dough rise 30 to 45 minutes, or until it has doubled in size, and bake. In a conventional oven bake loaves at 375° for about 45 minutes. Robin's loaves go into the solar oven around noon (1:00 P.M. daylight saving time) and bake until 2:00 or 2:30 P.M., when they're eaten warm for lunch. They can't really burn if left to bake until dinner, but they do take twice as long to bake later in the day when there's less sunlight.

Amaranth Breads

David Cavagnaro has had a great deal of experience with amaranth. His recommendations on working with this versatile grain are as follows. Harvest whole heads and any major side heads when the seeds begin to shatter (this is also when the seeds fall into the hand with gentle shaking or abrasion of the heads). The heads will appear plump and full of seeds. The plants are not at all dry at this time, but they look mature and their leaves may be beginning to turn color. In David's experience in both California and Iowa, harvest time is about the end of August.

Remove the seeds by alternately beating and rubbing the heads between your palms. Be vigorous. David processes large quantities at once on a sheet spread in the bed of his pickup truck. He piles the harvest onto the sheet and beats the grain heads against the side of the pickup bed. For small harvests he does the same thing in a wheelbarrow.

When most of the seeds are free from the chaff, David picks out the large pieces of debris and spreads the remaining seeds and chaff on a sheet to dry in the sun or in a dry place for a few days. He stirs the grain once in a while and lets it dry until it's ready to store. To eliminate the large chaff after drying, he screens the harvest through an ordinary piece of window-screen-size mesh. (He made a wood-framed screen that he places over the wheelbarrow.) For a large harvest, he rubs the seeds through the screen two or three gallons at a time. Seeds and hulls go through the screen. To clean the seeds further and separate them from the hulls and small chaff, he uses an old vacuum cleaner motor, stirring with one hand and holding the blower with the other. Another option is to use a fan, pouring the seed and hull mix in front of it over a sheet. David can thresh and clean a two-year supply (approximately eight gallons of amaranth seed, equal to about twelve gallons of flour) in half a day of work. A small harvest takes an hour or so.

Once the seeds are clean, they are ready to be ground into flour. David has ground white-seeded grain amaranths in the Corona hand mill, but he reports that the seeds of the black-seeded amaranths are almost too small to be ground in the hand mill. Thus, he grinds the black seeds in an electric grinder attached to his Champion juicer.

AMARANTH BREAD

Joanie Cavagnaro, David's wife, perfected this recipe using David's harvest. I fell in love with this bread on a visit, when Joanie made it for me fresh.

MAKES 6 LOAVES.

3 tablespoons dry yeast
10 cups warm water
3 tablespoons brown sugar
2½ tablespoons salt
½ cup molasses or honey
8 cups amaranth flour
6 cups whole-wheat flour
12 cups unbleached white flour
6 large loaf pans

Preheat oven to 350°.

Dissolve yeast in warm water; add sugar. Let sit 30 minutes. Add salt, molasses or honey, and enough of all three kinds of flour proportionately to make mixture stiff and too thick to blend with a spoon.

Spread dough on a floured board. Knead in approximately 4 or more cups of white flour until dough is a good consistency (not too sticky). Knead more. Let rise 45 minutes or until dough has at least doubled in size. Punch dough down and form loaves. Knead each loaf, adding any additional white flour needed. Let rise another 30 to 45 minutes. Bake for 35 minutes.

The first delicious loaf must be eaten hot out of the oven. This bread is best toasted once it has cooled. For a nice glossy crust, brush tops of loaves with beaten egg 5 minutes before removing from oven.

AMARANTH BREAD FOR THE FOOD PROCESSOR

This wonderful, aromatic bread with a spicy molasses flavor was created by William Phelps. It took William several tries to get the proportions right for this recipe, converting from the technique of kneading in flour to using a processor. He tested this recipe with freshly ground amaranth and whole-wheat flours; purchased flours may require more liquid. If adding additional water, have extra flour on hand to add if the machine bogs down during processing.

Note: Not all food processors can be used to make bread dough. Be sure yours can before trying this recipe.

MAKES 2 LOAVES.

1 package dry yeast
1 tablespoon brown sugar
¼ cup warm water (105 to 110°F)
2 tablespoons molasses or honey
1¼ cups cold water
2¼ cups amaranth flour
2¼ cups unbleached white flour
1¼ cups whole-wheat flour
2 tablespoons butter
1½ teaspoons salt
2 small loaf pans

Preheat oven to 350°.

Dissolve yeast and sugar in ¼ cup warm water to activate yeast. In a container good for pouring into processor's feed tube, dissolve molasses or honey in 1¼ cups water. Install dough blade in machine. Add flour, butter, and salt. Process to combine—about 20 seconds. With machine still running, pour in yeast mixture. Then pour water and molasses mixture through the feed tube in a steady stream. (Do not pour too quickly or flour will not absorb liquid. If this happens, stop machine and stir by hand to combine; then resume processing.) After all liquid has been added, continue processing until dough begins to form a ball; let machine run for about 40 to 60 seconds until dough becomes smooth and barely sticky and cleans the sides of the bowl. Do not overprocess.

Follow the procedure for "William's Food-Processor Whole-Wheat Bread," above, for making the dough with a food processor.

Sources

Seed Companies

Only a few seed companies carry grain seeds. See the ones listed below or try your local feed store or natural foods store.

1. Bountiful Gardens
   Ecology Action
   5798 Ridgewood Road
   Willits, CA 95490

   The Bountiful Gardens seed catalog lists a number of kinds of grains: hard red spring wheat, an old-variety 'Early Stone Age' wheat, bearded barley, rye, and oats. This company sells wheat in packages large enough to sow 100 square feet.

2. Johnny's Selected Seeds
   Foss Hill Road
   Albion, ME 04910

   Johnny's carries 'Roughrider' winter wheat, 'Polk' spring wheat, 'Aroostook' winter rye, and new 'Freedom Hulless' oats as well as grain amaranth. For the grains, you must buy a minimum of four pounds, enough for 1000 square feet, and pay for shipping, so buying for a small patch is expensive. The firm carries an inexpensive Corona hand mill for making flour.

3. Redwood City Seed Company
   P.O. Box 361
   Redwood City, CA 94064

   This seed company prides itself on carrying many useful plants. Among them are four types of amaranth and an 'Early Stone Age' type of wheat. In addition, it carries bread-seed poppies. Catalog: $1.00.

Suppliers' Catalogs

Sears and Roebuck Farm Catalog

Sears's mail-order farm catalog carries tools for harvesting and grinding grains. The catalog is available from local Sears stores.

Whole Earth Access Catalog
2950 Seventh Street
Berkeley, CA 94710

The Whole Earth Access catalog lists some basic milling equipment. It also lists the Corona hand mill and a grain mill attachment to the Kitchen Aid mixer. The catalog costs seven dollars, but five dollars are refunded when you make a purchase.

Books

Brown, Edward Espe. *The Tassajara Bread Book,* revised edition. Boston: Shambhala Publications, 1985.

Edward Brown's classic covers whole-wheat bread and pastry cooking from the ground up. This is a great resource for real bread-making basics.

Duhon, David. *One Circle*. Willits, Calif.: Ecology Action, 1985.

This book explains how to grow a complete diet in less than 1000 square feet. One chapter covers in detail the Ecology Action wheat-growing method at the Common Ground Minifarm.

Jeavons, John. *How to Grow More Vegetables Than You Ever Thought Possible on Less Land Than You Can Imagine*. Berkeley, Calif.: Ten Speed Press, 1982.

This is a basic primer on the Biodynamic/French Intensive Method. Jeavons covers soil preparation and double-digging to increase yields greatly in a small area.

Lawrence, James, ed. *The Harrowsmith Reader*, vol. 2. Camden East, Ontario: Camden House Publishing, 1980.

An anthology of country living and basic self-sufficiency. One section gives an overview of grain growing on a modest scale and another gives the complete rundown on grain mills.

Logsdon, Gene. *Small-Scale Grain Raising*. Emmaus, Pa.: Rodale Press, 1977.

This is the definitive book on grain. However, by my standards it covers fairly large-scale, not small-scale, grain growing. Logsdon discusses all the grains in detail and also deals with grain growing in harsh climates.

Pitzer, Sara. *Whole Grains—Grow, Harvest, and Cook Your Own*. Charlotte, Vt.: Garden Way Publishing, 1981.

A valuable book that covers large-scale grain growing in detail. It contains photos and many good recipes not only for wheat flour but also for cooked wheat berries.

Robertson, Laurel, Carol Flinders, and Bronwen Godfrey. *The Laurel's Kitchen Bread Book—A Guide to Whole-Grain Breadmaking*. New York: Random House, 1984.

An extensive book covering just about everything that can be made with whole wheat and other grains. The authors provide both detailed instructions for beginners and challenging recipes for experienced bread makers.

Rodale Press editors. *Amaranth Round-up*. Emmaus, Pa.: Rodale Press, 1977.

This booklet is extremely valuable if you are interested in growing and cooking with amaranth. The Rodale people have collected a great deal of information about the subject by actually growing and cooking with amaranth for many years.

Cajun Gardens

I WAS ON A CAUSEWAY in Avery, Louisiana, in the very heart of Cajun country. Snowy egrets were flying overhead, the moss was hanging off the trees, and it was hot—104 degrees! I was on my way to Avery Island, the home of the McIlhenny Company, one and only maker of Tabasco sauce. Edmund McIlhenny, vice-president of the company, and Tee Bruce Broussard, longtime McIlhenny family friend, a company foreman, and dedicated Cajun cook, had promised to teach me about Cajun cooking.

Happenstance plus some frantic networking the year before had turned up the perfect locale—and the perfect grower—for the book's Cajun garden. The plantation on Avery Island was rooted in history, extended-family feeling, and the all-encompassing hospitality the South is famous for. And Tee Bruce Broussard, a demon gardener as well as an expert cook, couldn't have been more enthusiastic about sharing his garden in the book.

Now I was heading to the island, anxious to see the garden I had been told so much about over the last year. I crossed the bridge onto the island, passed through a tunnel of live oak trees, went through a bird sanctuary (established by the

OPPOSITE: *Some of the basic Cajun vegetables are pictured under a magnolia blossom. From left to right clockwise are mustard, half of a mirliton, okra, red beans, 'Jalapeño' pepper, mirliton, green bell pepper, and a beefsteak tomato.*

McIlhennys many years ago to protect the snowy egrets), and drove straight to the company's magnificent old brick warehouse.

Once I was settled in Edmund McIlhenny's office, I asked the obvious question: What was the story behind Tabasco sauce? Edmund was clearly pleased that I had asked and launched right into the company's history. He told me that his great-grandfather had planted some hot pepper seeds brought to him from Mexico in the 1850s and grew them until the beginning of the Civil War, when the family moved from New Orleans to the Avery Island plantation. He started a pepper garden on the island too, but the war intervened. "The Yankees came and took the place over," said Edmund, "and after the war, when they moved out and we moved back again, it was just a shambles." During the course of renovating the farm, Edmund's great-grandfather poked around until he found a couple of the old pepper plants and started a new pepper garden. Soon he was making up a pepper sauce to spice the plantation's very limited table fare.

"Ironically," said Edmund, "the Yankees actually lent us a hand at that point. The local general, who visited periodically, became very fond of my great-grandfather's pepper sauce. And as it turned out, the general's brother was the largest wholesale grocer in New York State. The general mentioned the sauce, and the grocer told him to have my great-grandfather send some on up. Before doing that, great-grandfather wanted to come up with a trademark for the sauce, and what crossed his mind was *tabasco*, a native Mexican word meaning 'land where the soil is hot and wet.' Well, that kind of fit Avery Island, and the word had a nice lilt to it, so he named the sauce Tabasco. And the rest is history."

Indeed it is: today Tabasco is used worldwide. Still, to my mind, I told him, this distinctive pepper sauce is most closely associated with the slight hotness of many Cajun dishes. "Right," said Edmund, taking my cue, and he headed off on a thumbnail history of his favorite cuisine. Hot peppers, he told me, presumably entered Cajun cooking by way of the Native Americans of the region, who cooked with the local wild hot peppers. But while the peppers came from south of the border, the Cajun people themselves originally came from France—via Nova Scotia. In the 1600s they settled in an area of Nova Scotia called Acadia, but the British drove them out and they sought refuge in southern Louisana. Here they settled along the waterways and became fishermen or set up farms and produced the foods that grew well in Louisana's warm climate. Eventually, as Edmund summed it up for me during our delightful visit, they evolved a style of cooking that relied heavily on the abundant seafood, incorporated native foods and locally grown vegetables and rice, and became widely known for its richness of flavor and careful preparation.

Given the Cajuns' French heritage, it isn't surprising that Cajun dishes take a lot of careful attention and require lengthy cooking times. Where the English might boil up some snap beans and serve them with butter and a little salt and pepper, the Cajun cook is more apt to combine the beans with bacon, onions, cayenne peppers, and perhaps, after the mixture has cooked for a long time, some new potatoes for thickening. The epitome of this approach is represented by a rich gumbo (generally a seafood-and-meat stew thickened with okra), a jambalaya (a complex rice dish filled with seafoods and many kinds of vegetable seasonings), and a rich sweet potato pie covered with caramelized pecans. These dishes carry their history proudly, and unlike those of most American cuisines, which have evolved over time, they have remained relatively unchanged over the centuries.

Vegetables are not the focus of most Cajun dishes, but they are usually treated as important ingredients or seasonings. For instance, okra is frequently combined with shrimp. Mirlitons, or chayotes—wonderful, dense, squashlike vegetables with a nutty flavor—are mixed with crab. And red beans are cooked with hot sausage. Yet Cajuns feature some of their vegetables too, cooking them in truly unique ways. Sweet potato pie and smothered corn are notable examples. In this chapter, to begin to understand how vegetables are treated in Cajun food, we'll look at how some of them are grown, study a Cajun garden, and then examine individual varieties before turning to the cooking section for some authentic Cajun recipes and food-preparation techniques.

How to Grow a Cajun Garden

A Cajun garden is typically, though not necessarily, grown in the southeastern United States, where the summer temperatures are high and the winters fairly

An overview of one of the South's most famous vegetable gardens—Callaway Gardens, home of television's "Victory Garden South."

mild and short. These are ideal conditions for growing the vegetables enjoyed in Cajun cooking, particularly heat-loving okra and sweet potatoes. Other vegetables that make their appearance in Cajun fare are sweet and hot peppers, tomatoes, summer squash, eggplants, and mustard greens—all vegetables that can be grown fairly easily in most parts of the country. So don't turn the page if you live above the Mason-Dixon line. Your Cajun garden can grow nearly anywhere.

Still, if you want to grow okra and sweet potatoes in a northern climate, you will have to do a little planning and will need to choose the right varieties. Both vegetables will probably need cold protection at some point in the growing season, so plant them against a warm, south-facing wall, or surround them with heat-absorbing materials such as a black-plastic mulch. Note that one vegetable enjoyed in Cajun

cooking that won't cross into the North is the mirliton or chayote. This tender perennial will grow only in the mildest-winter areas.

Regarding the rest of the vegetables listed here, gardeners in cooler climates will need to seek specific information on short-season varieties, starting vegetables inside, and season-extending techniques and aids such as row covers and cold frames. The whole idea is to provide cold protection or to increase heat around the growing plants. For information on short-season vegetables, see the "German Gardens" chapter and Part Four, "An Encyclopedia of Superior Vegetables." Southern gardeners probably already grow many of the wonderful vegetables listed above and can readily find seeds or plants in their local nurseries. For more information on those vegetables and growing conditions in the South, consult *Southern Living: Growing Vegetables and Herbs.*

The author's Cajun garden includes red beans, cutting celery, tomatoes, corn, and three varieties each of hot peppers and okra. On the trellis in the back is a mirliton vine. The flowers include pink verbena and begonias, and 'Gold Nugget' calceolaria.

The Broussard Cajun Garden

After I left Edmund McIlhenny's office, Tee Bruce Broussard took me to see his garden. What a wonderful day I spent! Tee Bruce shared his garden and cooking experience generously, and his wife, Miss Alice, drove me around Avery Island to show me the Tabasco pepper fields and the wild preserve areas. And all day long we talked cooking and gardening, gardening and cooking. What a feast of words! I was certainly in my element.

It was in the afternoon after it had started to cool down that we toured Tee Bruce's garden. The plot is large, about thirty by forty feet, and Tee Bruce grows *lots* of food. "I like to have enough to share with my daughter and friends," he told me, "but it's probably double what most families would need." The garden is planted in long, forty-foot rows, with nearly whole rows given over to 'Louisiana' tomatoes, bush snap beans, 'Purple Hull' crowder peas, 'Pot du Poulos' cream peas, 'Black Beauty' eggplants, and green bell peppers. There's also a double row of 'Blue Lake' string beans and a triple row of Tee Bruce's favorite okra, 'Texas Longhorn'. At the end of the beds is a strip planted in cucumbers and white-and-yellow pattypan squash. The garden is surrounded

Emery Tee Bruce Brous-sard is a longtime friend of the McIlhenny Tabasco sauce family and a foreman in their company. When an occasion arises to entertain dignitaries, the McIlhennys often call on Tee Bruce to create a memorable meal with a Cajun flair. When I asked Edmund McIlhenny if he knew any Cajun cooks who loved to garden, he immediately thought of Tee Bruce. "He's your man!" Edmund said. "Tee Bruce loves to garden, and he loves to cook."

While touring Tee Bruce's garden, I discovered that he had a particular enthusiasm for okra, one of the unusual vegetables that characterize Cajun cooking. After we had talked for a while, I finally confessed: I thought okra was slimy, and I didn't like it. That certainly led to an animated discussion. Finally Tee Bruce took some gumbo from his refrigerator and served me a big bowl of it. "Okra isn't slimy if you cook it right," he told me. Sure enough, the shrimp gumbo— filled with okra—was delicious. And it wasn't slimy! The secret, he said, was to add a little vinegar when cooking the okra.

Newly interested in okra, I asked Tee Bruce to explain how he grows it. "When you plant okra, the temperature at night has to be at least 65 degrees," he said. "You'll have problems getting the plants to come up if you put them out too soon. In a cold climate, you have to start them inside as you would tomatoes.

"To plant okra outside, till the soil and soak your seeds in lukewarm water the night before you plant them. The next day, dig holes about two inches deep and eighteen inches apart and plant two or three seeds in each hole. As the okra come up, thin them out, leaving only the best plant in each hole. Apparently none of the seeds rot; they all seem to germinate

Emery Tee Bruce Broussard

sooner or later, maybe even six months later.

"I find okra can grow without fertilizer, but they won't be as healthy—so when they're about a foot tall, I fertilize them. I grow a long, velvety white variety called 'Texas Longhorn'," Tee Bruce says. He particularly likes this variety because it grows to be very large and flavorful before it becomes woody. While other varieties need to be cut when they reach three to four inches long, 'Texas Longhorn' will still be good to eat when it's eight inches long— or sometimes as long as a foot and a half.

"Years ago I got my first 'Texas Longhorn' from a feed store in town, and I've been keeping the seeds. I've never seen them in a catalog," Tee Bruce explains. "To save the seeds, harvest a few mature pods from the bottom of the plant, dry them, and put them in a sack for the winter. In spring, beat the sack until the seeds separate from the pods— and you're ready for planting.

"To harvest okra, watch it until the flowers form, followed by inch-long okra. When 'Texas Longhorn' gets to be about eight inches long [or other varieties three to four inches long], you can cut it. Sometimes this variety reaches a foot and a half long and is still edible, but you have to test it. Take a knife and see if it goes in easily. If it doesn't, then the okra is too old and you should leave it for seeds. The bigger okra gets before it gets tough, the more flavor it will have."

Tee Bruce certainly made a believer out of me. After enjoying okra with him, I planted some in my own garden. Unfortunately, we had an unusually cool summer and I didn't get much of a crop, but I'm determined to grow it again—and make some gumbo—next year.

Tee Bruce Broussard harvests tomatoes from his Cajun garden. In the foreground are crowder peas.

with a tall wire fence to keep out the deer and other animals, and the lush mirliton vine is trained over an arbor that helps shade the dog run. I was very impressed to see how much food was being produced in this relatively small area. The tomato vines were loaded with large, ripe tomatoes; the eggplants and peppers were covered with large, glossy fruits; and the crowder and cream peas and snap beans were all ready for a large harvest.

The soil in this garden is rather sandy, and over the years Tee Bruce has added manure. He starts his tomato, eggplant, and bell pepper plants in the greenhouse about mid-February. "But," he says, "I plant the rest of the garden during Holy Week, the week between Palm Sunday and Easter. That's an old Cajun planting time; that's when my daddy always planted."

My visit fell in mid-July, and the time was approaching for the tomato plants to be pulled out because the heat was slowing them down and they were about to stop producing. The okra, eggplants, and bell peppers were to be left intact, though, since they would produce until the frost, usually in late September. Tee Bruce was now thinking about his winter garden—in August he plants turnips, mustard, and sometimes cabbage.

As we toured the garden, I recalled my useless worry at how I would track down the perfect Cajun garden for the book. I couldn't have been more pleased with the way things had turned out. Tee Bruce was a gardener whose planting matched his cooking needs precisely. The garden before me was a perfect expression of the idea behind the book: that the selecting, planting, growing, harvesting, storing, cooking, and *eating* of produce were all aspects of one deliciously satisfying experience. I could hardly believe my luck, and I was suddenly impatient to move on to Tee Bruce's Cajun kitchen.

Recommended Cajun Vegetables

Cajun cooking means sausages, shrimp, and crayfish, but it also means okra, mirlitons, hot peppers, sweet potatoes, southern peas, greens, and big, juicy tomatoes. The following is a list of vegetables and Cajun-style cooking suggestions. The numbers in parentheses after variety names correspond to the seed companies listed in "Sources" at the end of the chapter. Where no number is given, the variety is available from most of the sources listed.

GREENS (including collards, kale, and mustard) *Brassica* spp.   These three leafy vegetables are used somewhat interchangeably in Cajun cooking.

How to grow: See the Part Four Encyclopedia for growing information.

How to prepare: Often these greens are simply steamed and served with butter. Alternatively, they are given a bacon and sweet-and-sour dressing or cooked with a little diced ham. They are also used in soups.

MIRLITONS (chayote)   *Sechium edule*   In Cajun cooking this green, pear-shaped vegetable is called a mirliton, and in Mexican cooking it is referred to as chayote. The mild flavor of the mirliton resembles that of summer squash but is both richer and sweeter.

How to grow: Mirlitons, which grow on huge (twenty-to-forty-foot) tropical-like vines, only thrive where the winters are nearly frost free. To start your mirliton plant, buy the fruit in a produce-oriented market in spring and plant it in full sunlight in fertile, well-drained soil, leaving the stem half of the fruit out of the ground. The vine, which needs strong support, will start to flower in the fall and to fruit six to eight weeks later. Once the fruits have reached three or four inches in length, you can start to harvest them. The small fruits can be eaten as is, but mature ones must be peeled. Be aware, though: when you peel them, mirlitons exude an adhesive-type substance. You might want to either wear rubber gloves or, as Cajun chef Paul Prudhomme recommends, parboil the fruit for a few minutes before peeling.

How to prepare: Mirlitons are wonderful steamed and served with butter as a side dish. They can also be fried, pickled, or cooked in casseroles and soups. A famous Cajun way to serve them is as pirogues (canoes) stuffed with shrimp, crawfish, Andouille sausage, or vegetables.

OKRA (gumbo)   *Abelmoschus esculentus*   If any vegetable is synonymous with Cajun cooking it is okra. This heat-loving member of the hibiscus family produces succulent and flavorful green, white, or red pods. Okra has a slippery consistency that is used to thicken soups and gumbos. It is just this quality that aficionados love and detractors find objectional.

How to grow: See the Part Four Encyclopedia.

How to prepare: There are many ways of preparing okra: it can be deep-fried, smothered in a sauce of tomatoes, green peppers, and onions; pickled; fried up with tomatoes, onions, green peppers, and herbs; combined with seafood; or made into gumbo.

PEPPERS   *Capsicum* spp.   The most famous peppers used in Cajun cuisine are the cayenne and tabasco varieties.

How to grow: See the Part Four Encyclopedia for basic growing information on peppers and the "Chili Gardens" chapter for details on hot peppers. Tabasco peppers are harder to grow than most easily available hot peppers. They need very warm, long summers to produce well. Hastings carries a variety of tabasco called 'Greenleaf Tabasco', but if you want to grow the authentic 'Tabasco' used in the famous sauce, order the seeds from the McIlhenny Company, Avery Island, LA 70513. The cayenne hot peppers

The harvest from Tee Bruce's garden includes 'Black Beauty' eggplant, 'Louisiana' tomatoes, cucumbers, white and yellow pattypan squashes, 'Texas Longhorn' okra, and 'Purple Hull' crowder peas.

grow more readily than tabasco peppers; try 'Long Red Cayenne' (1, 2, 4). Other hot peppers used in Cajun cooking are 'Jalapeño', 'Banana' (2), and the bird types, tiny peppers discussed in the "Chili Gardens" chapter and available from the sources cited there.

How to prepare: Green peppers are used in many vegetable side dishes as well as gumbos and jambalaya. Hot peppers are used to give bite to a great number of Cajun seafood, meat, and vegetable dishes.

SOUTHERN PEAS (black-eyed peas, cow peas, cream peas, crowder peas, field peas) *Vigna unguiculata* The common names given to peas vary greatly with geographical region, but in this case the designation is completely off the mark, since southern peas are actually more closely related to beans. They are borne on long pods that in some varieties stand upright on the plant and in some hang downward. They can be eaten in their fresh state as you would peas or shelling beans, or they can be dried and stored.

How to grow: Southern peas grow on bushy, drought-tolerant plants. These hot-weather annuals produce poorly in cool-summer areas but can withstand much drought and heat. Varieties of interest are the particularly flavorful 'Calico Crowder' (1, 3); 'Mississippi Silver' (2, 3, 4), a widely adaptable variety; and 'Zipper Cream' (1), which has easy-opening pods. Hastings carries sixteen varieties. Plant southern peas at least two weeks after your last expected frost date, sowing the seeds one inch deep in clay soils and two inches deep in very sandy ones, four to six inches apart. Thin the seedlings to between six and twelve inches apart.

Southern peas produce best if kept fairly moist. Fertilize sparingly, since too much nitrogen will result in lush growth but few peas. Pest and disease problems are minimal, and harvest will begin in sixty to ninety days, when the pods start to change color and fill out. For best production pick the pods as they ripen. The plants will produce enough pods for three to four harvests. For dried peas in winter, let the last flush ripen and dry, and then pick the pods and process as you would dry beans (see the "Baked Bean Gardens" chapter).

How to prepare: While not always considered a Cajun vegetable, southern peas are widely enjoyed in the South. A classic way to serve them is boiled with chopped tomatoes, onions, and green peppers, and seasoned with vinegar, salt, and pepper. Here's another popular preparation method: brown bacon in a Dutch oven, add three or four cups of peas and maybe a pound of okra or an onion or two, almost cover with water, and then simmer for fifteen to twenty minutes. Or try cooking southern peas with ham and diced green peppers.

SWEET POTATOES *Ipomoea Batatas* Sweet potatoes, sometimes called yams, are particularly appreciated in the South and are prepared there in many different ways.

How to grow: See the Part Four Encyclopedia.

How to prepare: Cajuns bake sweet potatoes, boil them, or use them for casseroles, often with some form of sweetening. Other popular serving methods are to candy them or to make them into pies covered with pecans and serve with whipped cream.

TOMATOES *Lycopersicon Lycopersicum* Big, juicy, ripe tomatoes are grown in the rich bottomland of the Mississippi River, where the warm sunlight makes them extra sweet. Their flavor adds both a sweetness and a slightly acidic touch to many dishes.

How to grow: See the Part Four Encyclopedia.

How to prepare: The distinctive sweetness of southern tomatoes makes them popular served plain or cut in great thick slices in a vinaigrette dressing. Cooked tomatoes are one of the primary seasonings in Cajun cooking.

Cooking from the Cajun Garden

To me the distinctive characteristic of Cajun cooking is its depth of flavor, a quality that Paul Prudhomme, renowned Louisiana chef, describes as "round." In one forkful of a typical Cajun dish you experience sweetness, a sharp bite, and maybe even a nutty flavor all at once. To achieve this fullness, Cajun cooks orchestrate a wide variety of seasonings, and above all they take their time when they cook. As Tee Bruce Broussard says, "I never like to cook anything fast.

OPPOSITE: *Gumbo—filled with crayfish, oysters, and fish; seasoned with onions and hot and green peppers; and thickened with okra—is one of the South's claims to fame.*

I cook on a slow fire. So whatever I'll cook in two hours, maybe you'll cook in a half an hour, but to me it won't taste as good." Terry Thompson, food writer and teacher, describes Cajun food as "stead-fastly untrendy" and notes that it has remained relatively unchanged over the decades. Cajun food has the authority of history behind it—all that long, slow cooking has proved itself over time.

When the Cajuns settled in southern Louisiana, they incorporated into their cooking the produce the countryside had to offer. It's true that there are many similarities between Cajun and Creole cooking, the region's more "citified " cuisine. The latter is centered in New Orleans and reflects Spanish, French, Native American, and African influences. But in its distinctively "country" quality, Cajun cooking reveals its origins in French country cooking. Cajun fare is considered more "down home" than its Creole counterpart.

Let's look specifically at how garden produce is used in the Cajun kitchen. Terry Thompson describes the five most important vegetables in this cuisine as onions, celery, bell peppers—known as the holy trinity—plus green onions and parsley. Other vegetables to make a frequent appearance are tomatoes, squash, mirlitons, eggplants, different types of greens, okra, and hot peppers.

Vegetables play a slightly different role in Cajun cooking than in other American cooking styles. While corn on the cob and sliced raw tomatoes are often offered up plain, vegetables Cajun-style are more apt to be served in combination with other ingredients—such as bacon, onions, seafood, or other vegetables. Many of us might quickly steam a vegetable and serve it with butter to accompany a main dish, but Tee Bruce Broussard might fix snap beans, for example, by first browning some bacon and chopped onion; then adding water, a little Tabasco sauce, and cut-up snap beans; and then cooking the mixture a bit. After a while he might add some peeled new potatoes to the beans and keep cooking the mixture until the potatoes are tender. In the end the snap beans will be cooked to the point of falling apart, the potatoes will have thickened the dish, and the bacon, onion, hot-sauce, potato, and bean flavors will have all blended together. Other vegetable combinations Tee Bruce cooks up are mustard greens with onions, mirlitons or okra served with shrimp, and turnips or carrots cooked with pork chops.

The idea of combining vegetables with seafood and meats receives its fullest expression in two famous Cajun dishes: gumbo and jambalaya. Gumbo is a thick soup usually filled with shrimp, crayfish, or meats and a tasty combination of onions, bell peppers, celery, and hot peppers. It is thickened and flavored with okra, filé powder (the ground-up young leaves of the sassafras tree), or a roux. Jambalaya is a spicy, rice-based dish containing a combination of meat, seafood, and some variation of onions, bell peppers, and tomatoes.

A few cooking techniques are especially associated with vegetables in Cajun cooking. One is a pirogue, named for a canoe used in the bayous. As the term suggests, in a vegetable pirogue the insides of the vegetable are scooped out and the hollow is filled with a stuffing or sauce. The vegetables most often treated this way are zucchinis, eggplants, and mirlitons.

Another Cajun approach to vegetables is the smother technique. According to strict definition, smothering means cooking vegetables in a covered pan with very little water (or sometimes oil) over low heat. This definition hardly hints at the somewhat caramelized blend of flavors that results when, say, onions, corn, tomatoes, and Tee Bruce's snap beans, mentioned earlier, are smothered. This very common Cajun cooking technique differs from the boiling and overcooking of vegetables described in the "Heirloom Gardens" chapter in that where water is used the amount is very small. And because numerous seasonings are added, smothered dishes become richly flavorful. Paul Prudhomme likes to add some less well cooked vegetables to the smothered ones at the end of the cooking time to give a contrast of flavors plus more color and crunch.

Still, not all modern Cajun cooks consider it proper to "cook the daylights out of their vegetables," as Paul Prudhomme describes the method. In fact, when serving, for example, summer squash, baby carrots, and greens as a side dish in his restaurant, he prefers to sauté them lightly in butter rather than smothering them. "That way you maintain the juices and crispy texture, which gives a light, fresh contrast to the rich, highly seasoned meat and seafood dishes."

Another cooking technique common in Cajun cooking is the use of a roux. A roux is a cooked mixture of flour and fat that is used to thicken soups and sauces and to add richness of flavor. Paul Prud-

Chef Paul Prudhomme, of K-Paul's Louisiana Kitchen in New Orleans, has done much to spread enthusiasm for Cajun cuisine.

homme gives detailed directions for making a roux in his *Chef Paul Prudhomme's Louisiana Kitchen* along with suggestions for using the different variations. Paul prefers a fast-cooking method of making roux, yet Terry Thompson favors the traditional, slow way. Making a roux, like making a pie crust, takes some practice, but using roux in your Cajun recipes will add much flavor to vegetables and gumbo and will lend body to the final dish.

Vegetables are often used as seasonings in Cajun cooking. A great example is an eggplant dressing that Tee Bruce likes to serve with fried chicken: the eggplants are combined with onions, sweet and hot peppers, and celery. The following vegetables show up as seasonings time and time again in Cajun recipes, though in varying proportions: bell pepper, celery, chopped onion, and a little tomato. Used as seasonings, these vegetables give a highly characteristic flavor to this cuisine.

As you add the following recipes to your repertoire of vegetable-cooking ideas, you'll notice that altering the proportion of aromatic vegetables only slightly or adding a little bacon or cayenne pepper will give a new lift to your table fare. Even if you don't become a complete Cajun convert—and many, many food lovers have—you'll find techniques here to borrow from that will give a new slant to your fresh produce.

GUMBO

This recipe for a traditional gumbo is from Tee Bruce Broussard. It features okra that is smothered before being cooked with the meat. Another, more spicy variation of gumbo thickened with a roux follows Tee Bruce's recipe. In preparing these gumbos, you might want to omit all or part of the meat and add more seafood (toward the end, to prevent overcooking it) to make a seafood gumbo. Sausage makes a good addition as well. Experiment to find out what you like.

SERVES 8.

> 2 pounds brisket or 1 frying chicken or 3
>   pounds short ribs of beef
> Salt and pepper to taste
> 1/2 to 2 hot peppers, minced, or ground hot
>   pepper or Tabasco sauce to taste
> Oil as needed
> About 6 cups water
> 2 pounds okra, finely sliced
> 2 onions, chopped
> 1 bell pepper, seeded and chopped
> 1 tablespoon vinegar or 2 tomatoes, chopped
> 1 to 2 pounds raw shrimp, shelled and
>   deveined

Cut meat into large pieces and sprinkle with salt, pepper, and hot pepper. Cover and refrigerate for several hours or overnight. Use enough oil to cover the bottom of a large, heavy skillet and brown meat well. Remove meat to a plate, pour excess oil into a small bowl, and add 2 cups water to skillet to boil and scrape drippings from bottom of pan. Pour off into a separate bowl. Add reserved oil back to pan and then add okra, onions, and bell pepper. Sauté over medium-high heat until golden brown. Add vinegar or tomatoes and continue cooking over low heat about 1 hour, stirring occasionally. Return water with pan drippings and meat to vegetables, adding enough water to barely cover. Simmer until meat is done, 30 to 45 minutes, and check for seasoning. Add shrimp and cook 5 minutes longer. Serve over rice in bowls.

Gumbo Variation

> 2 pounds brisket or 1 frying chicken or other
>   meats, as desired

¼ cup oil
2 cups water
1 pound okra, finely sliced
2 onions, chopped
1 bell pepper, seeded and chopped
1 cup chopped celery
3 cloves garlic, minced
½ to 2 hot peppers, minced, or ground hot
    pepper or Tabasco sauce to taste
2 cups peeled, chopped tomatoes
2 bay leaves
1 tablespoon minced fresh thyme or 1
    teaspoon dried thyme
Salt and pepper to taste
½ cup oil
¾ cup flour
About 1 quart water or stock
1 to 2 pounds raw shrimp, shelled and
    deveined (plus other seafood if less meat is
    used above)
2 tablespoons filé powder

Brown meat in oil; then remove meat, reserve oil, and boil water with pan scrapings as in the recipe above. Pour off water into separate bowl, add reserved oil back to pan, and sauté okra with all vegetables except tomatoes. Add tomatoes, bay leaves, thyme, salt, and pepper and smother for about ½ hour.

Meanwhile, make a roux by combining ½ cup oil and flour in a large, heavy pot and stirring constantly with a whisk or wooden spoon over medium-high heat until red-brown, about 15 minutes. Stir vegetables into roux. Add meat and water with pan drippings, along with enough water or stock to barely cover, and simmer until meat is done, 30 to 45 minutes. Check for seasoning, add shrimp (and other seafood, if desired), and cook about 5 minutes. Serve over rice in bowls.

SWEET AND BROWN SQUASH

This recipe, also from Tee Bruce Broussard's files, is a wonderful example of the Cajun cook's proclivity for creating unique blends of flavors. The squash is nearly caramelized here—surely one of the most decadent ways of cooking summer squash you'll come across. Use this preparation as a preserve or chutney with roast meat (especially pork), rice, and gravy. Note that for this recipe, Tee Bruce uses large, mature

pattypan squash, peeled and seeded, but younger pattypans can be used unpeeled, and yellow crookneck squash are good too.

SERVES 8 TO 10.

¼ cup corn oil
2 to 3 pounds pattypan squash, sliced or diced
½ cup sugar
¼ teaspoon salt
½ teaspoon nutmeg

Put oil in a large pot or frying pan, add squash, cover, and sauté on medium heat until it starts to cook and brown, about 5 minutes. Gradually sprinkle on sugar, stir, and cook until well done, brown, and sweet, 20 to 30 minutes. Add salt and nutmeg.

MAQUE CHOUX (SMOTHERED FRESH CORN)

This is another recipe from Tee Bruce Broussard. Note that it involves smothering the corn or, in the variation at the end, smothering the okra.

SERVES 6 TO 8.

15 to 20 ears fresh sweet corn (or field corn at
    the milk stage, as described in the "Native
    American Gardens" chapter)
¼ cup corn oil
½ teaspoon salt
Black pepper to taste
1 large onion, chopped
4 large ripe tomatoes, peeled and quartered
1 or 2 bell peppers, seeded and chopped
¼ cup butter
1 teaspoon Tabasco sauce
1 tablespoon sugar

Cut kernels off corn cobs and scrape milk off cobs with the back of a knife into a bowl. Put oil in a large skillet, add corn, salt, and pepper, and fry on medium heat for about 5 minutes. Add remaining ingredients and the corn milk, and cook and stir on low heat for ½ hour. Check for seasoning and serve.

Variation: To make smothered okra, substitute about 6 pounds of sliced okra for the corn in this recipe. Omit sugar and add 1 tablespoon vinegar. Do not use a cast-iron pan. Serve as a side dish or freeze for later use in gumbo.

PICKLED OKRA

Tee Bruce Broussard offered this recipe as well. This is an easy way to preserve okra.

YIELD VARIES WITH AMOUNT.

Fill clean pint jars with fresh, young okra, 3 to 4 inches long, and add 1 or 2 small hot peppers and ¼ teaspoon of salt per jar. If desired, add 1 slice of garlic and/or 2 or 3 whole cloves per pint. Bring white vinegar to a boil and fill jars to within ½ inch of top. Cover and seal immediately; process in a boiling water bath for 5 minutes. See *Joy of Cooking* or a book on canning for detailed instructions.

EGGPLANT DRESSING

Tee Bruce Broussard usually serves this dressing with fried chicken.

SERVES 6 TO 8.

> 2 tablespoons oil
> 1 pound ground pork
> 1 large onion, chopped fine
> 1 bell pepper, seeded and chopped fine
> 1 stalk celery, chopped fine
> Hot pepper, fresh, or dried, or Tabasco sauce
> to taste
> 2 large eggplants, peeled and cut to about 1-
> inch cubes
> Salt to taste
> 2 cups raw rice, cooked (to be used hot)

Put oil in a large skillet and cook pork on medium heat until it is whitish. Add onion, pepper, celery, and hot pepper, and sauté until tender. Add eggplant and salt and cover tightly. Cook over medium heat, stirring occasionally, until eggplant is soft. Place hot rice in a large bowl and stir eggplant mixture into it.

CANDIED YAMS

Here is Tee Bruce Broussard's version of a classic Cajun dish. This sweet side-dish vegetable verges on a dessert.

SERVES 4.

> 4 medium sweet potatoes
> ½ teaspoon cinnamon
> ¼ teaspoon salt
> 3 tablespoons butter
> ¼ cup each white and brown sugar
> ¼ cup pecans

Preheat oven to 375°.

    Boil sweet potatoes in water to cover until just tender. Drain, peel, slice, and place in a shallow, buttered baking dish. Sprinkle with cinnamon and salt and dot with butter. Melt sugars over a very low heat in a heavy pan, stirring constantly. Allow to boil to make a thick syrup, pour over yams, and bake for about 15 minutes, or until bubbling. Sprinkle with pecans and bake 5 minutes longer.

A MESS O' GREENS

Greens have long been a tasty and nutritious staple in the rural South. I find it unfortunate that most urban people are unfamiliar with eating greens. Most gardeners know that this is one of the easiest crops to grow in abundance. Here is a variation on a traditional preparation method that opts for a minimum of water and cooking time to retain nutrients and flavor. Note that the two-pound equivalent in cups for the raw, packed greens appears in parentheses following each kind. When preparing greens, remove all tough stems unless you are using chard—its stems are tender and tasty.

SERVES 6 TO 8.

> ¼ to ½ pound bacon or salt pork, coarsely
> chopped
> 2 pounds or so of greens—mustard (12 cups),
> collards (14 to 16 cups), kale (16 cups),
> dandelion (12 to 16 cups), or chard (16
> cups)—washed and torn or chopped
> ¼ cup cider or wine vinegar
> ½ cup water
> ⅛ to ¼ cup sugar
> 1 teaspoon dry mustard
> Freshly ground pepper to taste

In a large skillet, fry bacon or pork until crisp. Add greens, cider or vinegar, and water. Then cover skillet and cook on medium heat 3 to 5 minutes, until greens have wilted. Stir in sugar, mustard, and pepper. Cover and simmer on low heat 5 minutes longer or until greens are tender. Uncover pan and cook off excess liquid, or serve it in the Louisiana way as "pot likker," in a separate bowl as an accompaniment to the vegetables. Also good with some parboiled, diced potatoes added in with the greens.

STUFFED MIRLITONS WITH SHRIMP AND CRAB BUTTER CREAM SAUCE

This recipe comes from *Chef Paul Prudhomme's Louisiana Kitchen*. Paul says, "I like to use margarine in this dish because it has more oil than butter and reacts better in the caramelization process."

SERVES 6.

Note: See Paul Prudhomme's book for directions on making the seafood stock. Or use your own recipe, but omit any salt or pepper.

> 2 teaspoons EACH white pepper and ground
>   red pepper (preferably cayenne)
> 1 teaspoon dried thyme leaves or 2 teaspoons
>   chopped fresh thyme
> 1 teaspoon dried sweet basil leaves or 1
>   tablespoon minced fresh basil
> ½ teaspoon black pepper
> 2 whole bay leaves
> 7 medium mirlitons (chayotes) (or substitute
>   zucchini or yellow squash)
> ¼ pound (1 stick) margarine
> 2 cups finely chopped onions
> 1¼ cups seeded and finely chopped green bell
>   peppers
> 1 cup finely chopped celery
> 6¼ cups seafood stock
> 1 tablespoon minced garlic
> ¼ pound (1 stick) unsalted butter
> 2 teaspoons salt
> 1½ cups very fine dry bread crumbs
> 1 recipe of shrimp and crab butter cream sauce
>   (see below)
> 6 tablespoons finely chopped green onions

Preheat oven to 350°.
   Combine the first four ingredients in a small bowl to form a seasoning mix and set aside. Alternatively, substitute 6 to 6½ teaspoons of the commercial preparation called Cajun Magic Seafood Magic.®

Peel and finely chop 4 mirlitons. Peel, cut in half lengthwise, and remove seeds from remaining 3 mirlitons. (The seeds make a nice addition to a salad.) Set aside.
   In a large skillet (preferably not a nonstick type) combine margarine with 1 cup of the onions, ¾ cup of the bell peppers, and ½ cup of the celery. Sauté over high heat until most of the onions are browned, about 15 minutes, stirring occasionally. Add ¼ cup of the stock, the remaining 1 cup onions, ½ cup bell peppers, and ½ cup celery plus seasoning mix and garlic. Stir well and continue cooking for 2 minutes, stirring frequently. Add butter and continue cooking until it melts, constantly stirring and scraping the pan bottom well. Stir in chopped mirlitons and cook 5 minutes, stirring occasionally. Stir in salt and continue cooking for about 2 minutes to reduce some of the liquid. Remove from heat and transfer mixture to an ungreased 13 × 9-inch baking pan. Bake uncovered until mushy, about 35 minutes. Stir in bread crumbs and continue baking until browned, about 30 minutes. Remove from oven and discard bay leaves.
   Meanwhile, place mirliton halves and remaining 6 cups stock in a 4-quart saucepan. Boil mirlitons until tender, about 40 minutes. (Add water to pan as necessary to keep them covered with liquid.) Drain mirlitons, reserving 1½ cups stock to make shrimp and crab butter cream sauce (see below). Shave a thin slice from the rounded side of each mirliton half so it will sit level (seed side up) on a plate.
   Warm the plates in a 250° oven. Make the sauce and serve immediately.
   To serve, place a mirliton half on each heated plate and mound ⅔ cup stuffing in the cavity. Spoon about ⅔ cup shrimp and crab butter cream sauce over the top and sprinkle with 1 tablespoon green onions.

SHRIMP AND CRAB BUTTER CREAM SAUCE

This sauce is served over stuffed mirlitons (see above). It's also great over stuffed fish, vegetables, pasta, and omelettes.

MAKES ABOUT 5 CUPS.

> ½ pound (2 sticks) unsalted butter

¼ *cup finely chopped onions*
3 *tablespoons all-purpose flour*
1½ *cups reserved seafood-mirliton stock from recipe above or seafood stock*
1 *cup heavy cream*
½ *teaspoon salt*
½ *teaspoon ground red pepper (preferably cayenne)*
2 *dozen (about 3/4 pound) medium shrimp, peeled and deveined*
1 *cup (about ½ pound) packed lump crab meat (picked over)*

In a 1-quart saucepan melt 1 stick of butter with onions over medium heat; sauté about 1 minute. Add flour and blend with a metal whisk until smooth. Reduce heat to low and continue cooking and whisking constantly for 1 minute. (If mixture starts to brown, remove from heat—it will start to brown more quickly if salted butter is used.)

Meanwhile, bring stock to a boil in a 2-quart saucepan. Add butter-flour mixture and remaining 1 stick butter. Cook over high heat till butter melts, whisking contantly. Gradually add cream, whisking constantly; then mix in salt and red pepper. Lower heat to medium and stir in shrimp and crab meat. Continue cooking just until shrimp are pink and plump, about 1 to 2 minutes, stirring occasionally. Remove from heat.

CAULIFLOWER WELCH

SERVES 8.

This recipe also comes from Chef Paul Prudhomme and makes a festive holiday dish because of the presentation: the pecans and raisins make it really special. Some bacons are saltier than others, so if you use unusually salty bacon, cut back slightly on the amount of seasoning mix you use.

Note: See Paul Prudhomme's book for directions on making chicken stock, or use your own recipe but omit any salt and pepper.

1⅛ *teaspoons salt*
¾ *teaspoon sweet paprika*
½ *teaspoon* EACH *white pepper and onion powder*
¼ *teaspoon* EACH *garlic powder, ground red*

pepper *(preferably cayenne), black pepper, and dried thyme leaves or* ½ *teaspoon chopped fresh thyme*
⅛ *teaspoon dried sweet basil leaves or* ½ *teaspoon minced fresh basil*
2 *heads cauliflower (each about* 1½ *to 2 pounds)*
1 *quart chicken stock*
½ *pound sliced bacon, minced*
¾ *cup raisins*
½ *cup pecan pieces, dry roasted*
¼ *cup very fine, dry bread crumbs*
1 *cup finely chopped green onions*
½ *can diced green chilies (or use fresh 'Anaheim' peppers, roasted, peeled, and diced)*
1 *cup heavy cream*
3 *cups grated Cheddar cheese*

Make a seasoning mix by combining the first five ingredients. Alternatively, substitute 3 to 4 teaspoons of the commercial preparation called Cajun Magic Vegetable Magic.®

Remove any leaves from the base of the cauliflowers and trim stalks if necessary so heads will sit level. Place them side by side in a large pot containing stock. Sprinkle ½ teaspoon of seasoning mix evenly on top of each head. Cover pan and cook over high heat until cauliflower is fork tender, about 15 minutes. Drain well, reserving 1 cup of stock, and place cauliflower on a large-lipped serving platter. Set aside in a warm place.

Meanwhile, fry bacon in a large skillet over high heat until very brown. Add raisins, pecans, and remaining seasoning mix; mix well. Let cook about 1 to 2 minutes, stirring occasionally. Remove from heat and stir in about 2 tablespoons bread crumbs (if after stirring you still see a lot of bacon grease, add remaining bread crumbs). Stir in green onions and green chilies. Return to high heat and cook for 5 minutes, stirring occasionally and scraping pan bottom well. Add reserved 1 cup stock and cream, stirring until any sediment stuck to pan bottom has dissolved. Cook about 2 minutes, stirring occasionally. Remove from heat, add the cheese, and stir until cheese is melted. Serve immediately.

To serve, spoon half the sauce over each cauliflower and place platter on the table before dividing into portions.

...FISH TASTING & TRADE...

...AFAYETTE, LOUISIANA   ...UARY

Sweet potato pie with pecans is a scrumptious way to end a meal.

FRENCH-FRIED OKRA

This recipe is from the McIlhenny Company, creator and manufacturer of Tabasco sauce.

SERVES ABOUT 15 AS AN APPETIZER OR 8 AS A SIDE DISH.

> *2 pounds fresh, young okra*
> *2 eggs, beaten*
> *1 tablespoon Worcestershire sauce*
> *1 teaspoon garlic salt*
> *1/4 to 1/2 teaspoon Tabasco sauce*
> *White cornmeal*
> *Vegetable oil for frying*
> *Salt*

Cut ends off okra and discard. Boil okra for about 8 minutes; drain. In a small bowl beat eggs, Worcestershire sauce, garlic salt, and Tabasco sauce together. Dip okra first into egg mixture then into cornmeal, completely covering with cornmeal. Pour enough oil into a deep-fat frier or heavy saucepan to measure 1½ to 2 inches deep. Heat oil to 375°. Fry okra 2 to 3 minutes or until golden. Remove and drain on paper towels. Sprinkle with salt and serve hot.

CAJUN RED BEANS

SERVES 8 TO 10.

> *1 pound dry red beans*
> *2 to 3 pounds ham hocks or 1 pound smoked or Andouille sausage, sliced*
> *1 large onion, chopped*
> *2 bell peppers, seeded and finely chopped*
> *4 bay leaves*
> *1 to 2 cups finely chopped celery or 1/2 cup leaf celery, chopped*
> *1 tablespoon fresh thyme, chopped*
> *Hot pepper to taste (use more if using ham hocks, less if using sausage): choose from 1/2 to 2 fresh hot peppers, minced, 1 to 2 teaspoons dried pepper, or 1 to 2 tablespoons chili powder*
> *Salt and pepper to taste*

In a large pot or Dutch oven, soak beans overnight in plenty of water. Add all other ingredients, cover, and simmer for about 2 hours, stirring occasionally and adding water if necessary to keep everything moist. Cook until meat and beans are tender. If using ham hocks, remove bones, adding meat back to beans. Serve over rice.

SWEET POTATO PIE

SERVES 6 TO 8.

> *Enough sweet potatoes (about 1 1/3 pounds) to measure 2 cups when baked until soft, peeled, and mashed*
> *1/4 cup butter*
> *2/3 cup sugar*
> *2 large eggs*
> *1/4 cup bourbon and 3/4 cup milk, or 1 cup milk and 2 teaspoons vanilla*
> *1 tablespoon grated orange or lemon rind*
> *1/2 teaspoon nutmeg*
> *3/4 cup milk*
> *A 9-inch unbaked pie shell*
> *Pecan halves, optional*
> *Whipping cream*
> *Bourbon to flavor*

Preheat oven to 425°.

Bake sweet potatoes until soft; then peel and mash. With an electric mixer, cream butter until soft.

Gradually add sugar and blend well. Beat in eggs, sweet potatoes, bourbon and milk or milk and vanilla, and seasonings, beating between additions. Pour into a 9-inch unbaked pie shell and, if desired, decorate the top with carefully placed pecan halves. Bake at 425° for 10 minutes. Reduce heat to 350° and bake 45 minutes longer, or until set. Let cool at least ½ hour before serving. Garnish with whipped cream flavored with bourbon.

Sources

Seed Companies

1. Hastings
   434 Marietta Street NW
   P.O. Box 4274
   Atlanta, GA 30302
   This firm specializes in vegetable varieties for the South.

2. Park Seed Company
   Cokesbury Road
   Greenwood, SC 29647
   Park carries a large selection of vegetable seed varieties for southern gardens.

3. Southern Exposure Seed Exchange
   P.O. Box 158
   North Garden, VA 22959
   This seed company carries many open-pollinated heirloom varieties of vegetables and more-modern ones as well. All varieties have been selected to grow well in the Mid-Atlantic region of the country. Catalog: $3.00.

4. Wyatt-Quarles
   P.O. Box 739
   Garner, NC 27529

This seed company specializes in vegetable varieties for the Southeast.

Demonstration Garden

Callaway Gardens
Pine Mountain, GA 31822
   Callaway Gardens is a large recreational garden that contains one of the most extensive demonstration vegetable gardens in the country, comprising more than 400 varieties of fruits, vegetables, and herbs.

Books

Angers, Trent, and Sue McDonough. *Acadiana Profile's Cajun Cooking*. Lafayette, La.: Angers Publishing, 1980.
   This book contains a collection of recipes from cooks of southern Louisiana, the heart of Cajun country.

Prudhomme, Paul. *Chef Paul Prudhomme's Louisiana Kitchen*. New York: Morrow, 1984.
   Prudhomme's book is one of the most comprehensive and enjoyable books on the subject of southern cooking.

Southern Living magazine staff. *Southern Living: Growing Vegetables and Herbs*. Birmingham, Ala.: Oxmoor House, 1984.
   This marvelous book offers a comprehensive look at vegetable growing in the South and contains many basic and creative recipes.

Thompson, Terry. *Cajun-Creole Cooking*. Tuscon, Ariz.: HP Books, 1986.
   This is a colorful book on both Creole and Cajun cooking that contains many wonderful recipes.

Burpee All-Time-Favorites Gardens

IT WAS EXCITING TO DRIVE through the gates of Fordhook Farms in Doylestown, Pennsylvania. This stone-faced pre-Revolutionary house is now an inn, and I was going to stay the night. For nearly a century Fordhook Farms was the Burpee family home and, from 1888 until fairly recently, the site of the seed company's main experimental plot.

Once inside the house I was not disappointed. The lovely living room with its majestic mirrors and wealth of antiques, the study filled with the memorabilia of founder W. Atlee Burpee and his son David—everything was fascinating. I found scrapbooks full of letters from Luther Burbank and other dignitaries, family photo albums, and—oh, the books! How I was going to love poring over those old horticultural books. For the night, I was given the room of the late Lois Burpee, David's wife, and I found it moving to sleep in her four-poster bed. Her presence was all around me, and I wondered, as I drifted off to sleep, whether she and David, had they still been alive, would have stayed up far into the night talking with me of vegetables, gardening, and cooking—the good old American way.

OPPOSITE: *Antique Burpee catalogs surrounded by some of Burpee's popular vegetables, including 'Burpee's VF Hybrid' tomato, 'Burpee Yellow Globe Hybrid' onion, and 'Sweet Basil'.*

For years I have felt a strong emotional connection to Fordhook Farms and the W. Atlee Burpee Company. One of my earliest and most vivid childhood memories is of taking big 'Fordhook' lima bean seeds out of my father's hand and carefully putting each one in the ground. I can still see my handprint in the fluffy soil where I patted them into place. I was three or four years old, and my father had probably chosen lima beans because their large size made them easy to handle. I can still recall, too, seeing the first seedlings, tending the plants, and picking the pods with my father and then feasting on the lima beans at supper. The limas we ate were always 'Fordhook', and I know the seeds were always from Burpee, because the Burpee catalog was the only one my father ever ordered.

As my plans for this book advanced, and filled out more and more with unusual varieties and specialized gardens, it became clear to me that I needed a chapter that would highlight the familiar vegetables that form the core kitchen garden for most of us regardless of our special growing and cooking interests. I had to have a "standard" garden that would showcase the tried-and-true favorites of American gardening in the same way the heirloom garden drew attention to unusual and historical varieties. This garden would reflect the good work of American plant breeders and seed people in addition to gardeners and cooks, giving credit where it was due for the hybrid and other selected varieties that we often tend to take for granted. The chapter, then, would celebrate the kitchen garden as we have known it for the last thirty or forty years.

With this need in mind, though I could have approached a number of other seed growers, I asked the Burpee company if it would grow an all-time-favorites garden for my book. The firm's national scope and its consistent interest in home gardening combined with my sentimental attachment to influence my choice. I proposed the project to Steve Frowine, Burpee public relations manager and staff horticulturist, and he said the company would be delighted—but he threw in a caveat. Two years earlier, the growing ground at Fordhook Farms had been crossed by a new highway and put out of commission. Burpee had relocated its growing grounds to a new site with terrible soil, and even though the firm had been rebuilding the soil over that period, Steve still wasn't sure how well the garden would grow.

The W. Atlee Burpee Company is the largest mail-order seed business in the United States. Thousands and thousands of American gardeners share my emotional connection with it and enjoy the midwinter ritual of perusing the Burpee catalog. Since 1876 the company has focused on the home gardener and has introduced such varieties as 'Better Boy' tomatoes, 'Big Max' pumpkin, 'Golden Bantam' corn, and my old favorite, 'Fordhook' limas, all of which became old standbys. Unlike most seed companies, Burpee breeds and produces a number of its own seeds. In fact, you'll see variety names in other mail-order catalogs that contain the name Burpee—'Burpee's Golden Beet', for example, or 'Burpee's Improved Bush' lima.

As noted, the Burpee garden is intended here to represent the traditional American garden and to introduce for discussion some of our favorite types of vegetables and most beloved ways of preparing them. In comparison with some of the other chapters, this one might seem deceptively small. The vegetables described and recommended are only a few of hundreds I could have chosen. But detailed information on many more varieties makes up the bulk of Part Four, "An Encyclopedia of Superior Vegetables." For more information still on our national favorites, see the garden books and cookbooks listed in "Sources" at the end of this chapter.

How to Grow All-Time-Favorite Vegetables

In contrast to some of the other gardens in this book—for example, where corn varieties are grown for flour and tomatoes for their golden color—the vegetables in the Burpee all-time-favorites garden are typical of those you'll find in most people's gardens across the United States. Quite a few hybrids are represented, and the corn is for eating fresh. The eggplants are big and purple, the tomatoes red and round, and the beans long, straight, and green—just the way they're "supposed" to be. For detailed information on growing these vegetables, see Part Four, "An Encyclopedia of Superior Vegetables," and Appendix A, "Planting and Maintenance." For additional information, seek out the National Gardening Association's book *Gardening* and Derek Fell's *Vegetables: How to Select,*

Grow, and Enjoy (both listed in "Sources"), and talk with your local nursery people.

If you'd like to see first-hand how some of these varieties perform in your area, visit university extension variety-trial grounds. Look also for public gardens that contain All America display gardens. These are gardens created when the All America Selections committee, a professional growers' association, chooses promising vegetable varieties to be grown in existing gardens across the country to see how well they do.

If you are new to gardening, this chapter will serve as a good introduction to mainstream American gardening. You couldn't find a more secure way to learn than to study the Burpee garden and the list of recommended varieties later in the chapter. The varieties have been documented and information on them is easy to find. For the experienced gardener, the garden and its list provide a back-to-basics refresher course in designing a dependable kitchen garden.

The Burpee Garden

The new Burpee garden is a couple of miles from Fordhook Farms. The day after my arrival, Steve Frowine and I toured it together. I asked Steve to talk to me about its different aspects, and he started by saying, "I'm sure people think we would have the most perfect soil at Burpee, but the area for our new garden site was, when we moved to it, a most dreadful piece of ground. It was used for years by a candle factory for its corporation yard, where heavy vehicles had been parked, leaking oil and compacting the soil. As if that weren't bad enough, the topsoil had been stripped off to be put around the foundation of the office, the drainage was bad, and the ground had a high clay content. So when we took over the property three years ago, the soil was really in terrible condition. Of course, we knew going into it that it would take a lot of time and persistence to rebuild the soil and create a truly prime piece of gardening ground."

Obviously, before the Burpee staff did any gardening they had to add organic matter, and in the first two seasons they grew a cover crop of annual rye. The next year, when Steve started the garden for me, the soil was still poor in nutrients, and he had to apply a high-nitrogen slow-release fertilizer and mulch heavily to keep things growing well.

In planning the garden for this book, we had

Vegetable and flower gardens planted by Burpee employees at Fordhook Farms in Doylestown, Pennsylvania.

decided that the major objective was to develop a model garden that home gardeners could plant and maintain easily, and Steve had suggested we limit our vegetables to Burpee's Bull's Eye varieties. These are proven varieties that have done well for many years for gardeners all over the country. Said Steve, "Sometimes I think there is so much emphasis on what's new that some of the excellent older varieties get

Steve Frowine, Burpee public relations manager and staff horticulturist, tends the Burpee garden grown especially for this book.

passed by. A good example is 'Kentucky Wonder', with its proven performance and good taste. I think it's worth mentioning that some of our hybrids have been around since the early 1900s and are still very popular—simply because they do the job."

We had planned the garden so it wouldn't produce too much of any one thing at once and staggered the harvest from spring through fall. Steve had estimated the potential quantities produced in terms of a family of four. He chose a good combination of peppers, tomatoes, cucumbers, lettuces, and beans. The bean varieties were mostly pole types put on trellises, and the cucumbers were bush, not vine, types because they take up less space. We also included okra, rhubarb, both yellow and white bunching onions, and sweet potatoes, too, because they are traditional in many American gardens. For herbs we chose dill, parsley, and sweet basil, because they seem

to be the most popular. There was to be intercropping—with quick-growing lettuce interspersed among the slower-growing carrots—and succession cropping of peas followed by beans.

The dimensions of the garden were twenty feet by twenty feet, mostly laid out in rows two feet wide. A dozen tomato plants lined one side, and the south end of the garden was planted with hills of zucchini, winter squash, and melons. A separate garden measuring twelve feet by twenty feet was planted with corn.

We all know what can happen, though, to even the best-laid plans. Our garden was subject to the usual number of uncontrollable conditions, and a good number of them fell into the adverse category. Besides the poor soil, the summer proved to be very dry, and this caused stunting in some of the early cool-season crops, many of which went to seed and bore poorly. A related problem was irrigation: Steve hadn't had time to put in a drip system for watering.

Further, as Steve reported, pest problems during the growing season were formidable. "We had terrible problems with woodchucks, rabbits, and mice. I think the drought this summer drove the animals into our garden. Woodchucks wiped out the whole planting of peas and a second planting of beans. The mice nested and hid under the mulch of shredded wood clippings and came out to eat the corn seeds after we planted them. Next time I'll use a repellent on the seeds. We had a few flea beetles on the eggplants, but other than that we really didn't have much insect damage."

Amazingly, for all its problems, the garden still bore a tremendous amount of food. It wasn't picture perfect, as we might have wished, but it did its major job, which was to produce food for the table.

The varieties Steve chose for the garden all are Burpee's Bull's Eye varieties except where mentioned. You might think of this list as an introductory lesson in traditional gardening, American style. And consider how smoothly these varieties fit with typical American table fare, as the cooking section will reveal.

BEANS   Steve chose the 'Kentucky Wonder' pole snap bean, an old variety carried by most American seed companies. 'Kentucky Wonder' is noted for the distinctive flavor of its pods both fresh and dried, and its light-brown seeds make good shelling beans. The vines are early and heavy producers of large, thick, green pods that are meaty and tender, stringless when young, and fine for freezing.

For lima beans, Steve chose 'Burpee's Best Pole' and, at my request, 'Fordhook No. 242', a modern version of the old 'Fordhook' variety. Both these heat-resistant plants set pods well under adverse conditions and have an excellent flavor both fresh and frozen.

BEETS   Steve selected 'Burpee's Red Ball' beet, a sweet-flavored beet with uniform dark-red flesh that's free from any woody fiber. Its roots are globe shaped, grow to three inches in diameter, and have a smooth, deep-red skin. The tops, green touched with red, are erect.

I had asked Steve also to include one of my favorites, 'Burpee's Golden Beet', even though it's not a Bull's Eye variety. I like it because it has a rich beet flavor but its golden roots do not bleed like red

beets. It is excellent in salads and stir-fries and makes great pickles. The fact that its germination rate is lower than other beets probably accounts for the fact that these beets are not a Bull's Eye variety.

BROCCOLI   Steve chose 'Bonanza Hybrid' because it bears a bonanza of side shoots after the large central head is harvested. You'll pick delicious broccoli for weeks in spring and again in fall if you grow a second planting. Actually, Steve has had it produce all through the summer. It's good raw or cooked, fresh or frozen.

CANTALOUPE   Steve and I were unanimous in our choice of 'Burpee's Ambrosia' cantaloupe. I thoroughly agree when Steve says, "Any home gardener who has the space and doesn't grow 'Ambrosia' cantaloupe is really missing something." He also notes, "We have enthusiasts for both 'Ambrosia' and 'Burpee Hybrid', though, and they're just as strong on both sides." I'm partial to 'Ambrosia' for its rich, fruity taste. It's extra sweet and juicy. The fruits are of medium size, averaging from four and a half to five pounds. The vines are resistant to powdery mildew and produce a bumper crop.

CORN   Steve chose 'Golden Cross Bantam' instead of one of the supersweet varieties. 'Golden Cross Bantam' is a standard yellow-kerneled high-quality hybrid. It is versatile and can be used for freezing as well as fresh from the garden.

CUCUMBERS   Because many gardeners have small plots, Steve selected a small variety, 'Bush Champion'. It was developed at Cornell University and bears delicious, streamlined, well-formed, bright-green fruits over a long season. Vines are short, compact, mosaic resistant, and very productive.

EGGPLANT   Steve chose the 'Burpee Hybrid' eggplant. It has been a reliable favorite among Burpee customers for a number of years. It produces many medium-size purple fruits and holds them well off the ground so that they don't rot.

LETTUCE   Steve planted 'Green Ice', a long-time favorite Burpee lettuce. It holds up pretty well in the heat, keeps going for a long time without bolting or getting bitter, and has good flavor. According to Steve, this is one of the most popular lettuce varieties Burpee has ever carried.

Steve also included two other popular lettuces: 'Burpee's Royal Oak Leaf', one of the most beautiful lettuces in the garden, and the succulent 'Burpee Bibb'.

PEAS   Because few Americans sit down and shell peas nowadays, snap peas seemed the obvious choice to Steve and me. While newer varieties of sugar snaps are bush types, not long vines, Steve chose the original 'Sugar Snap' for its proven record of production. Its succulent, edible pods are crunchy and sugary sweet. The wilt-resistant vines are extremely productive over a long season, reach four to eight feet in height, and need strong support.

PEPPERS   'Crispy Hybrid' was Steve's choice for an all-around variety. It produces early and sets a heavy crop of delicious bell peppers all season. This is a blocky, thick-walled pepper that turns from green to red fairly early.

SQUASH, SUMMER   'Burpee Hybrid Zucchini' was chosen by Steve, but as he said, "As soon as our zucchini really started to bear, everyone locked their car doors in the Burpee parking lot. We couldn't pawn them off at the speed they were coming on. I even tried to let a few grow to baseball-bat size to slow down the rest, but even then they were hard to control. We wish we could breed that kind of vigor into every other vegetable we produce."

SQUASH, WINTER   Steve put in 'Burpee's Butterbush', a space-saving winter squash. It was the first bush-type butternut squash developed and was introduced by Burpee in 1978. It's ideal for home gardens since it takes one-quarter the space of the usual vine type. Each plant grows only three to four feet long and bears butternut-shaped fruits.

TOMATOES   For tomatoes, Steve tried to include a broad range of different types, starting with a very compact variety, the 'Pixie Hybrid'. The plant grows to be only eighteen to twenty-four inches tall and produces golf-ball-size fruit. It produces early and is good both for containers and greenhouse growing. For a standard tomato, he selected the 'Burpee's VF Hybrid', his favorite middle-size tomato. The fruits have good uniform shape, don't crack, and are good for slicing. And the plant is disease resistant.

Steve also planted 'Burpee's Supersteak Hybrid VFN'. The extra-meaty, red fruits have a rich, full flavor and a good flat-round, smooth-shouldered shape. Most of the fruits weigh in at one to two pounds. The plants are productive and resistant to wilts and root-knot nematodes. As Steve said, " 'Supersteak' is for someone really into he-man tomatoes—real big ones. Some people like to com-

The 'Burpee's Supersteak Hybrid VFN' was developed for those who enjoy large, meaty tomatoes.

pete with their neighbors to grow the biggest tomato. That's what 'Supersteak' is there for."

Finally, for a paste tomato, he included 'Roma VF'. He chose this one instead of 'Roma', the standard, because it was more disease resistant.

The Burpee garden represents the meat and potatoes of American vegetable gardening as we've all known and enjoyed it. The vegetables it contains are the ones generations have voted in by consent—fresh eating corn, great big tomatoes, blocky bell peppers, and all the rest. No matter which exotic ideas you choose to explore and express in your theme gardening, your main kitchen garden will undoubtedly look a lot like the Burpee all-time-favorites vegetable garden.

Steve Frowine is public relations manager and staff horticulturist for the W. Atlee Burpee Company. Unlike many administrators at companies that work with plants, however, Steve is a gardener—an avowed and enthusiastic gardener. "I love to garden," says Steve. "I've gardened every since I was a child, and I never get tired of it. There are always new things to learn. Gardening covers the complete spectrum; in fact, it's almost an international language. People from all parts of the world can get together and compare the size of their tomatoes."

Steve Frowine

more and more organic matter until you get a lighter soil and better growing conditions. I've gardened in sand, too, and that also has its problems: not enough nutrients and continually dry plants. The solution to this is the same: add lots of organic matter."

Even with lots of organic matter added, though, Steve finds that plants sometimes dry out. To solve this problem he recommends drip irrigation. "I have all my home garden plants on drip irrigation," he says. "Gardeners in the East and Midwest figure drip is okay for the arid West

Steve has both a bachelor's and a master's degree in horticulture, but he's learned the most about gardening by growing things himself. As he says, "There's no substitute for going out and digging in the soil and seeing what the problems are. Sometimes we lose touch; we're all so specialized and involved in horticultural science that we lose track of the 'how to grow-it' aspect. That's what most home gardeners need to know.

"At Burpee, we're most concerned with the home gardener," Steve says. "We don't produce hybrids that ship well or tomatoes that won't bruise if you throw them against a wall. We're interested in the tomato that tastes best when it's fresh and properly ripened. We breed varieties that are resistant to disease so home gardeners don't have to spray much, and we produce hybrids that bear over the whole season."

I asked Steve to share a few of his ideas about American home gardening, and he said, "It's funny. I've gardened all over the United States and everywhere you go, gardeners curse their clay soil. In Hawaii, the soil is terrible. The heavy red clay there is just like glue, and when it dries, it becomes as hard as brick. In the West, gardeners have adobe; in the Midwest, they have thick brown clay; and even here in Pennsylvania, we have a heavy clay. Fortunately there's a solution, and it's the same everywhere: just add

but shouldn't be necessary in their humid climates. I don't agree. All over the country I find that plants can be growing beautifully, but if they go into stress because they don't have enough water when they fruit, the yield will drop dramatically. Drip irrigation can also help prevent disease problems because soil with fungal spores doesn't get splashed up on the foliage. In addition, most fungal diseases thrive in humid conditions, and drip irrigation makes the air less humid than overhead watering does."

As we concluded our conversation about American gardening, Steve shared an insight. "I did a variety comparison not too long ago," he notes. "I sent for all the variety information I could get from universities, garden writers, and extension offices all over the country, and I was amazed to see that the same varieties showed up on list after list. Varieties growing in Florida were often the same ones successful gardeners grew in Kansas. It seems to me that a good variety is a good variety is a good variety. The difference seems to be determined more by cultural care than by climate restrictions. Certainly gardeners in Alaska have to start corn inside in peat pots, for example, and folks in the South have to plant lettuce in winter, but basically, varieties that are genetically superior and are given good care will consistently perform."

Recommended Popular American Vegetables

This selection of vegetable varieties is a representative sample from the best offerings of this country's largest seed companies. I could never have given here even a small percentage of the many varieties available, though many of them are covered in detail in Part Four, "An Encyclopedia of Superior Vegetables." What this section provides is an overview of the breeding characteristics—as I perceive them—that universities and seed companies have stressed since the beginning of this century. In this emphasis, this list of recommendations differs markedly from those in the other theme garden chapters, which primarily contain detailed descriptions of individual varieties.

It's important to note that Burpee is by no means the only seed company to carry most of the described varieties—even when those varieties have Burpee in their names. Other seed companies that carry the varieties mentioned here are listed in the "Sources" section of this chapter.

BEANS Over the years, stringlessness has been a major breeding goal with snap beans, so today few modern snap beans have strings. Uniformity and tenderness have also been stressed, as well as greater production and resistance to bean diseases such as rust and mosaic virus. 'Kentucky Wonder' and 'Blue Lake' are snap bean varieties that have been around for a long time, and they and their improved offspring are still among the best.

For the shelling varieties, ease of shelling has been a goal, though as yet an unrealized one. Burpee, for one, has tried to breed for an easy-opening lima, but so far to no avail.

BEETS Modern breeding in beet roots has been toward a uniform dark-red color, no woody center, no zoning, and fresh, sweet eating. The plants have been selected for taller, glossier foliage and overall good eating. These goals contrast with those of our ancestors, who selected for very large beet roots with good winter-keeping characteristics. Look for 'Ruby Queen' and the Detroit and Early Wonder types.

BROCCOLI It seems to me that much of the modern emphasis in broccoli breeding has been for one large, uniform head and uniform plants in a crop that ripens all at once. While this suits the market gardener or the home gardener who freezes lots of broccoli, those of us who do not freeze it only get a month's worth of intense broccoli eating. I prefer a variety that produces many offshoots over a long period. If you have the same preference, look for modern varieties such as 'Bonanza Hybrid', 'Green Goliath', 'Pac Man', or 'Green Comet Hybrid'. But if you want a good harvest for preserving, choose 'Premium Crop Hybrid'.

CORN Corn is America's specialty. Ours is one of the few cultures that grows corn for fresh eating. And, boy, what those that don't are missing! Corn varieties have been bred for resistance to diseases such as smut, bacterial wilt, and leaf blights and for tight ears resistant to corn borers. But for the last decade or so, sweetness seems to have been the most important goal for breeders. The new supersweet varieties are so sweet that some folks, myself included, actually don't like them. The kernels of these varieties just don't have enough corn flavor for me. Supersweet corn has its virtues, though: it stays sweet for a few days after it's picked, which means you no longer have to get the pot boiling before you harvest. It also stays sweet on the plant longer, so you can harvest over a longer season and still enjoy the corn. There are two possible drawbacks with some of the extra-sweet varieties, though: they must be isolated from other sweet corns to prevent cross-pollination, and they need very warm soil to germinate. Some of the supersweet varieties are 'How Sweet It Is', 'Burpee's Sugar Sweet', and 'Illini Extra Sweet'.

CUCUMBERS Cucumber breeders have been working to produce a high-quality "burpless" cucumber. In addition, they want plants that are smaller, more disease resistant, more productive, and varieties that will grow well in greenhouses. Disease resistance is probably the most important characteristic of many modern cucumbers. However, the breeding for greenhouse growing has gotten so specialized that you can actually choose varieties for greenhouses with different temperatures. Bush-type cucumber varieties are also a boon to some gardeners, because they don't sprawl as vines do. Choose from 'Pot Luck', 'Space Master', 'Bush Champion', and 'Park's Burpless Bush'.

In my opinion, the most successful new cucumbers bred for eating quality involve crosses with some of the Japanese varieties. The results are sweet and burpless varieties such as 'Sweet Success Hybrid' and 'Sweet Slice Hybrid'.

PEAS, SNAP   Over the years breeders have been selecting peas for compact plants, stringless pods, high production, and disease resistance. Today, however, few home gardeners want to sit and shell peas. Fortunately, Calvin Lamborn, an Idaho breeder, developed the now famous 'Sugar Snap' pea from a mutant pea with thick-walled pods. While there was a thick-walled edible pea, called the 'Butter Pea', grown in the 1800s, it never caught on and became extinct. Luckily, we have 'Sugar Snap', and nowadays gardeners seem to grow this variety more than any other. Along with 'Sugar Snap', 'Snappy' is among the best varieties; both are great producers on long, vigorous vines. 'Sugarbon' and 'Sugar Mel' are short-vine varieties that are very productive and among the tastiest variations.

PEPPERS   Most bell pepper breeding has been for a blocky shape, early bearing, good production, and cool-weather tolerance. For a very large, green bell pepper, try 'Park's Whopper Improved'. Other blocky bells are 'Crispy Bell', a popular performer, and 'Bell Captain', a productive midseason variety. 'Gypsy' represents a big breakthrough; it will set fruits in unusually cool and damp weather and in short-summer areas. Another variety for short seasons is 'Ace Hybrid'. Gardeners who want more decorative vegetables for the patio and flower borders should try 'Tequila Sunrise'; it holds its fruits on top. Of the bell peppers of different colors currently being bred, try 'Golden Bell Hybrid', 'Golden Summer Hybrid', and some of the purple varieties.

SQUASH, SUMMER   Most summer squash breeding must have been for productivity. As one who is forced to leave orphan zucchinis on the neighbor's doorstep, I'm not sure breeders have done us a favor in this case. For instance, my experience with 'Burpee Hybrid Zucchini', touted for its amazing hybrid vigor, gives me two or three zucchinis a day, whether I want them or not. Some years I can't face the problem, so I plant 'Gold Rush' or 'Yellow Crookneck', which are less productive. And there are a few new varieties available—'Spineless Zucchini Hybrid' is one—that have no stickers to scratch your arm as you reach into the plant.

SQUASH, WINTER   Modern breeding in squash seems to be for a bushy habit and away from the monster vines of yore. And according to Rob Johnston of Johnny's Selected Seeds, the American and Japanese breeders are doing some of the best winter squash selecting. Their goal seems to be for sweet and dry flesh. 'Sweet Mama' and 'Green Hokkaido' are representative. 'Table Ace' has been a good performer, and you might also want to try a newcomer called 'Jersey Golden Acorn', a gold-colored acorn squash of high quality that can be eaten both immature as a summer squash and in its mature stage.

TOMATOES   Americans have been conducting a love affair with the tomato for more than a hundred years. The 1888 *Burpee Farm Annual* used a full page to describe Burpee's seven-pound red tomato, called the 'Turner Hybrid'. Breeders at universities and seed companies have worked to make tomato plants more disease resistant and to produce bumper yields of uniform, large, red, round fruits. Critics say breeders have gone too far and have given the public a tasteless pink store tomato that doesn't deserve its name. However, according to Derek Fell, one of the nation's best garden writers and photographers, this is an exaggeration. He defends the breeders by saying that the average store tomato is tasteless not because the variety is flavorless but because the tomato was picked green. Modern varieties are valuable both for their productivity and their disease resistance. There are hundreds of varieties to choose from, so try a few each year and see which ones you like best. If you prefer not to stake your plants, choose a determinate, or self-limiting, variety such as 'Celebrity' or 'Bitsy VF'. For a more traditional tomato that will need staking but bear over a longer season, try, for example, the tried-and-true 'Burpee Big Boy', 'Better Boy FM', 'Early Girl', or 'Quick Pick'. And for novelty, try some of the new golden and yellow varieties.

Cooking from the All-Time-Favorites Garden

One of my summer rituals is to make a bacon, lettuce, and tomato sandwich—not the kind of BLT you get at a highway restaurant, but a real one. I harvest the best-looking big, red-ripe tomato in the garden and cut it into thick slices. Then I take some leaves from the heart of an 'Oakleaf' lettuce, four or five crisp pieces of good bacon, and spread mayonnaise on two slices of fresh, crusty Italian bread. I put it all together, carry iced tea and my sandwich out to a sunny place in the garden, and feast away. The juice from the tomato always runs down my chin and arms making a mess, but I don't care. Now, that's great garden eating, American style.

Toasted zucchini bread spread with cream cheese; chicken pot pie made with a flaky crust, plump chicken, fresh peas, and baby carrots; fresh, butter-dripped corn on the cob; strawberry shortcake—all these are true American classics. It seems a shame to me that what is called standard American cooking is overlooked so consistently by contemporary food writers and enthusiasts. Is it because TV dinners and franchise restaurants have made our food so banal, so tasteless? Is it that most of our produce is store-bought and lacks the flavors these dishes were based on? Whatever the reason, once you have a garden, you can create some real gems in the kitchen, and you won't be disparaging American cooking after that.

This section offers a few classic ways of preparing some of America's favorite garden vegetables plus recipes for some of them. It is really just an overview meant to jiggle your memory, in case you've forgotten how these vegetables *really* taste. For more recipes and classic preparation methods, see the recommended cookbooks in "Sources" at the end of this chapter.

ASPARAGUS   This member of the lily family needs no gilding. For me the most elegant way to prepare fresh, sweet asparagus from the garden is simply to steam and serve it with butter. If you're lucky enough to have a large harvest, use it in a cream soup or cold in a salad.

BEANS   Fresh snap beans are a delight steamed and served with butter or in a mushroom casserole. Try a casserole with baby-tender 'Kentucky Wonder' snap beans, fresh mushrooms, and a sauce made with heavy cream instead of canned soup. Three-bean-salad is another classic, one many of us remember none too fondly from the school cafeteria. Try it with fresh garden beans for a treat and wipe out that soggy memory.

BEETS   I grew up on Harvard beets and still love them for a cold winter supper. Pickling is another way to enjoy beets from the garden. And see the "Heirloom Gardens" chapter for a recipe for red-flannel hash.

BROCCOLI   One of America's favorite vegetables, broccoli is delicious straight from the garden, dewy fresh, and steamed with butter. But it's also good in a cream soup or raw in a salad or dip.

CABBAGE   Coleslaw is probably one of this country's favorite cabbage dishes. Fresh, sweet Savoy cabbage is garden cabbage at its best, but all types of cabbage are good in soups, stuffed, or as part of a New England boiled dinner.

CARROTS   Fresh-pulled from the garden when they are still sweet and tender, carrots are best served steamed with butter, glazed, or just plain raw, nibbled out in the garden. Enjoy the denser storing types in soups and stews or raw in carrot slaw, gelatin salad, and carrot cake.

CORN   No matter how I cook it, corn is my all-time summer favorite. It's wonderful steamed on the cob or roasted on the cob over coals. It's also great creamed and in relish, soups, chowders, stews, fritters, and, of course, succotash. Fresh, sweet corn is one of the garden's greatest pleasures.

PEAS   Nowadays when Americans cook fresh peas, they are usually some variation of 'Sugar Snap'. These peas are great in stir-fries and used raw for dips, but they are being so rapidly assimilated into our cuisine that they crop up unexpectedly in all kinds of other dishes, from salads to casseroles.

POTATOES   Fresh, new potatoes boiled with butter or mashed and covered with gravy, hashbrowns served with eggs, and baked potatoes served with sour cream—all are classic American dishes. Whether incorporated into salads, stews, or soups, or served on top of a shepherd's pie, the potato is certainly an all-time staple—and to me one of the world's most comforting foods.

TOMATOES   The tomato is king of the American vegetables. Big slices of raw tomatoes in sandwiches or salads and sweet cherry tomatoes in salads or used for dipping are both delicious. We enjoy tomatoes cooked, too—stewed, in soups, or even as fresh-made tomato juice. American gardeners don't cook tomatoes in very fancy ways; we mostly enjoy them as they are, fresh off the vine. Maybe that's why we get so frustrated by the pale, tasteless versions we find in grocery stores.

OPPOSITE: *Shepherd's pie with mashed potato crust—a variation on chicken pot pie—and strawberry shortcake, the classic American dessert.*

SHEPHERD'S PIE WITH CHICKEN AND FRESH TARRAGON

The recipe for this all-American favorite was contributed by Jesse Cool, chef and owner of the Flea Street Cafe and Late for the Train restaurant in Menlo Park, California. Jesse explained, "One night, I whipped up this dinner and my whole family loved it so much that I'm still trying to figure out how to integrate it into the restaurant menu. On second thought, maybe it's meant to remain one of those special family dishes my children will tell stories about, as I do about the dishes that made me feel loved and nurtured in my childhood in Greensburg, Pennsylvania.

"Since I always make them two at a time, this recipe is for two pies—one for dinner and one for the freezer."

EACH PIE SERVES 6 TO 8.

Pastry for 2 single 9-inch pie crusts
2 quarts water
1 medium to large whole chicken
2 sprigs parsley
1 onion, chopped (save the skin)
2 tablespoons butter
1 raw carrot cut into chunks
½ cup fresh or frozen peas
½ cup fresh or frozen snap beans, sliced
½ cup carrots, diced

Potato Topping

2 pounds boiling potatoes
¼ cup butter
½ cup sour cream
Enough milk to thin to a thick puree
Salt and pepper to taste

Cream Sauce

½ cup butter
¼ cup flour
2 cups chicken stock
1 cup milk
¼ cup fresh tarragon, chopped
½ teaspoon nutmeg
⅛ cup sherry
Salt and pepper to taste

Preheat oven to 375°.

Roll out pie crusts, line 2 9-inch pie pans, and put in refrigerator until ready to fill.

In a large pot, place chicken in 2 quarts water, cover, and simmer for about 30 to 45 minutes until chicken is done. Remove chicken, drain, and cool. Skin and bone chicken, saving remains. Cut meat into bite-sized pieces and set aside. To make stock, add chicken skin, bones, giblets, parsley sprigs, onion skin, and carrot to remaining broth in pot. Simmer uncovered and reduce to create a rich broth, adding water every once in a while if it boils down too fast. You'll need to end up with 2 cups of chicken broth (the more flavor you can extract from carcass, the more intense the flavor will be in finished pie). Drain and set aside.

While chicken is simmering, prepare vegetables. Put 2 tablespoons butter and chopped onion in a frying pan and cook over medium heat for about 5 minutes until onions are tender and translucent. Steam diced carrots, green beans, and peas for 5 to 8 minutes and set aside (use shorter time if you like crunchy vegetables).

Peel, boil, and mash potatoes. Mix in butter and sour cream, add enough milk to bring mixture to spreading consistency, and set aside.

Prepare cream sauce by melting butter and whisking in flour. Cook mixture for 2 or 3 minutes, stirring constantly. Slowly add milk and then chicken stock, whisking constantly as sauce thickens. Stir in tarragon, nutmeg, sherry, salt, and pepper. Add steamed vegetables, onion, and cooked chicken to cream sauce. Allow to cool. When cool, put vegetable and chicken mixture in pie shells. Cover with mashed potato mixture. Smooth with wet knife. Cover one pie with aluminum foil and freeze. Bake remaining one for 45 minutes or until crust is brown. Let sit for 15 minutes, garnish with paprika and chopped chives if you wish, slice, and serve. For the frozen pie, defrost, then cook and serve as above.

RHUBARB CHARD FRITTERS

This recipe is from Lois Burpee's book, *Lois Burpee's Gardener's Companion and Cookbook*. In the introduction she says, "I'll never forget the year the beautiful rhubarb chard plant was introduced. Garden writers were at Fordhook for lunch, and Mr. Burpee

Spaghetti squash serves as a tasty garden substitute for traditional pasta noodles.

wanted them to see and taste rhubarb chard fritters. My ovens were full of corn puddings, and the top of the stove had others being kept warm in pans of hot water, so I had to revitalize a kerosene stove to cook the fritters. I served them right from the pans—quite a rush! These fritters make a good hot hors d'oeurve."

SERVES 6 TO 7.

    8 stalks rhubarb chard
    1 cup flour
    ½ teaspoon salt
    ⅛ teaspoon paprika
    1 egg, slightly beaten
    2 tablespoons oil or melted butter
    ⅔ cup milk
    Oil for deep frying

Cut green leaves off chard stems and save for boiled

greens. Cut stems in 3-inch lengths, wash, and dry. Mix flour, salt, paprika, egg, oil or butter, and milk. Dip pieces of stem in this batter, covering them well. Fry in deep fat heated to 375° or until hot enough to brown a 1-inch cube of bread in 1 minute. Fritters should be cooked through and delicately brown in 3 minutes. Drain on brown paper in a warm oven.

BASIC SPAGHETTI SQUASH

Spaghetti squash is a rich, mellow, highly versatile vegetable. Serve it simply with a little butter or dress it up for an entree with a rich tomato or pesto sauce. Here's Lois Burpee's basic recipe.

SERVES 4 TO 8, DEPENDING ON SIZE.

Place whole squash in pan and bake for 45 minutes

at 350°. Or pierce squash in 4 or 5 places and put in a pot of boiling water; cover and boil for 30 to 45 minutes until a fork can pierce it easily.

Remove squash from oven or water and cut in half across the center. Scoop out seeds and stringy fibers. With a large spoon scoop out flesh into a bowl. Using two forks, pull apart flesh so that it separates into slightly crisp spaghettilike strands. (If it doesn't separate, the squash was either too young or not cooked quite enough, but it's still good to eat.) Put the squash in a heavy pot or double boiler, add seasoning, and heat (this will help fibers separate if squash needs more cooking time). If you have too much squash for one meal, refrigerate the extra before heating.

Seasoning

Your seasoning will vary depending on the other dishes you're serving. For about 3 cups cooked squash, use these basic seasonings and the additions that follow:

> ½ teaspoon salt
> ¼ teaspoon nutmeg
> 1½ tablespoons butter
> Choices to add to above: 1 teaspoon lemon
>   rind when serving with fish; 1 teaspoon
>   grated fresh orange rind and 1 rounded
>   tablespoon brown sugar when serving
>   with poultry or ham; ½ teaspoon mace
>   when serving with beef

Spaghetti squash is also delicious with your favorite spaghetti sauce or any other pasta sauce. Or try it as a salad with a vinaigrette dressing.

All prepared dishes of spaghetti squash freeze well. Thaw first if they are to be heated. Frozen spaghetti squash salads are good both cold and heated.

STEWED RHUBARB

Stewed rhubarb has been a spring favorite in this country for many, many years. Here is a basic recipe from *Lois Burpee's Gardener's Companion and Cookbook* that allows the rhubarb to retain its shape and color through baking rather than slow cooking on top of the stove.

SERVES 4 TO 6.

> 10 stalks rhubarb (about 1¼ pounds) cut into
>   ¾-inch-long pieces

> 1 cup sugar

Preheat oven to 300°.

Pour boiling water over rhubarb and let stand for 5 minutes. Drain and spoon into a glass or ceramic baking dish that can be covered. Do not fill to the top. Shake sugar over rhubarb and place in oven. After 15 minutes, stir gently so all pieces are in the juice. Cover and return to oven for 15 minutes more. Remove rhubarb from oven, taste, and add more sugar if needed.

Additions to stewed rhubarb: raisins (preferably golden) are good. Strawberries—even just a few—are nice, but a good proportion is 1 cup berries to 4 cups rhubarb added after the first 15 minutes of cooking. Use strawberry syrup or strawberry jam for some of the sweetening.

CREAMED CORN

Here are Lois Burpee's comments on an easy way to scrape corn for creaming—which simply means serving the scraped corn warm. "This is a way to have corn without the hard-to-digest skin of the kernels. Put ears in boiling water, a few at a time, and remove them as soon as it has returned to a boil. Cool the

The late Lois Burpee has shared some favorite all-American recipes in her book Lois Burpee's Gardener's Companion and Cookbook.

ears under cold water. Take a scorer and run it up and down the ear. Hold the ear tip down on a plate and, with the back of a firm knife, scrape the insides of the kernels out, starting at the tip and working up. If you don't press too hard, the skins remain on the cob like an empty honeycomb.

"It is easier to scrape out raw corn, but the milk in the corn will spurt all over your kitchen. If you choose to do it raw, spread plenty of newspapers around.

"Warm the scraped corn in a double boiler or, if the oven is being used anyway, in a casserole in the oven. If your corn is a bit old, some milk and a little sugar will revive it.

"I like creamed corn with chicken and turkey. It's also good with ham. Include a green vegetable in the meal."

MOTHER'S BREAD-AND-BUTTER PICKLES

Bread and butter pickles are an American institution. Lois Burpee certainly appreciated them, as her introduction to her recipe indicates: "These pickles spread over bread and butter were a treat for my mother when she visited her grandmother on the family farm in Connecticut. They are my favorite to serve with any meat and also to add to a green salad to give it a surprise touch when I have no tomatoes or aspic to use. I also make golden beet pickles in a similar way. (Other vegetables are good preserved this way, too, such as zucchini and cauliflower.)"

MAKES ABOUT 12 PINTS.

> *2 dozen unpeeled cucumbers no more than 1½*
> *   inches in diameter*
> *8 medium onions*
> *½ cup salt*
> *1 cup water*
> *5 cups white vinegar*
> *5 cups sugar*
> *1½ teaspoons tumeric*
> *½ teaspoon ground cloves*
> *2 teaspoons mustard seed*
> *1 teaspoon celery seed*

Thinly slice cucumbers and onions and layer in a bowl, sprinkling salt between layers. Add 1 cup water

and let stand for about 3 hours. Strain.

Cook remaining ingredients over low heat, stirring until sugar dissolves. Add cucumber and onion mixture. Heat very slowly until hot but not quite boiling. Put in sterilized jars while hot and seal at once.

GREEN TOMATO PIE

In many American homes the beginning of fall is heralded by a green tomato pie, made with the fruits that were saved from the first frost and served as a dessert. This is another recipe from *Lois Burpee's Gardener's Companion and Cookbook*.

SERVES 6 TO 8.

> *4 to 5 really green tomatoes*
> *Pastry for an 8-inch 2-crust pie*
> *1½ cups brown sugar*
> *3 tablespoons flour*
> *Grated rind of 1 lemon*
> *6 tablespoons lemon juice*
> *½ cup golden raisins*
> *¼ teaspoon salt*
> *¼ teaspoon allspice*
> *¼ cup minced candied ginger*

Put tomatoes through a coarse grater or a food processor's large shredder. There should be 2½ cups. Put in a colander and let drain overnight. Or prepare tomatoes in the morning and press out their juices from time to time throughout the day.

Prepare your favorite double pie crust, roll out half, and put in an 8-inch pie pan. Roll out the other half and set aside. Mix remaining ingredients with tomatoes, place in pie shell, and cover with top crust. Prick holes in crust. Bake in a 450° oven for 10 minutes; then reduce heat to 350° and bake 40 minutes longer.

SCALLOPED POTATOES

Vary the flavors and colors of this simple and classic dish by adding to the layers other thinly sliced vegetables and/or fresh herbs, such as dill, basil, or chives. Other appetizing additions are thinly sliced smoked ham, cheese, onion, or leeks, a bit of cayenne, or a dusting of paprika.

SERVES 6 TO 8.

*2 pounds potatoes (about 6 medium), peeled
    and thinly sliced
3 tablespoons flour
4 tablespoons butter
Salt and pepper to taste
Approximately 2 cups milk*

Preheat oven to 350°.

Butter a flat-bottomed casserole or baking dish approximately 7 by 12 inches and at least 2 inches deep. Make 3 layers of the ingredients, starting with ⅓ of the potatoes. Sprinkle with 1 tablespoon flour, dot with 1 tablespoon butter, and season with salt and pepper. Repeat with next 2 layers, finishing with 2 tablespoons butter. Add just enough milk to cover potatoes. Cover casserole and bake for 1 hour. Remove cover and bake ½ hour longer to brown the top.

VEGETABLE FRITTERS

Traditional fritters are made with fresh sweet corn that is mature but not doughy (delicious!), but you can also make excellent fritters with other vegetables, such as zucchini, minced green beans, grated broccoli, asparagus, carrots, or winter squash. You might need to vary the amount of flour used slightly in accordance with the moisture content of the vegetables.

SERVES 4.

*3 cups scraped sweet corn (see scraping
    directions in creamed corn recipe above,
    or scrape raw) or other vegetables
2 eggs, separated
¼ teaspoon salt
1 to 2 tablespoons flour
Approximately 1 tablespoon oil or butter
Recommended additions: Choose from black
    or cayenne pepper, minced fresh hot or
    sweet peppers, minced fresh herbs, grated
    sharp cheese, minced ham or clams,
    minced onion or shallots*

Mix vegetables with egg yolks in a medium bowl; add salt and flour. Add chosen additions. Beat egg whites stiff and fold into vegetable mixture. Drop by spoonfuls into hot oil or butter in skillet or on griddle, browning on each side, 3 to 4 minutes per side. Serve as a side dish or for breakfast or dessert with maple syrup (for the latter, omit additions).

HARVARD OR ORANGE BEETS

Famous Harvard-red beets are sweet and sour, and beets in orange sauce are tangy too. One recipe will do for both, since the technique for preparing them is the same.

SERVES 6 TO 8.

*1 cup orange juice and 2 tablespoons grated
    orange rind OR ⅓ cup vinegar, ½ cup beet
    cooking water, and ⅓ cup sugar
1 tablespoon cornstarch
3 tablespoons butter
¼ teaspoon each salt and pepper
4 cups cooked beets, diced or sliced*

In the top of a double boiler over hot water or in a pan at a very low heat, combine all ingredients except beets (dissolve cornstarch in some of the liquid before combining). Cook, stirring often, until sauce is thickened. Add beets, heat thoroughly, and serve.

GLAZED CARROTS

I generally don't peel garden carrots; a gentle scrubbing promptly after picking is all the cleaning they need. But peeling is important in this recipe to keep the thin skin from separating and muddying the dish. The cooking time necessary for carrots to become tender varies enormously, depending on their age, growing conditions, and size; watch carefully and don't overcook.

SERVES 3.

*2 cups carrots, peeled and cut into a
    convenient eating size; if small, leave
    whole
1½ tablespoons butter
2 to 3 tablespoons brown sugar or orange
    marmalade
Pinch of nutmeg or mace and salt
Parsley to garnish*

Boil or steam carrots until they just start to become tender, 3 to 10 minutes. Drain and reserve cooking water. Put carrots in a pan on low heat to evaporate moisture. Add remaining ingredients and coat carrots. Then add ½ cup reserved cooking water and roll carrots around until nicely glazed and hot. Pour into a bowl, garnish with parsley, and serve immediately.

FRIED GREEN OR RIPE TOMATOES

It's a rare gardener who doesn't have green tomatoes left at the end of the growing season. Here's a tasty way to prepare them—so tasty, in fact, that I sometimes prepare them early in the season before I have my first ripe tomato. If you use ripe tomatoes, they must still be quite firm.

Cut into ½-inch-thick slices and coat on both sides with cornmeal, flour, or bread crumbs, or a combination of these, which have been seasoned with salt and pepper (and herbs, too, if you like). Fry over medium heat in butter, oil, or bacon fat until lightly browned on both sides. You can make a gravy out of what's left in the pan by stirring in a little milk, bringing to a simmer, and pouring over the tomatoes.

STEWED TOMATOES

These are great hot or cold. Serve with a chunk of fresh garlic bread or croutons.

To peel tomatoes, drop each one into a pot of boiling water for about 15 seconds. Remove and let cool or rinse in a pan of cold water, and the skins will come off easily. Cut in half and gently squeeze out the seeds into a sieve over a bowl. Cut halves again and place in a pot along with the sieved juice. If you like, add some chopped peppers, onion, garlic, celery, herbs, salt, pepper, and sugar. Simmer, uncovered, stirring frequently for 15 to 30 minutes to thicken slightly.

ZUCCHINI BREAD

This traditional way of using some of that extra zucchini has become an American classic.

MAKES 2 LOAVES.

3 eggs
1½ cups white or brown sugar
1 cup vegetable oil
1½ teaspoons vanilla

3 cups flour, unbleached, whole wheat, or a
*   combination*
1½ teaspoons baking powder
1 teaspoon baking soda
2 teaspoons cinnamon
½ teaspoon nutmeg
½ teaspoon ginger and/or ¼ teaspoon allspice
*   (optional)*
3 cups grated zucchini
½ to 1 cup each raisins and/or chopped nuts
*   (optional)*
2 standard loaf pans

Preheat oven to 350°.

In a large bowl, beat eggs. Beat in sugar and then oil and vanilla. Sift dry ingredients into mixture and stir. Add zucchini (and nut and raisins, if desired) and stir well. Pour into 2 well-greased loaf pans and bake 45 to 60 minutes.

STRAWBERRY SHORTCAKE

No summer should go by without at least one strawberry shortcake from the garden—a treat almost as American as apple pie. Another traditional strawberry dish, strawberry-rhubarb cobbler, is made in a similar way; the recipe follows that for shortcake here.

SERVES 4 TO 6.

Biscuit Dough

2 cups sifted all-purpose flour or whole-wheat
*   pastry flour*
1 tablespoon baking powder
1½ tablespoons sugar
½ teaspoon salt
⅓ cup butter or margarine
¾ cup milk
Additional melted butter

Filling

3 cups strawberries
1 cup heavy cream
1 teaspoon vanilla
1 tablespoon powdered sugar
¼ cup sugar

Preheat oven to 425°.

In a large bowl, sift first 4 ingredients together. Cut in butter or margarine with a pastry blender or knife and fork. Make a well in center and stir in milk. Stir briefly to mix, then turn onto a floured board and knead gently and briefly. Divide into 2 equal parts and roll and pat each one to the size of an 8-inch round cake pan. Place first layer in pan, brush with melted butter, and then place second layer over it and bake for 15 to 20 minutes. Let cool in pan 15 minutes, then remove and finish cooling on a rack.

Stem and slice strawberries, reserving 10 to 15 beautiful ones for garnish. Just before serving, whip cream with vanilla and powdered sugar. Sprinkle sliced strawberries with sugar, and mix gently. Place bottom half of shortcake on serving plate, spread with about half the whipped cream and all the sliced strawberries. Add top layer, remaining whipped cream, and reserved berries, halved or whole.

STRAWBERRY-RHUBARB COBBLER

SERVES 8.

> *4 cups strawberries, washed and halved*
> *4 cups rhubarb, cut into ½- to 1-inch pieces*
> *1 cup sugar*
> *2 tablespoons cornstarch, flour, or tapioca*
> *(use 1 tablespoon if fruits are particularly dry)*
> *1 recipe biscuit dough for strawberry shortcake (see recipe above)*

Preheat oven to 350°.

Butter a 9-by-13-inch baking dish (or one of approximately the same size) that is at least 2 inches deep. Mix fruits with sugar and thickener and pour into dish. Make biscuit dough (but do not divide), roll it out, and place over fruit. Or use ½ cup less flour and drop dough evenly over fruit. Brush with melted butter and bake for about 30 minutes. You may substitute 8 cups of any other fruit for strawberries and rhubarb. Serve with vanilla ice cream.

Sources

Seed Companies

1. W. Atlee Burpee Company
   Warminster, PA 18991

Burpee carries all the varieties mentioned in this chapter. The firm publishes a 180-page general seed catalog that lists both flowers and vegetables.

2. Gurney Seed & Nursery Company
   Yankton, SD 57079
   Gurney has a large catalog full of vegetable varieties for the home gardener. It carries many hybrids as well as both familiar and unusual open-pollinated varieties.

3. Harris Seeds
   Moreton Farm
   3670 Buffalo Road
   Rochester, NY 14624
   Harris is a large seed company that does much research. It carries a large array of varieties for the home gardener, including many hybrids. If you are a beginning gardener or are particularly interested in disease-resistant varieties, select your varieties from Harris's "Vegetables of Special Merit" list.

4. Twilley Seed Company
   P.O. Box f65
   Trevose, PA 19047
   Twilley is a large seed company that offers many varieties, including many hybrids, for the home gardener. See the map in the front of its catalog for recommendations on varieties well adapted to your particular climate.

5. Park Seed Company
   Cokesbury Road
   Greenwood, SC 29647
   This family-owned seed company carries many of the vegetable varieties mentioned in this chapter, as well as many other varieties for small gardens. Park uses a "High Performer" designation to indicate varieties it considers the most potentially successful.

6. Stokes Seeds, Inc.
   P.O. Box 548
   Buffalo, NY 14240
   Numerous varieties mentioned in this chapter are available from Stokes.

Books

Burpee, Lois. *Lois Burpee's Gardener's Companion and Cookbook*. New York: Harper & Row, 1983.
    In this book, Lois Burpee, wife of David Burpee

and hostess at the Burpee home for many years, assembled many of her favorite recipes from the garden.

Fell, Derek. *Vegetables: How to Select, Grow, and Enjoy.* Tucson: HP Books, 1982.

A basic book on vegetable growing written by one of this country's most knowledgeable gardeners. The author gives detailed growing instructions and much variety information.

Hawkes, Alex D. *A World of Vegetable Cookery.* Rev. ed. New York: Simon & Schuster, 1984.

A comprehensive cookbook covering basic vegetable cooking and containing many unusual vegetables and recipes.

Morash, Marian. *The Victory Garden Cookbook.* New York: Knopf, 1982.

This cookbook is a must if you have a garden. Morash tells in the greatest detail how to prepare vegetables and gives numerous recipes for all the basic ones.

National Gardening Association. *Gardening: The Complete Guide to Growing America's Favorite Fruits and Vegetables.* Reading, Mass.: Addison-Wesley, 1986.

A comprehensive guide for growing edible plants, this book contains basic growing information as well as details for individual vegetables and fruits. This one's a must for the vegetable gardener's library.

Rombauer, Irma S., and Marion Rombauer Becker. *Joy of Cooking.* Rev. ed. Indianapolis: Bobbs-Merrill, 1975.

If you have only one cookbook in your kitchen, this should be it. It covers just about every aspect of basic cooking you can imagine and certainly contains all the standard American recipes.

PART
TWO

INTERNATIONAL
GARDENS

I T HAS TAKEN A WHILE for my image of myself to catch up with reality. I remember squirming as a child when my best friend's mother put raisin sauce on my ham or mustard seeds in the coleslaw. It was usually worth suffering through these indignities, however, because that nice lady made a fabulous lemon meringue pie that followed most meals. How do you suppose someone who would guiltily leave a pile of raisins at the side of her plate turned into a food adventurer?

For decades now I have listened to friends recount the adventures they have had going white-water rafting or hiking in the Great Smoky Mountains. Only recently has it dawned on me that I have had adventures, too—vegetable adventures. Once, in Rome, I was seeking out agricultural bulletins on unusual Italian vegetables and fruits. Arriving at the Depart-ment of Agriculture building, I asked the guard by the door to let me in. Probably viewing me as the typical American tourist and thinking I was in the wrong place, he said politely, "Agriculture, Madam." "*Si*, agriculture," I said. "No, Madam, agriculture." "*Si*," I said. Some frustrating minutes later, he finally led me inside to find someone who could speak English. As it turned out, the only person in this cavernous building who could converse with me at that moment was the minister of agriculture himself. I described what I was looking for to the minister; he seemed intrigued by my project and invited me to sit down for a moment. He was busy getting ready for a Common Market summit, he told me apologetically, but his aide would see what he could do. After spending some time on the phone, the aide handed me a list of people to see and directions on

Like many of the new seed company owners, Renee Shepherd, owner of Shepherd's Garden Seeds, has selected a number of specialty vegetables for her catalog. Renee offers many European vegetables in particular and includes recipes featuring them in her catalog.

Pallavi Fancy holds a platter of East Indian vegetables, including two kinds of green beans, eggplants for stuffing, warty bitter melons, and turmeric rhizomes.

how to find them. Needless to say, the red carpet was out. Anything I wanted to know about Italian agriculture was mine that day.

On another occasion, my quest for food information led a friend and me to the Cairo bazaar. While there, we were approached by a gentleman who could only be described as Charles Boyer with a missing front tooth. His name was Solomon, and with great charm he offered to show us the bazaar—the *real* bazaar. I made a snap judgment that I was too old to be sold into slavery, assessed my guide as being knowledgeable by asking him a few questions about Egyptian vegetables, and followed the fellow into the *real* bazaar. We were soon certain of being far from the tourist path when Solomon led us into an alley and kicked a dead cat out of the way. The grime of centuries made the footing underneath uneven, and the narrow passageways, sometimes only two or three feet wide, set a dramatic stage. But soon we were threading our way among piles of Egyptian white eggplants, utterly unfamiliar turbaned melons, piles of fresh ginger, baskets and baskets of flower petals—lavender, orange, and rose—huge baskets of saffron, ground turmeric, and chilies, and jars of rose water for teas and pastries. Solomon showed us how to make mint tea. He explained how the tea merchants made their rounds down the alleys, keeping track of their deliveries by making chalk marks on the ancient walls. I learned much about Egyptian foods that day, but more than that, I came away with indelible exotic memories. Frankly, I wouldn't trade my morning with Solomon for any rafter's rapids or any hiker's exhilarating climb.

I'll always be open to food adventures. I'm eager to visit the markets and gardens of the Caribbean to learn more about 'Habanero' peppers. I hope to spend more time someday harvesting an English garden and sampling different pea and leek varieties. I've fallen in love with the way Thai cooks use combinations of lemon grass, mint, and hot peppers, and I want to learn more about their vegetables. And I've found that you needn't travel far to have "foreign" experiences. I spent one of my most exciting days ever visiting the community gardens in Sacramento, California, and talking with Laotian and Hmong gardeners there. I saw round, white eggplants the size of golf balls with delicate green-lace markings, fluted pumpkins, and numerous herbs I've yet to identify in English. On another occasion, I spent hours with Mexican-American gardeners in their community plots discovering their burgundy-colored corn varieties and timidly tasting chilies. I needed a translator to help me with the actual words and variety information, but not for the sharing of the garden. A big tomato is a big tomato worldwide, and a giant bell pepper will elicit a smile in any country.

There is no better way to begin to know other peoples and cultures than through their gardens and food. The chapters in Part Two cover a wide range of ethnic gardens and cuisines—Italian, French, German, Mexican, and Oriental—including unusual as well as familiar vegetable species and varieties, along with myriad vegetable preparation and exotic cooking techniques. You'll find some real culinary treasures as you peruse these chapters—baked sweet fennel, mouth-watering Alpine strawberries, a *Römertopf* brimming with pheasant and sauerkraut, tamales stuffed with fresh corn, and a stir-fry made with home-grown fresh ginger. Let your garden and your kitchen carry you round the world!

Italian Gardens

M Y TAXI DRIVER IN ROME was sure it was a mistake and sent me back into the hotel to have someone translate the note I had handed him. It was six o'clock in the morning, and my note said, in Italian, "Please take me to the Rome produce market." Once there, I understood immediately why the driver thought I had made a mistake. The place was alive with people, verbal abuse was being exchanged all around, and utter chaos reigned. I was a little on edge, but after one glimpse at the stacks of spectacular and unfamiliar vegetables everywhere in sight, I relaxed. I had dedicated more than ten years to edible plants, and it was exciting to see some I didn't know. And now I'd find out why vegetables and fruits I'd been eating in restaurants throughout Italy had been so outstanding.

I was intimidated at first by all the shouting, but within minutes, the passion both vendors and buyers showed for the produce put me at ease. Besides, how can a food lover be cool in front of a waist-high pile of purple artichokes? The men beamed at my continued delight as I wandered through the stalls and exclaimed over sculptured chartreuse broccoli, purple

OPPOSITE: *Italian vegetables can be beautiful as well as delicious. The chartreuse broccoli with the sculptured turrets is a rich-tasting variety called 'Romanesco'. It is accompanied by radicchio, artichokes, and a spray of redbud, which is sometimes pickled in Italy.*

cauliflower, and stalks of miniature fava bean plants covered with pink flowers. "Do you eat the leaves *and* the flowers?" I tried to ask, eliciting shrugs and loud laughter. I wondered about the contorted stems of what looked like celery and marveled over bright magenta spheres. "Radicchio!" the vendor cried. We all exchanged fabulous gestures as I tried to put English words to vegetables and varieties I'd never seen before.

Prior to my trip to Italy, Italian vegetables had meant mostly zucchini and tomatoes to me. The herbs were garlic and basil, and Italian cuisine was primarily pizza and spaghetti. Now I know that while these items are Italian, they make up only a small part of the cuisine. I learned about marinated vegetables—bright red peppers and sweet onions with fennel, all bathed in olive oil and herbs. I came to love deep-fried cardoon (a close relative of the artichoke) and to savor slices of sweet cantaloupe wrapped with prosciutto, and bagna cauda, a vast range of raw vegetables dipped in cream and olive oil flavored with anchovies and garlic. I consumed loads of pesto and memorable salads made with endive, tangy arugula, and radicchio. And the pasta! I sampled sauces far more imaginative than our nearly mandatory tomato sauce. In Italy, pasta is made in a wide variety of shapes and might be served with a cream sauce and crowned with fresh baby peas or string beans. What revelations! What bliss!

I returned from Italy filled with enthusiasm and, already missing the food, determined to track down the vegetables and herbs I had seen and learn how to cook them. I visited Italian markets, perused specialty seed catalogs, and interviewed Italian gardeners. The latter two sources yielded the most information. A love of gardening is part of the Italian cultural heritage, and, together with frustration at the limited selection and quality of supermarket vegetables, this had inspired many of the Italian-Americans I had met to plant extensive gardens filled with unusual vegetables. The owners of the specialty seed companies, too, had often begun their businesses out of frustration with the limited varieties of European seeds generally available here. They had discovered the Italian vegetables and were as excited about them as I was.

No wonder Americans, using supermarket produce that often tastes like the cardboard it's packed in, simply can't duplicate the "taste of Italy." Americans might have recently discovered fresh pasta, and some American gourmets are spending eight dollars

a pound on radicchio. But it looks like anyone who wants to achieve the rich spectrum of tastes of true Italian cooking is going to have to plant a garden!

How to Grow an Italian Garden

Most of the vegetables and herbs planted in an Italian vegetable garden are grown in the same way American vegetables and herbs are, and both gardens commonly contain tomatoes, peppers, lettuce, beans, and zucchini. There are differences, though. Italian tomato varieties are often paste types, the sweet peppers frequently long and thin rather than short and blocky, the green beans often flat romanos, and eggplants generally smaller and either elongated or round. The seeds of these varieties usually must be ordered from specialty seed companies and are readily grown in American gardens. Other Italian vegetables that are easily grown in America gardens include arugula (rocket), broccoli raab, sweet fennel, and large- and small-leafed basils.

Because Italy is on the Mediterranean, its climate is characterized by long, hot summers with very little rain, fairly mild winters, and a long spring and fall. The long growing season gives the Italian gardener the opportunity to plant slow-maturing plants, such as some of the chicories (radicchios), garlic varieties, and some varieties of sweet peppers; to plant vegetables that like a long, cool spring, such as fava beans and cardoon; to enjoy the tender perennial artichoke; and to sun dry tomatoes with ease. In the United States a similar climate can be found in parts of California, Texas, Arizona, and New Mexico. American gardeners in other states who want to grow these plants will have to make cultural changes in some cases or choose similar varieties that need less heat or long, cool weather.

See the California garden of Vicki Sebastiani to learn how Italian varieties are planted in a Mediterranean climate and the Gilberti garden in Connecticut to see how they are grown in a more northerly climate. See "Recommended Italian Vegetables" for specific variety information for all kinds of climates. Finally, for a detailed guide to growing unusual Italian vegetables, consult *Gourmet Gardening,* by the editors of *Organic Gardening* magazine.

The Sebastiani Vegetable Garden

Vicki Sebastiani and her husband, Sam, are vintners and food enthusiasts who live in the Sonoma Valley of California. Vicki has been a vegetable gardener since the age of four. Her current garden is unusually large, because she and Sam entertain great numbers of visiting dignitaries throughout the year. I visited Vicki to talk specifically about Italian gardening. Her garden contains a hundred varieties of vegetables and herbs (most of them Italian), including red and yellow varieties of Italian tomatoes, white eggplant, Italian yellow and light-green zucchinis, giant cau-

liflowers, variegated and red chicories, and her favorite, yellow romano beans.

Vicki's vegetable garden is a special place. It is designed with long stone planter boxes arranged in a somewhat informal oval-shaped area. The garden has benches and wrought iron archways and is bordered by a low stone wall and rose garden on one side and an inlaid stone patio and a small pond on the other. The vegetable garden is the focal point of the area, and visitors enjoy wandering through the garden as well as viewing it from the patio tables when dining. Vicki says most people have never seen many of the vegetables she grows and enjoy both seeing them and tasting some of them at mealtime.

To plant her Italian vegetable garden, says Vicki,

The Sebastiani vegetable garden includes dozens of Italian varieties of vegetables and herbs, such as tomatoes, chicories, cardoon, zucchini, basil, eggplants, broccoli, and salad greens. The paths are lined with stone to reduce weeding and to create a beautiful focal point for the patio area.

Vicki Sebastiani is a stickler for authenticity. Her huge garden in Sonoma County, California, doesn't merely resemble an Italian garden; it *is* an Italian garden. Vicki imports many of the seeds herself. This marks her as a true adventurer among the relatively few dedicated American gardeners bent on ignoring geographical boundaries in selecting their seeds.

Over the last few years, as I talked with gardeners and restaurateurs, I became more aware of unusual vegetables I had never seen before. Many were heirloom American varieties, but still others were from Europe and Japan: radicchio, mâche, yellow romano beans, and dwarf pac choi, for instance. I also found that the gardeners and seed people who were going beyond our tried-and-true American bush beans, corn, and tomatoes sometimes even ordered seeds from abroad. Because of their experimentation and the public's growing interest in foreign vegetables, most of these varieties are now available through a number of small seed companies, whose addresses are given in "Sources" at the end of this chapter. However, while it is quite expensive, if you'd like to contact some of the foreign seed companies and try some varieties not yet available in the United States, you could benefit from Vicki Sebastiani's experience.

Vicki found that she couldn't get seeds from American companies for all the varieties of Italian vegetables and herbs she wanted. Furthermore, some of the vegetables she grew here in America didn't taste the same as what were supposedly the same vegetables in Italy. So Vicki brought seeds home with her after a trip to Italy; then, when she wanted more, she started ordering directly from Italian companies.

Vicki's favorite Italian supplier is Fratelli Ingegnoli. "I've found you can write your catalog request letter in English," she notes, "since they seem to have someone in the office who speaks English. When you receive the catalog, you'll find that it contains many

Vicki Sebastiani

full-color pictures to help you select the items you want. I just love going through it and seeing the pictures of yellow romano beans, purple artichokes, the colorful borlotto and cannellone beans, many varieties of radicchios, paste tomatoes, pink eggplant, and all the unusual zucchinis.

"The catalog includes an order blank, and since it's somewhat similar to those in American catalogs, you can sort of figure it out. If you feel intimidated, or your order is complicated, I'm sure you could find someone who speaks a little Italian, or take the order blank to a local high school and ask someone in the language department to help you. Once you've totaled your order, go to a full-service bank and get an international money order in lire. Send the completed order blank, together with the money order, in the envelope the company provides, to Fratelli. They usually send your seeds within a few weeks."

Vicki had some words of advice about your Fratelli order: "Fratelli used to carry only Italian varieties but now has seeds from all over the world. Since it doesn't make sense for you to order seeds that the company has imported from the United States, avoid those described in the catalog as '*seme originale americano.*' The seeds arrive in the mail, having no apparent problem with Customs. They come in small, brown packets printed entirely in Italian. I clip out the color photo of each vegetable I order from the catalog and attach it to the seed packet so I know what I'm planting." (For information on Vicki's experience with particular Italian vegetable varieties, see "Recommended Italian Vegetables" later in this chapter.)

Following Vicki's lead, I ordered my own Fratelli catalog, and, once I overcame the anxiety of not being able to read the order blank, I found the company quite easy to work with. They did understand what I wanted. Here are some tips, gleaned from my own ordering experience. Note that variety names in the Fratelli catalog are bracketed by the symbols ⟨⟨⟩⟩. Also, be aware that other gardeners who have ordered from Italian seed companies suggest that many of the Italian varieties are apparently not as widely adaptable as some of our hybrids; so, from our experience, Vicki and I recommend that you grow such varieties as an experiment, not as your main planting. Be aware, too, that variety names sometimes differ in their spellings, and even in their wordings, owing to diverse regional usage.

For Vicki, who specializes in Italian influences in her cooking, authentic Italian vegetables offer an exciting challenge both in the garden and in the kitchen.

"in late winter I send away to specialty seed companies for authentic varieties of Italian vegetable seeds. I order my American varieties from Gurney and Burpee, and I glean the Italian varieties from some of the large American companies, plus poring over some of the specialty seed company catalogs, such as Le Marché and Shepherd's Garden Seeds. I purchased a few of the Italian varieties when I was in Italy and ordered others from an Italian seed company, Fratelli Ingegnoli. But now that quite a few Americans are ordering from Fratelli, the price of the catalog has gone up to ten dollars." (See the profile of Vicki in this chapter for details on how to order seeds from Italy.)

To get a jump on the season, Vicki starts her tomatoes, peppers, eggplant, squash, basil, and the forcing chicories and cardoon in flats early in the spring so that she can transplant them into the garden after all chance of frost has passed. As the soil starts to warm up in spring, she plants the seeds of some of the early vegetables, such as lettuce, beets, carrots, fava beans, endive, arugula, and fennel. In early summer she starts the leaf chicories for fall harvest and a little later the broccolis for the next spring harvest.

The plants Vicki grows reflect a rich heritage of vegetables that are at the heart of Italian cuisine. To give you a idea of this vast range of vegetables, as well as the huge selection of Italian varieties unfamiliar to Americans, these are some of her favorites: romanesco broccolis, both the bronze and the chartreuse types; a purple spouting broccoli; 'Pepperoncini' peppers for pickling; 'Roma' and 'San Marzano' tomatoes for sauce; white and green varieties of pattypan squash; brown salsify (*scorzonera*); the peppery arugula; many chicories, including 'Palla Rossa', 'Castelfranco', 'Treviso', and a Catalonian type; three varieties of Italian chard; white and purple eggplants; Italian parsley; yellow and green romano beans; and a type of large vining zucchini that produces long, meaty fruits with almost no seeds. For detailed descriptions of most of these vegetables, see "Recommended Italian Vegetables" later in this chapter.

Vicki uses her garden vegetables for everyday eating, as well as to create meals for the many visitors the Sebastianis have from all over the world. The vegetables become part of an antipasto or minestone or, in many cases, are simply steamed or boiled lightly and served with olive oil and parmesan cheese. As Vicki says, "When you start with superior vegetables picked at the peak of perfection, they're very special in themselves." For details on how Vicki prepares many of these vegetables, see "Recommended Italian Vegetables" later in this chapter.

A Miniature Italian Herb Garden

You needn't plant a large Italian garden such as the Sebastianis' to get a strong sampling of authentic Italian flavors. Perhaps a miniature Italian herb garden—maybe even one planted in Italian olive oil or cookie cans—would better suit your needs and space limitations. This small garden can fit on an apartment balcony, on a sun porch, or in a greenhouse in the winter. A few basil plants alone can produce enough herbs to garnish tomatoes and enliven salads throughout the season. And one small oregano plant can make a big difference in homemade spaghetti sauce or pizza.

Last summer my closets bulged with beautiful but bulky empty cans, once filled with Italian olive oil, coffee, and amaretti cookies. I could never bring

If you want only a small garden, try planting a miniature Italian herb garden. The author's herb garden includes 'Spicy Globe' basil, Italian parsley and oregano, rosemary, and thyme, all planted in Italian olive oil and amaretti cookie cans.

myself to throw them away; they were too pretty. Then I realized I could use them as containers for herbs. They would be perfect for decorating the front steps of my garden.

You don't need Italian cans to create this garden—any good-size garden container will do—but they're not hard to find. When I visited a few Italian delicatessens and restaurants to see how easily I could find empty olive oil cans, the proprietors said they would be happy to save some for me. To get coffee and cookie cans, buy them full and empty them yourself.

Once you have the cans, use a can opener to remove the tops of olive oil cans and a church key to make a few drainage holes in the bottoms of all of them. Then fill the cans with a good potting mix and plant the herbs as you would in any other container. In hot weather, the sides of the cans will get hotter than clay or wooden pots would, so you will need to water your plants often and shade the sides of the cans. (See the list of herbs in the "Culinary Herb Gardens" chapter for more information on growing herbs.)

Choose the Italian herbs you will use the most. If you look through recipe books, you will find the following among those most frequently used in Italian cuisine:

BASIL   *Ocimum Basilicum; basilico*   Basil is the queen of Italian herbs. In fact, it is used in such quantities that you might call it an Italian vegetable. One plant of this easily grown warm-season annual will produce enough leaves to use as seasoning in soups and sauces and now and then for sliced tomatoes. For five to six pints of pesto, grow at least three plants. The variety I find best for growing in containers is 'Spicy Globe'. Start basil seed in the spring or buy plants of regular sweet basil from a nursery. Grow standard basil in the larger olive oil cans or the medium-size amaretti cans; 'Spicy Globe' can be planted in coffee cans.

BORAGE *Borago officinalis; borragine* Borage is another easily grown annual herb. Its blue starlike flowers and cucumber-tasting foliage make it a pleasure to grow. Only the very young tender leaves and the flowers are edible, so keep borage well watered and fertilized to continually stimulate new growth in containers. Start borage seeds in the spring and grow them in medium-size cans.

CHIVES *Allium Schoenoprasum; erba cipollina* Chives are perennial herbs that provide tasty leaves for about six months and grow very well in containers. Both the leaves and the flowers are edible; the flowers are delicious separated into florets and sprinkled over soups and salads. Buy plants in the spring or start your own from seed; grow chives in coffee cans.

FENNEL *Foeniculum vulgare; finocchio* Fennel is an annual herb noted for the sweet anise flavor of its leaves and seeds. Start it from seed in the spring. Fennel is a large plant (two to three feet tall), so plant it in at least a one-gallon olive oil can or a large amaretti cookie can.

OREGANO, ITALIAN *Origanum vulgare; origano* Oregano is a perennial herb used frequently in Italy, particularly in the southern regions. One plant provides all of the herb you need. Some specialty herb nurseries carry a very pungent variety, referred to as Italian oregano, which you might want to try. Buy oregano plants in the spring or summer and plant them in medium size cans.

PARSLEY, ITALIAN *Petroselinum crispum; prezzemolo* Italian parsley is a flat-leafed plant that is more pungent than what Americans commonly use. Seek it out; it makes quite a difference in the taste of Italian cooking. Put in two or three plants to produce a generous amount and grow in the same way you would grow standard parsley. Buy seeds or plants in the spring and use medium-size containers.

ROSEMARY *Rosmarinus officinalis; rosmarino* SAGE, *Salvia officinalis; salvia* THYME *Thymus vulgaris; timo* These are sturdy perennials used sparingly in Italian cuisine. Purchase plants any time of the year.

You don't need much of any of them; so if you don't have many cans, combine two of them in a medium-size can, as I do, or plant singly in smaller cans.

The Gilbertie Vegetable Garden

When you visit Tresa Gilbertie's Connecticut garden, you can't help but be impressed by her tomatoes, neatly trained plants laden with the largest plum tomatoes you've ever seen. When I visited Tresa in August, her garden was nearing its peak production: in addition to tomatoes, her peppers and eggplants were covered with fruits, Italian parsley and basil plants needed to be harvested again, and a second planting of bush beans was about to go into full production. A square bed of lush New Zealand spinach looked as if its enthusiasm were being carefully controlled by harvesting, and leeks, escarole, and garlic would also soon be ready. If I had visited in the spring, I would have seen rows of arugula, Catalonian chicory, and salad greens. And because Tresa's garden is in the middle of her son Sal's herb nursery, lots of herbs grow all season long. Many years ago, Tresa helped her husband grow vegetables and cut flowers for the trade, and she later became active with his herb nursery, now run by their son. Tresa still helps in the nursery as well as maintaining her own vegetable garden.

Tresa's main garden area measures twelve by fifty feet. Everything is planted in manageable short rows, kept weed free, and bordered by garlic chives, which Tresa feels help keep pests away. In an adjacent plot she grows arugula, melons, and zucchini. The gardens have been in place for many years and are now in fine shape, so she only adds perlite or peat moss occasionally to maintain them. Every spring, though, she digs and loosens the soil again. As she says, "You have to keep the soil around the plants loose in order to have them really produce for you." During the growing season, she fertilizes every month with superphosphate and 5-10-5. Tresa never uses pesticides and asks, "Why would I want to eat any of those chemicals?" To control her major pest, the Japanese beetle, she places traps around the garden. "The traps really help," she says, adding with a smile, "but of course you have to tie the bags securely when you throw them away or the beetles just fly out."

Tresa Gilbertie grows wonderful plum tomatoes in her Connecticut garden. Her aunt brought the seeds from Italy years ago, and to keep them going, Tresa saves her seeds every year.

Tresa really lights up when you mention her outstanding tomatoes—mostly huge, bright red plum (or paste) tomatoes from seeds her aunt brought from Italy years ago. As I caressed a perfectly ripe tomato, smelled its rich aroma, and wondered how many seeds were in it and if I could get some, she offered to give me a few fruits. She had obviously encountered people who covet before. These flavorful tomatoes are the foundation of Tresa's cooking; she uses them to make a rich sauce (or "gravy," as she calls it) and soups. "I can't get used to what comes from the store; it doesn't even come close," she says. She cans only fifty or sixty jars of sauce a year now because she cooks mostly for visiting children and grandchildren, but she used to can many more. Because her plum tomatoes have so much flavor and pulp, she uses them in her sauce, making sure they are very ripe. She cuts them in quarters, cooks them in a large pot without any added liquid for about fifteen minutes, runs them through a sieve to remove the skins and seeds, pours the sauce in canning jars, adds a little salt, and processes them in a canner.

"Of course this makes great gravy, but if you want it really rich, you make it the way my mother used to, by drying the tomato sauce instead," Tresa notes. "We don't do that today, but nothing beats the flavor. You cook your tomatoes for fifteen min-

utes or so, put them through a sieve to remove the seeds and skins, and then put the sauce out on a board in a sunny place, like on a porch. Stir the mixture off and on for a few days until it gets thick and is still soft but starting to get a little leathery. Then take it off the board, mix it with olive oil, put it in a crock with a little fresh basil, and cover it. When you take it out to use it, it will be like paste, the very essence of tomatoes."

Tresa grows the vegetables and herbs that are the heart and soul of Italian cuisine. Talking with her can only make you envy her children and grandchildren as she describes her garden-fresh minestrone, her eggplants and pasta smothered in her own tomato sauce, her spinach pie, and her marinated vegetable salad. She also describes a garden sandwich that gave my secretary such a wave of nostalgia that, as she typed, she determined to have one for supper. Her grandmother had made garden sandwiches for her when she was a child, and she remembered them as luscious and filled with sweet cooked onions, peppers, and garlic. See "Cooking from the Italian Garden" for some of Tresa's tastiest recipes.

Recommended Italian Vegetables

Listed below are some of the most popular Italian vegetables along with recommended varieties and seed sources. I give both the Italian and Latin names in case you want to select seeds from an Italian catalog. The numbers in parentheses next to most variety names correspond to the seed companies listed in "Sources" at the end of the chapter. For varieties carried by most of the nurseries listed, no numbers are given.

Most Italian vegetables and herbs, such as beans, eggplant, tomatoes, and basil, are grown as are their American cousins, and you can consult Part Four, "An Encyclopedia of Superior Vegetables," for cultural information. For the more unusual vegetables, basic growing instructions are included here. If you need more detailed information about these vegetables, consult *Gourmet Gardening*, by the editors of *Organic Gardening* magazine.

ARTICHOKES *Cynara Scolymus; carciofi* The usual variety offered in this country is 'Green Globe', but if you want to grow an authentic Italian variety for novelty's sake, order 'Violetto' artichoke seeds (5, 7). 'Violetto' produces purple artichokes, not the usual green ones.

How to grow: See the Part Four Encyclopedia.

How to prepare: According to Paul Bertolli, chef at Chez Panisse in Berkeley, California, purple artichokes are sliced very thin as a chiffonade and eaten raw in Italy. See the recipes in "Cooking from the Italian Garden" for more ideas.

BEANS *Phaseolus vulgaris; fagioli (rampicanti,* pole; *nani,* bush) Many types of beans are beloved in Italy. Choose from green, cannellone (white kidney-shaped), and borlotto (similar to white or pink pintos) beans, as well as favas.

While Italians use varieties of green beans similar to our American ones, they also favor broad, flat types of green and yellow beans called romano beans and coiled ones called anellino beans (5, 7). The romano and anellino beans seem to have a richer bean flavor than most green-bean varieties and are worth seeking out. These Italian beans come in both bush and pole varieties, and all are grown as are the green beans to which you are accustomed.

Shelled beans are also widely grown in Italy, particularly cannellone (5) and borlotto (5) beans. Use these beans fresh or dried. Both are traditional ingredients in minestrone soup and antipasto salads.

Vicki Sebastiani's favorite Italian variety is the pole bean 'A cornetto largo giallo Burro d'Ingegnoli' (5, 7). This is a variety of yellow romano beans. Vicki describes this bean as very tender and almost buttery in flavor. She also favors the bush bean 'Cannellone bianco' (5), a variety of cannellone beans.

How to grow: See the Part Four Encyclopedia.

How to prepare: In Italy green beans are usually steamed and served al dente, often with olive oil instead of butter. Sometimes Parmesan cheese or garlic is added. The romano beans, particularly the yellow ones, must be watched carefully during cooking, as they will turn to mush very quickly. Vicki Sebastiani recommends flash steaming the yellow romanos and serving them drizzled with olive oil.

Fresh shelling beans are usually served with olive oil, Parmesan cheese, and garlic or as a bean salad.

BROCCOLI *Brassica oleracea; cavoli broccoli* In addition to the familiar heading green broccolis, Italians grow ancient sprouting broccolis (7, 8), useful to the home gardener because they produce numer-
ous small heads over a long season. Also popular are broccolis of different colors— there are purple and white varieties of both the heading (5, 7) and sprouting (8) types. The green and purple sprouting types have proved more vigorous in my garden than the white one I tried. While I love sprouting broccoli, my favorite broccoli is 'Romanesco' (2, 5, 7, 8, 9). This truly beautiful cool-season broccoli is chartreuse and grows in sculptured, conical turrets. There seem to be a number of strains of this vegetable that vary greatly in vigor and climate adaptation. Though 'Romanesco' is sometimes temperamental about heading up, if you get a strain that is suitable for your climate, its sweetness and rich texture will spoil you for ordinary broccoli.

How to grow: See the Part Four Encyclopedia.

How to prepare: The sprouting and romanesco types of broccoli are very tender and cook more quickly than standard types of broccolis. Small florets of both can be marinated and used in antipasto or steamed and served over fettucine.

BROCCOLI RAAB *Brassica campestris; broccoletti di rapa, cime di rape, sparachetti* (3, 7) Broccoli raab is actually the flower shoot of a type of turnip. This easily grown vegetable deserves wider recognition.

How to grow: The seeds are sown in spring and grown as turnips are, but with one big difference: the plants are wintered over and the shoots harvested the next spring.

How to prepare: In its second spring the plant sends up shoots and then flower stalks. These are eaten blanched or steamed, served with olive oil and garlic.

CARDOON *Cynara cardunculus; cardoni* Cardoon is a wild relative of the artichoke, but unlike the artichoke, the cardoon's stalks, not its flower buds, are eaten.

How to grow: Sow seeds of cardoon (3, 5) in early spring, inside in cold climates and outside in mild-winter ones. Plant the seedlings or seeds in a trench about a foot deep in which the soil has been well prepared with organic matter. Keep the plants very well watered and fertilized to produce vigorous growth or the stalks will be bitter and tough. In the fall, to make the stalks sweeter and more tender, blanch them as you would celery. Gather up the leaves, tie them together, wrap them with plastic or paper, and put three or four inches of straw around them to prevent rotting. Then mound the plant with soil.

After a month, harvest the stalks by cutting them off at soil level. Alternatively, bend them to the ground and cover them well with a mulch to protect them from freezing; then harvest later. Another option for cold climates is to dig up the roots before the nights get too cold and place them in a box in the basement and blanch them there.

For more general information on climate considerations and cultural requirements, see the Part Four Encyclopedia under "Artichoke."

How to prepare: Remove the tough outside stalks and string as you would with celery stalks. Cut the stalks into three-inch pieces before cooking. To prevent discoloration, preblanch for five to seven minutes in water to which a couple of tablespoons of vinegar or lemon juice have been added, then discard the water. This will remove some of the bitterness. Steam until tender. Serve the steamed stalks with olive oil or herb butter. Or cook as a fritter, use in tossed salads, or marinate and use as a dramatic part of your antipasto presentation.

CHICORY   *Cichorium Intybus; cicoria*   Chicory is a leafy vegetable that has a much appreciated, mildly bitter taste. No cuisine in the world does as much with chicories as the Italian. Italian seed catalogs usually list many different types. This diversity can make the subject of chicories very confusing for the novice. All chicories are botanically *Cichorium Intybus,* but we eat the root of some and the leaves of others. (To further complicate things, chicories are sometimes confused with their close relatives the endives, *Cichorium Endivia.*)

The leaf chicories are more popular in Italy than the chicories grown for their roots, those that are used in coffee, or Witloof (also known as Belgian endive). In Italy, leaf chicories are one of the staple greens of the winter table. Red chicories are preferred in the north, and green varieties are preferred in the south. In fact, many of the chicories are identified by the areas they come from—for example, Verona, Treviso, and Chioggia.

In the United States we usually refer to the red chicories as radicchio, but in Italy it is common to refer to all chicories by that name. The red chicories can be braised or roasted but are usually eaten raw; they make a colorful addition to an antipasto dish or a green winter salad. There are two types of red chicories, or radicchios: forcing and nonforcing. (See the information on forcing—also called blanching—

in the "French Gardens" chapter.) 'Treviso' (2, 5, 7, 9) and 'Rouge de Verona' (2, 5, 7, 9) are the best known of the forcing types. Of the nonforcing types, 'Castelfranco' (2, 5, 7) and 'Chioggia' (5, 7) are both variegated red and white, and 'Palla Rossa' (2, 7) is green on the outside and red inside. A new type of radicchio, developed for spring planting, is 'Giulio' (7, 9). It will turn red even in warm weather and is resistant to bolting. All radicchios are strikingly beautiful.

Among the green chicories are the Catalonian, also called dandelion or asparagus chicories. These are particularly prized for their stems. Varieties to look for are 'Catalonian Puntarella' (2, 5), with its strangely twisted stems, and 'Catalonian Dentarella' (2, 5), which looks something like a large dandelion plant. Two other green chicories are less well known in this country: 'Grumolo' types (5), which look like deep-green lettuce and are quite bitter, and 'Pan de Sucre' types (5, 7, 9), upright light-green types that look something like Chinese cabbage. The 'Pan de Sucre' types are considered the sweetest of the chicories.

How to grow: My experience with growing chicories suggests that they are definitely cool-season crops; in warm weather they are much too bitter to eat. Besides, most of the red ones are actually red for only a short time—after a good frost. Start the nonforcing types of chicories from seeds in June or July and enjoy them after the weather cools down, when their bitterness decreases. In most climates they can be wintered over to produce another crop in the spring. Plant the forcing varieties in July and harvest them in the fall. (In cold climates start forcing chicories in late spring.) For the best quality, cut off the foliage in early fall and let the heads resprout and produce their firm rosettes for early winter. For a mild flavor, wrap the heads to prevent light from reaching the leaves, as you would with Belgian endive. Wrap the heads of the red varieties, too, to produce the white-veined, intense magenta colors you see in the produce market. Forcing varieties can be harvested again in the spring if they make it through the winter.

American gardeners still have a lot to learn about growing chicories. Most of our climates are quite different from those in Italy, and we have to inform ourselves on which of the various types grow best in which part of the country. Tresa Gilbertie says she gets the best Catalonian dandelion-type chicory by planting it in the fall and harvesting it in the spring.

It winters over well in Connecticut and is sweeter in the spring than in the fall. Shepherd Ogden (see the "Gourmet Salad Gardens" chapter), who lives in Vermont, reports that some of his chicories will winter over in his garden if he gets a good snow cover. Growers in California are finding they can grow chicories in much the same way the Italians do.

How to prepare: Most of the leaf chicories are served raw in salads or as part of an antipasto, and sometimes they are grilled. The Catalonian types are used as pot herbs, usually seasoned with oil and lemon juice or sautéed with garlic after parboiling.

EGGPLANT   *Solanum Melongena; melanzana*   Eggplant is one of Italy's favorite vegetables. Try some of the Italian varieties for a change—a white variety (5, 8), say, or my favorite, 'Rosa Bianco' (7, 8), with its large, deep-lavender, creamy-textured, and mild-tasting fruits.

How to grow: See the Part Four Encyclopedia.

How to prepare: Eggplants absorb flavors well and may be browned and served with Parmesan cheese or tomato sauce, used in lasagne, sautéed with garlic, and used in casseroles and even salads.

FAVA BEANS   *Vicia Faba; fava*   Ancient Romans relied on the broad fava-type beans as one of their staples, and while modern Italians still enjoy them, these beans were generally displaced a few hundred years ago when New World string- and kidney-type beans were introduced. Favas are cool-season beans that are shelled and used fresh or dried. For Americans in northern climates, they can be an interesting substitute for limas. In Italy, their special sweetness is prized, particularly when they are harvested very young. Once these tasty beans are fully mature, though they are very flavorful, their skins must be peeled off before preparation, and this is a real labor of love.

How to grow: In mild-winter areas plant favas in the fall. These beans need a long, cool growing period of about ninety days and can even take repeated light frosts. To plant, prepare the soil well and plant seeds two inches deep, about two to three inches apart, in rows about a foot and a half apart. The plants will grow quickly to three to four feet in height. Favas are sometimes bothered by black aphids and bean beetles. See Appendix B, "Pests and Diseases," for pest-control information. For young, tender beans, harvest when they first start to fill out the pods. Or let the beans mature and use them fresh or dried.

How to prepare: Fava beans are eaten as you would limas. Simmer or stir-fry the young ones and use the older beans in hearty soups or with meats.

Caution: Some males of Mediterranean descent are allergic to favas and should be wary when trying them for the first time.

FENNEL   *Foeniculum vulgare; finocchio*   Sweet fennel is a favorite Italian vegetable and is often included in antipasto dishes and salads. This ferny-topped plant, about two feet tall, looks a little like a swollen white celery. It is easy to grow and generally requires cool weather, but Vicki Sebastiani has had much success growing it in the summer.

How to grow: In areas of the country that have hot summers and cold winters, fennel is started in summer for fall harvest. In mild-winter areas, it is started in fall and harvested in spring. It requires from 80 to 110 days to mature. Plant seeds one-half inch deep—preferably in soil with a pH of about 7—and thin to about six to eight inches apart. Keep the plants well watered. Fennel plants are relatively resistant to pests and diseases. Harvest the plant when the "bulb" at the base is three to five inches across.

How to prepare: Use the slightly anise-flavored stalks as you would celery. Vicki Sebastiani recommends braised fennel drizzled with olive oil and sprinkled with anchovy bits. Serve as part of an antipasto, use the leaves and stalks in salads (combine with oranges and pine nuts for a refreshing salad), or just steam the stalks and sprinkle with melted butter and Parmesan cheese.

PEPPERS   *Capsicum* spp.; *peperoni*   The 'Pepperoncini' (1, 7) pepper is among the most traditional of Italian pepper varieties. It's great pickled and used in antipasto. Another Italian classic is a slightly hot pepper marinade using 'Corno di Toro' (7), a yellow pepper, and 'Corno di Toro Rouge' (7), a red one.

How to grow: See the Part Four Encyclopedia.

How to prepare: Many Italian sweet bell-type peppers are used raw, in salads and antipasto, or roasted and marinated. The spicier ones are sometimes pickled or used in soups and stews.

SALAD VEGETABLES   Lettuce, *Lactuca sativa; lattuga*   Rocket, *Eruca vesicaria* ssp. *sativa; rucola* (or *arugula*)   Corn salad, *Valerianella olitoria; valeriana*   Salads in Italy consist of more than our usual combination of iceberg lettuce and tomatoes. Lettuce is native to the Italian peninsula, and the home gardener can choose from dozens of varieties of Italian lettuces. Try 'Perella Red' and 'Perella Green' (7), the red-tipped 'Rossa di Trento' (2), the superior cutting lettuce 'Biondo a foglie lisce' (2), and a ruffled red lettuce variety called 'Lollo Rossa' (7, 9). To duplicate Italian salads, you could start by ordering a premixed package of seeds that includes the traditional combination called *misticanza* (2, 5) or *saladini*, a blend of four kinds of lettuce and five chicories.

How to grow: See the Part Four Encyclopedia.

How to prepare: Italian salads are generally a mixture of many different types of greens with complementary flavors—some tangy, some bitter,and some sweet. The ingredients of the Italian salad will change with the seasons. Salads are often dressed with a simple dressing of olive oil and vinegar or lemon juice. If wine is to be served with the salad, it's generally lemon, not vinegar, that is used. For more information, see the "Gourmet Salad Gardens" chapter.

SALSIFY, BLACK   *Tragopogon porrifolius; scorzonera* This black-rooted vegetable has a slightly oystery flavor. A close cousin is white salsify, called *scorzobianca* in Italian.

How to grow: Scorzonera (3) is as easily grown as its close cousin, salsify. A root vegetable, it is best grown in a deep, sandy soil. Plant in spring and harvest about 150 days later. Pull the roots up gently or you might break them off in the ground.

How to prepare: Many people enjoy the somewhat oysterlike flavor of *scorzonera* when the roots are steamed with the skin on, peeled, and then served hot with butter or a cream sauce. The roots are also nice in soups. But be warned: the black ones will stain your hands if you don't wear gloves when you work with them.

SQUASH   *Cucurbita Pepo; zucchetta* The most famous Italian summer squash is zucchini, and although many American varieties are available, the Italian types have unusual qualities you might enjoy. There are zucchinis of different colors, striped or white zucchinis, round ones good for stuffing, and some with flowers that are particularly well suited for sautéeing or stuffing—for example, 'Sardane' (9) and 'Romano F1' (7). One variety that Vicki Sebastiani raves about is the *zucchetta* 'Tromboncino' (2, 5, 8), a thin zucchini, twelve to eighteen inches long, that is light green and has a two-inch bell-shaped seed cavity at one end. The majority of its fruit is solid meat. This squash grows on long, vigorous vines instead of the usual bush, so you can grow it on a trellis.

How to grow: See the Part Four Encyclopedia.

How to prepare: In Italy summer squash is used in numerous ways. One of the easiest is to steam and serve it with Parmesan cheese and tomato sauce. Summer squash is used raw in salads and with dips, baked, or sautéed.

TOMATOES   *Lycopersicon esculentum; pomodori* The tomato is king in Italy. Its meaty red fruit is used in a great number of ways, particularly in the southern parts of the country. Many of the slicing-type tomatoes are similar to ours, though some varieties are fluted rather than round. In the many varieties we call paste tomatoes, Italians have perfected the tomato's taste. Paste tomatoes are used fresh in sauces and are also sun dried and reconstituted for winter use. Tomato varieties you might want to try are 'San Marzano' (5, 9), 'Roma' (7), and 'Super Italian Paste' (8). Vicki Sebastiani recommends trying any of the Italian varieties from Fratelli Ingegnoli. She recommends theirs over the varieties such as 'Roma' or 'San Marzano' that are commonly grown in the United States, because in her experience the Italians seem to be growing a different, more flavorful strain.

How to grow: See the Part Four Encyclopedia.

How to prepare: In Italy large slicing tomatoes are generally eaten raw, sometimes served with olive oil and fresh basil. The paste (or plum) tomatoes are preferred for cooking. See the recipes in "Cooking from the Italian Garden" and Vicki Sebastiani's and Tresa Gilbertie's comments on Italian tomatoes.

Cooking from the Italian Garden

Italian cuisine is glorious! Considered the "mother cuisine" for most of Europe, it has its roots in ancient Rome. Cabbages, artichokes, broccoli, peas, chard, lettuce, fennel, mint, parsley, melons, apples, as well as wine and cheese, many kinds of meats, and grains were all enjoyed by upper-class Romans. For feasts Roman cooks used many spices, developed recipes for cheesecake and omelettes, and roasted all types of meats. From this noble beginning, a sophisticated and flavorful cuisine has emerged.

OPPOSITE: *Antipasto is one of the most versatile ways to enjoy garden vegetables. Pictured here are 'Purple Sprouting' broccoli, baby carrots, fennel, roasted peppers, and artichokes.*

Paul Bertolli

Paul Bertolli has been chef at Chez Panisse restaurant in Berkeley, California, for five years and has also cooked and traveled in Italy. During his stay in Italy, Paul worked with vegetables from the Florence produce market while cooking at restaurants in that city as well as with vegetables from an extensive garden at Villa La Pietra, a private residence where he was chef. I asked Paul to comment generally on Italian vegetables and their preparation and then on some of the individual vegetables.

The vegetable garden at Villa La Pietra was staffed by four gardeners. While there, Paul saw a few vegetables he'd never seen before, such as Tuscan black cabbage (a green to black or forest green member of the cabbage family that sends up large, slightly curled leaves from a thick central stem), artichokes with purple buds, and a number of greens and herbs that were gathered from the wild. But he was most impressed that the vegetables—even those that might be considered common—"were just really so good; great little string beans, red and white shelled beans, and the tomatoes all were outstanding."

In Italy, "a common way to feature certain fresh vegetables, such as mushrooms, fennel, celery, and radishes, is to slice them very thinly," Paul explains. Italians do this, for instance, when making a salad. Back in the United States, Paul uses a refined method in which he shaves the vegetables with a mandoline, an implement that you can purchase from a cooking supply store or order by mail from a cooking equipment company (see Appendix C, "Suppliers"). Mandolines range in price from about six dollars for a plastic model to more than a hundred dollars for a professional model. To protect your hand when using a mandoline, be sure to wear an oven mitt or use a mandoline guard, which must be purchased separately.

One vegetable often sliced in Italy is the artichoke. "In Italy," Paul says, "I saw artichokes with purple buds. They were wonderful. I think they're probably the only artichokes suitable for eating raw, which is how they're often served. They were usually sliced very thinly." Paul cautions that you must pick fresh, small artichokes in which the chokes have not yet developed, or, for a different effect, use only the hearts of older artichokes. To prepare an artichoke, remove the tough outside leaves, cut off the top and most of the stem, pare the leaves remaining at the base, and slice very thinly or shave on a mandoline. Cut from the stem to the top of the artichoke. You'll end up with a pile of shavings that look similar to planed wood. Because artichokes discolor very soon after they are cut, be prepared to serve them immediately. Just before serving, drizzle with virgin olive oil, salt and pepper them, and add a few drops of lemon juice; then make thin shavings of Parmesan cheese with a cheese slicer and scatter them on top. For variation, top slices of *bresaola*, very thinly sliced air-cured beef, with dressed artichokes cut in a similar manner. Or for a fancy dish, try Paul's artichoke, fresh cèpes (porcini mushrooms), white truffle, fennel, and Parmesan cheese salad. To make this salad, layer the artichoke with shaved cèpes, shaved heart of fennel, and shaved white truffles. Dress as above and garnish with shaved Parmesan cheese.

One of Paul's favorite vegetables is fennel. When it's more fibrous, he likes to string it like celery. "Or, instead, you can just use the inner heart," he says. "In this country, I feel fennel isn't used enough. It has such a sweet flavor and goes well with so many other vegetables. It, too, can be served shaved, like the artichoke salad."

Paul says he experienced several different varieties of chicory when he lived in Treviso near Venice. "I think the best I ever had were 'Verona' chicories that were very bitter because they had been left growing at the sides of the fields since the previous season and had not been blanched, a growing process that mitigates their bitterness. You see them all over alongside the fields. Some people consider them to be weeds—rather too strong and bitter to eat at that point—but I used to pick them because I loved them. Many Italians in the countryside eat the bitter chicories, but what you generally see commercially in the markets are the milder blanched types of all those chicories. I don't care for the market varieties; I prefer a strong, bitter flavor. As a chef, you're always dealing with things that have these fine flavors. When I eat a strong chicory, I prefer to slice it very thinly. The dressing coats the sliced chicory more thoroughly, and this makes it seem less bitter. Sliced chicory is good combined with thinly sliced onions and drizzled with good red wine vinegar." Paul also likes the Catalonian-type chicory, which Italians tie up and grill. After grilling it, they usually serve it topped with anchovies, onions, and olive oil.

Cime di rape, or broccoli raab, Paul notes, is sometimes picked in Italy when it is tiny and leafy. Italians stew *cime di rape* and serve it with loin of pork that has usually been spit-roasted or braised. The pork is then served on a whole nest of these greens.

In Italy, arugula is used primarily in salads, but Paul sometimes likes to use it as a seasoner or herb. For instance, he uses it in ravioli: "I make pigeon ravioli and add a little arugula. I also use it on celeriac soup. It's a wonderful garnish."

If you'd like to try Paul's baked eggplant and tomato dish or his gratin of fennel and new potato creation, you'll find the recipes in "Cooking from the Italian Garden."

After the excesses of Roman banquets, where quantity was more important than quality, centuries of cooks on the Italian peninsula selected the best of the ancient cuisine and continued to pursue the art of cooking. Building on their Roman heritage, they adopted foods from Arabs who invaded them, learning to use sugar, for example, to make ice cream and almond-paste confections. In the late Middle Ages Italian cooks perfected bread making and started making pasta. In addition, Italian sailors, traveling the world for spices, brought back flavorings from the Far East. In the sixteenth century, the first modern cooking school was opened in Florence. Not until Catherine de' Medici and the then king of France, her father-in-law, Francis I, brought Italian chefs and many cooking techniques to France did the rest of Europe begin to catch up to Italy in the great art of cooking. Even though France became a great center of cuisine and eventually surpassed Italy in some of the very complex methods of food preparation, cooking remained a high art in Italy as cooks continued to explore new ways to prepare foods and new ingredients to add to them. In fact, it was Italian chefs who first embraced many of the foods of the New World in the early 1500s. Italians quickly learned to appreciate snap beans, tomatoes, peppers, squash, and potatoes, and eventually these wonderful vegetables found their way into much of European cooking.

Today, many of the staple foods of the last three or four centuries in Italy are still enjoyed. The vegetables—the foods I'm most interested in here—have been refined and selected over the years for their superior tastes and growing ease. And even though most Italians share a somewhat similar basis for their cuisine, the foods in one part of Italy can be quite different from those in another, because of regional differences in history, economics, and climate. For example, the foods of much of northern Italy are prepared with butter and cream. Pasta is often freshly made rather than dried, and it often contains eggs and is rolled out into flat noodles. A special dish of Piedmont, near the French border, is bagna cauda. This rich dish is a sauce made with cream, butter, garlic, and anchovies and is used as a dip for cold vegetables. Traditionally, the Piedmontese dip strips of cardoon, but they also enjoy using fennel, cauliflower, and peppers. Near Venice, in Treviso and Verona, the slightly to strongly bitter chicories (radicchios) are much prized; they are enjoyed as salad greens or sometimes roasted. In nearby Padua fritters are made with squash blossoms. Vegetables abound in the vicinity around Rome, where broccoli is cooked in wine, olive oil, and garlic; little peas are served in spring, sometimes cooked with tiny morsels of prosciutto ham and served on pasta; fennel is prepared as a cold dish with a dressing; and white haricot beans are baked with pork rind. Most of these dishes would not be found in more southern parts of Italy.

The dishes of southern Italy are, as a rule, more heavily spiced than those of the north, redolent of basil, oregano, and garlic. The primary cooking oil is made from olives, because butter is not easily obtained as cows do not produce well in the hot climate. Sauces are often made with sun-ripened tomatoes and olive oil. The primary pastas are dried and tubular in shape and usually do not contain eggs. A favorite dish of Naples, considered the heart of southern Italian cooking, is a sauce for pasta made with tomatoes, onions, bacon, and garlic. A fish soup from Abruzzi contains onions, tomatoes, garlic, bay leaves, and parsley for seasonings. Throughout much of southern Italy, favorite vegetables are red peppers, eggplants, tomatoes, spinach, and artichokes.

Over the years, as Italian cuisine has been refined, it has not evolved into a cuisine filled with complex dishes as is common in much of France. Instead, it has remained elegantly simple. Italian cuisine is often described as unadorned and honest, and, as Waverly Root comments, "The apparently simple cooking of the Italians is, in fact, more difficult at times to achieve than the more elaborate and refined French cooking. Things have to be good in themselves, without aid, to be exposed naked." In his book *The Cooking of Italy*, he adds, "Fruits and vegetables must be picked at the right time, neither one day too early nor too late. They must not travel far, must not be preserved beyond their allotted season by chemicals and refrigeration."

Given Waverly Root's comments, you can see why a garden of fresh, well-grown vegetables and herbs becomes a critical part of truly fine Italian cooking. In addition, since Italian cuisine is so unadorned, not only the vegetables and herbs, but all the starting ingredients must be the best. When you follow the recipes given here, use only the highest-quality olive oil—"extra virgin" for salads and a superior brand of "virgin" olive oil for cooking. Store the oil in the refrigerator so that it stays fresh. The Parmesan and other cheeses must also be of the best quality; canned versions will obliterate, not highlight, the flavor of your vegetables. Visit a a good Italian delicatessen and stock up. This may seem expensive at first glance, but you will use only small amounts of these ingredients and they will make a big difference in your cooking.

Experiment with new Italian recipes. In Italian cuisine more than any other, fresh vegetables and herbs have become *haute cuisine*. In Giuliano Bugialli's

Foods of Italy, for example, you can find recipes for vegetable compote with dry zabaione, pepper salad with capers, and carabaccia "of the full moon," made with fresh peas, carrots, and fennel. Bugialli states that "vegetables, even more than pasta, are the cornerstone of Italian cooking." With the produce from your Italian garden you can now truly create the tastes of Italy.

CAPONATA

Caponata is a wonderful way to use eggplant. The flavor improves if the dish is stored for a day or two in the refrigerator, but it's so tasty that you may have to make a large batch to keep it around that long. It's often served as part of an antipasto, but it also makes a lovely salad served on lettuce or endive and garnished with other vegetables.

SERVES 10 TO 12.

> *½ cup olive oil*
> *1 cup chopped celery*
> *1 large onion, chopped*
> *1½ pounds eggplant (1 large, about 3 cups), diced*
> *¼ cup wine vinegar*
> *1 cup chopped tomatoes*
> *2 teaspoons sugar*
> *2 tablespoons capers*
> *½ cup chopped Italian green olives*
> *½ teaspoon freshly ground black pepper*
> *2 tablespoons fresh minced parsley*
> *Salt to taste*
> *2 tablespoons each pine nuts and raisins (optional)*
> *2 tablespoons chopped fresh basil or 1 teaspoon dried basil (optional)*

In a large frying pan, heat oil, add celery and onions, and sauté over medium heat until tender. Remove with a slotted spoon to a large bowl. Add eggplant to same pan and sauté until golden brown and tender; then add to vegetables in bowl. Add vinegar, tomatoes, and sugar to pan; cover and cook 5 minutes, stirring occasionally. Return vegetables to pan with remaining ingredients and simmer uncovered (or, if not moist enough, cover pan) 10 to 20 minutes, until vegetables and seasonings are well blended. Cool and chill, but serve at room temperature.

MARINATED VEGETABLE ANTIPASTO

Antipasto means "before the meal," and its happy purpose is to excite the taste buds. Italians tend to eat small portions of a number of courses, and this is usually the first one. An antipasto straight from the garden can be stunning, showing off vegetables to advantage and opening the meal without being too rich or too filling. Garden vegetables good in antipasto include asparagus, artichokes, beans, beets, cardoon, carrots, chicory, eggplant, fennel, onions, peppers, and tomatoes.

Here are two antipasto combinations to get you started.

Marinade I

SERVES 4.

Vegetable suggestions, blanched and chilled, include cauliflower, broccoli, carrots, mushrooms, cardoon, and Catalonian chicory.

> 1 cup white wine vinegar
> 1 clove garlic, pressed
> 1/2 teaspoon mustard seeds
> 1/4 cup chopped fresh basil or 1 teaspoon dried basil
> 1/4 cup chopped fresh oregano or 1 teaspoon dried oregano
> 4 tablespoons olive oil
> 1 tablespoon fresh chopped parsley

In a nonaluminum saucepan, bring vinegar, garlic, and mustard to a boil. Add to remaining ingredients in a medium bowl. Add about 1 pound cut-up vegetables (amount depends on type of vegetables used and your taste) that have just been blanched about 3 minutes. Toss lightly, cover, and refrigerate at least 2 hours, stirring occasionally. Drain before serving.

Marinade II

SERVES 6 TO 8.

Use any of the vegetables above and/or the following: pickling onions, carrots, celery, sweet peppers, summer squash.

> 1/2 cup water
> 1 1/2 cups wine vinegar
> 1 cup olive oil

Fava beans are a treat served in the traditional Italian way—drizzled with a little virgin olive oil and sprinkled with fresh oregano and Parmesan cheese.

> 2 tablespoons sugar
> 2 teaspoons minced fresh oregano
> 1/2 cup pitted olives
> Freshly ground pepper and salt to taste

Wash vegetables and cut into bite-size pieces. In a saucepan, bring marinade ingredients above to a boil. Add approximately 2 quarts cut-up vegetables; cover and cook 3 to 4 minutes, stirring once. Uncover, cool, and refrigerate for at least 2 hours. Drain before serving.

BAGNA CAUDA

According to Teresa Candler, author of *The Northern Italian Cookbook: Vegetables the Italian Way*, this dish originated as a farmer's lunch during the grape harvest. It was cooked at home in an earthenware casserole and then taken to the vineyard and warmed over an open fire. The men would dip fall vegetables and crusty bread into it.

SERVES 4 TO 8.

2 cups heavy cream
1/4 cup olive oil or butter
2 teaspoons pressed garlic
6 to 8 anchovy filets, rinsed, dried, and finely
    chopped
Black pepper

In a small, heavy saucepan, reduce cream to 1 cup by simmering gently for about 15 minutes, stirring almost constantly. In another small pan, cook garlic in oil or butter on low heat until soft but not brown, about 5 minutes. Add anchovies; cook and mash them into garlic about 5 minutes longer. Gradually stir anchovy mixture into cream and bring to a low simmer. Season with pepper. Keep warm over a flame or hot tray and dip raw vegetables and crusty bread or bread sticks into the sauce.

MINESTRONE

As with many classic dishes, there is no set recipe for minestrone, and in Italy every region has its own version. The Genoese use lots of vegetables, including potatoes, and no herbs in the soup, but they top each bowl with pesto. The Milanese use rice as the starch. The Tuscans first ladle small pasta or stale bread rubbed with garlic into each bowl, then fill it with soup fragrant with rosemary, thyme, bay, and parsley. The idea is to make a hearty, flavorful vegetable soup that contains beans and a starch. When cooking from the garden, let your harvest be your inspiration, and feel free to substitute and vary proportions in accordance with what you have. The recipe below can be used as a basic guideline.

SERVES 8.

1/2 pound cannellini or borlotto beans (or
    substitute other dried beans, such as
    white, kidney, garbanzo, pink, OR fresh
    shelling beans added with the vegetables)
2 quarts water
1 pound beef, ham, and/or chicken bones,
    with or without meat
2 tablespoons olive oil
1 large onion, chopped
2 cloves garlic, minced
1 to 2 stalks celery, chopped
1 1/2 to 2 cups chopped tomatoes, fresh or
    canned
1 medium potato, diced

1/2 cup chopped carrots
1 cup chopped zucchini
1 cup chopped romano beans
1 cup chopped cabbage
1 cup chopped Swiss chard
1/4 cup small pasta
Salt to taste
Pesto sauce (see next recipe)

Soak dried beans overnight in water to cover; drain. In a large kettle, combine water, bones, and beans. Cover and simmer for 2 hours or until beans are very soft. Remove bones and reserve any meat. In a frying pan, heat olive oil and sauté onion, garlic, and celery for about 5 minutes. Add tomatoes and simmer for about 10 minutes. Add this mixture to kettle along with potato and carrots. Cover and simmer 10 minutes longer. Add remaining vegetables, reserved meat, and pasta and cook 10 minutes more. Garnish each serving with pesto sauce.

PESTO

MAKES 1 TO 1 1/2 CUPS.

3 cloves garlic
2 cups fresh basil leaves
1/4 cup pine nuts or walnuts
1 1/2 teaspoons salt
1/4 teaspoon pepper
1/2 to 1 cup olive oil
3 ounces freshly grated Parmesan cheese (or 2
    ounces Parmesan and 1 ounce Romano)

In a blender jar or food processor, combine garlic, basil leaves, nuts, salt, pepper, and half the oil. Puree, slowly adding remaining oil. Transfer to a bowl and add grated cheese, mixing thoroughly. Use immediately or cover with plastic wrap, since pesto turns brown if exposed to air. If you're a garlic fan, increase the quantity to taste.

Serve as a sauce for tagliarini or fettuccine noodles. Try combining cooked French-cut string beans with the noodles, or use pesto to flavor soups, spaghetti, grilled fish, or stews. Pesto may be frozen and kept for four to six months. When freezing, leave out cheese and add it before serving.

Herb substitutions: You can use up to 1 cup of parsley leaves instead of basil with similar results. However, many cooks today are experimenting with pestos of different herbal flavors—thyme, tarragon, or parsley with hazelnuts, for example. See the recipe for cilantro pesto in the "Culinary Herb Gardens" chapter.

PIZZA

MAKES 1 12- TO 14-INCH PIZZA OR 2 SMALLER ONES.

Dough

> ³/₄ *cup warm water*
> *Pinch of sugar*
> *1 tablespoon dry yeast*
> *2¹/₄ cups unbleached flour (or 1 cup whole*
> *wheat and 1 cup unbleached flour)*
> *1 teaspoon salt*
> *3 tablespoons olive oil*
> *Cornmeal*

Preheat oven to 450°.

Pour warm water into a small bowl. Add sugar and sprinkle yeast over mixture; let stand about 5 minutes. Pour flour and salt into a large bowl. Make a well in the center, stir yeast mixture and pour it in, add olive oil, and mix in flour with your fingers until almost all flour has been incorporated and you can form dough into a ball. Turn it out onto a floured board and knead until smooth and elastic, about 10 minutes. Do not knead in too much flour. Oil a large bowl and place dough in it, turning dough to oil all sides. Cover with wax paper and a clean dish towel and set in a warm place to rise until it has doubled in bulk, about 1½ hours.

Punch dough down and knead briefly. You can make a 12- to 14-inch pizza, or divide the dough for 2 smaller ones. Flatten dough into a circle. Gently stretch dough with your hands by turning and pulling on all sides. Lay it down and roll it gently from the center to the edge, making a quarter turn after each roll. Dough may be ⅛ to ½ inch thick, to your preference. Dust a baking sheet or pizza pan with cornmeal. Place pizza on pan, readjusting shape if necessary and crimping edge to form a little rim. Add sauce and toppings (see below) and bake on lowest shelf of oven (or on pizza bricks) at 450° until crust begins to brown, about 15 minutes. (If you'd like to have a frozen pizza ready to use at a later date, make 2 smaller pizzas and top one with sauce and cheese only. Remove the extra pizza from oven before completely done, cool thoroughly, wrap well, and freeze. To use, thaw, add toppings, and bake for about 10 minutes.)

Fresh Tomato Sauce

You will need only a cup or so of this sauce for the pizza, but you can refrigerate the rest for up to a week or freeze it. The sauce can be used in many other dishes (or for another pizza).

> *4 tablespoons olive oil*
> *1 onion, finely chopped*
> *1 tablespoon minced garlic*
> *3 pounds ripe paste (plum) tomatoes, chopped*
> *½ teaspoon sugar*
> *½ teaspoon salt*
> *Freshly ground pepper to taste*
> *1 tablespoon minced fresh oregano and/or 2*
> *tablespoons minced fresh basil and/or*
> *parsley*

In a large, heavy skillet, heat 2 tablespoons of the olive oil. Add onions and sauté until soft but not brown. Add garlic and cook for 2 minutes longer. Add tomatoes, sugar, and salt and cook over medium heat, stirring occasionally with a wooden spoon, until thickened, 30 minutes or longer. Pass through a food mill to eliminate seeds and skins. (Do not blend.) Return to pan and continue cooking if necessary to achieve desired thickness. Add herbs, pepper, and remaining olive oil.

Toppings

Spread about 1¼ cups sauce evenly over dough. Then sprinkle on 1 to 2 cups (8 to 12 ounces) grated mozzarella cheese and any other toppings you like. Be creative and try whatever appeals to you from your garden. (Do not exceed 3 cups of extra toppings; use much less of heavy or juicy ingredients.) Drizzle 2 tablespoons olive oil over assembled pizza before baking. Suggested toppings include the following:

> *¼ cup grated Parmesan, Romano, or pecorino*
> *cheese*
> *1 cup Italian sausage, cooked and crumbled*
> *1 cup pepperoni, sliced*
> *Thinly sliced vegetables: peppers, onions,*
> *mushrooms, zucchini, olives, fennel*
> *Vegetables that have been precooked and*
> *drained: spinach, chard, eggplant,*
> *artichoke hearts*
> *Chopped herbs: oregano, basil, rosemary*
> *Omit tomato sauce and spread pizza with*
> *pesto (see preceding recipe); cook as is or*
> *use other toppings sparingly*

PASTA

Although we are told that noodles were first invented in the Orient, most of us in the United States associate pasta with Italy. And most grew up eating spaghetti and a tomato sauce of some sort. Those of us who have made spaghetti sauce half a dozen times have discovered that we don't need to stick to the recipe exactly, but can sometimes have more fun and get more interesting results by adding ingredients that appeal to us. This becomes even more exciting and delicious when our garden harvest inspires our pasta creations.

For Italians, pasta is a daily staple, but with the infinite variety of noodles, sauces, and additions, it is an ever-changing creative experience. Some classic pasta preparations are offered below to give you a start with your Italian-garden pasta.

A useful rule of thumb regarding quantity of pasta is two ounces of dried or four ounces of fresh pasta per person. (A kitchen scale is handy for this.) If you are ambitious, making your own pasta is fun and satisfying. Fresh pasta has become widely available, and the good brands of dried Italian pasta are still an excellent choice, as they hold their shape and texture beautifully. Whatever you choose, cook to directions and enjoy!

Pasta with Tomato Sauce

The tomato sauce described in the pizza recipe above is a good basic sauce to use with any type of noodles, including lasagne. If desired, after sieving the sauce, add chopped vegetables such as sweet peppers, summer squash, eggplant, or fennel, and cook (or add them precooked). You might also add more herbs in addition to the rosemary and basil, such as thyme, sage, and bay leaves. Ground beef, sausage, or meatballs may be cooked and added. Serve with a good Italian cheese, grated, and a green salad.

Pasta with Cream Sauce

Fresh, shelled peas are an especially good complement to a rich cream sauce, although many other vegetables do beautifully, too. Use tortellini or ravioli filled with cheese, spinach, or meat, or a delicate pasta such as linguini, tagliarini, or fettuccine.

SERVES 6.

2 tablespoons butter
1/4 teaspoon freshly grated nutmeg
1 1/2 cups heavy cream
12 ounces dried pasta or 24 ounces fresh
    pasta, cooked and drained
3 cups shelled peas, cooked for 3 minutes and
    drained
1 egg, beaten with 1/4 cup of the cream above
1 cup freshly grated Parmesan cheese
Optional: dash of cayenne, white or black
    pepper, and/or fresh thyme

In a large skillet, melt butter; then add nutmeg (and other seasoning to taste) and cream, pasta, and peas. Bring to a boil and stir for about 1 to 2 minutes. Remove from heat and evenly stir in egg mixture and cheese. Serve immediately.

Pasta with Vegetables

In creating a pasta dish with vegetables, it's best to use a short noodle, such as shells, macaroni, or spiral noodles. Almost any vegetable or combination of vegetables can be tossed with the pasta and served hot or cold.

To make an easy pasta salad, use leftover or freshly cooked vegetables and a vinaigrette dressing and toss with cooked pasta that has been rinsed in cold water and drained. If you like, add herbs, olives, cheese, hard-boiled eggs, diced cold chicken, and so on.

One option for hot pasta is to cook vegetables in the same boiling water as the noodles (watch the timing carefully so that both are done at the same time). Drain together and toss with a warm sauce of butter or olive oil and garlic, to which you might add herbs, a little tomato sauce, hot or sweet peppers, nuts, and the like. Alternatively, sauté onion and garlic in olive oil and then add vegetables and cook them until tender but crisp. You might also add a few tomatoes or some leftover sauce, a little wine, and seasoning to taste. Toss with cooked, drained pasta and serve with grated cheese.

Baked Pasta

Lasagne is familiar to us, but many pasta dishes can be totally assembled ahead of time to avoid last-minute preparations before servings. Baking gives these dishes a solid texture and unique flavor that you might enjoy. Use tomato or cream sauces to keep the pasta moist and top with cheese before baking.

GRATIN OF FLORENCE FENNEL AND NEW POTATOES

Paul Bertolli, chef at Chez Panisse, contributed this recipe.

SERVES 6.

3/4 pound sweet fennel, bulbs only; reserve
  feathery leaves
1 pound new red potatoes
6 cups water
1 1/4 teaspoons salt
4 large cloves garlic (1 ounce), peeled
Juice of 1/4 lemon
1 cup heavy cream
1/4 cup Reggiano Parmesan cheese
Freshly ground pepper
3/4 cup fresh sourdough bread crumbs
1 tablespoon unsalted butter

Trim the root of the fennel flat with the base of the bulb, remove any tough or discolored outer leaves, and slice the bulbs lengthwise into 1/8-inch-thick pieces. Peel potatoes and slice similarly into 1/8-inch-thick rounds. Place fennel slices in a 2-quart sauce pot. Add 3 cups water, 1/4 teaspoon salt, garlic cloves, and lemon juice. Bring to a boil, reduce to a simmer, and cook gently for 15 minutes.

In the meantime, place potatoes in another pot with 3 cups water and 1 teaspoon salt. Bring to a boil, reduce heat, and cook for 5 to 8 minutes or until potatoes just lose their crunch; do not allow them to soften beyond this point. Drain potatoes through a colander, discarding water, and let them cool.

Remove fennel from water with a pair of tongs, letting garlic remain in pot, and transfer slices to a plate to cool. Raise heat and reduce liquid until it has nearly evaporated. Add heavy cream and whisk well. Turn off heat and pass cream mixture through a medium sieve, using a spatula to push as much of the soft garlic through as possible.

Assembling the gratin: Preheat oven to 350°. Pour several spoonfuls of cream mixture into a small baking dish (8 inches by 8 inches) or oval gratin, just covering the bottom. Alternate slices of fennel and potato, using all the fennel in this first layer. Spoon a little more cream over the layer. Lightly sprinkle with 1/3 of the Parmesan cheese and a little freshly ground pepper.

Use remaining potato slices to form the top layer, arranging them in a scalloped pattern. Lightly press gratin with the palm of your hand so that it is evenly flat. Pour the rest of the cream over, making sure to cover the potatoes. Grind pepper over the top and sprinkle the remaining Parmesan evenly. Bake for 1 hour and 15 minutes.

While gratin is baking, fry bread crumbs in butter to a golden brown. Five minutes before gratin is to come out of the oven, distribute crumbs over the top along with some chopped fennel leaves. Let gratin cool slightly before serving. This dish is delicious with grilled veal chops.

BAKED EGGPLANTS AND TOMATOES WITH BREAD CRUMBS AND BASIL

This is another of Paul Bertolli's recipes.

SERVES 8.

3 globe eggplants (2 pounds)
3 large beefsteak tomatoes (2 pounds)
2 1/2 cups lightly packed sourdough bread
  crumbs
4 tablespoons unsalted butter
2 tablespoons grated Parmesan cheese

Vinaigrette

2 large garlic cloves, minced
1 tablespoon plus 1/2 teaspoon red wine
  vinegar
1/8 teaspoon salt
1/8 teaspoon freshly ground pepper
1/4 cup extra-virgin olive oil
4 tablespoons fresh basil, chopped

Preheat oven to 400°.

Put on to boil a pot of water large enough to contain tomatoes. Peel eggplants with a sharp knife or peeler. Slice eggplants into rounds approximately 1/2 inch thick, discarding hard end pieces near stems. Lay slices on a cutting board and sprinkle with salt and pepper; then turn slices over and arrange them, slightly overlapping, in a nonreactive baking pan approximately 16 × 10 inches. Pour in enough water to come ⅛ inch up sides of eggplant. Lightly salt and pepper second sides of slices. Cover and bake approximately 1 hour or until eggplant is soft but not mushy.

Core tomatoes and drop into the pot of boiling water for 15 seconds. Remove tomatoes from water and place on a plate to cool.

Melt butter, add to bread crumbs, and mix well so that all pieces are coated. Spread crumbs on a baking sheet, place in 400° oven with eggplant, and bake for approximately 20 minutes or until golden brown, turning crumbs every so often with a spatula so that they brown evenly. While bread crumbs and eggplant are baking, skin tomatoes and cut into slices ½ inch thick. Prepare vinaigrette by whisking garlic, vinegar, salt, and pepper together until salt is well dissolved. Add olive oil and 2 tablespoons of the chopped basil and whisk until blended.

Remove eggplant from oven, transfer to a plate to cool, and discard any juices remaining in pan. Cut eggplant and tomato slices in half, producing half-moon shapes. Layer them, alternating and overlapping, in the same pan used for baking the eggplant. Fit any extra pieces into the cracks. Stir vinaigrette again and spoon it over eggplant and tomato slices, distributing basil and garlic evenly. Lightly salt and pepper the vegetables and sprinkle with Parmesan cheese. Put vegetables in the oven, reduce heat to 350°, and bake for 30 minutes. Evenly sprinkle bread crumbs over the top with the remaining 2 tablespoons of chopped basil and bake 15 minutes more. Let cool slightly and serve.

SPINACH PIE

Tresa Gilbertie makes a pie from New Zealand spinach using bread or pizza dough. Traditionally, this recipe is made with regular spinach or chard. If you keep your New Zealand spinach well watered and succulent, and if you pick only the very young leaves, it makes a fine summer substitute for regular spinach.

SERVES 6 TO 8.

3 to 4 pounds spinach
Salt and pepper
Olive oil
1 to 2 cloves garlic, minced
1 to 2 Bermuda onions, diced
Enough bread dough (use your favorite recipe)
*   to line a 9-inch pie pan*

Preheat oven to 375°.

Wash spinach, squeeze out all water, and add a little salt and pepper. Heat olive oil and sauté garlic and onions until tender. Add spinach and cook down until completely limp. Prick dough lining the pie pan, add spinach mixture, and bake for about 40 to 45 minutes. When crust is good and brown, it is done. Serve with beef, chicken, or veal.

TRESA'S GARDEN SANDWICH

This sandwich is a family favorite from Tresa Gilbertie and makes a wonderful lunch.

SERVES 1.

Olive oil
1 sweet pepper, cut into strips
1 clove garlic, minced
1 onion, chopped
3 or 4 fresh basil leaves, chopped
1 large tomato, chopped, or 2 eggs
Pinch of oregano (optional)
1 or 2 thick slices Italian bread

Heat olive oil in a frying pan. Add sweet pepper, garlic, and onion and cook them until wilted. Add basil leaves, tomato, and, if you like, oregano. Cook down just long enough to blend flavors. Remove mixture and spread on a large slab or two of Italian bread. Alternatively, substitute two eggs for the tomato; beat eggs as you would for an omelette, pour over pepper mixture, and cook until firm.

ITALIAN OPEN-FACE SANDWICHES

One of the respected Italian chefs of Los Angeles— Celestino Drago of Celestino's—shares a recipe for his delicious open-face Italian sandwiches. He prefers to make this sandwich on an Italian roll called a *michetta*, but any high-quality roll will do. Begin by covering one side of the roll with slices of tomato and *mozzarella di bufala* (buffalo-milk mozzarella), a few roasted peppers, arugula, and fresh basil. With some more basil make a light pesto sauce with a touch of garlic, a few pine nuts, basil, and olive oil. Serve open face.

Inspired by our conversations on fresh garden

vegetables, Celestino recommends other fillings too. One is made with raw, thinly sliced fennel that has been marinated with oil and lemon, white pepper, and a little salt. You can put a little smoked prosciutto or salami on top of the fennel. Or try cooked artichokes with grated Parmesan cheese and cucumbers. Deep-fried cardoon can also be used on top of a layer of pâté, or you may want to try radicchio and goat cheese. Celestino's favorite, though, is zucchini flowers made into an omelette, put on a roll, and garnished with fresh sage.

NONNA'S OLD-WORLD ARTICHOKE

Jesse Cool is chef and owner of the Flea Street Cafe and Late for the Train, both in Menlo Park, California. When Jesse was a little girl, her grandmother used to create very special ethnic dishes, and one of Jesse's favorites was this artichoke recipe. Her Italian grandfather liked to eat it with a big salad of hand-picked dandelion leaves, garlic, chopped eggs, and olive oil. Jesse serves this artichoke at her restaurant

Chef Celestino Drago's open-face sandwich is made of tomatoes, mozzarella di bufala, and arugula, dotted with a mild pesto sauce, and served on a michetta roll.

and says that sometimes people have a hard time figuring out how to eat it. Simply pull off the leaves as you would any other artichoke and scrape off the meat with the stuffing. You can make a whole meal out of it, but be sure your friends share your enthusiasm for garlic. Jesse recommends it with a glass of hearty zinfandel.

SERVES 6.

> 2 cups fresh bread crumbs
> ½ cup chopped parsley
> ½ cup chopped basil
> 2 tablespoons chopped fresh oregano
> 6 cloves garlic, minced
> ¾ cup freshly grated Parmesan cheese
> Salt and pepper to taste
> ¼ to ½ cup olive oil
> 6 artichokes

Toast bread crumbs in a 350° oven for 10 minutes to brown. Combine with herbs and garlic in a bowl. Add Parmesan cheese, salt, and pepper and drizzle olive oil over all until mixture sticks together.

Trim off tips of artichoke leaves. Into a wide-based pot with a lid, put about 3 inches water, 3 tablespoons olive oil, and a few lemon slices. Add artichokes, bottom side down; then cover and simmer about 15 minutes. Remove from water with tongs and let cool enough to handle. Gently pull back leaves from center of each artichoke and scrape out hairy choke with a spoon. Stuff breading into centers and leaves as evenly and as far down as you can. Pour off enough water in pot to leave 1 inch. Return artichokes to water and simmer until leaves pull away easily, about 30 minutes. Remove from water and serve at room temperature.

DON SILVIO'S VEGETABLE DESSERT TART

Vicki Sebastiani contributed this recipe for a surprisingly rich and delicious dessert made with vegetables.

SERVES 6 TO 8.

Tart Shell

> 2 cups all-purpose, unbleached flour
> ½ cup walnuts, ground
> 1 cup butter, chilled

Combine flour and nuts. Add butter, 2 tablespoons at a time, and mix well in food processor (or use your usual pie-crust method) until dough forms a ball. Spread dough with your fingers into a quiche, tart, or pie pan (9 to 10 inches) to ⅛-inch thickness along the bottom and sides and at least ¾ inch up on the sides. Chill while making filling.

Filling

> 2 cups coarsely chopped raw chard leaves (1 bunch)
> 2 cups grated zucchini (2 medium-size zucchini)
> 1 cup golden raisins
> 8 leaves chopped fresh basil or 1 teaspoon dried basil
> 8 leaves chopped fresh mint or 1 teaspoon dried mint
> ¼ cup honey
> 4 eggs, lightly beaten
> ½ cup chenin blanc or chardonnay wine

Preheat oven to 375°.

In a large bowl combine all filling ingredients. Pour half the filling into a food processor or blender and puree briefly. Combine with nonpureed half of filling and pour into shell. Bake approximately 45 minutes or until filling has set (inserted knife comes out clean). Cool 30 minutes before serving. Serve at room temperature accompanied by chenin blanc or chardonnay wine.

Sources

Seed Companies

1. W. Atlee Burpee Company
   Warminster, PA 18991
   Burpee has a wide selection of American vegetable seeds plus some Italian basics.

2. The Cook's Garden
   P.O. Box 65
   Londonderry, VT 05148
   This company specializes in salad greens and European varieties of seeds, including many of the Italian varieties discussed in the text.

3. DeGiorgi Company, Inc.
   P.O. Box 413
   Council Bluffs, IA 51502
   This nursery imports seeds of many of the Italian vegetables and carries many of the standard American varieties as well.

4. Epicure Seeds
   P.O. Box 450
   Brewster, NY 10509
   This seed company specializes in European seeds.

5. Fratelli Ingegnoli
   Corso Buenos Aires 54
   20124 Milano
   Italy
   See the text for more information on this seed company. Catalog: $10.00 in lire.

6. Gurney Seed & Nursery Company
   Yankton, SD 57079
   Gurney carries a large collection of unusual vegetable varieties.

7. Le Marché
   Seeds International
   P.O. Box 190
   Dixon, CA 95620
   Le Marché carries the largest selection of the Italian varieties mentioned in the text. Catalog: $2.00.

8. Seeds Blum
   Idaho City Stage
   Boise, ID 83706
   This seed company specializes in open-pollinated and old-time varieties, including some of the old Italian ones. Catalog: $2.00.

9. Shepherd's Garden Seeds
   7389 West Zayante Road
   Felton, CA 95018
   This seed company specializes in European varieties. Catalog: $1.00.

Mail-Order Sources of Ingredients

Balducci's
Mail Order Division
334 East Eleventh Street
New York, NY 10003
Balducci's carries a very large and sophisticated selection of Italian ingredients.

Books

Bianchini, Francesco, Francesco Corbetta, and Marilena Pistoia. *The Complete Book of Fruits and Vegetables*. New York: Crown Publishers, 1975.

This gorgeous book is translated from Italian. A small amount of text accompanies masterful paintings of many of the vegetables and herbs described in this chapter.

Bugialli, Giuliano. *Giuliano Bugialli's Foods of Italy.* New York: Steward, Tabori, and Chang, 1984.

This book is a celebration of Italian cooking. Its magnificent photos and detailed recipes are an inspiration.

Organic Gardening editors. *Gourmet Gardening.*

Anne Moyer Halpin, ed. Emmaus, Pa.: Rodale Press, 1981.

This book contains detailed information on how to grow many unusual and superior vegetables, some of which are mentioned in this chapter.

Scaravelli, Paola, and Jon Cohen. *Cooking from an Italian Garden.* New York: Holt, Rinehart and Winston, 1984.

The best book on how to cook Italian vegetables—a must for your cookbook library.

French Gardens

ON MY FIRST TRIP TO FRANCE many years ago, my husband and I spent a whole day at Versailles, and when we left the grounds in late afternoon we were famished. In vain we looked for a café, and we were finally so desperate that even an ice cream vendor stationed outside a large park looked promising. I hopped out of the car, and when I asked for some ice cream in my high school French, the vendor replied, *"Grand Marnier ou Chartreuse, madame?"* I must have looked puzzled, because he then said what sounded like *"Esqueemoo pie Grand Marnier ou esqueemoo pie Chartreuse?"* Taking a stab in the dark, I held up two fingers and said, *"Grand Marnier."* He handed me two Eskimo pies, flavored with Grand Marnier. Only in France! I thought. The bars were out of this world, coated with a wonderful rich chocolate (not chocolate-flavored paraffin), made with buttery-smooth ice cream, and flavored with real Grand Marnier.

That vendor's ice cream treat became a symbol to me of how much the French care about their food. On that trip, we couldn't eat enough onion soup filled with melted cheese and crispy garlic bread. We woke up to fabulous flaky croissants served with ripe, fragrant melons and wild strawberries. For

OPPOSITE: *Popular French vegetables—endive, tomatoes, shallots, leeks, and small cornichon pickles—accompany a French pâté.*

dinner we savored leek and mussel soup, veal medallions with a shallot cream sauce, breast of duck with a garnish of tiny filet beans, and celeriac mousse. Whether we were eating a snack or full meal, in the city or the country, the food was superb. For years I had cooked from Julia Child's recipes and loved them, but it wasn't until I went to France that I fully realized it was the culture the book reflected, not Julia alone, that made the food so good.

Back in the early 1960s, *Mastering the Art of French Cooking,* by Julia Child, Louisette Bertholle, and Simone Beck, along with Julia's television program first interested me in cooking. Were I to start someone cooking today, I would probably point them to the same book. What a great introduction to the basics this book is and what wonderful food it presents. When I pick up my dog-eared copy, I can still tell which recipes I followed by running my hands over the pages and feeling the tiny splatters and crumbs. As I page through, I read the penciled-in notes that say, "Fantastic, Robert loved it!" or "Needs more onions." Given our newlyweds' tight budget in those early days, my cooking was light on the meat and heavy on the vegetables, cheese, and eggs. I would make spinach soufflés, asparagus with hollandaise sauce, quiches with leeks or mushrooms, potatoes mashed with garlic, and, for a splurge, the spectacular molded dessert called Charlotte Malakoff, its almond butter cream layered with strawberries and homemade ladyfingers dipped in Grand Marnier.

As with the other chapters in this book, I have chosen to explore here a particular aspect of cooking or gardening. While the French are great gardeners and have added many fine vegetables and herbs to the world's repertoire, it is their superior cooking techniques I most want to emphasize in this chapter. The many hours I spent practicing the basics gave me a good foundation in French cooking, but in the last few years, while concentrating on French gardens, I have gathered more specific information from many cooks, so this chapter is a wealth of specialized material on French cooking techniques.

Still, French gardening methods are well represented here too. Actually, the first garden grown for me for this book was Nancy Welch's bare-bones French garden in Woodside, California. Nancy took a small section of her patio and planted French varieties of tomatoes, summer squash, little French beans, mâche (corn salad), basil, leeks, eggplant, and melons. She proved that you can grow quite a bit in a small space.

The little French beans were too stringy for her, but she really liked the leeks and eggplants. Poetically enough, her French goat got out of its pen and harvested much of the garden, so we had less to evaluate than we would have liked.

For this chapter I had two prototype French gardens grown, one on the East Coast and one on the West. Jeanne and Dan Will were my gardeners in Brookside, New Jersey, and Georgeanne Brennan and Charlotte Glenn grew the California garden. The Will garden represents a somewhat formal kitchen garden popular in France for centuries. The garden grown by Georgeanne and Charlotte, owners of Le Marché seed company and, having lived in France for many years, greatly experienced, depicts the *potager,* or less formal kitchen garden.

My research sources for this chapter were diverse. To re-experience a formal nineteenth-century kitchen garden like those I had seen in France, I visited the E. I. du Pont estate in Maryland. And to examine the common French vegetable varieties in detail and cook with them, I grew many in my own garden. To gather the cooking information, I interviewed countless growers and cooking professionals about their favorite preparations and presentations. Emily Cohen, French-trained sous chef and pastry chef at the San Benito House in Half Moon Bay, California, helped assemble and review cooking information. Tom McCombie, chef at Chez T. J.'s, in Mountain View, California, was of special help and contributed a number of recipes. And, of course, I drew on my visits to France and the many unforgettable meals I had there.

How to Grow a French Garden

Most of the vegetables commonly used in France are also popular in the United States, and detailed growing information on them is covered in Part Four, "An Encyclopedia of Superior Vegetables." One aspect of growing numerous French varieties that needs special mention here, however, is harvesting. With some French specialty vegetables, the timing of the harvest is critical, more so than with equivalent American varieties. For instance, the French filet beans *(haricots verts)* are exquisitely tender if harvested when tiny (a sixth of an inch across) but tough and stringy if larger or more mature. To achieve perfection, one must harvest them at least once a day. Other French edibles for which optimum harvest time is critical are petits pois, charentais melons, and many salad greens.

Another aspect of French gardening that deserves highlighting is the garden blanching of vegetables, sometimes referred to as forcing. While not exclusively French, this technique seems most appreciated in France and is necessary for a few of the popular French vegetables. Because blanching requires detailed attention, it warrants a special section.

Garden Blanching Vegetables

Blanching vegetables involves a technique whereby light is excluded from all or part of the growing vegetable to reduce the vegetable's strong taste. Vegetables that have been blanched are lighter in color than nonblanched ones and in most cases more tender. Vegetables most commonly blanched are asparagus, cardoon, cauliflower, celery, dandelions, some lettuces and Oriental greens, and the chicories, including Belgian endive (Witloof chicory), radicchio, escarole, and curly endive (frisée).

We can trace the concept of blanching back several centuries to the time when vegetables were more closely related to their primitive ancestors—which meant they were often tough, stringy, and bitter. Blanching made them both less strong tasting and more tender. Nowadays, most modern vegetable varieties are more refined and seldom need blanching, and because forced vegetables are less nutritious and take more hand labor than nonforced produce, they are generally less favored. So why blanch vegetables? Basically, because some vegetables have yet to be completely civilized. Cardoon, some radicchios, dandelions, and some heirloom varieties of celery and cauliflower are all preferable blanched, and Belgian endive can be eaten no other way. And sometimes gardener-cooks blanch vegetables simply to alter the taste for a treat. Thus, one might blanch asparagus in order to savor a plump, white version of this vegetable, which makes an unusual and historic dish. Or, for elegant salads, one might blanch endive to make its curly leaves light green in the center, or dandelion leaves to make them creamy colored, tender, and sweet.

The blanching process consists of blocking light from the part of the vegetable you plan to eat, be it leaf, stem, or shoot. The blockage keeps chlorophyll from forming, and the vegetable part will therefore

This magnificent garden at Eleutherian Mills, Delaware, is the restored garden of E. I. du Pont, who designed it in the early 1800s. It is a classic French garden open to the public with formal parterres (flowerbeds) and intersecting paths and beds filled with vegetables, flowers, and espaliered fruit trees.

be white, very pale, or, in the case of red vegetables, pink. A few general principles cover most blanching techniques. First, you must be careful to prevent the vegetable from rotting, since the process can create fungus problems. Select only unbruised, healthy plants to blanch and make sure you do not keep the plants too moist. Such vegetables as cardoon and celery need air circulation around the stalks. Make sure you only blanch a few plants at a time and stagger your harvest, since most vegetables are fragile and keep poorly once they have been blanched. Thus, you would not blanch your whole crop of cardoon, celery, or endive at one time. After you harvest your blanched vegetables, keep them in a dark place or they will turn green and lose the very properties you worked to achieve.

Let's go through the blanching process in detail first with a vegetable that *must* be blanched to be edible—Belgian endive, one of the many types of chicory. To produce those expensive little forced shoots called chicons, you grow the plants as you would regular chicory. (For details on growing chicories and additional information on forcing them, see the "Italian Gardens" chapter.) In the fall cut off the tops of the plants to within an inch of the crown and dig up the roots. Take the roots and plant them in about ten inches of loose soil in a bucket, orange crate, or wooden box deep enough to give five or six inches of head room (you will probably have to cut off their bottom halves to get them to fit). Cover the crowns with five or six inches of moist fine sand or sawdust; this material will hold the emerging leaves in a tight head. Then put the container in a completely dark place or cover it and put it in a cool (50 to 60 degrees Fahrenheit) basement or garage. Check occasionally to make sure the sand is still moist and water sparingly when it gets dry. Within a month or so the crowns will start to resprout and produce beautiful little white chicons. These should be harvested as they reach four or five inches in height. The plants will usually resprout at least once, and sometimes you can harvest a third or fourth time. Some of the "forcing" radicchios can be blanched in the same way. In mild-winter areas, both types of chicories can be blanched in the garden. Start the plants in midsummer and blanch them by covering the garden bed with six to eight inches of sand.

The most prized curly endives (frisées), also chicory species, are the ones with creamy golden centers and finely cut leaves. According to Georgeanne Bren-

nan, many curly endive varieties will develop a light heart without extensive blanching, especially if they are planted closer together than usual so that they shade each other's leaves. Georgeanne reported that in France you still see boards stretched across the tops of the curly endive rows a few weeks before harvest. This use of boards is a simple but effective way to blanch the centers of these endives.

You can also blanch celery and cardoon using boards, but in this case after the plants start to mature you prop boards up against the sides of the plants to exclude light from the stalks. This is most effective with celery planted in rows. An alternate way to treat celery and the preferred way to blanch cardoon stalks is to wrap the stalks with burlap or straw, surround the bundles with black plastic, and then tie them with string.

To blanch asparagus, you need to plan way ahead. First plant your asparagus bed much deeper than you would ordinarily—twelve to eighteen inches deep instead of the usual six to eight inches. Then you'll have to wait a few years for the plants to mature. To blanch the asparagus, in the spring before the shoots have come out of the ground you mound up three or four inches of earth or sand around the area, and when the tip comes up through the soil, reach down into the soil and cut it off six or eight inches below the soil line. The shoot you take out will be perfectly white. To experiment with blanching asparagus in an already established bed, before they emerge in the spring, cover the beds with eight inches of sand. Harvest as above.

To blanch cauliflower, after the curds start to show through the leaves, gather the leaves together and tie them up with soft string or plastic strips to cover the emerging head. Other vegetables can be blanched in a somewhat similar way. Blanch dandelions by loosely tying up the leaves and covering the plant with a flowerpot for a week or so, or cover the bed with four or five inches of sand. The flowerpot process will also work well with some of the leaf chicories and is occasionally used on romaine lettuces.

Serve these blanched vegetables with ceremony and give them special treatment. Most are quite mild in flavor and are best featured with light sauces and, because they are so tender, short cooking times. Imagine the luxury of sitting down to a dinner of thick, white, fresh asparagus spears and a salad filled with tender, succulent frilly endive.

The Le Marché Potager Garden

Georgeanne Brennan and Charlotte Glenn, owners of Le Marché seed company, carry numerous French varieties in their seed catalog and have spent a lot of time in France seeking out special varieties and recipes. When I asked them to grow a garden for this book, they agreed enthusiastically and, after thinking it over, decided to grow a *potager* garden. They had both gardened for years but had never set out to create a garden of this traditional French style. I was unfamiliar with the term *potager* but not, as it turned out, with the concept. *Potage* is the French word for soup, and in a gardening context a *potager* is a garden containing whatever is necessary for soup at any time throughout the year. Traditionally, the *potager* garden is planned in little three- or four-foot-square or rectangular plots, which rotate with the seasons, along with a nursery area for young seedlings.

Georgeanne and Charlotte's *potager* garden was duly planned, I remained in touch throughout the spring, and in late June went out to the garden near Davis, California, to visit. Georgeanne welcomed me and gave me a thorough briefing on the garden before showing me around. She explained that for centuries the *potager* had been part of most French families' lives, whether in the country or the city. "When I lived in France," she told me, "it was to me an absolutely astonishing idea that everything I needed was right there in the garden. In fact, this was necessary, because there weren't any stores nearby. But it was tremendously enjoyable as well. Part of the daily experience was to go out in the morning and pick whatever I was going to have for the noon meal. Then in the evening I would go out and choose vegetables

Georgeanne Brennan plants beans in her potager garden. Her traditional French-style garden contains small plots of different vegetables that are at varying stages of development and are planned to give a continuous harvest.

W orking on a book about food can be dangerous to your figure. For days, as I transcribed the information on French cooking from Georgeanne Brennan, co-owner of Le Marché seed company, I would eat and eat. As Georgeanne described dipping French bread into sun-ripened tomatoes mashed with garlic and basil, off I went to the kitchen. When she described a chard tart with Sultana raisins, pine nuts, and honey, I found myself needing a snack. We all know how deeply the French value good food, but Georgeanne's recollections emphasized the fact.

Georgeanne Brennan

Born in California, Georgeanne went to school in France, where she later married and settled in an old farmhouse in the country. There, far from the supermarket, she and her husband raised goats, and she grew and cooked the family's food. Eventually they moved back to the United States, but Georgeanne still retreats regularly to her old farmhouse in France for weeks at a time to research vegetables for Le Marché and recipes for the books she writes with her partner, Charlotte Glenn.

One of Georgeanne's recollections of living in the French countryside exemplifies the French respect for food: "The first time I had fava beans, a local farmer came to the door and said, 'Here are some favas for you.' He saw my blank look, and, transported by the first favas of the season, proceeded to show me how to use them. He shelled the beans and asked for a skillet. Then he heated up a little butter and oil and soon stood over my stove cooking away. He just popped those beans into the oil and butter, added a little salt and pepper, and shook the skillet around for a while. Then he said, 'I'm going to cook my own,' and left me to feast on the ones he'd prepared. They were delicious!"

The average French person is passionately involved with good food and, often, with cooking as well. Part of this involvement is because of a great respect for the garden/table connection—whether the produce comes from a local farmer or from an indi-vidual's plot. Mesclun, a mix of perishable salad greens, is a good example. Instead of sitting down to a head of lettuce and a few tomatoes at dinner, the average family in southern France will eat a mixed salad that includes baby lettuce leaves, young chicories, and herbs. "Through the centuries," Georgeanne explains, "different kinds of greens were grown in the garden—lettuces, chickweeds, and herbs —and the French refined these combinations. While many French people still grow their own salad greens today, market gardeners offer mesclun to the general public. When you go to the markets in Nice, you see piles of different little mixed greens and herbs for sale by weight. One seller might offer a mix with nine ingredients, another five, and so forth, but the principal selections will include romaine and butterhead lettuce, chicory, chervil, *roquette*, or any variation thereof. All the elements are there: peppery rockets, bitter chicory, tender butterhead, somewhat crunchy romaine, and slightly anise-tasting chervil. Because I miss mesclun in the States, I grow the mix myself. It's actually very easy to grow and can be harvested within about twenty to thirty days of planting. Just about anyone can grow it—it even works well in a window box.

"I miss French leeks and chervil, too. I think the leeks you find here in supermarkets are all wrong. They're two inches in diameter. In France, they're usually very small, maybe a few pencil widths, and they're more mild, tender, and flavorful. I love to harvest little ones from my garden and steam and serve them warm with a simple vinaigrette. Or cover them with béchamel sauce, or serve them Italian-style in a tomato sauce. When I do have large leeks I sometimes use the leaves to make little packets around pieces of fish. I serve them with a sauce made with shallots and cream, a dish that reminds me of northern France. Small or large, the rich yet mild flavor of the leek is unique."

Chervil appears in one way or another in French

sauces, soups, and salads, particularly in northern France. Because it's so perishable, though, it almost never appears in produce markets in the United States. Georgeanne likes to use chervil, with its aniselike flavor, with fish, white wine, and cream. "It tastes refined and doesn't overpower," she says, "so it's very good for delicate dishes."

When Americans spend time in France, they often become smitten by French melons. Undoubtedly, the melon they've had is charentais, a type of muskmelon with a smooth, pale-green skin. Traditionally, these melons are eaten as a first course, often with a thin slice of salt-cured ham. "This is one melon," Georgeanne reminisces, lighting up as she speaks, "that you'll never forget if you ever have it in its perfect state. You'll crave its taste and smell long afterward. These melons are so perfumed that if you go through French towns where they're being harvested in the summer, you'll notice the scent permeating the air as the lavender fields do."

Those who have grown charentais know, however, that a charentais not in its perfect state is less than distinguished. If underripe, it will be flavorless; if overripe, it becomes fibrous and fermented. These melons are difficult to grow, particularly in a damp climate. They need heat for high quality, and they crack open easily if watered near harvest time. The French barely water them for the last six weeks before harvesting. To complicate matters further, they're difficult to harvest at peak perfection. As Georgeanne says, "They're tricky. You can pick a perfect one in the morning, and by evening it's begun to ferment. Charentais don't slip from the vine when they're ripe like other muskmelons do. You have to judge ripeness by the feel and aroma of the melons instead.

"In France, people who specialize in melons, mostly charentais, walk the fields at five or six o'clock in the evening to see which of the fruit will be ready in the morning; then they return at four or five to find those selected and look for the next ones to be ready. They can choose which will be best in a few hours or a few days. When you go shopping in the market in France, you tell the melon expert when you want to eat the fruit—in a few hours, say, or the next day—and he or she will select the perfect one for you. Despite these difficulties, though, if you live in a part of the country with a Mediterranean climate, it would certainly be worth growing charentais with a hope that you will get at least one perfect melon."

Picking and serving produce at the peak of perfection is a crucial element woven throughout French cuisine. When you have your own French garden, you, too, will be able to savor these vegetables and fruits at their best.

---

for the evening meal. The light and sounds would all be different. Those daily vegetable gatherings slowed the whole day down."

The point of the *potager* garden is to make available a continual harvest. This means that seedlings are continually being started to fill in spaces as they appear in the beds. Sometimes, as with carrots and beets, the seedlings are begun in the beds themselves, but with most vegetables, and for better supervision, they are started in the nursery area or in flats, pots, cold frames, or, most often, an earthen hotbed. Seedlings are then transplanted into the beds. This may sound tedious, but actually the plots are very small and manageable. As Georgeanne put it, "This garden fits into your life; it doesn't dominate it. Once the garden area is prepared, an average of twenty minutes a day is required to keep it up. For instance, a typical day might include harvesting a handful of snap beans and a few herbs, cleaning up the spent chard plants in one of the small beds, and seeding that bed with beans."

Cooking from the *potager* garden varies both seasonally and regionally. "When you drive through the mountain villages in July," said Georgeanne, "you will see beautiful leeks and cabbages, but 300 kilometers to the south ripening tomatoes and eggplants appear. The regions differ that distinctively." Here, too, such gardens will vary from place to place. Thus, if you live in a cold climate, to maintain a continual harvest you will need to use row covers and cold frames for protection, and you will have to mulch heavily in the fall. Such a garden will actually be similar to those in northern France. On the other hand, if you live in a mild climate, chances are your summer garden will resemble a Mediterranean French garden.

The Le Marché *potager* garden is near Sacramento, California, on the edge of the great Central Valley. Summer temperatures in this part of the country are high, often hovering at 100 degrees for many days. The winters are mild and seldom dip below the mid-twenties. In the Le Marché garden, then, heat is the problem. When summer really moves in, it is too hot to start lettuce, or to use an enclosed nursery, and the seedlings of broccoli and cauliflower and other fall and winter crops must be started in one of the beds under shade cloth. Lettuce will survive the winter if started in October, as will other cool-season crops such as mâche (corn salad), dandelions, leeks, cabbages, and the root vegetables.

When Georgeanne and Charlotte selected vegetables for their garden, they chose primarily French heirloom varieties, those popular in the nineteenth century but still carried by French seed houses. Georgeanne explained: "France is having some of the same variety-erosion problems afflicting most other modern nations. By using nineteenth-century varieties, we could do our share in addressing this problem while still growing exceptionally tasty varieties." Also included in the garden was one old-fashioned vegetable, the crosne, now nearly forgotten in France. Crosnes, also known as Chinese artichokes, are small, crunchy, tuberlike vegetables that were brought to France from Japan in the 1800s and simply went out of fashion.

Georgeanne's descriptions of and preparation techniques for most of the varieties she and Charlotte grow should give you a good overall view of the *potager* garden. In her detailed explanation to me, Georgeanne started with the two varieties of radishes: 'Flamboyant', a long, red-and-white French breakfast type, and 'Sezanne', a round one with a magenta top. According to Georgeanne, radishes in France are often served as an appetizer with French bread and butter, and for centuries this has been a favorite midmorning snack for farmers. Next, she pointed out the two bean varieties: 'Coco Prague', a French horticultural shelling type with splashy red-and-white pods and one of the traditional beans used fresh in *pistou,* and 'Aiguillon', a thin filet-type snap bean. The two varieties of tomatoes were 'Super Marmande', a development from the old 'Marmande' and a good French stuffing tomato, and 'Oxheart', a flavorful, meaty tomato. Georgeanne's excited anticipation of the coming summer garden became obvious as she talked of the tomatoes. "They'll

be ready in high summer, and there's absolutely nothing better than going out to the garden and picking a few before dinner. They are still warm from the day's heat then, and all their flavor and aroma are at the maximum. As you can see, like the French, I love tomatoes and feel that life without them is inconceivable."

Also included in the garden is a winter squash, 'Musquée de Provence', which looks like the pumpkin pictured in nineteenth-century childrens' stories. It has a very deeply ridged buff-orange skin and is filled with thick, dense, orange meat. Charlotte and Georgeanne keep the squash in the garden until the first frost and then put them in the garage for winter. One of Georgeanne's favorite ways to prepare this squash is to cube it and cook it slowly with olive oil, garlic, herbs, and grated cheese.

About the vegetables soon to be started for the fall garden, Georgeanne said, "I have to plant cabbage; it's one of my favorite vegetables. We'll put in 'Quintal d'Alsace', the standard French sauerkraut cabbage since the nineteenth century. It's very big, very dense, and makes excellent sauerkraut. Most Americans think of sauerkraut as exclusively German, but it's very popular in France. I have friends there who live in a wonderful sixteenth-century stone house and have a sauerkraut party every year. Our sauerkraut cabbages will go into the nursery part of the garden in August and September. Then we'll transplant them to the main garden, and we should be making sauerkraut by next February or March.

"Peas are another of my favorite vegetables," Georgeanne went on, "and I want lots of them. We'll plant a French *mangetout,* a type with edible pods. The particular variety will be 'Bamby', a pea similar to a sugar snap but twice the size and flavor and one that seems to tolerate the heat here a lot better than other peas. We'll plant them in both fall and very early spring. In late spring we serve them in a traditional dish, *navarin,* made with turnips, carrots, peas, and the first spring lamb." Carrots and shallots were going into the fall garden too—a flavorful old carrot variety called 'Red Muscade', whose plants tend to produce large, misshapen, nearly red, dense carrots, and two different varieties of shallots, a small gray and a long red one.

I asked Georgeanne to explain in detail how the *potager* garden was harvested. In the typical American garden, full-size vegetables are gathered sporadically, but a large harvest of even one vegetable from the *potager* garden would be unusual. The idea is to do a daily mixed harvest, taking what is necessary for the day's soup, salad, stew, and/or vegetable side dish. Certain vegetables are planted with specific, and sometimes a number of, purposes in mind. For example, the *potager* gardener might sow chard, beets, and maybe lettuce and mâche thickly in a bed and then partially harvest most of them in a few weeks as thinnings. And some leeks and onions might be harvested young and eaten small and braised, while months later the larger vegetables are picked and cooked in a different way. And there might be a gathering of a large number of certain vegetables—cabbages for sauerkraut, or tomatoes before a first frost for some sauce—but usually for specific purposes. Mostly the harvest is determined by the needs of the day. For instance, potatoes, after reaching new-potato size, are harvested only as needed, not all at once. A leaf or two of broccoli or a head of cabbage might be picked from the garden and added to a soup. Preserving for the next season is not a primary goal, as the garden produces for most of the year, yielding vegetables and herbs in their ideal state—garden fresh.

I was enchanted with the *potager* garden, not only for its versatility but also for its individuality. In just about any yard and climate, a variation of a *potager* garden can be created to reflect the gardener-cook's personal taste, and the rotation of just two or three little beds will yield fresh salad greens and herbs for most of the year. The *potager* garden is infinitely expandable, since it's really more of a concept than a specific garden plan. It can even be expanded for those delicious, rare periods when you have unlimited time for cooking and gardening.

The Will Garden

Jeanne and Dan Will are avid gardeners, and their beautiful herb garden in Brookside, New Jersey, inspired many gardeners in the area. When I called the Wills in midspring to ask if they'd grow a French garden for this book, they plunged right in with the intention of growing a kind of garden they hadn't tried before. Their usual vegetable garden was an area off the greenhouse surrounded by a wire fence. It was very utilitarian but not designed with aethetics in mind. On the phone I had mentioned the beautiful kitchen and *parterre* (flowerbed) gardens in

France, and the Wills became inspired enough to look into the history of the French garden. That work plus an earlier visit to Rosemary Verey's garden at Barnsley House in England, fashioned after a famous Renaissance French garden, inspired them to plan their own variation of the classic French garden, distinctively geometric and decorative in character. With dedication above and beyond anything I expected, in one season they set about to create a miniature latticed garden filled with flowers and French vegetables and herbs.

To help them get started with the vegetables, I recommended a selection of French varieties from Shepherd's Garden Seeds and some French herbs with which they were already familiar. I kept in touch with Jeanne, who would be doing the day-to-day gardening, throughout the spring and early summer, and in midsummer I went to New Jersey to visit. The garden was simply glorious. It gave a true French feeling, and the vigor of the plants spoke to both the care they had been given and the wonderful condition of the soil. The vegetables, of course, were the primary focus, and they were planted throughout the garden in long, rectangular beds. The flowers of the garden were the fragrant flowering heliotrope, an unusual nicotiana (*Nicotiana sylvestris*), a few varieties of French roses, and the graceful clary sage. Herbs were both interplanted in the beds and grouped in containers under a gray lattice gazebo, which served as a focal point. A lattice fence, also painted light gray, surrounded the whole garden.

The French vegetables from Shepherd's Garden Seeds included 'Lorrisa' and 'Marmande' tomatoes, 'Cadice' bell peppers, 'Arlesa' zucchini, 'De Carentan' leeks, 'Vernandon' haricot beans, 'Paros' chard, 'Cornichon' cucumbers, 'Oak Leaf' and 'Mantilla' lettuces, and 'Giniac' eggplants. Jeanne tried 'Planet' carrots and 'Pharo' charentais melons too, but was disappointed with their performance. Also included were 'Palla Rosa' radicchio, mâche, French sorrel, arugula, a frisée chicory a friend had brought from France, and, of course, lots of herbs. The herbs were chervil, French thyme, tarragon, rosemary, and a selection of basils including cinnamon and regular basil.

Jeanne herself was delighted with the appearance of the plants compared with that of the standard American varieties she was used to planting. "And I was pleasurably surprised with the *flavor* of the produce," she told me. "Many of the varieties

Jeanne and Dan Will's garden in Brookside, New Jersey, is filled with French vegetables. Leeks, endive, and fennel are planted on the left side of the path and sorrel, eggplant, and tomatoes on the right.

were distinctly superior to those I'd grown in the past. I noticed that some of the plants were smaller, but they seemed equally productive." All in all, Jeanne and Dan Will were very pleased with their French garden and intend to keep growing many of the vegetables in the future.

Recommended French Vegetables

Most of the vegetables and herbs used in France are well known to us and in some instances are the same varieties as our domestic ones; you'll find growing instructions for these in Part Four, "An Encyclopedia of Superior Vegetables." However, some French garden produce and herbs are seldom seen here—for instance, celeriac, some varieties of shelling beans, Alpine strawberries, chervil, and sorrel. In addition,

the French enjoy miniature versions of some of our common vegetables—petite varieties of peas, snap beans, and carrots—which in this country we sometimes refer to as "baby" or "gourmet" vegetables. If the baby vegetables are of particular interest to you, see those mentioned below as well as ones covered in the "Rainbow Gardens" chapter.

The following list discusses French garden vegetables as well as many of the cooking terms you will find defined in the "Cooking from the French Garden" section. Notice the considerable overlap between the French vegetables and the Italian, and to some extent, the German. The numbers in parentheses after variety names refer to seed companies listed in the "Sources" section at the end of this chapter.

ALPINE STRAWBERRIES   *Fragaria vesca; fraises* These are small, conical-shaped wild strawberries much prized in France for their particularly intense strawberry flavor.

How to grow: Alpine strawberries are delightful perennials that, unlike our standard strawberries, tolerate much shade and do not produce runners. See "Strawberries" in the Part Four Encyclopedia.

How to prepare: Alpine strawberries are highly perishable and must be used within hours of being harvested. They are glorious in crêpes, compotes, and sorbets, and served in puff pastry or with a little Grand Marnier and whipped cream, and they are commonly featured in tarts. Because of their softness and intense flavor, they are generally used whole and raw, savored plain as a garnish, or served with other mild foods.

ARTICHOKES   *Cynara Scolymus; artichauts*   Artichokes are popular in France. There are many varieties, including a purple one from Provence, which when very young and tender, before the choke has really developed, is eaten raw as a crudité.

How to grow: See the Part Four Encyclopedia for specific growing instructions. For information on a purple variety see the "Italian Gardens" chapter.

How to prepare: Whole artichokes or artichoke hearts are popularly served warm with hollandaise sauce or lemon butter, or cold with a vinaigrette or mayonnaise. In France very often the hearts alone are used, and these are stuffed and served hot or cold by themselves or with other dishes. A typical dish is artichoke hearts stuffed with *duxelles* (a mixture with finely chopped mushrooms) and covered with béchamel sauce. In southern France, two appetizers of note use artichoke hearts. In one the heart is served cold with olive oil, garlic, and herbs. The other involves the immature purple artichoke served raw: the slightly bitter bud is cut into quarters, the stem end is dipped in salt, and the dish is accompanied by bread and sweet butter.

ASPARAGUS   *Asparagus officinalis; asperges*   Asparagus are a passion in France. The French eat green, purple, and blanched white asparagus.

How to grow: See the Part Four Encyclopedia. For information on blanching to create the famous French white asparagus, see "How to Grow a French Garden" earlier in this chapter and the "German Gardens" chapter. 'Larac' (5) is a French hybrid that is prolific and disease resistant.

How to prepare: French cooks usually peel asparagus before cooking. Peel the skin off with a knife or vegetable peeler up to where it becomes tender. Asparagus are usually prepared in a simple manner and served unadorned to allow the elegant flavor of the vegetable to come through. When asparagus are dressed, the accompaniments are most often hollandaise sauce, lemon butter, or a vinaigrette. Asparagus are also used in quiches, crêpes, salads, soups, soufflés, and timbales.

BEANS   *Phaseolus vulgaris; haricots*   The bean most closely associated with France is the *haricot vert,* the famous thin French filet-type string bean. Another famous French bean is the flageolet, eaten fresh-shelled the way we enjoy limas. Standard green beans, yellow wax beans, fresh fava beans, and all types of dry beans are also used in France.

How to grow: See the Part Four Encyclopedia. Varieties of the classic French *haricot vert* bean are eaten very young and are best when the bean is a sixth of an inch wide at harvest. If allowed to mature past this width, they can have strings and be tough. To keep the plants producing, harvest daily. Varieties to try are 'Aiguillon' (4, 5); 'Fin de Bagnols' (1, 4, 5), one of the heirloom varieties; and 'Vernandon' (6).

The flageolet is a rich-tasting, white to light-green shelling bean shaped something like a squat kidney bean. Harvest these beans as the pods fill out noticeably and before they get dry. If they get too mature, allow them to dry for winter use. Two bush varieties to try are 'Green Flageolet Chevrier' (1, 3, 4) and 'Coco Prague' (5) (while not a true flageolet, the latter is closely related). See also the "Baked Bean Gardens" chapter for more information on shelling and dry beans.

How to prepare: To retain the color and get the best flavor and texture from all types of filet and standard snap beans, the French blanch them (used in the cooking sense of the word to mean boiling them in a large pot of salted water). The beans are cooked until almost tender and then drained. They are then reheated in butter just before being served as a separate course or a side dish, and may be garnished with lemon juice, parsley, or heavy cream. The cooked beans are also sometimes served in salads and terrines (molded main dishes) as well. In southern France green beans are popular served with a sauce of tomatoes, garlic, and herbs.

Flageolets—meaty, rich-tasting shelling beans— are a special treat well worth the work and are eaten as are limas, with butter and salt and pepper. Or they can be used in salads or soups, particularly the classic vegetable soup known as *pistou*. When mature, the shelling beans can be dried and used in soups, stews, and baked in the traditional cassoulet. See the "Baked Bean Gardens" chapter.

CARROTS *Daucus Carota* var. *sativus; carottes*
Carrots are popular in France, and you will notice that many of the variety names familiar to you, such as 'Nantes' and 'Chantenay', reflect their French breeding.

How to grow: The French enjoy a wide range of carrots, covered in the Part Four Encyclopedia, and also grow miniature varieties of carrots meant to be served whole, such as 'Nantaise à Forcer' (3) and the small, round varieties of carrots 'Round Paris Market' (5) and 'Planet' (1, 6).

How to prepare: Large carrots are used sliced in soups and stews. They are also cooked, as are other root vegetables, with a small amount of stock, sugar, and butter to glaze them and then served as a side dish. And they are included in a basic minced-vegetable mixture called a *mirepoix,* which includes onions, celery, and leeks and is used to flavor many French sauces and stews. Carrots are also pureed for a side dish or soup and are commonly eaten grated fine with a vinaigrette dressing. The miniature carrots are usually prepared as a side dish or a garnish with a glaze or sauce.

CELERIAC *Apium graveolens* var. *rapaceum; céleri-rave* The knobby, brown celeriac is a vegetable used far more in Europe than here.

How to grow: See "Celery" in the Part Four Encyclopedia.

How to prepare: Most commonly, celeriac is julienned and used as a salad with a mayonnaiselike sauce called a rémoulade. It is also pureed with cream and butter and used in a mousse, or is sometimes combined with potato puree. Occasionally it is used as a French-fry-type vegetable. In a stunning dish I had in Avignon, the chef used celeriac in a dough to make a ravioli-like pasta and stuffed the pasta with scallops.

CHARD *Beta vulgaris* var. *cicla; poirée* or *bette à carde* Chard is very popular in French gardens and is grown most of the year.

How to grow: See "Greens" in the Part Four Encyclopedia for specific growing information. Standard French varieties are two slow-bolting varieties: 'Paros' (6), a mild chard, and 'Blonde' (3, 4), a light-

'Round Paris Market' carrots and baby leeks are favorites in France.

colored variety. Or try 'Chard de Nice' (5), selected for fall planting in mild-winter areas.

How to prepare: In France chard is made into a popular soup containing carrots, onions, and other seasonal vegetables and herbs. Young chard leaves are used in salads, and chard at any stage is used for a gratin or as a substitute for spinach in many recipes. Georgeanne Brennan reports that chard is featured in a tart made with raisins, pine nuts, and honey, and is a specialty of the region around Nice.

CHICORY *Cichorum* spp.; *chicorée* Numerous forms of the chicory plant are used in France: curly endive, called frisée; broad-leaved, or Batavian, endive, called *scarole*; leaf chicory or radicchio, called *sauvage*; and Belgian endive, called Witloof or endive.

How to grow: See "Greens" in the Part Four Encyclopedia for information on escarole and endive, two of the chicories, and the "Italian Gardens" chapter for the leaf chicories and radicchios.

To grow Belgian endive, start seeds in the spring. Varieties to choose from are 'Zoom F1' (1, 3, 5) and 'Chicorée de Bruxelles' (3, 4). Set plants out in full sun, about a foot apart in soil that is deep, porous, and well drained so the roots can fully develop. Grow as you would the other chicories. In the fall dig up the roots and blanch them. See "How to Grow a French Garden" for instructions on blanching Belgian endive and some of the other chicories as well.

How to prepare: Common in salads, frisée is most often used as you would lettuce, but it is also served with warm *lardons* (little slices of bacon) and with a little goat cheese as a first course in Parisian restaurants. Other common ways to serve it are in a salad with walnut or hazelnut oil and roasted nuts or as a bed for smoked duck.

The red-leaf chicories, known as radicchios in this country, are popular in France and are used primarily in salads. Use the large leaves in composed or mixed green salads, as a garnish, or braised. Immature leaves are often harvested and used in a mesclun mix (see the "Gourmet Salad Gardens" chapter). There is much overlap in France with the Italians' uses of leaf chicories; see the "Italian Gardens" chapter for more information.

Like the other members of the chicory family, Belgian endive's elegant white chicons have a rich, bitter flavor. Georgeanne Brennan recommends the leaves as an excellent complement to citrus fruits and suggests that they be cooked and served with capers, butter, or a béchamel sauce topped with Gruyère cheese. She also recommends cooking Belgian endive with chicken or pheasant. Like the vegetables we cook with a pot roast, the Belgian endive blends well with chicken or wild game, plus a potato, perhaps, and a turnip or two. All the vegetables absorb the juices of the poultry when they cook, and the slightly bitter flavor combines well with the rich juices. Georgeanne also speaks highly of using the leaves raw in salads. Try serving them with walnuts or toasted almonds, or, in a French version of our Waldorf salad, with celery, apples, nuts, and homemade mayonnaise.

CROSNES (Chinese artichokes) *Stachys affinis* Crosnes are small, crunchy tubers that Jan Blum, owner of Seeds Blum, describes as looking like strings of white pop beads. They were a popular vegetable in France at the beginning of the century, when they were first imported from Japan and grown not far from Paris. (Today, there is still a suburb called Montgeron-Crosne).

How to grow: Grow these perennial members of the mint family from tubers planted in spring. They require fairly moist but well-drained organic soil. The plants grow to about eighteen inches high and spread as wide. Harvest the tubers in about five months and dig up and save some for the next year's planting. Tubers are available from Seeds Blum and Le Marché.

How to prepare: Peel and use the crunchy tubers as you would water chestnuts, boil, and serve with a béchamel sauce. Alternatively, peel and pickle crosnes.

CUCUMBERS *Cucumis sativus; concombres* The French enjoy both the large "English"-type cucumbers and the small cornichons.

How to grow: See the Part Four Encyclopedia. For cornichon varieties, try 'Vert de Paris' (3, 4, 5) and 'Fine Meaux' (3, 4).

How to prepare: The most common use for large cucumbers is for salads. The cornichons are pickled and are traditionally served with a pâté.

EGGPLANTS *Solanum Melongena* var. *esculentum; aubergines* Eggplants are very popular in France and are served in many ways.

How to grow: See the Part Four Encyclopedia. 'Ronde de Valence' (5) is a round eggplant about the size of a baseball and good for stuffing. 'De Barbentane' (5), which has an elongated shape, mild flavor, and thin skin, is an heirloom French variety. Georgeanne Brennan believes it is probably one of the original varieties for ratatouille.

How to prepare: The usual preparation method for eggplants is to first blanch them in boiling water for a few minutes or salt them and then let them exude water for thirty minutes. The point of these steps is to keep them from absorbing copious amounts of oil or becoming bitter. They are then sautéed or broiled, and prepared with bread crumbs, herbs, a tomato sauce, or a combination of all three, or baked and served with a béchamel sauce. They are also stuffed, often with mushrooms, or used in a soufflé or a gratin. The most famous French treatment of eggplants is the Provençal dish ratatouille, a casserole containing tomatoes, onions, peppers, zucchini, and garlic.

FENNEL *Foeniculum* spp.; *fenouil* The French use both wild and "domestic" (what we call "sweet") fennel. The bulb of sweet fennel is eaten, whereas wild fennel is used as an herb for the flavor its leaves can impart to dishes.

How to grow: See the "Italian Gardens" chapter for information on sweet fennel and the "Culinary Herb Gardens" chapter for information on herb fennel.

How to prepare: Use sweet fennel braised, gratinéed, in soups and fish stews, or steamed and served warm or cold as a salad. In Provence sweet fennel is often baked with olive oil, garlic, tomatoes, and grated cheese. Georgeanne Brennan reports, "My neighbor in France taught me to make fish soup, and we would just take whatever the fish was and put it in a pan with garlic, potatoes, carrots, and other garden vegetables. Then she would direct me to go out and get a *bâton de fenouil,* which means a large stalk of fennel, and put it in the soup."

LEEKS   *Allium Ampeloprasum,* Porrum Group; *poireaux*   Leeks have their own special taste—rich but mild and oniony—and are much honored in French cooking.

How to grow: See "Onions" in the Part Four Encyclopedia. French varieties include 'Blue Solaise' (1, 3, 4, 5), a flavorful, hardy heirloom variety that turns blue-green to violet in freezing weather, and 'De Carentan' (3, 6), a delicate-flavored leek for spring planting and fall harvest.

How to prepare: In France, leeks are not used merely as invisible flavoring in soups and stews, as we use them, but are also served alone as a salad with vinaigrette. The baby ones are served hot with a cream sauce, and all leeks can be used as a filling for tarts, quiches, or pastry squares.

PEAS   *Pisum sativum; pois*   Peas are a delicacy in France. The French serve standard garden peas, pea pods, and the famous petits pois, those tiny morsels of intense pea flavor. They even use the empty green pods to make soup.

How to grow: See the Part Four Encyclopedia. French varieties of petits pois are 'Proval' (3), 'Fabina' (3), 'Waverex' (5), and 'Precovil' (6). For a climbing petit pois for fall planting, try 'Frizette' (6).

How to prepare: Standard peas are enjoyed as a side dish and in soups, stews, and salads. A pureed pea soup with fresh mint is a classic French dish, as is braised fresh peas with lettuce and onions. The petits pois are almost treated as a different vegetable. They are harvested when tiny, less than a third of an inch in diameter, and are best eaten within hours of picking. They are usually given a very simple treatment that features their specialness. They are cooked as the filet beans are, above, with great care to prevent overcooking. They are then served immediately with a little butter as a side dish or as a garnish for spring lamb.

POTATOES   *Solanum tuberosum; pommes de terre*
The French are creative with potatoes and consider them to be a separate vegetable, not merely an adjunct to the meal.

How to grow: See the Part Four Encyclopedia. Like the Germans, the French favor some of the waxy-type potatoes, and you will find much information on those in the "German Gardens" chapter, as well as on the more mealy types that we call baking potatoes.

How to prepare: Like most cooks in the West, the French prepare potatoes by boiling, baking, roasting, frying, and using them in soups and stews, but they hardly stop there. They also scallop potatoes with heavy cream, cheese, garlic, carrots, or combinations thereof, or prepare them in a Provençal manner with onions, tomatoes, herbs, and anchovies. In another dish from southern France, salade Niçoise, potatoes are boiled and served with a tarragon vinaigrette on a platter with beautiful vegetables. The French also transform potatoes into elegant fare by pureeing them and then mixing them with eggs and butter and piping this mixture into rosettes around a platter of roasted meat.

SALAD GREENS   See the "Gourmet Salad Gardens" chapter for information on the basic French ingredients for a salad, including mâche (corn salad), *roquette* (rocket), and the mix mesclun. Many French lettuce varieties are also covered there and in the Part Four Encyclopedia.

SHALLOTS   *Allium Cepa,* Aggregatum Group; *échalotes*   Shallots are members of the onion family but are milder and sweeter than most onions; their flavor is sometimes described as falling between that of garlic and onion.

How to grow: See "Onions" in the Part Four Encyclopedia.

How to prepare: Shallots are an integral part of French cooking. The rich, subtle, and complex flavor is considered important in *duxelles, mirepoix* (the carrot mix mentioned above), and many sauces. Use shallots in cream soups, stuffings, and wherever you want a mild onion flavor.

SQUASH, SUMMER   *Cucurbita Pepo* var. *Melopepo; courgettes*   Summer squash, particularly the zucchinis, are much used in France. Also sought after are squash blossoms. In some parts of France markets offer whole bouquets of squash blossoms for stuffing.

How to grow: See the Part Four Encyclopedia. For a modern French variety, try 'Arlesa' (6), with its glossy green fruits and productive plants. Also try two heirloom varieties: the small, pale-green 'Small Green Algerian' (5), narrow at the top and wider at the bottom and with good blossoms for cooking, and the round 'Ronde de Nice' (1, 5). The latter can't be shipped because its thin skin is too tender, but its fine flavor and creamy texture are much prized by home gardeners and local farmers and its round shape lends itself well to stuffing.

How to prepare: Use summer squash in ratatouille, stuffed, grated, in soups, steamed, or sautéed. Or serve it with a tomato sauce or gratinéed. The flavors of summer squash go perfectly with olive oil, garlic, tomatoes, and fresh basil. For more information on squash blossoms, see the "Italian Gardens" and "Native American Gardens" chapters.

TOMATOES *Lycopersicon Lycopersicum; tomates*
While we tend to think of tomatoes more in terms of Italian cooking, they are an integral part of French cooking as well, especially in southern France.

How to grow: See the Part Four Encyclopedia. French varieties of tomatoes to choose from include 'Marmande' (4, 5, 6), the most frequently planted tomato in France; 'Saint Pierre' (3); and 'Carmello' (6). The French also grow the meaty paste types of tomatoes that are covered in the "Italian Gardens" chapter, and according to Georgeanne Brennan, they also grow an old variety popular in this country for years: the 'Oxheart' (5), or what they call 'Coeur de Boeuf'.

How to prepare: Tomatoes are relished in France, and as soon as they are in season they are used stuffed, for juice, in salads and soups, in casseroles, baked (a very common side dish), and, of course, in sauces. As Georgeanne explained, "Tomatoes will find their way into almost everything. And a really wonderful way of having them is in a soup—for example, a chard or bean soup or a *pistou.*"

The French use many herbs. The most unusual ones and those treated most notably in their cuisine follow.

CHERVIL *Anthriscus cerefolium; cerfeuil* This delicate, lacy-looking herb is used quite commonly in France. Its slightly anisey flavor is a favorite in salads. Also, chervil is one of the herbs that make up the chopped mixture called fines herbes.

How to grow: Chervil is an annual herb that grows best in cool weather, and because it doesn't transplant well it is generally sown in place in early spring and again in fall. Give it filtered shade and rich soil and keep it well watered. The plants are short-lived, so, as with radishes and lettuces, to keep a supply, sow seeds every few weeks during the cool part of the year. In some climates, if you allow the plants to go to seed they will readily reseed themselves.

How to prepare: Chervil wilts readily, so harvest it fresh as close to preparation time as possible. The delicate leaves of chervil are used fresh in salads, with eggs and cream soups, and chopped in many classic sauces.

SORREL *Rumex scutatus; oseille* Sorrel, sometimes called French sorrel, is a slightly lemon-flavored green herb sometimes used as a vegetable.

How to grow: Sorrel is generally planted from divisions, though it can also be planted from seeds in the spring. It is a perennial plant that grows to about two feet. Locate plants in full sun or with some afternoon shade in rich, well-drained soil that is kept fairly moist. As sorrel can sometimes spread and become a weed, put it in the garden where it can be contained by paths or retaining walls or grow it in a container.

How to prepare: Sorrel leaves are used fresh in salads and sauces, particularly for fish. Sorrel can also be made into a delightful light cream soup.

TARRAGON *Artemisia Dracunculus; estragon* Tarragon, sometimes called French tarragon, is a rich but delicately flavored herb with an anisey flavor.

How to grow: Tarragon is a tender perennial that grows to about two feet. The plant is started from divisions, not seeds, and in very cold climates must be either brought indoors in the winter or started new with a fresh plant every spring. Grow in full sun (though the plant can tolerate some afternoon shade) and in rich, very well drained soil. When ordering plants, do not confuse with Russian tarragon, which is much inferior in flavor.

How to prepare: Harvest leaves and use fresh any time during the growing season. The tarragon flavor does not preserve well, but if you want to try, put the leaves in vinegar or freeze them. Tarragon adds richness and a slight anisey flavor to sauces, particularly béarnaise sauce, and salad dressings, and the French have used it with poultry and veal for centuries.

Cooking from the French Garden

A passionate interest in food binds much of French culture. All over France one senses the deep appreciation for good wines, cheeses, meats, and vegetables of all types. But traditional French meals differ markedly from region to region. Near the German border in the northern regions of Alsace and Lorraine, for instance, people grow cabbages and leeks and make wonderful sauerkraut, which they serve with hearty sausages, and they fill their well-known dish the quiche with cream and bacon. The wines there are most apt to be fruity and white. In southern France, near the Italian border, however, the flavorings are much bolder, with garlic and basil the main seasonings, and the vegetables are more apt to be artichokes, eggplants, and tomatoes. Here the basic oil is olive, made from the trees that grow in the area, and it is used in many dishes, including salade Niçoise, with its lovely potatoes, tomatoes, and snap beans, and ratatouille, a vegetable stew made with eggplants and zucchini. In the more central parts of France, in Touraine and around Paris, the vegetables are typically little *haricots verts,* peas, and asparagus, and the dishes are seasoned with tarragon, chervil, and shallots. Because the cows of this central area produce so well, the region is world famous for its Brie cheese, and its dishes are often made with sauces laced with butter and cream. It is the food from this last area, in fact, that is sometimes called *grande cuisine* and that we think of as most characteristically French.

Not only is French cooking regional, it is also quite seasonal. For example, in spring when lamb is at its best, a popular treatment is to roast it with young thyme shoots and serve it with tender, succulent peas and lettuce, also at their peak in spring. In Paris people eagerly await the first asparagus of the season and the summer's first wild strawberries. In late summer in southern France people prepare a celebratory *grande aïoli,* or *aïoli monstre.* As Georgeanne Brennan describes it, this is a harvest feast at which the area's new potatoes, snap beans, beets, and whatever else is at its best is cooked and put on large trays. Long tables are set up in the village square and the vegetables are served with codfish, great bowls of garlic mayonnaise (aïoli), and lots of wine, and the entire village participates.

Certainly, changes are coming about. The homogeneous modern supermarkets and presures of two-career families are taking their tolls on gardening and cooking within the modern French household. Still, the appreciation of fresh-picked beans, basil, chervil, and tomatoes in their prime is still alive throughout France. The kitchen-garden tradition is still vigorous, and dooryard herb, *potager,* and salad gardens are thriving all over the country.

Overall, the French have explored the chemistry, flavor combinations, and presentation of food with a depth unmatched in other cultures. Even the lowly egg is treated with subtlety and careful thought: in one instance as an omelette stuffed with artichoke hearts, in another puffed up in a cheese soufflé. Strawberries might be served in a simple manner folded into a custard or served over a magnificent *savarin,* a raised cake soaked with rum and painted with an apricot glaze. Meats are served in pastry, for example, or made into pâtés. There is no end to the ways the French prepare food, and space considerations limit the examples I can cite. Therefore, I will restrict myself here to the French cooking techniques that feature vegetables.

The French appreciate the perfect vegetable unadorned—for example, garden-fresh petits pois are often cooked simply and given homage as a course by themselves. But the French are also known to manipulate vegetables much more than other cultures—for instance, pureeing spinach and serving it in crêpes, filling a molded terrine with rows of asparagus, baby carrots, and mushrooms; or, in one of France's most extraordinary dishes, using the famous flageolet beans as the basis of a stew called cassoulet (see the "Baked Bean Gardens" chapter).

To do real justice to French cooking, one must master a dozen or so basic techniques. Nowadays, if I want to make a quick meal, I can whip up an omelette, crêpes, or vegetables with a hollandaise sauce in just a few minutes, but the first few times I made these dishes I had to put so much energy into learning the techniques that they seemed to take forever. This section contains a number of basic recipes that involve a few of the traditional methods, but I heartily suggest that you consult one or more of the wonderful

OPPOSITE: *Salade Niçoise is a marvelous way to enjoy vegetables fresh from the garden. Shown here are vine-ripened tomatoes, waxy boiling potatoes, filet beans, and small boiling onions.*

The meal at Chez T. J.'s took me back to France. The bread was crispy and the butter firm and fresh—and when it ran out, more appeared as if by magic. We started with a velvety white and green bean soup with a slight hint of garlic and cool fresh mint. Next came salmon, moist and sweet-fresh, covered with crème fraîche and served with beautiful filet beans. The wine suggestion was perfect—a buttery Chardonnay. Next we were refreshed by a salad of pristine greens and shredded radicchio with walnut oil dressing. And for dessert? A sinful

Tom McCombie

chocolate mousse and wonderful coffee. Attempting to convey the perfect preparation and presentation of the meal leaves me feeling trapped in a shallow world of words. I'll just have to settle for telling you that, besides experiencing the sensual pleasure of the food, I felt for a few hours as if some unseen person cared passionately that I was happy.

The chef behind the scenes at Chez T. J.'s in Mountain View, California, is Tom McCombie. Tom had been recommended as an expert on French cooking, and I was so enthused after interviewing him that I made a reservation at his restaurant for a birthday celebration. Actually, I also wanted to reassure myself that he "cooked as good as he talked." I had no further doubts after our meal.

Tom became interested in cooking while studying psychology at the University of California at Berkeley. A friend brought him a copy of *Mastering the Art of French Cooking* one night, and Tom says, "I thought, this looks pretty interesting. Let's cook something. Six hours later we'd made beef Burgundy and I was hooked on cooking. It started as a hobby, but months later I noticed that Simone Beck, one of the authors of *Mastering the Art of French Cooking*, was teaching a cooking class in the Napa Valley, so I took a week off to attend. I seemed to have an aptitude for it, and Simone suggested at the end of the week that if I were interested in proper training

in French cuisine, I should come to France so she could oversee every aspect of my training." Six weeks later Tom quit school, and he and his wife sold their house, took their life savings, and moved to Paris. "We lived in Simone's flat in Neuilly," Tom says. "She was a strict taskmaster, and she made sure I was trained in the most appropriate French restaurants and the best the world had to offer. It was so difficult that my wife and I often questioned our wisdom in going, but when we returned to the States, it was all worthwhile. After working in a few other restaurants, George Aviet and I put together Chez T. J.'s in 1982."

Tom had been recommended to me not only for his expertise as a chef, but also because he has a small garden at the restaurant. When I asked him why the restaurant had its own garden, he answered, "Well, I think it states very clearly that care goes into the cuisine. I don't grow much—lettuces, endive, and some of our fresh herbs—but if I have to run out and get more chives in the middle of the evening, people at the tables notice and think, 'Gosh, that's fresh!'"

Next the conversation turned to how the French view vegetables. Tom explained, "The French integrate vegetables into their cuisine. I think a timbale—a molded custard of asparagus or carrots—is probably one of the most elevated ways that the French use vegetables, and I don't really know of any other cuisine that includes that kind of dish. A pâté made of asparagus is another example, or a terrine of leeks, and crêpes made with spinach are also elegant. The whole concept of French cuisine is to manipulate food and explore all its aspects, and certainly their vegetable cookery is as complex as any in the world except, perhaps, the Chinese."

Tom went on to say, "A look at classic French dishes reveals good examples of how the French integrate vegetables. Traditional dishes must have specific, appropriate vegetable garnishes. For example, beef Burgundy would never, under any circumstance, have a potato in it. It would only be made from a base of celery, onion, and carrots, and it would have only onions and mushrooms for a garnish. That, by definition, *is* beef Burgundy. Roast of chicken, *bonne femme,* on the other hand, must have onions and potatoes, and no mushrooms; and lamb *printanier* cannot be made without what are considered the 'spring vegetables'—little carrots, beans, turnips, and onions. There are unwritten laws that are a product of tradition—the appropriate vegetable must be there. That's the way the French are with so many of their dishes.

"The French care and respect for vegetables and the way they explore the finest qualities a food has to offer are reflected in the way they prepare green beans. They take pride in the little French green bean—a *haricot vert.* Their use of that single bean as a garnish is very lavish and implies a lot of care. The beans are very expensive because labor costs are high and yield is small. They're picked very tiny, at the peak of perfection, and great care is given to cooking them properly. To prepare them, you plunge them into boiling water and salt the water only when it comes back to a boil, then boil them only briefly and remove them when still crisp. A perfectly cooked green bean is crisp and green and fresh; it sets the standard for all other cooked green vegetables, like asparagus or peas. Beans are then further prepared by reheating in butter, or they're used in dishes like gratins, à la Mornay, or an elegant salad with foie gras."

Tom went on to say that soups are probably among the most popular uses for vegetables in France. "There are all kinds of soups in French cookery that are entirely meatless and depend on vegetables, not only for flavor but also for liaison, or blending: potato soup, much like vichyssoise, called *potage Parmentier*; watercress, carrot, asparagus, Brussels sprout, and broccoli soups; and, of course, onion soup, a classic among classics."

In conclusion, Tom discussed the direction modern French cuisine seems to be taking. "I think the emphasis in modern French cooking is on a lighter taste. Crêpes filled with pine nuts or hazelnuts and vegetables are in vogue these days, and vegetable purees are being used for liaisons in sauces. These purees are much like tomato paste, but you may use chive, turnip, celery, or spinach paste to thicken the dish instead of cream or butter and flour." So some French chefs are moving away from traditional rich, heavy sauces and the confines of the classic cuisine and are including more unusual ingredients and vegetables in innovative ways.

---

books listed in the "Sources" section for much more information. Concentrate on learning to make basic French stocks, sauces, and pastry—not only so you can prepare authentic and flavorful French dishes, but also to ensure better eating from the garden of any style. Practice making béchamel, with milk, and velouté, with stock, both sauces thickened with flour. And make hollandaise, a butter sauce bound with egg yolks, and beurre blanc, a foamy butter sauce. Also learn to make mayonnaise in a technique related to that for making hollandaise. Once you have mastered these techniques, vegetables in your house will never be the same.

Before we look at the techniques and recipes in detail, let's set the tone by considering some of the traditional French seasonings. The most traditional of all is the herb mixture known as bouquet garni. This is a small bundle of fresh herbs—bay leaf, thyme, celery leaves, and parsley—used in stews, soups, and stocks. The bundle is used like a tea bag, allowing the herbs to infuse the dish before being removed. Fines herbes is another mixture often called for in French recipes. This classic mixture usually consists of chopped tarragon and chervil but can also include parsley and chives. It is a mixture that is almost impossible to duplicate in this country if you don't have a garden. Consequently, frustrated French chef-authors here are reduced to calling for parsley, chives, and dried tarragon in their recipes, a poor substitute. As Tom McCombie says, "I never saw a box of dried herbs in any of the restaurants I worked in in France."

Because herbs are very important to the flavors of the dishes, the French also make great use of fresh chives, mint, rosemary, sage, basil, sorrel, shallots, garlic, and fennel. See the "Culinary Herb Gardens" chapter for more infomation on how they are used in French cooking. And be aware as you continue that many of the basic food-preparation techniques used in France are also used in other countries. In this regard, see many of the cooking techniques in the "Italian Gardens" and "German Gardens" chapters.

Cooking Vegetables in France

The French have two standard methods of cooking vegetables. The basic technique for green vegetables is to blanch them. See "Beans" in the "Recommended French Vegetables" section for this method. This procedure is used for snap beans, asparagus, artichokes, broccoli, cauliflower, peas, Brussels sprouts, chard, and spinach. In blanching, great care is used to prevent overcooking the vegetables so that they keep their fresh color. Root vegetables such as carrots, beets, turnips, and onions are slow cooked in a covered pan with a small amount of liquid, butter, and seasonings. The liquid is evaporated away until the vegetables end up being almost sautéed in the butter. Other vegetables cooked this way are cabbage, lettuce, celery, fennel, and endive. Some of these slow-cooked vegetables—most typically, small onions, turnips, and carrots—are also glazed in France. *Glacer à brun* or *à blanc* is a technique of glazing cooked vegetables of small uniform shapes in a butter and sugar mixture that gives them a sheen (*brun* [brown] and *blanc* [white] refer to whether or not the sugar caramelizes and colors the vegetable).

Preparation Methods for Vegetables

What follows is an overview of the standard French treatments of vegetables. For more detailed instructions, consult one or more of the books listed under "Sources" at the end of this chapter.

Crêpes: These delicate pancakes, a specialty of Brittany, are stuffed with all varieties of vegetables and served with sauces. Crêpes stuffed with fruits make a spectacular dessert.

Custards: A custard is a dish in which ingredients are bound with milk and eggs, a common cooking technique in France. Included in this category are timbales, made with vegetables that have a relatively low water content. Broccoli, corn, asparagus, spinach, onions, zucchini, and cauliflower are often used to make these molded custards. Here a custard mixture is poured over the vegetables and the dish is baked in the oven in a water bath. Although the word *pain* ("loaf") designates something quite sim-

ilar, in general *pains* have a higher proportion of vegetables than a timbale. An example is a spinach puree bound together with eggs and a bit of béchamel sauce and then baked.

Gratins: These are vegetables cooked and then sauced or topped with cheese or bread crumbs and butter and put in the oven or under the broiler to brown. Vegetables often gratinéed are eggplants, leeks, onions, and potatoes.

Mousselines and purees: Mousselines are vegetable purees lightened with a lot of cream and butter. Typical vegetable purees are those of peas, carrots, potatoes, celery root, and turnips.

Mousses: Mousses are light dishes bound together with whipped egg whites, cream, or gelatin. While usually a dessert, a mousse can be made with vegetables and without sugar as a main or side dish. Red pepper mousse, made with a bell pepper puree and whipped cream, is an outstanding example. Try making a mousse with green beans, tomatoes, or garlic.

Salads: The French make wonderful and diverse salads, using both raw and cooked vegetables. Fennel can be used raw, as can the violet artichokes from Provence. Beets are used both raw and cooked. Other salad ingredients are radishes, peppers, endive, frisée, lettuce, mâche, radicchio, cucumbers, tomatoes, carrots, celery, yellow and green beans, dry beans, asparagus, cauliflower, celery root, broccoli, eggplant, onions, and leeks. See the "Gourmet Salad Gardens" chapter and the profile of Georgeanne Brennan in this chapter for more information on the basic French green salad.

Soufflés: A soufflé is a sweet or savory dish containing beaten egg whites that puffs up into an elegant preparation when baked. Soufflés can be made with a vegetable puree of artichokes, watercress, snap beans, leeks, onions, asparagus, eggplant, spinach, escarole, tomatoes, or zucchini, and flavored with fresh herbs and cheeses.

Soups: Soups fall into specific categories in France: purees, which are self-evident; *potages taillés,* containing little pieces of cut-up vegetables; cream soups thickened with cream or béchamel; bean-based soups; and consommés made with meat stock and sometimes flavored with vegetables or containing floating vegetables.

Stews and ragouts: Vegetables are often used in meat-based stews or in stews of their own such as ratatouille or a mushroom ragout. Other forms of stew are cassoulets, in which beans are the base of the stew; lentil stews, which are mixed with sausages and pork; and sauerkrauts, in which cabbage is the stew base.

Stuffed vegetables: Vegetables eaten stuffed are served raw or cooked, hot or cold. They may be stuffed with a vegetable soufflé made from the scooped-out insides of the vegetable or with fish, meat, or other vegetables. Tomatoes, peppers, artichokes, mushrooms, zucchini, eggplant, potatoes, cabbage, and onions are all vegetables that are commonly stuffed.

Tarts and quiches: Tarts are open-faced pies usually filled with fruits; quiches are similar but the filling is a savory custard mixture. As with timbales, the vegetable used must have a low water content or the water must be removed through cooking to protect the crust or custard. Besides pie shells, puff pastry shells or cases (flaky-thin layers of dough and butter) are filled with vegetables and sauce. Vegetables that are common in tarts and quiches are asparagus, onions, bell peppers, broccoli, and leeks.

Only a few fragrant Alpine strawberries are needed to richly flavor a French cream tart.

Terrines: A terrine is a molded main-course dish. The base is usually ground meat or fish, but the emphasis in presentation is on the rows of vegetables, such as peas, carrots, asparagus, snap beans, and mushrooms, baked into the loaf.

Like the world's other cuisines, French cuisine is changing. Fancy appliances, the ubiquitous supermarket, and the fast pace of modern life are nudging it more in the direction of streamlined dishes, fast meals, and convenience foods. Other basic changes, however, stem from nutritional information. For centuries a classic tradition dictated combinations of foods, sauces made with butter and flour, and strong seasonings, and the resulting dishes could be heavy in taste and on the stomach and the circulatory system. However, in the last twenty to thirty years a style of cooking called nouvelle cuisine has become popular. This style tends to vary the taste of some of the classic dishes and emphasizes lighter sauces thickened with butter or vegetable purees and vegetables that are less throughly cooked. And the meals, while sometimes less fattening, are usually about the same in caloric value and generally easier to digest. More recently, in 1976, three-star chef Michel Guerard created cuisine minceur and wrote a book of that name stressing techniques for cooking French food without all the calories—the original "spa" cuisine. (For more information on spa cuisine, see the "Spa Gardens" chapter). In the media and in the public's eye the nouvelle and minceur cuisines are often confused, but they are really quite different. Minceur emphasizes caloric consciousness while nouvelle primarily stresses lighter, subtler tastes and elegant presentation. The information presented in this chapter is drawn from the classic- and nouvelle-style French cuisines. It is directed more to those who will eat cottage cheese and salads for days to prepare for a glorious, calorific meal than those who are watching their calories. *Bon appétit!*

CREAM OF CARROT TOP SOUP

I had never heard of eating carrot tops until I met Tom McCombie, owner and chef of Chez T. J.'s, a French restaurant in Mountain View, California. I was actually a little skeptical, so before I asked Tom for the recipe, I checked the resources on edible and poisonous plants in the herbarium library at the University of California at Davis to make sure carrot tops were edible. The reports deemed them safe to eat, and after I tasted and loved them, carrot tops became a must for the book. This soup is an absolute delight. The orange carrots are pureed in their creamy base and the green tops done in a separate base; the two soups of different colors are then poured into the bowl separately to wonderful effect.

SERVES 6 TO 8.

> 1 large yellow onion, diced medium
> 3 mashed cloves of fresh peeled garlic
> 2 tablespoons butter
> 1 teaspoon whole fresh thyme leaves
> 4 cups chicken stock
> 6 large carrots, peeled and coarsely chopped
> 2 medium potatoes, peeled and coarsely
>   chopped
> 1 bay leaf
> 1 teaspoon salt
> ½ teaspoon ground white pepper
> About 1 cup milk or half-and-half
> 2 tablespoons softened butter
> 2 tablespoons chopped parsley
> 3 cups tender young carrot greens
> 1 quart boiling water
> 2 teaspoons salt
> 1½ cups lightly whipped cream

Sauté onion and garlic in butter until golden. Add thyme leaves and cook 1 minute more. Add chicken stock, carrots, potatoes, bay leaf, salt, and pepper, and simmer for 30 minutes. Remove bay leaf and put mixture through a food processor fitted with a steel blade or a blender by batches and puree to the desired consistency.

Return puree to soup pot. Thin to consistency preferred with the milk or half-and-half, and bring soup to a simmer. Stir in the softened butter by bits and chopped parsley. Keep warm.

Pick over carrot tops, removing any stems or yellow leaves. Plunge greens into the boiling water and when the water reboils add the salt. Remove from heat, drain, and puree greens in the blender or food processor with 2 cups of pureed carrot soup.

To serve the soup, fill soup bowls ⅔ full with orange carrot soup. Ladle green carrot soup in the middle of soup bowl to fill it. Top soup with dollops of whipped cream.

PISTOU SOUFFLÉ

Tom McCombie responded with this when I asked him for a recipe for a vegetable soufflé. Here the flavors come primarily from the *pistou*, a classic sauce of garlic, basil, tomatoes, and cheese. With this as a flavor base, a soufflé becomes a versatile way to prepare mild-flavored vegetables, such as zucchini and eggplant.

SERVES 4 TO 5.

Pistou

> 3 cloves garlic
> 1 large, ripe, red tomato, peeled, seeded,
>   chopped, and drained
> 1 cup fresh basil leaves
> ½ cup grated Parmesan cheese
> ⅓ cup chopped almonds or pine nuts
> ½ cup olive oil
> Salt and black pepper to taste

In a food processor fitted with a steel blade, combine garlic, tomato, basil, cheese, and nuts. Process the mixture until smooth. In a thin stream, add olive oil. Set *pistou* aside and proceed with soufflé.

Soufflé

> 4 tablespoons butter
> 1 minced shallot
> 1 cup finely grated zucchini, squeezed in a
>   cloth until absolutely dry
> 4 tablespoons flour
> 1 cup milk
> Salt and white pepper to taste
> The pistou above
> 4 egg yolks
> 5 egg whites
> Pinch of cream of tartar
> 1 cup of grated Parmesan cheese
> ½ cup warm cream
> 6-cup soufflé mold

Preheat oven to 425°.

In a sauté pan, melt butter. Add shallot and cook until translucent. Add zucchini and cook until tender and dry. Stir in flour and cook a moment longer. Off heat, stir in milk and cook mixture until smooth and thick. Season with salt and pepper. Stir in ½ of the *pistou* and the egg yolks.

In a bowl, beat egg whites with cream of tartar until very firm but not dry. Pour the warm base from above over whites, and with a large rubber spatula fold base and whites together until no trace of white is left. Pour resulting mixture into a well-buttered 6-cup soufflé mold. Top soufflé with grated Parmesan cheese. Put soufflé in the middle of the oven, turn heat down to 375° and bake for 30 minutes.

Use cream to thin remaining *pistou* to the consistency of sauce. Remove soufflé from oven and spoon a little of the sauce over the top of the soufflé. Serve immediately and pass sauce on the side.

FILET OF SALMON WITH TOMATOES, ROCK SALT, AND CHIVES

A beautiful showcase for garden-ripe tomatoes, this is one of the most requested dishes at Tom McCombie's restaurant. As Tom says, "This dish comes as close to chemistry as most people experience in eating because the range of tastes fills your mouth."

SERVES 6.

> *6 salmon filets, 4 ounces each*
> *3 cups dry white wine*
> *1 shallot, minced fine*
> *2 tablespoons sherry vinegar*
> *¼ cup softened butter*
> *3 large, ripe, red tomatoes, peeled, seeded, and chopped*
> *¼ cup dry white wine*
> *White pepper to flavor*
> *Salt, cayenne pepper, and white pepper to taste*
> *¼ cup fresh chives, minced fine*
> *1½ teaspoons rock salt*

Place salmon filets in a shallow pan and cover them with 3 cups white wine. Heat wine to the barest simmer. It will take 4 to 6 minutes to cook the salmon. When filets are cooked, drain off cooking liquid into an enameled saucepan, add shallot and vinegar. Keep filets warm while you reduce the liquid to ¾ cup. In another skillet, melt ¼ cup of the butter and add chopped tomatoes. Toss for a minute or so and add white wine and pepper. Do not overcook tomatoes. Now finish sauce over gentle heat by whisking the

rest of the remaining ½ cup melted butter into the reduced wine. Adjust seasoning with very little salt and peppers.

To serve, divide warm tomatoes among 6 serving plates. Place a salmon filet on top of tomatoes. Spoon some sauce over each filet and sprinkle sauce and fish generously with chives. Top each serving with a scant ¼ teaspoon of rock salt and dash of white pepper. Serve immediately.

GREEN AÏOLI

Jesse Cool, chef and owner of Flea Street Cafe and Late for the Train restaurant in Menlo Park, California, uses this herbed version of the classic sauce (most famous in the French *grande aïoli*) on fish or as a dip for vegetables. Careful! You might be tempted to put it on everything.

MAKES ABOUT 1½ CUPS.

> *¼ cup scallion greens, cut into ½-inch slices*
> *¼ cup loosely packed basil leaves*
> *2 to 3 large cloves garlic*
> *1 whole egg plus 2 egg yolks*
> *⅔ cup olive oil*
> *½ cup vegetable oil*
> *2 tablespoons lemon juice*
> *Salt and pepper to taste*

In a food processor, chop scallions, basil, and garlic. Add egg and yolks. Through feed tube, add oils slowly in a steady stream until sauce thickens to the consistency of light mayonnaise. Add lemon juice and salt and pepper and process until well blended. Chill. Use as you would a mayonnaise.

FRENCH ONION SOUP

Mastering the Art of French Cooking has long been my bible for French cooking, and I've used it to prepare many classic French dishes, including onion soup. Over the years, and particularly since visiting Les Halles, a market section of Paris where this soup is served in many restaurants, I've been developing my own recipe, one with a more pronounced onion flavor than that in the book. The careful browning of the onions is the secret to rich flavor here.

SERVES 8.

*8 to 10 medium onions (8 to 10 cups), thinly
  sliced*
4 tablespoons butter
1 teaspoon sugar
3 tablespoons flour
8 cups beef stock or bouillon
¾ cup dry white vermouth
Salt and pepper to taste
3 tablespoons cognac or brandy
1 tablespoon grated raw onion
1 clove garlic
8 slices toasted French bread
2 cups grated Swiss cheese
1 tablespoon olive oil
8 ovenproof ramekins or soup bowls

Preheat oven to 325°.

In a large saucepan, melt butter and stir in sliced onions, cover, and cook slowly for about 15 minutes, stirring occasionally. Uncover, stir in sugar, and cook on low to medium heat for 30 minutes or until well browned. Stir often, scraping bottom of pan to prevent burning. Sprinkle in flour and stir for 2 to 3 minutes. Off heat, slowly stir in stock, vermouth, and seasoning (if bouillon is salted, do not add more salt). Then cover and simmer on low heat for 30 minutes. Stir in cognac or brandy and raw onion.

Rub garlic clove over toasted bread. Place a little soup in each of 8 ovenproof ramekins or soup bowls. Divide ¼ of the grated cheese evenly among the bowls. Put 1 slice of bread in each bowl; then cover with more soup and the remaining cheese. Dribble oil over each and place in oven for 20 minutes; then set under broiler to lightly brown the top. Serve immediately.

GREEN BEANS LYONNAISE

Lyon is a French city famous for its gastronomic heritage, and the phrase *à la Lyonnaise* has come to mean "with browned onions," which indeed can be a tasty addition to many dishes. These onions go particularly well with fresh snap beans, as in the recipe below.

SERVES 4.

2 tablespoons butter
1 to 2 medium onions, thinly sliced
1 pound (3 cups) fresh snap beans, trimmed

*and cooked according to the recipe for
  blanched green beans in the "Rainbow
  Gardens" chapter*
Salt and pepper to taste
1 tablespoon wine vinegar
1 tablespoon minced parsley

Heat butter in a skillet and sauté onions until transparent. Add beans, salt, and pepper and sauté until onions and beans are lightly browned. Add vinegar, pour into a serving bowl, and garnish with parsley.

SALADE NIÇOISE

This classic salad is from the south of France; olives and anchovies betray the Mediterranean influence. The beauty of the dish is in the arrangement, which can be done on a serving platter or individual plates.

SERVES 6.

*3 to 5 medium potatoes (new potatoes
  preferred)*
*1 cup vinaigrette (see recipe in the "Gourmet
  Salad Gardens" chapter), preferably made
  with fresh tarragon*
*1 pound (3 cups) fresh snap beans, trimmed
  and cooked according to the recipe for
  blanched green beans in the "Rainbow
  Gardens" chapter*
*1 head butter lettuce, washed, dried, and
  chilled*
3 ripe tomatoes, quartered
*1 cup high-quality canned or cooked tuna,
  chilled*
3 hard-boiled eggs, halved
½ cup Mediterranean-style olives
Approximately 6 canned anchovy filets
Tarragon or other fresh herbs for garnish

Boil whole potatoes until just tender. Drain and rinse in cold water and slip off skins. While still warm, cut into ⅛-inch slices and gently toss with about ⅓ cup of vinaigrette in a bowl. Place blanched beans in another bowl and toss with enough dressing to coat. Just before serving, toss lettuce leaves with vinaigrette to coat and arrange on platter or plates. Arrange all ingredients in distinct clusters on lettuce, drizzling on remaining vinaigrette and garnishing with herbs. Serve with French bread.

BRAISED PEAS WITH LETTUCE IN THE FRENCH STYLE

This is Marian Morash's version, from *The Victory Garden Cookbook,* of the traditional French dish. She describes it by saying, "Here's the classic way to cook peas. The long braise gives a totally different taste and texture to the peas. Use older peas and see how mellow and creamy they get. You can almost eat them with a spoon."

SERVES 4 TO 6.

1 head Boston or butterhead lettuce
½ cup chicken broth or water
8 tablespoons butter
1 to 2 tablespoons sugar
2 to 3 sprigs parsley
½ teaspoon salt
3 cups shelled peas
3 to 4 tablespoons heavy cream (optional)

Clean and trim lettuce, cut into quarters, and place in a saucepan along with chicken broth, 6 tablespoons butter, sugar, parsley, and salt. Bring to a boil, stir in peas, cover, and return to a boil. Reduce heat and cook slowly for 15 to 20 minutes or until peas are very tender, tossing several times. (When peas are done, cooking liquid will be almost evaporated.) Remove lettuce and parsley. Toss peas with remaining butter. Serve with the lettuce if desired.

As a variation, use shredded lettuce, and when the peas are tender and the juices evaporated, add 3 to 4 tablespoons heavy cream and cook until cream is thickened, lightly coating the vegetables.

GARDENER'S SPRING LAMB (Navarin Printanier)

Georgeanne Brennan, of Le Marché seed company and co-author of *The New American Vegetable Cookbook,* contributed this and the next two recipes. She drew on her years in France to create them. Of this one Georgeanne says, "This is a very simple stew or ragout that acquires its excellence from the quality of the ingredients used, and the main ingredients are the very young, very fresh vegetables of

A simple, elegant salad of butter lettuce and fresh garden chervil is a French tradition.

spring. Of course, the best place to obtain these is in one's garden."

SERVES 4 TO 6.

2 pounds boned shoulder of lamb
Salt and pepper
2 tablespoons butter
1 tablespoon olive oil
2 tablespoons flour
3 to 4 cups beef stock
2 cloves garlic
4 sprigs parsley
4 sprigs chervil
2 bay leaves
16 very small new potatoes
16 small (2-inch-long) new carrots
16 small onions or 8 new shallots or 16 scallions
12 small new turnips
2 cups shelled peas (petits pois preferred)

Cut the lamb into ½-inch cubes. Toss with salt and pepper and set aside for an hour or so. In a heavy casserole, melt butter and add olive oil. Brown lamb; then remove to a platter. Off heat, stir in flour to make a thick paste. Return to heat, gradually adding half the beef stock, stirring all the time. When sauce is smooth, add garlic, parsley, chervil, and bay leaves. Add lamb, cover, and simmer for 1 hour.

Meanwhile, scrape the root vegetables, but leave them whole. Peel onions or shallots; if using scallions, trim the roots and cut off tops, leaving only the white plus 1 inch of green. Add root vegetables and onions to lamb and cook for 45 minutes, uncovered. Skim any surface fat or foam. Add peas and cook until they are tender, about 5 minutes. Serve in a hot dish.

FALL GREENS WITH CHICKEN LIVERS

This is a zesty way to do yourself some good nutritionally.

SERVES 6.

> ½ pound kale
> ¼ pound mustard greens
> ½ pound chard, red or white
> ¼ pound beet greens
> 1 clove garlic
> ½ onion
> 6 chicken livers
> Salt and pepper to taste
> 3 tablespoons olive oil
> 1 small dry red chili, seeds removed and crumbled
> 3 tablespoons red wine vinegar
> 1 tablespoon Dijon mustard
> ¼ cup olive oil

Wash greens twice thoroughly in bowls or a sink of water. Discard stems (or save for another purpose), chop greens, and steam 2 minutes in the water remaining on leaves (add a little more if necessary). Rinse quickly with cold water.

Peel and chop garlic and onion. Rub livers with salt and pepper. Heat oil in a skillet and sauté onion and garlic until just golden. Add livers and cook just until they are pink and firm; do not overcook. Remove

livers and chop or crumble. Combine remaining ingredients in skillet and heat. Add greens and livers; toss and serve warm.

GRATIN OF CROSNES

This dish displays a wonderful contrast between the nutty flavor and crunchy texture of the crosnes and the velvety sauce. It makes an elegant side dish with a fancy roast.

SERVES 4.

> 1 pound crosnes
> Juice of 1 lemon
> Pinch of salt
> 2 tablespoons butter
> 2 tablespoons flour
> 1 cup milk
> ¼ cup grated Gruyère cheese
> Salt to taste
> ½ teaspoon white pepper
> ¼ cup rich pan juices from a roast chicken or beef
> ¼ cup dry French bread crumbs
> 1 tablespoon butter

Preheat oven to 400°.

To prepare crosnes, remove the tiny tips and tails. Rinse and put them in a pan with just enough water to cover, lemon juice, and a pinch of salt. Bring to a boil, cover, and cook 10 minutes or until tender. Drain and place in a shallow, buttered casserole dish.

To make sauce, melt butter. Off heat, blend in flour, stirring constantly. Return to heat and slowly add milk, stirring constantly until sauce begins to thicken. Add cheese, salt, and pepper, and continue to cook over low heat until flavors have blended. Pour sauce over crosnes. Drizzle with pan juices and top with bread crumbs and dots of butter. Place in oven for 5 minutes, then put under broiler until top is nicely browned. Serve with roast chicken or beef.

WORKING WOMAN'S CORNICHONS

Georgeanne and her partner and coauthor, Charlotte Glenn, developed this quick and simple recipe for their mail-order vegetable seed catalog. They advise cooks to "use very small cornichon cucumbers (2 inch or less) and prepare the night before you plan on serving them. The next day you will have crisp and delicately flavored cornichons. Traditionally served with pâté, try them anytime you would serve other pickles."

MAKES 30 PICKLES.

> 30 tiny cornichon cucumbers
> 1 cup water
> 1 cup white vinegar
> 1 teaspoon salt
> ½ teaspoon sugar
> 2 cloves garlic, peeled
> 1 tablespoon fresh tarragon leaves

Scrub cucumbers and set aside. If you don't have enough at one time, you may store them refrigerated in a sealed plastic bag for 2 or 3 days. Combine water, vinegar, salt, and sugar in a saucepan and bring to boil. Add garlic and tarragon and pour over cucumbers. Cover and let stand for 12 hours. Refrigerate for at least 2 hours before serving.

RATATOUILLE

This dish from southern France uses the summer garden harvest to make a fragrant vegetable stew with rich, satisfying flavors. Traditionally, the essential ingredients are eggplant, zucchini, tomatoes, green peppers, onions, garlic, and olive oil seasoned with salt and pepper only. French chefs insist that each ingredient be cooked separately until just done, then reassembled and heated through. But the summer abundance always inspires me to add other vegetables to my ratatouille; I cook all the ingredients together and am always pleased with the results—even if it isn't a "true" ratatouille.

SERVES 6 TO 8.

> ¼ cup olive oil
> 1 large onion, chopped
> 2 medium eggplants (or enough to make 4 cups) chopped into ½-inch cubes
> 3 cloves garlic, minced
> 2 to 3 cups chopped tomatoes
> 2 to 4 zucchini or other summer squash (4 cups) chopped into ½-inch cubes

> 2 to 3 green peppers, diced or sliced
> Salt and pepper to taste
> 1 cup chopped green beans (optional)
> ¼ to ½ cup chopped fresh basil (optional)

In a large skillet, kettle, or Dutch oven, heat oil and sauté onion until just starting to cook. Add eggplant and garlic, stir, and sauté for 3 to 4 minutes. Add tomatoes and cook for about 5 minutes, stirring occasionally. Add squash, peppers, and green beans if desired; cover and simmer 10 to 15 minutes or until vegetables are tender. If using basil, add during last few minutes. If too much liquid accumulates, uncover pan and reduce.

Serve hot or cold. Good with chicken, beef, or lamb; with cheese melted over it; in crêpes, quiche, or omelettes; topped with poached or fried egg; on pizza; or just eaten with a spoon.

Early spring asparagus served with hollandaise sauce has to be one of life's richest pleasures.

ASPARAGUS WITH HOLLANDAISE SAUCE

Perfectly cooked, fresh-picked asparagus is the gardener's reward for care and patience. For a special occasion, gild this lily-family vegetable with a rich hollandaise sauce.

Asparagus

SERVES 6.

> 2 to 3 pounds asparagus
> Salt

Take each spear and snap off lower end at point where it breaks readily. Use tough ends for soup or discard. Wash spears well to remove grit.

Select a large oval roasting pan or deep casserole and fill 3/4 full with water. For each quart of water add 1 teaspoon salt. Bring water to a boil.

Add asparagus to water and boil until done, about 3 to 6 minutes. Pierce a stalk with fork to test for doneness. Well-cooked asparagus is slightly tender, a bit crunchy, and bright-green. Remove asparagus from pan with tongs and drain well on a towel. Serve immediately, as is, or with the following hollandaise sauce.

Hollandaise Sauce

The velvety texture and richness of hollandaise is the result of the artful combination of egg yolks and melted butter. Making this sauce is somewhat tricky but exceedingly rewarding, since once you learn how to make it, related sauces such as mayonnaise and béarnaise sauce are easily mastered.

The trick to making hollandaise is to allow the egg yolks to slowly absorb the butter and seasonings and not have them curdle or separate. To avoid these problems, you must not let the mixture get too hot or you will scramble the egg yolks, nor add the melted butter too quickly.

Hollandaise can be made by hand with a wire whisk or made in a blender or food processor. The first few times you make it, I recommend doing it by hand so that you have more control. If you want to use a blender or food processor, check the manufacturer's guide to your machine.

MAKES 1 TO 1½ CUPS.

> ⅓ to ½ cup butter
> 3 egg yolks
> 1 tablespoon water
> Salt and pepper
> 1 to 2 tablespoons fresh lemon juice

Melt butter in a saucepan. Keep warm but not boiling. Put egg yolks and water in top of a double boiler and whisk together. Place over water simmering in bottom of double boiler and whisk until eggs start to thicken. Do not let water in bottom of double boiler boil or touch top of boiler that holds eggs. Have a bowl of cold water nearby in case eggs start to curdle so that you can quickly submerge bottom of pan to cool it.

Once eggs have thickened, remove double boiler from heat. Beat sauce well and start adding warm butter a few dribbles at a time while continually beating mixture. The process takes 3 to 4 minutes. As sauce thickens you can add butter more rapidly. Do not include butter's milky residue in the sauce. When all butter has been absorbed, add lemon juice and seasonings to taste. Keep sauce warm over hot, not boiling, water and prepare asparagus.

Serve sauce in a small pitcher or make up individual serving plates and spoon a few tablespoons of sauce over asparagus spears.

Sources

Seed Companies

1. The Cook's Garden
   P.O. Box 65
   Londonderry, VT 05148
   This seed company carries numerous superior varieties of vegetables, many of which are European.

2. Fox Hill Farm
   444 West Michigan Avenue
   P.O. Box 7
   Parma, MI 49269
   This firm carries one of the nation's largest selections of herb plants, including the primary French ones.

3. Herb Gathering, Inc.
   5742 Kenwood
   Kansas City, MO 64110

This seed company specializes in seeds of French vegetable varieties.

4. Le Jardin du Gourmet
   West Danville, VT 05873
   This firm carries a large selection of French vegetables plus seeds for herbs. Catalog: $.50.

5. Le Marché
   Seeds International
   P.O. Box 190
   Dixon, CA 95620
   This seed company carries numerous European vegetable varieties, including many French ones. Catalog: $2.00.

6. Shepherd's Garden Seeds
   7389 West Zayante Road
   Felton, CA 95018
   This seed company offers many varieties of European vegetables, including many French ones. Catalog: $1.00.

Mail-Order Sources of Ingredients

Balducci's
Mail Order Division
334 East 11th Street
New York, NY 10003
While specializing in Italian foods, Balducci's carries many French specialty ingredients, particularly those of Provence.

Williams-Sonoma
Mail Order Department
P.O. Box 7456
San Francisco, CA 94120

This company stocks a large selection of sophisticated cooking equipment and ingredients for French cooking.

Books

Child, Julia, Louisette Bertholle, and Simone Beck. *Mastering the Art of French Cooking.* 2d. ed. New York: Knopf, 1985.
This classic is a must in every cook's library. I can't imagine cooking without it.

Fisher, M. F. K., and the editors of Time-Life Books. *The Cooking of Provincial France.* New York: Time-Life Books, 1968.
This is another classic text on French cooking. It contains a great deal of cultural background on the food and many basic recipes.

Pepin, Jacques. *La Technique.* New York: Pocket Books, 1978.
A classic, this book is filled with hundreds of detailed pictures illustrating most of the basic French cooking techniques

Puck, Wolfgang. *Wolfgang Puck's Modern French Cooking.* Boston: Houghton Mifflin, 1986.
This book contains numerous innovative recipes from the well-known chef of Spago's restaurant in Los Angeles.

Willan, Anne. *Basic French Cookery.* Tucson: HP Books, 1980.
This is an approachable book on French cooking filled with simplified recipes and many photos.

German Gardens

HANSEL HAGEL REMEMBERS back to her childhood in Germany after World War I when inflation was so bad you needed a million marks to equal one of the old ones. Just before the monetary world collapsed completely, the cabbage wagon came through town, and Hansel's parents spent forty thousand marks (their whole life savings) on enough cabbage to get them through the winter.

Cabbage is a German staple, and like most of her compatriots, Hansel's mother relied on cabbage as a component of the winter meal, most commonly served as sauerkraut. To make sauerkraut, her mother would shave huge, dense, white cabbages into slivers and layer them in a barrel with salt, juniper berries, and dried elderberries, pounding each layer as she put it down. The resulting sauerkraut was quite a bit finer than most we are used to in this country today.

The family stored its sauerkraut in the root cellar, and Hansel remembers that every few days her mother would go down and check on what she called her "children down in the cellar." The cellar was cool, and in addition to the sauerkraut, it contained barrels of potatoes, carrots, beets, and apples; bags of walnuts, beechnuts, and dried elderberries; and bottles

OPPOSITE: *A German garden highlights cool-season vegetables, such as Savoy cabbage, German-type 'Lady Finger' potatoes, celeriac, red cabbage, and carrots.*

of honey and homemade liqueurs. The cabbages and the sauerkraut were stored off to one side so they wouldn't impart their flavor to everything else. On her visits to the cellar, Hansel's mother would sort through the potatoes and apples to remove the rotten ones, but her main concern was to check on the sauerkraut. This entailed removing the wooden top on the sauerkraut barrel and taking off the white muslin cloth to rinse it in salt water, thereby preventing mold and scum from forming on the sauerkraut. Another part of the routine involved checking the water level in the sauerkraut barrel, since evaporation caused it to vary. Remembers Hansel, "My mother said that when the moon was full the water stayed high over the cabbages, and when the moon was new it became low, and she always had to add a little water to cover it."

The cool weather in Germany is perfect for growing healthy, dense cabbages as well as peas, aromatic leeks, and waxy potatoes. And, as I learned from my husband's family, the Germans have rich and innovative ways to cook all these foods. I had decided when this book was in the planning stage that including a German garden would be the perfect way to explore cool-season-vegetable growing and to track down exciting ways to prepare such produce in the kitchen.

True to plan, in the garden sections of this chapter, I concentrate on cool-weather vegetables, crops that are often undervalued but are usually rewarding in both the cool-summer and mild-winter areas of the country. In the cooking section, in order to cover a large variety of methods and vegetables, I focus on the traditional German cooking of a bygone era, when root cellars were common and the produce came from the family garden or a local farmer. Modern Germany, though it still favors cabbages and root vegetables, is quite Continental in its cooking style, and its produce markets are now filled with imported tomatoes, radicchios, and eggplants; greenhouse-grown peppers and cucumbers; and the usual array of prepared convenience foods. To fully appreciate these garden vegetables, then, I had to do some research on the past, when the German people routinely cooked fresh produce out of the garden.

I also take the opportunity in this chapter to touch on the problems that often arise when, in our ethnic cooking, we attempt to locate vegetables and herbs from other countries. Suppose you wanted to grow something unusual that you enjoyed abroad or that you grew up with elsewhere, but you didn't know how to locate the seeds in this country. I mention the experiences my neighbors the Kuckeins have had with that problem, and, as in the other chapters, I include the native (here, German) names of some of the country's most common herbs and vegetables to make the seeds easier to locate.

To explore the German garden I had help from Carolyn and Paul Kuckein, my neighbors who have lived in Germany off and on over the years and who offered to grow a German-style garden for me. Hansel Hagel and Kaete Reimnitz, both gardeners who grew up in Germany, also helped tremendously. Hansel gave me historical information, and Kaete spent hours going over lists of vegetables and herbs with me and sharing both her current methods and her mother's old-fashioned methods of cooking the produce we discussed.

As Hansel's recollections suggest, German gardeners and cooks traditionally concentrate on the root vegetables, the cabbage family, and a few other assorted cool-season vegetables. This is in contrast to Chinese gardeners and cooks, who also cultivate cool-season vegetables but seem more interested in the green leafy types. For an in-depth look at many cool-season greens, see the "Oriental Gardens" chapter and Part Four, "An Encyclopedia of Superior Vegetables." It's my hope that the current chapter will inspire those who don't usually garden in cool weather to consider the possibilities. Cool-season vegetables have great potential in both the garden and the kitchen.

How to Grow a German Garden

The weather in most of Germany is ideal for growing cool-season vegetables. In most areas, springs and falls are long and summers are short, humid, quite rainy, and cool—rarely topping 80 degrees. In this hemisphere, the areas that would probably be most similar in climate are the maritime Northwest and parts of coastal Canada and New England. In such climates, gardeners can become frustrated at trying to ripen melons or attempting to produce eggplants and corn in the summer, but cool-season vegetables become the stars of the winter garden. The same is true in other parts of the country that have long, cool springs or falls or, in most cases, mild winters.

To begin with a definition, I consider the cool-season vegetables to be those that grow and produce best in temperatures between 40 and 70 degrees, and that often bolt, get tough or bitter, or die back in hot weather. To identify the cool-season vegetables easily, I use this rough rule of thumb: where the leaf, root, tuber, or flower of a vegetable is eaten, the plant prefers cool growing conditions; cabbage, beets, white potatoes, and broccoli are examples. Where the fruit or seed is eaten, on the other hand, the vegetable is a warm-season one—for example, tomatoes and corn. There are a few exceptions to this rule, but the only important ones are peas and sweet potatoes. We eat the seeds of peas, but the pea is a cool-season vegetable; we eat the tuber of the sweet potato, but it is a warm-season vegetable. Here's a list of cool-season vegetables that conform to my rule: the root vegetables—beets, carrots, parsnips, radishes, rutabagas, salsify, and turnips; the tubers—potatoes; the cabbage family—broccoli, Brussels sprouts, cabbage, cauliflower, kale, kohlrabi; and miscellaneous other vegetables—for example, celeriac, chard, leeks, lettuce, mâche, onions, peas, and spinach.

Remember, though, the rule above has its exceptions, and some of the vegetables listed can actually take quite a bit of heat—chard, carrots, and specific varieties of cabbage, for example. And many of these vegetables are started in summer and grown over the winter. But the distinctive characteristic shared by all the vegetables on the list is that they grow and produce most readily in cool weather. Further, most of the plants can take quite a bit of frost.

When selecting and working with cool-season vegetables, bear the following points in mind. First, variety selection can be critical. For example, there are spring, summer, and winter varieties of cabbages, and it is important that you choose the right varieties for your climate, since cool-weather conditions will differ notably between, say, an Alabama midwinter garden and an Oregon summer one. The greatest differences involve the amount of daylight the plants get and the point in their growing cycle at which hot or cold weather occurs. I remember being frustrated winter after winter in my attempts to grow onions in my mild-winter area. The varieties I chose always went to flower in the spring instead of bulbing up. I didn't know that onions are triggered to bulb up by the change in day length, and I had been planting summer varieties that bulbed up as the days got shorter, not longer. Cabbage varieties, too, need to

be carefully selected; the types are best suited for one time of the year or another. Diseases also vary with the different parts of the country. For example, enation, a virus disease in peas, is a problem in the Northwest but not in coastal California. The solution to all these differences and potential problems is to get a basic garden book geared to your part of the country and to buy your seeds from companies that specialize in varieties for your climate.

Seed companies that carry quite a few cool-season varieties are listed in "Sources" at the end of this chapter. Nichols Garden Nursery has a large selection, and Territorial Seed Company, because it specializes in vegetables for the maritime Northwest, is particularly valuable to that area. Territorial Seed carries peas resistant to enation, a large selection of all types of cabbages, many varieties of storage onions, and great old varieties of root vegetables. In addition, Territorial founder Steve Solomon has written a book on gardening in the maritime Northwest, called *Growing Organic Vegetables West of the Cascades,* that offers valuable advice for growing vegetables in that cool, moist climate.

Cool-season vegetables are not the only vegetables grown in Germany, of course, but the warm-season ones there are somewhat different from many of our mainstream varieties because the German summers are so short. In fact, most of Germany is of the same latitude as southern Canada. Consequently, like other gardeners in northern latitudes, or those at high altitudes, German gardeners need quick-bearing varieties of summer vegetables. For more information on such short-season, or early, vegetables, see the individual variety information in Part Four, "An Encyclopedia of Superior Vegetables." In addition, obtain a copy of the Johnny's Selected Seeds catalog, as that company carries many short-season varieties of eggplants, peppers, and tomatoes along with a great many cold-hardy vegetable varieties.

If you grow a German garden, you might want to think about preserving the root vegetables and members of the cabbage family so you can enjoy them through most of the year. In mild-winter areas you can do this in the open ground; in more severe climates you can preserve in a root cellar. To store root vegetables and cabbages in place in the garden if your winters are not too severe, heavily mulch the plants in place with straw or leaves. The vegetables will stay fresh and crisp, and often become sweeter as they sit. But a root cellar provides easy access and offers the most control over the elements. A root cellar can be made as part of an outbuilding or basement or dug out of the ground. For a detailed look at this subject, consult Mike and Nancy Bubel's wonderful book *Root Cellaring*.

The Kuckein German Garden

A number of years ago I designed the landscape for the backyard of my neighbors Carolyn and Paul Kuckein. As we worked together and became better acquainted, I became aware of their intense interest in cooking, and particularly in German cuisine, and I included in their yard a small vegetable and herb garden. They are both of German heritage and had lived and worked in Germany off and on throughout the years. A few years after I designed their yard they moved to Germany again, this time for almost three years, and when they returned they were even more involved with German cuisine. And this time they brought back some seeds of German vegetables to try here.

When I saw their enthusiasm, I asked if they would be interested in turning their vegetable garden into a prototype German garden so we could all learn more about the varieties of individual vegetables and herbs and how to cook them in more ways. They were delighted with the idea, and we planned a garden, using both the varieties they had brought from Germany and American equivalents that we ordered here. Carolyn had a friend in Germany send the few varieties we knew or learned about but couldn't find.

The area for the garden was too shady in the winter for a cool-season garden, so we planned a summer one. This coastal California garden actually gets quite cool in the summer, but not cool enough for growing cabbages and kales easily.

The main bed was planted with 'Detroit Dark Red' and 'Rote Kugel' beets, 'Saxa' bush beans, 'Hilda' and 'Wachs Neckargold' pole beans, and 'Desiree' runner beans. Also in the same bed were 'Moneta' cucumbers, 'Lady Finger' potatoes, and two herbs— summer savory and dill. A small planter box against a hot south house wall was planted with 'Super Marmande' tomatoes and 'Yolo Wonder' and 'Golden Bell' peppers. And a cool, shady raised box was planted with 'Butter' lettuce, 'Nantes' carrots, cress, curly

parsley, 'Münchener Bier' beer radishes, and corn salad, or mâche. The garden grew well with no major problems. The harvest of beans, beets, and mâche was generous, but the potatoes were very sparse, because the plants were too shaded.

After most of the season was over I sat down with Paul and Carolyn and asked them to share their experiences with German vegetables in general and their garden in particular. Carolyn, who had become a true expert in German cooking in the process, began by telling me that when she was in Germany she had had a lot of difficulty figuring out what some of the produce was. "For instance, whenever you bought green beans in the market," she said, "the salespeople would ask if you would like a sprig of *Bohnenkraut* [summer savory], and I would say sure, and take it home. At first I just threw it away. It was always about two feet long and I finally discovered from a friend that you folded it and put it on the bottom of the pot for flavoring before you put in water and steamed fresh green beans. I asked the Latin name for it but the ladies in the market were no help. They just called it *Bohnenkraut*.

"Corn salad, called *Feldsalat*, was something else we liked but couldn't identify. I had never seen it before. It was generally served with a sweetened vinegar or a sour cream dressing. Another unfamiliar vegetable was cress. The sprouts of cress are quite sharp and spicy and used in the same way we use alfalfa sprouts here. We grew both in the garden and have really appreciated having them here.

"Then there were vegetables we only vaguely knew here in the States," Carolyn went on to say, "but didn't learn how to prepare and enjoy until we lived in Germany. Kohlrabi is an example. I certainly had never eaten it here, but we really enjoyed kohlrabi the way the Germans prepared it. Any root vegetable, and actually any vegetable in the cabbage family, is very popular in Germany. We also loved what they call *Wirsing*, what I now know here as Savoy cabbage. It was good steamed and served in a cream sauce.

"Radishes, too, were a little different and of varying kinds. Paul particularly enjoyed the beer radishes. They were often served as hors d'oeuvres in the *Gaststätten* [best described as pubs or country inns], where there are many kinds of beer on tap. These radishes are traditionally served at Oktoberfest as well. They are peeled and sliced very thin with a spiral cutter, salted lightly, spread out on a board,

The Kuckeins' German garden is designed to fit into their landscape. Shown here are a sunny bed under a south-facing window for heat-loving vegetables, a shaded bed in the foreground for cool loving crops, and a large bed in the background for the rest of the vegetables.

and served with black rye bread and butter. It was wonderful having them in our garden here, because we missed them when we left Germany.

"I prepared the beets from our garden the way I had had them in Germany. I cooked and peeled them and then made up a sauce with a little sugar, a cinnamon stick, and vinegar. Then I put the beets in and just simmered them for a couple of minutes. The garden beans I cooked with summer savory. Then I marinated them in the sweetened vinegar and served them cold with chopped red onion. In both cases I used cider vinegar, though typically the vinegar in Germany was red or white wine vinegar. We also enjoyed the cucumbers with dill and have served them in the typical German fashion with a sour cream dressing.

"All in all, it has really been a pleasure being able to grow these vegetables and herbs we had learned to love in Germany. To go out and harvest the corn salad and summer savory helps bring back some of those wonderful memories."

While Carolyn refined her expertise in the kitchen, Paul worked in the garden and served as an enthusiastic translator. The result of our combined efforts was a garden that could continually revive the Kuckeins' warm memories of meals they'd had in Germany.

Recommended German Vegetables

Over the centuries, German immigrants have brought their vegetables and cooking methods to this country, and according to Jan Blum (of Seeds Blum), whose ancestry is German, so much of their cooking has been absorbed into the mainstream that we don't recognize it as German anymore. There are a few differences, of course. In Germany the potato varieties are denser, for example, and cooks use cabbage in many more ways. They also use herbs such as summer savory and dill a lot more than Americans do. And they use a few vegetables, herbs, and cooking techniques that have not surfaced in this country. It is these less familiar foods and techniques that I explore in this section. Following the list of vegetables is a brief list of herbs traditionally used in German cooking.

In the following list, the numbers in parentheses after variety names indicate the seed companies in the "Sources" section that carry those varieties. When no number is given with a variety name, it means that most of the seed companies listed carry it. For further information about the individual vegetables, see Part Four, "An Encyclopedia of Superior Vegetables," and see the "Heirloom Gardens" chapter for Jan Blum's discussion of some unusual old German vegetables.

ASPARAGUS   *Asparagus officinalis; Spargel*   Asparagus is considered a great delicacy in Germany. The most prized asparagus are the fat, tender, white ones that have been blanched in the garden. For information on blanching asparagus, see the "French Gardens" chapter.

How to grow: The standard American varieties are fine for German recipes, but if you want to try one of the European varieties very similar to the German ones, try 'Lorella' (7), with its extra-thick stems. See the Part Four Encyclopedia for growing information.

Cool-season vegetables ready for a hearty feast: carrots, leeks, beets, red cabbage, new potatoes, and peas.

How to prepare: Germans delight in asparagus simply steamed and served with butter, but they also serve it with hollandaise, in soup, or cold in a salad.

BEANS *Phaseolus vulgaris; Bohnen (Stangenbohnen,* pole; *Buschbohnen,* bush) Germans enjoy both green and wax snap beans in many ways.

How to grow: See the Part Four Encyclopedia.

How to prepare: In Germany snap beans are steamed with summer savory, sometimes served with a bacon or a sweet-and-sour sauce, used in stew or soup, or served marinated in salads. Snap beans are also included in a few characteristically German dishes combining vegetables and fruits—namely, a dish called Blind Hen made with carrots, beans, bacon, and apples, and a Westphalian specialty made with pears, beans, and bacon.

BEETS *Beta vulgaris; Runklelrüben* or *Rote Beten* One of the favorite German vegetables, beets are used in many ways.

How to grow: See the Part Four Encyclopedia for growing information, and try the beet varieties recommended in the "Heirloom Gardens" chapter.

How to prepare: In Germany beets are frequently pickled in vinegar and sugar and then often seasoned with mustard seeds, cumin, or caraway. They are also grated and used in composed salads, and combined with cucumbers in a pureed soup.

CABBAGE *Brussica oleracea,* Capitata Group; *Kohlkopf* There are varieties of cabbages to grow throughout most of the year and ones that will store well in a cool cellar, so theoretically you can have cabbage almost all year round. But there are a few things to consider before choosing your cabbage varieties. The very early spring cabbages are generally loose-headed and poor storers; they are also usually more challenging to grow. The main-season cabbages—grown from midspring into fall, or in winter in the mild-winter areas—are easier to grow and give you a large selection of more specialized varieties to choose from. Some cabbage varieties store very well, some are quite winter hardy, and most have different uses in the kitchen. The rich repertoire of cabbage types and the many recipes for preparing them are fun to explore. Cabbages in Germany can be white, red, or green, smooth or wrinkled, and small-veined and flexible or large-veined and stiff. Each has its own optimum preparation style. The large, dense, velvety smooth cabbages are best for

sauerkraut. The flavorful red ones are good for slaw or for pickling with vinegar and sugar and flavoring with apples, prunes, cloves, and red wine. The wrinkled Savoy types are great in slaw with a creamy dressing, steamed, or, if very tender, sliced in a salad. The small-veined, flexible types are great for stuffed cabbage or recipes in which folded cabbage leaves are called for.

How to grow: Growing cabbages ranges on the effort scale from fairly simple to downright challenging, depending largely on the pest and disease problems in your area. See the Part Four Encyclopedia for more information. See the "Sources" section for seed companies that carry a large selection of cabbages. Varieties to look for are 'Red Head', 'Ice Queen', 'Roundup', 'Jumbo', 'Stonehead', and 'Salarite F1', all available from Stokes Seeds; 'Early Jersey Wakefield', 'Danish Ballhead', and 'Winter Keeper', available from Seeds Blum; and 'Hitstar F1', 'Red Rodan', and 'Savoy Monarch', all from Territorial Seed Company. If you are interested in Filder Kraut cabbage, the one Hansel Hagel reminisced about earlier in the chapter, the closest variety I can find is 'Quintal d'Alsace' (4), a huge, tall, pointed cabbage perfect for sauerkraut. This is a French cabbage from an area very close to southern Germany, where Hansel grew up.

How to prepare: German cooking has added much to the world's knowledge of how cabbage can be enjoyed. This vegetable can be made into a zesty soup with sausage or poultry; sliced into wedges and put in stews or roasted with meats, particularly pork; and steamed and served with butter or a cheese or cream sauce. Cabbage shaved or sliced thinly is versatile in salads and slaws, or it can be pickled or made into sauerkraut. Sliced cabbage is also wonderful steamed with onions, apples, pears, or prunes.

In addition, cabbage leaves are pliable and can be easily rolled or molded and stuffed with meats or other vegetables. And, finally, the rich sweetness of cabbage blends well with many flavorings—for example, the tartness of vinegar or lemon, the sweetness of honey and sugar, the smoky taste of bacon, the richness of game meats, and the varied tastes of herbs and spices such as mustard, caraway, cumin, sage, anise, fennel, dill, thyme, pepper, juniper, cloves, cinnamon, allspice, and nutmeg.

CELERIAC *Apium graveolens* var. *rapaceum; Knollensellerie* Celeriac is a close relative of celery but is much easier to grow. Instead of eating the stalks, you eat the swollen edible crown.

How to grow: See "Celery" in the Part Four Encyclopedia. A German variety, 'Alabaster' (4), is particularly prized because it does not discolor when cut open.

How to prepare: Celeriac is used cooked in salads and as a side dish served with a cream sauce. Try it in a Waldorf salad as well.

CRESS (Garden cress) *Lepidium sativum; Gartenkresse* This peppery salad green is popular in Germany.

How to grow: Cress is often grown as we do alfalfa sprouts, but it grows readily in the garden as well. Surface-sow seeds thickly in spring or fall in moist, rich soil. Thin to one-eighth inch apart. The plants grow very quickly, and the young seedlings can be cut back with scissors four or five times before going to seed. Once the weather turns warm, cress gets hot and tough. Varieties include 'Curled Cress' (4) and 'Extra Curled' (7).

How to prepare: Use sprouts or tender young seedlings in salads, in sandwiches, or as a garnish.

CORN SALAD (mâche) *Valerianella Locusta; Feldsalat* This salad green is very popular in Germany.

How to grow: See the Part Four Encyclopedia.

How to prepare: Germans use corn salad in a mixed green salad or combined with oranges or pears in a more formal salad.

KOHLRABI *Brassica oleracea,* Gongylodes Group; *Kohlrabi* This member of the cabbage family produces a swollen, aboveground protuberance that is succulent and sweet.

How to grow: Unlike most cabbage relatives, kohlrabi is seeded in place, rather than started indoors, in early spring. Plant seeds one-half inch deep in moist, rich soil, thin plants to four to six inches apart, and keep them growing vigorously with supplemental water and fertilizer. Start harvesting the kohlrabis once they are at least an inch across.

How to prepare: Choose young, succulent kohlrabis and steam or boil; then serve with butter or a cream sauce. Or grate them and use raw in a salad, where their natural sweetness can be shown off to advantage.

POTATOES *Solanum tuberosum; Kartoffeln* Germans classify potatoes into two types: *fest* (firm),

used for salads or soups, and *mehlig* (mealy), which are traditionally steamed or boiled and served, often parsleyed, with dishes having gravy. The firm ones are the most commonly used and are what we call boiling potatoes. They can be round but are usually cylindrical. They differ from most of our varieties, as most have yellow flesh and a waxy, dense texture.

How to grow: See the Part Four Encyclopedia for growing information. Try the boiling varieties, such as 'Ruby Cresent', 'Lady Finger', and 'Yellow Finn'; all are German fingerling types and can be ordered from Seeds Blum.

How to prepare: The dense, sweet, waxy potatoes used in Germany don't readily fall apart when cooked. They give substance to casseroles, pancakes, fritters, and salads, and their creaminess gives richness to dumplings and soups too. Do not substitute our baking-type potatoes for boiling ones in the German recipes, or your dishes will taste like wallpaper paste.

RADISHES *Raphanus sativus; Rettiche* or *Radieschen* Radishes are very popular in Germany. Germans use many of the same types of spring and summer radishes as we do, but according to Jan Blum, they also make more use of the "bitey" winter-type radishes than most cultures.

How to grow: See the Part Four Encyclopedia for growing information. Try some traditional German varieties, including the famous 'Münchener Bier' (7) radish.

How to prepare: Radishes can be thinly sliced and used as snacks, appetizers, in salads, or added to soups. The 'Münchener Bier' radish, sliced very thin and served on black bread, is the traditional radish of Oktoberfest. The seed pods of this variety can also be eaten fresh or pickled and used in salads.

A few major herbs and flavorings are characteristic of German cuisine, and these are described below. In addition, thyme, fennel, caraway, sweet bay, parsley, paprika, anise, and horseradish are all used in German cooking.

DILL *Anethum graveolens; Dill* This distinctively flavored herb is widely known for giving zest to pickles.

How to grow: See the "Culinary Herb Gardens" chapter.

How to prepare: Dill is most commonly used fresh with cucumbers, in a salad with sour cream or

Kaete Reimnitz

I'll always be grateful to Kaete Reimnitz for introducing me to the *Römertopf*, a German cooking pot from which I've enjoyed countless delicious winter meals. Kaete, a garden expert at my local nursery, grew up in Germany. When I needed help with my German garden, I asked her to share some of her experiences and recipes with me.

"Until I go back to Germany and taste my mother's home cooking," Kaete says, "I don't miss some of the food I grew up with. What I miss most then is what we called *Beifuss*. My mother used a little *Beifuss* in practically every sauce she made, with most vegetables, and with roasts. This herb, called mugwort in English or *Artemisia vulgaris* in Latin, is sometimes available from specialty herb gardens in the United States or from Richters in Canada.

"My mother cooked roasts in a *Römertopf*, a large clay pot that's sealed with all the ingredients inside and opened when the meat and vegetables are cooked. I remember she used to select rump or sirloin tip beef roast, pork loin, or sometimes even chicken to cook in the *Römertopf*. She added nice, waxy Germany potatoes, celery root, tiny carrots, beans, or whatever other garden vegetables she wanted and sprinkled them with small amounts of fresh *Beifuss*, thyme, parsley, or sometimes sage or marjoram. Then she made a sauce from the meat and vegetable juices. It was wonderful with a little cream added, too, and the vegetables were so good penetrated with meat juices. And it's so simple, she could go about her washing or gardening while it was in the oven.

"Cabbages, of course, are a German favorite; the average German cookbook probably has forty recipes for cabbage. Americans eat stuffed cabbage rolls, sauerkraut, and cabbage soup, but Germans even have cabbage pudding—layers of cabbage leaves alternated with ground beef and spices, steamed, inverted, and unmolded on a plate. Germans cook this dish in a traditional fluted pan called a *Gugelhupf*. The finished pudding looks like a cake; you slice it and serve it with noodles or rice. It's delicious. Whenever I ask my children what they want for their birthday meal, they always say *Gugelhupf!*

"I also enjoy dill from the garden. As a child in Germany, I had the luxury of fresh dill only in the summer. I particularly remember it in cucumber salad with sour cream dressing made with a little lemon juice, salt, pepper, and a pinch of sugar. In northern Germany, they add a lot of sugar and make a very, very sweet dressing. In East Prussia, where I'm from, we prefer a more lemony taste."

Other German dishes are also seasonal. For example, celery root salad, another of Kaete's favorites, is served in the winter on *Feldsalat* (corn salad). "Unless you have a garden, though, you can't find corn salad in this country," Kaete says. "And Americans don't eat string beans cooked with fresh summer savory, either. In Germany, summer savory and beans have a short season and are very special. Summer savory doesn't dry well, though, and while winter savory is good, it's more bitter than summer savory is. Lovage also loses much of its flavor when dried; it becomes like straw. I use very small amounts of fresh lovage because it's so strong, but it's great in vegetable soup."

Like many other people who move to another country, Kaete finds comfort in using the foods of her native land. Having a garden enables her to enjoy some of the vegetables and herbs that are not readily available here.

yogurt dressing, or in pickles. It is also used with fish and combined with other cooked vegetables.

LOVAGE *Levisticum officinale; Liebstöckel* Lovage (3, 4, 7) is a strong-flavored herb that tastes a bit like celery or parsley.

How to grow: Lovage is an attractive, easily grown perennial that reaches six feet in height. Plant seeds in fall, in sun or part shade in a rich, moist soil. Make sure you collect the seeds or this plant will spread all over your garden. Harvest the leaves as you need them throughout the growing season.

How to prepare: Because of its strong flavor, fresh lovage is used sparingly in soups, stews, salads, and vegetable and meat dishes.

MUGWORT *Artemisia vulgaris; Beifuss* Mugwort (3) is a pungent herb frequently used in home-style cooking in certain areas of Germany.

How to grow: This six-foot shrubby perennial grows and spreads so readily, quickly becoming a weed, that you need to ask yourself if you want it in your garden. If you really like mugwort and decide to plant it, you'll have to work to control it. Start it from seeds or, if you can find a neighbor who has planted it, from divisions. Plant mugwort in sun and give it minimal care.

How to prepare: Use the leaves sparingly, fresh or dried, in stews, soups, with meats, as a tea, or—the most well known use of mugwort—as a flavoring in the stuffing in roast Christmas goose.

ROOT PARSLEY (Hamburg parsley) *Petroselinum crispum tuberosum; Petersilie* This parsley is grown not for its leaves but for its roots, which look and taste a lot like parsnips.

How to grow: Grow as you would parsley. Make sure to seed root parsley in loose soil so the roots can form uniformly. 'Hamburg Root' (3, 4, 5, 7) parsley is the most readily available variety.

How to prepare: Cook this parsley as you would parsnips, steaming it until tender and serving it with butter or a cream sauce.

SUMMER SAVORY *Satureja hortensis; Bohnenkraut* Summer savory (3, 4, 7) is a mild, sweet-tasting herb that does not keep its flavor well when dried.

How to grow: See the "Culinary Herb Gardens" chapter.

How to prepare: The fresh leaves of summer savory are used traditionally with snap beans but can also be used in salads, soups, and stews.

Cooking from the German Garden

Meat in its myriad forms is the most important ingredient in a German meal. Hundreds of kinds of wursts and roasts abound to vary the typical heavily laden German table. But in addition to the hearty flavors of the sausages, the tanginess of the sauerkraut and the sweetness of the winter vegetables characterize these spreads. And the complexities of sweet and sour in the same recipe, plus the mellow tastes of caraway and dill, are often woven throughout many dishes. Another dimension is produced by the depth of the cabbage flavors and the richness of the waxy German potatoes. The fats used in German cooking are generally butter and some sort of pork fat, and the seasonings are most often vinegar, sugar, and herbs. But first and last, it is basic meat and potatoes that comes to mind when one thinks of German fare.

As the preceding section suggests, there is not a great array of vegetables in German cuisine. Still, the Germans enjoy the vegetables they do use in many different ways worth exploring. Kaete Reimnitz showed me the pages and pages of cabbage and potato recipes in her German cookbook. The cabbages might be stuffed and rolled, made into soups, or served as sauerkraut. Often the vegetables are pickled or marinated, served with a rich sour cream dressing, or stewed with meat. Creamy soups using many of the vegetables, such as asparagus, cauliflower, and celeriac, are also popular. And salads, mostly marinated vegetables arranged in a pleasing manner, are a part of most main meals. A tossed green salad is less usual, but when served is made with butter lettuce.

GERMAN SALADS

YIELD VARIES.

The most common salads in Germany are simply grated or julienned raw or blanched vegetables marinated in a very light vinaigrette that is usually a bit on the sweet-and-sour side, or a light, creamy dress-

OPPOSITE: *A Römertopf is used to make some of the easiest and tastiest one-dish meals in the world. Here, roast beef has been cooked with peas, roasted leeks and onions, carrots, and cabbage and is accompanied by parsleyed new potatoes.*

ing, often with dill. Often, several different vegetables are prepared in this way and arranged as an assortment, or "a composed salad." Use the recipe for beet salad as a guideline; if a creamier dressing is preferred for some of the vegetables, add some mayonnaise, yogurt, or sour cream, or a combination of these. If desired, add fresh herbs, such as dill, parsley, or savory, omit the green onions, and use a little dry mustard. Vegetables to choose from include beets, carrots, kohlrabi, cucumbers, cabbage, fennel, and celeriac.

When using celeriac for salad, peel and julienne it and drop the strips into water flavored with a little lemon juice. Boil for 3 to 5 minutes, drain, and mix with the dressing. Celeriac is also wonderful either substituted for or combined with potato dishes.

Arrange the individual vegetables on a plate or platter in a decorative manner, as on a bed of greens. Greens to serve with the salads might be butter lettuce, mâche (Feldsalat), or small amounts of cress.

BEET SALAD

This recipe comes from the Shepherd's Garden Seeds catalog.

SERVES 4 TO 6.

> 6 large beets, peeled
> 1 bunch green onions, chopped
> ½ cup apple cider vinegar
> 2 tablespoons water
> ½ cup salad oil
> Pinch of sugar
> ¼ teaspoon salt
> ¼ teaspoon black pepper

Grate fresh beets on the finest grater you have—preferably one used to grate lemon peel. If you are using a food processor, use the disc with the smallest holes. Place grated beets in a bowl. Mix the remaining ingredients until blended and pour over beets. Toss and marinate in refrigerator for several hours before serving. For an interesting variation, substitute grated carrots and/or grated beer radishes for one-third of the beets.

RÖMERTOPF DISHES

The word Römertopf means Roman pot, and in this context it refers both to the pot itself and the food prepared in it. The pots are available in this country in most large department stores and kitchenware shops. They come in small, medium, and large. I prefer the large one, which holds a twelve- to fourteen-pound turkey, because I like to have enough leftovers to reheat them the next day. Before each use, you must soak the Römertopf in water so the porous clay can absorb water and seal the pot. This both prevents the contents from sticking to the pot and makes them juicy. See the profile of Kaete Reimnitz for more comments on the Römertopf.

Select vegetables and wash them and keep whole or in rather large chunks. Try just one vegetable or combinations. My favorite vegetables for cooking in the Römertopf are leeks and onions (fantastic), carrots and parsnips (so sweet), and new boiling potatoes (creamy and sweet with a touch of sourness to the skins). Beets are also great (use only the yellow or white varieties if you don't want everything to turn red), as are cabbage and cooked dry beans or fresh shelling ones. This cooking method enhances the rich flavors of some of the old keeper types of root vegetables and the old varieties of beans. If you want meat with your vegetables, try roasts of any type, chicken, or any kind of wurst. Put the meat on top of the vegetables so it will turn nice and brown and the juices will soak into the vegetables.

The standard cooking method for any Römertopf recipe is as follows: First soak Römertopf and lid in water for at least 10 minutes; then put vegetables and meat in the pot and put the lid on. Place in a cold oven and turn it on. Most of the baking is done at a very high temperature: 480° for roasting chicken or beef with vegetables. Most authorities recommend that wursts, lamb, meat loaf, fish, baked potatoes, and vegetable dishes such as stuffed cabbage be baked at 450°, and vegetable casseroles at 400°. Cooking times vary from ½ to 2 hours.

Pheasant and sauerkraut is a classic German Römertopf dish. Prepare the sauerkraut with white wine and a few juniper berries (see the sauerkraut recipe below, but in this case simmer the sauerkraut with wine for 15 minutes) and then put it in the presoaked Römertopf. Place a 4-pound pheasant on the sauerkraut with a few bacon strips over it, cover the pot, and place in a cold oven. Turn oven on to 480° and cook for 45 minutes to 1 hour. Check with a meat thermometer for desired doneness. Serves 4.

Beef roast is wonderful in the Römertopf. Select a 5- or 6-pound rolled roast of beef; 6 to 8 medium potatoes and carrots; 4 good-sized leeks that have been cleaned and split down the middle; and a handful of mushrooms. Soak the *Römertopf* for 10 minutes, add the meat and vegetables, and season with salt and pepper. Add a bay leaf or two or some thyme. Cover the pot and place in a cold oven. Turn oven on to 480° and cook for about 40 minutes for rare, an hour for medium. Check with a meat thermometer for desired doneness. Serves 6.

GUGELHUPF

Gugelhupf (*Gugelhopf* or *Napfkuchen*), like *Römertopf*, refers both to the name of a utensil and the dish that is cooked in it. This decorative baking pan, with its tube center, is usually used to bake a German cake bearing the same name. Here it is the mold for a meat and cabbage dish that is a traditional recipe of Kaete Reimnitz's family. If you do not have a *Gugelhupf*, you can substitute a Bundt® pan. I was delighted when I tried this dish. It's a delicious variation on meat loaf, because the cabbage and caraway flavor and sweeten the meat. I prefer it made with ground round.

SERVES 8.

> 1 large head cabbage, core removed from the
>   bottom inward
> 3 small rolls or 3 slices of stale bread
> 1 pound ground beef
> 1 large onion, finely chopped
> 1 egg, beaten
> 2 tablespoons minced fresh thyme
> 1 teaspoon caraway seeds
> ½ teaspoon nutmeg
> Salt and pepper to taste
> Few drops hot pepper sauce
> ¼ cup catsup (optional)

Preheat oven to 350°.

After coring cabbage, loosen leaves a little from the bottom; then set in a steamer or in boiling water and cook until the leaves just become limp. Remove, drain, and separate leaves. Soak bread in water to soften, squeeze out excess water, and mash in a large bowl. Add all other ingredients except cabbage and mix well. Line *Gugelhupf* with large cabbage leaves, covering the central core as well as the sides and bottom. Alternate layers of meat mixture in pan with layers of cabbage leaves until pan is filled; end with

cabbage. Place *Gugelhupf* in a large pot containing enough boiling water to come about halfway up the *Gugelhupf* pan. Put into oven and bake uncovered for 1 to 1¼ hours. The top leaves of cabbage will brown. Remove *Gugelhupf* and drain off excess liquid from the bottom of the pan; save as a tasty broth. Put the *Gugelhupf* on a board to cool slightly; then place a large serving plate over the pan and invert onto plate. Slice and serve warm or cold.

SAUERKRAUT

MAKES 5 QUARTS.

Sauerkraut has many variations. Try this one and vary it to your taste. I live in a mild-winter area, so I must make sauerkraut in the coldest time of the year and ferment it in the garage, where it is very cool. Once it is fermented, I can it and store it in a cool place. In colder climates canning is not necessary.

Select dense, fine-textured cabbages. For 10 pounds of cabbage, use ½ cup of pickling salt and a 2-gallon stoneware crock or jar. Quarter cabbages, cut out cores, and shred leaves very finely. Mix with salt in large bowls, then pack into crock, cover, and let sit a few hours or overnight for juices to form. (In Germany, the cabbage is pounded in place to give an even finer texture, and often a few juniper berries, bay leaves, or caraway seeds are added.) Press down hard on cabbage, and if juices do not cover it, make a brine using 2 tablespoons pickling salt per quart of water and add as needed. Cover cabbage with a clean cloth, then place a plate on top that exactly fits the inside of the crock. Weigh this down with about a 5-pound weight and leave in a cool place, 40° to 60° F, to ferment for 3 to 4 weeks. Skim brine, change cloth, and wash plate daily. Fermentation is complete when liquid no longer bubbles. Finished sauerkraut may be stored in a cold place (about 38° F) for up to 3 months, or it may be frozen or canned. Before using in recipes, taste sauerkraut to see how sour it is. If the flavor is too strong, soak it for 10 to 20 minutes and squeeze dry. Hansel recommends another alternative: finely slicing some fresh cabbage and cooking it with the sauerkraut.

If you cook a sizable quantity of meat with the sauerkraut, you'll have a hearty a one-dish meal. Otherwise, sauerkraut is generally served alongside meats, sometimes with dumplings or other dishes.

You can make a sauerkraut salad by first washing and draining the sauerkraut and then adding diced apple, cucumber, minced green onions, and some dill and/or parsley, along with some oil and a little salt and vinegar, if needed. This is served chilled.

BASIC COOKED SAUERKRAUT

My favorite way to serve sauerkraut is with pork chops or some type of German sausage. When I prepare it I first brown the chops or sausages, remove them from the pan, cook the onions, put sauerkraut and seasonings in the pan, put the meat on top, and then proceed as below, but omitting the fat.

SERVES 6.

> 1 onion, chopped or sliced
> 2 tablespoons butter, lard, or other fat
> 2 pounds (4 cups) sauerkraut
> 1/2 to 2 cups liquid (amount depends on how juicy you like it and whether the optional potato is added for thickener); choose from or combine water, stock, white wine, or beer; sometimes pineapple or tomato juice is used
> Optional: 1 or 2 apples, sliced; 1 raw potato, grated; 1/2 to 2 pounds fresh or smoked pork, ham, chops, ribs, hocks, or sausage; seasonings, such as bay leaves, 1 tablespoon juniper berries, caraway seeds, or sugar

In a heavy pot, sauté onions in fat until soft. Add sauerkraut, any seasonings, and apple, if using. Cover and simmer 1/2 hour, shaking pot occasionally to prevent sticking. Add liquid (and potato, if using), cover, and cook 1/2 hour longer.

GREEN BEANS WITH SUMMER SAVORY

This classic combination of flavors is timeless. Be careful not to overcook the beans.

SERVES 4.

> 1/2 small onion, minced
> 1 tablespoon butter
> Salt and pepper to taste
> 1 tablespoon fresh summer savory, minced
> 1 tablespoon flour
> 1 pound green beans, trimmed and cut to about 2-inch lengths

In a saucepan, sauté onion in butter until soft but not brown. Add salt, pepper, savory, and flour, and cook and stir a couple of minutes. Steam or boil the beans in a separate pot until just tender. Slowly stir 1/2 cup or so of the bean cooking water into the onion mixture and bring to a boil. Immediately add the cooked beans. Pour into a bowl and serve.

PEG'S GERMAN POTATO SALAD

This recipe is from Margaret Creasy, my mother-in-law, and was my first introduction to German-style cooking. It is more Pennsylvania Dutch than old-country German, however. (If you are like me, that name is confusing. For years I thought the word Dutch in this context referred to the Netherlands, not to *Deutsch*, meaning German.)

SERVES 6 TO 8.

> 8 medium potatoes
> 3/4 cup vinegar (cider or white)
> 1/2 cup water
> 3/4 cup sugar
> 1/2 teaspoon salt
> 1 rounded tablespoon flour OR *mixture of 1/2 tablespoon flour and 1/2 tablespoon cornstarch*
> 8 slices bacon, diced
> 3/4 cup diced onion

Boil whole potatoes until just tender. Then drain, peel, and cut into 1/4-inch slices. Put into serving bowl.

While potatoes are cooking, combine vinegar, water, sugar, and salt and bring to a boil in a small saucepan. Mix flour or cornstarch and flour mixture with about 1/4 cup water in a small bowl. Then stir into vinegar mixture and simmer briskly, stirring occasionally, until translucent and thickened.

Fry bacon with onions in a skillet until golden brown, then add, including bacon fat, to vinegar mixture. Pour over potatoes while they are still warm and fold gently. Let stand at room temperature about 2 hours, stirring every 1/2 hour or so. Refrigerate if not using at once, but serve at room temperature or slightly warmed.

Thinly sliced beer radishes served on dark German bread with butter and salt are the traditional accompaniment to beer at Oktoberfest. Grow your own and have a party next fall.

STUFFED NEW POTATOES

This recipe is from Norbert Schulz, chef and owner of Norbert's in Santa Barbara, California.

SERVES 4 AS MAIN COURSE, 8 AS SIDE DISH.

> *8 medium unpeeled new potatoes, washed*
> *6 ounces Appenzeller or Raclette cheese*
> *8 slices raw bacon*
> *8 toothpicks*

Preheat oven to 375°.

Use a melon baller or a paring knife and spoon to scoop out about a third of each potato so that it will sit with a cavity in its top side. Fill potatoes with cheese, then wrap each one horizontally with a strip of bacon and secure with a toothpick. Place on a

broiler pan to allow bacon grease to drip through, cover loosely with foil, and bake for 30 minutes or until potatoes are tender. Serve with a garden salad or steamed fresh greens.

YOUNG KOHLRABI IN CREAM

Kohlrabi is a common vegetable in Germany; Chef Norbert also contributed this delicious recipe.

SERVES 4 TO 6.

> *¼ cup butter*
> *About 8 young kohlrabi, peeled and sliced*
>   *thinly to make 3 cups*
> *½ cup chicken stock*
> *2 cups packed finely chopped kohlrabi greens,*
>   *stripped from stem*
> *¼ cup heavy cream*
> *Pinch each of sugar and nutmeg*

In a medium saucepan, heat butter, add kohlrabi and stock, cover and cook on medium-low heat until tender, about 10 minutes. Remove kohlrabi from pan, add greens, and simmer covered for 3 minutes. Remove lid, add cream, and simmer 3 minutes longer on medium-high heat, stirring. Add sugar and nutmeg, then kohlrabi, and heat through. Serve immediately.

AUSTRIAN KALE

This is an adaptation from a recipe in Shepherd's Garden Seeds catalog. The cooking time has been reduced to retain the kale's flavor and nutrients. Some people find that preblanching kale helps to tenderize it and "set" the color. I usually just use a high temperature for the first couple of minutes of cooking, and then reduce the heat to medium. This is a delicious side dish for roast pork, beef, or chicken; also good with sausage.

SERVES 4 TO 6.

> *2 bunches kale*
> *½ medium onion, chopped*
> *1 clove garlic, minced*
> *1 tablespoon salad oil*
> *2 cups chicken stock or bouillon*
> *4 medium potatoes, peeled and quartered*
> *1 stalk celery, chopped*
> *Salt and pepper to taste*

Cut or tear kale leaves into pieces. In a large pan, sauté the onions and garlic in the salad oil until lightly browned. Add chicken stock, potatoes, and celery. Cover and simmer until potatoes are just tender, about 10 minutes. While the potatoes are cooking, blanch kale in boiling, lightly salted water for 1 minute. Add kale to potatoes and simmer about 10 minutes longer. Stir, season with salt and pepper, and serve.

ROTE GRÜTZE (*Fruit-Flavored Blancmange*)

Carolyn Kuckein was given this recipe by a friend when she lived in Germany.

SERVES 4.

> 12 ounces mixed berries and cherries
> ⅔ cup dry red wine
> 2 tablespoons sugar
> 1 tablespoon cornstarch
> ¼ cup water

Wash fruit if necessary. Halve very large berries and pit cherries. In a small pot, mix fruit with wine and sugar. Simmer 10 minutes. Mix cornstarch with ¼ cup water until smooth. Add to fruit mixture, stir to blend, and bring to boil. Remove from heat and spoon into 4 serving dishes. Chill and serve with cream, ice cream, or plain yogurt.

Sources

Seed Companies

1. Johnny's Selected Seeds
   Foss Hill Road
   Albion, ME 04910
   This seed company specializes in vegetable varieties for northern climates.

2. Le Marché
   Seeds International
   P.O. Box 190
   Dixon, CA 95620
   Le Marché carries a large array of European vegetable varieties, many of which are similar to or the same as German ones. Catalog: $2.00.

3. Nichols Garden Nursery
   1190 North Pacific Highway
   Albany, OR 97321

This nursery in the Pacific Northwest carries varieties for cool climates as well as most of the German herbs.

4. Seeds Blum
   Idaho City Stage
   Boise, ID 83706
   This company offers many of the varieties of vegetables mentioned in this chapter. Catalog: $2.00.

5. Stokes Seeds, Inc.
   P.O. Box 548
   Buffalo, NY 14240
   Stokes Seeds carries a vast selection of vegetable varieties, many of which are acclimatized to northern gardens. It offers more than fifty varieties of cabbage.

6. Territorial Seed Company
   P.O. Box 27
   Lorane, OR 97451
   This seed company specializes in vegetable varieties for the maritime Northwest.

7. Thompson & Morgan, Inc.
   P.O. Box 1308
   Jackson, NJ 08527
   Thompson & Morgan is an English seed company with an American office, so you do not have to send abroad. The firm offers a very large selection of unusual vegetable varieties, including some German ones.

Books

Bubel, Nancy, and Mike Bubel. *Root Cellaring*. Emmaus, Pa.: Rodale Press, 1979.
> This is a thorough look at how to store foods in a root cellar, a rewarding pursuit that sure beats freezing or canning for ease.

Gessert, Kate Rogers. *The Beautiful Food Garden*. Charlotte, Vt.: Garden Way Publishing, 1987.
> This is a book on beautiful food plants, but there's more to it than that. The author ran an extensive vegetable-variety testing at Oregon State University, and the book contains much information on which varieties do particularly well in the Northwest.

Meyer-Berkhout, Eda. *German Cooking*. Tucson: HP Books, 1984.
> This book contains a vast selection of German recipes, all accompanied by photos. The range of recipes is notable.

Solomon, Steve. *Growing Organic Vegetables West of the Cascades*. Seattle: Pacific Search Press, 1985.
Much of the coastal Northwest is a perfect climate for growing many German vegetables, and this book covers that climate in detail.

The following two books are out of print but are worth seeking out in libraries or used-book stores.

Hazelton, Nika Standen, and the editors of Time-Life Books. *The Cooking of Germany*. New York: Time-Life Books, 1969.
This book is a classic that gives not only recipes but also cultural background for German cooking.

Schmaeling, Tony. *German Traditional Cooking*. Secaucus, N.J.: Chartwell Books, 1984.
This is one of the most authentic German cookbooks available in English today. It describes many wonderful ways of using vegetables from the garden.

Mexican Gardens

WHAT WONDERFUL TIMES I HAVE HAD visiting the community gardens in my area. Northern California is blessed with a thriving system of community gardens run by local and county parks departments, and these places are filled to overflowing with small plots cared for by dedicated gardeners. Entering these gardens often seems like visiting the United Nations. In one plot will be trellises covered with giant cucuzzi vines and paste tomatoes tended by someone with an Italian accent; in the next will be tropical beans, tiny green eggplants, and lemon grass lovingly cared for by a gardener from Thailand. And the ethnic mix changes in accordance with the garden's locality. In my area many of the gardens are created by Mexican Americans and are filled with many varieties of corn, beans, and chili peppers as well as cilantro, cactus, and chayote, all brought from Mexico. But the gardens provide more than fresh, authentic vegetables and herbs; they also function as social meeting places, particularly for the men, who build covered patio areas, picnic facilities, and barbecue pits. And the men are the primary gardeners. The women and children commonly join them for suppers and parties.

When I visited community gardens in my research, usually

OPPOSITE: *An ear of corn from Mi Tierra community garden in San Jose, California. Corn is the foundation of Mexican cuisine.*

with an interpreter, the men could give me much growing information but only the most rudimentary cooking advice. In the Mexican community, it seems, few men cook and few women garden. I finally had to make a concerted effort to find one person who was skilled at cooking from the Mexican garden. I called Joan Jackson, who edits the garden section of the San Jose *Mercury,* and she highly recommended Victoria Lomeli, who had a garden plot next to hers in a community garden. She knew that Victoria had a reputation as a great cook and was a wonderful gardener. I contacted Victoria and made a date to meet and talk about cooking.

When Wendy Krupnick, my assistant, and I entered Victoria's kitchen, we were overwhelmed by the wonderful smells. The table was set for lunch, and her family was feasting on pork seasoned with garlic, chilies, and the first harvest of chard from Victoria's backyard garden. Next to this dish stood a bowl of fresh salsa and a plate of tortillas. As we savored the spicy pork, we talked of hominy, chayote, and cooking from the garden. Wendy served as interpreter and, as a recent traveler in Mexico, updater. And she was full of questions about the vegetables and herbs she had researched for me there.

One thing Wendy and I had on our minds when we entered Victoria's kitchen was hominy (called *pozole* in Mexico). We were hoping to talk with someone who had actually made hominy. We had tried to make it ourselves a few times and never succeeded in completely getting the skins off the corn kernels. By the time we met Victoria, we were wrapping up our homework on the "Native American Gardens" chapter and needed to crack the secret. All the people we had already asked had seen their mothers or someone else make hominy but had never made it themselves, and they could give us only generalities. I kept seeing myself as driving backward down the street. I was getting there but knew there had to be a better way. On the ride over to Victoria's, Wendy and I had shared our hope that Victoria would be the teacher we had been seeking.

We weren't disappointed. Victoria's mother had schooled her thoroughly in the making of hominy—how to choose the right corn varieties (pick those with large, round kernels), when to add the lime (after soaking the corn overnight), and how to cook the hominied corn until it is tender (cook until the kernels open up like flowers).

"Can you grow out the corn you buy at the Mexican market?" we asked.

"Yes," Victoria said, "but it will take a few years for it to produce well and get used to its new garden climate. My Mexican corn now grows twelve to fifteen feet high."

"And do you grow your own chayote?" we asked, satisfied that we finally had hominy covered.

"Yes, but only at the community garden. When we grew it here in our backyard it climbed all over the trees, the house, and even the TV antenna!"

"Can you make fresh tamales from ripe sweet corn?"

"No, sweet corn will just disintegrate when you steam it. When you open up the husks there will hardly be anything left. You need a starchier corn."

Too bad for us. Wendy and I had thought we had come up with a great dish for over-the-hill sweet corn. But as Victoria closed one avenue of cooking from the Mexican garden, she opened up many others. She described a mole she made for her string beans with ground cloves, garlic, and chilies toasted in oil. She told us how to stuff chayote with cheese and fry it in batter. And she explained how to make barbecue, Chihuahua-style, by creating a sauce from garden tomatillos and cilantro.

With our visit to Victoria's, all the pieces of what was to me a Mexican-cuisine puzzle finally began to come together. Though I had started eating Mexican food when I moved to California years ago, what I tried initially—such as tacos and nachos—wasn't very diverse or authentic. (I recently learned that nachos aren't even made in Mexico.) I also found that, contrary to my experience in Mexican restaurants, there are many elaborate and complex dishes that haven't migrated northward. Slowly, though, I became familiar with the particular dishes, the unusual herbs, and the many ways of using corn that distinguish Mexican cooking. When I decided to write this book, I knew I had some extensive garden research before me concerning the vegetables used in Mexican food.

I had already been gathering information on Mexican vegetables for a year when I visited Victoria. I had talked with many Mexican gardeners and cooks by then and had visited both the Mi Tierra community garden in San Jose, California, and the Mexican markets in Redwood City and Los Angeles. Mi Tierra is one of the largest and most active Hispanic community gardens on the West Coast. John Dotter, San Jose's community-gardening program manager, set up meetings for me with some of the gardeners

Mexican gardeners and cooks use many types of corn. Saul Vera holds a purple corn he uses for roasting over coals because of its tough husks, an orange ear of grinding corn, and a sweet corn variety for eating fresh.

and served as a valuable translator. I wound up with the equivalent of a short, intensive course in cooking from the Mexican garden. José Cerrillo spent an hour showing me all the ways of folding corn husks to make tamales. Saul Vera and his friends patiently shared all their ways of preparing chayote; they also told me how the many kinds of corn in the garden were used and in which dishes. "In my garden," he said, "the variety with the tough, purple husks is for roasting on the barbecue—after the ears have been soaked in salted water. The corn with the deep-orange kernels is used for making *pozole,* and the yellow one is for eating fresh."

In combing the Mexican markets during my research, I inventoried rack upon rack of unfamiliar herbs, spices, and chilies. Routinely I asked shop owners where their dry corn came from. And I always asked for lime *(cal)* for making hominy. This request was usually met with pleasant smiles but no lime, since few modern Mexicans make their own hominy. Wendy and I finally tracked down some lime at a restaurant that made its own tortillas, and the hostess sold us a small bag. We also called tortilla factories to ask what kind of corn they used, and we called seed companies to ask what grinding corns they carried.

In the middle of my research, I spent some time with Kit Anderson, managing editor of *National Gardening* magazine, and she mentioned that she was fascinated by Mexico and had spent much time there visiting the markets and researching some of the vegetables and corn varieties. When she told me she was interested in growing some Mexican vegetables, I suggested we plan a Mexican garden together. Excitedly, she agreed. To see how folks far from the Mexican border can grow many of the ingredients for great tamales, squash soup Mexican-style, or a tomatillo and cilantro barbecue sauce, read her garden description later in the chapter.

I wanted to actually get my hands on the chilies, corn varieties, and herbs I'd been hearing about, so I undertook to grow many of them myself. My Mexican garden turned out to be one of my favorite theme gardens; it overflowed with exuberance and great-tasting edibles. I planted epazote and chia (both herbs), grinding corn, amaranth, sunflowers, lima beans, runner beans, tomatoes, tomatillos, and three kinds of chili peppers.

To round out my research, I felt compelled to talk to one of the most respected authorities on Mexican cuisine, one who, I knew, had explored many styles of cooking from all parts of Mexico. This was Diana Kennedy, author of the definitive book on the subject, *The Cuisines of Mexico.* Diana was most enthusiastic and helpful, carefully reviewing my ideas and generously sharing her own experiences and recipes.

The gardens and recipes that follow should serve as a good starting place for adding Mexican zest to your garden cooking. And as with the Native American gardens, you'll find lots of information here on that wonderful food, corn. To begin, let's look at the basics of growing a Mexican garden.

How to Grow a Mexican Garden

Most of the vegetables in a Mexican garden are grown in a routine manner. The tomatoes, onions, green peppers, pumpkins, and sunflowers, for instance, are

The author with a harvest from her Mexican garden. Pictured are blue corn, lima beans, amaranth, onions, chili peppers, tomatillos, sunflowers, epazote, and tomatoes.

often the very same or similar to those we usually grow in the States. For information on selecting, growing, harvesting, and preparing other Mexican vegetables, see, for grinding corns, the "Native American Gardens" chapter; for dry beans, the "Baked Bean Gardens" chapter; and for chilies, the "Chili Gardens" chapter.

Mexico is a huge country that has many climates, from tropical to temperate. Most gardeners in the United States can grow a good number of Mexico's vegetables and herbs, but the nearer one lives to the Mexican border the more options there will be for growing Mexican varieties.

Let's start by surveying options open to north-ern gardeners. They can grow numerous varieties of common vegetables used in Mexican cooking, such as tomatoes, bell peppers, and snap beans. They can also choose vegetables less common in the States but characteristic of Mexican cooking, such as many kinds of dry beans, the dent corns, the jalapeño peppers, purslane, tomatillos, round, light-colored zucchini-type squash, and the important herbs cilantro and epazote. Nurseries with a good selection of short-season varieties are Johnny's Selected Seeds, Stokes Seeds, and Abundant Life Seed Foundation.

For more southerly gardeners, the array of authentic Mexican varieties is larger. Because the fall stays warm longer, they can grow day-length-sensitive varieties (varieties that don't set fruits until the days get short in early fall) of winter squash, runner beans, and chili peppers. Other options are tender perennials, such as jicama and chayote, which need a long, warm growing season and mild winter.

It's important to realize that even when you grow these vegetables and herbs successfully, in some cases geographical factors such as humidity and soil pH can influence their flavor. For example, a humid climate and frequent rainfall will make chilies less hot than those grown in an arid region. In this same vein, Diana Kennedy reports that, for whatever reason, the epazote grown north of the border that she has cooked with usually lacks the pungency and depth of flavor characteristic of that from her garden in Mexico.

To obtain seeds of Mexican vegetables and herbs, consult the seed companies given in the "Sources" section of this chapter. Mexican seed companies are not cited, since they carry mostly commercial varieties of standard vegetables common in this country. In Mexico, gardeners let the plants seed themselves or obtain their seeds locally and keep them from year to year. If you visit Mexico you can shop in the markets for seeds, but Mexican corn seeds will be confiscated at the border, for it is illegal to bring them into the United States. A worthwhile venture, if it's convenient, is to visit a Mexican market in your own region to shop for seeds of grinding corns, cilantro, and dry beans. But when you grow the seeds of Mexican edibles you buy in a grocery store, be prepared to baby them for a few years. Remember that Victoria found it took two or three seasons to acclimatize the Mexican corn she bought at the market to her home garden, and be aware that there's a possibility that in wet, cold climates it may never acclimatize.

The Anderson Mexican Garden

The fact that I grew a Mexican garden in California wouldn't be big news to most gardeners. But I knew most Mexican vegetables and herbs could be grown in northern gardens, and I needed a demonstration garden to prove it. Vermont sounded convincingly northern, so I approached Kit Anderson, my good friend and managing editor of one of this country's finest gardening magazines, *National Gardening*, in Burlington, Vermont. Kit and I have worked on many

projects together, and I knew of her great interest in both Mexico and, of course, gardening.

We did some initial planning together, Kit did the ordering and the labor, and after the harvest I asked her to write up a detailed account of her Vermont Mexican garden. It tickled me to invite one of the country's premier gardening writers to contribute an essay to this book. Kit loved the idea. Here's what she wrote:

"The eighteen-inch-tall statue of the Mexican corn god must have suspected something when I wrapped him in a blanket for the trip back from his native land to icy Vermont. Little did he know, but he had his work cut out for him. After all, our New England climate is not exactly suited for tropical crops. That's why we started planning the garden by crossing off those vegetables that wouldn't mature in a brief season. That meant we had to leave out chayote, jicama, and some of the southwestern flour corns and day-length-sensitive chilies. But we still had plenty to choose from: many chili peppers, tomatillos, bunching onions, cilantro, Mexican pinto beans and corn for drying, plus such necessities as tomatoes and squash.

"Growing heat-loving crops in Vermont isn't as absurd as it sounds. We grow fine peppers and tomatoes just about any year, and I've even had okra produce some summers. I live in a relatively warm part of the state, the Champlain Valley, which extends all along the western border and is almost at sea level. Our frost-free season often lasts close to 150 days as compared to the 90 to 120 usual in the mountains to the east. And it gets hot in midsummer.

"Nevertheless, we had to choose varieties carefully. After scanning a number of catalogs, we found a number of suitable varieties. Then came the design of the garden. I wanted it to have a Mexican feel to it, not be simply rows of crops that happened to be from that part of the world. Tropical gardens tend to be much less organized looking than the typical American garden. They're liable to consist of fruit trees, flowers, vegetables, and herbs all growing in apparent disorder in the area around the house. Where sunshine is abundant, layered gardens make sense, with some crops growing in the shade of others. But without avocado trees and tamarind for shade, and with crops that would need all the sunshine they could get, our Vermont garden wasn't going to be layered—that approach just wouldn't work.

"I compromised. The plan became a puzzle, with

Diana Kennedy

My greatest awakening about Mexican food came a few years ago, when Diana Kennedy, author of the definitive book *The Cuisines of Mexico*, orchestrated a most wonderful Mexican breakfast. I was attending a cuisine seminar in San Diego, and her breakfast was the hit of the conference. We oohed and aahed over light-textured meatballs flavored with herbs and served in broth. We came back for more *molletes,* a dish made with *bolillos* (crusty, bobbin-shaped rolls) filled with creamy beans and covered with cheese and salsa. We had huevos rancheros served with fresh salsa and refried beans. And all through the meal, a murmur of contentment hummed in the background as people returned to the buffet table.

Experiencing the wide range of dishes at that breakfast awakened me to the diversity of Mexican cuisine and its many subtle uses of herbs and spices, far beyond the limited tomato, corn, and pepper flavors I had previously associated with Mexican cooking. Later, I was able to talk with Diana about Mexican varieties of vegetables and herbs and how they grow in the United States; you will find much of her information throughout this chapter. As we spoke, Diana continually referred to her own garden in Mexico, and I found myself wanting to know more about it. Given Diana's unbounded enthusiasm and what I knew of Mexican gardens, I envisioned an exuberant tangle of exotic and productive plants spilling over walls and paths.

My speculations proved accurate as Diana described her garden: wild, rambling, and filled with flowers and plants that reseed themselves. Located about a hundred miles outside of Mexico City, her garden has two distinct sections, which she refers to as the lower and upper gardens, and she has a separate area just off her kitchen that's filled with culinary herbs. "My pride and joy—my passionfruit that I love—I have climbing over every wall," Diana says. "My gardener keeps wanting me to cut it back, but

I love to let it run. All over the garden, nothing goes in straight lines—I think that probably reflects my character. My chayote vine—the huge, spiny variety—grows wild and climbs all over my loquat trees. And I have marvelous, rich-tasting avocados, both the little black ones and some local green varieties.

"At this point the artichokes are huge, taking over my lower garden," Diana says. "But then my garden comes and goes with the variations in the weather. It can be destroyed by too much rain, but this June we're battling very hot, dry conditions. The carrots and onions are going to seed, and the chervil is also running to seed after a marvelous season. The wonderful cilantro continually reseeds itself, too, and comes back so I have cilantro most of the year. The cherry tomatoes are just riotous at the moment—but then the birds haven't found them yet. There's a little chili bush growing wild and some zucchini bushes struggling with the dry conditions. And of course I have epazote. I don't have to plant that; it grows wild in the pasture—it grows wild everywhere.

"I'm closing off the upper garden by the house for the dry season. It's supposed to be irrigated, but we can't get enough water—we didn't get our winter rains to help this year. Of course, I still have my herb garden just outside the kitchen, and I have sage, thyme, marjoram, and a huge pot of tarragon there."

When I asked Diana what she recommends the average gardener in the States grow for use in Mexican dishes, she began by cautioning against trying to duplicate a garden like hers because the climate here is so different from that in Mexico. Many of the things she grows—especially some of the chili peppers—won't grow well in the States because of the different growing conditions. "If you try to grow 'Habanero' chilies, for instance," Diana says, "you might get peppers, but they won't taste right [as they would in Mexico]. But if you're making a dish that just needs to be hot [not like chiles rellenos, which feature the flavor of the particular chili], you could use most any of the hot varieties."

After discussing herbs and vegetables with Diana for some time, and through my own experience with Mexican gardening in the States, I've discovered that certain varieties that contribute to authentic Mexican cuisine do grow well in the States. Cilantro seems to be particularly successful here, but you could also try epazote, little round green zucchinis, sharp varieties of onion (not our usual sweet ones), and local field corns for some of the corn dishes (see "Rec-

ommended Mexican Vegetables" for specific varieties). And, of course, you can also experiment yourself. Visit Mexican grocery stores in your area and try the tastes of the chilies and herbs from Mexico; then try to match those tastes in your own garden.

After trying some of Diana's recipes and tasting the many flavors of Mexico previously unknown to me, I've concluded that we're just beginning a long and wonderful adventure exploring the tastes of Mexico from our gardens.

---

irregularly shaped beds, each containing a combination of vegetables and flowers of different heights, and all planned so that sunshine would get everywhere. At the center, of course, would be the corn god.

"The next major challenge was the heavy clay soil in my garden. Even after adding a lot of organic matter, I can only harvest carrots after a heavy rain (and then I bring up huge globs of soil along with the roots). Combine that with a cool, wet spring and you have about the worst possible conditions for heat-loving crops.

"Fortunately we had a wonderful, early, relatively rain-free spring that year, so I was able to get in and till in April and incorporate much composted manure. I still had a long wait before I could plant most of the crops. Our average last frost date here is May 15, but peppers hate to be cold. It does no good to set them out early; they'll only be stunted. In late April I started cilantro, tomatillos, and 'Lemon Gem' marigolds in pots in my cold frame (a simple affair made of plastic).

"Encouraged by the warm weather, I set my pepper plants outside, let the young plants harden off [acclimatize outside] for a few days, and then put them out in the garden on about May 7, with individual wax-paper hot caps [little individual shelters] to protect them. The poor things needed all the help they could get, because the weather turned cool and rainy for several weeks. Finally it warmed up again, and I uncovered the peppers, since they were pushing up the hot caps. That night a ferocious storm blew in. My children watched in amazement as I screamed at the hail that was pounding the kitchen window. But even that storm didn't phase those peppers. Except

for a few ragged leaves, they looked just fine the next day.

"The little cilantro plants and the tomatillos went in next, along with a few cilantro seeds, a row of bunching onion seeds, and a few rows of pinto beans. By May 31, everything was planted, with the corn god occupying a place of honor in the center of the garden.

"To keep down weeds, I mulched with grass clippings around everything. The paths were covered first with newspapers, at least sixteen pages thick, then with shredded bark. Finally I set up a combination sprinkler and drip system. This last step proved unnecessary, though, for we headed into the coolest, wettest summer I've ever experienced in Vermont. Eggplants everywhere languished. Tomatoes ripened late. Squash, even zucchini, produced poorly. We had great lettuce for tacos but not much else to go with it. It seemed impossible that the Mexican garden would make it, but it plugged right along. The peppers started bearing fruit by late July and kept up through September. The corn grew (slowly) and matured beautiful ears. The cilantro, especially the batch started early, made a lot of greens before going to seed. I cut it all back once, freezing the leaves, and then let it go. The plants allowed to mature produced seeds, and from these I got another crop of leaves later in the season. The beans were fine until September; then I had to take them into the barn to dry because they started to sprout during a few late rains. The tomatillos grew like mad, overwhelming everything near them, getting much larger than I'd planned. The tomatillo is a low-growing, hulking sort of plant that needs its own space. The amaranth I'd carefully

Kit Anderson, managing editor of National Gardening magazine, harvests cilantro from her Vermont Mexican garden.

planned as a backdrop—with the supposedly smaller yellow strain in front and the red in back—did not cooperate; the yellow turned out to be much more vigorous, dwarfing the dramatic red plants, which just peeked through from behind.

"The garden was at its best in late July, although the marigolds had been slow to begin flowering, so things weren't as colorful as I'd hoped they'd be. Tithonia, the Mexican sunflower, was a disappointment, too; it had lots of green foliage but flowered only late in the season.

"When corn harvest time came, my son and I had a wonderful time picking the ears and pulling off husks to reveal the richly colored kernels, everything from blue to red and yellow. Some of the ears are still displayed in a basket in our kitchen.

"Unfortunately, I never had time to develop great gourmet recipes with all these crops. We did feast on lots of tacos with chopped fresh tomatoes and cilantro, and had salsas made of tomatillos, hot peppers, and green onions. I discovered I liked cilantro

as a garnish and have also used the frozen leaves for soups and in *esquite,* a corn dish sold on street corners that I had learned to love in Mexico."

Despite the problems, Kit's enthusiasm for her Mexican garden was constant and infectious. When I visited in July the garden was beautiful, and I was reassured to see everything doing so well. Even though I'd heard garden experts talk about growing chili peppers, cilantro, and tomatillos in northern climates, I found it much more convincing to see and touch the thriving plants myself.

Recommended Mexican Vegetables

The following list contains some of the most popular Mexican vegetables and herbs along with recommended varieties and seed sources. The numbers in parentheses next to the variety names correspond to those of the seed companies listed in "Sources" at the end of the chapter. No numbers are given for varieties carried by most of the seed companies listed.

Most Mexican vegetables and herbs, such as beans, corn, and squash, are grown the way our own common varieties are; for cultural information on them consult Part Four, "An Encyclopedia of Superior Vegetables." Basic growing instructions are included here for the more unusual vegetables.

BEANS (snap and dry)   *Phaseolus* spp.; *frijoles*   Fava beans, *Vicia Faba; habas*   All types of beans are enjoyed in Mexico. Fresh beans, particularly the fava beans during Lent, are served in a number of dishes, but cooked dry beans are the most common.

How to grow: For basic growing information on snap beans see the Part Four Encyclopedia; for specifics on dry beans see the "Baked Bean Gardens" chapter. For Mexican-type varieties used in their dry state, try 'Aztec Bean' (5), a large, white "potato" bean; 'Black Turtle' (3), 'Delgado Black' (2), 'Mexican Black' (6), and 'Mitla Black' (5), all black bean varieties; and 'Pinto' beans. For information on growing fava beans (3, 5), see the "Italian Gardens" chapter.

How to prepare: Fresh snap beans can be cooked with chilies, onions, garlic, and oil, or used in pork dishes and soups. Dry beans are eaten in soups, stews, tostadas, burritos, and, of course, as refried beans. Fava beans can be used dry or fresh and are delicious served with garlic and/or chilies.

CHAYOTE   *Sechium edule; chayote*   This green, pear-shaped vegetable is versatile, absorbs seasonings very well, and is much appreciated in Mexico. There chayotes are creamy white, dark green, thorny, or smooth, while the chayotes we usually see in U.S. markets are medium green and smooth. As with summer squash, some varieties are delicately sweet and somewhat watery while others resemble potatoes in their starchiness.

How to grow: See the "Cajun Gardens" chapter.

How to prepare: Chayotes are most often steamed or boiled, and seasoned with butter, salt, and pepper or flavored with garlic, chilies, and tomatoes. Victoria Lomeli enjoys steaming and cutting them in thick slices, making a sandwich of them with cheese in between, and dipping them in egg batter and cooking them as you would chiles rellenos. The men at Mi Tierra enjoy them steamed and mashed with milk and honey or baked in aluminum foil in the oven like baked potatoes.

Mexican vegetables are a wonderful way to enliven cooking from the garden. Here chili peppers, onions, and epazote are surrounded by tithonia and Mexican zinnias.

CORN   *Zea Mays; maíz* (dry corn), *elote* (fresh corn or corn on the cob)   Corn is the foundation of Mexican cooking. While the Mexican use of corn most familiar to us is in the making of tortillas, Mexicans have infinite uses for this versatile staple. Like the corn varieties mentioned in the "Native American Gardens" chapter, most Mexican varieties are intended to be used as dry corn. There are dent corns for grinding into meal and soft corns for grinding into flour. The grinding corns may be picked at the "milk" stage (when the kernels are mature but still juicy) for eating fresh, and certain varieties are preferred for this purpose. Dent corns predominate in Mexico, and there are numerous local varieties. Some have large, plump kernels best for *pozole,* a term that means both hominy and hominy-based soup in Mexico. The starchy-sweet ones are great for roasting and eating in their milk stage; the kernels of these can be scraped off the cob and made into fresh corn tamales or used in soups.

How to grow: See the Part Four Encyclopedia for basic growing information; see the "Native American Gardens" chapter for basic variety information. Also try two Mexican varieties of grinding corn used for tortillas: 'Amarillo' (2), a yellow combination of flint and dent, and 'Chishe' (2), a yellow and white combination corn. And for *pozole,* try 'Posole' (5) and 'White Posole' (3), two southwestern varieties. 'Papago' (5) is a good tamale corn. For the largest selection available in this country of varieties applicable to Mexican cooking, contact Native Seeds Search. Other varieties are 'Maiz Negro' (4) and, for green corn tamales, 'Yaqui June Corn' (4). In addition, if you live in southern latitudes, you might want to buy corn kernels from a Mexican market—these will probably be dent varieties—and grow them out. In this case, expect to wait several years for the plants to acclimate to produce well.

How to prepare: In Mexican cuisine corn appears at almost every meal in a variety of forms. See "Cooking from the Mexican Garden" for basic recipes and preparation styles.

HUAUZONTLI *Chenopodium nuttaliae; guauzoncles* The bushy spears of this tall plant's seed heads are edible.

How to grow: The *huauzontli* (2) is an annual plant that is started from seed and grows to two to three feet in height. Keep the plant fairly moist during the growing season. In autumn the leaves will turn reddish brown.

How to prepare: The mild-tasting shoots are eaten like spinach. A traditional way of cooking *huauzontli,* as described in Diana Kennedy's book *The Cuisines of Mexico,* is to harvest the tops (the top four to five inches) of the branches when they are covered with green seed heads and blanch them; then put

small bunches together with cheese, dip in egg batter, and fry. The dried seeds can be used for a flour.

JICAMA *Pachyrhizus tuberosus; jícama* Jicama is a crispy, sweet root vegetable commonly eaten raw.

How to grow: Jicama (1, 2, 6) is a tender perennial vine that reaches twenty feet in length and is grown as an annual in the United States. It is planted from seeds and takes eight to nine months to produce large tubers, but if you start it inside early and have a frost-free growing season of about five months, you can expect small but high-quality tubers. Plant in fertile, well-drained soil in full sun and keep plants fairly moist and well fertilized. Harvest the tubers when the plants have died back in the fall. *Caution: Do not eat the seeds or pods, as they are poisonous.*

How to prepare: This juicy, sweet vegetable is eaten either raw or lightly cooked. To prepare, peel off the brown skin and slice. In Mexico, jicama is often dipped raw in chili powder and/or lime juice and eaten as a crudité, eaten in a salad with cilantro, or combined with oranges.

ONIONS *Allium Cepa; cebollas* Both white onions and scallions are used in Mexican cooking.

How to grow: See the Part Four Encyclopedia and select a strong white variety. According to Diana Kennedy, sweet yellow or brown onions can ruin a Mexican dish.

How to prepare: Onions are one of the main seasonings in Mexican cuisine. They are used raw in salsas, burritos, tacos, and salads and are used in most cooked dishes.

PEPPERS *Capsicum* spp.; *chilis* (hot peppers), *morrones* (bell peppers) Peppers are native to Mexico and have added their delightful spiciness to Mexican cooking for centuries.

How to grow: For basic growing information see the Part Four Encyclopedia. For variety information and guidance in preparing chilies see the "Chili Gardens" chapter.

How to prepare: Large, mild chilies star in chiles rellenos (stuffed chili peppers), and both the mild and the hotter chilies are used in many Mexican dishes.

PURSLANE *Portulaca oleracea* var. *sativa; verdolagas* A wild form of this low-growing fleshy herb, one that many gardeners know as a pest, is pigweed. However, purslane can be a tasty green and is enjoyed in Mexico and many other parts of the world in many kinds of dishes.

How to grow: 'Large Leaved Golden' (7) is the most common cultivated variety of purslane. Seeds of this annual plant are started either in warm garden soil in spring or inside and then transplanted out when the weather warms up. If you are sowing the plants in place, either sow the seeds thickly and then thin and harvest the seedlings, leaving the remainder about six to nine inches apart, or sow less thickly (the former gives you the option of using the thinnings). Purslane also grows well in a cold frame in spring and fall. The object of growing purslane is to produce tender, succulent leaves, so keep the plants well watered and cut back often to force new growth. Harvest thinnings and young leaves. Remove flower stalks as they form or they will be tough and might go to seed.

How to prepare: The leaves of purslane have a slightly tart taste and are juicy. When eaten fresh they border on slippery, but this quality is less evident in the cooked leaves. In Mexico the preferred way of cooking this potherb is in a peasant stew with pork, tomatoes, tomatillos, and fresh chilies. Diana Kennedy provides a recipe for this dish in her *Mexican Regional Cooking.* Purslane is also used in soups and eaten raw in salads.

SQUASH *Cucurbita* spp.; *calabaza* Both summer and winter squash are used in Mexico.

How to grow: See the Part Four Encyclopedia. One of the most popular types of summer squash is the round zucchinilike 'Ronde de Nice' (3), which comes from France. Also popular are the light-colored zucchinis such as 'Greyzini' (available from many large seed companies) and 'White Lebanese' (3). For a winter type try *chilacayote (C. ficifolia)* (2, 3), an orange-fleshed squash used as are all winter squashes. This is a short-day perennial that can require more than 130 days to mature. A similar variety, 'Santo Domingo' (5), is a large, green squash with white flesh and black seeds that grows on large vines. When small—about six to nine inches long—it is used in Mexico as a vegetable; when large—eighteen inches or so in length—it is sometimes used as a *dulce,* which means it is put into sugar, boiled, and served as a sweet. Also used in Mexico are the cushaw types of squash, which are green with white stripes, and the popular 'Banana' squash. See the price list of Native Seeds Search for more varieties.

How to prepare: Summer squash is the perfect vehicle for absorbing the flavors of chilies, garlic, onion, tomato, and numerous herbs such as epazote, oregano, and thyme. Victoria Lomeli likes to prepare hers with cubed, sautéed pork, to which she adds sliced zucchini, garlic, tomatoes, green onions, and chilies. She serves it with corn tortillas. Sometimes she stuffs the squash with meat, and other times she cooks it like a chile relleno.

Squash blossoms, too, contribute to Mexican cuisine. They are a traditional filling for quesadillas and are also used in soup. Diana Kennedy gives recipes for both in *The Cuisines of Mexico.* The gardeners at Mi Tierra recommend using squash blossoms in chayote soup and in omelettes.

TOMATILLOS *Physalis ixocarpa; tomates verdes, tomates de cascara* This vegetable is related to and somewhat resembles the small, green tomato, but it has a paperlike husk.

How to grow: Tomatillos are grown very like tomatoes but the plants tend to be rangier and more brittle. Craig Dremann, of the Redwood City Seed Company, says that they ripen sooner and grow faster in cool weather than tomatoes. There are two varieties good enough to recommend: 'Rendidora' (3), the only named, large-fruited tomatillo readily available, and 'Purple De Milpa' (3, 6), a small one (the fruits are an inch and a half across) but considered one of the best flavored.

How to prepare: Before using tomatillos, remove the paperlike husks and rinse lightly. Use raw or, more often, cooked. To cook, put in a pot, cover with water, and simmer for about five to ten minutes; then proceed with your choice of a number of recipes. As an alternative, you might husk them and then roast them on a *comal* (a small griddle) until browned and slightly mushy when blended. Or you can stew tomatillos with chilies and onions, which complement their tart, slightly tomatolike flavor. Probably the most popular way to serve them is in *salsa verde,* the condiment, and in the sauce for *enchiladas verdes.* Victoria Lomeli makes her green enchilada sauce with tomatillos, garlic, chilies, and cilantro. Another idea is to use tomatillos in guacamole for an interesting alternative to tomatoes.

TOMATOES *Lycopersicon Lycopersicum; jitomates* Juicy, ripe tomatoes are celebrated in Mexican cooking. Native to the area, tomatoes are part of a multitude of dishes.

How to grow: See the Part Four Encyclopedia.

How to prepare: Tomatoes are the base of most

salsas and many stews and soups, and they are added to many vegetable and meat dishes.

Numerous herbs grow wild in Mexico and give distinctive flavors to native dishes. Few are available in this country's supermarkets or seed companies, and few are covered in our herb books. Some are available from Mexican grocery stores, but the only way to gain access to most is to grow your own.

CHIA *Salvia hispanica; chia* Chia is a traditional herb dating back to the Aztecs. While other plants are known as chia, according to Craig Dremann of the Redwood City Seed Company, this *Salvia* species (6) is the one commonly found in Mexican grocery stores in this country.

How to grow: This chia is an annual plant with blue flowers that grows to about four feet. Start seeds in the spring.

How to prepare: In chia's chief use, the seeds are stirred into water to make a refreshing cold drink. Less traditionally, chia leaves can be used to flavor poultry and meats, and the sprouted seeds can be sprinkled on salads to give a peppery taste.

CILANTRO (fresh coriander) *Coriandrum sativum; cilantro* This pungent herb looks something like parsley but its taste is different and much stronger.

How to grow: Cilantro is an easily grown annual herb that grows best in cool weather. Seed it in place in the garden and thin it to four to six inches apart. Keep it moist to ensure quick growth. The varieties most commonly available in this country are specifically grown for world trade; their seeds are used as a spice called coriander. However, you can grow varieties selected for their lush growth and used for their leaves. These are the "slow-to-bolt" varieties available from Johnny's Selected Seeds, Nichols Garden Nursery, and Shepherd's Garden Seeds. You can also use the leaves of plants grown from commonly available coriander seeds.

How to prepare: Cilantro leaves are most often used raw, generally chopped and sprinkled on a dish or mixed in at the end of cooking to give it a characteristic flavor. Add the leaves sparingly to salads, guacamole, and folded into cooked vegetable dishes and salsa or use whole leaves as a garnish. When you buy cilantro, choose fresh-looking, all-green plants, preferably with roots intact. To store, put cilantro in a glass of water in the refrigerator, cover with a plastic bag, and use within a few days.

EPAZOTE *Chenopodium ambrosioides; epazote* This herb is used in some areas of Mexico and Central America.

How to grow: Epazote (1, 5, 7) is so easily grown that it actually grows wild in many temperate areas of the United States. If you don't pick the seed heads off, the plant can become a weed in your garden. It is easily started from seed in spring, will grow to a height of three to four feet, and may need staking and some pruning to look tidy. Harvest leaves and shoots and use for a seasoning. Freeze leaves or bring a containerized plant inside for winter use.

How to prepare: Epazote has a very strong flavor that may take some getting used to. It has been used in Mexico for centuries, particularly with black beans, and can be used to season soups, quesadillas, and corn, mushroom, and seafood dishes. Mexicans use epazote to help control flatulence from eating beans.

JAMAICA (hibiscus) *Hibiscus Sabdariffa; jamaica* This plant is a hibiscus.

How to grow: See the "Edible Flower Gardens" chapter for growing information.

How to prepare: This acidic-tasting flower calyx is used to make a rose-colored drink called jamaica.

MEXICAN MARIGOLD *Tagetes lucida; anisillo* or *pericon* This traditional pungent herb, sometimes called Mexican tarragon, is used for an infusion (tisane) that has a strong marigold flavor with an anise overtone. The plant is also used to decorate the house in the Mexican equivalent of Halloween.

How to grow: Mexican marigold is an easily grown, tender perennial that reaches three feet in height and is grown as an annual in cold climates. Its ferny foliage sprawls if not continually cut back. In cold climates the plant is covered with small marigold-type flowers for much of the autumn; in mild-winter areas it can bloom all winter. Sow seeds in early spring indoors and plant in a sunny spot after the weather has warmed up.

How to prepare: Mexican marigold leaves are primarily used for an infusion.

MEXICAN OREGANO *Lippia graveolens; oregano* According to Craig Dremann, *L. graveolens* is common in Mexico and known as oregano, and its dried leaves are readily available in Mexican food stores in the United States. Still, this is only one of a variety of species you may get in Mexico when you ask for oregano: several other *Lippia*s plus a number of *Salvia* and *Origanum* species also fall under this heading. See the "Culinary Herb Gardens" chapter for information about *Origanum* oreganos.

How to grow: L. *graveolens* (6, 7) is a tender perennial that prefers part shade and quite rich soil in the garden. According to Richters seed company, it can grow in a bright window or solarium in cold climates.

How to prepare: In some parts of Mexico the leaves are toasted before using. Use the dried leaves in chili dishes and salsa; in fillings for burritos, tamales, and chiles rellenos; and as seasoning in such seafood dishes as stuffed fish and ceviche and such meat dishes as pork stew and tripe soup.

Cooking from the Mexican Garden

Mexican cuisine has its roots in the ancient Aztec civilization. When Cortés arrived in 1521, the native peoples in this part of the world were steeped in nature's bounty: corn, beans, tomatoes, squash, avocados, chili peppers, turkey, a vast range of seafoods, and two indigenous delicacies—chocolate and vanilla. Montezuma, the last Aztec emperor, had lobsters, shrimp, quail, bananas, guavas, and pineapples brought to him from all over the countryside. And a staple of the Aztecs was the tortilla, one of the world's most versatile foods. With the Spanish invasion, pork, beef, milk, wine, wheat, sugar, citrus fruits, and garlic entered Mexico. Over the centuries, the foods of both cultures blended into a unique cuisine.

In fact, the conquistadors affected cuisines in Europe as well by bringing home foods of the New World. The Italians embraced the tomato, the Germans the potato, and the Swiss, chocolate. In turn, Mexican cooks found ways of using garlic, lime, cheese, pork, and beef. However, according to the author of *A Treasury of Mexican Cuisine,* while North American cooking is basically an adaptation of European cooking to New World ingredients, Mexican cuisine as we know it can be traced directly to its pre-Hispanic origins. For this reason, those of us trained in any of the European-based cuisines come up against a number of unfamiliar ingredients and techniques when we introduce ourselves to Mexican cooking. For example, while many of us might have made pasta and bread, few of us in the United States have actually made tortillas.

Mexican cooks use such ingredients as cinnamon, black pepper, parsley, and mint, as do cooks worldwide, but they use much more ground corn and chili peppers than cooks in most other cultures. Within Mexico, we can discern regional characteristics as well, determined both by climatic and cultural factors—that is, by ingredients grown and the native peoples who originally grew them. Avocado leaves and epazote are examples; these seasonings are used in the south but seldom appear in the north.

To begin to get a feel for Mexican cooking, we can describe general characteristics of the food. First, corn is almost always present in any of literally hundreds of forms. Also, many dishes take quite a bit of preparation time; in fact, two cooking steps are often involved. And the food tends to be generously seasoned.

What follows is a rather general survey of the major vegetables used in Mexican cooking. This plus the recipes that follow will give you a good start in mastering one of the world's truly distinctive cuisines.

Beans

Beans and corn are the most important staples of the Mexican diet. According to Diana Kennedy, beans often appear in all three daily meals. As I discovered in my baked bean research, there is a great range of dry bean varieties to explore. The varieties differ subtly in both flavor and texture, and exploring the many preparation styles that have evolved to capitalize on these differences is great fun. The basic, traditional Mexican dry bean dish is *frijoles de olla,* beans cooked very slowly and with very little seasoning in an earthenware pot. Although the earthenware may be particularly helpful in bringing out the beans' flavors, any large pot used over a low flame will yield good results. *Frijoles a la charra* (translated by Diana Kennedy as beans made the way an elegant horsewoman would prepare them) are cooked with bacon, tomatoes, cilantro, and chili peppers. With the addition of a little beer, this dish becomes *frijoles borrachos* (drunken beans). Beans can be served as a side dish or in soup. Black beans, with a sprig of epazote added toward the end of cooking, are most common in the cuisine of the Yucatán and central Mexico. In the Yucatán they may also add mint to

the beans or sieve them to make a creamy puree. Beans are often refried with lard and garnished with cheese.

Here are some tips for making good Mexican beans. Do not presoak dry beans, but bring the water you will cook them in to a boil before pouring it over them. Then cook, covered, at a very low simmer and stir with a wooden spoon only. Do not add salt or acidic ingredients until the beans are done. Refrigerate beans after cooling. They actually taste best reheated the day after they are cooked.

Chilies

Chili peppers, of course, are used widely and distinctively in Mexican cooking. In this country we tend to view chili peppers as mostly hot and therefore ignore the range of flavors. This approach is analogous to enjoying wine but classifying it only in two categories—red and white—and therefore failing to experience the full range of flavors. In the "Chili Gardens" chapter I detailed the primary chili pepper varieties plus their tastes and uses in stew-type dishes and how to roast and dry them. In Mexican food chili peppers are used as the basis of salsa (the main Mexican condiment), moles, and sauces for meat and seafoods; in the stuffing for rellenos; and as a seasoning in the majority of cooked dishes. For a detailed rundown on the types of chili peppers and their uses in Mexican cooking, see Diana Kennedy's *The Cuisines of Mexico*.

Here are some general comments on chilies as used in Mexican cooking. Most Mexican cooks prefer fresh chilies in their green, not red-ripe state. The ripe peppers are usually used dried. The flavors of the chili peppers are as important as their hotness. Thus, for the average Mexican cook the variety of the chili used depends on the dish being prepared. Another factor influencing the variety used is geographical region. Thus, the 'Habanero' (a somewhat challenging chili pepper to grow) is preferred and used fresh or toasted in sauces in parts of the Yucatán and Campeche. On the other hand, the long, slim, black-green 'Chilaca' is used often in Baja and is particularly popular in fresh corn tamales in Jalisco.

OPPOSITE: *Chiles rellenos covered with a cream and nut sauce and sprinkled with pomegranate seeds and cilantro (chiles rellenos en nogada) are served on patriotic Mexican occasions.*

Grow some of the chili peppers recommended in the "Chili Gardens" chapter and experiment with the varying tastes to see which ones you prefer. Since most chili experts agree that climate and soil influence the taste of a chili, however, you may have to experiment to achieve the authentic flavors of some of the Mexican dishes you find in your cookbooks. You'll need to grow the varieties of chilies called for and then, if possible, buy the same varieties from a Mexican or Puerto Rican market to compare the tastes. Authenticity aside, whichever chilies you grow are guaranteed to give you more flavor than the canned ones.

Corn

Corn is Mexico's single most important food. The day can start and end with a corn dish of some sort. Mexican fresh corn, *elote,* generally a bit starchier than our sweet corn, is used quite a bit—for example, in a fresh corn soup with tomatoes, onions, and garlic, or in tamales made from fresh corn scraped off the cob. Street vendors sell fresh corn on the cob, which their customers can dip in cream and season with grated cheese.

Most of the corn consumed in Mexico is ground dry corn. It is used primarily in masa, a dough made from ground, lime-treated kernels. Masa is most often formed into tortillas, which are then used in many ways. In their versatility, tortillas resemble both bread and pasta. Tacos, for instance, are tortillas filled with meat and a little salsa and often garnished with lettuce and tomatoes. In Mexico, the tortillas for tacos are frequently soft rather than crisp, as they are here. Enchiladas are tortillas rolled around fillings of various types, primarily meats or cheeses, and then covered with a sauce and cooked. Quesadillas are made with tortillas or masa that has been folded and stuffed with cheese, squash blossoms, cactus, or other filling and then fried or cooked on a griddle. Tostadas are tortillas that have been fried crisp and then topped with beans, chopped meat, salsa, lettuce, tomato, and cheese. And you can imagine, with all those tortillas around, that uses are found for the stale ones too—for instance, in soups and casseroles and served in appetizers.

Because tortillas are so versatile, you can always put together a quick meal from the garden around them. Some of my uses of tortillas are hardly authentically Mexican, but I don't see how I ever cooked without these flat little cakes. Give me a batch of tortillas, a pot of beans, and some salsa (a garden staple I always put up), and I can take care of my meal planning for days. I roll tortillas around beans and garnish with tomatoes one night, with cabbage and grated carrots another. For another meal I put a little chicken in tortillas and add lettuce, guacamole, and cilantro. And I might finish the week by cooking up a mixture of zucchini, green peppers, onions, garlic, cumin, tomatoes, and grated cheese, and serve it with tortillas and beans on the side.

Tortillas are available commercially in most parts of the country, although in some places only frozen. As with bread or pasta making, it's worth the effort to make your own tortillas, but not as an everyday undertaking. If you want to make tortillas from your own garden-grown grinding corn, first see the section in the "Native American Gardens" chapter under hominy. Once you have your corn hominied, consult the books by Diana Kennedy listed in the "Sources" section.

Tamales, too, are a Mexican invention that can benefit from fresh garden produce. When I first had tamales in local restaurants my reactions were distinctly negative, but then I learned what wonderful creations tamales can be when properly prepared with fresh ingredients. The aroma of freshly ground masa steaming in fresh corn husks mingling with that of roasted peppers and a seasoned filling drew me to a whole aspect of Mexican cuisine that I had previously considered not to my taste.

The *uchepos* made in Mexico today are modern versions of an ancient preparation of cornmeal cooked in a corn leaf. But tamales don't stop there; they can have fillings of all kinds—meat, poultry, seafood, beans, and chilies, not to mention the sweet tamales filled with fruit, nuts, or sweet spiced beans and served for breakfast or snacks. In tropical regions, tamales are often wrapped in banana leaves rather than corn husks, and sometimes a ground avocado leaf is added to the filling for flavor. Tamales, in fact, are a basic fact of life in Mexico, knit into the social fabric. Because the traditional methods of preparation are very time consuming, the *tamalada* is a festive event in which families and friends, young and old, get together to make tamales—and then, of course, to feast on the results.

For the adventurous cook who wants really superior tamales, I suggest making your own hominy

José Cerrillo of Mi Tierra community garden demonstrates how to fold corn husks in making tamales.

and masa from home-grown corn. See the "Native American Gardens" chapter for directions. If there is a large Mexican population in your area, you might be able to buy fresh masa. Otherwise, take Diana Kennedy's suggestion for using Quaker instant grits as the next best substitute and combine it with packaged masa harina. For even greater convenience, though less flavor, masa harina can be used alone.

Seasonings

In addition to the herbs described in the "Recommended Mexican Vegetables" section, other seasonings used are cinnamon, cloves, and chocolate in meat sauces, and, occasionally in southern Mexico, avocado leaves in tamales and sprinkled over refried beans. When dried and ground up, avocado leaves give a somewhat anisey-nutty taste. (If you want to grow these yourself, choose among the Mexican varieties of avocados, for they have the most flavor. Best of all are the thin-skinned black avocados. Even one grown on a windowsill from a seed will give you leaves for your Mexican meals.)

Salsas

Although *salsa* means sauce, here we are referring to the primary condiment used in Mexican cuisine. Chili peppers are the predominant seasoning used in salsas, although tomatoes and onions are usually used too. But beyond that there are infinite variations, ranging widely in flavor depending on the technique and ingredients used. In the United States we are most familiar with tomato-based salsas, but in Mexico one might encounter a salsa of roasted, chopped chilies mixed with a little lime juice. A fresh, raw salsa made entirely from tomatoes, chili peppers, and herbs from the summer garden is a delight. Cooked salsas are equally delicious and have the added advantage of keeping longer refrigerated or frozen. Raw or cooked salsas may be canned, too. Check a recipe designed for canning; vinegar may have to be added for acidity to prevent botulism.

That covers the red salsas, but there are two types of green salsas as well. One consists of mild green chilies, roasted and peeled, plus garlic, onion, cilantro, perhaps hot chilies, some parsley, *pepitas* (pumpkin seeds), and oil. The other uses tomatillos, which are easy to grow and have a refreshing, tart flavor that blends well with hot chilies and other Mexican flavors.

Once you master a few basics, such as making salsa, fixing up a pot of creamy beans, and working with tortillas in a few different ways, you'll be able to prepare many a Mexican meal from your garden. These techniques plus the recipes that follow will take you a long way in exploring the rich relationship between garden-fresh vegetables and Mexico's distinctive cuisine.

SALSAS

Zesty sauces and relishes, with chili peppers as a key ingredient, are the primary condiments used in Mexican cuisine. Here are two variations on this theme.

Fresh Tomato Salsa

MAKES 2–3 CUPS.

> 2 to 4 fresh 'Serrano' or 'Jalapeño' chilies (or use milder varieties or a combination)
> 1 medium onion, quartered, or about 6 green onions, chopped
> 2 cloves garlic
> 4 large, ripe tomatoes, quartered
> 1/8 to 1/4 cup cilantro leaves
> 1/2 teaspoon salt

A food processor is especially useful for salsa. (If you don't have one, finely chop all ingredients and mix.) Stem peppers (seed, too, if you desire a milder salsa). Place several peppers at a time in food processor and pulse with metal blade until finely, but not overly, chopped. Use a rubber spatula to remove to a bowl. Place tomatoes, cilantro, and salt in processor and pulse to chop coarsely. Add to chili mixture, stir, and serve. Best used promptly, but leftover sauce can be brought to a simmer and then refrigerated to keep about a week.

Tomatillo Salsa Verde

MAKES 2–3 CUPS.

This traditional green salsa made with tomatillos can be served raw or cooked. Try it over barbecued pork and in tacos.

> 2 or 3 fresh 'Serrano' or 'Jalapeño' chilies, halved (seeded for a milder sauce)
> 1 medium onion, quartered
> 1 clove garlic, quartered
> 2 tablespoons minced fresh cilantro
> About 20 tomatillos, husked, washed, and boiled in a little water until just tender, to yield about 2½ cups
> 1/4 teaspoon sugar
> Salt to taste
> 2 tablespoons oil

In food processor or blender, chop chilies medium fine. Add onion and garlic and chop as above. Add remaining ingredients except oil and blend briefly, just until uniform. Heat oil in a skillet, add sauce, and cook over medium heat, stirring, for about 5 minutes. Cool and serve.

COOL WHITE SALAD

This recipe was created especially for this book by Carole Saville, a professional food writer and gardener. Carole designs culinary gardens for restaurants, styles food for photographs, and shares her vast knowledge and enthusiasm for foods with many professionals.

SERVES 6.

> 2 tablespoons lime juice
> ½ teaspoon Southwestern Originals' Sonoran Seasoning (see note) or ¼ teaspoon cumin
> Salt to taste
> Freshly ground white pepper to taste
> Pinch cayenne pepper
> 6 tablespoons light, extra-virgin olive oil
> 2 tablespoons cilantro, chopped fine
> 1 large or 2 small jicamas
> 1 slice red onion, one-half sliced orange for garnish

Note: Sonoran Seasoning, a blend of herbs and spices, is a product marketed by Chef Alan Zeman of the Tucson Country Club in Tucson, Arizona, and can be found at better shops across the country.

In mixing bowl combine lime juice, Sonoran Seasoning or cumin, salt, white pepper and cayenne pepper. Slowly whisk in olive oil until dressing is emulsified. Add cilantro and mix again. Peel jicama and cut into thin, matchstick-size slices. Pour dressing over jicama and mix well. Garnish with onion and orange. Place salad in refrigerator to chill.

SHRIMP CEVICHE FIESTA SALAD

This is another dish created by Carole Saville. Use your garden peppers and greens to show off the shrimp in all its glory.

SERVES 6.

> ¾ cup lime juice
> ¾ cup lemon juice
> ½ cup orange juice
> 1 clove garlic
> 2 teaspoons dried coriander seeds, crushed
> 1 'Jalapeño' pepper, roasted, peeled and chopped (but not seeded)

> 1 teaspoon salt
> Freshly ground black pepper to taste
> 1 pound very fresh shrimp, peeled and deveined (if large, cut in half)
> 1 red onion, sliced thin
> 1 purple pepper, 1 yellow pepper, 1 red pepper, 1 green pepper
> 2 tablespoons fresh cilantro, chopped
> Six iceberg lettuce leaves

In flat glass or ceramic bowl large enough to hold the shrimp in one layer, combine lime juice, lemon juice, and orange juice. Peel garlic, crush with the back of a knife, and add to juice. Add coriander seeds, 'Jalapeño' pepper, salt, and freshly ground black pepper. Combine well. Add peeled shrimp to mixture and cover with red onion slices. Make sure all ingredients are covered with marinade. Cover and place dish in refrigerator. Marinate for about six hours or until shrimp becomes opaque.

Cut peppers decoratively into strips or into thin rings and set aside. Remove shrimp from marinade,

Ceviche is a Mexican dish of seafood marinated in lime juice. Shown here is a nontraditional shrimp ceviche created by Carole Saville. The large poppies are matilijas from her yard.

reserving liquid. Toss shrimp with fresh cilantro. Coat cut-up peppers with reserved liquid. Drain. Place shrimp on a lettuce leaf on salad plates and decorate each plate with 1 slice of each of the colored peppers.

ENSALADA DE CHAYOTE

The people at Guaymas, a wonderful restaurant in Tiburon, California, popular for its unusual, authentic, fresh Mexican cuisine, contributed this recipe for chayote salad.

SERVES 6.

Dressing/Marinade

> ½ cup white distilled vinegar
> 1½ cups salad oil
> 2 cloves garlic, chopped
> Salt and pepper to taste

Mix all ingredients together.

Salad

> 2 chayotes, peeled and cut in 1-inch wedges
> 6 cups chicken stock
> 3 medium tomatoes, cut into 1-inch wedges
> 1 medium white onion, thinly sliced
> ½ head iceberg lettuce, cut into strips
> 6 olives, cut into strips
> ½ bunch fresh cilantro

Bring chicken stock to a boil, add chayote, and boil until tender, about 5 to 8 minutes. Cool.

In separate bowls, place chayote, tomatoes, and onions in marinade for about 10 minutes.

Toss lettuce with some of the dressing and arrange on individual serving plates. Place chayote and tomato wedges over this, place onion rings over the wedges, sprinkle with olives, and top with a sprig of cilantro.

CALABACITAS GUISADAS, ESTILO MICHOACÁN

This recipe for squash cooked Michoacán-style and the following recipe are from Diana Kennedy's *The Cuisines of Mexico,* revised edition. Diana writes, "Of the many versions of recipes for squash cooked with tomatoes, this, from the eastern part of Michoacán, is a favorite of mine. It is quite strongly flavored

with epazote. If this herb is not available do not try to substitute anything else. The vegetables will be delicious anyway. In Mexico either the elongated 'Calabacita Italiana' (zucchini) or the small round 'Criollo' squash is used.

"This is eaten as a separate course, and when sprinkled with cheese can supplant a meat dish."

SERVES 6.

> 3 medium tomatoes (totaling 12 ounces)
> 4 tablespoons safflower oil
> 2 pounds zucchini (see above), trimmed and diced
> 4 heaping tablespoons finely chopped white onion
> 4 tablespoons roughly chopped epazote leaves
> 1 teaspoon salt, or to taste
> 2 'Serrano' chilies, charred (see "Chili Gardens" chapter for technique)
> 2 cloves garlic, peeled
> 4 tablespoons finely grated cheese (queso anejo, Romano, or Argentinian Sardo; optional)

Place tomatoes on a cookie sheet and put under broiler at medium heat. Turn frequently for about 20 minutes until cooked through. They will blister and char a bit. Set aside.

In a heavy frying pan, heat oil and add squash, onion, epazote, and salt. Stir well, cover pan, and cook over a medium flame, stirring occasionally, until just tender, about 10 minutes.

Blend together whole broiled tomatoes, chilies, and garlic and stir into squash mixture. Cook over a medium flame, uncovered, until squash is soft and tomato puree has been absorbed. The vegetables should be moist but not too juicy. Adjust seasoning and serve immediately. You may top with cheese just before serving.

UCHEPOS

If you are growing dent corn (field or grain corn) for grinding or hominy, you may want to try these delicious, traditional fresh corn tamales using the corn when it is at the milk stage—mature but still juicy. (See the "Native American Gardens" chapter for recommended varieties.) Diana gives us this information on preparing to make these tamales: "The *uchepo* is a small tamal of fresh corn, a specialty of central

Michoacán. Many people just grind the corn, add sugar, salt, and sometimes baking powder or soda, and fill the fresh corn husks for steaming as with any other tamales. A food processor is ideal for this recipe, but you can also use a blender: grind the corn in several small batches and let the froth subside a little before stirring in the rest of the ingredients. Select 6 ears with the husks still wrapped around them. Using a very sharp knife, carefully cut around the base of the husks just above the spot where they are attached to the stalk. Carefully unfurl the husks, rinse them well in cold water, and shake them dry (or spin in a salad spinner), and set aside.

"Line the top part of a large steamer with the toughest outside husks and set the rest aside for covering the *uchepos*. Fill ⅔ of the bottom section of the steamer with water and throw in a heavy coin [so you can monitor the boiling water by ear without having to open the steamer to look]. Set the steamer over a low heat while you make the *uchepos*."

MAKES ABOUT 20 UCHEPOS.

> *Kernels from about 6 ears field corn (see note*
>   *above), shaved off cobs, to yield 5 cups*
> *¼ to ⅓ cup whole milk*
> *1 rounded teaspoon finely ground sea salt*
> *3 tablespoons sugar*
> *3 tablespoons unsalted butter, softened but*
>   *not melted*
> *3 tablespoons natas (clotted cream from milk*
>   *that has been scalded), crème fraîche, or*
>   *thick cream*
> *Corn husks*
> *Terry cloth toweling*

Put half the corn and all the milk into container of a food processor and process until corn has been reduced to a textured pulp, about 2 minutes. Add remaining kernels and continue processing until mixture is reduced to a fairly loose but textured paste, about 4 minutes more. Add salt, sugar, butter, and cream, and process only until well mixed.

Shake husks once more to make sure they are dry. Place 1 heaping tablespoon of mixture in middle of each husk, measuring from just below cupped end, to cover an area roughly 2 inches long and ¾ inch wide. Do not flatten or spread mixture. Roll husk loosely around it and turn up pointed end just beyond the dough.

By this time the water in the steamer should be boiling and the coin rattling away.

Set 1 layer of *uchepos* horizontally, folded tip down, over lined surface of steamer. Cover with extra husks and toweling before placing lid on steamer. Steam over high heat for 10 to 15 minutes, then lower heat to medium, uncover, and place the rest of the *uchepos* in horizontal layers in steamer. (This keeps the bottom layer from flattening out.) Cover as before and cook for about 1½ hours or until dough separates cleanly from husk.

Uchepos freeze well. To reheat, just place them, still frozen, into a steamer and heat for about 10 to 15 minutes.

Serve with a hot, pureed tomato and chili salsa or meat in a sauce.

ESQUITES

Kit Anderson, managing editor of *National Gardening*, bought this snacklike dish from a street vendor in Chapingo, Mexico, when she was visiting Professor Garrison Wilkes, a geneticist specializing in preserving corn varieties. She liked it so much we asked Professor Wilkes to track down the recipe. *Esquites* can be made with either field corn picked at the milk stage or fresh, ripe sweet corn. In some versions the corn is not fried in oil first, as it is here. Vendors sell it in cups with a spoon.

MAKES "ENOUGH FOR FIESTA."

> *1¼ cups oil or lard*
> *4½ pounds corn kernels cut off the cobs*
> *½ pound longaniza sausage, optional*
> *2 to 5 'Serrano' chilies, finely chopped, to*
>   *taste*
> *8 tomatillos, quartered*
> *Half a handful epazote*
> *1 to 2 tablespoons salt*

Heat oil or lard in a large, heavy pot and fry corn, sausage, and chilies over medium heat, stirring occasionally, until corn is slightly browned. Add remaining ingredients and enough water to moisten slightly, cover, and simmer until corn is tender, 10 to 15 minutes.

CHILES CON CREMA

Craig and Sue Dremann, owners of the Redwood City Seed Company, obtained this recipe from friends in Michoacán, Mexico.

SERVES 4.

> 12 ripe (red) 'Ancho', 'California', mild
> 'Anaheim', or 'New Mexico' chilies,
> roasted and peeled (see "Chili Gardens"
> chapter for technique)
> 2 cups sour cream
> ⅛ teaspoon minced fresh oregano (preferably
> Mexican)
> Dash of salt

Stem and seed chilies and cut into slices. In a frying
pan on low heat, add sour cream, chilies, oregano,
and salt. Stir to mix and heat just to warm sour cream
(overheating will curdle it). Serve as a side dish with
meat, rice, and tortillas.

CHILES RELLENOS
EN NOGADA

This traditional dish is made in Mexico in late August
and September, when nuts and pomegranates are ripe,
in conjunction with several patriotic occasions. There
are many variations, but in all of them the dish is
arranged beautifully to show the green of the peppers
and cilantro, the white of the sauce, and the red of
the pomegranates—the colors of the Mexican flag.
(At other times of the year, spiced crabapples can be
substituted for pomegranates for the red color.) This
dish makes a wonderful main meal served with beans,
tortillas, and a salad.

SERVES 8.

Nogada Sauce

> 1¼ cups walnuts or almonds (for almonds,
> first blanch and remove skins)
> 1¼ cups half-and-half
> 1 small piece white bread, without crusts,
> soaked in the cream
> ⅓ cup (3 ounces) cream cheese, farmer's
> cheese, or fresh goat cheese
> 1 tablespoon sugar
> Pinch of cinnamon
> 2 tablespoons sherry or brandy, optional

In blender or food processor, grind nuts fine. Add
half-and-half with bread, and then remaining ingredients. Blend smooth, remove to a bowl, and refrigerate if not using soon.

*Jicama salad served with lime juice and cilantro is a
refreshing Mexican dish.*

Picadillo Filling

> 4 tablespoons lard or oil
> 1 onion, finely chopped
> 2 cloves garlic, minced
> ½ teaspoon each cinnamon and cumin
> ¼ teaspoon cloves
> 1½ pounds (boneless weight) chicken, pork, or
> beef that has been boiled until done and
> shredded or chopped finely to give about
> 3 cups
> Salt and pepper to taste
> 1 cup meat cooking broth
> 2 small or 1 large tomato, chopped
> ¼ cup raisins, citron, or other dried fruit
> 1 large apple or pear, chopped

In a large skillet, heat oil or lard and sauté onion and
garlic until soft but not brown. Add spices and meat

and sauté for 1 to 2 minutes. Add remaining ingredients, cover, and simmer 15 minutes, stirring occasionally. Uncover and cook until almost all the liquid is gone.

To Assemble

> 8 large 'Poblano' or 'Anaheim' chilies, roasted and peeled (you may need more with smaller chilies; see "Chili Gardens" chapter for technique)

Preheat oven to 350°.

Carefully slit 1 side of each chili top to bottom and remove seeds but leave stems intact. Fill each with picadillo filling and place in a baking pan. Cover and place in oven until heated through, 10 to 20 minutes. Place chilies on plates or a serving platter, pour unheated nogada sauce over them, and decorate with pomegranate seeds and cilantro leaves. Serve immediately.

BAKED CHILES RELLENOS

This variation of the common chile relleno, which is fried, is easier to make and uses less oil than the standard dish.

SERVES 3.

Sauce

> 2 tablespoons oil
> ½ small onion
> 2 cloves garlic, crushed
> ½ hot or 1 mild chili pepper, chopped, OR 2 tablespoons salsa
> 2 medium tomatoes, peeled and chopped
> ½ teaspoon chicken bouillon concentrate or ½ cube
> 2 tablespoons minced fresh oregano (Mexican oregano preferred)

In a medium saucepan or skillet, heat oil and sauté onion, garlic, and chili (if using) until soft, about 4 minutes. Add remaining ingredients (including salsa, if using), cover, and simmer ½ hour, stirring occasionally, until tomatoes are well cooked.

Chilies

> 6 fresh 'Anaheim' or 'Poblano' chilies, roasted

> and peeled (see "Chili Gardens" chapter for technique)
> 6 ounces mild cheese, such as Monterey jack, cut into 6 slices
> 2 eggs, separated
> 2 tablespoons each oil, flour, and milk

Preheat oven to 350°.

Carefully slit 1 side of each chili top to bottom and remove seeds but leave stem intact. Stuff with cheese.

In a small bowl, beat egg yolks, add oil, flour, and milk. Beat egg whites until stiff but not dry; then fold yolk mixture into them. Grease a shallow baking dish and spread ½ of egg batter over the area the chilies will cover. Set chilies on batter and cover with remaining batter. Bake ½ hour or until lightly browned. Pour tomato sauce over chilies and serve with rice, beans, and tortillas.

FRIJOLES

The basic, traditional method of cooking beans is to make *frijoles de olla,* beans cooked in an earthenware pot with minimal seasonings. The beans in this recipe are nicely seasoned and can be a delicious side dish or filling for tostadas or burritos. Or simply eat them by themselves with tortillas.

SERVES 8 TO 10.

> 1 pound (2½ cups) dry beans (choose from pintos, red beans, pinquintos, boletas, or black beans)
> 10 to 12 cups boiling water
> 2 tablespoons oil or lard
> 1 onion, chopped
> 3 cloves garlic, chopped
> 2 cups peeled, chopped tomatoes
> 1 to 3 medium to hot chilies (large 'Anaheim' or 'Poblano' varieties should be roasted and peeled; see "Chile Gardens" chapter for technique), minced or chopped
> ¼ cup minced cilantro leaves
> 2 teaspoons ground cumin
> 2 large sprigs epazote (if using black beans)
> Salt to taste
> A soft, melting cheese (optional)

Place first 5 ingredients in a large pot on low heat, cover, and cook for 1½ to 2 hours or until beans are tender, stirring occasionally. (Cooking time will vary greatly depending on variety and freshness of beans.) Add remaining ingredients except cheese and cook ½ hour longer, stirring frequently. Serve hot and garnish with cheese, if desired.

Sources

Seed Companies

1. Horticultural Enterprises
   P.O. Box 810082
   Dallas, TX 75381
   This company specializes in peppers and carries thirty sweet and hot varieties. In addition, it carries tomatillos, jicama, and epazote.

2. J. L. Hudson, Seedsman
   P.O. Box 1058
   Redwood City, CA 94064
   This seed company carries many unusual vegetable and herb varieties including some Mexican varieties. Catalog: $1.00.

3. Le Marché
   Seeds International
   P.O. Box 190
   Dixon, CA 95620
   Le Marché carries many types of chili peppers and various Mexican varieties of squash, beans, and corn. Catalog: $2.00.

4. Native Seeds Search
   3950 West New York Drive
   Tucson, AZ 85745
   This organization is dedicated to saving seeds from the native peoples of the United States and northern Mexico. It carries a broad range of Mexican vegetables. Price list: $1.00.

5. Plants of the Southwest
   1812 Second Street
   Santa Fe, NM 87501
   This company carries seeds of plants adapted to the Southwest, including eight varieties of chili peppers. Catalog: $1.00.

6. Redwood City Seed Company
   P.O. Box 361
   Redwood City, CA 94064
   Redwood City Seed Company carries twenty-five varieties of Mexican vegetables. Catalog: $1.00.

7. Richters
   Goodwood, Ontario
   Canada LOC 1AO
   Richters is a company that carries many unusual herbs, including Mexican ones. Catalog: $2.50.

Mail-Order Sources of Ingredients

Casa Moneo
210 West 14th Street
New York, NY 10011
   Casa Moneo carries dried peppers and spices for Mexican cooking.

Santa Cruz Chili and Spice Company
P.O. Box 177
Tumacacori, AZ 65640
   This company is a source for chili powders, pastes, and salsas.

Books

Greer, Anne Lindsay. *Cuisine of the American Southwest*. New York: Harper & Row, 1983.
   This beautiful book contains an array of wonderful southwestern recipes, including many that are authentic Mexican.

Kennedy, Diana. *The Cuisines of Mexico*. Rev. ed. New York: Harper & Row, 1986.
   This is the definitive text on Mexican cooking, a must for your library.

Kennedy, Diana. *Mexican Regional Cooking*. New York: Harper & Row, 1984.
   Here Diana Kennedy goes beyond her first book and presents many more recipes.

Schildreff, Marjorie, and Clyde Schildreff, eds. *Adventures in Mexican Cooking*. San Francisco: Ortho Books, 1978.
   This comprehensive book on Mexican cooking is filled with photos and is particularly helpful in explaining how ingredients from the garden are used.

Sloan, Sarah. *A Treasury of Mexican Cuisine: Original Recipes from the Chefs of the Camino Real Hotels, Mexico*. Chicago: Contemporary Books, 1986.
   This elegant collection of recipes was assembled under the auspices of the Camino Real hotels.

Oriental Gardens

TEN YEARS AGO, in preparing for a trip to Hong Kong, I wanted to become proficient at eating with chopsticks so as not to embarrass myself. I practiced by using them to pick up dry macaroni until I thought I had acquired some skill. For our first dinner in Hong Kong, my husband and I arrived at the restaurant starving. To begin the meal the waiter placed a bowl of shiny, round Spanish peanuts in the middle of the table. Ah, food! I glanced around and discovered that the other diners were eating these nuts with their smooth, tapered chopsticks. Gamely, I plunged in—and onto the table went my peanut. Discreetly, I tried again and again in vain. Finally I snared a nut but squeezed too hard and, just as the waiter looked our way, "spronged" it against the wall! So much for saving face!

Chopsticks aside, we had a wonderful time eating our way through Hong Kong. We dined on familiar stir-fries made with baby corn and pac choi, eggplants with garlic sauce, and asparagus with shrimp. But we also tried the unfamiliar—eels, sea cucumbers, and all sorts of vegetables, mushrooms, and innards we couldn't identify. Regardless of what dish we ordered, the seafood and vegetables were always fresh and the preparation impeccable, and we thought the food we had there,

OPPOSITE: *Oriental ingredients from the garden include Japanese mustard, mizuna, a miniature winter squash, pea pods, and pac choi.*

with very few exceptions, the best we had ever eaten in our lives. I decided that if I were shipwrecked on an island and could have only one type of food for the rest of my life, this is what it would be—not my own native fare, not even French cuisine, but the food of the island of Hong Kong.

In fact, although we shopped, visited museums, and wandered around the waterfront, food in all its forms became our main interest in Hong Kong. We spent hours selecting restaurants from among the Japanese, Korean, and Chinese choices, and more hours choosing our food. We made numerous visits to the old part of the city, where herb stores abounded and produce markets lined the sidewalk. There we saw people walking down the street carrying water-filled plastic bags containing swimming fish, and string bags bulging with fresh bamboo shoots and unusual mushrooms. And we saw all sorts of fresh greens—I couldn't get over the variety. Everywhere I looked were green, leafy vegetables I'd never seen before. And much to the shopkeepers' amusement (probably because we looked so puzzled as we hovered over the bins), we'd buy all sorts of unfamiliar fruits and vegetables and bring them back to our hotel to taste and photograph them. After laying out a towel to provide a neutral background, I'd set down a spoon to give the picture scale, lay out the edibles, and then photograph them one by one. Then, with the produce well documented, we'd taste everything and make notes.

That long-ago trip to Hong Kong opened my eyes to a whole new world of vegetables and cooking. It became obvious to me that the main focus of Chinese cuisine was on vegetables, and that the varieties far exceeded my limited experience. It also became clear that the Chinese food I had had in restaurants at home only hinted at the heart of that cuisine. Since fresh Oriental vegetables are the cornerstone of Chinese cooking, and since restaurants in the United States generally can't obtain them, what I had come across in the States was only a very limited sample of Chinese cooking as a whole.

Once home I began to research Oriental cooking in earnest. I visited the community gardens of nearby Southeast Asian neighborhoods and began to frequent Japanese and Thai restaurants to learn about tempura and carved Thai vegetables. I also visited natural food stores in my area to purchase and learn about serving tofu and miso in all their forms plus the many types of rice and beans used in Oriental cooking. And by lucky chance, I found myself with new neighbors, Arvind and Bhadra Fancy, who grew up outside Bombay. In exchange for my help in locating and planting Indian vegetables for their garden, they generously served me innumerable delicious meals and taught me all sorts of things I didn't know, especially about spices. It was under their guidance that I acquired my taste for cilantro and bitter melon and, among other things, learned how to stuff baby eggplants, make raita, and grind chilies.

By now I've identified all the vegetables and fruits I saw in Hong Kong, though it took more than ten years and many people's help. I've visited the man who is probably this country's best-known Chinese gardener, Peter Chan, author of *Better Vegetable Gardens the Chinese Way.* And I've visited seed companies, such as Tsang & Ma International and Sakata Seed, that specialize in Oriental vegetables, as well as some American companies that are beginning to become very interested in these plants. I've grown many Oriental vegetables myself and spent time with gardeners actively exploring and experimenting with these vegetables. One such gardener is David Cunningham, staff horticulturist at the Vermont Bean Seed Company; he grew a demonstration garden for this book and talked with me extensively. And in my pursuit of information on individual vegetables and herbs, I spent some very informative hours with Geri Harrington, author of *Grow Your Own Chinese Vegetables;* Steve Frowine of the W. Atlee Burpee Company; and Holly Shimizu, curator of the National Herb Garden.

Few other people on earth celebrate the many flavors of vegetables so fully as those of the Oriental countries. In my effort to grasp the vast repertoire of edibles they draw from, I've experimented for many hours in my own kitchen. I've attended seminars on the medicinal aspects of Oriental cooking and talked with people from the Orient about how they cooked with this vast bounty. And in gathering information on Chinese and Japanese cuisine—the two most important cuisines to the gardener—I've spoken with Chinese chef-authors Ken Hom and Lawrence Chu and Japanese cooking expert and author Elizabeth Andoh.

Throughout this chapter I refer to the vegetables and herbs of Japan, India, Korea, Thailand, and the Philippines. However, the Chinese use the greatest variety of vegetables in their cooking, and the seeds of their plants are the easiest of all Oriental varieties for American gardeners to obtain. Further, of all the Oriental cooking styles, that of the Chinese is most accessible to cooks in this country. Therefore, I concentrate mainly on Chinese food here. Before you lies a whole new range of vegetables and herbs: Shanghai flat cabbages, Chinese chives, Japanese mitsuba, and the East Indian bitter melon. In reading this chapter, you could well be embarking on a lifetime of exploration, and it's none too soon to start!

How to Grow an Oriental Garden

Many of the vegetables and herbs used in the Orient are familiar to Westerners. In fact, we enjoy many cucumbers and winter squash varieties without even being aware that they come from Japanese breeding programs. Many of the so-called English cucumbers are examples. When you peruse seed catalogs looking for varieties, keep an eye out for sweet, "burpless" cucumbers such as 'Sweet Slice', 'Suyo Long', and 'Sweet Success' and for dense, flavorful, nonstringy winter squash varieties such as 'Honey Delight', 'Sweet Dumpling', 'Red Kuri', and 'Green Hokkaido'. Oriental gardeners also grow such familiar vegetables as eggplants, carrots, onions, and cauliflowers. Information on some varieties of these vegetables is given in the "Recommended Oriental Vegetables" section later in this chapter and in other chapters in this book, and basic growing information is covered in Part Four, "An Encyclopedia of Superior Vegetables."

Still, the majority of Oriental vegetables are unfamiliar to Western cooks and gardeners, and because the Orient comprises many different climates, these diverse plants grow under many different cultural conditions. These less common vegetables and

Peter Chan's Chinese vegetable garden in Portland is the focal point of his beautifully landscaped back yard.

herbs and their basic growing information are covered in "Recommended Oriental Vegetables."

In much of the Orient, land for cultivation is scarce and highly revered. Unlike Western gardeners and farmers, who often "mine" the organic matter out of the soil and then rely on chemical fertilizers, Eastern gardeners recycle nutrients. In fact, they are responsible for having developed some of the techniques sometimes referred to collectively as intensive gardening. My conversations with Peter Chan, whose garden is in Portland, Oregon, contributed much to my understanding of Oriental growing methods. Peter is a proponent of this intensive style of vegetable gardening, which he discusses in his book *Better Vegetable Gardens the Chinese Way.* Raised in China and trained in agriculture there, Peter writes of cultural techniques used in China for centuries, including the raised-bed system for good drainage, supplementing soil with organic matter, and composting. To this information he adds detailed instruction on growing techniques he himself has perfected in his many years of gardening, teaching, and as a practicing plant pathologist here in the United States. For me, Peter has served as a bridge between two cultures. Many of the gardeners referred to in this book use modifications of the intensive gardening method, and Peter's book offers a succinct synopsis of these cultural practices.

For another view of Oriental gardening, I visited with Geri Harrington, author of *Grow Your Own Chinese Vegetables,* in her Connecticut home. Over the years, Geri has experimented with most of the Oriental vegetables, and I asked her to recommend a good way to start becoming familiar with them. She immediately recommended Japanese cucumbers and Japanese eggplants as some of the best in the world. "Multiplier onions," she went on, "are handy, too. You don't have to replant these onions continually throughout the year. Instead, once they are established in spring, they put out all sizes at once and even come up the next year." As for the Oriental varieties in general, Geri had this to say: "With most of these vegetables, you don't have to feel compelled to cook in the Oriental style just because you're growing them. They're all amazingly versatile. For instance, I use many of the greens in soups and raw in salads. Sometimes I serve broccoli with hollandaise sauce and cook long beans the way I would regular snap beans." She went on to recommend that first-time Oriental vegetable growers might consider

beginning with a few plants each of most of the greens varieties to get an idea of which ones grow best in their climates and which ones they like to cook with. To these, gardeners might add a few snow pea, mizuna, and sesame plants, plus some Chinese chives and an eggplant or two. This grouping, she said, would make a good selection to experiment with, but there's a further advantage as well: most of these plants are so attractive that they can be successfully interplanted in a flower border.

With few exceptions, Oriental vegetable varieties grow easily and under the same conditions as their Western cousins. Obtain the seeds from the sources listed at the end of the chapter and have a wonderful time experimenting.

The Cunningham Garden

I met David Cunningham through Guy Thomas, owner of the Vermont Bean Seed Company. It was February and I was visiting Guy to plan the baked bean garden with him. As we chatted, I remarked that I needed an East Coast gardener to grow an Oriental garden for this book, and he immediately suggested David, the company's staff horticulturist. I called David, who loved the idea, and arranged to visit him at the family farm to discuss the plan in detail.

David's farm was absolutely beautiful. It sat on a knoll with a breathtaking view of the Vermont countryside. David had grown up there, and I couldn't help thinking that he was clearly destined to go into horticulture. We sat down to plan the Oriental garden together as soon as I arrived. Though I didn't pay much attention at the time, David mentioned that his mother was a wolf preservationist and that the garden was surrounded by a wolf run.

I returned in midsummer to see the garden, and at that time the wolves were much more in evidence. In fact, to visit the garden we had to exchange places with them: the two wolves went into the house while we went to the garden. Actually, though the idea of being in close promixity to these creatures unnerved me a bit, the wolves were actually quite lovable and shy.

In the garden, which is protected by an electric fence to keep out the wolves, David's horticultural skills came sharply into evidence. The soil was beau-

David Cunningham's Oriental garden, set in the middle of scenic Vermont, is filled with Chinese cabbages, pac choi, and edible-podded peas. Unlike most gardeners, David never has four-legged pests as the garden is surrounded by a run for his mother's white wolves.

tiful—crumbly and dark—and obviously well cared for, and row upon row of healthy Oriental vegetables attested to its quality. David told me that long ago the soil had been clay based but that in the early fifties it started receiving care as a vegetable garden. In winter the area is planted with winter rye, which in spring is grazed by sheep, and over the years the soil has been amended with mulches and compost. And a few years earlier David had incorporated twenty-five bales of peat moss into the plot. Always careful about keeping the soil healthy, the Cunninghams have kept planks on the paths to avoid packing down the soil because they plan to use the soil on the paths for beds sometime in the future.

The overall vegetable garden is about thirty by forty feet in size, and David had planted a little less than half with Oriental vegetables. We started reviewing the garden at the north end, which was planted with three varieties of edible-podded peas: 'Dwarf Gray Sugar', 'Mammoth Melting', and 'Oregon Sugar Pod'. "If I had to pick a favorite," David told me, "I think it would be 'Dwarf Gray Sugar', because it's such a vigorous grower. It has reddish-purple flowers and the pods are very tasty. At one point I thought I was going to lose all the peas, because we had a week of temperatures topping ninety. All the varieties looked pretty sad for a while, but they all perked right up again after it cooled down."

David went on to describe the six different varieties of cabbage-type greens he had planted in the next few rows. 'Pac Choy' has white stems, an open form, and doesn't make heads. 'Tyfon', a cross between Chinese cabbage and turnips, has a mild mustardlike flavor that, according to David, is good in salads. 'Spring A 1' is a cabbage with a medium-tight head, and 'WR 90' an upright cabbage with a very tight head. 'Winter Queen' is a cabbage good for fall harvest, and 'Tah Tsai' is a dark-green nonheading plant with spoon-shaped leaves growing out of its base.

In the next rows David had planted the Japanese herb mitsuba, an aromatic parsleylike herb, and 'Green Lance', a Chinese type of broccoli that David likes using in stir-fries. The head of this broccoli is open and the plant's stem is mainly what you eat. He had also planted two types of mustard: 'Red Giant', a striking, somewhat spicy vegetable, and 'Savanna' mustard spinach, a mild-flavored green. The variety of daikon, or Chinese radish, in the garden was 'April Cross'. David described it as very tender and uniform with no pith, woodiness, or hollowness to it. "When you start eating it," he said, "it doesn't seem hot, but it builds up. We eat it in stir-fries, but we've had it raw in salads too and are really happy with it."

David was about to start his fall garden during my visit and was so pleased with the summer's Oriental experiment that he wanted to try more varieties of the cabbages. This time he was planning to plant the cabbage varieties 'Green Rocket', 'Tsoi Sim', and 'Taisai' plus garland chrysanthemum and a mustard spinach called 'Osome'.

I asked David about pest problems, and he told me he had had flea beetles on some of the daikon plants and greens and an occasional problem with moles. He remarked that at one time the family had had problems with occasional rabbits, deer, and woodchucks and a serious struggle with raccoons whenever corn was growing. "But," he added in what I considered a masterful understatement, "since the wolves have been here things have settled down a bit."

I left this Vermont pastoral scene with my concern about the adaptability of at least some Oriental plants put to rest. Many of these wonderful vegetables could be well adapted to a non-Oriental kitchen, and David was obviously enjoying both growing and cooking with them. In fact, as far as I was concerned, a fair number of these vegetables had passed the true cooking gardener's test, since David was interested enough to try even more varieties the next season.

Recommended Oriental Vegetables

The countries of the Orient encompass diverse climates, so it is not surprising that the vegetables and herbs grown there are an extremely varied lot. For the sake of practicality, I have concentrated in this chapter on the vegetables and herbs most easily grown throughout the United States, those that interested cooks have been seeking out, and those that are either the most versatile in the kitchen or most characteristic of the cuisine. The foods covered are predominantly Chinese, but I certainly could not discuss the Orient without mentioning some of the edibles from Japan, India, Korea, the Philippines, and the countries of Southeast Asia. The result is a collection of vegetables ranging from those that are well known to those wholly unknown in the United States.

Filipino people here are frustrated because they can't purchase hyacinth beans or the shoots of bitter melons and pumpkins. Japanese cooks long for mitsuba and succulent varieties of daikon. Thai gardeners, to have a taste of "home," must grow their own long, green eggplants, lemon grass, and coriander for its roots. Chinese cooks seek out—but seldom find—Oriental chive shoots, Shanghai flat cabbage, and an amaranth called Chinese spinach. And East Indians—as I learned in designing a landscape for my neighbors the Fancys—long for any number of foods: small stuffing eggplants, certain kinds of beans, cilantro, chili peppers, Chinese okra (luffa), cucuzzi squash (bottle gourds), tumeric, and a particularly aromatic variety of cardamom. To enjoy these vegetables and herbs they need to grow their own.

For vegetables used in Oriental cuisine not covered in the following list, see the index listings for chayote, jicama, purslane, crosnes (Chinese artichokes), and lemon grass, covered in other chapters. Owing to space limitations, numerous other vegetables, such as adzuki beans, kudzu, Malabar spinach, hyacinth beans, sesame, Chinese okra, and cucuzzi, are not covered but are all easily grown, available through most of the seed companies in the "Sources" section, and well worth exploring. Certain plants, such as water chestnuts, rice, taro, and lotus root, are not on the list because they need special growing conditions. Others, particularly certain wonderful seasonings such as wasabi, myoga ginger, tumeric, and many Japanese herbs, are not included because there are no reliable commercial sources of seeds or plants in this country. To learn more about these plants, visit local community gardens in your area or try to obtain seeds or seedling plants from Oriental gardeners.

Notice that in many entries the edible parts of the plants are called out. This reflects an American, not an indigenous, approach to the vegetables. Often, Oriental cooks use more of the plant than American cooks do. For instance, the pea shoots as well as the pods are eaten in the Orient, as are ginger shoots as well as ginger roots.

The format of the entries calls for a few words of explanation. Each vegetable is listed under its most common name, which is followed by any alternate common names in parentheses, the Latin name, the Chinese name in Cantonese, and, where pertinent, the Japanese name. Regarding the spelling of Chinese names, there is great confusion, primarily because the English words are transliterated from Chinese characters. The result is a diversity of spellings approximating the original sounds. Pac choi, for example, might also be spelled pak choy, bok choy, bok choi, and baak choi.

Finally, note that the numbers in parentheses following the vegetable or variety names refer to the seed companies in the "Sources" section at the end of this chapter.

Cabbage family members are the staple among Oriental vegetables, particularly in China. For this reason, I start with them before reverting to the alphabetical format of the "Recommended" lists in other chapters. Be aware, though, that many other families of plants besides the cabbages are represented in the cuisines of the Orient, particularly the numerous greens that take warm growing conditions and many members of the cucumber family. These are covered following the overview of cabbage family varieties.

Cabbage Family Members

As chef Ken Hom, author of *Ken Hom's Chinese Cookery*, says, "In China, the word for meat is the same as that for pork, and the word for vegetable is the same as that for cabbage—*choi*. Cabbages are so important in China that in the fall all over China you will see cabbages piled up to be pickled in preparation for winter. They are so ubiquitous that they almost become a nuisance. People put them under their beds and everywhere, and the streets are filled with them."

In the Orient, as in the West, members of the cabbage family come in many forms. Some are heading cabbages; others, like pac choi, are loose leaf. With most it is the leaves that are used, but with others the stems or flower stalks are prized. Many of these vegetables are mild in flavor; still others are peppery or strongly cabbagelike. There is much overlap from group to group, and the various names make up a frustrating tangle. Under any circumstances, it would be impossible to cover all the varieties of cabbage family vegetables grown in the Orient, as in China individual villages and even communes often have their own varieties, but the following overview will give you years' worth of testing and enjoyment.

CHINESE CABBAGE (napa cabbage, Michihili cabbage) *Brassica Rapa,* Pekinensis Group; Chinese, *bow sun, siew choy;* Japanese, *nappa, hakusai* Chinese cabbage, a heading type of cabbage with wonderful mild, tender leaves, is a relative of our common garden cabbage. There are two major types: one is round and light green and often referred to as a napa cabbage; another is tall and cylindrical with lacy Savoy-type leaves, and is sometimes referred to as Michihili cabbage. According to Rob Johnston, of Johnny's Selected Seeds, napa cabbages are the easiest of the Oriental cabbage types to grow. Rob describes them as combining the thin, crisp texture of lettuce with the fresh mustard tang of juicy cabbage.

How to grow: See "Cabbage and Brussels Sprouts" in the Part Four Encyclopedia. With most varieties of Chinese cabbage, growing them for fall harvest reduces disease and insect problems and decreases the tendency to bolt. A few varieties, designated as spring or slow bolting, can be planted in the spring and harvested in early summer. Spring varieties include 'Spring A 1' (3, 10), a bolt-resistant, mild, sweet, light-green cabbage with three- to four-pound heads; 'W-R 55 Days' (6), a napa type resistant to heat and common wilt; and 'Tip Top' (10), also a napa cabbage and one that performs well in high temperatures. Fall types include 'Wong Bok' (6, 9, 10), an old Chinese favorite that is a vigorous grower with cannonball heads; 'W-R 70' (6), similar to 'W-R 55' but later maturing; 'N-R Green 60' (3), which is resistant to multiple diseases and has sweet, juicy four-pound heads; 'South China Earliest' (2, 8), with small one-pound heads that can take hot summers; and 'Winter Giant' (10), with excellent keeping qualities and large heads to ten pounds. Many of the older Michihili types are coarse and not very tasty, but a good new variety is 'Monument' (3), which has graceful, firm, twelve-inch-tall heads.

How to prepare: In China, these cabbages are most commonly prepared with meat in soups and stir-fries. They absorb flavors well and are often combined with oyster and black bean sauce, garlic, and seafood to be used as a stuffing for pot stickers and spring rolls. As for preserving cabbages, there are many techniques. In China the cabbages are often dried in the sun and used in soups in the winter. Most types are also pickled in brine, brine vinegar, or salt and—in Korea and some southern parts of China—hot peppers. In Korea, pickled cabbages are the basis for most kim chee, a vegetable pickle seasoned with garlic, red pepper, and ginger that is the national dish. Ken Hom talks about enjoying pickled cabbages stir-fried with beef. Japanese cooks use Chinese cabbage in soups; in sukiyaki, where it is braised with meat; in shabu-shabu, a one-pot meal cooked at the table; and pickled.

CHINESE MUSTARD   *Brassica juncea;* Chinese, *gai choi;* Japanese, *sum*   MUSTARD CABBAGE   *B. juncea* var. *rugosa;* Chinese, *kai choy*   MIZUNA   *B. japonica;* Chinese, *shui tsai;* Japanese, *kyona, mizuna*   *Chinese mustard* is a blanket term covering mustard cabbage and mizuna as well as mustard plants per se. Oriental mustards are mild to pungent leafy vegetables that grow one to three feet in height. They are loose-leafed plants, and most prefer cool growing conditions. Mustards range from mild to strong. Some can be slightly bitter; others have a hot bite.

How to grow: See "Cabbage and Brussels Sprouts" in the Part Four Encyclopedia. 'Green in Snow' (snow cabbage, 5, 9, 10) is one of the most popular mild Chinese mustards, and, as the name implies, it can be grown in very cold weather. 'Swollen-stem' (10) mustard is a leafy mustard that develops enlarged stems with maturity. 'Broadleaf Mustard Cabbage' (11) and 'Namfong' (7) are fairly strong tasting mustards popular for soups. Some mustards with bronzy-red leaves are quite peppery; these include 'Aka Takana' (4, 10), 'Red Giant Mustard' (5, 12), 'Osaka Purple' (2, 9), and 'Miiki Giant Japanese' (2, 5). An unusual green mustard is 'Horned' mustard (5), a Japanese mustard with bright-green, frilly leaves and a plant that flairs into a horn.

Mizuna (pot-herbed mustard) is a strikingly beautiful cut-leafed vegetable related to the other mustards that is very popular in Japan. The mild-flavored leaves of mizuna are dark green on top and silvery white underneath. Mizuna (4, 7, 10), though heat tolerant and not a lettuce, is grown in much the same way as lettuce. See "Lettuce" in the Part Four Encyclopedia for cultural instructions.

How to prepare: In China, mustards are most often combined with ginger and used in soups; it is generally the strong-flavored ones that are used in this way. Mustards are also blanched and served with oil or oyster sauce or stir-fried with meat and bean sauce. In Japan, the mustards are sometimes braised, used as salt pickles, or cooked in soups and stir-fries. I enjoy mustards served in nontraditional ways: the red mustards added sparingly to salads and sandwiches for their pungent, wasabi-like taste, and the leaves of mizuna raw mixed into salads for their texture and mild flavor.

PAC CHOI   *Brassica Rapa,* Chinesis Group; Chinese, *pac choy, boy choi, baak choi;* Japanese, *pac choi* or *taisai*   Pac choi is a delightful nonheading type of green that looks something like our white-stemmed Swiss chard. Varieties differ with regard to leaf shape: some leaves are swordlike, some spoonlike, and others open and flat. The most common varieties have white stems, but less common varieties have green stems, and some have been bred for their flowering leaf stalks.

How to grow: See "Cabbage and Brussels Sprouts" in the Part Four Encyclopedia. Standard, green-leafed varieties of pac choi resembling chard include the easily grown, slow-bolting 'Lei Choi' (1, 4, 6, 9); 'Kwan-hoo Choi' (8), a midsummer variety that pickles well; and 'Prize Choy' (3), a compact plant and one of the most popular pac choi varieties. Choice varieties of pac choi prized by gourmet restaurants include a compact, vase-shaped plant with misty-green, mild-tasting stalks sometimes referred to as Shanghai pac choi. Varieties available include the bolt-resistant, uniform 'Mei Qing Choi' (3); 'Pak Choy Green Stalk' (5); and 'Shanghai' (6, 7, 10). Two varieties of flowering pac choi are 'Chinese Tsai Shim' (7, 10), which has light-green leaves, and 'Flowering Purple Pak Choi' ('Hon Tsai Tai') (9, 10, 12), a cool-weather plant.

How to prepare: In China, pac choi is most commonly—and delightfully—used in stir-fries and soups with meat and seasonings. In Canton, it is served with roast pork or a black bean sauce. Chef Laurence Chu makes the green Shanghai pac choi into a beautiful banquet dish. He blanches the whole head; lays out the tender, succulent hearts on a platter; and then covers the hearts with black mushrooms and a flavorful gravy. I enjoy pac choi in vegetable soup, in omelettes, and raw in salads—by no means traditional uses but delicious.

MISCELLANEOUS CABBAGE FAMILY GREENS CHINESE FLAT CABBAGE *Brassica chinesis;* Chinese, *tatsoi, tai go choi,* or *tah tsai* CHINESE BROCCOLI (Chinese kale) *B. oleracea,* Alboglabra Group; Chinese, *gai lon* These two are considered some of the most choice cabbage family greens.

How to grow: Chinese flat cabbage is a rich, dark-green, almost rosette-shaped cabbage that grows low to the ground. The leaves are spoon-shaped, tender, and mild-flavored. Try the flat cabbage available from Sunrise Enterprises and the variety 'Tah Tsai' (3, 12). Both are easily grown in spring and fall and tolerate fairly cold temperatures. Flat cabbages are used full size but are also popular with some finer restaurants when immature, in their "baby" stage.

Chinese broccoli, sometimes referred to as Chinese kale, is somewhat similar to our Western kale but the leaves are smooth. Also, because the plant is allowed to flower before it's eaten, cooks treat it as a broccoli. These greens are grown in the spring and summer. Varieties to try are 'Green Lance' (7), 'Fat Shan' (2), 'White Flower Kale' (10), and the smaller 'Yellow Flower Kale' (10).

How to prepare: Stir-frying is a popular way to prepare both Chinese flat cabbage and Chinese broccoli. Some Chinese consider Chinese broccoli the most noble of the cabbages and enjoy it in soups with noodles, mushrooms, and pork, squid, or chicken. The flat cabbages are delicious braised and served with peanut oil and oyster sauce.

Other Oriental Vegetables

There are many families of plants represented in the cuisines of the Orient other than the cabbage family. Numerous greens that require warm growing conditions are important, as are many cucumber family members and beans.

BEANS, SOY *Glycine Max;* Chinese, *soy;* Japanese, *soy, eda mame* Soy beans are a powerhouse of nutrition. Sometimes called the "cow of the Orient," soy beans are rich in protein, calcium, and vitamins A and B.

How to grow: Grow soy beans as you would regular bush beans. Plant in rich, well-drained soil after the soil temperature has reached 60 degrees.

Most of the numerous varieties of soy beans are sensitive to day length, so it is best to grow varieties selected for your climate. Buy your seeds locally or ask your university agricultural extension agent for suggested varieties. Also, before ordering be aware that there are different kinds of soy beans. Green soy beans can be eaten fresh in their shelled state as you would lima beans or as a snack, or they can be allowed to mature and used as dry beans. Black soy beans are the richest in protein and are generally dried and then eaten when reconstituted. Yellow varieties are best used in soy products such as tofu. Johnny's Selected Seeds has a good selection of soy bean varieties.

How to prepare: The great majority of soy beans in the Orient are made into soy products or consumed as sprouts. The latter use is particularly prevalent in Cantonese dishes, where the sprouts are

A Hmong woman who gardens in Sacramento, California, carries a basket of vegetables grown from the seeds she brought with her from Southeast Asia. She grows fluted green eggplants, yard-long beans, and a cushaw-type squash. The fruits, blossoms, and shoots of the squash are all used in cooking.

stir-fried or used in soups. (*Caution:* Soy sprouts are not edible in their raw state and are always eaten cooked.) The Japanese enjoy the green-colored varieties of soy beans in a traditional fall snack consumed with beer. The beans, pod and all, are boiled in salted water and drained, and then the snackers shell their own, as we do peanuts in the shell. For a nontraditional use, boil the green varieties in the pods for about five minutes, cool, shell, and then cook the soy beans again in a little broth or soy sauce for fifteen minutes. Or use soy beans in dishes as you would shelled beans.

BEANS, YARD-LONG (asparagus bean) *Vigna unguiculata* var. *sesquipedalis;* Chinese, *dow gauk;* Japanese, *ingen, sasage* These beans are related to southern peas but produce very long pods.

How to grow: See the information about southern peas in the "Cajun Gardens" chapter. Note, however, that unlike bushy southern peas, the yard-long beans grow on tall vines and need trellising. There are two different types: the very dark, thin, green-pod type with black seeds (2, 4, 5, 8, 10) and the larger, light-green one with thick, spongy pods and red seeds (10). While these varieties are called yard-long beans, they are tastiest when twelve to eighteen inches long.

How to prepare: In a very popular Szechwan dish called dry-fried beans, the red-seeded yard-long beans are deep-fried, drained, and while still warm put in a wok and stir-fried with seasonings. The dark-green variety is best in a simple stir-fry with a bit of ginger. These beans are pencil-thin and a little like the French *haricots verts.*

BITTER MELON (bitter gourd) *Momordica* spp.; Chinese, *foo gwa;* Japanese, *nigauri, rei shi* Bitter melons are warty vegetables that resemble cucumbers and have a distinctive, quininelike taste. They are popular with most Oriental cultures where bitter tastes are appreciated. In the Philippines, the juice from a bitter melon is sometimes rubbed on babies' lips to accustom children to the bitter taste at an early age.

How to grow: Bitter melons are handsome vines that grow in warm conditions similar to those under which their relatives the cucumbers thrive. See "Cucumbers" in the Part Four Encyclopedia. There are two types: round varieties, called balsam apples (one variety is 'Hong Kong' [9, 10]), and long ones, called balsam pears (9).

How to prepare: This versatile vegetable is eaten in many forms and at different stages of its growth. Among some of the Oriental cultures, the young tendrils are considered a great delicacy and are prepared by quick-frying. Or they are incorporated at the last minute into simple egg dishes. The tendrils have little bitterness but possess a distinctive, quite pleasant vegetable taste. The taste of the fruits varies in flavor and bitterness depending on maturity. The fruits start out deep green and mild and grow increasingly yellow and bitter with age. Chef Hom recommends that young melons be used in soups and the more mature ones be used in stir-fries or stuffed with meat. Chef Lawrence Chu, author of *Chef Chu's Distinctive Cuisine of China,* comments that in China bitter melon is considered a tonic to be taken for its cooling effect in hot weather. For this purpose, it is usually cooked in a soup with pork and black beans. In India, bitter melon is often cooked with potatoes and numerous spices or pickled with garlic. Before cooking with bitter melon, to remove much of the water and some of the bitterness, my neighbor Bhadra Fancy salts the slices and then squeezes the juice out.

BUNCHING ONIONS (Welch onions, multiplier onions) *Allium fistulosum;* Chinese, *Ts'ung fa;* Japanese, *negi, nabuka* Bunching onions, widely used throughout the Orient, are somewhat similar to what we call scallions here. But unlike most scallions, they usually grow in clusters.

How to grow: See "Onions" in the Part Four Encyclopedia. True Oriental multiplier onions that will continue to spread from year to year include 'Kujo Green Multistalk' (3, 8, 9), a tender onion that grows in clusters of three to four stalks, and 'Tsukuba' (5), a particularly heat-resistant variety that can be sown in midspring for summer use. Choice single-stalk varieties that are particularly well suited for blanching and are not true multipliers include 'Ishikura Long' (2, 3, 9) and 'Long White Tokyo' (10). Harvest the leaves as you would chives or, once the plants are established, separate one scallion from the cluster at a time. To produce white stalks, mound the soil to blanch the stems.

How to prepare: These types of onions can lose their shape and become slightly bitter if overcooked, so they are generally chopped and added to cooked dishes toward the end of the cooking process. In China, these green onions are used as garnishes or added to rice, noodle, and fish dishes and soups and stir-fries. Chef Chu explains that historically the nomadic tribes of Mongolia would gather the wild green onions, which grew profusely in that region. They would then quickly fry up thin strips of beef and add handfuls of the onions at the last minute, the object being to cook the green onions lightly while still keeping the "life" in them. In Japanese cooking, these onion family vegetables are widely used in numerous forms, including pickling, soups, and garnishes, and are popular in sukiyaki.

BURDOCK (gobo) *Arctium Lappa;* Chinese, *ngau pong;* Japanese, *gobo* This plant's brown roots—which are two to three feet long and an inch wide—and its young shoots are prized in the Orient, especially in Japan.

How to grow: In early spring, plant seeds of this annual vegetable in extremely soft, deep, rich soil. Thin seedlings to eight inches apart. During the growing season, treat with extra phosphate for good root development and keep mulched. A popular variety is 'Takinogawa' (3, 10, 13). Keep growing vigorously throughout the season and you'll be able to harvest the roots in approximately four months. The best way to harvest is to use a post-hole digger next to the plant to expose the majority of the root before you pull it out; otherwise the root will break off easily. Gobo can also be seeded in the fall and harvested in the spring.

How to prepare: The primary edible part of burdock is the root, but young, tender shoots are sometimes used too. The roots are sometimes used in stir-fries and soups in China, but they are more widely used in Japan, where they are pickled or cooked in soups, tempura, and stir-fries with slivered carrots. Roots are harvested and scraped before cooking and stronger-tasting roots are generally chopped into slivers and soaked in water for several hours to remove some of the bitterness. Keep cut roots in water to prevent darkening.

CELTUCE (stem lettuce) *Lactuca sativa* var. *asparagina;* Chinese, *woh sun;* Japanese, *celtus* This vegetable, which tastes like lettuce, its close relative, looks like a loose head of lettuce on a tall stalk about a foot high. Both the leaves and the peeled stems are eaten.

How to grow: See "Lettuce" in the Part Four Encyclopedia. In approximately six weeks you will get leaves of celtuce (1, 10, 12), and in two to three months the stems will be ready.

How to prepare: In China, the cooked stems and young leaves are considered a delicacy. Before the stem is cooked, its bitter, tough skin must be completely peeled off; then the flesh is cut into matchstick shapes or chunks. The pieces are stir-fried with other vegetables and meats or pickled with spices. A nontraditional use of celtuce is raw in tossed salads.

CHINESE CHIVES (Chinese leeks, Oriental garlic) *Allium tuberosum;* Chinese, *gau choi;* Japanese, *nira, hana nira* Chinese chives, which are related to common garden chives, have flat, grasslike leaves and white flowers. In Oriental cooking they are used as a vegetable, seasoning, or garnish.

How to grow: See "Onions" in the Part Four Encyclopedia. Chinese chives (11) are eaten in two different forms. The green leaves of all varieties are used as a seasoning, as you would common chives. Blanch these same long leaves by mounding soil around them in the garden to turn them yellow and use them as a vegetable. In addition, the flowering stalks of a close relative, *A. ramosum,* are harvested at the bud stage and used in cooked dishes. Two selected varieties of Chinese chives are 'Broadleafed' (10), which has been selected for its leaves, and 'Chinese Leek Flower' (10), a variety selected for its flowering heads. Once your chives seem well established, harvest the leaves a few at a time. When the plant is mature enough to produce numerous little bulbs, you can start harvesting more. If you allow these chives to go to seed, they will sometimes take over the garden. (In the winter, they can be put in a pot and brought indoors.)

How to prepare: Oriental chives are used like common chives but have a stronger taste, more like garlic than onions. They tend to get stringy and tasteless when overcooked. Ken Hom recommends chopping up the flower stalks and adding them to a stir-fry with beef, blanching and serving them with oyster sauce, or braising and serving them with bean curd. He notes that "the blanched yellow chives have a unique taste and are considered a great delicacy in China. To feature them and highlight their delicate taste, Chinese cooks often simply stir-fry them or put them into dumplings in a classic vegetarian dish from the south of China." Another popular way to serve these yellow chives is to chop them into two-inch lengths and combine them with noodles either fried or in soup.

The more mature leaves of the green chives are added to stir-fries, simmered in broth, or braised and served alone as a vegetable. In Japan, chives are used as a garnish, in soups, and with eggs in a dish somewhat akin to an omelette.

CHINESE SPINACH (leaf amaranth) *Amaranthus gangeticus;* Chinese, *hinn choy, een choi;* Japanese, *hiyu*   This nutritious leafy vegetable is commonly used as a warm-weather potherb.

How to grow: See "Greens" in the Part Four Encyclopedia for basic planting and soil culture but note that, unlike spinach, this leafy green grows well in warm weather. There are both all-green varieties, including a light-green one called 'White Round Leaf' (10), and varieties that look like coleus, such as 'Red Stripe' (9, 10), which has red veins and red coloring on the leaves. 'Tampala' (1), a vigorous grower with tender green leaves, is another variety of Chinese spinach; it is available from W. Atlee Burpee.

How to prepare: Chinese spinach should be cooked for a few minutes only or it will get mushy. Popular ways to cook it are by stir-frying or adding it to soup made with pork and garlic. The reddish varieties turn the soup pink. Ken Hom recommends preparing it with the stems on. As he says, "Westerners usually cut the stems off, but most Chinese love the texture even though the plant is kind of hollow and a little bit stringy. It is simply stir-fried and flavored with fermented bean curd to make a pungent, savory dish."

EGGPLANT *Solanum Melongena;* Chinese, *ai gwa;* Japanese, *nasubi*   The most common eggplant in the Orient is a long, thin, purple one. It is generally less bitter and seedy than the larger American types. Small, bitter eggplants are popular in Southeast Asia.

How to grow: See the Part Four Encyclopedia for growing information. Long, purple Oriental eggplants to try are 'Orient Express' (3), 'Chinese Long' (2, 8), 'Taiwan Long' (10), and 'Ichiban Hybrid' (12). Other nonbitter eggplants include a cylindrical green one called 'Thai Green' (9) and a beautiful lavender-colored one called 'Asian Bride' (5). Classic bitter eggplants are 'Small Ruffled Red' (9), which produces two-inch red fruits; 'Emerald Pearl' (9), which has tiny green fruits; and 'Thai' (5), which has small, round, lavender or white fruits.

How to prepare: The standard Oriental eggplants have tender skin and therefore needn't be peeled. Chinese cooking methods for eggplants are braising or frying. Says Ken Hom, "Eggplants are one of the few vegetables besides long beans that the Chinese

A collection of Oriental vegetables: pac choi, Oriental eggplants, bitter melon, and bunching onions.

fry. The idea is to fry them in batter, which makes them very oily, but the Chinese like them that way. We hardly ever steam vegetables in Chinese cooking, but we do steam slices of eggplant for a long time—until they are quite soft—and then serve them with a sauce or cold by themselves." In Japan, eggplant is used in a number of ways: for tempura; baked and served with a variety of sauces, including a dipping sauce of grated ginger and soy sauce; braised in sesame and bean sauce; and pickled. The Thai bitter eggplants are usually used in sweet-and-sour dishes.

GARLAND CHRYSANTHEMUM (chop suey green) *Chrysanthemum coronarium;* Chinese, *tong ho;* Japanese, *shungiku*   This is a close relative of the familiar garden chrysanthemums and is cultivated for its succulent and flavorful young leaves.

How to grow: See "Chrysanthemums" in the "Recommended" list of the "Edible Flower Gardens" chapter for general information. Unlike the standard flowering ones, these chrysanthemums are seeded in place; alternatively, the plants are set out in rich soil a few inches apart. The plants are harvested small, at about five or six inches tall. Both large-leaved (2, 4, 10) and small-leaved (2, 10, 12) varieties are used in cooking. Both kinds are best grown in cool weather, as the flavor of the leaves gets bitter in warm weather.

How to prepare: Harvest whole plants or individual leaves before they get strong-flavored and bitter. Use them stir-fried or make a traditional Cantonese soup with pork or chicken stock and other mild-flavored vegetables, such as lettuce or mushrooms. In Japan the most popular uses for this aromatic vegetable are in sukiyaki and other rich soups and braised dishes. Occasionally, the flowers are used for a garnish.

PEA PODS *Pisum sativum* var. *macrocarpon;* Chinese, *ho lan tau;* Japanese, *saya endo* The popular peas of the Orient are the edible-podded ones.

How to grow: See "Peas" in the Part Four Encyclopedia. Varieties to try are 'Dwarf Gray Sugar' (6, 8, 9, 10, 12), 'Snowflake' (3), 'Oregon Sugar Pod', and 'Mammoth Melting Sugar' (5, 6, 8, 9, 12).

How to prepare: Pea pods, which are succulent and sweet, are very popular in Chinese cooking. They are usually simply stir-fried until just cooked through, only a minute or two, and can easily be made mushy by overcooking. They go particularly well with shrimp. A real treat unfamiliar in the West is the pea shoot, or tendril. According to Ken Hom, "Pea tendrils are absolutely out of this world. In Hong Kong they cost a fortune, because it takes so much to make one basket and because they are very perishable. We just stir-fry them very quickly in a little oil and garlic. Sometimes we add a little hot pepper and fermented bean curd too."

PEPPERS *Capsicum* spp.; Chinese, *tseng jiu* (sweet peppers), *la chiao* (chili peppers) Hot peppers are common in the southern parts of the Orient. Sweet peppers are a recent introduction from the West.

How to grow: See "Peppers" in the Part Four Encyclopedia. 'Thai Hot' (5) is a popular Oriental pepper that grows well in the warmer parts of this country. Also see the chili peppers covered in the "Chili Gardens" chapter.

How to prepare: Traditionally, sweet peppers were not used in the Orient, but they are now being incorporated into Oriental cuisines. The peppers used in India and Southeast Asia are often the very hot ones. Most of the Chinese who use peppers live in the southern provinces; the spicy cuisines are from Hunan and Szechwan. Chinese cooks also use rather mild long peppers, such as the 'Anaheim' grown here. According to Ken Hom, "Most of the hot peppers in Chinese cooking are used in their dry, strong-flavored state. But a favorite dipping sauce in China is made by cutting open a fresh hot pepper, putting it in soy sauce, heating up some oil until it's very hot, and pouring it over the pepper mixture." Hot peppers are used in stir-fries; with dry, braised long beans; in hot-and-sour soup; and in oils used for dipping. Chef Chu recommends making a chili paste similar to the one explained in the "Chili Gardens" chapter. In this case, hot peppers are chopped and cooked over low heat, and garlic, salt, and sesame oil are added to give a characteristic Oriental flavoring. The paste is then used to flavor stir-fries.

In India hot peppers are used to give bite to curries, and in Korea they are used in kim chee, or pickled cabbage, the country's national dish. In Thailand hot peppers yield the spiciness characteristic of many dishes in this cuisine—in stir-fries, curries, marinades for seafood and poultry, and hot and spicy soups.

RADISHES *Raphanus sativus;* daikon, *R. s.* var. *Longipinnatus,* Chinese, *lo bok;* Japanese, *daikon* There are two types of radishes used in the Orient: the small spring radishes familiar to us here and the very large radishes generally called Chinese radishes or, in Japan, daikon. Radish roots are prepared either raw or cooked. With some varieties the leaves, seed pods, and seeds are also used. Certain varieties of the large radishes store well and are used as a winter staple. Varieties of the strong-flavored Korean radishes are used in kim chee. High-quality daikons are fine-textured, nonfibrous radishes with juicy flesh. While daikons are readily available in many markets here, some of the chefs I spoke with suggested that the varieties carried are usually of poorer quality than those you can grow in your garden.

How to grow: See "Radishes" in the Part Four Encyclopedia. Spring radishes used in the Orient include 'French Breakfast' and 'Icicle' (for sources of these, see the Part Four Encyclopedia). Winter radishes are used extensively in the Orient, and most are large, generally ranging in size from two to eight pounds and in length from two to twenty inches, though some varieties are much larger. Most of these radishes have white skin and white flesh, but some varieties have red, green, or black skin and others have red or green flesh. Most varieties are long and tapered, but some are round. As a rule, the long, blunt ones are preferred in China and the long, tapered ones in Japan, though occasionally the Japanese use the large, round ones. Compared with Western radishes, Oriental ones are juicy and flavorful, ranging in taste from mild and sweet to strong and pungent. Most varieties of daikon are planted in fall and mature in cool weather, but a few can be planted in the spring. Varieties to look for include 'All Season' (Tokinashi, 4, 5, 9, 10, 13), a long, white, tapered variety that can be grown in the spring as well as fall; 'Sakurajima' (4, 13), probably the largest radish in cultivation (sometimes attaining a weight of thirty pounds), round, pure white, and very mild; 'Crimson and Long' (10), approximately a foot long and red on the outside with white flesh; 'Shantun Green' (10), a long Chinese radish, less than a foot in length with green skin and flesh; and 'Miyashige' (3, 4, 13), a white, stump-rooted fall radish that has crisp, high-quality flesh.

How to prepare: Throughout the Orient, the young, tender green tops of Oriental radishes are braised or added to soups, and radish roots are washed, scraped, and cut up or grated for addition to soups and other dishes.

The Chinese use cooked radishes in many ways but rarely use the root raw. They often stir-fry radishes after first salting and draining them for awhile. The stir-fries include pork, shrimp, or shellfish or, in a traditional dish, pickled pigs' feet and black beans. Also, radishes are made into hearty winter soups and stews and are used in a traditional radish pudding called *lo bok go,* a rice-flour pudding made with grated radish and seasonings, steamed, sliced into squares, and slightly fried before serving. Chinese sauces sometimes contain grated radishes.

According to Elizabeth Andoh, author of many Japanese cookbooks, in Japan daikon is "the all-impressive, all-purpose, absolutely everything kind of vegetable. When it's in season, it would be hard to find anybody in Japan who hadn't eaten a daikon within three days. Daikon is generally finely grated or shredded and often mixed with soy sauce to make

a dipping sauce served with tempura and other dishes. The peel of the large varieties is sometimes braised and used as a vegetable, and the center chunks can be steamed and sauced with miso. Any method of cooking can be used with daikon except deep frying, as the water content is too high." A traditional New Year dish is julienned strips of daikon, carrots, and dried apricots served with a sweet-and-sour sauce. In Japan, daikons are probably most commonly pickled in rice vinegar or rice wine and soy sauce or prepared as salt pickles. They are also braised or used in fish dumpling stew, soups, and salads. See Elizabeth's books (a good one for beginners is cited in "Sources" at the end of this chapter) for recipes involving daikon.

WATER SPINACH   *Ipomoea aquatica;* Chinese, *ong choi*   This leafy vegetable has arrow-shaped leaves and hollow stems and tastes something like spinach.

How to grow: This leafy annual vegetable should be seeded in moist, rich soil; it grows best in hot and humid weather. Keep the new shoots harvested regularly to promote new growth. There are dark-leaved (10) and light-leaved (10) varieties.

How to prepare: In Cantonese cooking, this vegetable is used in soups or stir-fried with garlic and fermented bean curd or shrimp paste. Other Asian cooks use this vegetable batter-fried, in soups, or even raw. Wash the greens thoroughly and remove the bottom inch or two of stem if it is too tough to eat. Cut up as desired but keep the stems and leaves separate, as the stems take longer to cook. According to Ken Hom, in China cooks usually cut this vegetable into sections, leaving the leaves and stems in rather long pieces. As he says, "We eat the vegetable as you would spaghetti, and it's not considered rude to have it hanging from your chopsticks."

WINTER MELON   *Benincasa hispida;* Chinese, *dong gwa;* Japanese, *tougan*   Winter melon is one of the largest of the Oriental vegetables, averaging around twenty-five pounds at maturity. It is shaped like a squat watermelon. Its close relative is the fuzzy melon, in Chinese called *tseet gwa,* which is primarily eaten in its immature stage.

How to grow: See "Squash" in the Part Four Encyclopedia. Winter melon (11) grows best in hot weather and matures in about 150 days. One seed company, Sunrise Enterprises, carries both a long, green-and-white one and a large, light-green, round one. Like pumpkins, winter melons store well for at least three to four months. Fuzzy melon (10, 11), a close relative, is a light-green, medium-sized, squash-like vegetable that is covered with fuzz.

How to prepare: The white-fleshed winter melon is harvested at the end of the summer in China and is usually served as a soup. It can be cut up, but for festive occasions it is usually steamed whole. The top is cut off jack-o'-lantern style, the seeds are removed, and stock is poured into the cavity; then the melon is set in a pan and steamed for hours. According to Ken Hom, "The taste is bland with a slight bit of sweetness, so the cook usually adds things like mush-rooms, vegetables, and seasonings to the soup to give it texture and taste. When you eat this soup, you just reach into the melon and carve off a bit of the side to add to your serving."

The flavor of fuzzy melon, sometimes called hairy melon, is similar to that of a mild zucchini. This melon is mostly used in soups or pork and chicken stir-fries. Before using, peel the fuzz off.

Herbs and Seasonings

There are a number of herbs and seasonings used in traditional Oriental dishes.

CORIANDER (cilantro, Chinese parsley) *Corian-drum sativum;* Chinese, *yuen sai* This pungent herb is sometimes used in Chinese cooking but is indis-pensable in Indian and Thai cuisines.

How to grow: See the "Mexican Gardens" chapter.

How to prepare: In China the pungent leaves of coriander are sometimes sprinkled over stir-fried or cold chicken dishes just before serving. In India, how-ever, this herbal garnish is indispensable to some curry dishes, served on raita, and is an integral part of the taste of India. Indian and Thai cooks sometimes use the ground seeds to flavor curries. In Thailand, the roots of the coriander plant are also esteemed. These roots are small, and the whole plants are harvested when they are six to eight inches tall to obtain them. The roots are then removed and cleaned of dirt, grated, chopped, and used to flavor dishes. Almost impos-sible to find commercially, the richly flavored cor-iander roots give many Thai dishes their unique taste.

GINGER *Zingiber officinale;* Chinese, *geung;* Japa-nese, *shoga* This pungent flavoring is the "official" ginger, highly esteemed in the Orient and familiar to us in the United States. Another ginger, called *mioga*

(Zingiber mioga), is used primarily in Japan; its roots are inedible but its young shoots are harvested in the spring. Mioga is grown from rhizomes that are avail-able only through private sources. The following information refers to common ginger only.

How to grow: This pungent-rooted plant (actually a rhizome) is heat-loving and grows almost bamboolike to about three feet. It takes long, hot summers to produce the roots, and the plant can tolerate no frost. Growing ginger is worth a try in colder climates, but the rhizomes must be planted in a container there and kept inside in a sunny place in cold weather. Purchase the roots in the spring from produce markets, Chinese grocery stores, or Sunrise Enterprises and the Gurney Seed & Nursery Company. Plant the rhizomes in very rich soil, in a fairly shady spot, and keep the plants moist during the growing season. In five to eight months, the plant will produce tubers. Dig these up and enjoy them in foods or bring the plant in and treat it as a house plant. If your ginger is growing vigorously, you can harvest some of the young, tender shoots and use these in your cooking as well.

How to prepare: As Ken Hom says, "What would Chinese food be without ginger? In China the root is eaten freshly grated in cooked dishes, particularly stir-fries; pickled; or candied. Type of preparation depends on the maturity of the root. When the root is very young and the skin almost transparent, you can slice and stir fry ginger and eat it as a vegetable. When the root is a little more mature, you can use it as a seasoning in a stir-fry. Even more mature gin-ger—which has developed a thick skin—can be scraped and chopped fine and mixed with other con-diments. Very old ginger is strong in flavor and in China is steeped in a broth or used in a very highly flavored dish." A ginger grater is a useful tool; look for this inexpensive little implement in Oriental mar-kets and some gourmet cookware shops. Such a grat-er is also useful for grating hot peppers for Indian food.

In Japanese cooking, fresh ginger is often sliced and pickled for use in sauces or as a condiment. In India, it is used as a basic flavoring in most curries and chutneys and in many cooked dishes as well.

To preserve the rhizomes after you harvest them, store them in damp sand in a fairly cool, dark place. Grated ginger can also be frozen. Note that dried ground ginger is not a suitable substitute for fresh ginger.

MITSUBA *Cryptotaenia japonica;* Chinese, *sam ip;* Japanese, *mitsuba* Mitsuba—also called Japanese parsley, Japanese wild chervil, honewort, or trefoil—is a fragrant perennial herb important to Japanese cuisine.

How to grow: Mitsuba (4, 11, 12) looks a little like Italian parsley, with dark-green, trifoliate leaves and long stems. The plants eventually grow to three feet and are usually treated as annuals—started from seeds, planted ¼ inch deep, and thinned to six to nine inches apart. Plant in moist soil in shade or part shade and keep plants moist all through the growing season. Let a few plants go to seed for the next year's planting. For extra-tender, extra-mild stalks, blanch the stems in the garden as you would celery. See the "French Gardens" chapter for blanching instructions.

How to prepare: Mitsuba is used only occasionally in China, but in Japan it is an important herb. There the leaves and stems are boiled for a minute or two and eaten as a green, used raw in salads, pickled in vinegar, fried in tempura batter, or used in soups, including eggdrop soup, or for flavoring and as a garnish. When used in soups or as a garnish, the leaves and stems are generally chopped up and added in the last minute of cooking. According to Holly Shimizu, curator of the National Herb Garden at the U.S. National Arboretum, often on important occasions—a wedding or the finalizing of a business contract—three or four stalks of mitsuba are tied together in a knot and added to a dish for decoration. In Japan, the knot is considered an auspicious symbol.

PERILLA (beef steak plant) *Perilla frutescens* (green), *P. f. Atropurpurea* (purple); Chinese, *ao geeso* (green), *aka geeso* (purple); Japanese, *shisho* According to Holly Shimizu, the aromatic perilla is the most commonly used herb in Japan.

How to grow: See "Basil" in the Part Four Encyclopedia, as perilla is related to it and grown in the same manner. This herb is readily available from most of the sources listed at the end of the chapter. Both the green and purple varieties of perilla grow to about eighteen inches tall and are decorative, bushy annual plants. In some gardens they will readily reseed.

How to prepare: The young leaves, seedling plants, and seeds are used in different ways in the Orient. The flavor of the red perilla differs from that of the green: the red is considered stronger tasting and spicier and is often used for its red coloring. Green perilla is much prized in Japan, where its leaves, tender shoots, and flowers are used as a garnish. In fact, according to Elizabeth Andoh, "The flower stalks of the green perilla will very often be lying on a shashimi platter, in which case you will take your chopsticks and rub the lavender flowers off into your dipping soy sauce and they will cling to the fish as you eat it. The flowers have a very clean, meadowy taste." Holly Shimizu describes green perilla as having a somewhat cinnamonlike flavor and states that in shushi it is wrapped around rice or fish, and that the Japanese make an elegant tempura with its leaves and flowers. She also mentions that the red perilla leaves taste a little of anise and are dried and sprinkled over rice. Other research has turned up these uses: the tiny seedling plants of red perilla are used as seasoning for sliced raw fish, the leaves are used to flavor bean curd and as a garnish for tempura; and the seeds are used in tempura and in making pickles. Also, the fresh purple leaves give color to pickled apricots, plums, eggplants, ginger, and Chinese artichokes (see the "French Gardens" chapter) and flavor to cucumbers, pickles, tempura, and bean curd. Chinese cooks generally prefer the pungent red perilla to the green one and use it for flavoring seafood and in pickling.

Cooking from the Oriental Garden

Hanging side by side in my pantry are a cast-iron frying pan and a wok—both utensils blackened with use. When I set up housekeeping in the early sixties, I had never seen a wok, but once I became familiar with it, I made it one of my best-used tools. Other Oriental influences have gradually found their way into my kitchen as well. Stir-frying ranks with soup at the top of my list of ways to prepare garden vegetables, and tofu is an inexpensive protein source whose great versatility is comparable to that of cheese. I use tofu in stir-fries and cabbage soup, but I also have some nontraditional uses for it: added to vegetable soup, mashed up and mixed with such flavorings as curry powder or dill as a filling in a cucumber sandwich and even as a filling for burritos. The Jap-

OPPOSITE: *Marinated squid, Thai-style, with carved vegetables; and a Japanese vegetable tempura made with mushrooms, sweet potatoes, perilla, chard stems, and eggplant.*

Ken Hom

Ken Hom is one of the world's leading authorities on Chinese cooking, according to Craig Claiborne, food editor of the *New York Times*. Ken, who was raised in a San Franciscan family of Chinese-American restaurateurs, is author of three Chinese cookbooks and was host of a BBC television series on Chinese cooking. If Ken's kitchen is any indication, he certainly qualifies as an expert. As he took me to his office to talk, we passed through a kitchen filled with different types of chopping blocks, cleavers, and woks, as well as cans, boxes, and canisters filled with unfamiliar ingredients.

"I think a lot of people in this country, especially those who aren't familiar with Chinese vegetables, avoid Chinese cooking because they think it's a very elaborate process," Ken says. "But on the contrary, it's very simple. Vegetables are vegetables, and we just treat them as simply as possible, featuring their natural flavors and goodness. For me, that means blanching or stir-frying them. For example, I braise Szechwan eggplant in lots of garlic, scallions, and chopped ginger; add chili bean paste and stock; and cook for a long time. Or I stir-fry cabbage. I put a little oil, garlic, and seasoning in a wok, and when it's very hot, I add cabbage and quickly fry it.

"Chinese cooking, especially vegetable cooking, reminds me of Bach—there's a simple theme with endless variations. This is one of the most appealing aspects of Chinese cooking: as much as I explore it, I can never learn it all."

I asked Ken where someone unfamiliar with Chinese cooking and Chinese vegetables might begin. "I think you should begin very simply," he advised. "Vegetables are easiest to adapt to Chinese cooking techniques, particularly stir-fried vegetables. There are many wonderful Oriental vegetables, but I don't think you should feel you have to use a Chinese vegetable just because you're stir-frying it. Instead you might start with a familiar vegetable, like broccoli.

That's another great aspect of Chinese cooking: the Chinese have gone everywhere in the world and adapted their cooking to the vegetables and meats around them. For instance, the Chinese don't have a tradition of asparagus, but Chinese people who live in Western countries cook it all the time and love it. In fact, they've brought it back to Hong Kong, where there's a rage for it now. They've adapted the recipe for long beans stir-fried with fermented black beans to asparagus. So I always tell people not to feel hemmed in by the Chinese recipes—just adapt Chinese techniques to whatever vegetables are available."

While researching Chinese cuisine, I came across countless references to the "philosophical" properties of certain foods and the ways in which they should be combined according to Yin and Yang, considered in China to be the principles of life. The Yin, representing the negative force of the earth, is identified with darkness, passivity, and female qualities. The Yang, the positive force, represents activity, light, and male qualities. In Chinese cosmology, Yin and Yang combine, interacting to produce all that comes to be, a pleasant harmony. Incorporating these principles into their cooking and eating, for example, many Chinese look at sugar as Yin and vinegar as Yang; together, these tastes create a lively contrast.

When I asked Ken to comment on the Yin and Yang of Chinese cuisine, he hesitated. "It's very confusing because it's so intertwined with Chinese philosophy," he said. "It's a whole ordered way of looking at the world. I can only touch upon it and say that it has certainly influenced Chinese cooking; most Chinese incorporate the principles of Yin and Yang automatically. I find it makes sense, too. For instance, it doesn't make sense to have four hot dishes—with Yang qualities—at once. So, for a balance of Yin and Yang, you serve bland dishes with hot ones. For instance, the sweet and bland winter melon, considered Yin, is cooling to your body; so you use it to complement a rich, spicy Yang dish—maybe one filled with hot peppers."

In addition to tasting delicious, this balance of Yin and Yang foods is believed to be healthy for your body. In fact, there are even restaurants in Hong Kong that are classified as medicinal, not culinary. Applying Yin and Yang principles to medicinal prescriptions, for example, the Chinese believe that a pregnant woman should eat many Yang foods, while Yin foods are believed to help cool a fever.

"Another unique quality of Chinese cooking is that we use very few herbs for seasonings," Ken says. "In China, most herbs are dried and used for medicinal purposes, not culinary. For seasoning, we depend on what I call the holy trinity: garlic, scallions, and ginger. If you want to add a fourth seasoning, it would be hot peppers. But the first three are crucial to the cuisine of China. Occasionally you'll find coriander [cilantro], or, in the province of Hunan close to Thailand, Asian tropical basil with its intense anise flavor. You can find that basil in Hong Kong now, but because it's not traditional, it's sold in medicinal herb shops, not in vegetable markets."

When I talked to Ken about cooking from a garden, he said that, unfortunately, he had never had the luxury of doing so, but he knows what a wonderful adjunct it is to cooking Chinese dishes. He became particularly aware of the value of home-grown vegetables through classes that he teaches annually in Hong Kong. "There," he says, "people bring fresh vegetables from their gardens. Many Chinese vegetables are wonderful when picked young, but they're not produced commercially, so you're forced to grow your own if you want them. I'm talking about Chinese broccoli, or even pac choi, which is out of this world when very small. Pea shoots are also an incredible luxury. There's a large array of Oriental vegetables that most cooks in this country can't get at the market."

When I left Ken's office, I offered to bring him some pea shoots sometime. He lit up. Pea shoots might be his request for his last meal on earth, he said; if I brought him some he would cook them for me. I stored that piece of information in the back of my mind, and someday I hope to take him up on his offer.

---

anese soup miso has become my afternoon pick-me-up. And in recent years, my constant exposure to Oriental vegetables has led me to consider pac choi, bunching onions, fresh ginger, pea pods, and cilantro reliable staples.

In introducing Oriental cooking, it is important to point out that day-to-day Oriental cooking differs quite sharply from what Americans generally think of as Oriental fare. Consider that Asians and Europeans rarely know how Americans really eat at home—often believing we live on hamburgers and French fries and remaining unaware of the corn on the cob, chili, and zucchini bread that enrich our lives—and you will start to sense how bound we are by stereotypes. I, myself, who was raised on chop suey, crispy noodles from a can, and bottled curry powder, for instance, was surprised to learn that these "Oriental foods" were mere anglicized creations. Further, as I began to do some research, I discovered that even the Oriental food we eat in restaurants contributes to our distorted view of these cuisines, since these dishes are, first, tailored to American tastes, and, second, represent restaurant- rather than home-style cooking. Regarding the latter point, it is a fact that well-meaning Chinese chefs wanting to please their guests often use more salt, MSG, meat, and oil than in China. And because many Oriental vegetables are either unavailable or unfamiliar to Americans, many Chinese chefs limit themselves to only a few dishes, using only some of their treasured cabbage family greens and none of the fresh ginger shoots or Chinese chives enjoyed in China. Indian cooks in the United States also adapt their dishes to the American palate by using more meat and fewer fresh spices. And Japanese chefs here, who are usually unable to obtain a full array of Japanese herbs and, again, are catering to American tastes, have tended to avoid using seaweed and daikon and until recently have kept raw seafood, a Japanese staple, to themselves. Even recipes in some Oriental cookbooks published in this country have an American bias and, on the assumption that Oriental vegetables are unavailable, routinely substitute American vegetables for Oriental ones in recipes.

Significantly, gardeners can view the cuisines of the Orient differently from restaurant patrons or the users of Americanized Oriental cookbooks by concerning themselves with authenticity. We need not be limited by the supermarket or by the restaurateur's hopes of pleasing a timid, habit-bound clientele. Rather, we have the luxury of exploring the Oriental cuisines by growing the vegetables and herbs native to them. Of course, even with the parameters of our Oriental cookery pushed back by the existence of a garden, a thorough summary of Oriental cooking in the few pages available here is impossible. The subject is enormous, not only because of the many nationalities involved, but also owing to the strong influence of vastly differing religions and the great range of climates, from the tropics to the mountains, encompassed by the Orient. Because I must strictly limit my coverage, I have focused my attention in this section primarily on Chinese cooking. You will find descriptions of some cooking techniques and ingredients of Japan, India, and Thailand, and summaries of their cooking styles; but Chinese food dominates here because of all the Asian food cultures, that of China incorporates the greatest array of vegetables.

Although it is necessary to explain my emphasis on one culture's food over the others, it is equally important to point out common characteristics. Though the Asian land mass has long supported vast populations, only a small part of the land in these countries actually provides food. Out of necessity, then, Oriental cooks have had to maximize the use of their food, energy, and water, and this need has led to many similarities among cuisines. For instance, oven cooking, which wastes fuel, is found in none of the Oriental countries. And water, which is scarce, is often used over and over again throughout a meal—first for steaming, later for blanching, and perhaps finally for soup. Grazing land, too, is limited, so the flesh of large grazing animals such as beef and lamb is rarely used. And food itself is dear, so it is characteristic that all edible parts of both plants and animals are used—this results, for instance, in the regular use of organ meats and the shoots of bitter melon and squash. The lack of refrigeration, too, has had its impact across national boundaries, forcing a reliance on fresh, pickled, and dried foods. Fresh vegetables and herbs are usually grown at home or near the consumer, which means that typically they are garden fresh and not bred for transport.

Another explanation for the prevalence of pickling in cooking Oriental foods has to do with the age-old agricultural practice of using human waste for fertilizer. For health reasons, vegetables are seldom eaten raw, and if not cooked they are pickled either by salt curing or in vinegar. At first taste these pickled or salted vegetables are often too strong for many Western palates, but within the context of Chinese cooking in general, and particularly along with often neutral components of a Japanese meal or as an adjunct to rice, they can provide the adventurous with an enjoyable tang, a contrast of flavors, and an experience of novelty that is the real reward of seeking authenticity in exploring the world's cuisines.

Also common in much of the Orient but foreign to most Westerners, are dried foods such as fish and pac choi. The flavors of dried foods give a characteristic taste to much of the food from the Orient. For those unfamiliar with them, these flavors might be compared to that of raisins as contrasted with the flavor of fresh grapes: the original taste is intensified and altered in subtle ways. The trouble is, appreciating dried foods takes experience. To really enjoy them, you must put aside your first impressions and plunge ahead. When you open a package of dried shrimp, for example, the strong smell could discourage you permanently, but once cooked and combined with other ingredients, the shrimp will have quite a subtle taste. (For comparison's sake, think of the strong flavor of Parmesan cheese or dried mustard when tasted alone.) Dried foods do much to add interest to many vegetable dishes—interest you may never find in a restaurant dish. Once you have committed yourself to cooking authentic Oriental food, you will no doubt begin to seek out the surprisingly large variety of dried foods available in Oriental markets or health food stores.

A discussion of Oriental foods would be incomplete without coverage of their healthfulness. You are surely aware by now of the campaign against saturated fat and for fiber in the diet. Health theories come and go, but over the years evidence has been building to support the fact that we do indeed eat too much butterfat and not enough whole grains and vegetables. In this regard, Oriental cooking ranks high among cooking styles, particularly as practiced by those indigenous people who use no lard (and *not* by most American Oriental restaurants). The cooking oils are predominantly vegetable based; myriad vegetables make up a large part of most meals; protein sources are lean or, in the case of tofu, completely free of saturated fats; and butterfat-filled pastries and sauces are rare. So, unlike far too many of life's pleasures, authentic Oriental food is good for you. If its diversity and exoticism haven't converted you, how can you resist the sheer rightness of it all?

Oriental Cuisines

As the Orient is so large and the cultures so varied, it helps to look at a few of the cuisines in detail.

Chinese cooking: Chinese cooking is a rich cuisine for the gardener/cook not only because it uses a wide range of vegetables, but also because many Chinese cooking techniques treat vegetables beautifully and are easily mastered. Also, the appropriate utensils and many ingredients are usually easy to procure in this country. Be warned, however. The range of ingredients and style in Chinese cooking is enormous. Cooks in northern China make dishes and use vegetables that their neighbors to the south have never heard of, and the opposite is true as well. For space reasons, I have stayed within fairly narrow parameters in presenting Chinese recipes in this chapter. The ranges of possibility and variety are far greater than I can convey here.

In China, food is one of the major components of the culture. In fact, discussing China's cooking without considering the philosophical and medicinal aspects of the food is something like taking a diamond out of its setting: the stone is wonderful to look at but its true potential is hard to experience. Only in France do Westerners even begin to experience the importance of food as expressed in the Chinese culture. For thousands of years, food has been woven into the fabric of Chinese society, and chefs have been considered prestigious individuals—some have even been important members of the emperor's court. Throughout the ages, poets, politicians, and philosophers, including Confucius, have expounded in great detail on foods and food preparation. Each holiday, each event in a person's life, is associated with specific foods. But the cultural significance of food in China has long been matched by the minute attention paid to its nutritional properties. In China, food itself has always been treated as an integral part of personal health care. In fact, during some of the ancient dynasties, physicians who specialized in nutrition were often among the highest ranking doctors at court, and foods we now describe as high in vitamins and minerals were often prescribed for specific conditions—iron-rich foods following childbirth, for example. See the profile of Ken Hom in this chapter for more information on the cultural and nutritional aspects of food in China.

Daily fare in China consists of rice served with vegetable-based dishes in which meat or seafood is used primarily as a seasoning. It seems appropriate here to mention that while some Americans who dine at Chinese restaurants will order a number of dishes and omit the rice, to the Chinese diner that is akin to eating spaghetti sauce without the pasta. The strength of the seasonings in the dishes is based on the assumption that the food will be consumed with rice, and that is true of the recipes included in this chapter as well. As for meat, while it is greatly appreciated in China, most people can afford to serve it only on special occasions. Thus, stir-fries of greens or beans might contain pork, chicken, or shrimp, but only the smallest amount added for flavor. There might be meat in the stock base of a braised or steamed vegetable dish, and a small amount of meat might be added to the vegetables.

Throughout most of China, the myriad members of the cabbage family are the primary vegetables. Also common are members of the cucurbit family, including a wide variety of squash, gourds, and melons. Many types of beans are used too. Ginger, garlic, and onions are the basic seasonings. The use of herbs as we know them is unusual, since herbs are considered strictly medicinal, not culinary. But Chinese food draws intense flavors from other valuable ingredients: dried mushrooms, seafood, and fruits; sauces made from seafood, beans, and fruits; pickled vegetables; and soy sauce. While many wheat breads and noodles are consumed in China, rice is the predominant grain, and in most of China it is served in some form every day.

For the average American, delving into the cooking of China not only greatly expands the repertoire of familiar vegetables, it also helps reduce the reliance on using large amounts of meat in everyday cooking. For the gardener, this affords a way of turning uneven harvests into a positive advantage. A recipe for French carrot soup might call for two pounds of carrots, but perhaps your garden only produced one or two carrots, a few pea pods, and a little broccoli. "What's for supper?" asks your family. That's easy: stir-fry, custom-designed from the garden in your yard!

Japanese cooking: Limited agricultural soil and proximity to the ocean have greatly influenced the tastes of Japan. Japanese cuisine, elegant and highly stylized, is characterized by the use of dashi (a light fish stock), a variety of braised and one-pot dishes, sea vegetables, a distinct scarcity of fats, and elegant presentations. While the Japanese enjoy many meat dishes, in the average Japanese household everyday meals are vegetarian. The primary proteins are some form of soy bean and seafood, both prepared in many ways often unfamiliar to Western cooks. As to vegetables, a somewhat limited range is widely used in numerous variations. Most often, vegetables appear in soups, braised dishes, fried in tempura batter, served cold with a dressing of some sort, or as pickles, which in some of their many forms are served with practically every meal. Rice and noodles are the primary starches; seasonings include ginger and onion plus numerous herbs, some of which are native to Japan. Many forms of seaweed and dried fish complete the array of components.

Tightly woven into the religion and heritage of Japan is a deep reverence for nature, and this feeling is expressed in the country's art, gardens, holidays, and cuisine. For instance, throughout the centuries, traditional foods have been strictly linked with each new season: strawberries with spring, melons with summer, and persimmons with fall. In recent years, these associations have relaxed somewhat in the face of outside influences, but for centuries serving foods out of season was considered strange, rather as if we were to serve turkey and pumpkin pie on the Fourth of July.

In Japan as perhaps no other country, the visual presentation of the meal has the aesthetic value of high art. A simple, clear soup might be garnished with chrysanthemum petals or a perfect leaf of the herb mitsuba. The love of nature is often expressed in this medium—with daikon carved in the shape of a crane, for example, a slice of carrot carefully cut into the shape of a maple leaf, or layers of onion shaped into a calla lily. Table settings, too, are carefully thought out. For instance, a hand-wrought pottery dish might feature a few perfectly formed shrimp, or a simple plate might contain nothing but a few clean slices of crab-stuffed cucumbers and a sprig of red perilla. Appreciating the appearance of the food is an integral part of enjoying a meal in Japan.

In general, Japanese foods are light and somewhat subtle by American standards, and they sometimes taste quite salty to us as well. In fact, Americans visiting in Japan often say that after a few weeks they sometimes crave something rich and buttery. By the same token, I've heard Japanese visiting here say they crave a light meal and feel overwhelmed by the oils and fats in our food. But without going to extremes, American cooks can mine Japanese cuisine for techniques for lightening familiar dishes, recipes for easy one-pot dishes, means of polishing the appearance of the meal, and myriad ways of preparing tofu, the soy-based miracle food. In the garden, American gardener/cooks can give themselves access to Japanese herbs, the versatile daikon, Japanese-bred cucumbers and squash, and the numerous flowers valuable in Japan as garnishes. And by viewing the garden through Japanese eyes, Americans can renew their appreciation for the seasonality of gardening—and of cooking from the backyard garden.

Indian cooking: Indian cooks are the world's "flavorists." Boiled new potatoes with butter and a little salt and pepper happen to be a favorite dish of mine. But consider potatoes cooked with mustard seeds, ground cumin seeds, coriander, freshly grated ginger, red chili pepper powder, raisins, coconut, peanuts, and lemon juice—wonderful! The flavors envelope your being with the first bite. Served with chapatis, an unleavened whole-wheat bread, and raita, a yogurt dish made with shredded cucumbers and green chili peppers, and garnished with fresh cilantro leaves, this dish is close to heaven. Americans are just now discovering this world of flavors, and we are finding much to enjoy.

India is a huge country, and many religions, climates, cultures, and styles of cooking are found within its borders. But no matter what part of India you look to, one quality remains constant: spices and seasoning in a vast and varied array.

In many parts of India the people are vegetarian; in others the people eat some meats and seafoods but no pork or crustaceans. Dahl—a loose term covering various legumes such as dried split peas and lentils—and milk products, including yogurt, are primary protein sources, particularly for the vegetarian segment of the population. Vegetables common in India include eggplants, potatoes, beans, carrots, cauliflower, okra, peas, and many kinds of dried legumes. Wheat is made into numerous unleavened breads, the most common of which is the pancakelike chapati, served with most stewed dishes and soups. Rice, often mixed with spices and vegetables, is common throughout most of the country.

Gardeners who experiment with Indian dishes can gain new insight into the varying flavors of vegetables and can learn to work with a whole new source of proteins by exploring the many types of dahl. Try the Indian recipes in this chapter to experience a new way of enjoying eggplant and cauliflower, and see the books on Indian cooking listed in the "Sources" section of this chapter.

Ingredients

Many ingredients commonly used in the Orient are unfamiliar to American cooks.

Cooking oils: Cooking oils are particularly important in Oriental cooking. In China the country folks often use lard, but most Chinese chefs in the West prefer peanut oil for frying. In my forays into Oriental cooking, I have used all the high-quality cooking oils with good results. The exception is olive oil, which is too strongly flavored. Sesame oil, with its strong characteristic flavor, is used in China and Japan as a seasoning rather than a cooking oil and is usually added to the dish at the last moment. In India, vegetable oils, and occasionally ghee (clarified butter), are used in many curries and vegetable dishes.

Dried ingredients: Mushrooms are one of the most important dried ingredients in both Chinese and Japanese cooking. There are many types and they impart their rich, musky flavor to many dishes. Soak dried mushrooms for about half an hour in cold water before using them. Most cooks discard the stems. Other dried ingredients used to flavor stir-fries and soups of all types are dried lily buds (golden needles), shrimp, fish, seaweed, and pork. Most dried ingredients need to be reconstituted in water for fifteen to twenty minutes before use. Purchase these items in an Oriental grocery store or order them from the sources listed at the end of this chapter.

Pickled foods: Pickled foods are most closely associated with Japanese cuisine but are highly appreciated in China, Korea, and India as well. Historically, pickling has been a popular way to preserve foods in the Orient, and through the ages the sharp flavors it creates have become part of the cuisines. In Japan in particular, some meals are simply not complete without the accompaniment of a specific kind of pickle. You can make many of these traditional pickles from your garden produce; for recipes consult the books in "Sources" at the end of this chapter. Another alternative is to purchase pickles from specialty stores and mail-order sources.

Sauces and condiments: For many Oriental dishes characteristic flavor lies in certain sauces. Visit your local Oriental markets, natural food stores, or gourmet cooking shops and stock up on such key ingredients as oyster, hoisin, plum, and brown bean sauces for Chinese food; chutneys of all types for Indian cooking; and rice vinegar, sake, miso, and instant dashi for Japanese cooking. In her book *The Modern Art of Chinese Cooking,* Barbara Tropp gives detailed information on how to select and use the best of many kinds of Oriental seasonings. She recommends both specific brands of these products and local sources all over the country. As with commercial sauces and prepared seasonings in the States, numerous inferior products are on the market and her guidance is most valuable.

Soy sauce: Soy sauce is a pungent, salty brown liquid made from fermented soy beans, wheat, yeast, and salt. There are many grades and flavors, ranging from dark, heavy, and somewhat sweet brands to light and less salty. As a rule, Chinese cooks use the dark types for color and the lighter ones for salting dishes. Japanese cooks generally use light to medium strengths of soy sauce. A good brand available in most areas of this country is the familiar Kikkoman, a medium-strength soy sauce.

Tofu: Tofu, also called soy bean cake or bean curd, is a neutral-tasting, custardlike substance made from the curds of soy bean milk. The greatest virtues of tofu are its nutritional richness and its ability to absorb flavors. As with cheese, to which I liken it, tofu comes in different forms: the familiar white squares as well as dried, fermented, and even prefried forms. Of greatest interest to the gardener, and to the cook unfamiliar with tofu, are the different forms of the standard white squares. These come in a firm Chinese-style, a harder-to-come-by soft, or "silky," Japanese tofu, and a medium, or what I call "regular," custardlike type available in American grocery stores. Look for the latter in plastic square containers in the refrigerator section of your market. To buy firm and soft tofu or the dried and fermented types, you will need to visit Oriental or specialty markets.

Regular tofu, which is ready to use as is or cooked, will keep for four to five days in the refrigerator if rinsed in fresh water daily, but will become tough if frozen. Standard procedure is to drain the squares in a colander or on paper towels for half an hour. Simply cut the drained tofu into bite-size squares or strips and toss it into a soup, stir-fry, or egg dish. "Silky" tofu is usually served raw with a flavorful sauce. It can also be added to soups at the end of cooking since it will fall apart if stirred around much. In addition, of course, tofu can be served in dozens of nontraditional ways. I use it cubed or mashed in salads, sandwiches, omelettes, and casseroles.

Seasonings

Just as catsup, mayonnaise, and butter can be used to flavor American dishes, many seasonings are used to flavor Oriental foods.

In Chinese cooking: As mentioned before, the Chinese view of herbs is strictly medicinal and therefore few are used in day-to-day cooking. Instead, members of the onion family are used in abundance to flavor stir-fries, stuffings, and soups. Ginger and, in some parts of China, hot peppers are also popular. The other flavors of China are derived from the sauces and dried ingredients mentioned above as well as the hundreds of subtle variations and combinations of vegetables, seafoods, and meats.

In Indian cooking: The seasonings of Indian food give the cuisine its distinctiveness. While we have bastardized the term *curry* to mean the spice powder probably created by the British—and never used in India—true curries derive their flavor from a combination of particular dried and ground spices that is probably based on a traditional spice mixture called in India *garam masala*.

Far from using a premixed powder, the cook in India adds spices and herbs to a curry separately, some after fresh roasting and grinding them, others after grating or pounding them with a mortar and pestle. The seasonings, probably the richest selection in the world, are added in differing amounts depending on the dish and the artistry of the cook. Some of the many seasonings used are ginger, chili peppers, onions, garlic, holy basil, mint, lemon grass, black pepper, cardamom, nutmeg, cumin, coriander, fenugreek, fennel seeds, saffron, and cinnamon. Other seasonings, less well known here but available from Indian grocery stores, include rhizomes of tumeric, the sap of the asafetida rhizome, pomegranate seeds, curry leaf, *amchoor* (ground dried unripe mango fruits), and tamarind pods.

For a rough idea of which seasonings might be added to which vegetables, consider the cooking style of my neighbor Bhadra Fancy, a fabulous cook. In a cauliflower dish, for example, she uses a combination of ground cumin and coriander seeds, grated green chili, garlic, tumeric, and lemon juice, and she garnishes the dish with fresh coriander leaves. In preparing carrots and cabbage, she shreds the vegetables very fine before cooking them. Next, she sprinkles the cabbage with salt to extract some of the water and then rinses and drains it. Finally, she cooks both carrots and cabbage momentarily—just long enough to begin to wilt them—in a hot oil to which she has added mustard seeds, grated green chilies, salt, and lemon juice.

When Bhadra prepares eggplants, she roasts and combines them with chopped onions, garlic, and green chilies, and, again, she adds fresh coriander when she serves them. She cooks snap beans and peas together with green chilies, garlic, salt, and a pinch of sugar. Fresh garbanzo beans she cooks with onions, cumin seeds, and asafetida; then she adds ground cinnamon, cloves, nutmeg, coriander seeds, and *amchoor* before serving them. Okra is spiced with whole cumin or fenugreek seeds, asafetida, green chilies, garlic, ground cumin, and coriander, and the garnish is fresh cilantro leaves. As you can see, vegetables Indian style are bursting with delightful flavors.

In Japanese cooking: Dried fish and seaweed give the basic flavoring to many Japanese dishes. These two ingredients often take the form of the fish stock called dashi, which can form the base for soups, dressings, vegetable and seafood fishes, and sukiyaki. Dashi is similar in concept to our chicken or brown stock but is nearly omnipresent because it often takes the place of fats and therefore can be used in more than one way in the same meal. Other flavors come from rice vinegar, sugar, salt, soy sauce, sake, and the numerous herbs, such as perilla and mitsuba, that are unique to Japan.

In some cases the Japanese approach to seasoning food differs sharply from that of both Chinese and our own Western cooks. Although some seasonings—such as dashi and miso, a fermented soy bean paste—are incorporated into the prepared dish, other flavorings are lent by the many herbs and spices, pickles, and dipping sauces served as condiments or garnishes. For example, chopped scallions, grated or pickled ginger, or a salted plum might accompany a dish in the same way that horseradish or relish accompanies sausage or pork chops in our own cooking. The seeds and shoots of perilla might be served with shashimi, or an herb mixture might be dried and grated and sprinkled on noodle soup. In such cases, the garnish or condiment might be critical to the flavors of the whole dish in a way that most of our garnishes—for instance, a dusting of parsley leaves—are not.

In Thai cooking: The flavors of Thailand and many of the other Southeast Asian cuisines are derived both from the seasonings of China, with its vegetables and onion family flavors, and from the myriad spices of India. Curries in Thailand are often flavored with ground fresh spices and herbs made into a paste. The paste usually includes fresh chili peppers, lemon grass, cilantro leaves, and lime juice. Fresh mint, coriander root, and anise ('Thai') basil are also characteristic of many Southeast Asian dishes. Gardeners who want to lend authentic touches to their Thai dishes can grow their own.

Stir-Frying

Some basic techniques are used in Oriental cuisines. These range from the fancy carving of vegetables and the artistry of creating a rich and balanced curry, through Japanese braising and steaming, and on to versatile Chinese stir-frying. I recommend that you consult the books listed in the "Sources" section for specific instructions on most of them. Because no gardener should be without stir-fry techniques, however, I will conclude this section with a simple primer on the subject. Stir-frying allows you to take a varied harvest from the garden and create a wonderful meal within minutes.

The basic stir-frying technique is very simple. You fry a few ingredients together over a very high heat in a small amount of oil, stirring the contents of the pan continuously and vigorously for two or three minutes until cooked.

Fundamental to successful stir-frying is the use of the wok—a large, heavy, concave cooking pan that distributes heat evenly. The curved shape allows you to cook a little or a lot of food, depending on your needs, and to push foods to the side, away from the heat, to keep them from getting overcooked. The heat source for cooking a stir-fry in a wok should be very intense, so it's best to work on a gas stove. If you have electric burners you may want to use a wok with a flat bottom or a large, heavy, cast-iron skillet

instead. It is certainly possible to make successful stir-fries in a sturdy frying pan, but in this case you might need to cook the stir-fry in batches to keep the contents from overflowing. If only to avoid the fuss, purchasing a wok, an inexpensive and worthwhile kitchen tool, is a good idea if you don't already have one.

The first step in preparing a traditional stir-fry, and the most time-consuming and exacting part of the process, is cutting up the vegetables and meats evenly. Ingredients of uneven sizes will cook at different rates, which means that some pieces will be either over- or undercooked. Once your ingredients are assembled, put the wok over the flame and turn the heat up high. After the wok has completely heated, which might take a full minute, add three or four tablespoons of oil and your flavoring, such as hot peppers or ginger. Once you smell the perfume of the seasonings, remove them from the oil and, if you are using meat, cook it next, stirring continuously for the one or two minutes needed. Remove the meat to a plate when it's done; you'll add it to the vegetables after they are cooked. Next, add the vegetables that will take the longest to cook—for instance, carrots or stems of pac choi—stirring vigorously for a minute or two to keep the ingredients moving around. At the very end, add the more delicate vegetables, such as the leaves of pac choi, pea pods, and bean sprouts. Either continue to move them around or add a small amount of stock or seasoning, such as oyster sauce, plus a little water, and cover to steam them for less than a minute. Remove the contents to a large plate or platter and serve immediately.

If your stir-fry includes nonleafy vegetables that have a fairly long cooking time, such as carrots, broccoli stems, or peas, Chef Chu suggests that you blanch them in a few cups of broth or water in the wok before you start stir-frying. Cook them for a few minutes, and when they are almost tender remove them from the wok and pour off the liquid into a stock pot. Reheat the wok and then fry the rest of the ingredients in the normal manner, adding the blanched vegetables at the end. This technique allows you to control the cooking times precisely so you don't wind up with some of your vegetables burned and others raw. See the recipes in this chapter for more ideas on stir-frying and for an idea of the proportions of ingredients to use.

The hardest part of stir-frying is becoming familiar with the different textures and cooking times of the vegetables so you can determine the order in which to cook them. But rest assured that after a few sessions of stir-frying this will become second nature. Still, a few hints will help. Don't overfill the wok; cook in two batches if you need to. Also, keep the heat up very high, almost to the point at which the oil begins smoking. Always keep the mixture moving so that nothing will burn. But most importantly, relax and have a good time stirring your wonderful garden vegetables.

BHADRA'S HARVEST CURRY

My neighbor Bhadra Fancy contributed this recipe. The rich taste of the spices makes this a wonderful way to cook up many vegetables from the garden. Note that you can substitute or add eggplant and bell peppers to the vegetable mixture. Like many curries, this one is best eaten the day after it is made, when the flavors have blended.

SERVES 6 TO 8.

Vegetables

>   2 to 3 cups snap beans cut into 1-inch pieces
>   1 small cauliflower separated into large
>   chunks
>   4 medium potatoes cut into 1-inch cubes and
>   parboiled
>   2 cups sliced carrots
>   1 cup peas (optional)
>   6 tablespoons vegetable oil
>   2 cups chopped onion
>   4 medium tomatoes cut in wedges

Masala Paste

>   2 tablespoons poppy seeds
>   3 tablespoons dry grated coconut
>   1 tablespoon whole coriander seeds
>   1 tablespoon cumin seeds
>   1 teaspoon ground cinnamon
>   ¼ teaspoon ground cloves
>   6 whole cardamom pods
>   12 almonds or cashews or ¼ cup peanuts
>   10 peppercorns
>   2 teaspoons ground turmeric
>   1 cup chopped onions
>   8 cloves garlic

>   2 to 4 green chilies to taste
>   1½ inch fresh ginger, peeled
>   1 to 2 teaspoons cayenne pepper
>   2 to 3 teaspoons salt

>   4 cups water
>   2 teaspoons amchoor or 2 tablespoons lemon
>   juice

In a large pot, boil the first five vegetables until almost tender. Drain and reserve the liquid. In a large heavy-bottomed pot or Dutch oven, heat the oil and add 2 cups of chopped onions and cook over medium heat until transparent. Add the tomatoes and cook for about 3 minutes.

In a food processor put all the masala ingredients and blend for about 3 minutes or until mixture is a smooth paste.

Add the masala paste to the onions and tomatoes and cook for 3 minutes. Add the vegetables and 4 cups of cooking water and stir in. Season with salt and the *amchoor* or lemon juice. Cook for about 30 minutes. If the mixture gets too dry, add more of the cooking liquid and/or water.

Serve with chapatis or pita bread and rice and raita (see recipe below).

RAITA

Raita is a popular condiment in India. A simple dish, it offers a cooling contrast to spicy curry. This is Pallavi Fancy's recipe. To vary it you can add diced green chilies or fresh grated coconut, or substitute tart apple for the cucumber and add grated fresh ginger and ground cumin.

SERVES 6.

>   2 cups of shredded Armenian or "English"
>   cucumbers
>   1 teaspoon salt
>   2 cups yogurt
>   2 tablespoons fresh chopped mint or cilantro
>   Salt to taste

Shred unpeeled cucumbers on a grater. Sprinkle with salt and make a ball out of shredded cucumbers, then squeeze out the juice with your hands.

Put shredded cucumbers in a small bowl and stir in yogurt. Add herbs and then salt to taste.

STIR-FRIED PAC CHOI IN GARLIC OIL

Here is a common method of preparing one of the most popular Chinese vegetables. The recipe is from Ken Hom's book *Chinese Technique*. The variation using mustard greens makes a nice alternative.

SERVES 2 AS MAIN VEGETABLE COURSE OR 4 AS SIDE DISH.

> 3 tablespoons peanut oil
> 1 teaspoon salt
> 3 or 4 cloves garlic, lightly crushed and peeled
> 1½ pounds pac choi, cut into 1-inch pieces

Heat the wok over a high flame for 1 minute. Heat oil until very hot (this will take just a few seconds; pass your hand over it to feel the heat or look for a wisp of smoke). Add salt and garlic to flavor oil. Remove garlic when it has browned. Add pac choi and stir-fry, working smoothly and rapidly, keeping vegetables moving. Within a minute, taste a piece of pac choi to test doneness. It should be crisp but should not taste raw. When ready, transfer to a serving dish. Stir-fried vegetables should glisten with brilliant color; never let them fade in the wok.

Variation: Prepare Chinese mustard greens in a similar manner. Substitute 4 ¼-inch-thick slices of fresh ginger root for garlic and 1½ pounds of mustard greens, cut into 1-inch pieces, for pak choi and proceed as above.

DEEP-FRIED GREEN BEANS

Ken Hom recommends using "yard-long beans" in this recipe, also from his book, although any garden green bean can be used.

SERVES 2 TO 4.

> 2 cups oil
> 1 pound string beans, trimmed and cut into 5-inch pieces
> 1 tablespoon finely chopped garlic
> 1 tablespoon finely chopped ginger
> 2 tablespoons finely chopped scallions
> 4 dried red chilies
> 1 tablespoon bean sauce
> 1 tablespoon rice wine or dry sherry

Deep-fried yard-long beans prepared with garlic, ginger, and chili peppers.

> 1 tablespoon dark soy sauce
> 1 teaspoon sugar
> 1 tablespoon water

Heat the oil in a wok until it is fairly hot. A single bean dropped in the oil should bubble all over. Deep-fry half the beans until they are slightly wrinkled, about 3 to 4 minutes. Remove beans and drain. Fry the second batch in the same way.

Transfer about 1 tablespoon of oil to a clean wok or skillet. (You can save the rest for future use in cooking vegetables.) Add garlic, ginger, and scallions and stir-fry quickly. Add chilies and stir-fry them for about 30 seconds, until they turn black. Remove chilies and add all other ingredients. Stir-fry for a few seconds; then add cooked, drained beans and mix well. Serve when beans are heated through.

SPICY AND SOUR SQUID SALAD (Yum Pla Muk)

Areewan Fasudhani, of the Khan Toke Thai House in San Francisco, California, created this lovely dish, illustrated in the full-page photograph in this section. For the photo she added some Thai-style carved vegetables. Note that nampla, listed among the ingredients, is a salty fish sauce commonly used in Thai cooking. It is bottled like soy sauce and is available in Oriental markets.

SERVES 2 AS SALAD OR 4 AS APPETIZER.

> 1 cup shelled, cleaned, and sliced squid
> 1 tablespoon finely chopped lemon grass
> 2 tablespoons lime juice
> 1½ tablespoons nampla (fish sauce)
> 1 tablespoon sliced shallots
> About 1 teaspoon chili powder or finely chopped hot peppers, to taste
> 1 teaspoon finely chopped coriander root (if available)
> 1 teaspoon each chopped green onion and coriander leaves
> Lettuce or cabbage leaves
> 10 mint leaves
> Sprigs of cilantro

Dip squid into boiling water for 30 seconds and then put in bowl. Season with lemon grass, lime juice, nampla, shallots, chili powder, coriander root, green onions, and cilantro. Toss lightly. Place mixture on serving plate next to lettuce or cabbage; decorate with mint and cilantro sprigs. Serve immediately. Eat by scooping up squid and juice with lettuce or cabbage leaves.

PORK AND VEGETABLE POT WITH CLEAR BROTH (Mizutaki)

Elizabeth Andoh shares the Japanese customs that accompany this dish from her book *At Home with Japanese Cooking:* "An inviting array of vegetables and thinly sliced pork is brought to the table and cooked in a clear delicate broth. Bite-size pieces are scooped from the communal pot and dipped into individual bowls of piquant lemon-and-soy sauce or a fiery grated radish condiment. Mizutaki makes a perfect family or company dinner on a chilly day, served with hot white rice and assorted pungent pickles." Note that partially freezing the pork before preparing mizutaki will facilitate slicing. Also be aware that mizutaki made with chicken is equally delicious.

SERVES 4 TO 6.

> 1½ pounds lean boneless pork loin, partially frozen
> 1 cake yaki-dofu (grilled bean curd)
> 5 to 6 scallions with green tops intact
> ¼ pound fresh button mushrooms
> 1 small carrot
> ½ pound hakusai (Chinese cabbage)
> ¼ pound shungiku (chrysanthemum leaves), dandelion greens, or fresh spinach
> 1 lemon cut into wedges
> ¼ to ⅓ cup soy sauce
> 2 to 3 inches daikon (Japanese white radish)
> 1 togarashi (dried hot red pepper)
> 6 inches konbu (kelp for stock making)
> 1 quart fresh cold water

Slice pork into paper-thin slices about 2 inches square. Drain grilled bean curd (if packaged in water) and slice once lengthwise, then across 3 or 4 times to yield 8 to 10 bite-size blocks. Trim scallions and cut into 2-inch lengths. Wash and pat dry mushrooms, trim off and discard stems, and slice in half. Scrape carrot and cut into decorative flower shapes or ¼-inch thick rounds. Rinse cabbage, drain, and cut into 1-inch-thick wedges. Cut each wedge across into 3 sections. Rinse chrysanthemum leaves, greens, or spinach well under cold running water. For chrysanthemum leaves, trim bottoms of stems and cut off any flowering buds. If stalks are very long, cut in half. Pat leaves dry. Arrange these ingredients and lemon wedges attractively on a large platter or tray.

Divide soy sauce among 4 to 6 small bowls, one for each person. Peel radish and poke several holes in it. Then break open the dried red pepper pod and remove all seeds. Stuff pieces of pepper into the holes in the radish and grate radish. The white will be flecked with red and the mild radish will have a fiery accent. (The Japanese call this particular condiment *momiji oroshi,* or "autumn maple leaves.") Drain off any liquid from grating and mound the fiery radish in a shallow bowl. At the table each person adds lemon juice and/or radish to taste to the soy sauce.

Make a clear broth from kelp and water, discarding kelp once water has come to a boil. Lower heat slightly and start adding ingredients from platter. Begin with half the pork, adding it 1 slice at a time. Next toss in half the carrots and mushrooms. Let cook, partially covered, for 3 to 4 minutes, then add half the scallions, cabbage, and grilled bean curd and cook for another 3 to 4 minutes. Add half the chrysanthemum leaves and cook about 1 minute or until barely wilted. Remove pot from heat and let diners pick out whatever they wish to eat. Diners help themselves to bits of meat and vegetables, dunking these pieces lightly into their own dipping sauce before eating. Replenish cooking pot with remaining ingredients and cook as above.

Note: You can strain the broth remaining in the large pot and use it instead of plain water for cooking other vegetables.

BATTER-FRIED SHRIMP AND VEGETABLES (Tempura)

This recipe is also from Elizabeth Andoh's book. She says: "Tempura, one of the best-known Japanese dishes in the West, transforms shrimp and a variety of vegetables into delicate, crisp puffs. There are two schools of thought concerning the making of the batter; some chefs insist that just flour and water be used, and others always include some egg. It's really a matter of personal choice—the plain flour-and-water batter produces wispy, lacelike morsels, whereas the addition of egg makes for richer, more golden tempura. The recipe here allows for both options.

"Traditionally, each diner is provided with a shallow bowl of faintly sweet amber dipping sauce, to which he can add as much grated radish and/or fresh ginger as he wishes. Wedges of fresh lemon or lime make an attractive and delicious garnish, too—squeeze a bit of juice directly on the fried tempura.

"Unlike most Japanese main courses, this is a dish that should be served piping hot, a good reason for making it in small batches at the table if you've got the equipment. If not, keep freshly fried and drained pieces warm for up to 20 minutes in a 225–250 degree oven."

SERVES 4.

Shrimp and Vegetables

12 jumbo shrimp
1 small eggplant (weighing about ¼ pound)
2 green bell peppers or 8 okra pods
4 fresh white mushrooms
1 carrot
Note: Other vegetables, such as squash, green beans, broccoli, or sweet potato slices may be substituted.

Batter

1 cup flour (preferably low-gluten tempura ko, available in Oriental markets)
1 cup ice water or 1 egg yolk, beaten, plus enough very cold water to measure 1 cup liquid
Vegetable oil for deep frying

Dipping Sauce (Tentsuyu)

1 cup dashi (basic soup stock)
3 tablespoons soy sauce (preferably usu kuchi shoyu, light soy sauce)
1 tablespoon mirin (syrupy rice wine)
1 tablespoon sugar

Condiments

¼ cup peeled daikon (Japanese white radish)
2 teaspoons peeled and grated fresh ginger
½ lemon or lime, cut into 4 wedges, optional

Shell and devein shrimp, leaving tail sections intact. Lightly score underbelly to prevent shrimp from curling when fried. Remove stem and cut eggplant in half across its width, and then cut each half into 4 pieces lengthwise. Cut each of these 8 wedges into a fan shape. Cut each green pepper into quarters, lengthwise, and remove seeds, or wash okra pods well and pat them dry. Wash mushrooms; remove and discard stems. (Cut very large mushrooms in half.) Pat them dry. Peel carrot and slice into matchsticks.

To prepare batter, place all but 1 tablespoon flour in a large bowl. Make a well in the center of flour and pour in half the plain ice water or egg-water mixture. Stir with light, circular motions, incorporating about half the flour. The batter should be slightly thinner than that used for pancakes, and small lumps are of no importance. It is better to undermix than overmix batter.

Before frying tempura, make dipping sauce by combining all ingredients in a small saucepan and heating through.

To fry tempura, pour at least 1½–2 inches of oil into frying pan. Heat to approximately 360° and test a bit of batter in pan. It should sink slightly, then rise immediately, puffing out and coloring lightly.

Hold each shrimp by its tail and lightly dust it in a bit of flour. Dip into batter and then fry. Fry no more than 3 or 4 at one time to prevent oil from cooling down too much. The shrimp will puff, turn golden brown, and be cooked through in about 2 to 3 minutes. Turn shrimp once if necessary, halfway through frying. Drain well and skim oil with a net skimmer to remove batter spatterings.

Coat each eggplant piece in batter and fry, 3 or 4 at a time, skin side down, for 1 minute. Turn pieces and continue to fry for another minute or two until golden and cooked through. Drain vegetables and skim oil after each batch.

Pour a bit more liquid into bowl and incorporate more flour to make additional batter as needed. Dip pepper pieces or okra pods, one at a time, in batter and fry (less than a minute for peppers, about 1 to 1½ minutes for okra).

Dip mushrooms in batter and fry for about 1 minute. Toss carrot strips in batter and let 4 or 5 stick together, forming several small bundles. Fry bundles for 1½ to 2 minutes.

On each of 4 large individual plates (the Japanese often use woven bamboo trays), lay a sheet of plain white paper or a doily and arrange 3 shrimp, 2 eggplant pieces, 2 pepper pieces or okra pods, 1 mushroom, and 1 to 2 bundles of carrot.

Serve tempura hot, providing each diner with warm dipping sauce and condiments.

STIR-FRIED SHRIMP AND GREENS

David Cunningham, staff horticulturist at the Vermont Bean Seed Company, created this recipe in order to take advantage of the many Oriental greens he grows in his garden. Serve this stir-fry with steamed short-grain rice.

SERVES 6 TO 8.

Marinated Shrimp

> 1 tablespoon tomato paste
> 1 tablespoon cornstarch
> 1 tablespoon soy sauce

Stir-fries are among the most versatile vegetable dishes in the Orient, and those made with Chinese cabbage are among the tastiest.

> 2 tablespoons vinegar
> 2 tablespoons water
> ½ teaspoon Chinese mustard
> 1½ pounds raw shrimp, shelled, cleaned, and
>   deveined

Sauce

> ½ cup chicken stock
> 1 tablespoon cornstarch
> 1 tablespoon soy sauce
> 2 teaspoons honey
> 4 large cloves garlic

Stir-Fry Ingredients

> ¼ cup oil
> 2 large heads pac choi, stems sliced diagonally
> 4 green onions, 'He-Shi-Ko Long White
>   Bunching' preferred, sliced diagonally
> 4 cups Japanese greens, 'Tah Tsai' preferred

Mix marinade ingredients, add shrimp, and refrigerate for 3 hours. Mix sauce ingredients and add drained marinade liquid. Start heating the wok with about half of the oil. Sauté marinated shrimp very quickly in small batches, putting cooked shrimp and any juices into a separate bowl. Heat remaining oil and sauté pac choi ribs and green onion for about 1 minute; add greens and stir until wilted. Add sauce, lower heat, and stir until thickened. Add cooked shrimp and heat another minute.

STIR-FRIED CHICKEN WITH GOLDEN NEEDLES

Geri Harrington, author of *Grow Your Own Chinese Vegetables*, contributed this recipe, which features golden needles. These are usually tiger lily buds that are dried and sold in blocks in Chinese markets. Geri reports that dried day lily buds work just as well; just pick the buds before they open, dry them thoroughly, and store them in a closed container. They will keep a long time. You could substitute fresh lily buds though they would be inauthentic and less flavorful. To do so, use 1½ to 2 cups fresh lily buds and do not soak.

SERVES 4.

> *1 ounce golden noodles*
> *5 dried Chinese black mushrooms*
> *2 teaspoons rice wine or dry sherry*
> *2 teaspoons cornstarch*
> *1 pound boned chicken breasts, pounded flat and cut into 2-inch-long strips*
> *2 tablespoons peanut oil*
> *6 scallions, cut into 1-inch pieces*
> *½ pound snow peas, stemmed and stringed*
> *4 thin slices fresh ginger root*
> *2 whole hot chili peppers (vary according to taste)*
> *1 teaspoon fresh cilantro, minced*
> *1 tablespoon tamari sauce (a thick, mellow soy sauce)*
> *½ cup chicken broth*
> *½ teaspoon sesame oil*
> *4 tablespoons cornstarch*
> *¼ cup water*

Soak lily buds and mushrooms in warm water until soft, about 20 minutes; drain. If desired, tie each lily bud into a knot for appearance. Cut mushrooms into bite-size pieces.

Combine rice wine or sherry and 2 teaspoons of cornstarch. Add chicken breasts, stirring to coat. Marinate in refrigerator from ½ to 2 hours.

Set wok or skillet over high heat, adding 1 tablespoon oil. Drop in scallions, snow peas, and ginger, and stir-fry 30 seconds. Add chicken, hot chili peppers, golden needles, and mushrooms and stir-fry 30 seconds, adding more oil if necessary. Add tamari, broth, and sesame oil, stirring to blend. Cover and simmer 3 to 4 minutes. Mix 4 tablespoons cornstarch with ¼ cup water to make a paste. Stir gradually into wok mixture and cook for 1 minute.

Before serving, remove hot chili peppers, being careful not to break. Garnish dish with cilantro.

AUBERGINE (EGGPLANT) WITH YOGURT SAUCE

This classic recipe for eggplant is from Madhur Jaffrey's *A Taste of India*.

SERVES 3 TO 4.

> *2 tablespoons ground coriander seeds*
> *1½ teaspoons ground turmeric*
> *9 cloves garlic, peeled and mashed to a pulp (keep one of the mashed garlic cloves separate from the rest)*
> *Approximately ¾ teaspoon salt*
> *⅓ cup plus 3 tablespoons water*
> *¾ cup vegetable oil*
> *2 medium-size onions, peeled, cut in half lengthwise, and then cut crosswise into very fine, even, half rings*
> *1 pound eggplant cut into ½-inch-thick rounds*
> *1 cup plain yogurt*

Put coriander seeds, turmeric, and 8 of the mashed garlic cloves into a small bowl. Add ¼ teaspoon salt and ⅓ cup water and mix.

Line two dinner plates with absorbent paper towels and set aside. Heat 6 tablespoons of the oil in a frying pan, preferably a nonstick one, over a medium-high flame. When hot, put in onions. Stir and fry until onions have turned dark brown and crisp. Remove with a slotted spoon and spread out on one of the towel-lined plates.

Turn heat down to medium and put in as many

eggplant slices as pan will hold in a single layer. They will suck up the oil. Brown on one side lightly and then turn slices over. Add another 3 tablespoons of oil, dribbling it along sides of pan. Brown second side. Turn slices over once more, browning first side more thoroughly. Remove slices with a slotted spoon and put them on the second towel-lined dinner plate. Fry a second and, if needed, a third batch of eggplant slices and cook the same way, adding 3 tablespoons of oil after turning the eggplant slices over.

Put coriander seed, turmeric, and garlic mixture into oil. Stir and fry it for 2 minutes or so. The paste should dry up and the garlic should get properly fried. Now add 3 tablespoons of water. Stir once and turn off heat.

Put yogurt in a bowl. Add the 1 remaining mashed garlic clove and ¼ teaspoon of salt to it. Stir to mix.

Just before serving, sprinkle eggplant slices with about ¼ teaspoon salt and arrange them in a single layer on a large serving plate. Spoon some of the coriander spice mixture over each slice and spread it over the top. Now cover slices with large dollops of yogurt. Crumble browned onions and scatter them over yogurt. Serve at room temperature.

Sources

Seed Companies

1. W. Atlee Burpee Company
   Warminster, PA 18991
   Burpee, known for its large selection of American varieties, also carries a number of Oriental ones.

2. Gleckler's Seedmen
   Metamora, OH 43540
   This seed company carries a great variety of unusual vegetables, including a large selection of Oriental ones.

3. Johnny's Selected Seeds
   Foss Hill Road
   Albion, ME 04910
   Johnny's specializes in vegetable seeds for the Northeast but also carries many superior Oriental vegetable varieties.

4. Kitazawa Seed Company
   1748 Laine Avenue
   Santa Clara, CA 95051

   This company specializes in Oriental vegetables, including bitter melon, spinach mustard, and edible chrysanthemum.

5. Le Marché
   Seeds International
   P.O. Box 190
   Dixon, CA 95620
   This seed company has an international focus and carries many Oriental vegetable varieties. Catalog: $2.00.

6. Lockhart Seeds, Inc.
   P.O. Box 1361
   3 North Wilson Way
   Stockton, CA 95205
   This large seed company offers a good selection of Oriental vegetables.

7. Nichols Garden Nursery
   1190 North Pacific Highway
   Albany, OR 97321
   This firm carries a large number of unusual vegetable and herb varieties, many of which are Oriental.

8. Redwood City Seed Company
   P.O. Box 361
   Redwood City, CA 94064
   This firm sells seeds of many Oriental vegetables. Catalog: $1.00.

9. Seeds Blum
   Idaho City Stage
   Boise, ID 83706
   Seeds Blum offers many unusual open-pollinated varieties of vegetables and herbs, including many Oriental ones. Catalog: $2.00.

10. Sunrise Enterprises
    P.O. Box 10058
    Elmwood, CN 06110
    This seed company specializes in Oriental vegetables and herbs and carries one of this country's largest selections. It offers ginger and taro tubers and Chinese chive plants in addition to vegetable seeds.

11. Tsang & Ma International
    P.O. Box 294
    Belmont, CA 94002
    This company carries a large selection of Chinese vegetable seeds, including Chinese chives, bitter melon, Chinese parsley, and a selection of Oriental spices and cooking equipment.

12. Vermont Bean Seed Company
    Garden Lane
    Fair Haven, VT 05743
    This firm maintains an extensive list of beans and peas but also carries the seeds of some Oriental vegetables.

13. Dr. Yoo Farm
    P.O. Box 290
    College Park, MD 20740
    This company carries a large selection of Oriental vegetables.

Mail-Order Sources of Ingredients

Look for hard-to-find ingredients in your local Oriental community or inquire at local Oriental cooking classes. Alternatively, try the following mail-order sources.

Kam Man Food Products, Inc.
200 Canal Street
New York, NY 10013
    To order, write to the company and request specific items.

Oriental Food Market & Cooking School
2801 West Howard
Chicago, IL 60645
    The school carries a full selection of nonperishable foodstuffs and basic equipment. A catalog is available but does not give brands.

Orient Delight Market
865 East El Camino Real
Mountain View, CA 94040
    This market offers a good supply of specialty items, including meats, teas, tools, and nonperishable foodstuffs. Catalog available. Address inquiries to Robert Yin.

Books

Andoh, Elizabeth. *At Home with Japanese Cooking.* New York: Knopf, 1980.
    This detailed primer on Japanese cooking contains numerous recipes, both simple and complex.

Chan, Peter. *Better Vegetable Gardens the Chinese Way: Peter Chan's Raised-Bed System.* Rev. ed. Pownal, Vt.: Garden Way Publishing, 1985.
    This charming book outlines in detail Peter Chan's productive and soil-enriching garden techniques.

Chu, Lawrence C. C. *Chef Chu's Distinctive Cuisine of China.* New York: Harper & Row, 1983.
    This comprehensive book on Chinese cooking contains many photos and recipes.

Dahlen, Martha, and Karen Phillipps. *A Popular Guide to Chinese Vegetables.* New York: Crown, 1983.
    This little book, with its watercolor illustrations, is invaluable for sorting out the Oriental vegetables.

Harrington, Geri. *Grow Your Own Chinese Vegetables.* Pownal, Vt.: Garden Way Publishing, 1984.
    Offering extensive information on thirty-eight Oriental vegetables, this is one of the best books on the subject.

Hom, Ken. *Ken Hom's Chinese Cookery.* New York: Harper & Row, 1986.
    A marvelous book with detailed how-tos, inspirational photographs, and delicious recipes.

Hom, Ken, and Harvey Steiman. *Chinese Technique: An Illustrated Guide to the Fundamental Techniques of Chinese Cooking.* New York: Simon & Schuster, 1981.
    If you want to carve vegetables or make won tons or dozens of other Oriental dishes, here is the place to look for detailed instruction. Included are all the basic recipes and hundreds of black-and-white photos that illustrate the techniques described.

Hsiung, Deh-ta. *Chinese Vegetarian Cooking.* Secaucus, N.J.: Chartwell, 1985.
    This book contains a good selection of basic cooking techniques and a large array of very fine recipes.

Jaffrey, Madhur. *A Taste of India.* New York: Atheneum, 1986.
    This fabulous book covers both the cooking and the culture of India.

Nix, Janeth Johnson. *Adventures in Oriental Cooking.* San Francisco: Ortho Books, 1976.
    Here's a fine how-to book for beginners and experienced cooks alike on using Oriental vegetables.

Tropp, Barbara. *The Modern Art of Chinese Cooking.* New York: Morrow, 1982.
    This book, a compendium of information on Chinese food, can be a real help to American cooks. It contains numerous recipes, both authentic and adapted to American ingredients.

PART
THREE

AVANT-GARDE
GARDENS

CAN YOU PICTURE black squid-ink pasta covered with a yellow curry sauce and served on a black plate? When I visited the California Culinary Academy for a session on food photography, this was the dish prepared by the class. Oh, no. "Punk" food, I thought, as they offered me some. I've eaten many unusual foods, but everyone draws the line somewhere—and this was past my limit. Is this the future of food? I wondered.

From my point of view, the students who created this ominous-looking dish and served it in the starkest of settings were seeing only a small part of the future of food. My personal vision of food in the twenty-first century, particularly the produce and herbs, is much more colorful, and I think more inviting. It includes bowls filled with fresh arrays of little red and yellow tomatoes and florets of purple broccoli around a dip made with fresh herbs, vegetable terrines sauced with a puree of leeks, shrimp marinated in a lemon grass brew, salads filled with radicchio and young lettuce leaves, and baklava served with rose-petal honey and garnished with fresh rose petals. But, of course, we needn't wait for decades to realize such a vision. We need only step into the avant-garde by expressing, in our kitchens and gardens, today's most forward-looking trends.

We modern Americans probably have more food options than any people ever before. Even with respect to produce alone, we have a full spectrum to work with, not only because conscientious gardeners have saved our heritage of fruits and vegetables from extinction, but also because professional breeders are constantly creating new varieties. And given our melting-pot culture, we continually absorb the dishes of other nations into our cornucopialike cuisine. We have chili peppers and tortillas from Mexico, pac choi and fresh ginger from China, and basil and paste tomatoes from Italy. At present, we are in a great period of food exploration, not unlike the time in Europe when explorers were returning from the New World with ships full of potatoes, peppers, chocolate, and tomatoes. A high standard of living, extensive traveling, and a new breed of chef are all combining to spark a revolution.

Another element has particular significance in shaping recent approaches to food: a new emphasis on health and the importance of nutrition. Mounting medical evidence on the causes of heart attacks and strokes is finally being absorbed into our national consciousness, and diners are looking for ways to reduce salt and fats and to include more fresh produce in their meals. With chefs taking a keen interest in these matters, "spa" menus and "Heart Association–approved" menus have begun to make their appearances in fine restaurants and resorts.

My travels around the country have shown me that the spirit of experimentation has entered the private as well as the restaurant kitchen. I've been served a stir-fry in Idaho, garden tacos in Boston, and fruit salad and yogurt for breakfast in St. Louis. Plates of steak and potatoes have become noticeably fewer and farther between. Popular magazines are filled with recipes for lighter meals, and grocery chains are remodeling to make room for larger produce sections. Consumers, now aware that vegetables need no longer be relegated to side dishes, are traveling miles to seek out "boutique" produce stands.

It is the garden that is fueling the revolution—sometimes the market garden, where the new vegetables are grown for the public, but just as often the home garden, where bold gardener-cooks are reshaping their families' tastes and eating habits. Part Three covers newly emerging trends and explores the growing and cooking of everything from red, white, and blue potato salad to nasturtium butter pasta. Step out into the garden and join the avant-garde.

Flower petals can be minced or incorporated into sweet butter to make a delicious spread for biscuits and toast.

Rainbow Gardens

I LOVE BRIGHT COLORS! My dresses are red, bright blue, even deep purple. My house is decorated with primary colors, and sometimes you practically need sunglasses to look at my garden. I dream in Technicolor, and while I thrill to Ansel Adams's black-and-white photographs, I take pictures in color only. Intellectually I realize that not everyone feels about colors the way I do. I tell myself there are people who love beige and others who decorate solely with black and white, but in my heart I'm not sure these people really exist.

Given my predilection for colors, I guess it's not surprising that I'm enamored with colorful vegetables. Why should I grow only standard green beans or broccoli when I can have purple ones too—providing, of course, that they taste good. Why limit myself to green bell peppers when I can have yellow, orange, and violet ones as well? It's not the colors alone that I glory in; it's the infinite variety that nature offers. Just as I enjoy seeing exotic birds and insects and growing unfamiliar species of flowers, so I enjoy growing and cooking with vegetables of unusual colors. I love getting my hands on them and sharing them with others. When a neighbor's child helps me harvest some of my blue potatoes, we take pleasure in the

OPPOSITE: *A basket of rainbow-colored vegetables includes unusual-colored eggplants, peppers, tomatoes, cherry tomatoes, potatoes, and squash.*

color together, and I get a great kick out of serving lavender vichyssoise to a visiting gardener. All in all, color is a whole dimension of my edible garden that I can experiment with and enjoy.

I can trace my fascination with colorful vegetables back some years to my discovery of orange tomatoes and purple string beans. These vegetables were so much fun I started looking for other varieties in unusual colors. Soon I was growing all sorts, and always looking for more. Eventually I met Jan Blum, fellow color enthusiast and owner of Seeds Blum, and we started playing that great gardening game, "Have I Got Something for You!" I'd show her lavender eggplants and she'd tell me about blue potatoes and peas and red celery. I'd tell her about chartreuse broccoli and she'd show me red orach, red Brussels sprouts, and green radishes. I always thought I was on the cutting edge with my vegetables, but I was constantly getting outclassed!

When I first conceived of this book, I grew a rainbow garden to kick off the project. I conferred at the last minute with Jan, as well as with Renée Shepherd, owner of Shepherd's Seeds and another color enthusiast, to see if I had left out any obvious gems. In the spring I filled the raised vegetable bed in my back yard with yellow and white beets, white carrots, red lettuce and chard, green and 'Easter Egg' (multicolored) radishes, and blue potatoes and peas. As summer approached I planted purple and golden bell peppers, yellow tomatoes and zucchini, red chicory, blue corn, lavender eggplants, yellow cucumbers, red basil, purple snap beans, and scarlet runner beans.

In designing the garden I became so enthused that I selected a number of flowers, all in primary colors, to emphasize the theme. In the end, the garden turned out to be great fun, very beautiful, and a good learning experience as well. For example, I found that some of the unusual-colored vegetable plants were more decorative in the garden as well as in the kitchen than the standard varieties and, given my penchant for edible landscaping, this was information I could use. The bright lavender fruits of 'Rosa Bianco' eggplant, the scarlet runner beans with their bright-red flowers, the colorful pepper varities, 'Opal' basil, and 'Gold Rush' zucchini—all turned out to be especially beautiful in the garden.

With the success of my rainbow garden still fresh in my mind, I visited the New York Botanical Garden and mentioned my color experiments to Debra Lerer,

director of children's gardening. She was inspired immediately with the desire to grow a rainbow garden in the children's section of the botanical garden the next summer. This was perfect! I would have the opportunity to see how these vegetables performed in another climate, and even better, I'd be able to see another dimension added to the rainbow garden—children. Once we thought about it, it became obvious that children and colorful vegetables were a natural combination, and sure enough, the next summer the plot of rainbow vegetables was the hit of the children's garden.

As my research continued on the book, I added more and more colorful vegetables to my list. The heirlooms in particular were often quite colorful; so were some of the Italian and Oriental vegetables. And as I talked with other gardeners and chefs, I found many who shared my fascination. One of the most involved chefs was Doug Gosling, of the Farallones Institute in Occidental, California. He and I compared notes, and I discovered that he grew a lot of unusual-colored vegetables I had never tried. He harvested some for me to photograph and then prepared them for me. I also spoke on the phone to Ken Weslowski, a market grower in Scotia, New York, who is particularly interested in vegetables of unusual colors and in growing "baby" ones, too (serving up the babies is a good way to feature unusual-colored vegetables). Ken and a local chef, Jim Westerfelt, collaborate on using the unusual produce. Ken gave me a lot of information on how they prepare them and how the vegetables grow in his climate.

I hope you can become as involved with some of these vegetables as I have, because they're really great fun, and harvesting a rainbow garden can be an aesthetic experience in itself. Picture yourself toward the end of your growing season taking a large basket out to the garden. You start harvesting the red vegetables and flowers, placing red chard and pungent red nasturtiums into the basket. Then you move on to the golden beets and calendulas; your succulent yellow tomatoes and the yellow zucchini might be next. Add to them the green, sweet-ripe tomatoes and green radishes if you have some—these will make you chuckle. Dig up a few blue potatoes to put in the basket and finish the rainbow array with a luminescent 'Rosa Bianco' eggplant and some purple string beans. No matter how many times I do this with my rainbow vegetables, harvesting still makes me smile.

The author's rainbow garden. In the foreground, bordered by romaine lettuce, is an arc of yellow violas, lavender alyssum, violet lobelia, and red impatiens. In raised beds in the background is a rainbow vegetable garden with blue potatoes, purple snap beans and peppers, orange tomatoes, and yellow cucumbers, beets, and zucchini.

How to Grow a Rainbow Garden

With a few exceptions, most unusual-colored vegetables grow much as standard vegetables do. For detailed information on them, consult Part Four, "An Encyclopedia of Superior Vegetables." A few of the rainbow varieties are a little challenging to grow; for example, yellow beets are somewhat harder to germinate than the red varieties. Also, the all-red and all-blue potato varieties usually yield half as much as most modern hybrids, so you must plant more

than the regular amount. However, a few of the rainbow vegetables are downright advantageous. For example, purple beans, blue-podded peas, and gold zucchinis are easier for gardeners to find on the vines than the usual varieties. Thus, as unpicked peas and beans make the vines less productive, you need not wonder why your beans and peas have stopped producing or what to do with a three-foot zucchini that has grown unnoticed for a week or two. Also, 'Hopi Blue' corn needs less water than the average corn crop, 'Royalty' purple beans can be started in much cooler soil than standard string beans, and purple cauliflower varieties need no garden blanching to be tender and sweet. The only real problem you will encounter in growing a rainbow garden is locating seeds of some of the varieties, since they are not readily available from most seed companies or local nurseries. The seed companies listed under "Sources" at the end of this chapter are good places to start.

The color range of your harvest will be a major planning consideration. You'll need to pay particular attention to the number of plants you'll grow in your rainbow garden and to selecting and coordinating particular varieties. For example, the special effect for some colorful vegetables depends on numerous varieties of different colors being served together. Envision three colors, not one, of tomatoes or peppers arranged on a tray. To achieve the effect, you'll want to grow two plants of three or four varieties where possible instead of three or four plants of one or two varieties. For a mix of color with some of the root vegetables and lettuces, instead of planting a row of each color, you can mix the seeds of many colors of beets, carrots, or radishes and sprinkle them together in the planting bed. You'll be able to tell the colors apart when you harvest, since the foliage is different in the beets and the shoulders of most of these vegetables show about the soil.

It also seems appropriate here to talk about baby vegetables, because unusually colorful vegetables are popularly used in their immature stage. To set the record straight, not all vegetable varieties are equally good as "babies." For instance, some immature zucchini squash taste metallic when picked too soon, some baby carrots are tasteless, and some young lettuces are watery. Of the varieties of vegetables that do make good babies, some have been bred to be harvested as miniatures and others just happen to taste good that way. Examples of varieties bred for eating small are 'Little Ball' red beets, 'Tom Thumb' lettuce, 'Planet' carrots, French cornichon cucumbers, and most filet beans. Varieties of vegetables that just happen to be tasty when young are most varieties of sweet corn if they are harvested when the silks first appear, 'Minicor' carrots, and 'De Milan' turnips. A number of colorful varieties of vegetables are excellent as babies. Try 'Royal Burgundy' snap beans, 'Gold Rush' and 'Sunburst' scalloped summer squash, 'Burpee's Golden' beets, and 'Yellow Pear' and 'Green Grape' tomatoes. Some of these miniature vegetables are wonderful as side dishes or garnishes; others can be barbecued whole or used in salads. Seed companies with a large number of vegetable varieties appropriate for using as babies are Shepherd's Garden Seeds, Le Marché, and Nichols Garden Nursery.

The New York Botanical Children's Rainbow Garden

Though the New York Botanical Garden is in the city, as you walk through the garden you hear birds instead of taxi horns and see flowering shrubs and lush trees, not skyscrapers. I first visited the garden to give a lecture, and that was when I met Debra Lerer, director of children's gardening. As noted earlier, together we planned a rainbow garden for the botanical garden's children's garden. I suggested some vegetable varieties Debra might want to select and gave her the names of the seed companies listed under "Sources" in this chapter. The next summer I returned to talk with Debra again and to see how the rainbow garden had done.

The children's garden is a large, walled garden with numerous plots, each six feet across and fifteen feet long. Dozens of children participate, and two children share each plot, which they visit two and a half hours a week to plant, water, and weed. In the middle of the garden are a few demonstration plots of the same size as the children's plots. It was one of these that Debra designated as the rainbow garden.

The children plant their individual gardens in May. Debra and some of the garden staff started the rainbow one when the kids were busy with their plots. Only unusual-colored vegetables and herbs went into the rainbow garden. This early planting included white and yellow beets, 'Easter Egg' radishes, red lettuce, purple basil, and blue potatoes. Later on Debra and her assistants planted a series of peppers—purple, golden, and yellow—two varieties of lavender eggplants, yellow cucumbers, and several 'Yellow Pear' tomato plants. Behind the tomatoes they planted 'Royal Burgundy' bush beans.

All in all, the garden did very well. The yellow cucumber plant was lost to verticillium wilt; a few tomato hornworms, an occasional rabbit, and a number of greedy squirrels showed up; but the garden produced and was a source of delight and wonder for all the gardeners, big and small.

To make sure the children fully experienced the rainbow garden, Debra had them come in groups of ten or twelve to look at the different plants and talk about the unusual varieties and guess the colors of their produce. Later in the season she had them taste some of the vegetables. "Some of the vegetables in the rainbow garden actually shocked the children," she told me. "The kids were really surprised at the vegetables; they found some absolutely unbelievable. The children themselves had been growing red lettuces and the 'Easter Egg' radishes, so those weren't that thrilling, and the white beets weren't that dramatic either. But those kids had never seen anything like the blue potatoes or the purple string beans and lavender eggplants. They were very surprised to find that when you break open purple beans you find the insides bright green, and they liked the fact that the purple beans tasted like their own garden green beans. We gave at least one purple string bean to each child, and some were so entranced they started harvesting a lot of them. Some picked enough for dinner for the family. Their parents hadn't seen purple beans either. However, even before the bean plants produced, the concept must have been interesting enough for the children to talk about them at home. So I had parents coming back and saying, 'We hear you have purple string beans.' Or, 'Do you really have blue potatoes?' I guess children go back and say a lot of things that parents don't necessarily believe. So when the vegetables produced and the children showed them to their parents, *they* became excited too."

Our conversation drifted to the topic of working with children in the garden. Debra had much to share about gardening with her young charges. She remarked on the difference between working with young and older children. "The little children need very literal instructions, and you can't take anything for granted with them. We've seen some children just take soil and fling it over their shoulders because they don't know what digging means. So you really have to teach them a lot and never assume they understand certain basic things. You'll find that some children bury seeds down as far as they can dig or turn the hose full-blast on the garden. But those kinds of things are what they learn the first couple of sessions, and after that they're ready to go a lot further on their own. You also have to be careful to provide them with tools of the correct size. [A few of the garden-supply companies listed in Appendix C carry high-

Debra Lerer and Rachael DeJesus enjoy 'Yellow Pear' tomatoes from the rainbow vegetable garden at the New York Botanical Garden's Children's Garden.

quality child-size gardening tools.] You can give a lot more freedom and flexibility to older children. They get very involved in choosing varieties and, of course, they don't need as much supervision. They grow what they want and are responsible for their own plots. For them you're just there as an advisor."

Debra went on to talk about allowing for the children's individual differences. Some children, she mused, will not let one weed grow in their garden, while others don't seem to care about weeds. Some children want to cram in as many types of vegetables as possible while others want a whole garden full of tomatoes. Some find gardening at the children's garden a very social event and they share willingly with a partner. But others are really possessive and want half of every cabbage or feel they've made a personal claim to a plot simply by planting a seed. Those differences aside, however, children learn a lot about living from having a garden. "For instance," she said, "we had a drought this summer and had a big problem with water. We weren't able to water the garden for a very long time, and the children learned first-hand what that meant. They became aware of the weather forecasts, how important rain was, how much we needed rain, and how their plants suffered on a really hot day.

"I think this garden is very special to the children in all the age groups. Most of the children here are inner-city kids from the Bronx and had never tasted fresh vegetables before they grew their own. Very few have home gardens. Some of the children have had some limited gardening experience with a grandparent or in a classroom, but most have never tested vine-ripened tomatoes, raw snap beans, or fresh peas. No matter what the vegetables tasted like, the children loved them, even the bitter lettuce or carrots that were half an inch long. The fact that the children grew the vegetables themselves made the produce seem like candy. It's really a thrill to see the children taste their vegetables. They liked bringing the produce home, but they truly liked eating it better.

"I think children have a real affinity for and with plants," Debra concluded. "The plants are young growing things just like them, and they love the way they're tiny and cute like little pets. They get really involved. They love their own gardens, but they also loved the rainbow garden. We will definitely do it again, and I hope to make it larger with more vegetables and more colors next time. We'll also incorporate some of the unusual-colored vegetables into the children's individual gardens. Why should they grow only the routine colors?"

Debra, like most gardeners who work with people, knows that not just children, but all people who garden, learn certain lessons: in the garden, as in life, nothing is guaranteed, and the growing of a garden is not all up to you. We are dependent upon a lot of factors and are part of a greater cycle. Debra, like many of the children she teaches, grew up as "a total city kid." "When I was exposed to gardening, though, I fell in love with it completely. It gave life new meaning." Obviously, Debra enjoys spreading this love to "her" kids, and the rainbow garden gave her one more way to do it.

Recommended Rainbow Vegetables

There are hundreds of vegetables of unusual hues. For this list I chose varieties that were particularly bright and colorful, but I couldn't resist stretching the concept to include white vegetables too. In some cases the colorful vegetables will be enjoyed most in the kitchen. Blue potatoes and green radishes, for instance, grow underground and are not even visible in the garden. On the other hand, lavender or red eggplants will be enjoyed most in the garden, because in preparation the skin will be peeled off (if the eggplants are cooked with the skins on, they will discolor and will therefore add little color to the dishes you prepare).

Before we begin, a blanket apology is in order. In tracking down sources of unusual-colored vegetables in seed catalogs, I found that some varieties cropped up under a number of different names, because seed companies sometimes rename imported and, less frequently, heirloom varieties. Short of calling every seed company to make sure they haven't renamed anything, I have no way of knowing whether I've cited the same variety under two different names. Therefore, there may be some duplications on this list.

See Part Four, "An Encyclopedia of Superior Vegetables," or individual index entries for information on growing the vegetables listed. With a few exceptions, which are covered in another chapter or noted here, the varieties named have the same growing habits as their less colorful cousins. The numbers in parentheses after a variety name correspond with the numbers of the seed companies listed in the "Sources" section at the end of the chapter.

The vegetables in this list are grouped by color.

Red

AMARANTH   Amaranth leaves can be green, red, cream, or a combination of these colors. Red-colored varieties are 'Flaming Fountain' (5, 6), a leaf amaranth, and 'Burgundy' (6) and 'All Red' (6), both grain types. A tricolor variety—red, cream, and green—is 'Joseph's Coat' (5, 6).

How to prepare: To preserve the color best, select young, tender leaves and use raw in salads or as garnishes. All the amaranths may be cooked, although this will take some of their color, and may be used as a potherb.

BRUSSELS SPROUTS   'Rubine Red' (6) is a red Brussels sprout variety that produces clusters of miniature red cabbages.

How to prepare: Like red cabbage, if not cooked in water with salt, vinegar, or lemon juice, these sprouts will lose much of their color. Cook them al dente to keep them red.

CELERY   Red celery is more common in England than

it is here. 'Red' (6) has bronzy-colored green stalks until the frost brings out the redness. The stalks stay red after they are cooked. 'Giant Pink' (3) has pink stalks. You might need to string these varieties before serving them. If you blanch them in the garden (see the "French Gardens" chapter) they will be less stringy but much lighter in color.

How to prepare: Use raw or cooked in dishes where the pink color will add to the appearance.

CHARD   'Rhubarb' is a truly beautiful and rewarding chard, so vividly red that when the sun shines through the stalks they look like stained glass in the garden.

How to prepare: For the brightest color, use the stalks raw in salads or as a garnish. Prepare as you would any other chard for quiches and soups. You can even serve the leaves stuffed, as with cabbage. Some of the red color will bleed during cooking.

CHICORY (radicchio)   'Treviso' (1, 3, 4, 7), 'Rouge de Verone' (1, 3, 4, 7), 'Palla Rossa' (3), and 'Giulio' (3, 7) are red chicories. The first three become intensely wine red in cold weather. 'Giulio' can be planted in late spring or early summer and will color up in warm weather. For more information see the "Italian Gardens" chapter.

How to prepare: See the "Italian Gardens" chapter.

CORN   Both 'Strawberry' popcorn (2, 4, 6) and 'Bloody Butcher' grinding corn (6) are red-kerneled corns. 'Strawberry' popcorn has a small ear and deep-red kernels and is decorative for fall arrangements (good winter popping follows). 'Bloody Butcher' is an heirloom corn that makes very flavorful red-flecked cornbread.

How to prepare: Use as you would regular popcorns (as it pops white) or grinding corns. See the "Native American Gardens" chapter.

EGGPLANT   'Small Ruffled Red' (6) is a small, bright-red, bitter eggplant. Another red variety, 'Small Sweet Red' (6), is not bitter.

How to prepare: Eggplant is usually peeled before use, so the color is not evident in the final dish. The bitter red eggplant is used in Oriental sauces and a number of Cambodian and Thai dishes. The sweet red one is used as is regular eggplant.

KALE   'Coral Queen' (4) is a beautiful red-leafed variety of ornamental kale. When the temperature dips below 60 degrees the leaves turn a vibrant coral.

How to prepare: To keep its color best, use this kale raw in salads.

MUSTARD   The Japanese red mustards 'Giant Red' (3) and 'Osaka' (1, 6) are tangy, handsome mustard plants with crinkled, wine-red leaves. These are real showstoppers.

How to prepare: To keep the color, which dulls with cooking, use the leaves raw in sandwiches and salads.

OKRA   'Red' (1, 3, 5, 6) okra has red instead of green or white fruits. With its red stems and midribs and creamy yellow blossomns, this is a showy plant.

How to prepare: The red pods turn brown when cooked but keep their color when pickled. Use pickled and in marinades.

ORACH   'Red Orach' (4, 6) is a vibrant-red, leafy vegetable. In the garden this tall plant can brighten the back of a border.

How to prepare: Use raw in salads or cook as you would chard. The leaves will bleed and turn the cooking juices red.

PEPPERS   While most peppers eventually turn red as they ripen, 'Earliest Red Sweet' (8) ripens more quickly, so its color is more evident in the garden. Another variety that can be used the same way is 'Earlired' (6), which will ripen three crops in one season in Idaho and is one of the few peppers to turn red in the cool summers of the Northwest.

How to prepare: Ripe-red peppers are very sweet when ripe and are great raw or cooked.

POTATOES   'Blossom' (6) is a productive, red-fleshed potato whose plants produce large, petunialike flowers ranging from white to pink. 'Levitt's Pink' (2) is a pink- to red-fleshed potato. In my experience it isn't too productive in the garden but it's interesting to try.

How to prepare: Use as you would any other potato, but to feature the color, boil (do not overcook) and then slice and serve with a colorless dressing.

RADISHES   'Red Meat Chinese' (3) is a radish from China and is white to purple on the outside but bright-red inside.

How to prepare: Use raw to show off the color.

SCALLIONS   'Purplette' (6) is a red-skinned scallion with pinkish flesh.

How to prepare: Use as you would any scallions.

TURNIPS   'Scarlet Fall' (1) and 'Ohno Scarlet' (6) both have red skin and white flesh.

How to prepare: To show off their color, serve as babies raw with a dip.

Orange

BEETS   'Burpee's Golden' beet is a great vegetable with bright-yellow flesh and leaf midribs. But it is not as vigorous as most beet varieties, so sow seeds quite heavily and plant more than usual.

How to prepare: Use as you would red beets, but, because the color will not bleed, you can use them in dishes as you would carrots. To highlight the beets, serve them julienned with red ones or as baby beets. Note that pureed yellow beets sometimes oxidize, turning light brown. Other cooks report having used them to make yellow borscht with no browning problem.

PEPPERS   'Tequila Sunrise' (5, 6) is a small orange pepper that holds its fruits above the foliage and is beautiful in the garden. Most peppers go through a green stage and then turn orange on their way to red, but a few, such as 'Golden Bell' (5) and 'Tequila Sunrise', stay orange when ripe. Some gold peppers, such as 'Giant Szegedi' (8), start gold and never turn another color.

How to prepare: Use yellow peppers raw in combination with peppers of other colors. Rings or strips of different colors are beautiful together.

SQUASH   Most acorn squash are deep green, but 'Jersey Golden Acorn' (4, 5) is a flavorful, deep-orange acorn squash. The squash are yellow when young, but both the skin and flesh ripen to orange. Another unusual squash is an orange spaghetti squash, 'Orangetti' (4), which has orange skin and orange flesh.

How to prepare: Use young 'Jersey Golden Acorn' as baby yellow summer squash whole in a dip or braised and served as a side dish. Use the orange spaghetti squash mature for the best flavor; serve it as you would standard yellow spaghetti squash.

TOMATOES   'Golden Boy' (2, 5), 'Mandarin Yellow Cross' (1, 3), 'Golden Jubilee' (4), 'Persimmon' (6), and 'Goldie' (1) are large tomatoes ranging from gold to orange. 'Gold Nugget' (4) is a medium-size gold tomato. For cherry types of gold to orange, try

Wendy Krupnick holds a platter of rainbow vegetables ready for dipping, including purple peppers, yellow tomatoes, and blue potatoes.

'Ida-Gold' (6), 'Golden Pygmy' (3), and the tiny 'Currant' (6).

How to prepare: Serve raw to get the full benefit of the color. The gold-colored, large-fruited tomatoes are lovely sliced on the salad plate or on top of a fresh tart. Use the smaller ones in salads, with dips, or as hors d'oeuvres.

WATERMELON   Try 'Hybrid Pineapple' (2), a large, deep-green watermelon with sweet, golden flesh, and 'Sweet Siberian' (6), a watermelon with apricot-colored flesh.

How to prepare: Serve in slices, perhaps combined on a serving plate with red-, yellow-, and white-fleshed slices.

Yellow

BEANS (wax)   There are many yellow wax bean varieties, including the old favorite 'Pencil Pod Black Wax' and the more unusual yellow romano 'Merviglia de Venezia' (3).

How to prepare: Serve wax beans as you would any snap bean. Try them in a three-bean salad garnished with raw purple beans.

CUCUMBERS   'Lemon' is a popular round, light-yellow cucumber that is readily available. For best eating, do not let the cucumber get too yellow.

How to prepare: Use slices raw.

PEAS   'Golden Sweet' (6) is a beautiful yellow-podded pea.

How to prepare: Use in the pod on a dip platter with the green ones.

PEPPERS   'Gypsy' (2, 5), 'Sweet Pickle' (5, 6), 'Yellow Wax Hungarian' (2, 4, 5), and 'Yellow Cheese' (6, 8) are all sweet peppers that remain yellow for a long while before eventually turning orange or red.

How to prepare: Use raw or cooked, particularly with red, green, and gold peppers.

POTATOES   'Yellow Finnish' (4, 6), 'Lady Finger' (2), and 'Bintje' (6) are waxy, yellow-fleshed potatoes.

How to prepare: Some people consider these creamy potatoes "prebuttered" because they are so rich and yellow inside. They are at their best boiled.

SQUASH   'Sunburst' (3, 4, 5) and 'Yellow Scallop' (6) pattypans and 'Gold Rush' (2, 5) and 'Golden' (6) zucchinis are all bright-yellow squash that grow on large, bushy plants.

How to prepare: Use these yellow squash for a barbecue (see the recipe in the cooking section), raw in salads, with dips, stuffed with colorful ingredients, and in cooked dishes with green and white squashes for contrast. They are also great used as baby squash with their flowers left on and as a side dish.

TOMATOES   'Yellow Pear' (1, 3, 6), 'Ponderosa Yellow' (6), and 'Hybrid Lemon Boy' (2, 4) are tomatoes that are truly yellow rather than the more common golden tomatoes listed above under "Orange."

How to prepare: Use the way golden tomatoes, above, are used.

WATERMELON   'Tendersweet' (2), 'Gold Baby' (1), 'Golden Midget' (6, 9), 'Moon and Stars' (yellow fleshed) (6), and 'Yellow Baby' (3, 5) all have sweet, yellow flesh.

How to prepare: Serve sliced with red, orange, and white watermelon slices for a colorful presentation.

Green

RADISHES   'Martian' (8) is a white-fleshed radish with green shoulders; 'Green Meat Radish' (3) is the opposite—white on the outside with green flesh.

How to prepare: Use the green-fleshed radish sliced to appreciate the color contrast.

TOMATOES   'Evergreen' (1, 6) is a medium-size tomato; 'Green Grape' (3, 6) is a large, green cherry tomato. Both stay green when juicy and ripe.

How to prepare: Use as you would the other colored tomatoes listed above.

Blue

CORN   'Hopi Blue' (6) and 'Blue Tortilla' (3) are old Native American varieties famous for making tasty, light-blue to greenish cornbread and chips. Also available from Seeds Blum is a sweet corn called 'Sweet Baby Blue' (6) that is blue in the milk stage. See the "Native American Gardens" chapter for more varieties.

How to prepare: To intensify the blue color of blue grinding corns, the Hopis added culinary ashes before cooking. See the "Native American Gardens" chapter for more information. Most of the colored varieties of corn will be white to cream colored in the milk stage and will only turn blue when ripe for storing.

POTATOES   'All Blue' (2, 6) potatoes are deep-purple blue inside and out. The ones I've grown from Seeds Blum are much darker than those I obtained from Gurney.

How to prepare: To feature the color of these potatoes, boil (but don't overcook) them. Use colorless dressings in your potato salads. Also try lavender mashed potatoes and vichyssoise.

Indigo and Violet

ARTICHOKES   'Violetto' (1) and 'Purple Sicilian' (3) are artichoke varieties that produce bronzy-purple buds.

I met Doug Gosling a number of years ago while visiting the Farallones Institute, a nonprofit self-sufficiency demonstration community in Occidental, California. I was there for a gardening workshop and had wandered down to the kitchen for a cold drink when I found Doug preparing the evening meal—an extravaganza of homemade breads, colorful salads, and stir-fries from the garden with fresh sugar snap peas. Doug has been the Farallones garden manager for about five years; he's responsible for providing vegetables for the institute, selling specialty produce to area restaurants, and preparing meals for special events. Doug had started cooking in Michigan while teaching a course in wild edible plants. To make the course more interesting, he used wild edibles to create dishes for his students, and in the process, he got hooked on cooking.

Since our first meeting and that fabulous meal, Doug and I have spent hours discussing our favorite subjects: gardening and cooking. On one occasion, because he's one of the few chefs I know who is particularly interested in unusual-colored vegetables, I asked him which unusual vegetables he likes best and how he prepares them.

"Tomatoes," he said. "They're definitely on my list of favorites. For restaurants and specialty grocery stores, I market a basket of six miniature varieties that I call the Toy Box Mix. The baskets are a big hit with our customers. I fill them with oblong 'Yellow Pear' and 'Red Pear' tomatoes; round 'Yellow Cherry', 'Red Cherry', and 'Yellow Plum' tomatoes; and orange pea-size 'Currant' tomatoes." Doug is also partial to large 'White Beauty' tomatoes, which are a beautiful cream color and have a strong tart flavor. He likes to use orange tomatoes such as 'Persimmon', 'Goldie', and 'Mandarin Cross', and yellow tomatoes such as 'Lemon Boy Hybrid'. Doug slices large tomatoes for salads and open-faced sandwiches, but he's most famous for his tomato tart. To

Doug Gosling

make the tart, he slices different-colored tomatoes and arranges them in patterns to feature their colors on top of a savory pie.

Doug is also intrigued by blue potatoes and violet peppers. He got a chuckle when I told him about my lavender vichyssoise and my red, white, and blue potato salad. Because violet peppers turn green when you cook them, though, both he and I have only been able to feature their color by serving them raw in salads and on dip platters.

Doug's favorite use of colorful vegetables is in arranging salad greens. "The colorful 'greens' that come to mind first are deep red orach, coral-colored ornamental kale, and Oriental red mustard," he says. "All are beautiful used raw. 'Red Orach' is wonderful used in salads and for garnishing—and it keeps its color when cooked, so it's also good as a potherb. I make omelettes with it, too—pale yellow omelettes—and when you bite into them you see the deep, bright maroon color of the orach. I enjoy the ornamental kales, too—like purple, ruffled-edged 'Ragged Jack'—and the Japanese red mustards, and I feature them as baby greens in salads. I like the red mustards in omelettes, too, or stir-fried. And all these greens add life and color to winter salads. For color in summer salads, I enjoy the young leaves of red and tricolored [red, yellow, and green] amaranths. They're also good as cooked vegetables.

"For visual impact, I think the 'Dragon Longerie' snap beans are probably among the most exciting things we grew this year. They're an unusual flavorful bean available from Pine Tree Seeds—yellow, flat-podded beans with purple lacelike stripes. I especially like them raw, cut on the diagonal in salads. I also enjoy purple snap beans, which I use raw because they turn green when boiled."

Like me, Doug has been fascinated by blue corn for many years. The Farallones gardeners have grown 'Hopi Blue' corn for about ten years and, in fact, gave me my first blue corn seeds so I could grow it. Doug seems to find more uses for it every year; he makes 'Hopi Blue' French bread that retains its bluish-purple color when baked, traditional blue cornbread, blue tortillas, and blue tortilla chips. Lately, he's been adding 'Hopi Blue' cornmeal to pie crusts; he finds that combining it with white flour makes a nice bluish-gray crust with a nutty crunch.

I'm sure the next time I talk with Doug, he'll have tried some new vegetables. We'll probably jabber on about my latest find of purple carrots or a new way he's cooked some whimsical vegetable. We've only begun to scratch the surface of cooking with colorful garden vegetables, but when more cooks and gardeners get hooked, the artistry will come out in us all.

How to prepare: Feature their color by using them raw. See the "Italian Gardens" chapter for more information.

BASIL 'Opal' (3, 4, 7) and 'Purple Ruffles' (4, 5) are basils that have rich mahogany-colored leaves.

How to prepare: Use these basils raw in salads, sandwiches, and as a garnish. If you puree or dice them—for instance, for pesto—they will turn brown.

BEANS 'Royal Burgundy' bush, 'Cherokee' pole (6), and 'Royalty' bush (3) are deep-purple string beans that turn green when you cook them. 'Purple Yard-Long' (6), one of the Oriental long-bean varieties, stays purple even after it is cooked.

How to prepare: To take advantage of the deep purple of 'Royalty' and 'Royal Burgundy', serve the young beans raw in a dip or salad. Cooking, or even marinating them in vinegar or lemon juice, will turn them green. Use 'Purple Yard-Long' in colorful three-bean salads and cooked in soups or as a side dish.

BROCCOLI 'Purple Sprouting' (3, 6), 'Christmas Purple Sprouting' (9), and 'King Purple' (1) are all purple broccolis.

How to prepare: These purple broccolis mostly turn green when you cook them. To preserve their color, use them raw in salads and with dips.

CARROTS 'Afghanistan' (6), a carrot that is purple on the outside and yellow inside, has a mild carrot flavor.

How to prepare: Use raw to see the unusual colors.

CAULIFLOWER 'Violet' (3, 6), 'Purple Giant' (6), and 'Purple Cape' (9) all range from bronze to purple.

How to prepare: These cauliflower varieties turn light green when you cook them. For best color, use raw in salads and in dips.

EGGPLANT Numerous eggplant varieties fall into the lavender-to-rose range, including 'Rosa Bianco' (3, 6), which is round to almost heart-shaped and lavender to white; 'Black Prince' (9), deep-lavender and oval-shaped; and 'Pink Bride' (1) and 'Asian Bride' (3), virtually identical varieties that have long, thin, lavender-and-white fruits.

How to prepare: To feature the color of 'Rosa Bianco', use it as a hollowed-out shell for dips and eggplant caviar. Brush the inside with lemon juice so the flesh won't turn brown. Grill these lavender eggplants on a barbecue or stuff them and cook. Cooking will reduce the color somewhat.

KOHLRABI 'Early Purple Vienna' (8), 'Purple Vienna' (6), 'Purple Danube' (3), and 'Rapid' (5) are beautiful pink to purple kohlrabi varieties.

How to prepare: To appreciate the color, use them young and raw in dips and salads.

PAC CHOI 'Purple Pac Choy' (6) is a pac choi with purple stems and leaf veins.

How to prepare: To take full advantage of the color, use the flower shoots with their purple stems raw.

PEAS 'Blue Podded' (6) is a striking pea that produces purple pods and lavender blossoms.

How to prepare: While this is usually a shelling pea used for a creamy soup, the pods are edible too if harvested very young. Use pods in salads or on a dip platter.

PEPPERS 'Violetta' (3), 'Lorelei' (7), 'Pretty Purple Pepper' (1), and 'Purple Bell' (5, 8) are sweet peppers that are purple-black when small but eventually ripen to red. 'Aurora' (6) is a striking small, bright-lavender hot pepper.

How to prepare: These peppers turn green when cooked, so to keep the color serve raw. The sweet ones make beautiful arrangements on a dip tray or in salads.

RADISHES　'Easter Egg' (2, 4, 5) produces a mixture of purple, lavender, pink, and white radishes. 'Purple Plum' (2) is a mild, tender, deep-purple, round radish. All are white inside.

How to prepare: Serve these radishes sliced raw in salads, as garnishes, or on hors d'oeuvre platters.

SWEET POTATOES　'Burgundy' (6) is a sweet potato with deep-purple flesh. Its vibrant color does not fade in cooking.

How to prepare: Feature the deep-purple potatoes as you would the blue ones. Boil or bake them and serve them as they are or use them in casseroles. Or even make a purple pie!

WATERMELON　'Early Arizona' (6) has purple flesh.

How to prepare: Use sliced or in fruit salads with other colored watermelons.

White

BEETS　'Albino' (6, 8, 9) is sweet and white; 'Chioggia' (3, 6) is red outside but white with red rings inside. These varieties of beets will not bleed and discolor the other ingredients in a cooked dish.

How to prepare: Use in salads, cooked or raw, or cooked in soups and stews.

CARROTS　'White Belgian' (4, 6) is a white carrot variety. If grown in cool weather these carrots have a sweet, intensely carroty flavor. In my experience, if you grow them in hot weather they get too strong.

How to prepare: Serve them raw or cooked as you would any carrots and combine with the red and orange ones julienned on a plate or in a salad.

EGGPLANT　Some of the more primitive forms of eggplant were white; hence the name eggplant. White-skinned varieties available today are 'White Egg' (1, 6), 'White Beauty' (6), and 'Long White Sword' (6).

How to prepare: Use unpeeled in the same way you would use the lavender ones described above.

KALE　(ornamental) 'Christmas Fringed White Flowering' (1) and 'White Frizzy Hybrid' (5) are beautiful green kales with decorative white fringes or centers. They are classified here as white because they appear white in the garden.

How to prepare: Use raw in salads and as a garnish.

PEPPERS　'Albino' (6), 'Bullnose' (6), and 'Alwin' (3) are creamy-white peppers that eventually turn orange when ripe.

How to prepare: Use sliced or ringed with peppers of other colors on a dip tray, as a garnish, or in salads.

SQUASH　'Kuta' (5) is a winter squash that turns green when mature but is often eaten in its immature stage when it is almost white.

How to prepare: Use both raw or cooked as you would any summer squash.

TOMATOES　'White Beauty' (1, 6) is a large, white prolific tomato.

How to prepare: Use with tomatoes of other colors on a salad plate.

WATERMELON　'Cream of Saskatchewan' (6) has creamy-white flesh and 'Crystal' (6) has extremely white flesh.

How to prepare: Serve with slices of watermelon of other colors.

ZUCCHINI　'Greyzini' (8) and 'White Lebanese Zucchini' (3) are very light-green, almost white squash.

How to prepare: Use raw in salads or on the grill for a barbecue.

Cooking from the Rainbow Garden

It's great fun to cook with rainbow vegetables. They add their vibrant colors to everyday meals and their unusual hues lift any dish out of the routine. A plate of sliced red, orange, and yellow tomatoes becomes an artistic creation, and blue cornbread is guaranteed to give pleasure through both the tastebuds and the eyes. Of course, if you really want to go beyond the pale, mash up some 'All Blue' potatoes for lavender mashed potatoes!

As in the garden, colored vegetables bring certain benefits to the kitchen besides novelty and eye

OPPOSITE: *Using rainbow-colored vegetables in cooking can be not only delicious, but visually dramatic. Pictured here are red, white, and blue potato salad; a fresh tomato tart made with orange, gold, and red tomato slices; and a plate of brilliantly colored bell pepper rings.*

appeal. Yellow beets, for instance, add their sweetness to stir-fries, soups, and stews without discoloring broccoli and snow peas as red beets do. Purple string beans turn green when boiled for two minutes, a built-in timer that shows you when they are properly blanched for freezing. And some of the yellow tomato varieties are low in acid, which means that people unable to tolerate most red tomatoes can enjoy them.

Still, the most obvious advantage of the colorful varieties is their appearance. To make the most of these vegetables, take a cue from chefs interested in nouvelle cuisine, which emphasizes fresh produce. These cooks use the rainbow-colored vegetables as paints with which to highlight their creations. Sautéed whole baby vegetables featuring miniature yellow acorn squashes or golden beets, or salads with red chicory (radicchio), salad Savoy (ornamental kale), multicolored tomatoes, and edible flowers are now de rigueur with these chefs.

Before you start cooking with these colorful vegetables, be aware that some of them—such as red okra, red basil, purple snap beans, purple artichokes, some varieties of red celery, and purple cauliflowers—lose their color when cooked at all. So if the color is what you want to emphasize, these varieties are best served raw or, in the case of the okra, pickled. Others only partially lose their color when cooked— purple broccoli, red chard, red celery, and the ornamental kales are examples. In all cases, the longer you cook a vegetable—even the standard green snap bean or asparagus—the more color it will lose. So be careful not to overcook them, and whenever possible serve them al dente. Some of the colored vegetables—such as some of the radish, kohlrabi, and cucumber varieties—will lose all their color if peeled, so to enjoy the color, serve them with the skins on.

As with many vegetables, raw artichokes, carrots, beets, and all the potatoes, if peeled, chopped, or grated and thus exposed to the air, will turn brown within a few minutes. So if you are using these vegetables raw, keep them in water with some added lemon juice or vinegar to prevent discoloring. If you are using artichokes as a chiffonade, as recommended in the "Italian Gardens" chapter, prepare them at the very last minute and immediately sprinkle them with lemon juice. Another point to remember when cooking with colorful vegetables is not to muddy the colors with dark sauces or opaque dressings. Jim Westerfelt, chef at the Ritz in Schenectady, New York, uses a veal stock base to make a light sauce for colorful baby vegetables served as a side dish. I have found a chicken stock does well too, and for a colorful potato salad I use a vinaigrette instead of mayonnaise.

Colorful vegetables can be used in many creative ways to add nutrition and excitement to your table fare. For example, think about all the ways of dressing a plate besides using the standard parsley. For a summer garnish, try using a cluster of yellow and red cherry tomatoes; strips of violet, yellow, and red peppers; or a small slice of yellow watermelon along with some strawberries. Spring garnishes might include a few blue-podded peas, some baby lettuce leaves interspersed with red orach leaves, or some frilly leaves of red and green kale.

The many-hued vegetables make exciting appetizers too. Julienned bell peppers of all colors, red scallions, baby purple snap beans, red celery stalks, baby red turnips, and bright-yellow zucchini slices make a dip platter particularly festive. To carry the theme even further you might fill colorful bell peppers and stuffing tomatoes with the dips. Salads, too, lend themselves to the multicolor approach. Use red orach, ornamental kale, lavender radishes, and any of the vegetables mentioned above arranged on a plate to show off the many colors or added to a conventional tossed salad.

The colorful vegetables need not be limited to auxiliary status; they can also become the focal point of the meal. Try charcoal-barbecuing them, for example. Slices of golden zucchini and lavender eggplant, whole small red onions, and halved yellow, orange, and red peppers look as beautiful on the grill as on the plate. And grilling is one of the all-time tastiest ways of preparing vegetables. You'll find a recipe for grilling vegetables in this section.

The brightly colored vegetables should inspire your own creations as perhaps no other produce has. Here's a chance to treat your garden as an artist's palette. Make a fruit salad with red and yellow watermelons, make a multicolored quiche, or even make an outrageous purple sweet potato pie (yes, it really comes out purple!). I myself am planning to make a tricolored cornbread from my red, blue, and yellow grinding corns. One section of the loaf will be pink, one light blue, and the other yellow. Maybe I'll even use one of those cake pans with compartments to separate the batters to make checkerboard cornbread. With a rainbow garden, the sky's the limit.

DOUG'S TOMATO TART

Doug Gosling, garden manager and chef extraordinaire at the Farallones Institute in Occidental, California, is famous for his garden cooking. His tomato tart not only shows off different-colored tomatoes beautifully but is delicious as well. To quote Doug precisely: "Yummo!"

The full-page photograph in this section shows a variation on Doug's lovely cooked tart that uses cream cheese and is not cooked. For that variation we blended softened cream cheese with some fresh basil and cream, spread it in the cooked pie shell (recipe below), and arranged tomato slices that had been drained on paper towels over the filling. We then glazed the tart lightly with garlic-flavored olive oil.

SERVES 8 AS AN APPETIZER.

Pastry Crust

> 1½ cups unbleached white flour
> ½ cup finely ground toasted almonds
> 1 tablespoon brown sugar
> Pinch of salt
> ⅔ cup sweet butter
> 10-inch tart pan

Preheat oven to 450°.

Mix dry ingredients together throughly. Cut in butter until mixture resembles coarse sand. Work dough into a ball, wrap in waxed paper, and refrigerate for at least one hour.

Press pastry into tart pan until it is even and smooth (this pastry is too flaky to roll out) and prick it with a fork. Spread a layer of foil over crust and fill it with dry beans to keep the sides from slipping down. Bake at 450° for 10 minutes; reduce heat to 350° and bake an additional 15 minutes or until crust is golden brown. Set aside and cool. Turn oven up to 375° to preheat for tart.

Filling

> 9 to 12 medium-size rainbow-colored
>   tomatoes (a selection of yellow, orange,
>   pink, red, and white, if you have them)
> 1 cup virgin olive oil
> 3 cloves crushed garlic (or to taste)
> ½ bunch chopped parsley
> 3 tablespoons chopped fresh oregano or basil

> Freshly ground black pepper to taste
> ¼ pound mushrooms, sliced
> ½ sweet red onion, chopped
> 2 tablespoons butter
> 2 tablespoons Dijon mustard
> 5 tablespoons grated Parmesan cheese
> 3 tablespoons grated Swiss cheese

Cut tomatoes into thin slices and spread into a straight-sided bowl. Marinate for at least one hour in olive oil, garlic, parsley, oregano or basil, and pepper.

Sauté mushrooms and onions lightly in butter and set aside.

With pastry brush, paint baked crust with mustard. Scatter mushrooms and onions on crust; then sprinkle with grated Parmesan cheese. Drain tomato slices and arrange in a one-layered circular pattern over Parmesan. Sprinkle with grated Swiss cheese. Bake in a 375° oven until cheese just melts, about five minutes. Serve at room temperature.

LAVENDER VICHYSSOISE

Vichyssoise is an elegant but easy first course. Make it with blue potatoes and you'll really delight your guests. To get the lavender effect, you need to use the very deep purple varieties rather than the medium- or light-blue potatoes carried by some seed companies. The lighter-colored ones will give you a gray, not lavender, soup. The lavender vichyssoise, garnished with chives and chive florets, looks lovely in glass bowls.

SERVES 6.

> 2 tablespoons butter
> 3 cups sliced white part of leeks, preferred, or
>   2 cups chopped white onions
> 3 cups chopped deep-blue potatoes
> 3 cups chicken broth
> 1 cup half-and-half
> Salt and pepper to taste
> Dash of nutmeg
> Fresh chives and their flowers, if available, for
>   garnish

In a large saucepan, melt butter and sauté leeks or onions over medium heat to soften but do not brown. Add potatoes and broth; cover and simmer until potatoes are tender, 15 to 20 minutes. Add half-and-half and seasonings and puree in a blender or food processor. Chill and serve cold, garnished with chives and chive flowers (separate florets and sprinkle on soup).

SCALLOPS WITH RED CELERY IN A VINAIGRETTE SAUCE

We have adapted this recipe from *The Victory Garden Cookbook*, by Marian Morash, to feature the lovely 'Red' celery. This is the recipe for one of Marian's favorite appetizers; she likes the pleasant way the celery's crispness contrasts with the soft texture of fresh poached scallops.

SERVES 4.

> 1 lemon
> 1 pound baby sea scallops (or large scallops cut into halves or thirds)
> 1½ cups finely chopped 'Red' celery, stems and leaves (string celery if necessary)
> Vinaigrette made with lemon juice (see "Gourmet Salad Gardens" chapter)

Bring a saucepan of salted water (enough to cover scallops) to a boil and squeeze in juice of ½ lemon. Pull off small hard nuggets on sides of scallops; their rubbery texture is unpleasant to eat. Drop scallops into boiling water, lower heat to a simmer, and poach

Beautiful vegetables make a barbecue even more festive.

for 2 to 3 minutes. Drain. Coat scallops with juice from remaining lemon half. Before serving, toss scallops with celery and leaves and vinaigrette. Serve on red and green lettuce, endive, or chicory leaves.

BARBECUED VEGETABLES

One of the tastiest ways to prepare summer vegetables is a quick and easy adaptation of the ever-popular barbecue. Although meat, fish, or poultry can be a nice complement, the vegetables are so good cooked this way one is tempted to dispense with the rest.

If you are limited by the size of your grill you may have to do a couple of batches. Also consider that the eggplant needs a slightly longer cooking time than the squash and onions, and that the peppers need the least cooking time.

SERVES 4.

> 1 cup olive oil
> 2 cloves garlic, crushed
> ¼ cup minced fresh basil or 1 tablespoon minced fresh rosemary
> 2 medium to large eggplants, cut into ½-inch-thick slices
> 2 to 4 variously colored summer squash, depending on their size (if large, slice diagonally in ½-inch-thick slices; if small, slice lengthwise in halves or leave whole)
> 4 small red onions, whole, or 1 large onion, quartered
> 2 to 4 sweet red or yellow peppers, halved and seeded

In a jar or small bowl, mix oil, garlic, and herbs and let stand at least 2 hours (refrigerate if left to stand much longer). Place vegetable slices on a cookie sheet and brush with seasoned oil. Prepare barbecue, and when coals are ready spread them evenly and place vegetables oiled-side down on grill. Brush top sides of vegetables with oil and turn when first side is just starting to brown. Cooking time will vary in accordance with heat, distance from coals, and size and density of vegetables. Over medium coals, expect average cooking time to be approximately 4 minutes on the first side and 3 minutes on the second side, but watch carefully. Cook until just tender; if overcooked, vegetables will fall apart.

GOLDEN BEETS AND BROCCOLI STIR-FRY

SERVES 4 TO 6.

3 tablespoons vegetable oil, of which 1
  tablespoon may be sesame oil
1 cup golden beets in ¼-inch slices
2 tablespoons minced ginger
1 tablespoon minced fresh hot pepper or 1
  teaspoon dried hot pepper, to taste
  (optional)
2 cloves garlic, minced
½ medium onion, sliced
3 cups green broccoli, stems peeled and cut in
  ¼-inch by 1½-inch slices and flowers
  separated to bite size
1 cup diced firm tofu or cooked chicken,
  shrimp, or meat (optional)
2 tablespoons rice vinegar
3 tablespoons sherry or sweet sake
½ cup toasted whole cashews
Soy sauce, oyster sauce, or hoisin sauce (a
  sweet soy-based sauce) to taste

Heat oil in wok or skillet on medium to medium-
high heat. Add beets, ginger, and hot pepper (if used),
and cook 1 minute. Add garlic, onion, and broccoli
stems; cook and stir about 3 minutes. Stir in broccoli
flowers and tofu or meat, if used; cover for 1 minute
and then stir and add vinegar and sherry or sake.
Cover for 2 minutes. When vegetables are crisp-tender,
stir in cashews and seasoning sauces and serve over
rice.

STUFFED 'STRIPED CAVERN' TOMATOES OR 'SUNBURST PATTYPAN' SQUASH

Both the tomato and squash versions of this recipe
are favorites from the midsummer garden. Not only
are the varieties called for especially tasty and prolific, but they are the perfect size for stuffing and
serving as individual portions. 'Striped Cavern'
tomatoes are especially well suited for stuffing, as
they are already partly hollow, stand well, and are
very flavorful. The pretty yellow stripes on the toma-

toes and the vivid golden glow of the squash make
these vegetables stars of the rainbow garden. Of
course, you could use any other variety of large tomato
or summer squash of the appropriate size.

This recipe details the tomato version. To use
squash instead, cut off the top ½ inch of the stem
end and hollow out each squash with a spoon, leaving a ¼- to ½-inch-thick shell. Drop squash shells
into boiling water for about 3 minutes; then drain
and cool upside down on a rack until ready to fill.
Use the removed squash instead of zucchini in recipe.

SERVES 4 AS A MAIN COURSE, 8 AS A SIDE DISH.

1 medium onion, diced
6 tablespoons olive oil
4 cloves garlic, minced
1 small zucchini, grated
8 medium to large 'Striped Cavern' tomatoes
  or 'Sunburst Pattypan' squash
1 or 2 eggs
2 cups fresh bread crumbs
½ cup each grated Monterey Jack and
  Parmesan cheese
¼ cup each finely chopped fresh parsley and
  basil
½ 'Anaheim' pepper, roasted, peeled, and
  diced, or ½ small can diced green chili
  peppers, or a little fresh hot pepper,
  minced

Preheat oven to 350°.

In a nonstick pan on medium heat, sauté onion
in oil about 4 minutes. Add garlic and zucchini and
continue to cook, stirring occasionally, until onion
is transparent and zucchini tender but not mushy.
Remove from heat and set aside to cool while you
prepare tomatoes.

Cut just enough of the tops off the tomatoes to
allow you to remove the insides carefully using a
small paring knife and a spoon. Drain and set aside.

Beat eggs and add with remaining ingredients
to onion mixture in pan, reserving about three tablespoons Parmesan cheese to garnish tops. Mix well
and spoon into tomatoes, pressing in very gently.
Top with remaining Parmesan and place in shallow,
flat baking dish with about ⅓ inch of water in it.
Cover loosely with a hood of aluminum foil and bake
for about 20 minutes. Tomatoes should be tender but
not disintegrating. Uncover and brown tops slightly
under the broiler, if desired.

CONFETTI BEAN SALAD

This recipe, from the Shepherd's Garden Seeds catalog, features snap beans of three different colors. The purple ones turn green when cooked or even marinated, so I add them raw just before serving.

SERVES 4.

> 6 small green onions, finely chopped
> 2 tablespoons vinegar, tarragon preferred
> 1/2 teaspoon salt
> 2 teaspoons Dijon mustard
> 1/3 cup oil
> 1 cup each of yellow and green beans, cut into
>   1- to 2-inch lengths and cooked according
>   to blanched green beans (recipe below)
> 1 cup young, raw, purple beans, cut as above
> Chopped parsley or chives for garnish

Whisk together onions, vinegar, salt, and mustard; add oil and whisk to blend well. Let dressing stand until ready to use. *Just* before serving, put all beans in a serving bowl, stir dressing, and pour it over beans. Toss to blend and sprinkle with chives or parsley.

BLANCHED GREEN BEANS

Renée Shepherd shares a restaurant technique for keeping fresh beans bright green, tender, and flavorful.

Boil plenty of water in a large pot with 1 to 2 tablespoons of salt. (The salt sets the green color and is rinsed away by the cold running water.) Drop in fresh-picked beans and boil until just tender-crisp, 2 to 5 minutes. Drain beans in a colander and cool immediately under cold running water. Use in salads or reheat with butter or other combinations.

RED AND GREEN CHRISTMAS BRUSSELS SPROUTS

This recipe is similar to the one for Brussels sprouts in the "Heirloom Gardens" chapter. Blanching is a good method of cooking sprouts, and their flavor goes well with nuts. Salt and lemon juice or vinegar are added to the blanching water here to set the colors, and chestnuts are a special Christmas-time treat.

SERVES 8.

> 1 pound (about 3 cups) each green and
>   'Rubine Red' Brussels sprouts
> 3 cups water
> 2 tablespoons lemon juice or vinegar
> 1 teaspoon salt
> 4 tablespoons butter
> 1 1/2 to 2 cups roasted and peeled chestnuts
> 1/2 cup chicken or veal stock

Cut a small x in the bottom of each sprout for even cooking. Boil water with lemon juice or vinegar and salt in a 3-quart saucepan. Add green sprouts, cover, and boil for 3 to 5 minutes. Scoop sprouts out of water with a sieve or slotted spoon and plunge into an ice-water bath for 1 minute; then remove. Add 'Rubine Red' sprouts to boiling water and cook the same way. In a skillet or large pot, melt butter, add chestnuts and stock, cover, and simmer for 3 minutes. Add cooked sprouts and simmer uncovered until sprouts are heated through and liquid reduced to a light glaze. Pour (or arrange) into a warmed serving bowl and serve immediately.

Sources

Seed Companies

1. Glecker's Seedmen
   Metamora, OH 43540
   This seed company prides itself on its unusual varieties of vegetables, including numerous colorful ones.

2. Gurney Seed & Nursery Company
   Yankton, SD 57079
   Gurney's large general seed catalog lists flowers and unusual vegetables.

3. Le Marché
   Seeds International
   P.O. Box 190
   Dixon, CA 95620
   This seed company specializes in outstanding vegetables from all over the world. The firm carries numerous unusual-colored varieties. Catalog: $2.00.

4. Nichols Garden Nursery.
   1190 North Pacific Highway
   Albany, OR 97321

This nursery carries many vegetable varieties of unusual colors.

5. Park Seed Company
   Cokesbury Road
   Greenwood, SC 29647
   This large seed company offers a wide selection of different-colored vegetables.

6. Seeds Blum
   Idaho City Stage
   Boise, ID 83706
   Probably more than any other seed company, Seeds Blum is interested in unusual-colored vegetables.Catalog: $2.00.

7. Shepherd's Garden Seeds
   7389 West Zayante Road
   Felton, CA 95018
   This seed company carries many European varieties, some of unusual colors. Catalog: $1.00.

8. Stokes Seeds, Inc.
   P.O. Box 548
   Buffalo, NY 14240
   One of the largest seed companies in this country, Stokes carries a number of unusual vegetables.

9. Thompson & Morgan, Inc.
   P.O. Box 1308
   Jackson, NJ 08527

This English seed company carries many unusual varieties of vegetables.

Books

Hobhouse, Penelope. *Color in Your Garden*. Boston: Little, Brown, 1985.
   This magnificent book is filled with ideas on using color in your garden. It focuses on ornamental plants, not vegetables, but the concepts are useful if you are trying to combine flowers with your colorful vegetables.

Skelsey, Alice, and Gloria Huckaby. *Growing Up Green*. New York: Workman, 1973.
   This book is a must for parents who want to help their children enjoy the garden. It is more than a how-to; its tone is so warm and human it makes the experiences come alive.

Sunset Books and *Sunset* magazine editors. *The Best of Sunset*. Menlo Park, Calif.: Lane Publishing, 1987.
   This cookbook is full of marvelous recipes, and quite a few can be used with the unusual-colored vegetables.

Spa Gardens

I WAS HEADING FOR an afternoon at the Golden Door health spa in Escondido, California. I passed through the beautiful Oriental-style gates, drove around a Japanese garden, passed the famous shining golden doors, and parked my car. Once inside the office, I was welcomed and given a tour. Most people come here for a delicious week of revitalization, but I had come to see the spa's beautiful gardens. My guide led me past a huge bank of day lilies in bloom and up to a vegetable/flower garden that must have covered more than three acres. There I met the garden manager, Serena Wyatt. She was harvesting the frilliest of lettuces, surrounded by a gourmet cook's fantasy of vegetables: baby carrots and golden beets; baskets of plump, young snap peas; and huge heads of 'Romanesco' broccoli. Serena and I strolled around the garden and talked for a while, comparing variety information, and then she took me up to the kitchen to meet the chef. Afterward, we sat down to discuss the possibility of Serena growing a demonstration spa garden for this book. I wanted to include a garden that would focus exclusively on the nutritive value of vegetables. I knew from years of cursory reading that vegetables were healthful—didn't everyone know that?—but now I meant to examine the subject

OPPOSITE: *Healthful vegetables such as 'Ruby' chard, asparagus, and baby lettuces are emphasized at health spas and in spa cooking.*

in detail, with the particulars firmly rooted in the ground, so to speak.

As we conversed, people around us were busy preparing meals. They set large, crinkled, red lettuce leaves on edge and filled them with baby greens, fancy mushrooms, and flower petals. They prepared scallops for a leek sauce and poured frothy fruit drinks into chilled crystal glasses. As I was leaving the kitchen, the nutritionist, Linny Largent, was helping plan the menu for the next day. The careful attention going into the activity at hand seemed to confirm my initial hunch: a spa garden at the Golden Door would be the perfect vehicle for conveying the new look of nutrition to my readers.

The Golden Door offered a startling contrast to the way I learned nutrition and healthful eating. I still remember Miss Bryant, my eighth-grade home economics teacher. From her, my adolescent classmates and I learned to make, and unfortunately had to eat, creamed spinach, chipped beef on toast, and sunshine eggs (boiled eggs with a cream sauce). Miss Bryant never ate the stuff, as none of us failed to notice. She simply sat her paunchy self down at her desk and held forth on vitamins and food groups while we forced down the results of our efforts. The spa food at the Golden Door was the perfect antidote to Miss Bryant's killjoy approach to nutrition.

Healthful eating is not a new concept. In order to survive, all civilizations have had to determine which of the available foods give health to the populace. But time and higher standards of living seem to have yielded a number of questionable food practices, ones that now are being vigorously reexamined. It is an apparent trend that modern civilizations come to treat the feast foods of their ancestors as daily fare. As a result, high levels of fat, sodium, and protein plus low levels of fiber, complex carbohydrates, and vegetables have come to characterize modern diets. Though good nutrition has been highly valued for many years, most of us remain enamored of the calorific "goodies" all around us, particularly when faced with the "thou-shalts and thou-shalt-nots" of the world's Miss Bryants.

But over the last fifty years, changes, especially in the American approach to food, have become evident. In the sixties, when habits of every sort were broken, the steak, French fries, and overcooked peas and carrots of the forties and fifties began to fall out of favor. What emerged in their place as the nutritionist's diet of choice was a healthful but somewhat

somber set of foods centering on yogurt, sprouts, granola, and brown rice. While a definite improvement, healthwise, this approach failed to capture the imagination of the general public. A more joyful and elegant approach was needed that stressed flavor as well as nutrition. Enter spa cooking, with its endorsement from professional chefs and its myriad spices, vegetables, herbs, and cooking techniques gleaned from the world over. The term *spa cuisine* was coined by and is the trademark of The Four Seasons restaurant in New York City. Their chef, Seppi Renggli, describes spa cuisine as consisting of elegant, nutrient-rich foods low in sodium, saturated fats, and calories that are served in a strikingly flavorful and aesthetic manner. Other chefs and nutritionists have taken up the cuisine and lent their own variations and emphases, but the three key words are still *healthful, flavorful,* and *attractive.*

Spa cooking is generally considered to have originated in the cuisine minceur created by Michel Guérard in France in the early 1970s. Chef Guérard developed a light version of the famous French gourmand cuisine and became its advocate in his restaurant, Eugénie-les-Bains, and in his book *Cuisine Minceur.* In the same spirit, many health spas in this country—for example, Gurney's Inn at Montauk, Long Island; the Heartland spa in Gilman, Illinois; and the Lake Austin Resort near Austin, Texas—have employed fine chefs to help make their meals both healthful and exciting. Other advocates of a lighter cuisine abound, among them the American Medical and Heart Associations and the American Cancer Society. But few medical and dietary professionals have been able to give to lighter eating the style and appeal that the professional chefs convey in their cookbooks and restaurants.

For our purposes here, and to further clarify what I consider to be the major aspects of this light cuisine, I use *spa food* to refer to foods low in saturated fats and sodium and high in vitamins, complex carbohydrates, proteins, and fiber. Many of the advocates of spa cooking encourage elaborate dishes and sophisticated cooking techniques, but given the busy lifestyles of most Americans, I have downplayed this emphasis somewhat. Many sophisticated recipes are included in this chapter, but I also provide some down-to-earth, everyday staples. And one further comment is called for here: while people are often drawn to this style of cooking for the purpose of losing weight, this nutritious cuisine is not necessar-

The courtyard at the Golden Door health resort in Escondido, California, is a restful retreat.

ily low in calories, though certainly it can be easily tailored to that goal and that is the emphasis given at the spas. Weight control aside, the twin goals of this form of eating are longevity and good health, with a strong emphasis on good taste.

On my quest for information for this chapter, I spoke with Serena Wyatt and Stephen Disparti, garden managers at the Golden Door; other specialty organic growers; and my assistant, Wendy Krupnick, long a serious student of nutrition. For spa recipes and information on their nutritional aspects, I talked with a number of chefs, including Seppi Renggli, and university nutritionists around the country, particularly Dr. Helene Swenerton.

Theories of nutrition vary throughout the years and change from culture to culture, with some gaining and some losing favor. However, as Dr. Lou Gravetti at the University of California notes, "Regardless of how information might vary, there is indisputable evidence that modern Americans are eating too much fat and not enough vegetables." Both

the American Heart Association and the American Cancer Society agree. Despite this certainty, the problem remains: how can we change our society's lifelong eating patterns to conform to our scientific knowledge? Spa-style dishes seem to offer a solution by reaching the diner through pleasureful, not didactic, Miss Bryant-type means. My foray into spa cooking has convinced me that the way to a human's health, as well as heart, is through the well-fed, but not overfed, stomach.

How to Grow a Spa Garden

The goal of growing a spa garden is to produce highly nutritious, tasty produce free from questionable chemicals. To grow the most healthful foods, you must provide plants with the most healthful and nurturing conditions. This idea embraces the concept of organic growing: the garden must be as free from chemicals as possible. In spa cooking—as contrasted with German or American cooking, for example—vegetables are major components of the meal. And since the vegetables play a starring role, they should be as tasty, nutritious, and appealing to the eye as they can possibly be.

Like many of today's fine restaurants, spa kitchens are set up to use organically grown produce from their own gardens or those of specialty growers certified to use purely organic means. I am in complete agreement with the majority of spa owners when they assert that vegetables and herbs grown without chemical sprays and synthetic fertilizers are the most healthful and flavorful.

Regarding specific how-tos, it suffices to say that spa gardening is organic gardening. Appendixes A and B cover organic practices in detail, and numerous individual techniques practiced by professional growers are explained throughout the book. See in particular the profile of Andrea Crawford in the "Gourmet Salad Gardens" chapter, the description of the Common Ground Minifarm garden in the "Grain Gardens" chapter for information on basic bed preparation, coverage of the Cunningham garden in the "Oriental Gardens" chapter regarding soil preparation, and the section on the Golden Door garden in this chapter. Hundreds of specialty growers all over the country use absolutely no artificial chemical pesticides or fertilizers, and under most circumstances you can too. For sources of the many specialty vegetables and herbs mentioned in this chapter, see the chapters recommended in "Sources" at the end of this chapter.

The Golden Door Garden

When you enter the famous golden doors and cross the long footbridge that passes over the creek and under ancient oaks, you enter a world of tranquility. Japanese landscape designer Takendo Arii has combined a serene setting of moving water, mossy rock outcroppings, and tall bamboo with classic Japanese architecture to give the Golden Door health resort the feeling of a Zen monastery. Surrounded by beauty, visitors meditate, dine elegantly—mostly on foods grown on the grounds—and learn new ways to enjoy exercise and health-promoting food.

The spa's three-acre kitchen garden is one crit-

ical part of the nutritional program. Another is a small demonstration garden used to teach visitors how to grow some of their own fresh produce at home. When I first visited the Golden Door four years ago, the demonstration garden occupied a little corner of the larger garden, and according to Serena Wyatt, garden manager at that time, it needed to be revamped. In our discussion she mentioned that a new site would be in order and, when we agreed to use the demonstration garden for my book, she resolved to make it the garden she had always envisioned it to be: more prominent and large enough to demonstrate the garden's full potential. However, Serena left the Golden Door soon afterward to run her own market garden, and Stephen Disparti took her place. It was with Stephen that I ultimately helped to plan the demonstration garden.

Through the years, Serena had made good soil preparation and encouragement of soil-microbe activity priorities for the Golden Door vegetable garden. Like many of the market gardeners of today, Serena had developed a sophisticated composting system, built raised beds for good aeration, and used only organic soil amendments. To encourage the development of high-nutrient soil, she rotated crops with legumes and added much compost. When Stephen took over the spa garden, he was as enthusiastic as Serena had been about this emphasis—and, fortunately for me, about using the demonstration garden for the book as well. To Serena's criteria for building rich organic soil and choosing only superior vegetable varieties he added his philosophical conviction that self-sufficiency was an important goal for the garden. It was his idea that, given the existence of a well and a great deal of compostable material on the property, very little material should be brought in to maintain the garden.

The area chosen for the demonstration garden was on the side of a little hill above the main garden. The design encompassed an abandoned Oriental-style chicken coop that served as a drying and storage building. The garden was fenced to protect against rabbits and was of a manageable size—a little under a thousand square feet. Stephen started the demonstration garden in October by digging six inches of mushroom compost into the top two feet of soil. All the beds except those built on the steepest part of the hill were raised to six inches to give good drainage and aeration to the soil, and, owing to the arid climate, an irrigation system was put in place. This irrigation system was a variation on a drip system: instead of using emitters to drip water directly into the soil, it used microjet spray heads spaced two feet apart that enveloped the plants in a mist. The drip emitters, Stephen had found, led to a build-up of salts on the top of the soil, but these tiny emitters watered as well without leaving the salt crust. The microjets were about a quarter-inch in diameter and were set upon six- or twelve-inch risers.

Once the garden was prepared, Stephen started by planting some of the perennial herbs the chefs find most valuable. These included Greek oregano; lemon, caraway, and English thyme; tarragon; marjoram; and numerous types of lettuce, beets, and carrots. All these plants could produce through the winter, since the weather seldom went below 25 degrees Fahrenheit. On the steepest part of the hill, he planted a strawberry bed; the idea was to use the strawberry roots and leaves to provide constant protection against soil erosion. It was October when he started planting, too late to put in broccoli and cauliflower, green onions, and daikon. But those vegetables would go in the beds the next fall to replace summer vegetables such as tomatoes and bush beans.

In February, Stephen started the warm-season vegetables and herbs in the greenhouse. His choice of varieties was determined by the specific needs of the kitchen. For instance, he selected bell peppers, tomatoes, and summer squash in an array of colors so they could lend eye appeal to the dishes and also be used as colorful garnishes. For the summer herbs, Stephen planted many varieties of basil—including anise, cinnamon, and lemon—to be used to flavor mousses, salads, and vegetable terrines.

Spring vegetables included snap peas trained on the fence and, for beautiful and tasty salads, green onions, radishes, and a great variety of greens. The latter included spinach, endive, Oriental greens, and numerous kinds of lettuce. Stephen chose certain varieties, such as 'Cybele Batavian', for their large, cupped-shape leaves—for holding individual salads or lining salad plates—and others, such as 'Marvel of Four Seasons' and 'Red Salad Bowl', for their red-tinged leaves. Other lettuces, such as 'Lollo Rossa' and 'Oak Leaf', were planted to lend their contrasting textures to a mixed salad, and some romaines were seeded in as well. As for carrots, varieties were chosen for both baby carrots ('Amstel') and more mature ones ('Toudo'). Finally, Stephen added in valuable spring herbs—cilantro, dill, and chervil.

Stephen was bursting with hints on producing the largest selection of the finest vegetables for the kitchen—just the kind of information I was after for the book. For instance, he recommended continually planting new lettuce every few weeks for a constant supply, adding organic matter with every planting. For fertilizer, he relies on compost, green manuring (see the "Grain Gardens" chapter for information), and occasional applications of blood meal, fish emulsion, and, for micronutrients, Maxicrop. He also suggested constantly trying new varieties in the search for improved taste and disease resistance. "That's how we found some of my favorites like 'Sun Drop' and 'Sweet 100' tomatoes, and 'Toudo' carrots," he told me, "and how the kitchen came to appreciate 'Cylindra' beets, with their long, easy-to-slice shape." Another garden technique he relies on is using the floating polyester row cover called Reemay. With

Serena Wyatt displays a selection of lettuces grown in the Golden Door garden.

Stephen Disparti in the demonstration garden at the Golden Door.

when the growth slows down, not at the baby stage and not when old. Finally, get into the habit of planning menus with the harvest in mind. Garden/kitchen coordination is what it's all about." Since this is the message my book was to bear, I was delighted to hear that it guided the approach at the Golden Door.

The larger Golden Door garden contained a tremendous array of varieties, those Serena and Stephen selected for specific kitchen uses, not a representative sample, as in the demonstration garden. Here you might find up to twenty varieties of tomatoes and thirty varieties of lettuce at one time. As an example, Stephen showed me the tomatoes mentioned before plus 'Yellow Cherry', 'Yellow Pear', 'Red Plum', 'Celebrity', 'Mandarin Cross', 'Champion', 'Striped Cavern', and 'Better Bush'. Lettuce varieties when I was there included those mentioned above plus 'Rouge d'Hiver', 'Erthel Crisp Mint', 'Craquante d'Avignon', 'Valmaine', 'Cybele Batavian', 'Augusta', and, for hot weather, 'Black-Seeded Simpson', 'Canasta', and 'Oakleaf'. The generosity and specificity of varieties are directly linked to the spa's highly varied, ever-changing menu.

Recommended Spa Vegetables

Unlike the lists of recommended vegetables in other chapters, this discussion of the best vegetables for a spa garden emphasizes vitamin and mineral content. Other aspects of nutrition in vegetables are covered in the cooking section of this chapter.

We all grew up hearing about vitamins, but if you're like me you've forgotten most of what you learned, or simply turned a deaf ear during school lectures. I am here to tell you, though, that vitamins can actually be fascinating, serving as a window into the workings of the human body. As my space is limited, my goal here is to convey only a little of the information I turned up in my research and to inspire you to explore the subject further.

For better or worse, our parents were right when they admonished us to eat our vegetables or else. The sad part was that the stuff often tasted so bad and was served in such unimaginative ways that force was necessary. Vegetables are important because they contain vital vitamins as well as minerals, fiber, and complex carbohydrates. But not all vegetables are

Reemay, he said, in winter lettuce will grow almost twice as fast as that out in the open.

Stephen had some helpful suggestions for kitchen use, too. For instance, "When you pick your vegetables, use them within hours; don't just let them sit in the refrigerator. One of the reasons you have a garden is to eat vegetables as fresh as possible. Also, learn to pick vegetables at their particular peak of flavor—each variety has its optimum time of harvest. Most carrots, for example, are best at a midpoint created equal. Some, such as kale, are filled with nutrients, while others, such as cucumbers, are mostly empty crunch. And a few should be enjoyed only in moderation. Celery, for instance, is fairly high in sodium, and spinach contains quite a bit of the toxin oxalic acid. But vegetables as a group are an essential part of our nutrition and are a central component of spa cooking.

Let's start the discussion of vitamins with a rather dry definition from *Webster's New Collegiate Dictionary:* "any of various organic substances that are essential in minute quantities to the nutrition of most animals and some plants." This is useful information, but a comment out of the richly informative *Laurel's Kitchen* means more to me: "Part of the job of vitamins is to help speed up the millions of reactions that life depends on by bringing the right things together at the right time. Vitamins are enablers. Without them you can fill the body with platters of proteins and energy foods but most of it would be eliminated without being used. While few of us are going to die from lack of vitamin C or some of the B vitamins as happens to peoples on starvation diets, instead we suffer vague symptoms of fatigue, slow healing, dry skin, premature aging, and myriad other nonfatal maladies."

Some vitamins, specifically A, D, E, and K, are fat soluble; they are stored in the fatty tissues and need not be ingested every day. Others, such as vitamin C and the B vitamins, are water soluble; they cannot be stored in the body for long periods and are best included as part of the daily diet.

The most important aspect of vitamins, aside from the fact that they are vital to functioning, is that they do not stand alone. Many of the vitamins must be ingested with other nutritive substances to become accessible to the body; conversely, some must be present to allow other nutrients to be available to the body. It is critical to understand that nutrients are not absorbed as single units but as part of an interlocking system. And just as a dose of 10-10-10 fertilizer doesn't begin to substitute for a rich soil filled with organic matter, so vitamin pills are no substitute for a diet composed of all the nutritional necessities. For example, to absorb vitamin A, necessary for healthy mucous membranes and good night vision, you need some fat in your diet; to absorb calcium, required for strong bones and teeth, you need vitamin D. Without vitamin D, the body simply flushes out the calcium and it is wasted. Similarly,

without certain water-soluble B vitamins, our bodies are unable to use the energy in food fully, and as a consequence we may feel listless even though we have consumed plenty of fuel. The body uses vitamins in countless ways. Vitamin B_6 is needed for converting certain amino acids into hormones; riboflavin helps the body repair itself, as does vitamin C. Vitamin C also helps combat infections and is an essential component of connective tissue and healing. Vitamin K is necessary for normal blood clotting.

The "best" vegetables—those containing the most vitamins and minerals—are listed and described in detail below. But these starring foods aside, there is still a remarkable range of vitamins in garden produce. Most vegetables contain many vitamins and minerals in differing amounts. To gain a sense of the spectrum of vitamins in vegetables, consider these facts: sweet potatoes, sorrel, and cantaloupe contain substantial amounts of vitamin A; wheat and oats contain vitamin E and the B vitamins thiamin and niacin; leeks are strong in vitamin E; cantaloupe, strawberries, tomatoes, sweet potatoes, and okra are all good sources of vitamin C; okra and asparagus of riboflavin; and dry beans and potatoes of vitamin B_6. Asparagus, beets, celery, corn, cucumbers, lettuce, sweet potatoes, cantaloupe, and wheat are sources of folacin (a B vitamin); and lentils, sweet potatoes, and cantaloupe contain pantothenic acid (also a B vitamin).

Minerals are inorganic substances that, like vitamins, are critical to the functioning of the human body. At least twenty minerals are generally considered to be needed in varying amounts. Six of them are often called the macrominerals, as they are needed in fairly large amounts. These are sodium, potassium, chloride, calcium, phosphorus, and magnesium. The remaining minerals, needed in minute quantities, are referred to as trace minerals. Minerals are constituents of nerves, hormones, the cells of the body, and the bones and teeth. Unlike some of the vitamins, individual minerals need not be consumed every day, as they remain in the body over time. A balanced diet that includes numerous vegetables and fruits will provide most sufficient minerals for healthy functioning.

Certain vegetables are mentioned below as particularly high in minerals. For other good sources of minerals, look to dry beans, cantaloupe, parsnips, and potatoes for potassium; pak choi, okra, soy beans, and rutabagas for calcium; dry beans, wheat, and corn for phosphorus; and legumes, wheat, parsnips, and potatoes for magnesium.

For in-depth, readable information on vitamins and minerals, see both *Laurel's Kitchen* and *Jane Brody's Nutrition Book*. They contain detailed information on the vitamin and mineral content of many vegetables, grains, and starches, and *Laurel's Kitchen* is filled with recipes.

The fresh vegetables listed below are particularly high in vitamins, minerals, fiber, and other constituents that promote good health. Where several vegetables have very similar nutrient levels, I have grouped them together.

Lima beans and peas are the only legumes listed, first because they are the legumes most commonly eaten fresh, and second because they are very high in nutrients. Legumes are the vegetables highest in protein, which is most highly concentrated in their mature, dry state. See the "Baked Bean Gardens" chapter for more information on the nutrients in dry beans.

There seems to be a curious parallel between concentration of nutrients and intensity of flavor in vegetables. How fortunate that the vegetables that are best for us are also some of the tastiest! For information on growing the individual vegetables, see Part Four, "An Encyclopedia of Superior Vegetables."

BROCCOLI *Brassica oleracea,* Botrytis Group Broccoli is one of the most nutritious—and most popular—vegetables in the garden. It contains the vitamins A, C, K, riboflavin, thiamin, and niacin and the minerals calcium, potassium, and phosphorus. It's also high in fiber.

How to prepare: To prepare broccoli in the most healthful manner, avoid serving it with butter, margarine, and mayonnaise. Steam or blanch it at high heat with just enough water to cook it adequately. (Always boil the water before adding any vegetable. This reduces cooking time and helps preserve the vitamins. And always save the water to use in sauces, soups, or as a refreshing beverage.) Another way to prepare broccoli is to stir-fry it with chicken in a small amount of vegetable oil. However you cook it, remove broccoli from the cooking pot when barely tender, as the internal heat will continue the cooking.

Lemon juice or a good vinegar goes well with broccoli. Other good fat-free seasonings are mustard, curry, dill, thyme, black pepper, leeks, and ginger. Yogurt works well for simple sauces or as a garnish.

If you want to use an oil of some type, try a small amount of olive oil.

For spa recipes, try broccoli pureed in a soup or sauce, in a light soufflé, as a filling for crêpes, or in a vegetable terrine. Serve raw or blanched and chilled broccoli with a cottage cheese or tofu dip flavored with fresh herbs. Leftover broccoli is wonderful in salads, with dips, or as a snack.

BRUSSELS SPROUTS and CABBAGE   *Brassica oleracea,* Gemmifera Group, and *B. o.,* Capitata Group   These vegetables have been popular for eons, and cabbage has been the staple vegetable for much of China and Germany. Both vegetables are rich in vitamins C and K; the primary minerals found in them are calcium and potassium.

How to prepare: Brussels sprouts and cabbage are tasty additions to our diets. They are very nutritious, although not quite as vitamin-packed as some of their close relatives. As with broccoli, Brussels sprouts can be steamed, blanched, or stir-fried. Cook them until barely tender and chill for an unusual addition to crudités or salads. Cabbage, a much more versatile vegetable, can be used in an infinite number of ways: in salads and slaws, steamed, stir-fried, in soups and casseroles, stuffed, and when young and tender in place of lettuce on sandwiches.

In addition to the seasonings mentioned for broccoli, apples, caraway or fennel seeds, dill, and nuts go well with Brussels sprouts and cabbage.

CARROTS   *Daucus Carota*   A favorite staple in most households, carrots are renowned for their vitamin A content. They also contain much potassium.

How to prepare: Pureed carrot soup, flavored with a little almond, is my favorite cooked carrot dish, although carrots are indispensable in many other soups and stews. Raw carrots are wonderful grated or diced in salads, sliced for crudités, and marinated, but nothing beats a just-pulled carrot munched in the garden. Some favorite seasonings include chives, tarragon, dill, marjoram, nutmeg, curry, almonds, and orange.

CHARD and BEET GREENS   *Beta* spp.   These closely related leafy vegetables are powerhouses of nutrition and are filled with the vitamins A, E, K, folacin, riboflavin, and biotin and the minerals magnesium and potassium.

How to prepare: These greens are closely related to spinach and have similar nutrients, flavor, and

This market gardener's display of unusual vegetable varieties highlights our country's growing interest in a wide spectrum of vegetables.

cooking requirements. They should be thoroughly washed, chopped (I usually put the chard stems under the greens in the pot), and placed in a pot with a close-fitting lid. Use only about a quarter-inch of water and set at a medium heat. Check after a few minutes, and if they have started to wilt, stir occasionally and cook for only a couple of minutes after all are wilted. Remove the greens from the pot when done; they will keep cooking even when off the heat. A light touch is best for seasoning: garlic, leeks, onions, nutmeg, curry, mustard, lemon, and yogurt all go well. If you want to use an oil, try a little olive oil instead of butter. These greens are favorites with chefs as wrappers for fish, chicken breasts, and vegetable stuffings.

KALE and COLLARDS *Brassica oleracea,* Acephala Group Kale and collards are certainly among the most nutritious vegetables you can grow. When grown during the cool season and with proper preparation, these sometimes maligned greens develop a sweet, rich flavor and may become your favorites. They contain the vitamins A, C, E, K, folacin, riboflavin, thiamin, niacin, and biotin and the minerals calcium, iron, magnesium, potassium, and phosphorus.

How to prepare: To retain the nutrients, you must cook these vegetables rapidly at a high temperature. This also helps to set the color and flavor and to tenderize them. Blanch or steam with minimal water until just tender—for only a few minutes after they have wilted—or stir-fry using a little broth, water, or other liquid, and then cover the wok to allow the greens to steam a bit (dry heat will scorch them). High temperatures will ensure tender greens, but do not overcook. Very young kale leaves are good raw in salads.

Many recipes for these greens call for bacon or salt pork, but a little olive or safflower oil with some garlic or onion may be substituted for a more healthful approach. The seasonings mentioned for broccoli go well with kale and collards as well.

LIMA BEANS and PEAS   *Phaseolus limensis* and *Pisum sativum*   Lima beans and peas are high in complex carbohydrates, fiber, and the vitamins folacin, niacin, riboflavin, thiamin, and B_6. They are also high in minerals, especially calcium, iron, phosphorus, and potassium. And they are fairly high in protein.

How to prepare: When still green and freshly shelled, these legumes require nothing more than brief steaming or simmering in a little water or broth until just tender. For peas, this may only take one or two minutes. As the beans and peas become more mature, their protein content increases, as does the time needed for cooking. Both are wonderful plain and also good chilled and added to salads, in succotash and other vegetable mixtures, and in soups, where they can be pureed to make a thick, rich, nutritious dish that is still low in calories. The latter technique can also be used to make a delicious and unusual dip or spread.

As for seasonings, lima beans go well with onions, leeks, garlic, black pepper, most herbs, and lemon. Peas combine well with mint, dill, chives, and nutmeg.

PARSLEY   *Petroselinum crispum*   This common herb, described in the "Culinary Herb Gardens" chapter, is too frequently treated as an inedible garnish. But parsley has lovely green leaves and a mild, refreshing flavor, and it is packed with nutrients. It contains the vitamins A, C, folacin, and riboflavin and the minerals calcium, iron, magnesium, and potassium.

How to prepare: Use chopped parsley abundantly in tabouli and other salads; blended into bright green dressings, dips, and sauces; and in soups. Parsley goes well with almost all other foods, herbs, and seasonings.

PEPPERS   *Capsicum* spp.   Peppers are another example of the high correlation between flavor and nutrients: ripe peppers are among the richest sources of vitamins A and C and have a pungent, zesty sweetness that puts them in high demand.

How to prepare: As vitamin C is easily destroyed by exposure to heat and air, retain most of it by freshly slicing the peppers and using them soon afterward, raw as a snack, with dips, or in salads. However, cooking intensifies the flavor of peppers, which

enhance many dishes diced and sautéed, roasted, stuffed, and pureed into soups and sauces.

SPINACH   *Spinacia oleracea*   If Popeye got strong and healthy from eating canned spinach, imagine the results if the spinach he had been eating was garden fresh and properly cooked! Spinach contains the vitamins A, E, K, folacin, riboflavin, and biotin and plenty of the minerals magnesium and potassium.

How to prepare: This tender, flavorful green is, of course, wonderful in salads. In cooking, the water remaining on the leaves from washing may suffice; use a medium heat and cook only until wilted. Cooking and seasoning recommendations are similar to those for chard, above.

TURNIP, MUSTARD, and DANDELION GREENS   *Brassica Rapa*, Rapifera Group; *B. juncea;* and *Taraxacum officinale*   These greens are among the most nutritious of the garden vegetables. They contain the vitamins A, C, E, K, folacin, riboflavin, thiamin, and niacin, and are important sources of such minerals as calcium, iron, magnesium, potassium, and phosphorus.

How to prepare: These greens are similar in nutrients to kale, but are thinner-leaved, requiring less cooking time. They should be cooked with moisture and high heat initially, but as they are more tender than kale, the heat should be reduced to medium and not prolonged much beyond wilting. All three greens can be used raw in salads when young; cooking reduces the sharpness of turnip and mustard greens. And all three types go well with the seasonings suggested for broccoli.

WINTER SQUASH   *Cucurbita* spp.   Another staple historically, winter squash is experiencing a comeback as a wide assortment of beautiful and delicious varieties become available to both the gardener and the shopper. Winter squash is a rich source of potassium, and the darker the orange of the flesh the higher the concentration of vitamin A.

How to prepare: Winter squash is so delicious baked whole until soft and eaten plain or with nut butter that I only recently discovered its other culinary uses. This vegetable is great diced or julienned and sautéed until crisp-tender, sliced and layered in a casserole, stuffed, and diced or pureed in soups or pasta sauce. *The Victory Garden Cookbook* contains some wonderful suggestions in both the winter squash and pumpkin chapters. Seasonings are similar to those for carrots.

Cooking from the Spa Garden

There are two major components to spa cooking: the nutrition and visual appeal. Here the marriage between health considerations and the love of food reaches its zenith by way of the garden, with fresh garden produce the critical element. Specialty vegetables such as fancy lettuces, fresh sweet pea pods, juicy tomatoes, and tangy basil lie at the heart of the spa meal, boosting the experience from the healthful and satisfying into the realm of elegance.

However, spa cuisine embraces down-home cooking as well as haute cuisine. As you learn its techniques and ingredients, you can modify both your day-to-day and special-occasion cooking with an eye to increasing their healthfulness. Happily, most changes involve moderation and substitution, not deprivation. Spa chefs have improved modern cooking by eliminating some of the problem ingredients, such as butterfat and refined flour and sugar, and have developed alternative techniques that still produce smashing meals.

Before the chef at a spa creates recipes, he or she must be well versed in nutrition, and that is where we must start as well to get a firm grasp on this cuisine. I make no claims to being a nutritionist; in fact, I'm somewhat skeptical of food dos and don'ts, having lived long enough to see a few theories and numerous guaranteed diets come and go. And I'm certainly guilty of occasional ice cream binges and other food sins too decadent to mention. But experience and research have convinced me that one fact is irrefutable—namely, a diet full of fatty meat, rich pastries, butter and margarine, and cheeses takes its toll on our bodies by depositing fat in the arteries, causing obesity, and even possibly contributing to the development of some types of cancers. In the last hundred years or so, we Americans have replaced the wasting diseases of deficiencies with the "clogging" diseases of plenty.

Some of our information on diet and health has come from studying other cultures. Two examples are the home cooking of China, with its reliance on rice, vegetables, and minimal amounts of seafood and meat, and of southern Italy, where the primary oil is olive and large amounts of pasta and numerous vegetables and, again, only small amounts of meat are consumed. Note that I am referring to the home-style cooking, not the feast foods, of these countries.

Nor does this observation apply in regions where large amounts of lard are used, or in the Chinese and Italian restaurants in this country where foods are tailored to American tastes to include fatty meat and saturated fats and to de-emphasize vegetables. These cuisines are confirmed as healthful because in both cases decade-long studies have found that people in these countries have a lower incidence of heart attacks, strokes, diabetes, obesity, and certain kinds of cancers than our own population. Scientists also found that when these people changed their diets—often when they became more prosperous or moved to the United States—the incidence of all the conditions under study increased. To me these results were compelling reasons for taking a new look at my family's food-intake patterns.

Basic Nutrition

In the list of recommended spa vegetables, I focused on vitamin and mineral content. Here the goal is to give an overview of other aspects of nutrition. Again, for highly detailed, readable, and valuable information on nutrition, see the books recommended in "Sources" at the end of this chapter.

Carbohydrates: Carbohydrates are the sugars and starches that serve as fuel for our bodies. Sugars are called simple carbohydrates and are quickly absorbed by the body. Starches are classified as complex carbohydrates and are changed into sugars in our bodies before they are absorbed. Before the invention of food-refining processes, most carbohydrates were bound in complex forms that contained valuable nutrients and allowed a measured release of sugars into the bloodstream. Today's refined sugar and flour provide concentrated energy but lack nutrients. And as stated in *Laurel's Kitchen,* "Since the body needs certain vitamins to metabolize foods for fuel, eating large amounts of carbohydrates devoid of vitamins is a little like gathering the logs and kindling for a fire but not having any matches with which to light it. Since the body's appetite is satisfied by calories alone, large amounts of 'empty calorie' foods crowd out other foods needed for decent nutrition."

Foods containing complex carbohydrates give us sustained energy, satisfy our hunger, and supply many important nutrients. The American Heart Association recommends that we take 50 to 60 percent of our daily calories from the complex carbohydrates contained in such foods as legumes, whole-grain breads and cereals, and vegetables and fruits. At present, most Americans average only about a third of the recommended amount.

Fiber: Dietary fiber, a carbohydrate sometimes called roughage, is defined by Jane Brody in her nutrition book as "the components of foods that cannot be broken down by enzymes in the human digestive tract." There are two types of fiber in foods, both found only in plants: insoluble fiber, which keeps the digestive tract running smoothly and foods moving along the intestines, and soluble fiber, which helps regulate swings in blood sugar levels and has been shown to lower blood cholesterol. A lack of fiber in the diet may cause constipation, contribute to hemorrhoids, and cause the intestinal wall to thicken and weaken, creating pockets in a painful condition known as diverticulosis. There is also a suggestion that such a lack may be associated with some forms of cancer. In so-called peasant societies where large amounts of dried legumes, whole grains, and vegetables are eaten, the incidence of colon cancer is relatively low.

The average American diet is composed largely of meat, fats, and refined carbohydrates, and our daily average fiber quota is therefore less than half of that usually recommended. To increase the amount of fiber in your diet, try to include numerous whole grains, fresh fruit, and varied selection of vegetables, particularly all types of legumes, carrots, chard and other greens, cucumbers, broccoli and other members of the cabbage family, eggplant, leeks, okra, onions, parsnips, peas, peppers, potatoes, pumpkins, rutabagas, salsify, winter squash, sweet potatoes, and turnips.

Fats: Fats provide concentrated amounts of energy and carry the fat-soluble vitamins. Although small amounts are necessary for good health, fat is a problem in the American diet in two major ways. First, fats are a concentrated source of calories and are easy to overconsume, which leads to overweight. Second, excessive fats, especially saturated fats, may contribute to a build-up of cholesterol in the arteries. As the media continually remind us these days, there are different kinds of fats and they affect the body's cholesterol level in different ways. Saturated fats are considered by most medical professionals to be one of the major contributors to arteriosclerosis, commonly known as hardening of the arteries. Unsaturated fats, which may be monounsaturated or polyunsaturated, contain the essential fatty acids important in our diet,

which makes them the good guys. Saturated fats are found in animal products such as butter, most cheeses, egg yolks, lard, fatty meat, whole milk, and a few vegetable products, particularly cotton, palm, and coconut oil, and hydrogenated solid vegetable shortenings. Overall whole grains, vegetables, and fruits contain very little fat, but plants are important sources of unsaturated fats.

Many of the foods our society loves are culprits in overweight and many other of the health problems we battle. Butter and fatty meats are fairly obvious fat sources, but the great array of snack foods and nondairy substitutes—made with cottonseed, coconut, or palm oils—are hidden repositories of saturated fats. To most people, fats taste good and give a richness to food. Hence, the average citizen in this country consumes twice the amount of fat generally recommended. However, once one is awakened to the intense and diverse flavors of fresh foods unmasked when dietary fat is reduced, the old favorites often begin to seem greasy and unappealing. One of the greatest challenges of spa cooking is to help us make the transition by creating satisfying and beautiful low-fat meals.

Proteins: Proteins are complex combinations of the twenty-plus amino acids the body needs for growth and repair. Once the pet prescription of nutritionists, high protein consumption has come under scrutiny in the last decade or so. Professionals now think that a moderate intake of protein is preferable and that the body functions better if more of the diet consists of complex carbohydrates such as whole grains, fresh fruits, and vegetables.

To manufacture the proteins it needs, the body must have access to specific combinations of amino acids. Meats, fish, poultry, eggs, and dairy products provide "complete" proteins, meaning that the full complement of amino acids is present. However, vegetarians and those who want to cut down on meat and dairy-product consumption may want to investigate the wide variety of plant protein sources. At the top of this list is the soy bean, both high in a complete protein and low in calories and fat. All the other legumes are high in protein too, but they lack

OPPOSITE: *Spa food is both beautiful and healthful. Shown here are chef Gretchen Gunther's fish timbale with a red pepper sauce, fancy-cut steamed vegetables, and fruit from a summer spa garden.*

some of the essential amino acids. Thus, legumes must be combined in the diet with proteins from other plant sources, such as whole grains, or with animal products, to make adequate amino acids available for protein building. For excellent discussions of vegetable proteins and how to use them in your diet, see *Laurel's Kitchen,* listed in "Sources" at the end of this chapter.

Health Issues

With the various components of nutrition covered, two important health issues deserve special comment in a discussion of spa cuisine: salt and cholesterol.

When a chef puts together a spa menu, she or he tries to keep the intake of salt to a minimum. The culprit in salt is believed to be sodium. The body needs a certain amount of sodium to function properly, but in the modern diet consumption far exceeds need. In some individuals too much sodium is thought to contribute to high blood pressure, which in turn has been linked to heart and kidney problems and strokes. In cultures where little or no salt is consumed, the incidence of high blood pressure is relatively low.

The kidneys are the regulators of sodium in the body, excreting the excess into the urine. According to *Jane Brody's Nutrition Book,* "in a significant percentage of people, perhaps as a result of having to dump excess sodium for years, this machinery fails to operate properly and the kidneys don't get rid of enough sodium. The retained sodium holds water, and the volume of blood rises." Suffice it to say, without going into detail, that the extra fluid seriously taxes the circulatory system. In addition, a critical balance between sodium and another element, potassium, is disturbed.

People accustomed to large amounts of salt from an early age seem to crave it, and foods with little or no salt taste flat to them. The manufacturers of processed foods, aware of salt's appeal, often use it liberally. And salt is not the only source of sodium in the diet. Besides occurring naturally in most vegetables, meats, and dairy products, sodium is present in baking powder and soda, MSG, some forms of nitrates and nitrites, and milk products. In fact, because sodium is so pervasive and unobtrusive, cutting down on it can be more of a challenge than cutting down on fats. Even such foods as packaged cereals and muffins as well as fast-food milkshakes and apple pies contain significant amounts of sodium.

While some consider salt a flavor enhancer, those who cut down on it while focusing on the flavor in garden-fresh foods often find that salt actually detracts from other flavors. In fact, their increased appreciation of the clear, fresh taste of high-quality foods can come to spoil the enjoyment of "junk" foods— not a bad thing if you're an addict trying to break the habit.

The suggested safe and acceptable range for sodium for adults is 1100 to 3300 mg, or 3 to 8 grams of salt, a day. The average adult American consumes more than double the recommended amount, and most children take in even more, so there is much room for cutting down. To reduce your salt intake, try some of the following techniques: eliminate the saltshaker from the table; reduce the amount of salt when cooking foods by half; read labels on prepared foods carefully and purchase foods low in sodium; whenever possible buy products labeled as low sodium; experiment with substitute seasonings such as lemon juice, chili peppers, and fresh herbs; and, if you're using butter or margarine, substitute unsalted for salted.

Cholesterol intake is the other demanding health issue I want to tackle. Cholesterol, a fatlike substance, is an essential part of animal cells and fluids, but excess amounts are apparently deposited in the arteries, where they clog blood flow. Past infancy, the liver manufactures all the cholesterol the body needs.

Cholesterol intake is one of the most controversial of the food health issues. Since the discovery of cholesterol more than sixty years ago, the negative effects on the body of ingesting large amounts of fat have been widely studied. Unfortunately, some of the results of the studies have conflicted. The question is, Do ingested fats contribute to the elevated amounts of cholesterol in the blood and arteries or not? As yet, there is no firm evidence that the amount or type of fats consumed adds to cholesterol accumulation in the arteries and leads to arteriosclerosis. But according to *Dietary Guidelines for Americans,* published by the United States government, it makes sense for the American population as a whole to reduce the daily intake of total fats, particularly saturated fats, because there is enough solid evidence that it may be beneficial to a number of individuals.

A subissue of the cholesterol controversy relates to the different kinds of fats and their effects. As suggested earlier, there are three major types of fatty acids, the constituents of fats: saturated, monounsaturated, and polyunsaturated. Space limitations allow me only to sum up the complex prevailing theories on the effects of these different fats. Saturated fats seem to contribute to the build-up of cholesterol in the arteries, monounsaturated fats seem to be primarily neutral, and polyunsaturated fats might actually help in some cases to lower the cholesterol level. Related to the consumption of saturated fats is the question of whether eggs are a problem in the diet. The yolk of an egg contains a large amount of cholesterol, typically between 250 to 275 milligrams per egg. Since most health professionals recommend a daily cholesterol-intake limit of 300 milligrams, an egg a day nearly uses up the allowable cholesterol before you've buttered your morning toast. However, because eggs contain so many other high-quality nutrients and have such versatile uses in our cooking, few professionals would eliminate them altogether. Rather, the general consensus is that we should cut down on our consumption and use eggs sparingly.

In conclusion, most medical and nutritional professionals believe that the evidence is sufficient to justify our reduction of all dietary fats. As my neighbor the heart surgeon says, "If you've read as many studies and seen as many clogged heart arteries as I have, it's hard to enjoy consuming much fat." For a more comprehensive treatment of this subject, send away for the pamphlet *Dietary Guidelines for Americans*, Home and Garden pamphlet #232 (Human Information Services, USDA, Room 325A, Federal Building, Hyattsville, MD 20782).

Spa Cooking Techniques

Dietary changes are difficult. Foods don't simply feed our bodies; they nurture our spirits as well and have a powerful effect on our emotions. Here and there people may alter their diets owing to a warning signal from their bodies or a particularly effective nutrition class, but resistance to change is still formidable among us. At this point in history, though, the coming together of nutritionists and some of the world's greatest chefs makes sweeping dietary change throughout society a distinct possibility. At The Four

Seasons in New York, for example, or at the Golden Door, chefs are sitting down with nutritionists to plan meals. The chefs then work their creativity within agreed-upon nutritional parameters—low butterfat and no salt, for example—and might spend hours perfecting a technique to whip skim milk and make it tasty or trying many combinations of spices to season the dish with originality. If the meal is lacking in protein, perhaps nuts or julienned turkey breast will be sprinkled on the salad. If the entree is low in complex carbohydrates, an herbed bean dip with a few special, beautifully arranged raw vegetables might be planned as a first course. In short, the sublime pleasures of eating are now being coupled with serious nutrition principles, and it is finally becoming possible to indulge our appetites in good conscience with respect to our health.

Spa chefs prepare many dishes borrowed from classic international cuisines, adapting techniques and ingredients to principles of nutrition. For example, they might make an Italian pasta primavera, with its crown of fresh vegetables, with a little olive oil and serve it with pasta or spaghetti squash. A French bouillabaisse full of lean seafood in a light, flavorful broth might be served with whole-grain bread and a salad with lemon-herb dressing. Mexican salsa makes a zesty sauce for eggs or potatoes. Japanese, Indian, and Chinese ingredients and techniques are all invaluable in spa cooking. Chefs have even found creative ways to translate classic French sauces, pastries, and basic techniques into less caloric alternatives. And to make mealtime an aesthetic high point of the day, they have drawn from the Japanese and French in their style of presenting meals.

The Aesthetics of the Spa Meal

Most restricted diets deprive us of some of the social and visual niceties of a meal. But far from the spartan, low-cal TV dinner or the hurried bowl of cottage cheese eaten on the run, the spa dinner is inevitably a special occasion served with grace and flair. A dinner table set with linens and flowers stands on a summer porch or before a fireplace hearth to capture the mood of the day. A picnic basket might be filled with intriguing little containers of crudités, flowers, and lovely dishes and the repast moved to a sunny spot of lawn. The place settings are carefully chosen: sometimes they are earthenware pottery, other times

The Manhattan taxi driver made a mistake and let me out on the west instead of the east side of Fifth Avenue, so I was blocks away from The Four Seasons restaurant. I had an appointment with chef Seppi Renggli and, figuring he must have a very tight schedule, started running. I was twenty minutes late as I ran up the regal stairway to the chandeliered dining room and announced myself between gasps for breath.

Seppi came out of the kitchen to join me at a corner table. He gave me time to catch my breath and immediately put me at ease with his warm voice and easy manner. Seppi is one of the chief creators of spa-type cooking and author of *The Four Seasons Spa Cuisine,* and I was interested in how he coordinates his menus with a nutritionist and in what techniques he uses to create his famous meals.

After The Four Seasons decided to feature a low-calorie, high-nutrition menu, Seppi told me, he began commuting to Columbia University to learn nutrition from Joyce Leung at the Institute for Human Nutrition. Armed with the basics, "I was possessed," he says. "I came back and cooked like crazy. I wanted to create exciting meals that would have less than 700 calories and be balanced nutritionally." At first, he sent the recipes to Joyce for review, and they would come back with changes. "For instance, I had a lot of trouble including enough calcium," he says. "I can't use much cheese or cream because of their high fat content, so I had to come up with a calcium source. I began to include high-calcium vegetables, and I came to rely on dry beans, split peas, and lentils in sauces and soups. Now that I've cooked this way for a long time it's become second nature, so I seldom need help anymore."

An example of how one of Seppi's menus is analyzed nutritionally is his tomato-mozzarella salad served with steamed breast of chicken in romaine lettuce. Altogether the meal provides more than fifty

Seppi Renggli

grams of protein; nineteen grams of fat, of which seven are saturated; nearly forty grams of carbohydrates; five grams of fiber; five hundred fifty milligrams of calcium; eleven milligrams of iron; and three hundred milligrams of niacin. It has a total of 632 calories, much of which is in the cheese.

I asked Seppi to name some of his favorite vegetables for spa cuisine. "I love leeks," he says, "because they're so beautiful and taste so sweet. I steam and serve them fanned out on a plate with a vinaigrette sauce with crayfish. I also use the leaves to make a wrapping for red snapper seasoned with jalapeño peppers, minced orange rind, and horseradish. I like broccoli, too, especially in a stir-fry with other vegetables. I use the sprouting type when I can get it; it seems to have more flavor. And sweet fennel. I love to cook with the sweet licorice flavor of fennel. I serve it with fish, in soups, and in sauces."

Seppi is known for his creative use of herbs and spices, particularly chili peppers. Because no salt or butter is used in spa cuisine, seasonings are critical. Popular ways to use seasonings include sauces, soups, stuffings, and marinades. "I often use what I call the warm spices," Seppi says. "Chili peppers being one kind, of course. Years ago I used to buy a small box of chili peppers for the restaurant, but now I buy cases—mostly jalapeños. I also use quite a bit of fresh ginger, coriander seeds, and garlic, as well as cumin, caraway, fennel, and dill seeds. For the most flavor, I work with the whole seeds, roasting and grinding them in a coffee grinder just before I use them. The fresh herbs I use frequently are chervil, cilantro, basil, mint, arugula, and watercress. A nearby herb grower provides most of the fresh herbs for our kitchen. I also like to use lemon juice, orange peel, and juniper berries."

Poultry, fish, vegetables, tofu, and mousses of all types wrapped in the leaves of green vegetables are some of Seppi's signature dishes. These dishes are full of vitamins and contain few calories. "I like to take the different colors of leafy vegetables and combine them—maybe a few leaves of dark-green chard, light-green Savoy cabbage, and the almost-chartreuse Chinese cabbage—and use them to wrap around a filling," he explains. "To prepare these rolled entrees, I first blanch the leaves and lay them out by color on a sheet of plastic wrap or parchment paper. On top of them I might put finely sliced cooked carrots, a few spears of asparagus, or some yard-long beans; then I press in some mashed tofu. I roll up the leaves and steam them. When cooked, I cut them in slices, fan them out on a plate, and serve them in a pool of spicy garlic, shallots, and chili sauce. It's beautiful! I make another dish that's similar using cabbage leaves and a spiced rabbit-meat filling."

Steaming is a technique Seppi uses often because it cuts down on fat in a recipe. In fact, as he says, "When I stir-fry I use mostly a steaming process with chicken stock. Another change in my stir-fry is that I use light soy sauce or lemon juice instead of regular soy sauce, which is very high in sodium. I also make timbales—little ramekins filled with fish, poultry, or vegetables mixed with seasonings, steamed and then served unmolded with a sauce of some sort. One of my favorites is a timbale with carrots and eggplant served with a peanut sauce."

I commented to Seppi on his use of many Oriental ingredients. "My wife is from Indonesia, and that's had an impact on my cooking," he says. "I use a lot of lemon grass, preferably fresh, and fresh cilantro. In some of my dishes, I also include *ulek sambal,* a red chili paste, and *ketjap manis,* a sweet, syrupy soy sauce. Lately, though, I've been busy working with Thai food because it features so many flavors. I've been creating dishes choosing from five different kinds of curry paste." Seppi also uses Japanese ingredients, such as soba (buckwheat noodles), kombu, (dried seaweed), enoke mushrooms, and dried bonita flakes, and some of his rolled dishes are reminiscent of shushi.

Seppi loves to garden, and we touched on that subject several times during our discussion. "Gardens are fantastic," he says. "I can't wait to go out to my garden. It's the best of all possible ways to cook. Besides, I'm happiest when I'm digging and making compost. That's one of the ways I relax. Sometimes that's when I get some of my most creative ideas."

Seppi says about 25 percent of the people who come to The Four Seasons order from the spa menu. The number has grown over the years as people become more aware of this style of cooking. "Of course," he says, "there are always people who order the spa meal and then follow it with a large piece of chocolate cake."

fine china and crystal. It's not a large budget that's needed, only a generous amount of creativity.

Inevitably, the chef shows a special artistry in arranging the food. Plates are garnished with a miniature rosebud or a carved vegetable or two. Even the hackneyed cottage cheese plate is given new life when the chef whips the cheese with fresh mint or tarragon from the garden and tucks a scoop of it, sprinkled with flower petals, into a shell of lacy red lettuce. And instead of tomato slices, the chef might offer a whole tomato stuffed with a frothy mousse of spinach. Protein shakes are served with a few fresh raspberries in a chilled goblet with a violet floating on top. The point is to use all the senses to help indulge, not deprive, the diner.

Other visual techniques are used to camouflage the size of small portions or to slow down and draw out the meal. For instance, a strawberry or raspberry sauce is folded into whipped egg whites to give it more volume. Portions of sliced vegetables such as zucchini and artichokes are fanned out to fill the plate or shaved with a mandoline to create a nest for a piece of poached salmon (see the profile of Paul Bertoli in the "Italian Gardens" chapter). Think of the time it takes to consume a selection of roasted cherry tomatoes and mushrooms on a skewer—much more than forking up a serving on a plate. The same is true for a selection of baby garden vegetables with a dip or a bowl of clams in their shells in a broth. For pages of inspirational photographs that detail many of these presentations consult Edward Safdie's *Spa Food.*

Meal Planning with Spa Food

Good nutrition involves a global, not a meal-by-meal, approach to food. The spa cook considers a whole day's consumption in terms of recommended quotas of nutrients. This section is meant to illustrate some of these ideas and give you a place to begin. You'll find references here to numerous recipes throughout the book (use the index to locate them).

Breakfast: This can be a simple meal and an easy one to plan in terms of nutrition. Rely heavily on whole-grain breads or cereals (see the "Grain Gardens" chapter), nonfat milk, and fresh fruit. Low-fat and low-sugar granolas and cooked whole-wheat cereals make a hearty start to the day. To cut down on butterfat if you're hooked on whole milk for your cereal, try mixing 2 percent (lowfat) milk with skim milk; gradually, then, whittle the proportions down to all skim milk. Another easy breakfast is plain yogurt with fresh fruit. Vary it by adding granola to the yogurt. Homemade yogurt is often milder than the store-bought varieties and hence needs less sweetening when served with fruit (by the way, the mildness makes homemade yogurt acceptable to some yogurt-refusing children). Make a low-fat cream-cheese-type spread for bread by draining your homemade yogurt in cheesecloth for twelve to twenty-four hours. Other wonderful spreads for bread or toast are the nut butters—for instance, almond, hazelnut, and sunflower seed. These are anything but low in calories but the fats aren't saturated—and, after all, not everyone needs to lose weight. *Spa Food* contains a recipe for cashew date butter made from tofu, ground cashews, and dates that is absolutely luxurious on any kind of whole-grain bread. And by the way, tofu can be included in fruit smoothies or "custards."

This no-nonsense approach to breakfast is fine for everyday, but what will substitute for eggs Benedict, fried potatoes, and pastries when we want something special for a brunch for company or to begin a vacation day with a more elegant meal? Since eggs, the foundation of many special breakfasts, are high in cholesterol, most spa chefs minimize their use. And when they do make them they never fry them in fat, as that process compounds the fat problem. Rather, eggs in spa breakfasts are usually boiled or poached. For an omelette, the spa chef might use two whole eggs and two egg whites where four whole eggs might ordinarily be used. (When you do this, give the yolks to your cat or dog; animals don't seem

to have cholesterol problems.) The omelette itself is cooked in a nonstick pan or with spray-on nonstick oils to avoid the addition of more fat. Fresh peaches or mangoes make a grand filling, and an omelette so filled might be dusted with powdered sugar. A variation on the traditional Mexican huevos rancheros is poached eggs with warm salsa and a little Jack cheese. Other festive ideas are fresh fruit kabobs, broiled grapefruit, and homemade whole-wheat and blueberry bran muffins. Make cheese blintzes with low-fat milk and fill them with low-fat cottage or ricotta cheese and grated apples and spices.

For an American, a completely nontraditional approach to a special breakfast is to center the day's first meal on vegetables. How freeing it was for me to discover I could actually serve vegetables for breakfast! I grew up starting the morning with grain products, eggs, and fruit, and it just never occurred to me to have vegetables at that time of day. Many other cultures routinely start with vegetables. For instance, in Latin America corn and bean stew or refried beans are popular for breakfast, in Japan miso vegetable soup is routine, and in Germany and Holland grated vegetable salads and pumpernickel bread are not unusual.

After being around my assistant, Wendy Krupnick, who sees no boundaries on vegetables, I often break the fast midmorning with leftover vegetable soup or a pac choi and chicken stir-fry warmed up in the microwave oven. Other dishes can be made up fresh or from leftovers from the dinner menus described below. The vegetable soufflés are spectacular for company breakfasts, and the eggs in them go farther per serving than if served singly. See the recipe for *pistou* soufflé in the "French Gardens" chapter and cut down on the butter.

Lunch: For lunch ideas, see some of the suggestions above plus the soups in this chapter. Luncheon salads, either hot or cold or in the form of an antipasto, can be very satisfying. See the "Italian Gardens," "Gourmet Salad Gardens," "Mexican Gardens," and "Rainbow Gardens" chapters for salad ideas. Any of the entrees likely to be left over are convenient for lunch—for example, garden and seafood chili, and Italian-style baked beans. Tofu or bean purees as sandwich fillings are absolute winners. Try them with fresh salad herbs, minced red peppers, celery, cucumbers, tomatoes, and carrots. To cut down on calories and make the meal dramatic, serve sandwiches Danish-style—that is, open face—and use lots of vegetable garnishes, including fancy lettuces, mizuna, Japanese mustard, and mâche.

Dinner: Although it's important to think of balanced nutrients throughout the day, we usually end up giving most attention to a complete meal at dinner. This is also a time to tally up the intake to see if there are any major gaps, and to add ingredients to help balance the deficiency.

Dinner is where the spa chefs' artistry finds its fullest expression. Here, whether it be for home cooking or entertaining, they have come up with an enormous range of substitute ingredients and techniques, especially for sauces and soups ordinarily made with butter and cream. One simple substitution is low-fat yogurt for sour cream as a garnish for borscht, cream soup, or a crêpe. And a baked potato might be topped with salsa, not sour cream. In *Cuisine Minceur,* Chef Guérard uses powdered skim milk in a garlic sauce for chicken and vegetables and a rich chicken stock to make a flavorful béarnaise sauce. A vegetable puree can effectively thicken a velvety sauce for fish or meat, and sauces can be wonderfully flavored with beef and chicken stocks. A good homemade meat, fish, or vegetable stock, in fact, is a most valuable spa food component. It will give extra flavor to your vegetables when used in sauces, soups, and stews and allow you to cut down on salt in the bargain. For another substitution, use whipped egg whites with pureed vegetables folded in for making a low-calorie, high-nutrient mayonnaise.

An ingenious spa cooking technique is to replace filo dough pastry, and all its massive amounts of butter, with the leaves of ruby chard or pac choi. And why give up poultry stuffing? Make a stuffing with whole grains such as brown or wild rice and vegetables. Instead of using pastry dough to line an entree or appetizer tart, use mashed or grated potatoes or squash. All such changes cut down calories and add nutritional value while preserving the pleasure in the meal.

Spa meat dishes are made with lean meats such as poultry and beef, pork, and veal cuts with little fat. Since fat adds flavor to meat, these cuts are often marinated in herbs and wine or given varied vegetable or herb sauces to compensate for the loss. In a novel approach, Chef Guérard marinates and cooks fish in apple cider. Spa chefs seldom fry meat or fish, preferring to roast or broil. And to add interest, they often cook over coals.

Many spa chefs do not use red meat, but often use alternative dishes such as low-fat cheeses, tofu, and fish. Entree ideas are meatless lasagna with ricotta cheese and spinach, black-bean burritos, scallops with sorrel sauce, trout with dill and lemon sauce, baked stuffed onions, stewed leeks with mint, frittata with herbed vegetables, and stir-fried vegetables with tofu and sunflower seeds. See the "Native American Gardens" chapter for a recipe for a native squash stew made with turkey and winter squash. *Spa Food* contains a wonderful recipe for pesto that uses very little oil and is great on vegetables and pasta. Sushi, with its raw fish, is a wonderful spa food as well. Literally hundreds of exciting recipes are available in the books recommended in the "Sources" section.

Spa chefs, besides helping us reduce our reliance on meats, have worked hard to find more ways to increase the complex carbohydrates in our diets. Wherever possible, they use foods such as whole-wheat bread, pasta, and brown rice, and avoid white rice, refined flour, and refined sugar. They serve brown rice or pasta salads filled with peppers, tomatoes, snap beans, and scallions. Tabouli, with its many variations, is used for lunch and dinner, even occasionally as a stuffing for vegetables. Rice pilaf is made with stock and minced vegetables. The traditional succotash is used to incorporate legumes. Beans are incorporated in salads and soups and pureed for dips. Split peas and lentils find their way into salads, soups, stuffing, and curries and are pureed for sauces. Though all these legumes are somewhat high in calories, they contain valuable nutrients and satisfy the appetite. Potatoes are also valuable in these ways and are included pureed, as shells for vegetables, to line pastry dishes, as new potatoes in stew, or as potato salad marinated in a small amount of olive oil and herbs, as in salade Niçoise.

Desserts offer a wonderful opportunity to work more fruit into the diet. Try fruit mousses and sorbets, apple crisp with a minimum of butter, and dried fruits used for sweetening. Instead of adding heavy cream to your desserts, consult *Spa Food* for its method of whipping skim milk into a frothy topping. *Cuisine Minceur* contains recipes using egg whites or gelatin for other whipped toppings.

Your nearest natural foods store or Oriental market are the places to look for ingredients for this cooking style. Shop there for nut butters, a selection of whole-wheat baked goods, low-salt chips, cheeses, vegetable juices, tofu, unsaturated oils, herbal teas, low-sodium canned goods, and snack foods that contain no cottonseed or coconut oils. If you are particularly lucky, your local stores might have a delicatessen offering prepared casseroles, tabouli and tofu salads, and fresh bran muffins.

You'll need little special equipment for spa cooking, but a food processor will be very helpful for many of the vegetable dishes, a blender for many of the pureed drinks, a nonstick pan to cut down on fats, a salad spinner to help wash all the greens, and a large stock pot. All in all, spa cooking offers a new perspective on your food, one that will yield new pleasures along with its health advantages.

STEAMED TURKEY BREAST WITH CABBAGE, CORN, AND PEAS

This recipe is from *The Four Seasons Spa Cuisine* by Seppi Renggli. Seppi says, "This is one of the best ways to cook turkey I know. It picks up all the flavors of the marinade and stays moist from the steaming."

SERVES 4.

- 1 tablespoon minced jalapeño pepper
- 1 dried red chili pepper, minced, or 1 teaspoon flakes
- 1 teaspoon dried rosemary (or 2 teaspoons minced fresh rosemary)
- 1 cup minced fresh parsley
- ¼ cup minced shallots
- 2 cloves garlic, minced
- 1¼ pounds boneless turkey breast, skin still attached
- ½ pound green cabbage, cut into 1-inch strips
- 1 cup (¼ pound) corn cut from 2 medium ears or substitute 1 cup frozen corn, defrosted
- 1 cup (5½ ounces) shelled peas
- 1 tablespoon white wine vinegar
- 1 tablespoon almond or olive oil
- 12 cherry tomatoes

With a sharp knife or a food processor, chop peppers, rosemary, parsley, shallots, and garlic together to make a fine mixture.

Loosen skin from turkey but leave it attached at one end. Stuff some herb mixture between skin and turkey. Loosen filet from underside of the breast.

Stuff more of herb mixture there. Use about ⅔ of herb mixture on the turkey.

Bring water to a boil in the bottom of a steamer or wok. Line a steamer basket with cabbage. Put turkey, skin side up, over cabbage. Sprinkle remaining herb mixture over cabbage that shows. Cover steamer and cook over boiling water for 15 minutes. Remove cover and sprinkle corn over cabbage. Cook 10 minutes longer; then add peas over cabbage and corn. Cook 5 minutes more.

Remove from heat and uncover steamer basket. Put turkey on a plate to cool. Put cabbage, corn, and peas in a bowl. Toss them with vinegar and oil.

When everything has cooled to room temperature, remove skin from turkey and discard. Cut turkey into thin slices and arrange them, overlapping, on one side of a platter. Spoon vegetables down the other side. Garnish with cherry tomatoes.

VEGETABLE TIMBALE WITH PEANUT SAUCE

This is another recipe contributed by Seppi Renggli, and it's absolutely delicious. The thinking that goes into these types of recipes is reflected in the nutritional information Seppi provides along with them. In this case, the data per serving are as follows: calories, 191; protein, 9.1 g; carbohydrates, 16.1 g; fat, 10.9 g; saturated fat, 2.1 g; cholesterol, 3.4 g; fiber, 2.2 g; calcium, 144.8 mg; zinc, 2.4 mg; iron, 1.9 mg; folic acid, 51.4 mcg; sodium, 303.4 mg; sugar, 0 g.

SERVES 6.

Timbale Mixture

- 2 6-ounce Oriental eggplants
- 1 6-ounce carrot
- 6 Chinese cabbage leaves
- 1 clove garlic
- 1 large jalapeño pepper
- 1 4-ounce onion
- 1 4-ounce zucchini
- 1 4-ounce red pepper
- 1 4-ounce green pepper
- 6 ounces tofu
- 6 small ramekins (4 to 4½ inches across)

Slice 1 eggplant unpeeled and one large carrot into

6 long slices. Blanch eggplant 3 minutes and Chinese cabbage 2 minutes. Cover with cold water to cool, drain, and pat dry.

Chop garlic and jalapeño pepper fine, dice the rest of the vegetables into ½-inch cubes, and steam in a small, covered sauté pan with ¼ cup of water for 3 to 5 minutes. Remove lid and reduce liquid completely. Add diced tofu. Cool.

Line each ramekin with 1 Chinese cabbage leaf (trim to fit if necessary), 1 carrot slice, and 1 eggplant slice. Fill center with steamed vegetables, cover each ramekin securely with aluminum foil, and steam for 5 to 7 minutes in a roasting pan or large pot with rack and cover. (Or cover ramekins with plastic wrap and microwave at full power for 2 minutes.)

Prepare peanut sauce, below, and pour 2 tablespoons on each of 6 preheated plates. Turn hot timbale out on sauce. Serve at once.

Peanut Sauce

1½ teaspoons sesame oil
⅓ cup minced shallots
1 clove garlic, minced
1 teaspoon chopped fresh lemon grass or ¼
    teaspoon dried lemon grass (sereh)*
1 teaspoon ulek sambal*
1½ tablespoons ketjap manis (Indonesian soy
    sauce)*
1½ teaspoons grated ginger root
½ teaspoon ground cumin
½ teaspoon ground coriander
2½ ounces (5 tablespoons) unsalted peanut
    butter
2 to 4 tablespoons water
1 cup unflavored low-fat yogurt

* If you cannot find these ingredients,
    substitute 1 teaspoon lemon juice for
    lemon grass, ¼ teaspoon ground cayenne
    for sambal, and Japanese soy sauce for
    Indonesian soy.

Heat oil in a saucepan. Add shallots, garlic, lemon grass, and sambal. Cook over medium heat until lightly brown. Stir in ketjap manis, ginger root, cumin, and coriander. Once smooth, add peanut butter and water. Whisk until smooth. Whisk in yogurt and continue cooking until sauce thickens enough to coat a spoon.

BROCCOLI/BROCCOLI

This and the next two recipes come from the *Golden Door Cookbook* by Deborah Szekely with chef Michel Stroot. When I visited the Golden Door, the chef made the following recipe using 'Romanesco' broccoli, and it is probably the most exciting way I've eaten broccoli.

SERVES 4.

1 large onion, halved and peeled
2 pounds fresh broccoli
½ cup reserved vegetable broth (if necessary)
4 ounces low-fat Neufchatel cream cheese
½ teaspoon vegetable seasoning
¼ teaspoon grated nutmeg
1 teaspoon arrowroot
¼ teaspoon ground cardamom
Fresh lemon juice, to taste
Cayenne pepper, to taste
1 hard-cooked egg, chopped
2 tablespoons scallions, chopped
2 ounces Monterey Jack cheese, freshly grated

Grilled fish with an herbed sauce served with steamed baby vegetables and a side dish of marinated artichokes makes a delicious, healthful meal.

Place onion in saucepan and cover with water. Cook, covered, about 45 minutes, till onion is tender. Cool. Trim stems from broccoli, leaving flowerets with 1½-inch stems. Set flowerets aside. Peel stems, cut into 1-inch chunks, place in small saucepan, and cover with water. Cook, covered, about 25 minutes, until tender. Drain, reserving vegetable broth.

In blender or food processor, puree onion, broccoli stems, and (if necessary to blend) ½ cup reserved vegetable broth. Add Neufchatel cheese, vegetable seasoning, nutmeg, arrowroot, cardamom, squirt of lemon juice, and dash of cayenne pepper. Mix sauce well in blender until smooth and creamy. Place in saucepan and warm over low fire. Check seasonings. Before serving sauce, add chopped egg and scallions.

Quarter broccoli flowerets, and steam about 7 to 10 minutes, until tender yet firm. Place in individual serving casseroles. Coat broccoli with sauce; sprinkle with grated jack cheese. Broil until cheese melts and browns slightly. Serve immediately.

EGGPLANT FLORENTINE

This tasty eggplant dish is full of flavor and, at 166 calories per serving, is much less fattening than the customary preparation of this dish.

SERVES 4.

1 eggplant, small, sliced in 4 ¾-inch rounds
    (about 4 ounces each; discard ends)
2 teaspoons olive oil
¼ pound fresh mushrooms
1 small onion
1 garlic clove, large
2 tablespoons minced fresh oregano
Vegetable seasoning, to taste
¼ teaspoon black pepper, freshly ground
¼ teaspoon grated nutmeg
2 ounces Monterey Jack cheese, grated
2 tablespoons chives, scallions, or fresh
    parsley, chopped
1½ cups fresh spinach, cooked, drained, and
    chopped
2 tablespoons Parmesan or Romano cheese,
    freshly grated
1 cup fresh tomato sauce (see "Italian
    Gardens" chapter)
Watercress or parsley sprigs for garnish

Brush both sides of eggplant slices with oil. Broil on

both sides till lightly browned but not cooked. Place in nonaluminum baking dish just large enough to hold slices. Brush lightly with oil, and season with dash of vegetable seasoning and 1 tablespoon of the oregano. Set aside. Preheat oven to 350°.

Grate mushrooms, onion, and garlic in food processor or by hand. Put into heavy skillet; add remaining oregano, vegetable seasoning to taste, and black pepper. Cook, covered, over medium heat about 5 minutes, until all liquid has evaporated; stir occasionally.

Add nutmeg and jack cheese. Cook till cheese is melted and creamy. Stir in chives and spinach; blend in thoroughly. Spoon over eggplant slices; sprinkle with Parmesan or Romano cheese, and spoon tomato sauce around base of eggplant (not on top).

Bake about 30 minutes, till eggplant is tender. Garnish and serve.

FISH AND GREENS BAKED IN TIMBALES

This recipe, from chef Gretchen Gunther, is elegant enough for a dinner party yet will spoil no one's diet. Note that if you use fresh tomato sauce in this recipe, fresh dill makes a good addition.

SERVES 4.

1 to 1½ pounds fresh firm white fish filets,
    such as halibut or shark
1 red bell pepper, sliced into thin strips
Nonstick spray or oil
2 to 3 pounds trimmed greens (soft greens
    such as spinach, not chard or kale) to give
    3 cups cooked
3 tablespoons minced onion
1 clove garlic, minced
Pinch each salt, pepper, and nutmeg
1 egg
2 cups fresh tomato sauce (see "Italian
    Gardens" chapter) or sweet and spicy red
    pepper soubise sauce (recipe follows)
4 custard molds or timbales (about 4 inches in
    diameter)

Preheat oven to 350°.

If filets are thick, slice into ½-inch-thick strips and divide into 4 portions. Blanch bell pepper strips briefly and drain. Coat insides of custard molds or timbales with nonstick spray or oil. Place pepper strips in bottoms of molds in desired pattern. Carefully press fish to cover bottoms and sides of molds.

Wash and chop greens. Put a little oil or non-stick spray in a large skillet or nonstick pan and sauté onion until translucent. Add garlic, greens, and seasoning, and cook lightly for a few minutes until greens wilt. Cool, then whisk egg and mix with greens. Press mixture into centers of fish-lined molds and place molds in baking pan with boiling water to about halfway up molds. Bake at 350° for 20 minutes.

Remove from water bath and let stand for 5 minutes. Heat sauce and place ½ cup of it on each warmed plate. Run a knife around edges of each mold and invert onto sauce. Serve immediately.

SWEET AND SPICY RED PEPPER SOUBISE SAUCE

Jesse Cool, chef/owner of the Flea Street Cafe and Late for the Train restaurant in Menlo Park, California, says of this recipe, "This sauce is delicious and beautiful with steamed broccoli or cauliflower served as an appetizer or side dish."

1 cup chopped yellow onions
2 cups chopped sweet red peppers (peeled if tough)
2 tablespoons olive oil
Cayenne, salt, and pepper to taste

Sauté onions and peppers in olive oil over low heat until very soft. Remove and puree in blender or food processor. Add seasonings and serve hot or at room temperature.

VEGETABLE PÂTÉ

This pretty, 3-layer pâté is elegant, yet low in calories and high in nutrition. Serve as an appetizer, salad course, or side dish. Note that the seasoning here is up to you. Experiment with the flavor until you have matched your personal preference.

SERVES 8 TO 10.

6 eggs
1 cup milk
⅔ cup brown rice, cooked
2½ cups green vegetables: choose from

A vegetable pâté featuring layers of carrots, onions and rice, and snap beans.

blanched and finely chopped green beans, broccoli, asparagus, or peas (edible pod or shelled type) alone or mixed with up to 1 cup grated raw zucchini, and/or cooked, well-drained, and finely chopped greens (such as spinach, chard, or kale)
Salt and pepper, herbs and spices to taste (see below for suggestions)
1½ cup grated carrots or sweet yellow winter squash
2 cups diced white potatoes or cauliflower
¼ cup diced onion, shallots, or white part of leeks
1 clove garlic, crushed (optional)
Standard loaf pan

Preheat oven to 350°.

In a medium bowl, beat 2 of the eggs, add ⅓ cup of the milk, ⅓ of the rice, the green vegetable(s), and season to taste. Green herbs such as basil, dill, thyme, or summer savory are good with this mixture. Add crushed garlic, if you like. Stir well and set aside.

In another bowl, beat 2 eggs, add ⅓ cup milk, ⅓ of the rice, grated carrots or squash, and seasonings. With this mixture, try 1 to 2 teaspoons curry powder or 1 teaspoon nutmeg, mace, or coriander.

In a saucepan, cook potatoes or cauliflower with onion in 1 or 2 inches of water until just tender.

Process in food processor briefly with just enough cooking liquid to make mixture workable. Add 2 eggs, ⅓ cup milk, and seasoning, and blend very briefly. Use a small amount of dill or thyme, dash of cayenne, and/or salt and pepper. Pour into a third bowl and mix with remaining rice.

Butter a standard loaf pan and line with buttered wax paper. Carefully pour carrot mixture into pan, making an even layer. Follow with potato mixture, then green mixture. Filling should come to about ½ inch below top of pan. Place pan in a larger pan containing about 3 inches of hot water. Bake at 350° degrees for 1¼ hours. Check to see if firm; if not, bake 15 minutes longer. Let loaf pan cool on a rack ½ hour. Run a knife around edges of pan, put serving plate over it, and invert. Remove pan and wax paper and let cool ½ hour longer.

Serve slices warm on sweet and spicy red pepper soubise sauce (above), or at room temperature on a bed of chilled greens with a light dressing.

KALE PIE
WITH POTATO CRUST

Many people are unfamiliar with the virtues and delicious flavor of kale. A kale pie as a main course is a lovely way to introduce this leafy green to those who might be wary of it. This recipe was inspired by one for cauliflower cheese pie in *The Moosewood Cookbook* by Molly Katzen; there, too, the tasty, low-fat crust was made from grated potatoes. In Molly's other excellent cookbook, *The Enchanted Broccoli Forest,* she gives suggestions for more wonderful, innovative, and healthy crusts for main-dish pies.

SERVES 5 TO 6.

Crust

  2 cups grated raw potato
  ½ cup grated carrot (or parsnip)
  ¼ cup grated onion
  1 egg, beaten
  1 tablespoon whole-wheat pastry flour
  1 rounded teaspoon minced fresh thyme or dill
  Freshly ground pepper to taste
  10-inch pie pan
  Nonstick spray
  1 tablespoon oil

Preheat oven to 375°.

Put potato in a colander or strainer and set aside for about 15 minutes. Combine remaining ingredients except oil in a bowl. Squeeze potato with your hands to remove excess moisture; then mix into other ingredients. Pat firmly and evenly into a 10-inch pie pan that has been greased or sprayed with nonstick spray. Bake at 375° for 40 minutes; halfway through baking brush lightly with oil. Set aside to cool slightly. While crust is baking, make filling.

Filling

  1 onion, chopped
  1 tablespoon oil
  2 cloves garlic, minced
  1 rounded teaspoon minced fresh thyme or dill
  4 cups packed kale leaves, stripped from stems
      and torn up
  2 eggs
  1 cup low-fat milk
  Dash of cayenne
  ¼ teaspoon freshly grated nutmeg
  1½ cups grated part-skim mozzarella cheese
  1 tablespoon whole-wheat pastry flour

Reduce oven to 350°.

In a large nonstick skillet with a lid on medium-low heat, sauté onion in oil for about 5 minutes, covered, stirring occasionally. Add garlic, cover, and cook for 3 minutes; then stir in dill or thyme. Place kale in the skillet, add 2 tablespoons water, and cover closely. Cook for about 5 minutes to wilt kale slightly. Remove from heat, stir, and let sit with lid ajar. Meanwhile, beat eggs with milk, cayenne, and nutmeg. Toss cheese with flour and place half evenly over baked crust. Spoon kale over cheese and pat down, top with remaining cheese, and pour egg mixture over all. Bake at 350° for about 40 minutes.

GARDEN BOUNTY SOUPS

My favorite way of dealing with an abundant harvest is to make pureed soup. This concentration of nutrients and flavors makes for very satisfying food that is perfect for the "spa" diet. Although creamy in texture, these soups need not be made with cream. They are easy, versatile, and can be served hot or cold, rich or light, to suit any weather and occasion. The proportions of the recipes are flexible too. By decreasing the liquid measurement, a soup can be transformed into a delicious, low-calorie pasta sauce—in this case, increase seasoning with herbs, garlic, and pepper, and top with cheese. Or add a squeeze of lemon and use the sauce to dress a vegetable, pasta, or potato salad. For added protein, put in a slice of tofu when you puree the soup (this will thicken it). These soups offer another opportunity to let the garden spark your creativity.

Any of these soups freeze well, which means they're a good way to enjoy your harvest into the winter. But do not add cream, tofu, or milk before freezing (the soup can be thinned later).

ALL RECIPES MAKE ABOUT 6 CUPS.

Curried Squash Soup

3/4 cup chopped leeks, shallots, or onion
2 tablespoons butter, margarine, or oil
2 teaspoons curry powder
1/4 teaspoon pepper
2 pounds yellow squash, chopped
2 cups chicken broth
Suggested garnishes: yogurt, chive or
    nasturtium flowers, toasted sunflower
    seeds

In large pan, sauté leeks, shallots, or onion in butter until wilted. Stir in curry powder and pepper and cook a few minutes longer. Add squash and broth, cover, and simmer until squash is tender. Process in batches in blender (never fill blender more than 2/3 full). Good hot or cold.

Zucchini soup variation: Use any green summer squash, omit curry powder, add 2 to 4 cloves chopped garlic to onions, and add fresh herbs when pureeing: use 2 tablespoons minced fresh dill or 1/4 cup chopped fresh basil and 1 or 2 sprigs parsley for a bright green color. Garnish with Parmesan cheese.

Runner Bean Soup

For this soup, I like to use runner beans that are full sized but still quite flexible when bent.

3/4 cup chopped green onions, leeks, or sweet
    onion
1 clove garlic
1 tablespoon EACH butter or margarine and
    olive oil
Freshly ground pepper to taste

1 1/2 pounds runner beans, cut to 1- or 2-inch
    pieces
2 cups chicken broth
1 tablespoon minced fresh winter or summer
    savory
Suggested garnishes: runner bean flowers or
    savory sprigs

In large pot, sauté onions and garlic in butter and oil until wilted. Stir in pepper; add beans and broth. Cover and simmer until beans are just tender. Add savory and process in batches in the blender. If beans are quite stringy, strain mixture in colander and add a small amount of finely chopped savory.

You may add 1/2 to 1 cup milk, cream, broth, or water to enrich or thin the soup. *When heating a soup containing milk or cream, do not let it simmer.*

Greens Soup

Potatoes can give body to pureed soups made from leafy greens such as spinach, sorrel, lettuce, and chard. Begin as in the recipes above, cooking the onions and garlic. Then simmer 1 diced potato in 1 1/2 cups chicken broth until tender. Stir in at least 1 quart chopped greens and cook until wilted. Puree or blend, adding 1/2 to 1 cup milk, if desired (or more broth), and season with nutmeg and pepper.

Carrot Soup

Use squash soup recipe above, but substitute 1 1/2 pounds carrots. You may need a little more liquid. Good seasoned with tarragon or chervil instead of curry.

Sweet Pepper Soup

Use recipe for red pepper soubise sauce but add more liquid—water or chicken stock, a little white wine, or some milk—and puree in blender for a luscious soup.

TOFU DIP

This delicious and healthful combination will complement your garden beauties while it woos the most timid tofu skeptic. You can serve it with fresh vegetables or crackers or use it as a sandwich filling.

MAKES ABOUT 2 CUPS.

1 cup tofu (8 ounces)
½ large ripe avocado
2 cloves garlic, chopped
2 teaspoons minced fresh ginger
½ cup parsley leaves, stems removed
2 tablespoons lemon juice
*1 tablespoon tahini (sesame butter), sunflower
    seed butter, or peanut butter*
*1 tablespoon applesauce or a pinch of sugar or
    a little honey*

Blend all ingredients in a food processor until very smooth.

LEMON BASIL HERB-AND-SPICE-SEASONED SALT SUBSTITUTE

This flavor-filled seasoning comes from Shepherd's Garden Seeds catalog. It's wonderful to have on hand to add flavor to soups, sauces, and vegetables as a substitute for the taste of salt.

MAKES ABOUT 3 OUNCES.

*2 tablespoons dried lemon basil or dill weed,
    finely crumbled*
*1 teaspoon dried oregano leaves, finely
    crumbled*
*2 tablespoons onion powder or finely ground
    onion flakes*
1 teaspoon celery seed
2 tablespoons toasted sesame seeds
¼ teaspoon grated dried lemon peel
Pinch of freshly ground pepper
½ teaspoon paprika
½ teaspoon garlic powder

Combine all ingredients in a small bowl and blend well. Put into a shaker with large holes. Store in a cool dark place.

GARDEN GAZPACHO

This refreshing soup takes full advantage of vine-ripened tomatoes and fresh herbs. It makes the most sparkling gazpacho we know.

SERVES 8.

*About 7 medium fully ripe tomatoes or about
    7 cups cut up*
1 onion or several green onions
2 cloves garlic
½ hot or medium-hot pepper, to taste
*1 large or 2 small sweet bell peppers (green,
    yellow, or red)*
1 large or 2 small cucumbers
1 tablespoon olive oil
⅓ cup wine vinegar
½ cup red or white wine
*3 to 6 sprigs fresh herbs, choosing from
    parsley, dill, basil, cilantro, and oregano
    (use cilantro and oregano in moderation)*

Chop all vegetables coarsely for processing in a food processor or blender. The processor will give the soup some crunch; the blender will give a smoother texture. Process all ingredients in batches, pouring into a large nonaluminum bowl to mix. Refrigerate at least 3 hours before serving. Garnish each bowl with your choice of: avocado slices, sweet pepper slices, cucumber slices, chives, fresh herbs, slightly toasted sunflower seeds, or plain low-fat yogurt.

If a more traditional, tomato-based flavor and texture are desired, add 1 to 2 cups of tomato juice to the soup.

Sources

Seed Companies
For sources of seeds for your spa garden, see the seed sources in the "Gourmet Salad Gardens," "French Gardens," "Italian Gardens," "Baked Bean Gardens," "Chili Gardens," "Culinary Herb Gardens," and "Edible Flower Gardens" chapters.

Books
Brody, Jane. *Jane Brody's Nutrition Book*. New York: Bantam Books, 1987.
    This is an invaluable guide to a lifetime of healthy eating by the award-winning *New York Times* columnist.
Guérard, Michel. *Michel Guérard's Cuisine Minceur*. New York: Morrow, 1976.
    This is the basic text for spa cuisine translated from the French. Guérard covers classic French cooking fundamentals and then gives alterna-

tive methods and ingredients for cooking with fewer calories.

Health Travel International. *Spa Dining*. New York: St. Martin's Press, 1985.

This book features luscious, low-calorie recipes from America's great spas.

Renggli, Seppi. *The Four Seasons Spa Cuisine*. New York: Simon & Schuster, 1986.

Master chef Seppi Renggli gives a vast selection of delicious and healthful recipes in this book.

Robertson, Laurel, Carol Flinders, and Bronwen Godfrey. *The New Laurel's Kitchen: A Handbook for Vegetarian Cookery and Nutrition*. Berkeley: Ten Speed Press, 1986.

This is one of the best basic primers on nutrition, and it offers many fine natural food recipes as well.

Safdie, Edward J. *Spa Food: Menus & Recipes from the Sonoma Mission Inn*. New York: Clarkson N. Potter, 1985.

This book contains a sophisticated selection of healthful recipes.

Szekely, Deborah, and Chef Michel Stroot. *Golden Door Cookbook: The Greening of American Cuisine*. Escondido, Calif.: Golden Door, 1982.

This was one of the first cookbooks written on the subject of spa cooking. You'll find many fine recipes here.

Culinary Herb Gardens

WHAT A LUXURY IT IS TO have a garden full of herbs! Even this country's best chefs usually can't match the meals created from such a garden. Imagine having enough lemon thyme or fennel to be able to use the prunings for smoking pheasant or salmon. Think of creating a salad, as if from the heart of France, with fresh tarragon and chervil, or making an elegant plate of shushi with the traditional *shisho* leaves. Fresh herbs are the signature of a chef and often a specific cuisine, yet very few markets in this country offer more than a meager selection.

When I think back on my cooking of years ago, I seem to myself to have been working in black and white and monaural. The form was there and it was enjoyable, but the depth and richness were missing. Now that I regularly use fresh herbs, I'm cooking in full color and stereo. The zip of fresh mint or the many flavors of thyme give the dishes more dimension. Twenty years ago I started on my herb adventure by adding fresh chives to potato soup and fresh basil to spaghetti sauce. What a difference! I went on to use fresh dill on fish,

OPPOSITE: *Herbs harvested at the Farallones Institute include dittany of Crete, 'Opal' basil, chervil, golden thyme, fennel, tarragon, cutting celery, chives, summer savory, sorrel, basil, lemon balm, curly parsley, spearmint, marjoram, oregano, bronze fennel, green and gold sage, dill heads, chamomile, and golden oregano.*

pesto on pasta, and herb vinegars on salads. Now, after years of exposure to the full range of herbs, and thanks to many people's guidance, I use many more in my cooking, and almost all of them are fresh.

Herbs are the easiest to grow of all the edible plants. Therefore, of all the gardens in this book, for most people the herb garden is the best place to start. Another incentive is the fact that cooking with herbs can be a very healthful way to add excitement to meals. At a time when the safety of the salt and fats in our diets is being seriously questioned, it's a relief to explore enjoyable substitutes for them. I get so tired of being deprived in the effort to be "good." Using herbs is a way to deepen the pleasure as well as the healthfulness of food.

As I mentioned, my education in herb cookery started slowly. I was always an avid gardener, so years ago I put in a basil plant or two and some dill and chives, and that's still a good way to start. But my serious interest in herbs took hold when I visited the herb garden at Caprilands in Coventry, Connecticut. This extensive garden, fueled by the enthusiasm of Adelma Simmons, actually contains many different kinds of herb gardens: a butterfly one (a garden that attracts butterflies), an all-gray one, a garden full of scented geraniums, and another of herbs for drying. While at Caprilands, my sister and I enjoyed a meal in which herbs were used in each course, and Adelma came around while we ate to talk about the ones we were enjoying. That trip to Caprilands opened my eyes to the vast world of herbs and many of its possibilities.

Since then I have visited many public herb gardens, and I highly recommend them to other interested gardeners and cooks. Visiting these gardens is a great way to learn to identify the appearance, smells, and flavors of individual herbs. This country has hundreds of beautiful public herb gardens. Try a visit to our nation's herb garden in Washington, D.C., at the United States National Arboretum, or to the Cloisters, with its wonderful medieval garden, in New York City. Or sample herbs at the magnificent formal herb gardens at the Missouri and Chicago botanical gardens and the historical gardens at Old Sturbridge Village and Colonial Williamsburg. All grow a wonderful range of herbs and usually provide a guide to help you identify them.

Once I had a working knowledge of most of the herbs used in cooking, I found I needed the help of creative cooks to explore herbs in the kitchen. For every way I came up with to use an herb, someone like Carole Saville, a food authority in Los Angeles, and Rose Marie Nichols McGee, raised in the shadow of Nichols Garden Nursery, a well-known herb supplier, had created ten. And in the hands of master chefs such as Tom McCombie of Chez T.J.'s in Mountain View, California, and Ron Zimmerman of the Herb Farm outside Seattle, Washington, dishes came alive with herbs.

To put their creative information together and show us how simply and elegantly herb gardens can be created, both Carole Saville and Rose Marie McGee grew demonstration gardens for the book. In the process, they shared much information on how to cook from these gardens and how to maintain them.

One final comment before we proceed. You might be totally unacquainted with some of the herbs covered in this chapter. In my research I was struck by how much of the available information and emphasis on growing and cooking herbs comes from Europe, particularly England. This is a wonderful bank of knowledge, but it excludes the many cultures around the world that season their foods with native plants. Many of these exotic herbs have already been covered in the "Mexican Gardens" and the "Oriental Gardens" chapters, but I discuss a few here as well.

How to Grow an Herb Garden

Jim Wilson, owner of Savory Farms wholesale herb growers, came to visit me one day, and as he walked up my herb-lined front path, he became completely engrossed in the plants before I could usher him into the house. He kept leaning down and rubbing his hands over the foliage, first of the tarragon, then of the lemon and caraway thyme. "Your thyme and tarragon grow so much more lushly than ours," he said. "We have problems with nematodes and wilt diseases." And he couldn't get over the Greek oregano. He was clearly envious. Jim, probably best known to most gardeners as the southern host of the "Victory Garden" television show, grows his herbs in humid South Carolina in a climate very different from that of dry California. Actually, Jim was just refreshing his memory, because years ago he had gardened nearby. As we renewed our old friendship, the subject of herbs came up again and again, and we compared notes

Dayna Breedon harvests tarragon from the author's front-walk herb garden. On the left of the walk are burnet, oregano, winter savory, and lavender. On the right side are caraway thyme, tarragon, silver thyme, Greek oregano, and lavender.

about the different species and how they grew in the different parts of the country. In speaking with Carole Saville as well, she has often noted how an occasional herb grows so much larger in her Los Angeles garden than it would have in her New Jersey garden.

Growing Herbs

Variability aside, herbs are among the easiest plants to grow. The majority are perennial plants that need six to eight hours of sun daily, very well drained soil, little fertilizing, and some spring pruning for renewal. In areas of the country where the ground freezes they need mulching, and in arid areas summer watering. Tender herbs such as rosemary, lemon grass, and lemon verbena must be brought inside in the winter in cold climates; alternatively, these tender perennial herbs

can be treated as annuals and replanted every spring. As a rule, herbs are seldom targeted by pests and diseases. Herbs in the South are the exception, and there, where plants are bothered by fungus or nematodes, new perennial herbs can be planted every year in a new area of the garden or in containers. Where garden soil is poorly drained, containers are the solution for that as well; an alternative is planting in raised beds. In most cases, there are solutions to any cultural problem that might arise with herbs, and even gardeners with no yard at all can grow a few herbs on a sunny windowsill.

The annual herbs, such as basil, dill, chervil, and cilantro, are grown in a somewhat different manner, as they need annual planting and better soil than the perennials. Give these herbs fairly organic soil and moderate amounts of fertilizer and water. Chervil and cilantro grow better in cool weather and are short-lived plants. For a constant supply, reseed the beds every few weeks as you would for radishes. See "Basil" in Part Four, "An Encyclopedia of Superior Vegetables," for more growing information specific to annual herbs.

Herb plants can be planted in a simple dooryard cluster, in a flower border, in containers, or in a traditional formal knot garden. As a rule, because they need similar growing conditions, annual herbs are at home in a bed of annual flowers and/or vegetables or clustered together. Perennial herbs grow best surrounded by other perennial flowers and herbs. For ease of maintenance, the informal cluster of perennial herbs is hard to beat. On the other hand, if a formal knot garden has always been your dream, be prepared to give continual care, as the plants will need constant clipping to look their best. Whatever your choice regarding garden design, the most important factor concerning your herb garden is how close it is to the house. All the herb authorities I know agree that the closer your herbs are to the kitchen door the more you will use them in your cooking. See the "Sources" section at the end of this chapter for many good books on herb gardening.

Harvesting Herbs

For the average cook, harvesting herbs means a last-minute dash to the garden to pick a few leaves for flavoring. Harvesting larger amounts for preserving involves choosing a time when the herbs are at peak flavor and the plants are growing well enough to renew themselves. For the most flavor, harvest most herbs just before the plant starts to flower. Another good time to harvest a large amount is when the plants need to be cut back so they can renew. A wonderful way to use large amounts of leftover prunings is for smoking. When you smoke fish or meat, place branches of green herbs such as thyme, lavender, fennel, rosemary, or dill over the wet wood chips before you close up the smoker.

Preserving Herbs

Fresh herbs are best, of course, but not all herbs are available year-round, so good cooks over the years have learned ways to preserve the flavors. The best ways to preserve herbs are in oil, in vinegars, and by freezing. Information on these methods is covered in the "Cooking from the Herb Garden" section. Another time-honored way to preserve some herbs is by drying.

The following directions for drying herbs can be used for borage, marjoram, mint, parsley, rosemary, sage, bay, chives, dill, thyme, winter savory, and oregano.

Pick the leaves in the driest part of the day. Wash quickly, if necessary, and pat dry. Place the leaves in a single layer on a screen. For quick drying, put the leaves in an oven at a *very* low temperature (104 degrees) for a few hours. If you have more time, place the screen in a warm, dry place indoors, such as a garage or attic, and dry for five to seven days. Stir the leaves once a day. When they are dry, store in airtight containers in a cool, dark place.

The Saville Herb Garden

The first time I visited Carole Saville in Los Angeles, I went to see her herb garden. As we chatted she offered me some herb tea. I expected her to get out a jar of dried herbs, but instead she stepped out of her kitchen door and gathered some fresh leaves of lemon grass and peppermint. Her teapot was glass, and when she put the leaves in it and poured boiling water over them, I could see the water turn bright green. The steam that rose up had a clean, fresh aroma, and the cup of tea I drank with honey was the best I had ever tasted.

When the time came to prepare dinner, out Carole went to her herb garden again, this time to gather snippets of tarragon and winter savory. She proceeded to slip the tarragon under the skins of Cornish game hens and chop the winter savory and put it in with the snap beans. When dinner was about ready, she went out once more to gather some crisp, fresh herbs and a few edible flowers for the salad. The meal had such richness and there were so many flavors woven through it from course to course that I realized, not for the first or last time, that I had a great deal to learn about herbs.

Since that day five years ago, Carole has become even more involved with herbs. When I first met her she was writing about cuisine, styling food for photographs, and giving seminars on herbs. Since then there has been a real renaissance of herbs in this country, and the chefs of many of the best restaurants are expressing the need for guidance in growing them. Now Carole devotes herself full time to herbs and gourmet varieties of vegetables, designing culinary gardens for restaurants and private individuals.

When Carole and I agreed that I would use her garden in my book, I asked her for some background, starting with how she had become interested in herbs. She told me that when she moved from the city to a wonderful old house in New Jersey, she and her husband, Brent, decided to put in an herb garden because of her interest in cooking. After a few years, Carole became so involved she actually ended up with three herb gardens. The first was an informal one filled with culinary herbs, the next was an ornamental herb garden containing primarily plants with blue flowers, and the third was a traditional English knot garden.

Eventually, Carole and Brent moved to Los Angeles. On their cross-country flight they brought cuttings of some of Carole's favorite herbs, and once

the two moved in, they quickly installed the new herb garden. It was designed in a classic geometric pattern with a raised brick planter in the middle. And, of course, it was right off the kitchen. Today, because Carole is so busy designing herb gardens for other people, she has limited herself to this one herb garden of about twenty by twenty feet. It contains all the culinary herbs she finds indispensable, including all the popular herbs, such as thyme, basil, and sage. But Carole also enjoys exploring uses for the less common lovage, Mexican tarragon, lemon verbena, lemon grass, bee balm, costmary, sweet cicely, and scented geraniums. All in all, she grows more than seventy different varieties of herbs. In addition, she has a small corner of this garden full of edible flowers.

I asked Carole to describe a few of her favorite ways of cooking with herbs. "I like to use generous

Carole Saville's adventurous herb garden in Los Angeles.

When I visited Rose Marie Nichols McGee at her herb garden in Oregon, we shared our enthusiasm for fresh herbs and she commented that she's so dependent on her herbs that she brings some of the plants inside during the winter. Rose Marie has had much success growing herbs inside, she says, particularly in strawberry jars, pottery planters with many pockets protruding from their sides. "Most herbs tolerate a range of lighting," Rose Marie says, "though they probably couldn't survive year after year inside. They're not as productive and lush as in the summer, but they make it through the winter and are a pleasure to have."

I asked Rose Marie if she could assemble a strawberry jar herb garden for me so I could see the process. To demonstrate, she selected some of the herbs she's had the most success growing inside: parsley, oregano, French thyme, sage, dwarf basil, 'Opal' basil, winter savory, rosemary, and lemon thyme. Rose Marie recommends purchasing a fairly large strawberry jar and, toward the end of August or early September, selecting from your garden or a nursery the plants you'll use most during the winter. You'll need a plant for each pocket, plus one or two for the top of the jar.

"Begin by filling the base of your jar up to the first row of pockets with a very lightweight potting mix," she explains. "A little time-release fertilizer blended with the potting mix helps by providing long-sustaining, light fertilization throughout the winter; otherwise you'll need to fertilize lightly once a month. Because the jar is hard to water and the pockets dry out readily, I also put in a watering tube the depth of the jar. To make this, I take a one-inch diameter PVC pipe and drill holes about an inch apart in the sides of it, leaving the bottom open. When filling the jar with soil, I plug the top of the tube with a cork so it remains clear. Then, later, I water through the tube's opening as well as into the top of the pot.

Rose Marie Nichols McGee

Rose Marie recommends planning which plants will look best in which pockets and saving one or two of the best-looking for the top of the jar. Plant the bottom row and tamp the soil lightly around the roots; then proceed to fill the next level of pockets. Cover the roots of this level with soil, tamp in place, and continue the process up the pot. "Fill soil in from both the inside and the outside pockets so all roots are covered," Rose Marie says. "If you think a plant doesn't fit a pocket, try a smaller plant from your garden, or prune the roots and foliage of a large one. Keep working your way around from level to level, tamping in place until all of the pockets are filled. Finally, plant the top of the jar and remove the cork from the pipe. Gently water down the pipe and into each pocket, repeating two or three times until the entire jar is soaked. Place the jar outdoors in the shade for a few days so the plants have a chance to adjust. This way, they'll acclimatize to their new growing location in the pot before they're moved indoors, reducing shock and stress. After a few days move the jar to a sunny spot.

"Bring the jar inside before you expect your first frost. Place it in the brightest, sunniest spot you have in your house, but avoid locations near wood stoves or under air ducts, where forced air could dry the plants' leaves. Put the jar on some kind of a water barrier to avoid staining the floor, because you'll need to keep the jar moist—but not saturated—throughout the winter. A tray of pebbles and water beneath the jar will keep the air around it suitably humid and, together with misting, will usually keep spider mites from becoming a problem. If the plants become badly infected with either spider mites or whiteflies, you'll need to use a suitable pesticide or discard the plants."

Remember that your winter herbs will grow slowly, so you'll need to use them only a few sprigs at a time, not with abandon. Use rosemary and sage in vegetable soup or marinades. Or use a few clippings of thyme in salads, or a few leaves of fresh basil to brighten a bowl of stewed tomatoes or an omelette.

"I really appreciate having a little sprig of savory on hand when I make borscht or cook beans," Rose Marie told me as she finished her demonstration jar. "And it's a luxury to have fresh lemon thyme when I'm making a salad dressing or preparing chicken and look out the window to see snow on the ground. Besides tasting so good, the herbs are fresh reminders of summer."

amounts of chopped fresh thyme, marjoram, parsley, and dill in rice for herbed rice," she began. "And I enjoy serving herb butters made with basil or oregano with crusty breads. I slip leaves of basil, tarragon, lemon grass, or dill under the skin of chicken before I bake it. I substitute coriander or tarragon for basil in pesto and chop rosemary or sage up fine and add it to my cornbread batter before baking it. Lemon grass, *Hisbiscus Sabdariffa,* and spearmint I use in teas; and I make a lemon confiture [jelly] flavored with English lavender or lemon verbena. I use many of my herbs in salads: the mints, basil, thyme, chervil, tarragon, chives, in particular, and lots of salad burnet and many of the edible flowers. Sometimes I rub the salad bowl with lovage before I add the greens to give the salad a celery taste, and I often add basil or chervil to mayonnaise or add chopped herbs to the dressing. I could go on and on. I just can't imagine cooking without my herb garden."

After spending time with Carole and tasting her food, I'm left with the goal of weaving herbs into my daily life with the elegance and pleasure she achieves at the task.

The McGee Herb Garden

Rose Marie Nichols McGee grew up in Oregon next door to an herb nursery. Maybe I can be forgiven, therefore, when I say that she knows herbs from the ground up. For years I ordered herbs from her parents' company, Nichols Garden Nursery, and it seemed natural to contact them when I was searching for knowledgeable people to share information on herbs.

Rose Marie and her husband now own and manage the nursery, and she was very enthusiastic about growing a demonstration garden for me. She saw it as a great excuse to put in a small herb garden for her mother. Her mother has been hampered by arthritis for some years and missed having a garden. What a wonderful little garden the new one turned out to be! Rose Marie cut a modified kidney-shape area out of an existing lawn about ten by twenty feet in size and filled it completely with herbs. The idea, she told me, was to make "an informal and inviting little oasis, with paths so my mother—or anyone!—could get right in and enjoy it."

The bed preparation was rather straightforward. Rose Marie began in late spring by digging up the area, and then, to save a lot of weeding in the future, sifted through the soil to remove all the rhizomes of the weedy quack grass that had grown rampantly in the lawn. She then put on a layer of mushroom compost and hand tilled it in. Finally, to prevent another future problem and to give the garden a clean line, Rose Marie put in a black plastic edging to keep the lawn from growing into the herb bed.

One design objective was low maintenance, which meant making a perennial garden. She explained: "This year, because it's new, I've added many annuals, but by next year the perennials will fill it in and be in their glory. I enjoy having a constant supply of flowers and color in the garden for most of the season, so I chose many of the flowers to bloom at different times of the year."

Rose Marie decided to start the blooming season with sweet cicely, which blossoms in spring along with the daffodils and has white, lacy, very fragrant flowers. Other herbs that will bloom throughout the growing season include clary sage, which will produce great spikes of lavender flowers; regular chives, with their lavender blossoms produced in late spring; Oriental chives, with white flowers that smell like roses and that bloom in July and August; two varieties of lavender that bloom most of the summer; lemon mint, which will provide a lot of color in late August with its shaggy purple heads; and pineapple

Rose Marie Nichols McGee, of Nichols Garden Nursery, created this herb garden oasis in the middle of the back lawn of her mother's house. The garden includes sages, nasturtiums, thyme, lavenders, rosemary, and chives.

sage for late-fall color—its scarlet blossoms will brighten up the garden from September until it is cut down by frost and dies. During the first year, annual plants yielded much of the garden's color—the purple foliage of 'Opal' basil, orange and yellow nasturtiums and calendulas, and the large yellow heads of fennel.

The garden was designed with low edging plants in the front and along the paths, with a gradual increase in the height of the plants toward the middle and back. As focal points for the design, Rose Marie used a dramatic plant of angelica, with its large spreading leaves and handsome foliage, and two graceful statues of monks made by a local artist.

I asked Rose Marie to talk a bit about how she uses herbs from the garden. "I harvest angelica when it's just starting to bloom," she began, "because that's when it has the most flavor. I don't let the flower heads develop at all. I then simply take the large stems and cut them up and boil them in a sugar syrup. Once they're candied and dried, I chop the stems and add them to my favorite shortbread recipe. Another herb I enjoy is sweet cicely. I use the foliage in salads during the year and the seeds in fruit or green salads. The seeds are tender and have a sweet anise flavor."

There was a great deal of basil in the garden, and I asked her how she prepared it. She told me that she and her mother preserve it by chopping the leaves and layering them in a jar alternately with layers of Parmesan cheese and then freezing it. They find that it keeps very well that way and they sprinkle basil on sliced tomatoes and salads and use it in pesto and spaghetti sauce all winter long.

On my last day at Rose Marie's garden she laid out a marvelous tea party—the very vision of a childhood fantasy. All the confections were wonderful, and all were filled with herbs!

Recommended Culinary Herbs

The following is an overview of culinary herbs you can grow in your garden. Check the recommended vegetable and herb lists in many of the other chapters for more species of herbs and other ways to cook them. The numbers in parentheses after the herb names refer to the seed companies listed at the end of this chapter. When no number follows a name, the herb is readily available from most of the sources listed.

ANGELICA *Angelica Archangelica* Angelica is a large-leafed herb that in humid climates can be a dramatic backdrop to a flower border. Both the aromatic leaves and the stems are used in numerous dishes.

How to grow: This hardy herb is a biennial that produces huge clusters of yellow flowers in the summer, beginning in its second year. It is started from seeds in rich, well-drained, slightly acidic soil. Keep fairly moist during the growing season. In arid climates it generally grows less rampantly. Seed companies supply fresh seeds during midsummer, and these must be planted immediately, as they are short-lived.

How to prepare: The fresh stems can be used sparingly to flavor salads. Stems can be preserved, most popularly by candying. The fresh leaves can also be used in salads and cooked with fish or poultry.

ANISE *Pimpinella Anisum* Since ancient times, anise has been enjoyed for its slightly licorice taste.

How to grow: Anise is an annual plant started from seed in the garden. Thin seedlings to six inches apart. The plants will grow to about two feet and put out both lobed and feathery green leaves and umbels of cream-colored flowers. The ripe seeds are only produced in very warm summer areas. Anise is

fussy about its growing conditions and needs full sun and moist, well-drained soil. Pick the seed heads when they start to mature, clean, and store them in a warm, dry place.

How to prepare: Leaves can be used for seasoning soups, and seeds are used in baked goods, including the traditional German *pfeffernuss* cookies. Anise is also used in liqueurs and salad dressings and, my favorite way, in spaghetti sauce.

ANISE HYSSOP *Agastache Foeniculum* See the "Edible Flower Gardens" and "Gourmet Salad Gardens" chapters.

BASIL *Ocimum Basilicum* This is probably the queen of the culinary herbs. In fact, it is used in such large amounts that I categorize it as a vegetable in the Part Four Encyclopedia.

How to grow: See the Part Four Encyclopedia.

How to prepare: See the Part Four Encyclopedia plus recipes throughout the book.

BAY LAUREL (sweet bay, Grecian laurel) *Laurus nobilis* The aromatic leaves of the bay tree have been used in cooking since Roman times.

How to grow: Bay is a woody perennial. Purchase plants or (a slow way) grow from seeds. Plant in good, fast-draining soil. Bay laurel is not hardy; in cold-winter areas plant in containers and bring it inside to use as a house plant (watch for scale insects). Harvest leaves as you need them.

How to prepare: The strong, almost resinous-tasting leaves of bay are used in soups, stews, spaghetti, sauces, and marinades. The leaves dry well and keep their flavor.

BORAGE *Borago officinalis* See the "Edible Flower Gardens" and "Gourmet Salad Gardens" chapters.

BEE BALM *Monarda didyma* See the "Edible Flower Gardens" chapter.

BURNET, SALAD *Poterium Sanguisorba* This attractive plant produces leaves with a slight cucumber taste.

How to grow: Start plants from seeds or divisions. Plant in full or partial sun in poor soil, keep fairly moist, and cut off seed heads as they appear or they will reseed in the garden.

How to prepare: Use fresh leaves in salads, as a garnish in summer drinks, and in sauces or vinegars. Burnet does not retain its flavor when dried.

CARAWAY *Carum Carvi* The pungent seeds of caraway are a favorite seasoning in parts of northern Europe.

How to grow: Caraway is a biennial that produces carrotlike leaves the first year and flower heads and seeds the second year. Sow the seeds in spring in a sunny, well-drained soil and keep fairly moist. If the soil freezes in the winter, mulch the plants. Harvest the seed heads a month after they have blossomed and store them in a warm, dry place.

How to prepare: Caraway seeds give a distinctive flavor to many dishes. Use with vegetables, salads, breads, sauerkraut, and stuffed cabbage. See the "German Gardens" chapter for more information.

CHAMOMILE *Chamaemelum nobile; Matricaria recutita* There are two types of chamomile—the perennial type, which is low growing and moderately hardy, and an annual chamomile, which is a lovely short-lived garden flower that grows to about eighteen inches and produces a cloud of small white daisies.

How to grow: Start both chamomiles from seed in well-prepared soil in full sun. Keep fairly moist. Or plant perennial chamomile from plants available from the nursery.

How to prepare: Most cooks prefer the flavor of the annual chamomile. The perennial one usually tastes medicinal. Use the flower heads in herbal teas and the petals in salads. The heads dry well for winter use.

CHERVIL *Anthriscus Cerefolium* See the "French Gardens" chapter.

CHIVES *Allium* spp. See "Onions" in the Part Four Encyclopedia; see also the "Oriental Gardens" chapter.

CILANTRO *Coriandrum sativum* See the "Oriental Gardens" and "Mexican Gardens" chapters.

CUMIN *Cuminum Cyminum* Cumin is a distinctive-tasting herb whose seeds give characteristic flavor to curry powder and chili.

How to grow: Cumin is rather temperamental and needs a very warm summer to produce seeds. Start seeds in spring in full sun and well-drained soil when the weather warms up. Seeds are only produced in very warm summer areas. Harvest whole seed heads and let dry in a warm, dry place.

How to prepare: Use cumin seeds sparingly either whole or ground. Toasting slightly enhances their flavor. Use in curries, deviled eggs, pot roasts, and dishes containing beans and chilies.

DILL *Anethum graveolens* Dill is famous in pickles, but it's also quite versatile and enjoyable in many different dishes. Both the young leaves and seeds are used.

How to grow: Start these annual plants in spring from seeds after the weather has warmed up. Plant in full sun in well-drained soil. Make successive sowings for a continuous supply of fresh leaves. These ferny plants grow to three feet, so give them room to spread. Keep moist throughout the growing season and harvest leaves as soon as the plants get four to five inches tall. Save seed heads and dry in a warm, dry place. The varieties 'Aroma' (4) and 'Bouquet' (2, 3) are bushier and more vigorous than regular dill.

How to prepare: Use dill leaves fresh in salads, omelettes, vegetables dishes, fish sauces, and with mild soft cheeses. Use the seeds in pickling cucumbers, snap beans, carrots, and beets. Preserve the leaves of dill by drying or put in vinegar or oil. Harvest the seeds and keep them in a cool dry place.

FENNEL *Foeniculum vulgare* This herb has beautiful, ferny foliage reminiscent of that of licorice. See the "Italian Gardens" chapter for information on its close relative, sweet fennel.

How to grow: Though a perennial, fennel is usually grown as you would dill (see above). A coppery-colored fennel variety, 'Rubra' (3, 4, 5), is striking in the landscape.

How to prepare: Fennel leaves can be used in salads, sauces, fish, soups, stews, salad dressings, and pasta. Throw the dry plant prunings onto the barbecue when you are grilling fish to give a great, rich flavor. Use the seeds in spaghetti, soups, sauerkraut, and bread pudding. Preserve as you would dill.

GINGER *Zingiber officinale* See the "Oriental Gardens" chapter.

LAVENDER *Lavandula augustifolia* See the "Edible Flower Gardens" chapter.

LEMON GRASS *Cymbopogon citratus* An aromatic grass-family herb with a rich lemon flavor.

How to grow: Native to the tropics, lemon grass can be grown outdoors in very mild climates and in containers in cold ones. Purchase divisions from local nurseries or from Fox Hill Farm or Taylor's Herb Gardens. Plant in good, well-draining soil in part shade.

How to prepare: Harvest leaves of lemon grass

once the plant is established and use as a seasoning in Thai dishes, sparingly in light soups, and as a wonderful refreshing tea. The inner tender portion of the base can be used in soups and in chicken. To preserve lemon grass, either dry or freeze the leaves.

LEMON VERBENA *Aloysia triphylla* Lemon verbena is another of the tropical herbs that has a strong lemon flavor.

How to grow: Lemon verbena is a woody perennial shrub growing to ten feet in mild-winter areas and is hardy to about 10 degrees. In most areas it will lose its leaves in winter. In cold-winter areas it can be grown well in containers and brought inside in the winter or grown in a greenhouse. Plants brought in will lose their leaves and should be kept in a fairly cool place. Cut back and repot in the early spring. Purchase plants from Fox Hill Farm or Taylor's Herb Gardens or start from seeds obtained from the "Sources" list at the end of the chapter. Starting from seeds is a slow process, however. In mild climates, situate plants in a sunny area of the garden in good soil. Lemon verbena produces sprays of tiny pink flowers in summer.

How to prepare: Use the lemon flavor of this herb in fruit salads, jellies, fruit drinks, and as a tea or garnish, as well as with chicken or fish. The leaves dry well and retain their flavor.

LOVAGE *Levisticum officinale* This large herb has a strong flavor reminiscent of celery.

How to grow: Start seeds in the garden in fall. In coldest areas, start inside and plant out once the weather warms. Plant in full sun or partial shade in moist soil with good drainage. In moist areas, the plant can grow to six feet, so give it lots of room and keep seed heads cut off or it will reseed itself. Harvest leaves once the plants are a foot high. Collect seed heads and dry in a cool, dry place.

How to prepare: Use the leaves sparingly in salads, soups, and stews, or with meat and poultry dishes. The stems can be candied as with angelica or frozen for winter use, and the seeds used to flavor baked goods.

MEXICAN OREGANO *Lippia* spp. and *Origanum* spp. See the "Mexican Gardens" chapter.

MINT *Mentha* spp. There are many different kinds of mint. Among the most commonly used culinary ones are peppermint, spearmint, apple mint, and pineapple mint.

A chocolate cake made with fresh mint leaves can be the highlight of an afternoon tea.

How to grow: The mints are perennial plants, and most grow to two to three feet tall, have shiny green leaves, and are quite rangy and sprawling. If not controlled they can become pests. Mint spreads by underground runners, so it is best planted in containers or within rings of metal flashing in the ground to contain the roots. Most mints prefer moist, shady conditions. Set out plants in the spring; once they are growing vigorously they can be harvested anytime throughout the year. Under some conditions they are prone to whitefly infestations, but these can usually be controlled with a soap-based spray. Mints bloom in midsummer. The flowers in some varieties are white, in others lavender to violet.

How to prepare: All the mints have a characteristic clean "minty" flavor. The leaves are best used fresh, though they can be preserved by freezing or drying. Use them in cool drinks, in green salads, in Middle Eastern dishes such as tabouli, with cucumbers, in soups, and in savory sauces, particularly with mustard or garlic served with lamb. Also try mint in sweet dishes—desserts, jellies, sauces, fruit salads, and with chocolate.

MITSUBA   *Cryptotaenia japonica*   See the "Oriental Gardens" chapter.

OREGANO and MARJORAM   *Origanum* spp.   In European cooking, *oregano* is generally the term used for *Origanum vulgare hirtum,* though sometimes this herb is used interchangeably with its close relative marjoram. However, in Mexican cooking the term *oregano* is much more general and often represents a large number of herbs used for flavoring. For more information on the oreganos used in Mexican cooking, see the "Mexican Gardens" chapter.

How to grow: Oregano is a rangy perennial native to the Mediterranean. It must be planted in full sun in a light, fast-draining soil. Start the plants from cuttings or divisions. Cut plants back in late spring to encourage new growth so the plants do not become too woody. A particularly rich and pungent variety, called Greek oregano, is available from Taylor's Herb Gardens and Fox Hill Farm.

How to prepare: Oregano is most commonly associated with a number of Italian sauces used with pizza, spaghetti, and marinades. It can also be used in soups, stews, salads, and most meat dishes. It is best used fresh, though it can be frozen or dried or preserved in vinegar or oil.

PARSLEY   *Petroselinum crispum*   Parsley is a versatile herb whose leaves are used in most of the world's cuisines in one form or another. For information on the 'Hamburg Rooted' parsley, see the "German Gardens" chapter. For more information on Italian parsley, see the "Italian Gardens" chapter. For Japanese parsley (mitsuba), see the "Oriental Gardens" chapter.

How to grow: Parsley is a biennial generally treated as an annual. This beautiful plant has dark-green, curly, finely divided leaves and is neat and tidy looking in the garden. Use it in borders, herb gardens, and containers. Start seeds in the spring or buy plants from nurseries and set out. Parsley seeds take from two weeks to up to a month to germinate. Parsley grows very well in light shade when given rich, moist soil. It does not dry well, however, so move plants inside for winter use. The preferred culinary parsley for flavoring many European dishes is Italian parsley; varieties include 'Italian Parsley' and 'Flat Parsley', both available from all the companies listed in the "Sources" section. Standard parsley is used for flavoring and as a garnish. Varieties to try are 'Extra Curled Dwarf' (3), 'Moss Curled' (4), and 'Decora' (4).

How to prepare: Harvest the outer leaves of parsley during the growing season. They are best used fresh, though they will retain some of their flavor when frozen. Parsley, while commonly used as a garnish, is high in iron and vitamin C. Its refreshing, peppery flavor lends interest when its leaves are chopped up and served with new potatoes or added to soups, stews, sauces, salads, casseroles, and tabouli, the Middle Eastern salad.

ROSEMARY   *Rosmarinus officinalis*   Rosemary is a pungent herb native to the Mediterranean.

How to grow: Rosemary is a tender perennial grown from cuttings, divisions, and, occasionally, from seed. It needs full sun and fast-draining soil. In mild climates it can be used as a landscaping plant. In cold areas it is usually grown in containers. Most varieties of rosemary produce a profusion of blue flowers in the spring and a sprinkling of flowers throughout the summer. Flower colors include deep blue, lavender, pink, and white. The form of the plant can vary from strongly upright to completely prostrate. The standard culinary rosemary has light-blue flowers. Purchase the unusual varieties from Fox Hill Farm and Taylor's Herb Gardens.

How to prepare: Leaves can be harvested anytime during the growing season, though they will be most flavorful just before flowering. Preserve rosemary by drying or putting in vinegar or oil. Rosemary lends its almost pinelike flavor to many dishes containing pork, veal, and lamb and is a favorite herb to add to soups, stews, breads or biscuits, and pizza toppings. Use this herb sparingly, as the flavor is very strong.

SAFFRON   *Crocus sativus*   Probably one of the world's most expensive flavorings, saffron is the dried, pulverized stigmas of a fall-blooming crocus.

How to grow: Plant the corms of these crocuses in late summer. They are available from Nichols Garden Nursery. The plants prefer rich, well-drained soil with some afternoon shade. Plant these pretty, mauve to purple crocuses in large quantities if you wish to harvest for the saffron, since a suitable harvest requires many plants. Divide and replant every one to two years. *Caution:* Do not confuse with the autumn crocus, *Colchicum,* which is poisonous.

How to prepare: Remove the orange stigmas with

a tweezer, dry them for a few days, and store in a covered jar in a warm, dry place. Grind and use them in rice dishes, including paella, and in East Indian dishes.

SAGE *Salvia officinalis* Sage is a popular, pungent herb best known in the stuffing for Thanksgiving turkey.

How to grow: Most culinary sages are perennials that can be grown from cuttings or seeds. Plant in poor soil, in full sun, and with extremely good drainage. Sages die readily in heavy clay or if their roots stay damp. Plants range in height from two to four feet. Numerous sages can be used in landscaping situations, in traditional herb gardens, and in containers. Most have gray foliage and purple flowers, but a particularly striking one, tricolor sage, has pink, green, and white leaves. To keep these plants looking neat, trim them back once or twice during the growing season. Garden sage, which is a perennial, is the most commonly used culinary variety. It has gray-green leaves and lavender flowers. Other common varieties are purple sage and golden sage. Golden sage, *S. aurea,* while colorful in the garden, is somewhat less preferred in the kitchen. Purple sage, *S. purpurea,* has soft, purple, aromatic leaves and purple flowers.

Other sages to try are clary sage, *S. sclarea,* which is a spectacular biennial producing huge spikes of lavender-to-rose flowers the second summer, and pineapple sage, *S. elegans.* Clary sage is planted from seeds. Pineapple sage, which is propagated only by cuttings or divisions and is a very tender perennial, grows to four feet tall and produces spikes of bright-red flowers loved by hummingbirds.

How to prepare: Common garden sage is a favorite seasoning for all types of poultry, stuffings, sausages, and fish, as well as soup, stews, and tomato sauces. Clary sage's culinary use is generally limited to the making of tea from the leaves and the using of flowers in salads. The leaves of pineapple sage have a distinctive pineapple taste and are used for teas and cold drinks and in fruit salads, jams, and jellies. The flowers can be used in fruit salads too and as garnish for pastries. Dried, the leaves of garden sage retain their flavor well.

SAVORY *Satureja* spp. Summer and winter savories are other favorite herbs from the Mediterranean area. The most popular savory for culinary purposes is summer savory, famous for flavoring snap beans.

How to order: Summer savory is an easily grown annual plant that reaches eighteen inches in height. It has very small gray-green leaves and small lavender-to-white flowers that bloom all summer long. Use the plants in a flower border, in containers, or in an herb garden. Start seeds in the spring in a sunny place in the garden that has fairly good soil and keep plants moist throughout the growing season.

Winter savory is a perennial that grows from six to eighteen inches tall. It has compact, bright-green foliage and tiny spikes of white flowers and makes a handsome plant in the garden. Winter savory, while slow to germinate, can be started from seeds but is usually propagated by cuttings or division. It is hardy to about 10 degrees and grows very slowly. Plant in full sun, in sandy soil, and keep somewhat moist during the growing season.

How to prepare: Summer savory can be harvested throughout the summer and is best used fresh. Winter savory can be harvested throughout the season and is somewhat more successful preserved for winter use by freezing or drying. Better yet, keep the plant in a container and bring it inside in winter. Use savories in salads, soups, and poultry. See the "German Gardens" chapter for more uses for both savories.

SHISHO (perilla) *Perilla* spp. See the "Oriental Gardens" chapter.

SORREL *Rumex* spp. See the "French Gardens" chapter.

SWEET WOODRUFF *Galium odoratum* This fragrant plant is known especially for its traditional use in May wine.

How to grow: Sweet woodruff's dark-green foliage and tiny white flowers make an attractive ground cover in shade. The plant seldom grows higher than a foot. As its seeds are slow to germinate, it is usually propagated by division or by putting out new plants. Sweet woodruff prefers partial to full shade and a rich, well-drained soil. You may want to restrain it, as it is self-sowing and can become a weed. Mowing will help control sweet woodruff but will not harm it.

How to prepare: Dried sweet woodruff has a faint vanilla fragrance. Pick stems and dry upside down in bunches. Fresh woodruff freezes well. Fresh or dry leaves are used in tea or in May wine.

TARRAGON *Artemisia Dracunculus* See the "French Gardens" chapter.

THYME   *Thymus* spp.   Thyme is versatile in the garden and the kitchen and is used in cuisines throughout the world.

How to grow: This perennial reaches nine to twelve inches in height and has either gray-green, dark-green, golden, or silver foliage, depending on the variety. Some of the varieties are more useful in the landscape, while others are more useful in the kitchen. English thyme, *T. vulgaris,* is the most commonly used culinary thyme. Other choice varieties are lemon thyme, *T. citriodorus* (1, 3, 4, 5), which has a rich lemon taste and pink flowers; caraway thyme, *T. herba-barona* (1, 3, 4, 5), with a caraway taste, dark-green leaves, and pink flowers; and French thyme, *T. vulgaris,* a mild thyme with grayish foliage. All the thymes need full sun and fast-draining soil. In cold climates protect with mulches. In spring cut back the foliage by about one-third so the plant will stay lush. Start from seeds or with cuttings.

How to prepare: Thyme can be harvested anytime throughout the growing season. It is wonderful fresh, though stripping the leaves off the stems can be tedious. Simplify the process by drying the stems until just brittle and then gently rubbing them between your palms to remove the leaves. Small amounts of thyme complement many garden vegetables and most meat dishes. Thyme is one ingredient of the traditional French bouquet garni. Thyme leaves can be dried or preserved in vinegar or oil.

Cooking from the Herb Garden

I have an amber jar of magic in my refrigerator. It's a marinade of olive oil crammed full of slices of garlic and fresh basil leaves. When I add a spoonful of this oil to an omelette or a soup I feel like Tinkerbell spreading magic dust. Presto! The dish explodes with flavor. Everyday foods become instant decadence. Actually, *decadence,* with its negative connotations, isn't really the word, since by using this mixture instead of butter I dramatically cut down the amount of cholesterol in the dish. I spread this flavored oil on toast or in the pan before I cook a cheese sandwich. I use it with a baked potato, in a salad, or on green beans and zucchini. Preparing that little jar took, at the most, ten minutes of my time. I picked and sliced a cup of basil leaves, sliced eight or ten cloves of garlic, found a jar, put the basil and garlic in it, and poured olive oil in to cover. Sometimes I make the marinade with 'Lemon' basil or 'Cinnamon' basil. I'm sure I could make it with lemon thyme or tarragon, too. No matter which herbs I use, after a week or so of letting the flavors blend, I have a half-pint of pleasure waiting for me in the refrigerator. How did I ever cook before I learned to make this mixture?

Like most Americans, I grew up with few herbs in my food, and the ones I did know were dried. According to French chef Tom McCombie, "We Americans are so used to seeing our herbs labeled 'Schilling' or 'McCormick' that we expect them to be grown in the cans we buy them in. Most of us have no idea that basil and tarragon in their fresh form bear no resemblance to the dried products. In fact, most of our cookbooks call for 'tarragon or parsley' and 'chervil or parsley.' Well, they're all green, but that's really where the resemblance ends. In France, I worked in some of the greatest restaurants and I never once saw a can of herbs. I feel that's one of the main reasons French food is so good."

I know now that I grew up not color blind but "herb blind." And in doing my research for this book I discovered that cookbook publishers have unknowingly helped to perpetuate this problem in our society by discouraging authors from calling for fresh or unusual herbs in their recipes. Editors have seemed to assume that listing ingredients unavailable in markets would frustrate their users. This assumption is currently being challenged dramatically. The new chefs writing cookbooks refuse to knuckle under and are, in fact, creating a demand to which stores are responding. And, of course, more cooks are finding that most herbs are very easy to grow.

"Painting" with Garden Herbs

A good way to begin learning about herbs is to think of a garden containing a dozen varieties of fresh herbs as a kind of palette of paints to work with in the kitchen. As with colors, the possibilities are endless. Just pick your herb and then your medium. It's really hard to go wrong. Here are some ways to get started. But remember that in almost all cases fresh herbs are preferred over dried.

OPPOSITE: *Spicy sausages are marinated in a cinnamon basil and mustard sauce.*

Let's begin with the medium of vegetables. For asparagus, try adding some chopped fresh dill leaves or tarragon to the mayonnaise or the melted butter you serve it with. When you cook snap beans, add a little fresh chopped savory, basil, dill, or tarragon to the pan. If you are cooking dry beans in a recipe, add some thyme, oregano, basil, or, for Mexican-style black beans, epazote. See the "Baked Bean Gardens" chapter for more herb ideas for dry beans.

A brief overview of the world's cuisines turns up a wealth of simple, time-tested ideas. In Germany, for instance, beets are sometimes served with caraway or dill, particularly if they are pickled. You might also want to try adding lemon balm. For eons, people have enjoyed cabbage cooked with caraway, dill, mint, sage, or, in some parts of Germany, mugwort. The neutral flavors of the cabbage seem to soak up herb flavors readily. In France sweet, young carrots are often seasoned with dill, mint, thyme, or tarragon,

Herb and flower vodkas made with roses, lemon grass, dianthus, lavender, kumquats, sweet woodruff, and costmary. Serve them ice cold.

and all over Europe cucumbers are flavored with dill, chervil, tarragon, or basil. In the Middle East cucumbers are combined with mint and in India with cilantro. Eggplant, a favorite in southern parts of Europe, is often flavored with basil, thyme, oregano, fennel, or parsley. The famous peas of the English are served with mint, and in other parts of the world cooks use thyme, chervil, and basil with peas.

The sweetness of peppers combines naturally with the strong tastes of basil, oregano, or thyme, and spinach is complemented by dill or basil in an omelette. Also, try a dill and feta cheese filling for filo-dough pastries or in crêpes.

Certain vegetables seem to have been created as vehicles for herb flavors—namely, potatoes, tomatoes, and summer squash. Try potatoes cooked or sprinkled with parsley, tarragon, dill, chervil, or thyme. And have tomatoes or summer squash with basil, oregano, parsley, thyme, fennel, anise seeds, mint, bay, cilantro, borage, rosemary, tarragon, and cumin.

Of course, other foodstuffs are also good vehicles for herbs. Take breads, for instance. I've already described my method of spreading olive oil seasoned with basil and garlic on toast. Also try adding fresh dill to your white or potato bread dough before baking. Or add rosemary to your biscuit dough when you make dumplings, and use basil in your cornbread.

Herbs have many uses, of course, with meats and fish of all types. Herbs add a new dimension to marinades—try one made of Italian seasonings on a London broil or hamburgers. Soak pork in a sauce with sage, or chicken in a sauce with fennel or anise seeds. And sprinkle rosemary on lamb chops before putting them on the barbecue. A light sauce for fish is exquisite with just a hint of dill or chervil. A lamb stew is much more interesting when a handful of fresh chopped mint is added. Add chopped herbs of all types to sausage meat or hamburgers before cooking, or sprinkle them over a chicken before baking it. Glazes, too, made with herbs and jelly or mustard will spice up the blandest meat dish.

Cheeses and egg dishes respond gloriously to fresh herbs. Layering soft cheese with chopped herbs makes a fancy but easy hors d'oeuvre. Fill omelettes and soufflés with fresh herbs and build a special brunch around baked eggs served with a sauce containing chopped dill or tarragon. Or try eggs Benedict with an herbed hollandaise.

Garnishes make up another medium. Use sprigs

Carole Saville, herb specialist and food writer, designs herb gardens and uses herbs from her own garden to flavor teas and enhance main courses and side dishes alike. But I was surprised to learn that she also uses them in more unique ways—to flavor vodkas, for example. I had never heard of flavored vodkas before, but Carole quickly brought me up to date on them.

"Flavored vodkas are ones that have either herbs, spices, or fruits added to them," she explained. "They first became popular in old Russia, where distillation and filtering methods were crude and something was needed to mask the tastes. The solution? Flavoring the liquor with fruits, berries, or herbs. In fact, Peter the Great habitually peppered his vodka, a practice thought to draw impurities to the bottom of the glass.

"Flavored vodkas are very popular in Eastern Europe today," Carole says. Old World favorites include *Pertsovka,* reputedly Stalin's favorite, which has the spicy taste of hot chili peppers; *Okhotnichya,* or hunter's vodka, flavored with herbs and berries; and *Chesnochnaya,* vodka infused with garlic, dill, and peppercorns.

While Russians drink flavored vodka throughout a meal, commonly referring to it as "the little ray of sunshine in the stomach," Carole likes to serve it with the first course—a nice way to begin a meal, she says. And while imported flavored vodkas are available in the United States from ethnic markets catering to Eastern Europeans, Carole recommends making your own. Commercial vodkas taste much stronger and certainly not as fresh as homemade, and

Carole Saville

you can create your own combinations.

When I asked Carole which flavors she likes best, she said, "I personally like to flavor vodka with mint, rosemary, or sweet woodruff, or with edible flowers such as roses, lavender, or dianthus—alone or in combinations. But I think everyone should be an alchemist and experiment in the kitchen!

"I use only *good-quality* Polish, Russian, or Swedish vodka," Carole emphasizes, "because the primary flavor is still vodka. I put herbs in the vodka and keep it at room temperature for a day or two. Chefs and vodka aficionados have different opinions as to how long to infuse the herbs to achieve the best fragrance; the vodka will take on the flavor in just one day, but I like to leave it a little longer. Whatever your taste, the vodka is best if stored in a freezer because the liquid thickens slightly and the flavors become more pronounced.

"I save pretty bottles, about sixteen-ounce capacity, to transfer the vodka into when it's ready. I serve the vodka ice cold in ice cold glasses with smoked salmon or other smoked fish, or—if the pocketbook allows—caviar."

Carole likes to serve vodka in small, pretty glasses that she buys in antique shops. If the glasses are mismatched, she says, all the better. She prefers small glasses because they hold only small amounts; she thinks vodka should be sipped, and the smaller amount prevents people from getting drunk. As Carole says, "Drinking flavored vodkas, like using flavored vinegars and oils, is a way to enjoy the fresh taste of some of humanity's favorite herb flavors."

of fresh dill or fennel with fish and place the beautiful leaves of scented geraniums around a tea sandwich tray. Sprigs of mint are nice on cold drinks and fruit salads. Teas, too, constitute a medium for fresh herbs. In particular, try the mints and the lemon- and anise-flavored herbs.

Preserving the Fresh Flavors

The essential oils that give flavor to most culinary herbs don't always hold up very well when the leaves are dried. Therefore, creative cooks have developed the following ways of preserving the sparkle in the flavor.

Jellies: We are all familiar with fruit jellies, but for years imaginative cooks have been using jelly as a medium for diverse flavors. You can add all types of flavorings—for instance, lavender, the basils, and, of course, the mints—to a neutral-tasting fruit jelly such as apple. See the recipe in this chapter for making herb jellies. Use these jellies as condiments with meats, on crackers, or with cream cheese and crackers.

Pesto: Pesto is generally defined as a paste of olive oil, garlic, nuts, Parmesan cheese, and fresh basil and is a specialty of the area around Genoa, Italy. It is traditionally served as a sauce for pasta or flavoring for soup. But I prefer the broader definition of pesto that many modern chefs adhere to: a paste or sauce made with oil, nuts, and/or cheese and a fresh herb. Thus, for instance, chef David Schy's pesto is made with cilantro, peanuts, and peanut oil. Experiment with your own pestos. Someday I would like to make a mint pesto and use it with lamb. Pestos are very versatile as toppings for pizza, pastas, stews, and soups. They can be incorporated into sauces for meats and, mixed with yogurt, mayonnaise, or sour cream, into dressings for salads. And they can be mixed with softened cream cheese or goat cheese and spread on crackers as dips. Finally, because pesto freezes very well, it becomes a marvelous way to preserve the fresh flavor of the herb after the season is past.

Herb vinegars and oils: The flavors of many herbs are lost when the herbs are dried but can be preserved effectively in vinegar or oil. This method works well for dill, tarragon, thyme, lemon thyme, the basils ('Opal' basil gives a beautiful magenta hue to vinegar and 'Cinnamon' and 'Anise' basils impart pinkish tones), mint, or your favorite combinations. You may add other flavorings, such as garlic, onion, chives, hot peppers, or spices. Use a large, wide-mouthed jar or crock and pack loosely with herbs (the stems and flowers can go in along with the leaves). Fill the crock with white wine vinegar, usually available in gallon jugs through restaurant or institutional suppliers, or virgin olive oil. Cover and leave the crock in a dark place for one to two months. Strain the infusion through cheesecloth or a fine sieve, and then pour through a funnel into bottles (clear glass shows off the colors best; use pretty bottles for holiday gifts), leaving any sediment at the bottom of the crock. Decorate with a sprig of the herb you used for flavoring, and then cap or seal the tops.

Use these herb-flavored oils and vinegars in salad dressings, for marinades, for flavoring soups, or in just about any dish where you would use the unflavored ones. Try a mint vinegar in fruit salad or a tarragon vinegar in potato salad. A wonderful use for the oil is to marinate fresh miniature goat cheeses or fresh mozzarella cheeses. Try putting them into olive oils flavored with basil and garlic. When the cheeses are all gone, you can use the oil for sautéeing omelettes, vegetables, and potatoes.

You can also preserve some herbs by freezing. I do this with fennel, dill, chervil, chives, and mint. Just wash the herbs, pat them dry, and take the leaves off the stems. Put the leaves in a self-sealing plastic bag, press out the air, and freeze. Some herbs may be successfully dried; see "How to Grow an Herb Garden" for information on this method.

SCENTED BASIL JELLIES

This recipe for delicate, easy-to-make jellies comes from the Shepherd's Garden Seeds catalog. The clear, jewellike colors of these jellies—rose-pink, deep-garnet, and champagne—are quite beautiful. And the jellies themselves are delicious with cream cheese and crackers or bagels. They make wonderful presents for others—and yourself!

MAKES 4 8-OUNCE JARS.

> *1½ cups packed fresh 'Anise' or 'Cinnamon'*
> *or 'Opal' or 'Lemon' basil*
> *2 cups water*
> *2 tablespoons rice vinegar*
> *Pinch of salt*
> *3½ cups sugar*
> *3 ounces liquid pectin*

Wash basil and dry in paper towels. Finely chop by hand or in food processor. Immediately put basil into a large saucepan, and use the bottom of a glass to crush leaves. Add water, bring slowly to a boil, and boil for 10 seconds. Remove saucepan from heat, cover, and let steep for 15 minutes.

Pour 1½ cups of liquid from saucepan through a fine strainer into another saucepan. Add vinegar, salt, and sugar, and bring to a hard boil, stirring. When the boil can't be stirred down, add pectin. Return to a hard boil that can't be stirred down and boil for exactly 1 minute; then remove saucepan from heat.

Skim off foam and pour hot jelly into hot, sterilized 8-ounce jelly jars. Leave ½ inch of head space and seal at once with sterilized 2-piece lids or melted paraffin.

MAY WINE BOWL

This and the next recipe are from Rose Marie Nichols McGee of Nichols Garden Nursery in Albany, Oregon. German people use this traditional punch to celebrate May Day.

SERVES ABOUT 20.

5 bottles of Moselle or Riesling wine
Abundant sweet woodruff
1 cup brandy
1 cup sugar
A large ring mold of ice
1 cup strawberries, Alpine or wild, if available

Pour 2 bottles of wine into a large jar or crock, add 2 large handfuls of fresh, clean sweet woodruff, cover, and let stand 3 days. Strain infused wine into a large punch bowl and add remaining wine, brandy, sugar, and ice. Add strawberries to bowl and decorate around the base with woodruff.

GREEK MEATBALLS

I used to dislike making meatballs because I had to stand over the frying pan cooking and turning them while the grease spattered all over the stove. In this recipe you bake them, which makes it easier and also cuts some of the calories. And the seasonings help reduce the need for salt.

This is a great make-ahead dish, since these

meatballs are even better the second day. Refrigerate uncooked or bake and reheat before serving.

MAKES 30 MEATBALLS.

1 pound extra-lean ground beef
1½ cups minced parsley
1 egg
3 cups soft, fresh French bread crumbs
⅓ cup chopped fresh mint (spearmint preferred)
2 teaspoons minced fresh oregano
½ cup water
1 clove garlic, minced
1 cup chopped onions
1 fresh lemon

Preheat oven to 400°.

Mix all ingredients except lemon, form walnut-size balls, place on a nonstick baking sheet with at least a ½-inch-high edge, and bake for 30 minutes. Squeeze a few drops of fresh lemon juice over each meatball and serve.

GOAT CHEESE CHEESECAKE WITH HERBS

This is a contribution from Jesse Cool, chef and owner of the Flea Street Cafe and Late for the Train restaurants in Menlo Park, California. Jesse reports that this dish is a real hit with everyone, including those who don't usually like goat cheese. Try serving it as an hors d'oeuvre with crisp apples and warm, crusty bread or homemade garlic toast. The cheesecake must be refrigerated overnight, so plan ahead. However, it can keep for weeks, and a wedge wrapped for your guests to take home makes a wonderful offering.

SERVES UP TO 20 PEOPLE AS AN HORS D'OEUVRE.

2 pounds fresh goat cheese
1 pound cream cheese
3 eggs
2 tablespoons minced fresh rosemary, oregano, thyme, or a combination of these
¾ cup finely chopped sweet red peppers
About 1 cup pine nuts
8-inch spring-form pan

Preheat oven to 375°.

Soften cheeses and whip all ingredients together except pine nuts. Butter the pan and pour goat cheese mixture into it. Spread pine nuts evenly over the top and bake for 25 to 30 minutes. Cool to room temperature, cover, and chill in the refrigerator overnight. Slide a wet knife around outside of cheesecake to loosen. Remove spring and lift off ring. Slide onto a plate if you choose or simply serve from the pan bottom. Serve at room temperature.

SWORDFISH WITH ARUGULA SAUCE

This recipe is from Mark Stech-Novak, chef and consultant with the May Design Group, consultants to restaurants in California.

SERVES 4.

> 1 ounce (about ¼ cup) shallots, peeled and
>   chopped
> 1 teaspoon finely minced garlic
> ½ cup dry white wine
> Juice of 1 lemon ('Meyer' preferred)
> ⅓ cup cream
> 2 ounces (about ¼ cup) blanched, drained,
>   squeezed dry, and chopped spinach
> 4 tablespoons sweet butter
> 2 ounces by weight (1 to 1½ cups loosely
>   packed) chopped arugula leaves
> ½ cup fine virgin olive oil
> ½ teaspoon white pepper
> Salt to taste
> 1½ pounds swordfish filet
> 2 large heads radicchio, washed
> Calendula, marigold, or nasturtium petals for
>   garnish
> 4 ounces dry or 8 ounces fresh linguini,
>   cooked (optional)

Preheat oven to 450°.

Place shallots, garlic, white wine, and ½ of the lemon juice in a saucepan and boil until about 3 tablespoons of mixture is left. Over medium heat, add cream and boil and reduce until mixture is as thick as maple syrup. Place this while hot into a blender jar and add spinach and butter cut into little pieces. Blend to a puree, add arugula leaves, continue to blend, and add olive oil. Finish with pepper and some salt mixed with some more lemon juice, if needed.

Slice swordfish into strips as long as possible and ½ inch thick and wide. Cut each head of radicchio into 8 wedges, leaving leaves attached to core.

Drizzle radicchio with blended olive oil mixture and paint some onto swordfish strips. Grill radicchio over a low flame so that it is cooked and crisp but not burned. Grill swordfish quickly across bars of grill; leave them underdone. Assemble plates by placing radicchio in quadrants of the plate and draping swordfish pieces into a point at center of the plate. Pour sauce around the point and warm plates in oven for a minute. Sprinkle with calendula, marigold, or nasturtium petals. You can also place a very small swirl of fine linguini under the pile of swordfish at center.

ZUCCHINI WITH OREGANO

This and the next two recipes are from Ron Zimmerman, chef at The Herb Farm, a beautiful farm and restaurant in Fall City, Washington. This dish, which uses a small amount of cheese to serve as a flavor bridge between the zucchini and the oregano, makes an excellent accompaniment to lamb and pork and goes well, too, with chicken and beef. It is particularly attractive when made with a combination of green and golden zucchini.

MAKES 8 5-OUNCE SERVINGS.

> 2½ pounds young zucchini, sliced medium
>   (with older zucchini peel and cube)
> 1 small onion, minced
> 1 clove garlic, minced
> 7 tablespoons butter
> 1½ tablespoons Greek oregano, fresh and
>   chopped fine
> 1 teaspoon pepper, freshly ground
> ⅓ cup Gruyère cheese, grated
> Salt to taste
> 8 ramekins

Steam zucchini until tender. Drain well, saving the steaming liquid. Boil down steaming water until it thickens into a syrup; large, multilayered bubbles rising from the surface mean liquid is reduced enough.

Meanwhile, sauté minced onion and garlic in butter until translucent.

Add steamed zucchini and zucchini syrup to onions and cook over medium heat until all liquid has evaporated.

Add chopped oregano and cook for 3 minutes. Season with pepper. Just before serving, carefully stir in grated cheese—don't stir too much or you'll create string cheese. Check seasoning and salt to taste.

Spoon into small ramekins and rewarm or keep warm in a water bath. Garnish with a small sprig of oregano just before serving.

RACK OF LAMB WITH MUSTARD AND HERBS

Says Ron Zimmerman, "Half the secret to the success of this dish is the ruthlessness you must bring to the task of removing all (that's *all*) the fat from the meat. You must do this to appreciate the perfection this recipe approaches. Brace yourself and remember . . . the meat isn't getting any more expensive, it's just getting smaller!"

A few preliminary notes are in order. First, keep paper on garlic cloves or the flavor of the dish will be radically changed. In their wrappers, garlic will roast so sweet and mild that even the most staunch garlicphobe will fail to recognize it in the final dish. And regarding the mustard, Ron says he likes the flavor best with the grainy Pommery mustard that comes in pottery crocks, but results are good with English Pub mustards too. Finally, regarding utensils, you'll need a mortar and pestle, an instant-reading thermometer, and a fine-wire sieve to make this recipe.

MAKES 4 4-CHOP OR 8 2-CHOP SERVINGS.

*2 lamb racks, split, chined (backbone-split),
    trimmed, and Frenched by butcher and
    then further trimmed and Frenched as
    described below*
2 tablespoons rosemary, dry
2 tablespoons thyme, dry
*2 tablespoons green herbs (your choice of
    chives, parsley, chervil, or salad burnet)*
Salt and pepper
4 tablespoons olive oil
16 cloves garlic (in their paper)
Several small pats butter, unsalted
½ cup water
2 shallots, minced fine
½ cup Pommery mustard
1 tablespoon butter, unsalted
2 tablespoons yellow mustard seed
1 tablespoon parsley, chopped

Trim all fat from lamb rack. Start at small end of rack and peel back the overburden of fat and meat with your fingers; cut off this flap with a knife. Cut and remove fat from all areas, including back of bones. Cut between ribs all the way to remaining filet of meat and scrape bones until absolutely clean.

Grind rosemary and thyme with mortar and pestle. Mix with chopped green herbs. Salt and pepper lamb on both sides. Press herbal mix onto all meat surfaces. Heat 2 or 3 tablespoons of olive oil in a hot pan. Add garlic cloves and cook 1 minute. Add rack and sear on all sides—approximately 2 minutes on meat side, 1 minute on back, and 30 seconds on both ends.

Place rack in roasting pan meat side up. Put several small pats of butter on meat and pour hot oil and garlic cloves over butter. Recipe can be prepared to this point and refrigerated (bring back to room temperature before proceeding).

When ready for dinner, preheat oven to 500°. Roast racks 9 minutes. Turn over. Place another pat of butter on rack, return to oven, and roast another 4 to 6 minutes, or until an instant-reading thermometer reads just 125° for medium rare. Remove racks from pan, cover with foil, and let rest 10 minutes.

Meanwhile, deglaze roasting pan with water, stirring with wooden spoon to free brown bits. Strain liquid through strainer and press to push all the cooked garlic through strainer, leaving paper behind.

Add shallots and cook 1 minute. Add mustard and bring to boil until sauce thickens slightly. Add juices, which have drained from the resting rack of lamb. Stir in a tablespoon butter, mustard seeds, and parsley.

Carve rack by slicing between ribs. Ladle sauce onto plate, place chops on it, and top with a little more sauce.

Serve with the zucchini with oregano, above, and accompany with a wonderful well-aged, premium Cabernet Sauvignon.

PHEASANT SUPREMES WITH HONEY AND FRESH THYME

The stock and sauce for this dish are prepared in advance, and the actual cooking of the pheasant takes only a few minutes. The pheasant breasts come straight to the table warm, perfectly cooked, and oh-so-easy to eat. Candlelight is recommended.

It is often easiest to bone the pheasant breasts

the evening before serving and let the stock makings simmer very slowly overnight. That way, only 20 or 30 minutes' worth of work is left on the way to the grand event.

Pheasant Supremes

MAKES 2 LARGE SUPREMES; IF THIGHS USED (SEE BELOW), SERVES 4.

> 1 pheasant, 2¼–4 pounds, cleaned and drawn
> 2 to 3 tablespoons butter, unsalted
> 2 tablespoons honey
> 2 teaspoons thyme leaves, fresh
> Salt and pepper

Carefully cut breasts from pheasant and remove "tenderloin" strip from back of each supreme (a "supreme" is half of the breast). Skin supremes, dry, and wrap in waxed paper while you make rich pheasant stock from carcass (see below). (If desired, debone pheasant thighs and prepare in a similar manner. They will take about twice as long to cook as supremes.)

Ten minutes before serving, salt and pepper supremes on both sides. Melt butter in pan. Sauté skinned side of supreme for 1 to 1½ minutes over moderately high heat until nicely browned. Turn supreme and cook another minute. Cover each supreme with a light coat of raw honey and sprinkle thyme leaves evenly over surface.

Cook until done but still pink in the center, 2 to 5 minutes longer, depending on size. (To check for doneness, press your index finger on thickest portion of supreme from time to time while it cooks. From experience you'll learn to feel when it's done—the meat will offer resistance and spring back. First time around, though, you'll probably want to make a small knife cut and peek inside.) *Do not overcook.*

Cooked supremes can be kept warm for a *few* minutes on a plate set in a warm oven. Don't leave pheasant in sauté pan or it will overcook.

Serve whole supremes on warm plates and top with honey-thyme sauce (see below). Sprinkle on a few more thyme leaves if necessary. Accompany with a seasonal root vegetable.

Rich Pheasant Stock

> ½ yellow onion, diced
> 1 pheasant carcass after supremes and thighs
>   have been removed

> ½ bottle dry red wine
> Water as needed
> ½ carrot, chopped coarsely
> 4 juniper berries
> 3 peppercorns
> 1 bay leaf
> 1 sprig thyme
> 3 sprigs parsley

Stir onion around on the bottom of a hot stock pot. Chop pheasant carcass into medium-size pieces and add to pot. Stir and turn pheasant pieces to brown them somewhat.

Add wine; then add water until liquid barely covers pheasant pieces. Add all other ingredients and simmer covered for at least 3 hours, skimming surface occasionally and adding more water as needed.

Remove bones and strain stock into clean pot. Skim off layer of floating oil. Bring stock to boil and reduce volume by ⅓. If using later, cool and store covered in refrigerator. Remove thin layer of congealed fat before using for sauce.

Honey-Thyme Sauce

MAKES 1 CUP.

> ⅓ teaspoon thyme leaves
> ¼ cup honey
> ¼ cup red wine vinegar
> ½ cup rich pheasant stock, concentrated (see
>   above)
> 1 teaspoon salt
> Pepper to taste

Add thyme to honey and cook over moderate heat until honey turns dark and begins to caramelize. Add vinegar and mix well. Add stock and simmer at very low heat for 15 minutes to blend flavors. Add seasoning. Serve warm over pheasant.

CILANTRO PESTO WITH PEANUTS

This recipe comes from David Schy, a chef I met at an herb seminar in Los Angeles who is now working in a Chicago restaurant. Use this unusual spicy sauce over fresh pasta and soups or to flavor meat dishes. When I make it I double the amount of cilantro and I make it in a blender. Make this pesto only a few hours before using as the flavors deteriorate rapidly.

MAKES 1½ CUPS.

> 2 ounces (4 tablespoons) butter
> 1 ounce (3 tablespoons) roasted, unsalted
>   peanuts
> ½ cup loosely packed cilantro leaves
> ½ fresh 'Jalapeño' pepper (seeded if desired)
> 6 ounces (¾ cup) peanut oil or 3 ounces each
>   peanut and cottonseed oil
> 1 ounce (¼ cup) Argentine (or other)
>   Parmesan cheese, freshly grated
> Salt to taste

Place butter and peanuts in a food processor. Process until pureed. Add cilantro and 'Jalapeño' pepper and process briefly until incorporated. Drizzle in all of the oil while machine is running. Add Parmesan and salt. Process briefly. Remove from workbowl and cover until ready to serve.

SHORTBREAD WITH CANDIED ANGELICA

This unusual herbal creation comes from Rose Marie Nichols McGee of Nichols Garden Nursery in Albany, Oregon. Make this recipe when the angelica is growing vigorously and is best harvested—late spring or early summer. And be warned: making the candied angelica requires up to two weeks.

MAKES APPROXIMATELY 32 SQUARES.

Shortbread

> 1 cup butter
> 1¼ cups brown sugar
> 1 teaspoon vanilla
> 2½ cups all-purpose flour
> ½ cup candied angelica (see below), chopped
> 9 × 12-inch baking sheet

A tea party at Rose Marie Nichols McGee's includes herb tea, angelica shortbread, a caraway seed cake, and scones for lavender, 'Opal' basil, and rosemary jellies.

Preheat oven to 300°.

Cream butter and brown sugar together. Add vanilla. Sift flour and beat in until smooth. Add angelica. Roll or pat out onto baking sheet and bake for 20 minutes.

While still warm, cut into 1½-inch squares. Do not remove from pan until cool.

Candied Angelica

> 1 pound angelica stems
> Water to cover
> 2 cups sugar
> ⅔ cup water
> Additional sugar to coat

Slice angelica into 2-inch lengths, place in a saucepan, cover with water, and simmer 5 minutes. Remove from water and peel or slip the bitter outer membrane from stems. Return to water and simmer until stems become a bright green. Drain.

Put sugar and water in a heavy saucepan, stir, and boil until it becomes a syrup. Remove from heat, add angelica, and allow to sit overnight.

The next day, remove stems from syrup, which will be diluted by juices from angelica. Boil syrup until thickened. Remove from heat, add angelica, and repeat as above. Repeat this procedure about 4 times until all the sugar and juices have been reduced or absorbed by the angelica. This is a 5-day process.

Roll stems in sugar until well coated and allow to rack dry—up to 10 days. When thoroughly dry—about the consistency of candied ginger—place in an airtight container, separating the layers with wax paper. Sprinkle each layer with a spoonful of sugar as a safeguard against moisture. Check after a few days to make sure it is not damp. If it is, remove and air dry or put in a warm oven.

MANDALAY CUSTARD

Wendy Krupnick, my assistant, tasted this unusual treat several years ago at the Mandalay restaurant in Santa Barbara, California. Although chef G. Scott Brown is now at the Port Royal in Ventura, California, the Mandalay lives on in his recipes.

SERVES 6.

Custard

> 1¼ cups milk
> 1¼ cups heavy whipping cream
> ¼ vanilla bean (or substitute ½ teaspoon vanilla extract and add with eggs)
> 4 tablespoons freshly chopped 'Cinnamon' basil
> ½ cup sugar
> 3 eggs
> 3 egg yolks
> 6 buttered custard molds

Preheat oven to 350°.

Simmer milk, cream, vanilla bean, and 3 tablespoons of the basil for 5 minutes. Beat sugar into eggs and yolks until light and fluffy. Strain milk mixture and gradually pour into egg mixture while beating constantly. Add remaining basil and pour into buttered custard molds. Bake molds in a pan of hot water for 45 minutes. Let cool; then turn out of molds onto dessert plates lined with mint sauce.

Mint Sauce

> ¼ cup water
> ½ cup green crème de menthe
> ½ tablespoon freshly ground ginger
> ½ teaspoon ground cinnamon
> 1½ tablespoons freshly chopped mint
> 1 teaspoon cornstarch

Combine all ingredients in a blender. Pour 2 to 3 tablespoons of sauce on each dessert plate.

Sources

Seed Companies

1. Fox Hill Farm
   444 West Michigan Avenue
   P.O. Box 7
   Parma, MI 49269
   This company carries one of the nation's largest selections of herb plants. For example, it offers thirty-two types of thyme, eleven kinds of rosemary, and seventeen varieties of mint. A demonstration garden is open to the public and a basil festival is held annually.

2. Halcyon Gardens Herbs
   P.O. Box 124-M
   Gibsonia, PA 15044
   This seed company carries a large selection of herb seeds.

3. Nichols Garden Nursery
   1190 North Pacific Highway
   Albany, OR 97321
   This firm maintains an extensive list of herbs—plants as well as seeds—plus unusual vegetables and miniature flowering kale. Its demonstration garden is open to the public.

4. Richters
   Goodwood, Ontario
   Canada L0C 1A0
   Richters specializes in herb seeds and carries many unusual varieties. It has a retail store and offers classes in herbs. Catalog: $2.50.

5. Taylor's Herb Gardens, Inc.
   1535 Lone Oak Road
   Vista, CA 92084
   This company offers a very large selection of herb plants, including many that are quite unusual. There is a demonstration garden. Catalog: $1.00.

Demonstration Gardens

Caprilands Herb Farm
Silver Street
Coventry, CT 06238
   This wonderful garden shows the many ways herbs can be both grown and preserved. Reservations are needed for the herb demonstrations.

The National Herb Garden
U.S. Arboretum
3501 New York Avenue NE
Washington, DC 20002
   Our nation's demonstration herb garden is filled with specialty herb gardens, including a Native American and Oriental garden. Classes are given throughout the year.

Books

Boxer, Arabella, and Philippa Back. *The Herb Book*. London: Octopus Books, 1980.
   This valuable book is filled with wonderful herb recipes.

Esplan, Ceres. *Herbal Teas, Tisanes and Lotions*. Wellingborough, Northamptonshire: Thorsons, 1981.
   The book is a guide to growing, preparing, and using herbs to make stimulating tonics, soothing infusions, and refreshing drinks.

Garland, Sarah. *The Herb Garden*. New York: Penguin Books, 1985.
   This is a complete guide to growing scented, culinary, and medicinal herbs.

Lathrop, Norma Jean. *Herbs: How to Select, Grow and Enjoy*. Tucson: HP Books, 1981.
   This book is one of the best for the basics of growing and using of herbs of all types.

Tolley, Emelie, and Chris Mead. *Herbs: Gardens, Decorations, and Recipes*. New York: Clarkson N. Potter, 1985.
   This glossy book will inspire you to use herbs in all aspects of your life.

Gourmet Salad Gardens

H OW LIMITED MY SALADS have been throughout the years! Seeing a salad in the hands of someone with a completely different vision amazed me. It was sometime in the early 1980s, and I had just entered the kitchen at the Farallones Institute in time to see artistic salads being put together for an evening meal. First Doug Gosling and Mimi Fry went out to the garden carrying big baskets to choose a little of this and a little of that. It was late spring, and what a selection! This garden contained every herb, edible flower, baby vegetable, and salad green you could imagine. I think deciding what to include each night must have been the hardest part.

Doug and Mimi brought everything back and washed and spin-dried it. Next they set up five pottery bowls—some as big as two feet across—along a large counter, and then went to it. First Doug lined two of the bowls with baby leaves of 'Ragged Jack' kale, one with baby red lettuces, one with romaine lettuce, and a final one with frilly frisée. Mimi broke up five or six kinds of lettuce, some radicchio, and some endive and started adding their leaves to a few of the bowls. Into one salad went a little fennel, into another a little chervil, and into

OPPOSITE: *A basket of salad greens, herbs, and edible flowers includes, starting at top left, mint, butter lettuce, sorrel, yellow broccoli flowers, pink dianthus, blue borage, spinach, miner's lettuce, purple baby tree collard leaves, and curly parsley.*

A salad harvest of miniatures from the Chez Panisse garden that includes some of Andrea Crawford's favorites. From top to bottom are 'Yellow Finn' potatoes, endive, 'Lemon' cucumbers, baby carrots, petis pois, baby wax beans, 'Limestone' and 'Red Perella' baby lettuces, baby wax beans, and rocket (arugula) flowers.

another went red orach or some slices of baby kohl-rabi. The decisions weren't random; Doug and Mimi had done this many times before and had their favorite combinations. To garnish the salads, Doug julienned some stalks of red chard and sprinkled them over some chartreuse lettuces. Onto one of the simple lettuce salads Mimi scattered miniature roses, pea blossoms, borage flowers, and mustard blossoms. Deep-red nasturtiums were artfully placed on one, calendula petals scattered over another. Sunflower seeds went into one, pecans into another, and on and on went the assembly process. Within an hour the buffet table was covered with fabulous salads, and the appreciative diners were feasting.

Since watching Doug and Mimi, I have turned up in my research many other creative salads made with many unusual garden ingredients and in many styles. Obviously, there is more to making salads than tossing together a piece of iceberg lettuce and a few slices of tomatoes. From Andrea Crawford, at the Chez Panisse restaurant in Berkeley, California, I learned about baby cutting lettuces. From Shep Ogden in Vermont, I learned about growing specialty lettuce varieties—he and his wife served me a salad in February made of just-sprouted greens from their greenhouse. From Bruce Naftaly and Robin Sanders, chef-owners at Le Gourmand in Seattle, I learned about wild greens, fancy vinegars, and olive oils. But I gathered the most information over the last few years from the salad garden in my own back yard, just off the patio. Here my day-to-day experimentation with a large number of ingredients plus the vast restaurant and market-garden experience of my assistant, Wendy Krupnick, has added dramatically to my repertoire of salads.

Before I go much further, it's important to mention that, although just about any vegetable can be made into a salad, in this section I have chosen to concentrate on green, leafy salads in their myriad forms. This means that I set out to examine in detail most of the aromatic herbs and leafy domestic vegetables used worldwide in salads. I have included very few wild greens, however, since that subject could amount to a book in itself.

In doing my research I have certainly widened my definition of a salad, and I hope you will too. But in learning a great deal about salad greens, I also came to appreciate an important fact: nowhere else in your from-the-garden cooking will freshness and quality result in such dramatic improvements as with greens and herbs. In this regard, I discovered that most of the chefs in this country long for garden-fresh produce and have no commercial access to it. As Seppi Renggli, chef of the Four Seasons restaurant in New York told me, "I have a garden at home and get used to all these special fresh vegetables and unusual herbs, but I can't get many commercially for the restaurant." To treat yourself, and eat like royalty, put in a small salad garden.

How to Grow a Salad Garden

Salad gardening is largely cool-weather gardening. Our ancestors anxiously looked forward to the first greens of spring. After spending a winter eating root vegetables and dense cabbages, they savored those first succulent leaves of lettuce or, more often, wild greens as precious, tonic to the body and soul. Today, thanks to modern transportation, we enjoy salad greens all year round, and the cool-weather preference of these vegetables is less obvious to us. But when you eat from the garden you will find that the majority of your salad-garden production will come in the spring, fall, and, with extra protection, winter, because the majority of leafy salad greens prefer cool growing conditions. Consequently, garden books instruct you to start your lettuces early in the spring and guide you in preparing your fall garden, growing in cold frames, and preventing the plants from going to seed in hot weather. (For information on cold-frame growing, see Appendix A, "Planting and Maintenance.")

An easy way to plunge into salad gardening is to order a premixed selection of salad-green seeds. These seed mixes are traditional in parts of Europe and are called *mesclun* or *misticanza*. Mesclun Provençal is popular in the Provence region of France and consists of various mixes of lettuces, rocket, finely curled endive, and chervil. This is the most popular mix and a good choice for beginners. Another mesclun mix, mesclun Niçoise, is a more piquant variation reflecting the wild origins (they were collected wild for centuries) of these mixes and includes curly endive, 'Spadona' (a cutting chicory), dandelion, upland cress, and rocket. *Misticanza* (or *saladini*), an Italian mix of greens, is generally made up of four varieties of lettuce and five kinds of chicories. It is

quite a bit milder than mesclun Niçoise. Cook's Garden seed company carries all the mixes, and Herb Gathering and Le Marché seed companies each carry a mesclun mix.

You can grow a mix in one bed or buy seeds in individual packages and plant them in a conventional manner—in rows or a wide bed—mixing them in the salad bowl instead. An intensely grown garden bed of about fifty square feet will provide a generous amount of salad ingredients for two people. The salad greens for mesclun mixes are usually harvested when very young—when the lettuce leaves are about two or three inches long. Sometimes the greens are grown by the cut-and-come-again method, described in the profile of Andrea Crawford in this chapter.

All the salad greens need rich, moist, well-drained soil, and the majority benefit from regular applications of compost, small amounts of nitrogen, and supplemental watering. The secret to growing succulent greens is keeping them growing vigorously; otherwise most will get bitter or tough or go to seed prematurely. You can plant the salad greens in rows or cast the seeds over a well-prepared bed no more than four feet across. A wider bed is too hard for most people to reach across comfortably and too difficult to weed and harvest. Most greens are rarely bothered by pests and diseases, and most are started early in the spring, though some species and varieties are better started in the summer or fall. It is possible to have a wide selection of salad greens growing throughout most of the year, and if you get very involved with yours you will find yourself wanting to succession plant. This is a technique for keeping a constant supply of young plants coming along by continually seeding in flats or containers and then filling in the holes left by harvested plants with transplants. This technique is covered in Appendix A, "Planting and Maintenance." For individual growing instructions on the salad plants, see Part Four, "An Encyclopedia of Superior Vegetables," particularly the listings for "Greens" and "Lettuce," and the "Recommended Salad Vegetables" list in this chapter. All the major seed companies in this country carry a nice selection of lettuces and greens, but for the more unusual species and varieties you will probably want to obtain seeds from the companies listed in the "Sources" section at the end of this chapter.

All in all, a salad garden makes a wonderful beginner's garden and a good selection for busy cooks. Few edible gardens can be as beautiful or as useful

Many people grow lettuce, but few do so with as much passion as Andrea Crawford does. Andrea, who grows lettuce for some of the best restaurants in California—Chez Panisse in Berkeley and Spago's in Los Angeles—as well as restaurants like the Four Seasons in New York, takes pride in producing the incredibly succulent and dewy lettuces that are critical to the restaurants' reputations for having fresh, seasonal ingredients.

Andrea Crawford

Andrea oversees these large gardens devoted to what she considers the best vegetable varieties, the most important culinary herbs, and the tastiest edible flowers (see the "Edible Flower Gardens" chapter). Her real specialty, though, is lettuces. After many years of gardening experience, she has perfected a productive growing technique of leaf-picking baby lettuces. She recommends this method or another referred to as scissor-cutting, or cut-and-come-again, because she feels they help home gardeners obtain high-quality lettuces.

Andrea is eager to share her techniques for growing and harvesting baby lettuces. "People ask why I don't grow lettuce in the standard manner, why I bother with this intensive technique," she says. "My immediate answer is: aesthetics. People in restaurants love baby lettuces because they don't have to tear the leaves. My method allows them to preserve the shapes of individual leaves, unlike the more common and traditional pale fragments of 'Iceberg' lettuce. Garden lettuce is beautiful to look at; you can enjoy the lobed blades of 'Oak Leaf', the undulations of 'Salad Bowl', and the frills of 'Lollo Rossa'. If you're going to grow your own lettuces, why not enjoy them to the fullest? Big lettuces taste great, but the baby varieties, while milder and usually more tender, taste good too. This method is also an efficient way to produce lettuce in a small area—but aesthetics is the main issue.

"To grow baby lettuces using my methods, it's critical to start with optimum exposure and weather conditions and, most important of all, very rich soil. At the gardens I work with, we place a premium on compost, making it as rich as possible by composting continually and digging in at regular intervals. Three times a year we add soil amendments: blood meal and bone meal or cotton seed meal. I think organic soil amendments are best for growing anything—particularly lettuces, because lettuce can be very bitter if not grown in rich, humusy soil. We never have bitter lettuce because we use so much organic matter—and because the weather never gets very hot in my garden.

"The only pests we have are aphids and slugs. For the aphids we use an insecticidal soap. Slugs aren't a problem most of the year because we're out there all the time to control them, but the few times when they're really active, we use slug bait on the perimeter of the garden, never touching the food plants.

"For our intensive method of growing lettuce, we don't let plants get much bigger than three or four inches tall. When we sow the seeds, we space them about a quarter inch apart; then we never thin them. Because we pick them so fast and so often, we never have crowding problems as we would if we just left them to choke themselves and eventually self-thin.

"Optimum exposure and weather conditions are also essential to producing the best baby lettuce, so we take care to protect the plants in all weather. In cold weather, we create tunnels of clear plastic film spread over PVC [polyvinyl chloride] tubing hoops; the plastic is attached to the hoops with giant plastic clips available from plumbing supply houses. In warm summer weather, we shade the beds with commercial shade cloth. Of course, winter weather doesn't drop much below 30 degrees in either Berkeley or Los Angeles, and our summers are mild, but in cold-winter areas you could do the same thing in a greenhouse or cold frame.

"Because we produce so much lettuce for the restaurants, I've decided through the years against scissor-cutting; leaf-picking is easier on plants because the plants regenerate faster that way. We pick only the biggest leaves, which are still only two to three inches long, and leave the crowns to produce new leaves.

"Home gardeners can choose whichever method appeals to them, though. If you prefer scissor-cutting, take a knife or scissors and just go snip, snip across the plant about an inch or two above the crown. This won't kill the plant because enough growing information is left in the crown for it to produce new leaves. New growth will occur in a short time if the weather is right—not too cold or too hot. Cut as much as you need and then separate the damaged leaves from the good ones. Scissor-cutting is great for home gardeners because it's fast, but we leaf-pick each plant for restaurants and sort as we go so only the perfect leaves end up in the tub. Then all we need to do is wash the lettuce and serve it.

"Washing is an important part of the final presentation. Put the lettuce leaves in a sink filled with water, gently slosh them up and down, and then spin

several turns in a salad spinner until quite dry. It's important to dry baby lettuces thoroughly because they'll collapse under the weight of any water left on them. Put the leaves between damp towels and refrigerate immediately. Later, be careful to dress them very lightly with a delicate oil and vinegar mixture so they won't sag under the weight of a heavy dressing."

When asked which lettuce varieties she prefers most, Andrea said, "I think all varieties are interesting. There are all kinds of lettuces, and they're fun to grow because all look and taste slightly different. I've decided that the final product depends not so much on which varieties you choose as on how you grow them. There's no such thing as a bad lettuce or a terrific lettuce; it's entirely personal. Aesthetics are important; color, taste, and texture depend on what you want. If you like smooth, buttery, tender lettuces, go with limestone lettuce. For something slightly more crunchy and succulent, try bibb. And for the crunchiest choice, try romaine. Finally, in general, the reds may be a little more strongly flavored than the greens. All in all, it's entirely up to your individual taste."

in the kitchen. To get an idea of a working salad garden, read the following account of how my own salad garden grows from season to season.

The Creasy Salad Garden

In the middle of my small back yard is a huge but fruitless mulberry tree. In the past, I would stand staring at it every year asking myself the same question: With all that shade and all that root competition, what edible plants can I grow under that tree? One spring it occurred to me that the area would be a perfect place for a salad garden. Leafy salad greens would grow in the cool sun of winter and spring while the leaves were off the tree, and would do fine most of the summer and fall when the shade of the tree would protect them from the heat. The root problem would be solved by the continual disruption of the soil when it was dug and amended before every major replanting.

I was right. The patio salad garden turned out

to be the perfect solution to the problem. Not only did the salad vegetables grow well, but the leafy greens interplanted with annual flowers also made a beautiful garden next to the patio. As a bonus, with a salad garden right off the kitchen, I found myself using many more salad greens than in the past, since it was so easy to harvest leaves as I needed them.

To prepare the area for the lettuces and herbs, I had the soil under the part of the tree where the salad greens would go dug up to remove as many mulberry roots as possible. Then I added lots of compost and put in some low, pop-up sprinkler heads. To keep a continual supply of salad greens, my assistant Wendy set up a nursery area with starter flats so she could replant lettuce every six weeks or so. (We also bought seedlings from the nursery on occasion.) We found that starting lettuce plants by seeds in place in the garden sometimes resulted in spotty germination. Also, in warm weather, watering seedlings twice a day overwatered the more mature plants and contributed to fungus problems on the lettuce.

For more than two years we planted different

My assistant, Wendy Krupnick, in our salad garden. From left to right in the bed are Alpine strawberries, Corsican mint, pink begonias, curly parsley, 'Mantia' lettuce, 'Amstel' carrots, and 'Salad Bowl' lettuce. Across the path are chervil, a row of 'Red Salad Bowl' alternated with 'Oakleaf' lettuce, a large row of 'Limestone' lettuce, and romaine lettuces in the background.

lettuces and salad herbs recommended to me by restaurant gardeners and seed company folks. Here's a list of what we tried: chervil, parsley, corn salad (mâche), rocket (arugula), 'Planet' and 'Amstel' carrots, and the lettuces 'Salad Bowl', 'Oak Leaf', 'Red Salad Bowl', 'Marvel of Four Seasons', 'Summer Bibb', 'Buttercrunch', 'Limestone', 'Capitane', 'Brune d'Hiver', 'Mantilla', and 'Rouge d'Hiver' and 'Romance' romaine. In the cool seasons, all the lettuces, and the chervil, the corn salad, and the rocket did very well. On the other hand, for a short time in the hottest weather most of the greens did poorly; only the parsley and the 'Oak Leaf', 'Summer Bibb', and 'Salad Bowl' lettuces held up, though these lettuces did go to seed and turn bitter more readily than in the spring.

It was certainly handy to have a salad garden right off the kitchen, but even handier was the method of lettuce harvesting that Wendy showed me. First thing in the morning, when the lettuces are dewy and the temperature is cool, she goes out and harvests enough lettuce and salad greens for one or two days. She brings them in and washes and then dries them in a salad spinner. (The salad spinner, a basket inside a plastic bowl, with a cover equipped with a spinning device, has to be one of the most useful modern kitchen inventions.) Then she dumps the salad mix into a plastic bag and puts it in the refrigerator. Picking the lettuces at their peak in the cool of the morning means they are crisp and flavorful, and washing them up makes them available for use any time, whether you're grabbing a few leaves for a sandwich at lunch or making a salad in the evening.

I've found that I really enjoy the chervil and corn salad. I'm less enamored with the strong-flavored rocket and prefer to use it as an herb rather than a chief ingredient. But all the lettuce varieties have been lovely and tasty, and each gives its own look to the salads. The romaines have a crisp texture, the butterheads are velvety, and the leaf lettuces are beautiful and tender. If I had to pick favorites, though, I'd choose my old standbys, 'Oak Leaf', 'Salad Bowl', and 'Buttercrunch'; still, the others are all great for variety. In the next few years I'm going to see if I can control some of the wild greens, such as miner's lettuce and chickweed; maybe I can find a way to let them self-seed and keep going from year to year as the corn salad now does, without taking over the whole garden. I'm also planning to try some more lettuces, such as 'Lollo Rossa', 'Deer Tongue', and 'Tom Thumb', that other gardeners have told me about or served me.

A salad garden is without doubt one of the easiest and most rewarding gardens you can have. One great advantage is that it doesn't lock you in. When I'm real busy and don't have time to reseed or am going to be traveling for a while, I simply fill the beds with carrots, parsley, and begonias (or primroses, depending on the season) and then resume the salad garden whenever I want. And I actually resume quite often, since having such wonderful salad greens available has spoiled me for store-bought produce.

Recommended Salad Vegetables

The salad greens listed here represent a vast range to choose from. Just a few will enliven your salad bowl, and a large selection will knock the socks off the most blasé house guest. To give your salads that extra flair, see the "Edible Flower Gardens" chapter and select some flower petals—from roses to violets—to sprinkle on your greens.

As with the other recommended variety lists throughout this book, the numbers in parentheses after the name of the plant or variety refer to the seed companies listed in the "Sources" section at the end of the chapter. When most of the seed companies listed carry the named plant, no number is given.

CABBAGE *Brassica* spp.

How to grow: See the Part Four Encyclopedia. For a mixed green salad, I prefer the early loose-leaf cabbages and tender Savoy types or the mild, sweet-tasting cabbages bred for fresh eating, such as 'Grenadier' (9) and 'Early Jersey Wakefield' (8, 10). All these cabbages are more succulent than the dense storage types, which I prefer for coleslaw. For a succulent early cabbage try 'Salarite Hybrid' (6). For Savoy cabbages try 'Spivoy Hybrid' (7, 11) and 'Savoy King' (6, 7, 11). Also good in mixed salads are Oriental cabbages, with their mild flavor and crunchiness. To add color to winter salads try the red-and-white ornamental cabbages and red cabbage varieties such as 'Preko' (7).

How to prepare: Use both the leafy and ornamental cabbages in bite-size pieces in mixed salads and whole frilly leaves of the ornamental cabbages to line a salad bowl. For coleslaw, shave cabbage very thinly and, for a change, try mixing a little red cabbage in with the green. Some salad connoisseurs prefer that no mustard be used in dressings with cabbages, as they feel it overemphasizes the vegetable's natural sulfur taste. Creamy or sweet dressings are nice with cabbages.

CHICORY *Cichorium Endivia, C. Intybus.*

How to grow: See the "Italian Gardens" chapter for information on forcing and heading the chicories called radicchios. For the chicories referred to as curly endives (frisées) and escaroles, see "Greens" in the Part Four Encyclopedia. For the Belgian endives, known sometimes as Witloof chicories, see the "French Gardens" chapter.

All chicories are primarily salad plants and are somewhat bitter. The bitterness level of chicories, which varies from slight to extreme, is influenced by many factors, including the variety, whether the leaves have been blanched (see the "French Gardens" chapter), and the weather, as warm temperatures encourage bitterness.

How to prepare: These strong-flavored leaves are favorites in European salads. The red radicchios add their color and bittersweetness to mixed salads. As with the endives and escaroles, they are excellent used sparingly in light mixed salads. When used alone or with other strong greens, they can be paired with a hearty complement such as meat, poultry, seafood, nuts, or a rich and flavorful dressing.

Another of the chicories, Belgian endive, is certainly one of the noblest of salad vegetables, and its blanched shoots, called chicons, are sweet yet slightly bitter and crunchy. Their distinctively pointed, cupped-shape leaves lend themselves to fillings in formal salads and go well unfilled in mixed green salads.

CORN SALAD (mâche, lamb's lettuce) *Valerianella Locusta.*

How to grow: See "Greens" in the Part Four Encyclopedia.

How to prepare: The small, dark-green leaves have a mild nutty flavor and can be used in mixed salads or by themselves with a light vinaigrette. These greens are popular served with cooked beets or potatoes and are sometimes garnished with sieved, hard-cooked egg. They are particularly nice with pears and a walnut oil dressing in the fall.

CRESS *Barbarea verna, B. praecox.*

How to grow: There are dry-land and water cresses. See the "German Gardens" chapter for information on the land cresses. If you have a stream of *pure* running water, you can plant watercress (2, 8), though some people swear by a pot of soil put in a pan of continually freshened water. Watercress is easily grown in most parts of the country and, if its requirements are met, can even become something of a pest.

'Redhead', a red heirloom lettuce.

Cast seeds on the bank of a slightly moving stream or plant rooted cuttings you have started from store-bought watercress.

How to prepare: The peppery leaves of both cresses can be used sparingly in mixed green salads or sandwiches. Their refreshing, zesty flavor is excellent with rich foods ranging from cheese omelettes and sautéed wild mushrooms to lamb or venison. Sprouts of the dry-land cress can be used this way too.

DANDELION GREENS *Taraxacum officinale.*

How to grow: See "Greens" in the Part Four Encyclopedia and grow your own. Or gather dandelion greens from wild areas early in the spring, but make sure they haven't been treated with herbicides.

How to prepare: Dandelion greens are flavorful and add a slightly bitter richness to a salad. When gathered very young they can be used in large amounts, but if they are strong flavored they should be used sparingly. They are eaten cooked or raw and go well with hot-bacon or creamy dressings.

KALE *Brassica oleracea,* Acephala Group.

How to grow: For detailed growing instructions see "Greens" in the Part Four Encyclopedia. There are numerous types of kale: the large, blue-gray types; the tasty dwarf, dark-green, curly-leafed types; colorful, ornamental ones sometimes called salad Savoy; and a distinctive one called 'Ragged Jack' (7). The latter is an old-fashioned variety of ornamental kale that when used young is particularly well suited for salads with its mild taste, frilly notched leaves, and slightly purple coloration. The ornamental kales become more colorful in cool weather.

How to prepare: The coarse-leaved kales can be eaten raw when young and succulent; more tender-leaved ones can be eaten in salads unless very old. Use them for their rich, sweet, broccoli/cabbage flavor and, in the case of the ornamental ones, also for color in the salad. The kales can be combined with light lettuces for a light salad or with heavier greens for a heartier salad.

LETTUCE *Lactuca sativa.*

How to grow: See the Part Four Encyclopedia.

How to prepare: When most people think of a salad the first thing they think of is lettuce. The many different types of lettuces generally fall into these four categories, though there is a certain amount of overlap: loose-leaf, butterhead, crisphead, and romaine. Loose-leaf types do not form heads and are some of the easiest to grow. Butterheads, also called bibb types, form soft, buttery, loose heads. Crispheads are the most familiar to Americans as the iceberg type found in supermarkets. Romaines are crisp and dark green, and the heads and leaves are elongated. Romaines have more robust and sweeter flavors than most lettuces and stand up well to strong-flavored dressings. For more information on lettuces see the profile sections in this chapter.

MUSTARD *Brassica juncea.*

How to grow: See "Greens" in the Part Four Encyclopedia.

How to prepare: This fairly strong-flavored leafy green has a zesty mustard flavor that adds body and a little bite to a mixed salad. Use sparingly in light salads or pair with other strong-flavored greens in a heartier salad with a rich dressing.

ORACH *Atriplex hortensis.*

How to grow: Orach is an old-fashioned salad plant that can have red (2, 8), yellow (2), or green (2, 3, 6, 8) leaves two to three inches long. Plant seeds in spring in rich soil and thin to about eight inches apart. You can also plant again in fall for a quick crop before winter or for cold-frame growing. This plant will grow to at least three feet and provide leaves for salads and cooking well into hot weather. Generally it goes to seed in hot weather unless you keep the flower heads cut back.

How to prepare: Use young leaves in mixed salads or cook as a potherb. Orach is a mild-tasting, sweet, tender salad green that blends well in light salads or with strong-tasting ones. The red and yellow varieties add color to salads.

ORIENTAL GREENS See the "Oriental Gardens" chapter for detailed information on Chinese cabbages, mizuna, shungiku, pac choi, and the flowering mustards.

How to prepare: Use these greens in mixed green salads or by themselves with an Oriental-style dressing, which might include some of the following: cilantro, ginger, soy sauce, rice vinegar, and sesame oil.

PURSLANE *Portulaca oleracea.*

How to grow: See the "Mexican Gardens" chapter for information.

How to prepare: Purslane leaves are small and quite succulent. Used raw they have a slightly acidic tang; used cooked they tend to get quite slippery. Use tender young leaves in raw mixed salads for a contrast of texture and flavor.

ROCKET (arugula, *roquette*) *Eruca vesicaria.*

How to grow: Seed catalogs carry this annual under the names rocket, arugula, or *roquette*. Grow it in early spring and again in fall. The plants are short-lived; they get quite spicy and bolt in hot weather. Broadcast seeds in the garden or plant in flats and transplant out into the garden. In the fall plant some in a cold frame for winter salads. For succulent growth keep rocket well watered and fertilize lightly. Harvest individual leaves or cut plant back and leave a few inches of growth for a cut-and-come-again crop (see the profile of Andrea Crawford in this chapter for a description of this technique). Late in the season, use the flowers, as they are tasty long after the leaves have turned too strong.

How to prepare: Rocket leaves are lobed, pungent, and peppery and taste a bit like radishes. When only two or three inches tall, and very mild, they can be used in fairly large amounts in a salad. When strong-tasting, use as an herb in a mixed salad, in a dressing, or in a main course.

SORREL *Rumex scutatus* and *R. Acetosa.*

How to grow: See the "French Gardens" chapter.

How to prepare: Use leaves of sorrel sparingly in mixed salads and sandwiches. They have a somewhat lemony, "grassy" flavor.

SPINACH *Spinacia oleracea.*

How to grow: See "Greens" in the Part Four Encyclopedia.

How to prepare: Spinach is a hearty green good in raw or cooked salads. Use it by itself with a fairly heavy dressing such as blue cheese or the traditional bacon, or use it more sparingly combined with lettuces for a light salad. The flavor of spinach is complemented by rich olive and nut oils.

WILD GREENS Claytonia (miner's lettuce), *Claytonia perfoliata* Chickweed, *Stellaria media* Shepherd's purse, *Capsella bursapastoris* A wide array of wild plants can be used in salads. Many cultures regularly harvest from the countryside, particularly in Europe. Here I have focused on only a few of the most common ones, as the use of wild plants is a study in itself. These wild plants, usually referred to as weeds, are so widespread you may already have them growing in or around your garden. Before you

S hepherd Ogden and his wife, Ellen, own a seed company in Londonderry, Vermont, where they specialize in salad vegetables and carry the seeds of more than twenty varieties of lettuce. Shep's family has grown vegetables for many years, and in addition to the seed company, they operate a farm stand filled with "fancy" salad greens for local residents. Shep's enthusiasm for salad greens is obvious when he talks about them.

At one time, Shep supported himself while writing poetry by driving a cab in Cambridge. Then in the early 1980s, during a summer visit to his grandfather, Sam Ogden, a garden writer who had a small market garden, Shep planted the garden for him. The work was so satisfying that he took over the garden the next year and sold produce to local restaurants and vacationers. Unable to obtain some of the specialty lettuces he wanted from other American companies, he started his own seed company a little while later.

Shep talked to me about the different types of lettuces, dividing the many varieties into categories. First he discussed forcing lettuces, which are grown in greenhouses or cold frames. "We plant forcing lettuces in our heated greenhouse in mid-February and transplant them to the outdoor tunnels in mid- to late March," he said. "In Vermont, that means harvesting in the middle of May. These types will grow in temperatures as low as 14 degrees because they'll actually freeze, unthaw, and recover. My favorites for forcing are 'Magnet' and 'Akcel', two butterheads that force exceptionally well.

"Most lettuces are spring lettuces—except for the overwintering types," Shep explained. Spring weather is ideal for growing lettuces, and even summer and fall lettuces can be grown in the spring, although some spring lettuces will not tolerate the heat of summer or the cold of fall or winter. Shep particularly likes the spring variety 'Red Sails'. "We used to grow a lot of 'Ruby', but I prefer the big, beautiful heads

Shepherd Ogden

of 'Red Sails'," he says. "They have very open rosettes; we get them twelve to eighteen inches across—very nice, dark, and open.

"I also like 'Black-Seeded Simpson', which grows fast and tastes good. We've always grown it; in fact, it was the only variety my grandfather grew. 'Red Grenoble', another of my favorites, is a vigorous grower and can be cut as loose-leaf lettuce or left to head up. 'Four Seasons' is a good red butterhead and seems to grow a little longer into the summer than some around here do. And 'Reine des Glaces' is beautiful. I have a harder time getting it to stay in good condition in the summer than I do some other varieties, but I wouldn't leave it out because it has such beautiful lacey leaves and nothing else looks like it. My wife thinks it has a nutty taste.

"For the summer, 'Orfeo' is a great butterhead with big, beautiful heads. We've had good luck with that even in the middle of summer. Of course our summers aren't as hot as many; they're usually in the seventies with some days in the low eighties. Occasionally we get temperatures in the nineties, but they don't last long enough to really hurt the lettuce. And we always have cool nights.

"Other summer lettuces I like are 'Rigoletto' and 'Buttercrunch', which have very nice heads; 'Rigoletto' is the darker of the two. 'Continuity' is nice—it's similar to 'Four Seasons' but darker and holds better in the heat. 'Craquerelle du Midi' also holds well in the heat and is like 'Buttercrunch' but more open-hearted. I don't care for the texture that much, but it's popular among people in warm climates because it succeeds better than any of the other varieties do in the heat. People even write to us from Florida to tell us how well it does there.

" 'Little Gem', another summer variety, is my personal favorite at the moment. I first tried it after reading how well Joy Larkcom had done with it in her book *The Salad Garden*. I planted a lot of it and found it did really well. It's very heat resistant—so heat resistant it almost fouls up our successions, because it can sit in the heat longer than all of the other lettuce varieties in the same bed without going to seed. But that makes it a good home variety, and it's the best sandwich lettuce I know of.

"Of the fall/winter lettuces, I like 'Winter Density'. That's like a large 'Little Gem', but with row covers it overwinters here—or it grows well in the summer. 'Brune d'Hiver', another nice winter lettuce, is more brown than red and is real hardy. That one overwinters here with no problem, but it has to be planted late in the summer to prevent bolting.

"Of the cutting lettuces, I like 'Matchless' a lot—but I like 'Royal Oak Leaf', 'Salad Bowl', and 'Red Salad Bowl' even more. I grow large amounts of these three side by side because they're so beautiful and look so good in salads. The 'Royal Oak Leaf' gets bitter easily, though, and it's more susceptible to disease than the others. When it's very young, it lacks the vigor of the old 'Oak Leaf', but it's much better looking—less floppy and a darker green.

"For other greens, we do fine with escaroles and endives, but chicories, which should be planted in the fall for a spring harvest in a Mediterranean climate, are really chancy here. 'Sugarlof', 'Ceriolo', 'Spadona', 'Puntarella', and 'Dentarella' are all chancy, as are red chicories, the radicchios. We grow them on a spring/fall schedule rather than a fall/spring schedule, and I always leave some in the ground because I've discovered that they occasionally will survive the winter. We've tried forcing various radicchios as you would 'Witloof', but they haven't done well.

"Obviously, rocket also needs to be included on the list of other greens," Shep continued. "Its spicy flavor is a good addition to salads. I have no use for 'White Mustard', on the other hand; it has a hairy leaf. I much prefer 'Miike Purple', 'Osaka Purple', or mizuna. Mizuna has beautiful cut foliage and a mild flavor. I also like all of the cresses. I sow the seeds often and harvest when very small. I like corn salad, too, but I haven't found a lot of difference between the various varieties."

As Shep's strong ideas about varieties indicate, there are lots of options. Deciding which lettuces are best for your garden will depend on your climate and season and on which ones enchant you the most!

---

introduce them intentionally, see if you can find them in your own or a neighbor's yard. Make very sure you can properly identify these greens; consult an expert if you have the slightest doubt. If you are gathering your greens from the wild, to avoid lead contamination, make sure they're not growing by a heavily traveled road.

How to grow: Miner's lettuce (2) is native to the West Coast of the United States but grows readily in most parts of the country. Grow in partial shade in rich, moist soil. The stems, which grow to about six inches, emerge from the base and produce round to square, flat, fleshy leaves about two inches across that wrap around the stem. Little clusters of white flowers emerge from the center of the leaves. Plant seeds in spring in the garden or in late summer for winter use in cold frames or greenhouses. In mild-winter areas the plants take light frosts and winter over or appear in early spring from fall-planted seeds. Chickweed (I know of no source of seeds) is another common garden weed. Its light-green leaves grow on a rather disjointed stem that sprawls across the ground It appears in spring and dies back in the hot weather. Shepherd's purse (I know of no source of seeds for this plant either) is a low-growing plant (to two inches) with cut leaves. It produces a little seed stalk that has a spike of tiny heart-shaped seed pods.

How to prepare: Gather whole young plants or individual leaves of miner's lettuce. You can harvest young or mature leaves of miner's lettuce a few at a time or cut back the whole plant to an inch above the ground and treat it as a cut-and-come-again crop (see the Andrea Crawford profile in this chapter). Miner's lettuce has very succulent leaves and a slightly "grassy" taste. For chickweed, use only the very young leaves. They are tender, a little tangy, and have that characteristic "grassy" taste as well. Shepherd's purse has a taste all its own with a slightly sulfurous overtone. Use all three plants in a mixed green salad with other greens and flowers.

Cooking from the Salad Garden

If you occasionally enjoy pulling off a memorable coup when you entertain, a salad garden should be in your arsenal. Frankly, I've been known to purr when folks ooh and ahh over my salads, and some day I'm bound to get caught gloating. The discussion around the table can get quite animated. "Miner's lettuce—what's that?" Or "Look, I have a pea blossom. And what do you suppose this is?" And "Wow, this tastes great!"

A truly masterful salad is a work of art and is best achieved with a garden a few feet from the kitchen. To orchestrate a well-blended green salad, most experts recommend that you limit yourself to only a handful of ingredients; that way diners can savor the tang of the sorrel, the slight bitterness of the radicchio, and the buttery texture of the lettuces. The idea is to give clear flavors and not produce a muddy mix.

That's very fine advice for most of your salad making, but if "show biz" is what you want, I say throw out the rules. Try using, say, four or five varieties of red and green baby lettuces, some serrated burnet leaves ("What's this?" they'll ask), some tiny pink 'Ragged Jack' kale leaves, a little rocket, some tiny dandelion leaves, and a little purslane or miner's lettuce. Make a ceremony of it. Bring to the table a big bowl of your greens, a decanter of vinegar (maybe with a few raspberries in it), some light-green olive oil, and a small bowl of flower petals, and dress the salad at the table. Once the salad is annointed, sprinkle the petals over the greens. Voilà! A happening! It's fun when you can use food to please the eye as well as the palate. And sometimes an animated discussion of food is the perfect icebreaker for a dinner party.

Obviously, your everyday salads are not going to be as grandiose as the one described above. Simpler salads and clear flavor combinations will wear better on a daily basis. Nothing beats the lettuces as the backbone of your salad garden. Simple green salads made primarily with lettuces can be dressed up one day with dill, another with nasturtiums, and yet another with blue or goat cheese. The pristine fresh lettuces of all types can be used in an infinite variety of combinations. To the lettuces you can add some of the radicchios, endives, and chervil to create your own mesclun mix or gather wild greens and edible flowers for a completely different dish. As you exper-

iment, you might try some combinations that other cooks have enjoyed. For instance, serve the basic mesclun salad with garlic-rubbed croutons or smoked duck or quail. In *The Fine Art of Salad Gardening*, Annie Proulx recommends an autumn salad made with late-season endive combined with peppery watercress, chopped celery, and sliced russet apples and sprinkled with chopped hazelnuts. Other classics are a spinach or young dandelion-green salad topped with a hot bacon dressing, or the bitter chicories with a honey vinaigrette.

Before you begin creating your salads, take a look at the general guidelines on how to integrate a salad into the meal in this chapter's profile of the chefs at Le Gourmand restaurant and read the descriptions of the tastes and complementary flavors of the greens and herbs in the "Recommended Salad Vegetables" section. You will also probably want to glance through the "Edible Flower Gardens" chapter for suggestions of flowers to add to your salads.

To start making your salad, harvest your salad greens and flowers in the cool of the day, preferably in the early morning when they are the crispest and sweetest in flavor. Scan the garden to see what's looking best, or what needs to be picked, and taste as you go along. Has the rocket or mustard gotten too hot? If so, try some of their flowers instead. Does the kale need thinning? The little leaves are wonderful. Think of flavors to combine, but also visualize the colors and shapes you want in your salad. The greens, served with a simple dressing, can be the end in themselves or the foundation to build on and the vehicle for featuring baby beets or even fresh pears.

Look beyond the salad garden to the rest of your vegetables for ingredients. Have the radishes gone to seed? The pods are good in salads. Are the peas growing well enough to let you harvest a few of the sweet, young shoots? Do you have fava beans growing vigorously? Their young leaves are tender and flavorful. Is the apple tree or redbud in bloom? The

OPPOSITE: *Salads come in all different forms. At the top, right, is a Caesar salad with crisp romaines; at the left is a mixed salad with numerous greens and edible flowers; and in front is a composed salad with golden tomatoes, cucumbers, and baby 'Ragged Jack' kale around the outside. In the middle is a leaf of red orach. A small head of curly 'Fine Maraichere' endive is in the foreground.*

While visiting the Seattle area to explore new developments in vegetable cookery in the Northwest, I was told about Le Gourmand, a restaurant known for its creative use of fresh vegetables and local specialties. While there, I met with chef-owners Bruce Naftaly and Robin Sanders. They had begun experimenting with a variety of unusual greens, herbs, flowers, and wild edibles years before this was fashionable and have accumulated a vast knowledge of salad greens, producing dishes like asparagus with sweet cicely herb butter and salads of miner's lettuce, or pristine young dandelions, or the mixed flavors of kale, anise hyssop, and preserved duck, dressed with balsamic vinegar.

Over the years, Robin and Bruce have cultivated a network of hobby and market gardeners who supply them with fancy greens, fresh herbs, and flowers, and they've developed their own ideas about what makes a good salad. "First, it's a question of taste," says Robin. "Just as with colors—some people like red, others blue—if you like it, it's right. Next I ask, What's the purpose of the salad? To cleanse the palate after a meal? To balance a heavy course? And what comes next? If it's a light dessert, you don't want a pungent, heavy salad; that would be more appropriate as a luncheon meal or before a rich game dish. Finally, what's the high point of the meal: the salad or the entree?"

"A salad is a mixture of textures and tastes," Bruce says. "You need to taste everything, maybe even take notes on the characteristics of various ingredients for later combinations." For example, he says, you should be aware of ways in which ingredients complement each other. Mustard brings out one flavor in greens, vinegar accents another, and orange juice and honey have still different effects. "Notice everything," says Bruce. "Are the greens smooth, or fuzzy? Crisp, or soft? Hot and spicy, bitter, or sour?"

Bruce Naftaly and Robin Sanders

Most cooking is improvising, combining textures and flavors in ways that please, Bruce and Robin believe. "We all get better with practice," Robin says. "You shouldn't be afraid to try different combinations; don't be afraid to make a mistake. Of course, you don't want to get carried away filling a salad with everything in sight, either; too many ingredients tend to muddy the flavors. Try featuring just a few greens."

I asked Bruce and Robin what salad greens they like to use and how they might combine them. For a rich salad, they suggest arugula (rocket) and/or slightly spicy mustard greens; rich and tender mizuna, bitter radicchio, and/or edible chrysanthemums; and a small amount of slightly sweet anise hyssop. This kind of salad is best served with a fruity olive oil and balsamic vinegar or another heavy dressing.

For light salads they suggest lettuces, very young dandelions, grassy-flavored chickweed (used sparingly), and mâche (corn salad), a favorite because it's neutral, nutty, and slightly sweet. They also like lamb's-quarters and purslane because, as Bruce says, "they're not very strong and they give interesting flavor and texture contrasts—very nice with lettuces."

One of Robin's personal favorites is arugula— if it's not too sharp. "When it's really strong, I sometimes chop it up and use it like an herb in a dressing. But when it's not too strong, it has a full, nutty taste, and it's spicy. It makes my mouth come alive."

Bruce especially likes French sorrel. "It's lemony—tart, but still springy," he says. "It's one of the first greens to come up in the spring, so I often use a little in my spring salads." Bruce also likes anise hyssop, which he says "has an interesting licorice taste. It's a little fuzzy, and the flowers are very pretty and tasty as well. I like to use hyssop sparingly in warm salads, maybe with some kale and preserved goose or duck. It's nice with a balsamic vinegar; then it has a sweet-and-sour flavor that I like a lot."

Both Robin and Bruce like mild mustard greens in salad. They combine the mustard with heavy greens, add pork or lamb cured with red currant juice or red currant vinegar (which is very tart but fruity), honey, and a warm dressing. Served warm, this salad makes a light main course—or a nice appetizer if served in a small quantity.

Just as Bruce and Robin have personal favorites, they also have personal dislikes. Both, for example, avoid combining sweet dressings with members of the Brassica family. "We think that brings out the worst in the Brassicas," they say. "Instead we use a simple oil and wine vinegar dressing—not a sweet balsamic but a dry sherry."

"Through the years we've experimented," Bruce concludes, "and we've enjoyed creating all types of salads. We've put nasturtium leaves, tips of young pea vines, young leaves of salad burnet, and sweet cicely in our salads, and we've garnished them with chive, dandelion, and broccoli flowers."

After I left Le Gourmand, I felt compelled to look beyond my salad garden and start harvesting more from my flower border. I looked at my weeds in a new light and scrutinized my vegetable garden to find other parts of the plants that I could use in my salads. Bruce and Robin, part of a new breed of cooks, have not only diverged from routine produce selection; they have broken the shackles of the vegetable garden to include wild and ornamental plants in their edible horizon as well.

---

flowers of both are a rare treat. If you have nasturtiums, pick a few tangy leaves or flowers. And, of course, look over your "weeds." Are the *edible* ones young and succulent? As you can see, the boundaries of the salad garden really encompass the whole yard, and a "salad awareness" can stimulate you to look at your yard with new eyes.

Once you have chosen your salad ingredients, you need to prepare them. Wash the greens; it is critical to remove the grit and occasional insect that might have taken up residence there. The easiest way to wash a reasonable amount of greens is to fill your kitchen sink half full of cool water and gently slosh the greens up and down so the grit sinks to the bottom. You might need to do this a few times. Then dry the greens well. (Wet greens will shed the dressing and make it watery besides.) By far the easiest and most efficient way to dry them is to use a salad spinner. If you don't have one, pat the greens dry with paper or tea towels. Place your clean and dry greens in a plastic bag or between damp paper towels and refrigerate until you are ready to serve them. Keep any flowers you may have picked separate, because they are fragile; most should be preserved in water or on a damp towel.

If you are using only small baby lettuces and greens, they are now ready to be dressed and served. (Remember to have them very dry and dress them only lightly, as the dressing will easily weigh them down.) If you are using mature, full-sized greens, most people prefer that they be bite-size; tear them gently so as not to bruise them. Alternatively, serve whole leaves, as Europeans sometimes do. The diner, then, is expected to dexterously fold an individual leaf around a fork and eat it in its entirety or to cut the salad with a knife and fork.

The presentation of your salad can be anything as simple as putting the bowl with the dressed salad on the table and having everyone help themselves, to the downright ceremonial with all the trimmings. You can mix the greens together or arrange them on individual serving plates to accent the leaf shapes or colors. The choice is up to you, the artist. Some cooks prefer to dress the salad themselves; others let the diners dress their own.

While I've given much attention to the salad greens and herbs, another key ingredient to a masterful salad is the dressing. Dressings are usually a blend of some sort of oil, an acidic liquid such as vinegar or lemon juice, and flavorings. The dressing is an important element in a salad; it serves to meld the many flavors and textures and highlight the greens. Like your greens, it is important that the dressing ingredients be fresh, fresh, fresh and of the best quality. Off-tasting stale oils and vinegars will undo the delicate and sweet flavors of the greens and defeat the purpose of having superior salad vegetables.

For your dressing use cold-pressed oils and high-quality vinegars (discussed in detail below) whenever possible. Note that these ingredients must be stored well to maintain their freshness. Once opened, oils and vinegars should be kept in a cool, dark place or, if used infrequently, in the refrigerator. While some authorities might disagree with putting oil in the refrigerator, I recommend that you do so with oil kept more than six months. However, some oils will solidify when refrigerated and need to be brought up to room temperature to be used. Check your oil before using it, as a rancid, off-tasting oil can ruin your salad.

The secret to making a good dressing is to keep the proportions right and match the ingredients to the particular combination of salad makings. A vinaigrette is a time-honored and versatile dressing. You can dress it up or down and vary it from day to day. Most recipes for a vinaigrette call for three parts oil to one part vinegar. (Marinades for vegetables and meats can contain the same ingredients but usually with a higher proportion of vinegar.) If you use too much oil, the dressing will be bland and slick; too much vinegar will make it too sharp.

For other dressings, the proportions and ingredients will vary according to personal taste, the types of oils and vinegars used, and the kind of dressing intended. For example, a rich or creamy dressing is nice with the heartier greens; it might be made with an egg yolk, a heavy olive oil, or a cheese. Spices as well as herbs can be added for seasoning. For some reason, I used to be intimidated by the idea of making my own salad dressings, and for years I purchased bottled ones. Nowadays, I find making dressings quite simple and the results greatly improve my salads, especially since I use my own herbs. If you're hesitant, start with a vinaigrette, which is easy, and use the lighter oils and vinegars. For a basic vinaigrette and other dressings see the recipes that follow.

Earlier in the chapter I discussed the salad greens in detail. Other ingredients you might want to include in your salads are many of the herbs and edible flowers covered in the "Edible Flower Gardens" and "Culinary Herbs" chapters. Now let's look more closely at some of the other components of your salads.

Mustards

One of the most common flavorings for salad dressings is mustard. Like vinegar or lemon, it adds sharpness to a dressing, but has a zesty flavor as well. Mustard is made from the ground-up seeds of the white- (yellow-) or brown-seeded mustard plants, *Brassica alba* and *B. nigra*. Both mustards, in fact, can be grown in your garden, though harvesting and cleaning the seeds are rather time-consuming. Plant the seeds and grow as you would standard mustard but pamper the plants less. In about three months the plants will flower and go to seed. Harvest the yellow pods and thresh; then winnow to remove the chaff as you would with grains (see the "Grain Gardens" chapter) and strain through a kitchen strainer with holes just large enough to let the seeds go through. To make into a grainy mustard, grind up the seeds in a blender with a liquid such as wine or vinegar and then mix with other flavorings such as honey or spices. Experiment to see what combinations please you. Your homemade mustards will be hotter than the commercial brands.

If you do not grow your own mustard, buy seeds from a health food store and process them or, easier yet, buy already prepared mustard. The most common type of mustard used in salad dressings is a Dijon-type. Use mustard sparingly in your salad dressings and add to taste. Once opened, keep your prepared mustard in the refrigerator. It is best used within six months.

Oils

Oils are used in salads to coat the greens and carry the flavorings. They add richness and, in many cases, their own flavors. Many different kinds of oils are used in salads; they range from the heavy, fruity olive oil to the light, almost neutral safflower oil. While the choice of an oil is basically a matter of taste, the olive oils and some of the nut oils are most often used on strong-flavored greens or in combination with lighter oils. For everyday salads, the lighter oils are the most versatile. Whatever your choice, try to buy cold-pressed oils (check the label), which means they have not been heated and are consistently of high quality. Heating can destroy some of the vitamins in an oil. Store oil in a cool place.

Olive oils: There are many informal grades of olive oil. They range from "extra-virgin" (first cold pressing) and "pure virgin" to "pure" and "fine." The latter two ratings, though they sound distinctive, often indicate inferior quality; generally oils in these categories have a lighter and sometimes off taste. The meanings of these classifications are somewhat

inexact, but while the "extra-virgin" and "pure virgin" olive oils have been cold-pressed and the oil
poured off, the "pure" and "fine" oils are sometimes
made from batches containing imperfect olives, are
from second pressings, and/or are extracted by boiling or chemical means.

Olive oils can have quite a range of flavors. Those
of higher quality are generally green in color and can
be quite strong to mild. Some connoisseurs consider
the French olive oil made from ripe olives to be of
the highest quality. You'll need to taste many different kinds of olive oil to determine your own
preferences.

Salad oils: The most easily available and often-
used oils are what are called salad oils in this country. These include safflower, sunflower, and corn oil.
They range from light-flavored to almost neutral and
can be used with some of the lighter-flavored greens.
They combine nicely with the nut or olive oils in
varying amounts to taste and take added flavoring,
as with chilies, garlic, or herbs, very well.

Nut oils: Many oils are made from nuts, the
most common of which is peanut oil, frequently used
in Chinese cooking. Some of the peanut oils are heavy
tasting while others are quite light, so try different
brands.

In the last few years, walnut, almond, and hazelnut oils have come into favor for salads. They are
usually pressed in the fall and are best used very
fresh. These oils are elegant with some of the hardier
greens or with corn salad, where their nutty flavors
really come through. Walnut oil is particularly nice
with bitter salad greens or combined with raspberry
vinegar and served over a mixed lettuce salad. Or try
it with lemon juice in a spinach salad. The French
sometimes use walnut oil in making croutons. The
hazelnut and almond oils are particularly nice with
avocados and with spinach. For all the nut oils, the
taste is heightened by garnishing the salad with a few
roasted nuts.

Vinegars

The dictionary defines vinegar as a sour liquid consisting of dilute and impure acetic acid. This speaks
little to the wide range of flavors to be found in
vinegars. Basically, vinegar is fermented fruit juice
or, as with Oriental rice-wine vinegars, grain. A good
vinegar should be sharp but not harsh.

Wine vinegars: Wine vinegars are among the most
flavorful and popular for a mixed green salad. They
can be made from red or white wine grapes. Most of
the fancy restaurants and caterers use French or a
local winery's vinegar, as opposed to a common
commercial brand, which can be harsh or lacking in
flavor. Frequently, specialty stores stock high-quality, locally made vinegars. White-wine vinegars are
the most versatile for flavoring with herbs such as
tarragon and basil or with fruits and spices.

Sherry vinegars: The rich, dry flavor of vinegar
made from sherry wine seems to combine well with
the flavors of the nut oils. Sherry vinegar can be quite
expensive, since some brands have been aged for
twenty-five years. You can substitute a good red-wine
vinegar with a dash of sherry for sherry vinegar.

Balsamic vinegar: Balsamic vinegar (*aceto bal-
samico*) is another rich-tasting vinegar used on salad
greens. It is slightly sweet and quite rich. Balsamic
vinegar is aged for years in wooden vats, and each
brand has a slightly different taste, so try a few to
see which you prefer.

Cider vinegar: Cider vinegar, made from apples,
is a mild vinegar. It combines well with light oils and
in sweet-and-sour dressings.

Oriental vinegars: Another type of vinegar I like
to keep on hand is an Oriental rice-wine vinegar.
Oriental vinegars come in many forms and flavors,
but most are quite a bit milder than European vinegars. Oriental vinegars are particularly nice when
combined with a little soy sauce and used to dress
Oriental greens.

Flavored vinegars: You will probably see flavored vinegars in specialty stores. These are made by
steeping fruit (for instance, raspberries), herbs, hot
peppers, rose petals, or garlic in the vinegar. But it's
easy, fun, and certainly less expensive to make tasty
flavored vinegars at home. To make a fruit vinegar,
start with a very high quality wine vinegar and use
two parts fruit to one part vinegar. Soak the fruit in
the vinegar for a few weeks until you like the flavor
strength and then strain the vinegar. Put the strained
vinegar in a sterilized bottle and refrigerate. For more
information on herb vinegars see the "Culinary Herb
Gardens" chapter.

Doubtless, these ideas on oils and vinegars plus
the thought of a salad garden outside your kitchen
door have already sparked your creativity with respect
to salads. It should inspire you even further to

A Farallones Institute salad that includes three or four types of lettuces and edible flowers. Seen are yellow mustard blossoms, blue borage, 'Eglantine' roses, and white pea blossoms.

remember that of all the gardens described in this book, the salad garden could conceivably make the most profound changes in your family's eating, regarding both taste and nutrition. Read on for a diverse array of salad recipes and their variations.

VINAIGRETTE DRESSINGS

A basic vinaigrette is given below with suggested variations for each ingredient. Robin Sanders and Bruce Naftaly of Le Gourmand restaurant in Seattle like to use extra-virgin olive oil and a twenty-five-year-old sherry vinegar for mild, tender greens such as lettuces, corn salad, young mizuna, rocket, edible chrysanthemum, and miner's lettuce. Herbs for these salads include parsley, basil, chervil, tarragon, and thyme. Robin and Bruce use the heavy kalamata (Greek) olive oil and balsamic vinegar for hardier greens of autumn and winter such as chard, kale, and chicory. Rose geranium leaves, sage, rosemary, oregano, marjoram, and other strong-flavored herbs could also be used, though with discretion.

Chef John Downey, from Downey's in Santa Barbara, California, likes to use a vinaigrette with lots of garden-fresh herbs to marinate lightly cooked vegetables for appetizers. For this he uses a light combination of olive and corn oils and cider vinegar to let the flavors of the greens and herbs predominate. Just be sure that, whatever oils and vinegars you use, they are of the best quality. Your lovely garden vegetables deserve it!

SALAD SIZE FOR THIS AMOUNT VARIES WITH TASTE.

>   ¼ *cup wine or cider vinegar*
>   1 *to 3 teaspoons high-quality mustard*
>   1 *to 2 tablespoons minced shallots, dried or green onions, garlic, or a combination of these*
>   ⅓ *cup finely chopped fresh herbs*
>   *Salt and freshly ground pepper to taste*
>   1 *cup oil*

Combine all ingredients except oil in a bowl or process briefly in food processor. Slowly whisk in oil or add to processor. Let stand for ½ hour to allow flavors to blend; check seasoning. Refrigerate unused portion and use within a few days.

MESCLUN

Mesclun is a French Provençal term for a salad of many varieties of young red and green lettuces and herbs. This recipe comes from Warren Weber, a farmer who grows vegetables organically on his Star Route Farm in Bolinas, California. He has become known for his wonderful greens, used by some of the finest restaurants in the San Francisco area.

SERVES 5 TO 6.

Salad

Warren uses a seasonal selection of 6 varieties of lettuces and herbs chosen from the following: 'Red Salad Bowl', 'Oak Leaf', a red romaine, 'Cybelle', 'Marvel of Four Seasons', and butter lettuces, chicory frisée, Italian parsley, chervil, and dry-land cress. You may use any other young greens and herbs your garden offers as well.

Prepare enough leaves for 5 to 6 servings; gently wash well and spin dry. Chill in a plastic bag until ready to use.

Vinaigrette

>   2 *tablespoons wine vinegar*

Salt and pepper to taste
6 to 7 tablespoons virgin olive oil

Mix the vinegar, salt, and pepper and blend in the oil to taste. Toss gently with the salad and serve.

Variations

Use other vinegars, such as balsamic or herb-flavored; add a finely chopped shallot or crushed garlic clove to the vinegar and let it marinate for ½ hour before adding the oil; add a teaspoon of Dijon mustard and finely chopped herbs or anchovies. Garlic croutons are good with mesclun. To make them, brush thin slices of baguette with olive oil and toast on a baking sheet in the oven until golden brown. While still warm, rub croutons with a raw garlic clove.

SPINACH AND WATERCRESS SALAD WITH SAVORY MAYONNAISE

Robin Sanders and Bruce Naftaly at Le Gourmand contributed this recipe for cool autumn and early spring as well as the suggestions for winter salad garnishes that follow it.

YIELD VARIES WITH SALAD SIZE.

Salad

A generous amount of spinach and watercress
  leaves for each serving in a 2:1 ratio (or
  substitute young nasturtium or rocket
  leaves for the watercress)

Dressing

2 egg yolks
3 tablespoons balsamic vinegar
¼ teaspoon freshly ground white pepper
½ teaspoon salt
1 teaspoon chopped fresh sage (optional; very
  good with cold, moist, poached chicken
  added to the salad)
1 cup kalamata (or other virgin) olive oil (if a
  lighter flavor is preferred, substitute
  safflower, peanut, or corn oil for half the
  olive oil)
⅓ cup glace de viande (dark-brown reduced
  brown stock)

Calendula petals for garnish (during winter,
  use dried calendula petals)
Jerusalem artichoke pickles or red-chard-stem
  pickles (optional; see below)

All ingredients must be around 70° F. In a large bowl, use an electric beater on medium-high speed or a whisk to beat egg yolks well. Add 1 tablespoon vinegar, salt, pepper, and sage (if used). While beating, very slowly add oil and remaining vinegar by droplets until half the oil is used; add the rest in a slow stream. Beat in glace de viande and remove to a storage or serving container with a rubber spatula. Refrigerate if not using immediately, but warm to room temperature by beating in a bowl before adding the greens to toss. Dress the greens to taste and garnish with calendula petals and, if desired, Jerusalem artichoke pickles or red-chard-stem pickles (both given below).

SOME WINTER SALAD GARNISHES

Here are the optional additions to the spinach and watercress salad, above. Obviously, you can enjoy them in other salads too or on their own as crudités.

Jerusalem Artichoke Pickles

Scrub and very thinly slice Jerusalem artichokes and marinate in the finest vinegar (we use the 25-year-old sherry vinegar) for at least 2 days.

Red-Chard-Stem Pickles

Remove the thickest fibers from red-chard stems. Dice the stems small. Marinate in the finest red-wine vinegar (zinfandel vinegar is recommended) for at least 2 days.

SPINACH SALAD WITH HAZELNUTS AND FRESH RASPBERRIES

This recipe, from John Downey of Downey's, Santa Barbara, makes a fine summer appetizer or, with a little grilled duck, squab, chicken, or fresh goat cheese, a wonderful lunch entree.

SERVES 6.

Dressing

> 1 tablespoon raspberry jam
> ½ cup fresh raspberries
> 1 tablespoon Dijon mustard
> ½ cup raspberry vinegar
> Lots of fresh ground black pepper, to taste
> 1½ cups olive oil plus 1 tablespoon hazelnut
>   oil

Combine all ingredients except oils in a bowl with a whisk, mashing berries. Slowly whisk in oils. Allow to sit 30 minutes; then correct seasoning if necessary.

Salad

> ½ cup hazelnuts
> 2 bunches (about 2 pounds) young spinach,
>   washed and dried

Roast the hazelnuts in a hot oven for 15 minutes or until brown skin flakes away and nuts are lightly browned. Rub them with a dry towel to remove skins. Cool.

Crush hazelnuts and toss with spinach and dressing. Garnish with a few whole raspberries.

TOMATO AND BASIL SALAD

YIELD VARIES WITH AMOUNT OF TOMATOES.

This combination is inspired by a regular summertime feature on the menu of John Downey's restaurant, when local farmers bring John luscious, ripe tomatoes and fragrant basil. Simply make the best vinaigrette (see above) using virgin olive oil, red-wine vinegar, crushed garlic, sliced sweet red onions (optional), and lots of coarsely chopped fresh basil. Marinate sliced tomatoes in this for about ½ hour, then remove with a slotted spoon and serve.

CAESAR SALAD

Tijuana, Mexico, was the unlikely birthplace of this famous salad. It remains one of the best treatments for crisp, fresh romaine lettuce (my other favorite is to use inner leaves as dippers for tabouli salad). Worcestershire sauce, not anchovies, was part of the original salad. They are both listed here as optional; use one or the other.

SERVES 8.

> 1 large clove garlic, pressed
> ¾ cup olive oil
> 1 large or 2 medium heads romaine lettuce
>   (about 1½ pounds)
> 1½ to 2 cups cubed stale French bread
> 1 egg
> ½ teaspoon salt, if using anchovies; 1
>   teaspoon if using Worcestershire sauce
> 1 teaspoon Worcestershire sauce (optional)
> 6 to 8 anchovy filets, diced and mashed
>   (optional)
> Dash of Tabasco sauce
> ¼ cup fresh lemon juice
> ¾ cup freshly grated Parmesan cheese
> Freshly ground black pepper

Add garlic to olive oil in a small jar or covered bowl; refrigerate overnight. Wash lettuce well, dry, and refrigerate in a plastic bag until ready to use. Warm oil to room temperature and pour about 3 tablespoons into a skillet. Sauté bread cubes on medium heat, turning to brown all sides. Drain on paper towels. Boil egg for 1 minute, remove from water, and set aside. Break lettuce into 2-inch pieces in a large salad bowl. Add salt, Worcestershire or anchovies, and Tabasco sauce to oil; then pour over lettuce and toss well. Crack egg into salad, add lemon juice, and toss again. Add Parmesan and plenty of black pepper, toss, add croutons, and toss a final time.

GARDEN BOUQUET SALAD WITH LEMON-HERB VINAIGRETTE

Here's an elegant and exotic salad. This and the following recipe are from the catalog of Shepherd's Garden Seeds.

SERVES 6.

Lemon-Herb Vinaigrette Dressing

> 1 small green onion, chopped fine
> 1 teaspoon Dijon mustard
> 2 to 3 tablespoons lemon juice
> 1 tablespoon dry white wine
> 1 egg yolk
> 1 tablespoon minced parsley

*1 tablespoon minced chive flower petals or
    chopped chive leaves*
¼ teaspoon salt
Pinch of freshly ground pepper
¾ cup olive oil

With a whisk, combine all ingredients except oil.
Slowly whisk in oil, beating continually until thoroughly blended. Taste for seasoning. Chill until ready
to use.

Salad

*2 heads radicchio (or red-leaf lettuce as a
    second choice)*
2 heads corn salad
2 small heads bibb lettuce
*12 to 14 leaves (2 handfuls) young rocket or
    watercress*
¾ cup fresh green and purple basil leaves
½ cup calendula petals
¼ cup borage flowers
2 to 3 fresh sorrel leaves

Remove leaves from assorted vegetables; wash and
dry. Reserve 6 to 8 radicchio or red lettuce leaves.
Tear remaining radicchio, corn salad, sorrel, lettuces,
and rocket into bite-size pieces and combine with
basil leaves in center of salad bowl. Line outer edge
with reserved radicchio or red lettuce leaves. Sprinkle
with flowers around the outside border. Stir dressing
again and pour over salad after presenting it at the
table.

PETITS POIS SALAD

This salad makes a colorful and delicious side dish
or picnic take-along.

SERVES 6.

*3½ cups petits pois cooked in a little water
    until tender, drained and chilled*
*1 cup sour cream (or ½ cup yogurt or "lite"
    sour cream and ½ cup regular sour cream)*
2 green onions, finely chopped
*6 slices bacon, cooked crisp, drained, and
    crumbled*
½ teaspoon salt
Freshly ground pepper

Toss peas with all ingredients and serve.

*An Italian salad with red radicchio, fennel, rocket,
and mixed lettuces, served with olive oil and red basil
vinegar, and sprinkled with edible redbud flowers
(Cercis occidentalis).*

CONFETTI RICE WITH TWO BASILS

This is an adaptation of a recipe from the Shepherd's
Garden Seeds catalog.

SERVES 4 TO 6.

1 cup raw brown rice
¼ cup lemon juice
½ teaspoon salt
¼ teaspoon pepper
⅓ cup olive oil

2 scallions, finely chopped
3 tablespoons finely chopped green basil
    ('Lettuce Leaf' preferred)
¼ cup chopped 'Purple Opal' basil
2 tablespoons chopped parsley
½ cup finely chopped celery or fennel bulbs
1 sweet red pepper, chopped
Kernels of 2 ears fresh, young sweet corn
½ to 1 cup sprouted beans (optional)

Cook rice and let cool in pot. Gently spoon rice into serving bowl. Shake lemon juice, oil, salt, and pepper together in a small jar and pour over rice. Add remaining ingredients and fold together.

SAUCE VERTE

Here is a variation of the classic sauce verte. Alternately, any leftover cooked green vegetables can be pureed in a blender or food processor and mixed with vinegar or lemon juice, some mayonnaise, fresh herbs, and seasoning to make a lovely green salad dressing or dip.

MAKES APPROXIMATELY 2½ CUPS.

½ cup blanched and drained spinach
¼ cup chopped watercress leaves (or ⅛ cup young rocket or nasturtium leaves)
¼ cup chopped parsley leaves (Italian preferred)
¼ cup chopped sorrel leaves
1 scallion or 1 shallot or 2 tablespoons minced chives
1 small clove garlic, crushed
2 tablespoons minced fresh tarragon, dill, or chervil
1½ cups mayonnaise
½ cup sour cream or yogurt

Blend all ingredients in a blender or food processor.

Sources

Seed Companies
1. Bountiful Gardens
   Ecology Action
   5798 Ridgewood Road
   Willits, CA 95490

This seed company carries many open-pollinated vegetable varieties, including some interesting lettuces and other greens.
2. The Cook's Garden
   P.O. Box 65
   Londonderry, VT 05148
   This firm is particularly interested in lettuce; it carries twenty-two varieties.
3. Good Seed
   P.O. Box 702
   Tonasket, WA 98855
   This seed company carries many heirloom vegetable varieties and a range of salad plants.
4. Herb Gathering, Inc.
   5742 Kenwood
   Kansas City, MO 64110
   Herb Gathering carries many French salad greens.
5. Le Marché
   Seeds International
   P.O. Box 190
   Dixon, CA 95620
   Le Marché carries many unusual salad greens. Catalog: $2.00.
6. Nichols Garden Nursery
   1190 North Pacific Highway
   Albany, OR 97321
   This nursery carries a large selection of interesting lettuces as well as corn salad and various other salad greens.
7. Park Seed Company
   Cokesbury Road
   Greenwood, SC 29647
   One of this country's largest seed companies, Park carries many good lettuce varieties and numerous other salad vegetables.
8. Seeds Blum
   Idaho City Stage
   Boise, ID 83706
   This seed company is interested in heirloom vegetables and unusual salad greens. Catalog: $2.00.
9. Shepherd's Garden Seeds
   7389 West Zayante Road
   Felton, CA 95018
   This firm carries superior varieties of European salad greens. Catalog: $1.00.

10. Stokes Seeds, Inc.
P.O. Box 548
Buffalo, NY 14240
Stokes carries many varieties of lettuces, cucumbers, tomatoes, and other popular salad ingredients.

11. Thompson & Morgan, Inc.
P.O. Box 1308
Jackson, NJ 08527
This English seed company offers a good selection of lettuces, cucumbers, and miscellaneous salad vegetables to choose from.

Books

Larkcom, Joy. *The Salad Garden*. New York: Viking, 1984.
This volume is an absolute must for the salad gardener and cook. It contains full-color photos of many of the unusual salad greens and much culinary and gardening information.

Proulx, E. Annie. *The Fine Art of Salad Gardening*. Emmaus, Pa.: Rodale Press, 1985.
This book contains much in-depth information about salad greens and how to grow and prepare them.

Edible Flower Gardens

I T'S INCREDIBLE HOW MANY flowers or parts of flowers I've eaten in the last few years—lavender petals made into ice cream, zucchini blossoms stuffed with ricotta cheese, roses used in butter for scones, just to name a few. And I've gone out of my way to spread the natural wealth, serving unadorned blossoms of anise hyssop and an Art Deco–style cake with matte-finish candied pansies to unsuspecting guests. Not only do I eat edible flowers, but I've become a missionary in promoting them!

I'd love to be able to tell you about the first flower I ever ate, but I can't remember. It was probably a nasturtium, though, six or seven years ago. I'm certain I started slowly, since to eat flowers seemed odd to me, maybe even taboo. I remember eating rice garnished with calendula petals in Vermont and thinking that they made the dish colorful but didn't add much to the flavor. Later I tried a few pansy petals served in a restaurant salad and still wasn't won over. Not until I tasted lavender ice cream at an herb seminar did I become really enthusiastic. It was fantastic! There and then I determined to learn more about the subject of edible flowers.

OPPOSITE: *A harvest of edible flowers. Included are 'Alaska' nasturtiums, red gladiolas, 'Austrian Copper' rose, hollyhocks, Johnny-jump-ups, yellow calendula, lavender borage, yellow squash blossom, orange nasturtiums, yellow marigolds, lavender chicory, white and red runner bean blossoms, and violas.*

Since that time I've probably asked everyone I know to try eating flowers and to describe their reactions. There's been a tremendous range. A few people just plunge right in with delight, as if I've given them permission to enjoy a new pleasure. But most people are much more hesitant. One friend would only accept my dinner invitation with the warning, "But I won't try any of your darn flowers!" You'd have thought I was offering her fried caterpillars. I've tried to get people to explain their hesitation about eating flowers, but they seem to have a hard time doing it. I certainly have difficulty explaining why I had a problem initially. Why do others? Is it because flowers are a new food? Somewhat. Is it a concern about the safety of eating them? Maybe. But I've just about concluded that the main problem involves a belief that flowers are almost magical, so beautiful that only the eyes should feast on them. To those who hold this belief, eating flowers seems a bit greedy.

Since becoming involved with edible flowers I've read everything I could find about them. I've asked all the chefs I've interviewed about their experiences with them. And I've tasted, tasted, and tasted every edible flower I could get my hands on, even stooping, on occasion, to take a sly bite out of my hostess's centerpiece.

In doing my research I've found the available information on edible flowers to be the strangest hodgepodge I've ever run across. Much of what we know about edible flowers, it turns out, is based on the information in old herbals. But when I decided to see if I could expand on my knowledge by turning to the herbals themselves, my confusion mounted. In medieval Europe eating flowers was commonplace, but in those days foods often had medicinal as well as nutritional uses, and sometimes flowers with potent chemicals were included in the old recipes. Thus, a recipe might call for two or three blossoms of foxglove, which is classified as poisonous today. True, we use foxglove to make digitalis, a heart stimulant, but only in carefully measured doses. I started realizing, as I read the old recipes, that the term poisonous was more relative than I'd thought.

Also, as if the herbals' folk-medicine approach didn't make it difficult enough to determine which flowers were safe to eat, our forebears often called flowers by different names than we use. For instance, what we call calendula they called marigold; what we call cottage pink they called gillyflower. So I was faced with the challenge of making sure the flowers referred to in the recipes matched the flowers we grow today.

Another major question arose in the course of my research: of the flowers that are edible, which are palatable? I collected a number of modern lists of edible flowers and cautiously began my tasting. Some of the entries were absolutely horrible! Obviously, no one had tasted them before adding them to the lists. For example, some marigolds have a slight lemony taste, others are tasteless, but the taste of most falls somewhere between skunk and quinine. Furthermore, none of these lists gave much guidance as to *how* to eat the different kinds of flowers. I remember innocently putting an entire mullein petal into my mouth and finding it to be horribly astringent. I had the same experience with a carnation petal. Later I learned that before eating most flowers you need to remove the white part at the base of the petals, since it often tastes terrible.

I am sharing my frustration with you here because I want to gain your trust and break down any resistance you might have to eating flowers. I feel that flowers have a great future in our cuisine. We are looking for alternatives to salt and sugar as seasonings, and here we have one. And not only do flowers make interesting seasonings, but their aesthetic value as decorations is obvious. As you can see, my zeal for cooking with flowers is irrepressible!

Regarding cooking methods, I asked every gardener, chef, and food expert I could talk with how they prepared edible flowers. And I arranged for a number of edible flower gardens to be grown for this project: by Carole Saville, an herb specialist in Los Angeles; by Margaret Kinkaid, a dedicated gardener in New Vernon, New Jersey; and by the folks at the Chez Panisse restaurant in Berkeley, California.

Carole Saville helped me determine that an area as small as two feet by four feet filled with edible flowers could make an impact in the kitchen. And as Carole had already grown and cooked with many edible flowers and flowering herbs, she was able to give me a lot of detailed information. I learned from her, among other things, how to make tea from roselle and sorbet from gillyflowers as well as how to use fresh flowers in some quite original ways to decorate petits fours.

Margaret Kinkaid talked to me about which of the edible flowers grew in New Jersey. I had wondered whether the scarlet runner beans and nasturtiums would bloom in the hot summer weather (yes) and how an uninitiated family would react to eating flowers (Margaret's teenage daughter was particularly fascinated and experimented with many). And it was a pleasure to see how beautifully she integrated vegetables and edible flowers into the same garden.

Food professionals, too, helped with ideas and recipes. From Bruce Naftaly and Robin Sanders, chef-owners of Le Gourmand restaurant in Seattle, I learned how to use rose petal honey in baklava. From Renée Shepherd, of Shepherd's Garden Seeds, I found out how to make anise hyssop tea bread. And from Kerry Marshall, manager of Mudd's restaurant in San Ramon, California, I learned to match the flower garnish with the dish being served. Holly Shimizu, curator of the National Herb Garden in Washington, D.C., taught me how the arboretum there uses roses and how restaurants in Japan use flowers. The most concentrated knowledge about edible flowers, however, came from the people associated with Berkeley's Chez Panisse restaurant. All the information came together, both in the garden they grew for me and in the cooking knowledge they shared.

To me, this chapter on edible flowers is one of the most exciting in the book. It seems, more than the others, to break new ground (a forgivable gardener's pun, I hope) and to give gardeners materials to cook with that they might not have thought of on their own. But if you're still hesitant about jumping right in and starting to grow an edible flower garden, I urge you to read the following sections for inspiration. I'm counting on the fact that by the time you've finished the cooking section, the sheer anticipation of working with flowers in your kitchen will have you planning your edible flower garden.

How to Grow Edible Flowers

With the exception of some of the herbs, most of the edible plants I have covered in this book have been annuals, perennials treated as annuals, or biennial plants. This chapter is different; it covers perennial and woody plants as well, since so many edible flowers grow on them. Because the gardeners and chefs I met were so hungry for factual information, I decided not to limit myself in this chapter to specific plant categories.

Growing the average annual flowers, such as

The Kinkaid edible flower/vegetable garden in New Vernon, New Jersey.

nasturtiums, Johnny-jump-ups, or calendulas, is quite a straightforward procedure, similar to that for growing such annual vegetables as lettuce, bell peppers, and corn. You won't have any trouble finding information on growing them, and you shouldn't have any in growing them either. These annuals need rich, moist, well-drained soil and in most cases full sun or light shade. They are all started from seeds, but because I have selected unusual varieties, many of those listed in the "Recommended Edible Flowers" section will have to be ordered from the specialty seed companies listed under "Sources."

Many edible flowers are perennials produced on herbaceous plants, bulbs, shrubs, or trees. Day lilies, tulips, roses, and plum blossoms, for example, are all edible flowers. Because they grow for years—perennially—they need a permanent site in the landscape. They are planted from seeds, divisions, or grafted plant material, depending on the species and their availability, and they need good soil preparation and drainage, though they are usually not quite as fussy about soil fertility and moisture as the annuals. But many perennials need protection in severe winter areas. Tender ones, such as oranges, gardenias, and hibiscus, can be grown in containers in a greenhouse or on a sunny porch.

Consult the marvelous books on flower culture given in the "Sources" section for detailed information on growing the individual species. Be aware, however, that the authors of most of the flower-culture books in this country do not expect you to eat the flowers and therefore recommend pesticides that are unsafe for human consumption. If possible, grow your flowers organically. But if you must use a pesticide, always read the label carefully to make sure it can be used on edible plants.

The "Recommended Edible Flowers" section gives rudimentary growing information on all flowers mentioned—enough to get you started and to give you an idea of how much care the plants will need. However, there are some basic factors to consider before you select the edible flowers you will plant in your garden. First, unlike vegetable varieties, the flowers bred at the nurseries have been selected not for their flavor but only for their appearance and growing ease. Therefore, it will help to taste as many varieties as possible before you plant. Visit the gardens of friends and neighbors if you can and taste a few flowers at a time. But this step raises another cautionary note: *beware of poison!* Before you start tasting flowers, let alone planning your garden, you need a brief lesson on poisonous plants.

Poisonous Plants

What is poisonous, anyway? When I began my research I was naive enough to assume that I would be able to find a definitive list of poisonous flowering plants. No such luck. There are plenty of lists

A corner of Carole Saville's miniature edible flower garden. Pictured are cottage pinks, dwarf nasturtiums, Alpine strawberries, calendulas, and a salad garnished with a harvest from the garden.

of poisonous plants but none that completely resolves the issue of what is and is not poisonous. I had to do my own legwork, so I began at the beginning, with *Webster's Third:* "poison. substance that in suitable quantities has properties harmful or fatal to an organism when it is brought into contact with or absorbed by the organism." So there are two crucial factors: chemical contents and dosage. As to the former, plants containing alkaloids, glycosides, resins, alcohols, phenols, phytotoxins, and oxalates are potentially poisonous, but their toxicity depends on the amounts of these substances they contain. After all, many poisonous plants are also valuable medicines. As with foxglove, which contains digitalis, and the more familiar aspirin, a derivative of willow bark, it is the dosage that determines whether the end product will be medicinal or toxic. In fact, some lists of poisonous plants actually show spinach because it contains oxalic acid, which is poisonous in large quantities.

Still, determining the amount of a poisonous substance that makes a plant or serving toxic is a matter for chemists. Obviously, the more you ingest—say, by indulging in foxglove ice cream rather than a single petal on a salad plate—the greater will be the hazard. My advice and the rule I follow is, Don't take chances. I go on the premise that if a plant is on *any* list of poisonous plants, I don't eat it—not even a single petal.

To give you more help, here are some guidelines I have gathered from food technologists and environmental botanists:

1. Positively identify the plant—Latin name and all. As with mushrooms, the identification is crucial.

2. Birds and animals are unharmed by some plants that are poisonous to humans. For instance, the gray squirrel can eat the deadly amanita mushroom without harm, and birds regularly gorge on the irritating red elderberry berries. So don't depend on guinea pigs of any species to guide you.

3. In many cases, not all the parts of toxic plants are poisonous. For instance, rhubarb stalks and potatoes are edible but the leaves of both plants are poisonous.

4. Some plants, such as pokeweed, are poisonous only at certain times of the year.

5. Because individuals can be allergic to substances that are not generally poisonous—wheat and milk are examples—when you first taste a new food go slowly.

6. Just because most members of a particular plant family are not poisonous does not mean that there are no poisonous ones in the family.

7. Heating or cooking in water removes many toxins but not all.

To help you identify poisonous plants, here are a few of the major ones and the parts of the plants known to be dangerous:

AMARYLLIS *Hippeastrum puniceum* Bulb
ANEMONE *Anemone tuberosa* and other spp. All
AUTUMN CROCUS *Colchicum autumnale* All
AZALEA *Rhododendron* spp. All
BELLADONNA LILY (naked lady) *Amaryllis Belladonna* Bulb
BIRD-OF-PARADISE *Strelitzia reginea* Seeds and pods
BUCKEYE *Aesculus arguta* and *A. Hippocastanum*

and other spp. Seeds, flowers, and leaves
BUTTERCUP *Ranunculus* spp. All
CALADIUM *Caladium bicolor* and other spp. All
CARDINAL FLOWER *Lobelia Cardinalis* All
CLEMATIS *Clematis* spp. All
DAFFODIL *Narcissus Pseudonarcissus* Particularly the bulb
DATURA *Datura meteloides* All
DELPHINIUM *Delphinium* spp. All
GLORIOSA LILY *Gloriosa* spp. All
HYDRANGEA *Hydrangea* spp. All
IRIS *Iris* spp. Leaves and rootstock
JESSAMINE *Gelsemium sempervirens* All
LANTANA *Lantana* spp. All
LARKSPUR *Delphinium* spp. All
LILY-OF-THE-VALLEY *Convallaria majalis* All
LUPINE *Lupinus* spp. All
MONKSHOOD *Aconitum* spp. All
NARCISSUS *Narcissus* spp. All
OLEANDER *Nerium oleander* All
POINSETTIA *Euphorbia pulcherrima* All
RHODODENDRON *Rhododendron* spp. All
STAR-OF-BETHLEHEM *Ornithogalum* spp. All
SWEET PEA *Lathyrus* spp. All
TANSY *Tanacetum vulgare* All
WISTERIA *Wisteria floribunda* and *W. sinensis* Pods and seeds

The Chez Panisse Edible Flower Garden

A few years ago I invited Andrea Crawford, manager of the Chez Panisse restaurant garden, to join me in an experiment: to grow a prototypical edible flower garden and to have the chefs at the restaurant experiment in the kitchen with the types and varieties we included. Andrea was immediately interested. She and Alice Waters, the executive chef of Chez Panisse, had been growing and serving edible flowers for many years and were eager to know even more about them. In this garden we would grow flowers that none of us had ever used in the kitchen before.

To begin, we looked over my list of edible flowers, perused seed catalogs for unusual varieties of the individual species, and ordered a good selection of each. Both Andrea and I drew information from everyone we knew who had grown a few of our selections. Jan Blum, of Seeds Blum, sent us 'Fragrance' dianthus seeds to try; Renée Shepherd, of Shepherd's Garden Seeds, sent us 'Kablouna' calendula, anise hyssop, and 'Whirlybird' nasturtium seeds; and we both raided our own supplies of seeds and plants. We concentrated mainly on annual flowers, because we wanted to evaluate the flowers in the kitchen within a year, and because they are easiest for most gardeners to obtain. For the restaurant, Andrea had been producing the flowers of borage, Johnny-jump-ups, lavender, climbing nasturtiums, violas, mustard, radishes, chicory, scented geraniums, and herbs for a number of years, and she chose varieties from among her favorites to go into the demonstration garden. For years I had been growing scarlet runner beans, English daisies, and marigolds, but I had never tasted their flowers and was curious about them, so I chose the most promising varieties of those. I also selected 'Empress of India' and 'Alaska' nasturtiums, two particular varieties I had never used in the kitchen.

Summertime temperatures in Berkeley are moderated by morning fog, and few days exceed 90 degrees. The winters are mild, with temperatures seldom dropping below freezing. Though you might be hesitant at first about trying to duplicate much of this garden if you live in a northern region, almost all the flowers here are annuals and can actually be grown equally well anywhere in the country. As for the soil in the Berkeley garden, it is clay with a tremendous amount of organic matter added. The beds have been double-dug and are in wonderful shape after years of loving care. Andrea, like most good gardeners, is passionate about soil preparation and care, and her years of effort show. Her garden receives no rain from May through September, and summer watering is a constant necessity.

After a few seasons had passed in the edible flower garden, Andrea and I sat down to discuss both her experiences in the garden and the chefs' experiences with the flowers in the kitchen. She was eager to sum it all up. She reminded me that when I had suggested the garden, she and Alice Waters were planning a pansy garden for the restaurant and had already planted flats of them. It had seemed natural to expand to hollyhocks, scarlet runner beans, anise hyssop, gladiolas, 'Austrian Copper' roses, 'Adnami' chrysanthemums, Alpine strawberries, 'Lemon Gem' marigolds, and the rest and to make the new, expanded garden both an ornamental border and a productive garden. For purposes of the book, we had agreed to try to approximate amounts a home gardener would

use. "Well," said Andrea, "we planted far more than a person could ever use at home. In fact, that narrow strip, which was thirty feet by two and a half feet, produced more than the restaurant could use; but we viewed the thing as an ornamental garden that a person could also eat out of, and that was really very nice."

Seeds of the new varieties they tried were obtained from a number of sources, but in retrospect Andrea reported that Stokes Seeds had the best selection and that she could get just about all the varieties she needed from them. Thompson & Morgan, on the other hand, turned out to be really frustrating. They offered a large number of varieties, but Andrea found that they always seemed to be out of what she wanted and sent back credit slips instead of seeds.

In the end, the most successful and versatile edible flowers in this trial garden were the species Andrea had always grown for the restaurant—the nasturtiums, borage, and calendulas. Of the new things planted, the pansies—all the varieties—were probably the most useful, and they were a lot of fun as well. The chefs used them as garnishes and chopped them into butters. The anise hyssop was very flavorful. The runner blossoms were tasty too—the chefs mixed them with other flowers and put them in salads. "Of the nasturtiums," Andrea told me, "we liked 'Alaska' and 'Empress of India'. The flowers of these varieties are similar to those of most other varieties, but the leaves are beautiful and when they are small are quite delicious. We hadn't used those before. With nasturtiums, taste is the most important factor, and that's affected by how you grow them. If you start them without much water, they're quite hot to the taste. They grow best in really lush conditions, and then they're much milder."

On the other hand, the hollyhocks were a complete failure—they didn't have much flavor and had a slippery quality like that of okra. Still, Andrea thought they might be good dipped in batter and fried tempura-style. She went on to say, "Most of the calendulas we tried didn't impress me as much as our simple pot marigolds, which self-seed right here in the garden. They have large flowers and nothing seems to affect them. I don't like 'Kablouna' because you can't get the petals off the tight head easily. And I found Stokes's claims about their calendulas—all these so-called scarlet, gold, and apricot tones—to be an overstatement. The differences among them are very, very subtle."

A lice Waters is the chef and inspiration behind one of this country's most famous and revolutionary restaurants, Chez Panisse in Berkeley, California. Although I've worked with Alice casually through the years, I never appreciated her vast range of talent and knowledge until I interviewed her specifically on the use of edible flowers. While other chefs can talk about some of the most common edible flowers, Alice expounds on many with an excitement that's infectious.

How do patrons react to flowers on their plate? I asked. "The flowers are a fascination," Alice said. "People really focus on them and are very curious. Some people refuse to eat them, but about half will taste readily. I like to serve them in such a way that they're tasty and accessible to people; a large flower by itself is a little intimidating. I like to incorporate Johnny-jump-ups or nasturtium petals in salads—or serve them in ice cream or butter."

I gave Alice the list of edible flowers I had compiled and asked her to comment on those she had tried. Her face brightened as she perused the list; she seemed to be able to replay the tastes and feelings of those she had used.

"Calendulas have a real nice flavor," she began. "Not too strong, but kind of peppery—even a little grassy. I use fresh petals in salads, or I like to dry them and use them in soups in the winter. Honeysuckle is good too," she continued. "It's very sweet and tastes just like it smells; it's quite extraordinary in some desserts. You don't need much of it, though, just a little spoonful.

"Lavender is wonderful. You can use it in both

Alice Waters

sweet and savory dishes, as a marinade for meats, or for lavender ice cream. I'm crazy about nasturtiums, too. 'Empress of India', which has a dark-red color, has a spicy, peppery flavor. I enjoy using the 'Alaska' variety in salads because the foliage is so beautiful—variegated green and white. I also use nasturtiums to top soups, salads, or pizzas—for example, smoked salmon pizza. Just put them on top at the last minute so they won't wilt. In butters, the colors and flavors seem suspended.

"I've used the petals of plum blossoms many times. Eating plum blossom ice cream is like sipping nectar. I make a presentation of the event, a celebration of spring. I have sprays of blossoms around and let people smell them when I bring out the ice cream.

"And certainly we have to talk about roses and violets. Rose petals are fantastic; they have all different flavors, depending on the variety. On one special occasion I used 'Damask' roses in ice cream and garnished it with deep red-orange 'Joseph's Coat' rose petals that had been dipped in egg white and sprinkled with sugar. Another time I chopped candied rose petals so they looked like little sparklies— very special. I find brightly colored varieties most effective. And we use fragrant violets in late winter; we candy them and then use them to garnish sherbets, or we fold fresh violets into ice cream just before we serve it."

The day I interviewed Alice, a gentleman called from Texas to find out if this was the restaurant that served edible flowers; he wanted to come try some. It seems that people are finding delight in trying new tastes, and Chez Panisse is leading the way.

Andrea told me they did a lot of experimenting with the flowers in the kitchen. For example, she picked two deep tubs—that's probably about ten gallons—of nasturtium flowers. A lot! She then asked the chefs to get creative with them, and they made a soup with potatoes and the nasturtiums, but according to Andrea it turned out to be a total flop. "It was really awful," she said. "It had kind of a slimy texture. So we found out that you can't use nasturtiums in great quantities; they have to be used quite sparingly." Their most successful way of using nasturtiums was to chop them and mash the bits into butter. The butter then looks like it's been laced with confetti, especially when they chop up borage and pansies along with the nasturtiums to get blue and purple. "It's very pretty," said Andrea, "and you can put it on pasta, steak, or toast. Alice also found this to be a good way to use flowers that have started to wilt. Squash blossoms, too, are wonderful. The chefs stuff them with cheese, or chop and fry them and serve them over pasta. They also sauté them with vegetables. Squash blossoms are very versatile and have a pleasant, delicate flavor."

Chez Panisse chefs use flowers not only in salads and butter, but also in many of their famous desserts. They use fresh flowers on cakes and soufflés or candy them and use them whole or chopped to make a kind of glitter. "Very pretty on a chocolate cake," Andrea says. "The chefs sprinkle it on the sides and then, using a small doily as a stencil, over the top, making a little design all the way around of sparkling, multicolored glitter. This glitter idea came from using the delicate candied flowers. It turned out to be a great way to use the broken ones."

One of the most popular ways the chefs have of using flowers is as flavorings in ice cream. Before they make the basic custard mix, they steep the petals in milk for as long as it takes to flavor it—anywhere from a few hours to a day, depending on the intensity they want. Then they strain the flowers out. The idea is to flavor the custard slightly stronger than you want the end result to be, because some of the flavor is lost in freezing. The most successful flower ice cream, and Andrea's personal favorite, is the anise hyssop, but the chefs have made ice cream with everything from rose petals, lavender, and plum and almond blossoms to many of the scented geraniums.

"Over the years," Andrea concluded, "we've found that you really have to think about how you use flowers. They should enhance the meal, not just be thrown randomly onto the plate or into the salad. The flower garnishes, for instance, need to have some relationship to the food. So thyme flowers in a savory soup or chive blossoms in a salad instead of onion would be great, but just floating pansies by themselves on a soup doesn't make any sense.

"I would definitely grow all the edible flowers again, even the hollyhocks. They're so beautiful, and it's fun to share them with your friends. And there may be ways to use them that I just haven't discovered. I think having a flower border that's entirely edible is a good enough reason in itself to plant it. People who visit the restaurant are delighted with the edible flowers. All in all, it seems a great way to combine the beautiful flowers in the garden with what you enjoy on your table."

Recommended Edible Flowers

Following is a list of some edible flowers. There are many others to be explored, but these are the ones with which I've had the most experience. Others not discussed that you might want to try are chamomile (German chamomile), *Matricaria recutita*; chicory (radicchio), *Cichorium Intybus*; English daisy, *Bellis perennis*; gladiolus, *Gladiolus* spp.; hollyhock, *Alcea rosea*; hibiscus, *Hibiscus* spp., particularly *H. Sabdariffa* (roselle); hyssop, *Hyssopus officinalis*; mustard, *Brassica* spp.; sunflower, *Helianthus annuus*; rocket, *Eruca vesicaria*; red clover, *Trifolium pratense*; redbud, *Cercis canadensis*, *C. Siliquastrum*, and *C. occidentalis*.

The numbers in parentheses after the flower or variety names match the numbers of seed companies that carry the item given in the "Sources" section at the end of this chapter. Where no number is given the plant is widely available. *Caution:* Make very sure you identify your species correctly, as some look-alikes are poisonous.

ANISE HYSSOP   *Agastache Foeniculum*.
How to grow: This highly ornamental plant (3, 5, 9) is an easily grown herbaceous perennial that reaches two to three feet and has gray-green leaves and striking, dense, one- to two-inch flower spikes ranging from mauve to lavender. Start from seeds or divisions and grow in full sun. The plant dies down in the winter.

Edible flowers are gaining momentum in the produce world. Here is a Quail Mountain Herb Farm display of edible flowers at northern California's annual Tasting of Summer Produce.

How to prepare: The tiny petals of these sweet flowers have a flavor somewhat between anise and root beer and are very pleasant in salads, iced drinks, soups, tea breads, and dessert dishes. This is one of the tastiest of the edible flowers.

APPLE BLOSSOMS and PLUM BLOSSOMS *Malus* spp. and *Prunus domestica*.

How to grow: Most varieties of these fruit trees bear light-pink to white flowers in early spring. 'Pink Pearl', an old heirloom apple variety, bears deep-pink blossoms and is available from a few nurseries that carry old varieties and from Gurney Seed and Nursery Company. Buy your fruit trees bare root in late winter from firms specializing in fruit trees and consult a good fruit-growing text for your area for selection and planting. Remember to keep the blossoms free of chemical sprays if you are planning to eat them.

How to prepare: These fruit tree blossoms have a slightly floral taste, and the petals are nice in salads, as a garnish, or in ice creams. You can also crystallize the petals or make jelly with them. Flowers from all apple and plum trees are edible, and the more aroma they have the stronger they taste.

BEE BALM *Monarda didyma*.

How to grow: Bee balm (9) flowers are exuberant, shaggy heads of red, pink, lavender, or white that are two or three inches across. They bloom from midsummer to fall. The most popular variety, 'Panorama', is astringent and too strong to eat. For tasty flowers, choose these varieties: 'Cambridge Scarlet', 'Croftway Pink', 'Adam Red', and 'Snow White', all available only from local and mail-order nurseries that specialize in perennials—for example, White Flower Farm, Litchfield, CT 06759. This is a hardy, easy-to-grow perennial that reaches two to four feet in height. Start it with divisions and plant it in sun or partial shade in moist soil.

How to prepare: The recommended varieties of bee balm have a slight lemony-mint taste. Use the petals in teas and salads.

BEGONIAS   *Begonia Xtuberhybrida.*
How to grow: Begonia (1, 4, 6, 10) flowers are spectacular puffs of orange, yellow, white, pink, or red ranging in size from two to four inches across. To ensure safe eating you must either grow them using no chemicals or buy chemicals that are registered for edible plants. In some climates tuberous begonias are prone to mildew, but in many cool-summer areas these plants grow with ease. Start begonia tubers in flats or pots in spring in rich, moist, well-draining potting soil. When the plants are two or three inches high, replant in the garden or in containers. They need a slightly acid soil, filtered sun, and constant moisture and feeding. Dig up the tubers in late fall, knock off the dead and dying stalks, and store in a cool, dry, frost-free place. Do not lift the tubers until the foliage turns yellow.

How to prepare: The flowers of tuberous begonias have a delicious, light, lemon taste and are crisp in texture. Sliced petals can be used in salads and tea sandwiches. Dip whole petals in flavored yogurt as an appetizer that is sure to spark a conversation.

BORAGE   *Borago officinalis.*
How to grow: Borage is one of the easiest annual herbs to grow. It may even become a fairly manageable weed in your garden, so be forewarned. Borage will grow in poor soil but prefers better. Sow seeds in the spring when the soil warms up. Two or three plants are usually sufficient.

How to prepare: Borage flowers are deep-blue, half-inch stars that have a light cucumber taste. To make them edible, you must remove the hairy sepals from the flowers using the following simple procedure. With your left hand (if you are right-handed) grasp the stem of the flower. With your right hand gently pinch the middle of the star and pull. The flower (corolla) should separate from the sepals intact. The one-inch borage flowers can be used in salads, to garnish soups, or to decorate desserts. They can also be crystallized.

CALENDULAS (pot marigolds)   *Calendula officinalis.*
How to grow: These easily grown cool-season annuals are eight inches to two feet tall and have orange, yellow, or apricot daisylike flowers. Plant seeds in full sun eighteen inches apart in early spring

Calendulas can be dried and used throughout the winter. The 'Pacific Giant' on the right has very large petals and is the easiest to work with in the kitchen.

or late summer in mild-winter areas, or buy bedding plants. The large petals of the variety called 'Pacific Beauty' (1, 6, 10) are easiest to use in the kitchen. These plants are very attractive planted in masses, in flower beds, and in containers.

How to prepare: Calendula petals have a very slightly tangy taste. Remove petals from the two- or three-inch-wide heads before using them in salads, soups, soufflés, rice dishes, and omelettes. If you grow varieties such as 'Kablouna' (9, 10), with its tight rosettes, make sure to check for insects in among the petals. Dried petals can be used all winter long in soups and rice.

CHIVES, COMMON and ORIENTAL   *Allium Schoenoprasum* and *A. tuberosum.*
How to grow: The flowers on common chives

are lavender, an inch across, and produced in spring. The Oriental ones are white, flat umbels that bloom throughout most of the summer. See "Onions" in the Part Four Encyclopedia for growing information.

How to prepare: Harvest the flowers just after they open, and in the case of the common chives, before they get too papery. Pull the crisp, mild florets off the flower heads and use them where a mild chive taste is pleasant, as in butters, sauces, soups, egg and potato salads, and sandwich spreads. Use the flowers fresh or dry.

CHRYSANTHEMUMS   *Chrysanthemum Xmorifolium.*

How to grow: Chrysanthemums are perennial plants that bloom in fall. The flowers come in bronze, yellow, white, lavender, or pink, and range in size from one to five inches across. Some varieties are more bitter than others, so taste some to see which ones you prefer. Buy plants in spring (or in bloom in fall) from your local nursery and plant them in the garden or containers in good soil in full sun. For bushy plants, pinch back frequently until late summer to encourage branching. Water during dry weather. Aphids are an occasional problem. Garland chrysanthemum (shungiku) varieties are sold for eating the greens, but the ones that I have tried produce small flowers with very short petals.

How to prepare: The petals have a mild to strong bitter taste depending on the variety. Use petals in salads, in tea, and to sprinkle over clear soups. The varieties with large, open petals are the easiest to work with.

CITRUS BLOSSOMS (lemon and orange)   *Citrus Limon* and *C. sinensis.*

How to grow: Lemons and oranges are tender evergreen shrubs or trees that bloom at different times depending on the variety. Obtain plants from local nurseries and Logee's. Plant trees in spring in rich, well-drained soil or in containers. Keep well watered and fertilize with citrus fertilizer. Gardeners in cold climates can grow citrus plants in cool greenhouses.

How to prepare: Most orange-blossom varieties have a very strong rindlike taste, but others are wonderful in syrups, jams, and as a garnish. Taste to select. Lemon blossoms vary too. Some varieties have a strong rind taste; others, such as 'Meyer' (4), have a pleasant lemon taste. Use petals to flavor whipped cream, ice cream, puddings, and lemonade. These cream-colored petals can also be sprinkled on salads

and soups. If you want to candy whole citrus blossoms, use a mixture of confectioner's sugar and egg whites; the sugar will hide the brown tinge of the petals when it dries. Apply this mix carefully and paint toward the center of the blossom, as the petals come off very easily.

DAY LILIES   *Hemerocallis* spp.

How to grow: Lilies come in yellow, orange, and bronze, range in length from three to five inches, and grow to two to three feet in height. These wonderful plants, particularly some of the older varieties, are hardy perennials that just want to grow. Buy plants from local nurseries and Burpee, Country Garden, and Park. Although you can use all varieties, it is the old-fashioned wild tiger lily that is used in Oriental cooking as the source of "golden needles," the dried lily buds. These are available only from specialty nurseries. Give all lilies good soil in either light shade or full sun. Fertilize occasionally and keep fairly moist.

How to prepare: The taste of lily petals ranges from sweet floral to slightly metallic; be sure to taste for suitability. The buds have long been used in Chinese stir-fries and Japanese tempura. Petals can be sliced and used in salads and soups.

ELDERBERRY FLOWERS   *Sambucus canadensis* or *S. caerulea.*

Caution: Be sure to get the cultivated edible varieties, as some of the wild, red-berried varieties are poisonous.

How to grow: Elderberries are easily grown deciduous shrubs available from local nurseries or fruit tree specialists. It's best to plant them in out-of-the-way areas, because the berries are messy. The plants grow best where the winters are cold. They need full sun, good soil, and severe annual pruning.

How to prepare: The cream-colored elderberry blossoms grow in large clusters. Use either the whole cluster, which can reach ten inches across, or smaller florets to make fritters. Dried blossoms can be used for tea.

GERANIUMS   *Pelargonium* spp.

How to grow: The flower colors of scented geraniums are white, pink, or lavender, and the common garden and ivy varieties are red, pink, white, and lavender. Set out plants from the nursery after the weather warms up or start them from cuttings or seeds earlier in the spring. In mild-winter areas they can be grown outside year-round. Plant them in full sun or light shade in well-drained soil. Fertilize and water only lightly.

How to prepare: There are many different varieties of geraniums, and flavor differs with variety. Most hybrids have a strong metallic taste unsuitable for cooking, so taste the flowers when you're making your selection. The scented geraniums have the most potential; particularly try the rose, peppermint, lemon, and nutmeg geraniums for flavoring ice creams and desserts. Others are good for garnishes and salads. My greatest success at candying edible flowers has been with geraniums; they keep their color and are very flavorful.

HERBS   As with their leaves, all culinary herb flowers can be eaten.

How to grow: See the "Culinary Herb Gardens" chapter for growing instructions and varieties.

How to prepare: Herb flowers are a good place to start incorporating flowers in your cooking. The flowers of culinary herbs such as basil, coriander, fennel, oregano, sage, and thyme taste like milder forms of the herbs. The flowers are great to use as garnishes to complement the herbs used in the dish. Note that when an herb plant has grown too strong or bitter, the flower may still be palatable.

HONEYSUCKLE   *Lonicera japonica.*

How to grow: In warm climates this honeysuckle grows on evergreen vines; in cold climates it will lose its leaves. Wherever honeysuckle grows, its perfume will fill the air. Buy plants locally; many varieties are available. The vine is a rampant grower everywhere and needs a large trellis to support it. Plant in full sun and severely prune annually to control growth. Do not plant honeysuckle near wilderness areas or farmland, as it can spread and become a pest.

How to prepare: The flowers have a strong floral taste and are filled with nectar. The yellow or cream-colored blossoms can be used in syrups, puddings, and, sparingly, in ice creams.

LAVENDER (English)   *Lavandula angustifolia (officinalis).*

How to grow: Lavender (3, 5, 6) plants grow to a height of about two feet. Some varieties, such as the English, are quite hardy, but others are vulnerable to cold. In most varieties the foliage is gray and the flowers lavender. Plant lavender from seeds, cuttings, or nursery stock in full sun. In dry climates water only occasionally. Shear the plants back after they bloom.

How to prepare: With the strong lemon-perfume taste of the petals of its two-inch flower heads, lavender is one of the most useful culinary flowers. Heads can be steeped for use in drinks, jellies, soufflés, and ice cream. Use petals sparingly in salads, soups, and as a garnish. Most of the people I know in the culinary field use all species of lavender for cooking, but I can only find official references to *L. angustifolia.*

LILACS   *Syringa vulgaris.*

How to grow: Lilacs (1) are hardy deciduous shrubs. For eating, choose fragrant varieties at local nurseries. Plant in spring in full sun in alkaline soil. Prune only to remove the spent blossoms just above where next year's buds are forming or you will remove next year's flowers. Lilacs sometimes get mildew and leaf miners.

How to prepare: The blossoms have a light floral taste. Make the purple or white clusters into fritters, crystallize them, or use them as a garnish or in a flower butter. Remove woody stems and leaves before use.

MARIGOLDS   *Tagetes erecta* and *T. tenuifolia.*

How to grow: Marigolds are easily grown annuals. All marigolds are edible but most are unpalatable; the varieties best for eating are available only through mail-order seed companies. Start seeds in spring and set out in full sun after all danger of frost is over. Give plants fairly rich soil and adequate moisture to keep them growing well. Fertilize a few times during the growing season.

How to prepare: Most marigolds taste awful; I've suffered through many to taste them for the "cause." Only a few are mild. These can be used to add color and in some cases a light citrus flavor to a dish. Try the yellow variety 'Climax' (1, 10) and the white 'Snowbird' (1); both have a mild taste and their petals can be used as garnishes. Some of the small, single-flowered varieties—'Lemon Gem' (1, 5, 8, 11); 'Tangerine Gem' (8, 11); and 'Lulu' (10) (*tenuifolia* species)—have a pleasant citrus flavor. Petals can be used sparingly as a garnish and in salads.

NASTURTIUMS   *Tropaeolum majus.*

How to grow: Nasturtium flowers, about two inches across, are yellow, red, or orange. There are many varieties of this easily grown annual available, both climbing and dwarf. The foliage is attractive and in the 'Alaska' variety (10, 11) is variegated. The vining types can spread to eight feet. The dwarf varieties are usually a foot and a half tall and covered with blooms. See "The Chez Panisse Edible Flower Garden" for Andrea Crawford's comments on the different varieties. The fancy varieties are only available from mail-order firms; Stokes Seeds and Thompson & Morgan have a large selection. Start nasturtiums from seeds in the garden or in flats in early spring. After all danger of frost has passed, plant out six inches apart in full sun or, in hot climates, filtered shade. For a mild flavor, keep the plants quite moist, but give little fertilizer or they will bear few flowers. Nasturtiums are occasionally bothered by aphids. In mild-winter areas, nasturtiums are a winter and spring flower and often reseed themselves for years.

How to prepare: Nasturtiums have a peppery, watercress-type flavor that is great in salads, tea sandwiches, and butters. Use these flowers as a garnish or stuffed.

PEAS *Pisum sativum.*

Caution: Do not confuse peas with sweet peas, which are poisonous.

How to grow: See the Part Four Encyclopedia for information on growing peas. All the flowers of the pea varieties I have tasted are pleasant. Most are white, but the more decorative ones are the flowers of 'Dwarf Gray Sugar' (6, 8) and 'Blue-podded' (8), both with purple flowers.

How to prepare: The flowers of some varieties of peas have a "grassy" flavor; others have a mild, sweet, floral taste. Use them for salads or garnishes or crystallize them to make some of the prettiest candied flowers of all.

PINKS *Dianthus* spp.

How to grow: Of all the types of dianthus, pinks (2, 6, 10, 11) are the most versatile in the garden as well as the kitchen. Pinks are easily grown perennials that are at home in a rock garden, flower border, or containers. They are hardy, and some bloom most of the summer. They grow best in full sun and in rich, well-drained soil. Start them from seed or divisions or buy plants from the nursery. For the best eating use the small, fragrant clove pinks, *D. Caryophyllus,* or cottage pinks, *D. plumarius.*

How to prepare: Pinks (gillyflower is the old-fashioned name) have a pleasant, spicy, floral, clove-like taste. The one- to two-inch blossoms can be steeped in wine, made into syrup or sorbets, chopped and mixed into butter, and used to garnish cakes, salads, and soups. Taste your flowers first. Sometimes the white base of the petals is bitter; if it is, remove it. Though called pinks, the flowers come in pink, rose, white, or red.

ROSES *Rosa* spp.

How to grow: Rose flowers are red, white, pink, yellow, lavender, or orange. All are edible but the old varieties are usually the most fragrant and thus the most flavorful. To start, you might choose from the following: 'Cecile Brunner' (7), a small, pink sweetheart rose; 'Zephirine Drouhin' (7), a very fragrant, bright-pink rose; 'Austrian Copper' (7), a deep-orange single rose; 'Eglantine' (7), a small, deep-pink rose that smells like apples; 'Belinda' (7), a small, deep-pink rose particularly good for candying whole; and the versatile damask roses (7). All are quite disease resistant and need no spraying in most climates. Rose bushes are best planted bare root in early spring. Most modern roses need much care, so you should consult a good book on roses to keep them growing well. Remember, to keep roses edible you must be very careful about which chemicals you use on them. *Never* use florist-grown roses in the kitchen, as they may contain chemicals unfit for eating. The growers certainly don't consider the possibility that consumers might eat them!

How to prepare: Roses are among the most versatile flowers in cooking and have been used in Europe and Asia for centuries. Most varieties have a strong floral taste, and most of the older varieties have more taste than the modern hybrids. Some of the dark-red varieties are too strong and metallic tasting. With most roses you need to remove the white part at the base of the petals, as it is bitter. Petals are candied and used in jelly, rose sugar, rose water, vinegars, honey, butters, syrups, salads, and as a garnish. Individual petals or whole baby roses can be candied; for this try some of the old sweetheart types and the miniatures.

RUNNER BEANS *Phaseolus coccineus.*

How to grow: Flowers are red-orange, white, or, in the case of 'Painted Lady' (8, 11), salmon and white. The scarlet runner (5, 8, 9, 10, 11) varieties are the most common. See the Part Four Encyclopedia for information on growing runner beans.

How to prepare: These flowers have a sweet, bean/pea taste and a slightly crunchy texture. There's a sweet nectar in the base of each flower, so don't remove the base. Use runner bean flowers to top soups, in salads, and as a garnish.

SQUASH BLOSSOMS   *Cucurbita* spp.

How to grow: See the Part Four Encyclopedia for information on growing squash. All squash and pumpkins produce large yellow blossoms that are edible, but some varieties have larger and longer-lasting blossoms. Try in particular 'Sardane' (9) and 'Gold Rush' (5, 6, 10) zucchinis.

How to prepare: Squash blossoms have a slightly sweet nectar taste. Try to gather blossoms in the early morning before they close, and put their bases or stems in water in the refrigerator until you need them. The female flowers have an immature little squash at the base where they meet the stem; the male flowers end at the stem. Usually you gather only male blossoms, making sure to leave a few to pollinate the females. If you want to slow down summer squash production, want to thin your winter squash harvest, or are cooking them as baby squash, harvest females too. To prepare flowers, wash and gently dry them. (Watch out for bees if you are using closed blossoms; they sometimes get trapped inside and, contrary to reason, are not happy when you free them!) If you're using the blossoms for fritters or stuffing, keep the stems on. Otherwise, remove stems, stamens, and stigmas. Some cooks string the blossoms like celery, removing the veins that run down the outside of the flower. Cut up the blossoms and use in soups, omelettes, and salads. See the "Italian Gardens," "Native American Gardens," and "Mexican Gardens" chapters for more ways to serve them.

TULIPS   *Tulipa* spp.

How to grow: Tulips (1, 2, 6) can be red, yellow, orange, magenta, pink, lavender, or white; fluted or smooth; and large or small. Get bulbs at your local nursery or, for a large selection, contact one of the large bulb nurseries. Tulips are hardy plants grown from bulbs set out in fall. Before planting, prepare the bed well and add bone meal. In large drifts or even in containers, plant the bulbs two and a half times as deep as they are wide. Make the beds in a sunny area in well-draining soil. If rodents are a problem, plant the bulbs in wire baskets.

How to prepare: Tulip petals have a sweet, pea-like flavor and tender crisp texture. Delicious! Use them in salads or tea sandwiches. Try arranging petals on a platter around your favorite savory dip. Or better yet, stuff whole flowers with shrimp or chicken salad for a show stopper. Carefully remove the pollen and stigmas from the base of the flowers before stuffing.

VIOLAS, PANSIES, and JOHNNY-JUMP-UPS   *Viola cornuta, V. Wittrockiana,* and *V. tricolor.*

How to grow: The viola-type flowers come in various colors and are about half an inch to three inches across, depending on the variety. They are all annual flowers that grow best in cool weather. Plant seeds or bedding plants in moist, rich soil in partial shade. They can take light frost.

How to prepare: The petals have a very slight lettucelike taste. They are beautiful for decorating desserts and as garnishes, in salads, and candied.

VIOLETS   *Viola odorata.*

How to grow: Violets (4, 6, 11) are hardy perennials that grow well in a shady, moist corner of the garden in rich soil. They grow so readily that they can sometimes spread and become invasive. Choose from purple, pink, and white varieties. Buy them at a nursery or get divisions from a gardening friend. Spider mites can sometimes be a problem in dry climates. For the most flavor and for those that candy best, select the single fragrant violets over some of the double hybrids.

How to prepare: Violets have a strong, sweet, very floral taste. They're best for crystallizing or using plain in desserts, salads, as a garnish, and in tea sandwiches.

Cooking from the Edible Flower Garden

I remember the first time an artichoke was placed in front of me. I had never seen one before, and a knife and fork looked woefully inadequate. "How do you eat it?" I asked my hostess. Over the years I have had a similar feeling when restaurants put flowers on my

OPPOSITE: *Creative uses of edible flowers enliven the table. Shown here are a dip of peach yogurt with tuberous begonia flowers, a bowl of runner bean soup garnished with runner bean flowers, and a salad of shrimp, tomatoes, and nasturtiums.*

plate. Flower eating is not part of our culture, but in many other cultures, both ancient and modern, people grow up eating flowers without thinking it odd at all. Italians regularly use squash blossoms, the Japanese put chrysanthemum blossoms in tea, and Europeans have used roses and violets in numerous dishes for centuries. In fact, I drew the great majority of the information for species selection in the "Recommended Edible Flowers" section from historical documents and ethnic cookbooks.

I gathered the recipes that follow partly from these sources, partly from among this country's best chefs, and partly from my own experimentation. Unfortunately, I couldn't begin to incorporate all the ways of preparing edible flowers into this small section, but you'll find enough information here to give you a good foundation. You'll also discover that you can get very involved without using complicated cooking techniques and that the range of possibilities is exhilarating. Even very simple uses of flowers can be quite spectacular—chopping up nasturtiums and incorporating them into sweet butter, for example, or decorating baked pears with white lilac florets. Use your imagination, for there is much new ground to explore. Consider making such dishes as baklava flavored with rose petal honey, herb pizza sprinkled with nasturtium and herb flowers, a wedding cake strewn with fresh violets or orange blossoms, or sorbet made with gillyflowers or plum blossoms.

The primary contribution flowers make in the kitchen is indisputably decorative—their colors and shapes are truly spectacular additions to many dishes. American cooks are thinking more and more about how food is presented and are subscribing to the belief that beautiful meals are often more satisfying and life-enhancing than plain fare. Consider how much more festive and colorful are salads made with borage and nasturtium blossoms than those sporting the usual radish or red cabbage slices. Parsley has been done to death, so how about using mustard or scarlet runner bean blossoms instead? Or for an alternative to the usual frosting flowers on your next birthday cake, how about using apple or honeysuckle blossoms or large damask rose petals?

But eye appeal is not the only virtue of edible flowers. Many actually give us new flavors to cook with. Consider the rich, aromatic flavors of roses, lavender, orange blossoms, or anise hyssop. These underutilized flavors are as useful as the more familiar ones with which we enrich our cooking.

But before you start using edible flowers to any degree, you need to learn a few basics. As I mentioned before, eating flowers is not part of our heritage, so both the cook and the diner need direction. The list of edible flowers in the preceding section takes care of the most important issue—Which flowers are edible?—but some fundamental questions remain: How are the flowers prepared for cooking? What parts are edible? Which flowers go with which dishes?

Let's begin with the question of preparation. Start by choosing your flowers from the list and then tasting them to see if you like them. This step sounds obvious, but I've been served some pretty unpalatable flowers over the years and I'm sure the cooks hadn't tasted them before serving. Once selected, flowers are easy to prepare. Pick them in the cool of the day, preferably morning. Put those with long stems in water; pick short-stemmed blossoms, such as borage and orange blossoms, within three or four hours of using and put them between layers of damp paper towels or in a plastic bag and refrigerate. Flowers, of course, are perishable, and will wilt in a warm place. And they'll bruise almost instantly if they're roughly handled.

Most cooks gently wash flowers before using them. For candying especially, flowers must be thoroughly dry, so allow yourself enough time. While washing your flowers, look for "critters," such as baby slugs, earwigs, and aphids, that might be hiding down in the petals. There are more places for them to hide in flowers than vegetables, and many people get really upset when they see something crawl out of their salad.

With some flowers—such as roses, calendulas, tulips, chrysanthemums, and lavender—only the petals are edible. With others—Johnny-jump-ups, violets, and pea and runner bean blossoms—the whole flower can be eaten. If you are using only the petals, separate them just before using, as they will wilt within minutes. Some flower petals, such as those of roses, dianthus, and marigolds, have a white portion that can be quite bitter. If the flowers you are using have such an area, remove it. Also remove the stamens, styles, and sepals of large flowers such as tulips, open lilies, and squash blossoms.

It is important that the edible flowers you use actually fit your dish. While this is not an absolute rule, sweet flowers are best in or as garnishes to desserts and fruit dishes, while savory types are wonderful with soups, salads, and entrees. Examples of

What a hit the candied roses were on my son's wedding cake! Tucked among clusters of frosting flowers were sparkling pink miniature roses. In the last year or so, I've also decorated salmon canapés with candied white pea blossoms and petits fours with crystallized rose geraniums. These sparkling flowers are so striking and tasty that I now keep a stack of flat wooden boxes, nine inches square and an inch deep, filled with different kinds of candied flowers. I love to open them to smell the perfume—the flowers retain their original scent—and to see them arranged by color: purple violets, violas, and Johnny-jump-ups; pink and purple geraniums; little pink roses; red and blue sage flowers; green mint leaves; and white orange blossoms.

Candying (or crystallizing) flowers is an art that was common in Europe in the seventeenth and eighteenth centuries. Frosting flowers did not exist in those days, so they used crystallized flowers as dessert decorations and also ate them as candy. I became fascinated with the idea of crystallizing flowers while researching edible flowers and decided to try it myself. Bother! I found several different methods, but none of the directions was explicit enough for me. I tried using candy syrup, gum arabic, and egg white and sugar. The candy syrup is difficult to control because it forms crystals or hardens too fast. I had difficulty locating gum arabic, and although it's fairly easy to use, it leaves flowers with a thick, clumpy coating. Of the three techniques, egg white and sugar is the easiest and makes the most elegant-looking flowers.

To candy flowers with egg white and sugar, you'll need a fine camel's-hair brush, a small bowl, a cake rack, a small wire whisk, toothpicks, finely ground granulated sugar, and an egg white. Select flowers

Rosalind Creasy

from the "Recommended Edible Flowers" section.

In the cool of morning on a dry day, select and cut flowers that are perfectly shaped and newly opened. Keep enough stem so that you can put them in water and later hold them comfortably while working. Wash the flowers a few hours before candying so they will be dry when you begin work.

To candy the flowers, beat an egg white slightly in a small bowl. Holding one flower by the stem, gently paint a light coating of egg white on the petals. Cover the front and back thoroughly, because any part of the petal not covered will wither and discolor. At this point, most literature says to dip the flowers in sugar. I disagree with this advice, however, and instead recommend sprinkling the flowers with sugar, making sure to cover both sides of the petals thoroughly. If you dip the flowers, they're likely to end up looking like folded sugar lumps, not lovely porcelainlike crystallized flowers. An alternate method I've discovered uses a paste mixture of confectioner's sugar and a little egg white and gives a nice matte finish to citrus blossoms and large flowers. I paint this mixture on both sides of the petals.

When your flower is completely sugared, lay it on a cake rack, using a toothpick if necessary to carefully spread the petals in a natural position. Then go on to the next flower. After an hour or two, move the sugared flowers around so the petals won't stick to the rack and put them in a warm, dry place. After a few days they should be fully dry and ready to store in a sealed tin or similar container. Use them within a few hours of sugaring or a year later—but they'll have the most color if used in the first few days. Once they're candied, use the flowers to grace all sorts of cakes, cookies, ice cream, and hors d'oeuvres.

the latter are chive blossoms in sandwiches and on onion dishes, nasturtiums in salads, and mustard blossoms on ham-filled crepes. The sweet floral taste of roses, violets, and apple blossoms goes well with cakes, puddings, and pies. Still, bee balm petals are rather floral and sweet but make a good garnish to a lemon-flavored fish sauce. Use discretion with garnishes; the flavor of the flower shouldn't overpower the flavor of the dish. Lavender, for example, is very strong, and a whole flower on a light cream soup would probably cancel out the taste of the soup. In this instance, a few tiny lavender petals or mild calendula petals would be a subtle and elegant solution.

Here are some more simple adventures to introduce you to the world of flower cookery. Use squash blossoms in crêpes, light soups, and omelettes. You can steep lavender, plum, and apple blossoms as well as honeysuckle, anise hyssop, and violets in milk to extract the flavors from the flowers and then use the milk to make a custard for use in pies, puddings, ice cream, or as a filling for cream puffs. Imagine floating-island pudding with a violet-flavored custard and meringues decorated with candied violets. Even more lusciously decadent is a grand marnier chocolate cake decorated with orange blossoms. Make flower butters by finely chopping the petals of roses, nasturtiums, lilacs, calendulas, dianthus, or violets and mashing into slightly soft, unsalted butter with a fork. Use on pasta, bread, tea sandwiches, and tea biscuits. Use candied flowers throughout the year on mousses, soufflés, chiffon and cream pies, chocolate truffles, petits fours, hors d'oeuvres, ice creams, iced teas, and all kinds of cakes.

Cooking with edible flowers can become very involving. My conversation with Holly Shimizu, curator of the National Herb Garden in Washington, D.C., demonstrates this point. I asked her if she had had any experience with edible flowers, and she answered that she was particularly enthusiastic about roses. Her favorites are the *Rosa rugosa*, with its clovelike flavor, the 'Eglantine', and the damask and gallica roses. The gallica known as *Rosa gallica officinalis*, she said, is unique in that its petals are more flavorful when dried and have therefore been used more than those of other roses in conserves and confections and as dried roses as well. Holly is passionate about her rose-cake recipe: "I add an extract of roses to a standard angel food cake and cover with a pale pink icing. I then decorate the cake with fresh roses and violets and put rose geranium leaves around

Crystallizing edible flowers by coating them with egg white and sugar preserves them for winter use as decorations on cakes, canapés, and petits fours.

the base. I serve it with ice cream and a little bit of crème de cassis (a black-currant liqueur) so that everything is pale pink." Holly is so excited about flower cookery that she has added workshops on it to the herb garden program.

TULIP, CRAB, AND ASPARAGUS APPETIZERS

This dish is so beautiful it's absolutely eye-popping. I've used 'Red Emperor' tulips, but you can try any variety that has large, cup-shaped petals. As for the crab, use fresh or frozen, thawed; use canned, drained, only as a last resort.

MAKES 25 TO 30 APPETIZERS.

3 ounces cream cheese, softened
2 teaspoons lemon juice
1 tablespoon minced chives
1 teaspoon minced fresh dill or mint (optional)
Dash of pepper or cayenne
1 cup (about 5 ounces) crab meat, flaked
25 to 30 fresh asparagus spears
25 to 30 tulip petals

In a medium bowl, beat cheese with lemon juice, herbs, and pepper; stir in crab.

Break tough ends off asparagus. Blanch in 1 inch of boiling water in a large skillet with a lid, or steam standing upright in a couple of inches of water in a tall, narrow pot, until crisp-tender, 2 to 5 minutes, depending on thickness of stems. Plunge into an ice-water bath for 1 minute; then pat dry. Trim asparagus to about 5 inches; from the trimmings, cut as many ¼-inch-thick rounds as you have tulip petals. Save extra ends for salads.

Fill each tulip petal with about ½ a rounded teaspoon of crab mixture and garnish with an asparagus round. (If your petals are large and asparagus thin, you can use 3 rounds to garnish each filled petal.) Arrange asparagus in a fan on a serving platter and place tulip petals alternately (or create your own pattern).

RICOTTA-STUFFED ZUCCHINI FLOWERS

This recipe was created by Vicki Sebastiani, famous for her garden, her cooking, and her family vineyard and winery. The number of flowers needed will vary according to their size.

SERVES APPROXIMATELY 15 WITH OTHER HORS D'OEUVRES, 10 AS AN APPETIZER COURSE.

1 pound ricotta cheese
1 onion, minced
½ cup toasted almonds or pine nuts, finely
*   chopped*
½ cup grated Italian Asiago (or Parmesan)
*   cheese*
½ teaspoon ground pepper
1 teaspoon seasoning salt
2 tablespoons minced fresh basil or 1 teaspoon
*   dried*
2 tablespoons minced parsley

1 teaspoon melted butter
Approximately 20 to 30 medium zucchini (or
*   any other squash) flowers, freshly picked*
*   and rinsed in cold water*
Nasturtiums for garnish

Mix together all ingredients except butter and flowers. With filling at room temperature, use a pastry tube to carefully stuff flowers; do not overfill.

Drizzle melted butter over flowers and cook in microwave on medium power for 3 minutes, or at 350° in regular oven for about 15 minutes. Be careful not to let filling ooze out of flowers.

Garnish with nasturtiums stuffed with extra filling.

GARDEN SQUASH AND NASTURTIUM BUTTER PASTA

This recipe is from *Chez Panisse Pasta, Pizza, and Calzone*, by Alice Waters, Patricia Curland, and Martine Labro. This basic nasturtium butter is wonderful spread on fresh bread or crackers. The authors say, "The butter sauce is very beautiful on the pasta with all the flecks of color." For use in this recipe, make the butter several hours before cooking so the flavors of the nasturtiums and herbs permeate it.

SERVES 2.

18 to 20 nasturtiums
2 shallots, diced small
1 teaspoon EACH finely chopped fresh savory
*   and thyme*
2 teaspoons finely chopped Italian parsley
4 tablespoons sweet butter
Salt and pepper
4 EACH tiny yellow and green squash with
*   flowers*
½ cup chicken stock
Tagliatelle (ribbon-shaped noodles) for 2
Additional nasturtium blossoms for garnish

Separate nasturtiums from stems and chop them. Blend flowers, shallots, and herbs together with butter and season with salt and pepper. Slice squash into thin rounds and squash blossoms into ribbons. Keep each separate.

Gently sauté squash alone in half the nasturtium

A mandala of salad vegetables and edible flowers. Here David Cavagnaro used his artist's eye to lay out lilacs, calendulas, cottage pinks, clover, borage, dandelions, mustard, and violets.

butter for 2 to 3 minutes. Add chicken stock and squash blossoms and simmer while you cook the pasta. Drain pasta and add it with remaining nasturtium butter to squash; season and mix well. Serve garnished with additional nasturtium blossoms.

Variation: Delicate vegetables that won't overpower nasturtium butter—for example, whole shallots, fava beans, peas, or leeks—can be added or used in place of squash.

NASTURTIUM SHRIMP APPETIZER SALAD

This and the next two recipes are from the catalog of Shepherd's Garden Seeds. You'll see that anise hyssop is the favorite edible flower at Shepherd's.

SERVES 2 TO 3.

2 teaspoons fresh lemon juice
¼ cup olive oil
Salt and freshly ground pepper
1 cup cooked, shelled, deveined shrimp,
    coarsely chopped
2 tablespoons finely chopped onion
1 small tomato, cubed
½ avocado, peeled and cubed
2 tablespoons chopped nasturtium leaves
Lettuce leaves
Nasturtium flowers

Place lemon juice in small bowl. Whisk in oil and season to taste with salt and pepper. Add shrimp and onion and toss lightly. Let stand for 15 minutes so that flavors can blend.

Add in tomato, avocado, and chopped nasturtium leaves. Mound onto lettuce leaves and surround with fresh whole nasturtium flowers.

LEMONY ANISE HYSSOP TEA BREAD

The combination in this recipe of anise and lemon will especially please those who do not like things too sweet. This bread keeps well and actually tastes best after being wrapped in foil overnight.

MAKES 1 LOAF.

> 1 bread or loaf pan
> 2 cups flour
> 1 tablespoon baking powder
> ½ teaspoon salt
> ½ cup butter at room temperature
> ½ cup sugar
> Grated rind of one lemon
> ⅓–½ cup anise hyssop flowers, finely
>   chopped
> 2 eggs, beaten
> ½ cup lemon juice
> ½ cup chopped walnuts

Grease and flour the bread or loaf pan. Preheat oven to 350°.

Sift together flour, baking powder, and salt. In another bowl, cream butter with sugar until fluffy. Then add lemon rind, chopped flowers, and eggs, and beat mixture just until thoroughly combined. Stir in lemon juice. Gradually mix in dry ingredients and nuts, mixing until blended. Spoon into prepared pan and bake 50 to 55 minutes. Cool on rack.

SPECIAL TREASURE CHINESE BEEF WITH ANISE HYSSOP

The anise hyssop adds a subtle flavor that enhances all the other ingredients in this simple and delicious dish. Serve over fluffy white rice.

SERVES 4 TO 6.

> 1 pound flank steak, cut across the grain into
>   strips 3 inches long and ¼ inch wide
> ½ cup chopped anise hyssop flowers and
>   leaves
> ⅓ cup soy sauce
> 1 tablespoon brown sugar
> 2 tablespoons sherry

> 2 tablespoons vegetable oil
> ¼ cup chicken broth
> 2 teaspoons cornstarch dissolved in 2
>   teaspoons water

Combine chopped anise hyssop, soy sauce, brown sugar, and sherry, and pour over steak strips. Marinate several hours.

Remove meat from marinade, reserving any remaining sauce. Heat wok or large skillet, add oil, and stir-fry meat quickly over medium-high heat until brown. Add chicken broth and remaining marinade and heat through. Stir in cornstarch mixture and cook, stirring until thickened. Garnish with flowers if desired.

IOWA HAY FIELD STIR-FRY

David Cavagnaro, master photographer and gardener, shares this quintessentially midwestern treatment of edible flowers: "In Northeast Iowa, every hay field seems rimmed with borders of native wildflowers and agricultural escapes, giving a constantly changing series of hues and aromas to the landscape. Returning from the garden one day in early July, I

An Iowa hay field stir-fry made with heirloom varieties of pea pods and peas, served on rice, surrounded by strips of tofu alternating with lily buds, and garnished with other edible flowers, including clover blossoms and yellow mustard flowers.

was struck by the beauty of the masses of orange day lilies in flower among the pink crown vetch and remembered that their buds are a favorite ingredient in stir-fries and soups among the Chinese. I stopped to pick a handful to quick-fry with the edible pea pods and shell peas I had harvested in the garden. There I noticed a number of other tasty weeds and flowers, which I added to the collection. That night we cooked up our first Iowa Hay Field Stir-Fry."

The ingredients and quantities for your flower stir-fry will depend on your garden, so use your creativity in substituting based on David's methods and suggestions below.

Store-Bought Ingredients

> *Miso*
> *Orange juice*
> *Honey*
> *Oil (burnt sesame seed oil is best, but lacking that, and wanting to be patriotic to Iowa, we used corn oil)*
> *Tofu (firm)*
> *Rice*

Assorted miniature tarts decorated with fresh edible flowers, including clockwise from the top: Johnny-jump-ups, borage, miniature rose, lilac, strawberry, violet, rose geranium, red pineapple sage, and cottage pink blossoms.

Garden Ingredients

> *Fresh shelled peas*
> *Tender edible pea pods*
> *A fistful of day lily buds, ready to open the next day*
> *A few young pigweed plants (edible wild amaranth), chopped*
> *A smattering of the following edible flowers: alfalfa, pink clover, white clover, and wild mustard*

Make a simple sauce by dissolving some miso in hot water until it is of pea-soup consistency. Thin this out with a little orange juice and a touch of honey. Make enough sauce so that the stir-fry has a little juice for the rice.

Steam shelled peas until just tender. Sauté diced tofu in oil. Stir-fry pea pods and day lily buds lightly, leaving them a bit crisp; add chopped pigweed leaves and cook for 1 minute. Throw in steamed peas at the last moment and stir a few more times. Spread shelled peas, pigweed leaves, and sauce over a bed of rice and then arrange tofu, day lily buds, pea pods, and uncooked alfalfa, clover, and mustard blossoms into a pleasing mandala on top.

GILLYFLOWER SORBET

Carole Saville served this to me on a visit, and I told her I had to have the recipe for the book. The sorbet has a clovelike flavor but it's not too sweet.

SERVES 6.

> *1¼ cups water*
> *4 to 5 tablespoons sugar*
> *½ cup gillyflowers (clove pink—Dianthus Caryophyllus)*
> *Lemon verbena, finely chopped (optional)*
> *Juice of 1 lemon*
> *1 egg white, beaten to form peaks*

Make a simple syrup with the water and sugar. Bring to a boil and cook over low heat till sugar is dissolved. Add gillyflowers (and lemon verbena, if using) and remove from heat. Put a lid on the pot and leave it on until mixture is cool. When cool, pour into an ice cube tray without dividers and place in the freezer. After ice crystals have formed, transfer sorbet mixture from tray into mixing bowl, add lemon juice (to taste) and egg white and whip. Put back into tray,

Gillyflower sorbet has a lovely light clove taste.

freeze again, and whip again just prior to serving. Garnish each serving with one perfect flower, preferably a gillyflower.

ROSE PETAL HONEY

Robin Sanders and Bruce Naftaly of Le Gourmand restaurant in Seattle use this honey for making baklava, transforming an already delicious dessert into something divine. They also suggest using this honey in other desserts, meat glazes, and teas.

> 1 cup unsprayed rose petals, preferably the
>   fragrant old-fashioned types
> 1 cup honey

Rinse rose petals briefly in cold water; dry in a salad spinner. In a nonaluminum pan, slowly heat honey until runny. Stir in rose petals with a wooden spoon, cover, and steep over lowest heat for 45 minutes, stirring occasionally. Turn off heat and let cool 15 minutes. Strain out rose petals through a fine sieve.

Save "honeyed" rose petals to flavor ice cream, mustards, baked goods, and chutneys.

To use rose honey for baklava, make your favorite baklava recipe (*Joy of Cooking* has one; eliminate the orange water it calls for). When assembling the layers, sprinkle a few chopped, honeyed rose petals on nut mixture; garnish with fresh or candied roses.

LAVENDER ICE CREAM

This recipe was created by David Schy when he was executive chef at the El Encanto Hotel in Santa Barbara, California. At the seminar where I first had this dish, participants were reduced to bickering like children over who had the most. The ice cream has a unique lemony-perfume taste.

MAKES 1 QUART.

> 14 ounces milk
> 3 ounces fresh lavender leaves and flowers
> 2 ounces crystallized ginger, chopped
> 1 cup sugar
> 3 egg yolks
> 2 cups heavy whipping cream, cold
> Lavender flowers for garnish

In a saucepan, slowly heat milk to approximately 200°. Remove from fire and add lavender. Allow to steep for 15 minutes. Strain milk through cheesecloth while warm. Add crystallized ginger and sugar to milk. Place egg yolks into a small bowl; then put half the mixture from saucepan into the bowl to blend. Stir mixture with a spoon and pour back into the saucepan. Place over low heat and cook until mixture is approximately 200°. Add 2 cups cold heavy whipping cream and place into refrigerator until well chilled. Process in any ice cream machine. During the last few minutes of ice cream processing, sprinkle individual lavender flowers (stripped from flower heads) into the ice cream so they will be whipped into it.

Sources

Seed Companies

1. W. Atlee Burpee Company
   Warminster, PA 18991
     Burpee is a large seed company that carries both vegetable and flower seeds.

2. The Country Garden
   Box 455A
   Route 2
   Crivitz, WI 54114
      This company carries a huge selection of annual and perennial flower seeds and plants. Catalog: $2.00

3. Fox Hill Farm
   444 West Michigan Avenue
   Box 7
   Parma, MI 49269
      This nursery carries a vast number of herbs.

4. Logee's Greenhouses
   55 North Street
   Danielson, CT 06239
      Logee's specializes in unusual flowers and herbs. The firm carries many geranium and begonia varieties and many tropicals. Catalog: $3.00.

5. Nichols Garden Nursery
   1190 North Pacific Highway
   Albany, OR 97321
      Nichols maintains an extensive list of herbs—plants as well as seeds—and unusual vegetables and flowers.

6. Park Seed Company
   Cokesbury Road
   Greenwood, SC 29647
      Park is one of the major suppliers of vegetable and flower seeds in the United States.

7. Roses of Yesterday and Today
   802 Brown's Valley Road
   Watsonville, CA 95076
      This nursery specializes in old-fashioned roses. Catalog: $2.00.

8. Seeds Blum
   Idaho City Stage
   Boise, ID 83706
      This seed establishment carries seeds of ornamental, heirloom, and open-pollinated vegetables and edible flowers. Catalog: $2.00.

9. Shepherd's Garden Seeds
   7389 West Zayante Road
   Felton, CA 95018
      Shepherd's carries a large selection of European vegetables and a select offering of edible flowers. Catalog: $1.00.

10. Stokes Seeds, Inc.
    P.O. Box 548
    Buffalo, NY 14240
       This company carries a very large array of annual vegetable and flower varieties.

11. Thompson & Morgan, Inc.
    P.O. Box 1308
    Jackson, NJ 08527
       This seed company specializes in unusual vegetables and flowers.

Mail-Order Sources of Ingredients

Aphrodisia
282 Bleeker Street
New York, NY 10014
   This mail-order firm carries rose and orange water; dried petals of hibiscus, orange blossoms, peonies, primroses, red clovers, and rosebuds; and hundreds of dried herbs.

Books

Clifton, Claire. *Edible Flowers*. New York: McGraw-Hill, 1984.
   This beautiful little book is filled with flower recipes.

Diamond, Denise. *Living with the Flowers: A Guide to Bringing Flowers into Your Daily Life*. New York: Quill, 1982.
   This comprehensive book looks at the uses of flowers and contains many edible flower recipes.

MacNicol, Mary. *Flower Cookery: The Art of Cooking with Flowers*. New York: Fleet Press, 1967.
   This is one of the most complete books on cooking with edible flowers. It contains much lore and history.

Rohde, Eleanour Sinclair. *Rose Recipes from Olden Times*. New York: Dover, 1973.
   This is a complete look at cooking with roses.

Shere, Lindsey R. *Chez Panisse Desserts*. New York: Random House, 1985.
   This wonderful dessert cookbook contains modern flower recipes.

Smith, Leona Woodring. *The Forgotten Art of Flower Cookery*. Gretna, La.: Pelican, 1985.
   This is a knowledgeable book on cooking with flowers.

PART
FOUR

ENCYCLOPEDIA

ALL OF THE CHAPTERS in this book cover great numbers of vegetables and herbs. The emphasis there, however, is on unusual varieties specific to the individual chapter themes, and the use of these varieties in the particular cuisine. Thus, the "Italian Gardens" chapter covers many Italian varieties of vegetables and herbs and their use and preparation in Italian cuisine.

"An Encyclopedia of Superior Vegetables" is intended to supplement this information with a systematic approach to growing, harvesting, and preserving a number of our most popular vegetables and herbs. Controlling pests and diseases, seed saving, and purchasing these vegetables and herbs in your local market are covered as well. Each entry also includes a listing of the most common, proven superior varieties of the vegetable or herb. As in the chapters, seed sources are listed along with the varieties.

To fully utilize the growing and variety information given in both the main text and the encyclopedia, I recommend first looking up the vegetable or herb in the encyclopedia for basic information. Then follow the cross-referencing to the chapters given in the entry. For instance, if you are interested in growing tomatoes, first read the "Tomatoes" entry and then follow the cross-referencing to the "Italian Gardens" chapter for Italian varieties, the "Rainbow Gardens" chapter for unusual-colored tomatoes, and the "Burpee All-Time-Favorites Gardens" chapter for more information on hybrid tomatoes. For additional information, also check the index under "Tomatoes."

A Typical Encyclopedia Entry

Entry Title

Plants are listed alphabetically, generally under their most often used common name. Sometimes the entry title is for two or more related plants, such as broccoli and cauliflower. Plants so grouped are usually members of the same family and in most cases have similar growing conditions.

The common names of plants can be confusing and often vary regionally, so each common name is further identified by its botanical, or Latin, name. Botanical names are not always agreed upon, however. I have used the third edition of *Hortus*, the major reference of many American horticulturalists, as the authority for names and spellings. The names given in the entry titles include genus, species, and sometimes variety or subspecies.

A genus is a definable group of plants that are closely related and share certain characteristics. The genus is always the first of the plant's Latin names. For example, the genus name for all peppers—be they rounded, oblong, hot, or mild—is *Capsicum*. As you use the encyclopedia, you will notice that several seemingly distinct plants share the same genus name. One example is the genus *Brassica*, which includes cauliflower, Brussels sprouts, cabbage, broccoli, kale, and mustard. Knowing a plant's genus often helps you know more about that plant. For instance, the Brassicas are often bothered by the same pests.

The second of the plant's Latin names designates its species. Put simply, the species indicates an even closer relationship between plants in the same genus. A particular species of *Brassica*, then, would be *Brassica oleracea*.

Some species sharing certain characteristics, but not having a clearly defined relationship, are further differentiated by groups. Thus, various *Brassica oleracea* species are also designated by their group. Broccoli and cauliflower are *B. oleracea*, Botrytis Group, while collards, kale, and flowering kale are *B. oleracea*, Acephala Group.

Some entries have yet a third Latin name, indicating a particular variety or subspecies. Varieties retain most characteristics of the basic species while differing in some way. For example, corn—*Zea Mays*—has several varieties differing in such ways as kernel hardness and sugar content. Thus we have *Z. M.* var. *everta*, popcorn, and *Z. M.* var. *saccharata*, sweet corn.

Effort Scale

The degree of effort involved in growing and using edibles varies widely. My experience with students and clients has shown that newcomers to edible gardening sometimes get carried away. Overextension often leads to discouragement, so I have tried to quantify the size of your project by an effort scale.

The effort scale is a simple 1 to 4 ranking that reflects the sum of the various effort factors involved in growing a plant. The effort factors applying to the specific plant are listed below its ranking number and may include requirements for planting and thinning; soil and climate; watering, mulching, and fertilizing; weeding; pests and diseases; and harvesting. A ranking of 1 indicates that the plant requires minimal effort, while 3 and 4 indicate a need for continued maintenance.

The effort scale ranking assumes you have selected a plant variety appropriate for your area and will cultivate the plant at the appropriate time of year for your region. While no climate mapping is included, each entry contains much specific information on appropriate climate conditions and preferred growing seasons. Whenever possible, I have included a broad selection of varieties with a wide range of growing conditions to enable you to find the best variety for your area. For example, under "Corn," 'Sugar Dots' was especially chosen for cool, damp conditions, and 'Polar Vee' was selected especially for northern gardens.

Finally, please note that the effort scale is approximate and is meant only as a guide. Different households, yards, and climates add to the variables involved.

Thumbnail Sketch

Each entry begins with a brief sketch of the pertinent visual and cultural features of the plant. This sketch should prove particularly useful when you are selecting your plant materials.

Introduction

A few introductory paragraphs expand on the thumbnail sketch and offer culinary uses and landscaping ideas for the vegetable at hand. I've also included a few adjectives useful in evaluating the taste and texture of the particular vegetable. In the last few years I have attended a number of produce tastings and county fair produce "taste-offs." While evaluating the taste of wine has been traditional for centuries, few people except professional vegetable breeders have looked at vegetables in this way. But it is my belief that to really appreciate the different vegetable varieties, we must develop a taste (and a texture) vocabulary. For me, words help focus my perception. For instance, professionals sometimes describe a carrot flavor as soapy or parsleylike. Once I had this descriptive vocabulary, it helped me iden-

tify the qualities of carrot varieties I did or didn't like.

How to Grow

Here I have supplemented material found in Appendix A, "Planting and Maintenance," by focusing on the particular and sometimes unique requirements of each plant. More detailed information can be found in many of the general gardening books listed in the bibliography.

You will notice that my fertilizer recommendations are more conservative than those of many garden books. This reflects my conviction that for most crops, unless you have poor or sandy soil or are planting mostly hybrids, if you properly prepare the soil with much organic matter, only minimal supplements are needed. Here is where it is critical to learn to recognize nutrient deficiencies, particularly the most common one, nitrogen—in most species, yellowing or pale leaves or stunted growth. If you are a beginning gardener, to be sure your plants are getting enough nitrogen, you might want to fertilize a little more often than recommended, but leave a few plants minimally treated to observe the differences.

Pests and Diseases

Pests and diseases specific to the particular plant are covered here. A more detailed discussion of pests and diseases, along with some suggestions for their control, can be found in Appendix B, "Pests and Diseases."

Containers

Not all vegetables are suitable for container culture, but some do very nicely and can be very decorative this way. In this section I discuss the appropriateness of growing a particular plant in containers, as well as types and sizes. To help ensure success, make sure you have fairly large ones. I find containers less than eight inches across very difficult to maintain. And remember, when you grow plants in containers, watering and fertilizing become much more critical.

I particularly want to emphasize watering, because that is at the root of 90 percent of my clients' and students' failures. When you water a container, the first pass with the hose doesn't even count. It's like having to wet the sponge to get it to hold water. Most of the water drains out the bottom of the pot.

The second and *third* passes, applied a few minutes later, are what waters the soil! In addition, another key to successful container planting is to fertilize often and lightly.

Prolonging the Season

The various methods for elongating the production period of edible plants are discussed, and those particularly appropriate to the species at hand are described here.

Harvesting

This subject is self-explanatory. Where appropriate, specific directions on how to know when a vegetable is ready for harvest and the correct harvesting method are included.

Seed Saving

As more and more people have become interested in enjoying and preserving the old heirloom plant varieties, and as the population has become more sophisticated and demanding in its culinary tastes, the interest in seed saving is also expanding. Each encyclopedia entry contains information on the particular plant's reproductive method and directions on saving and storing its seeds. Two subjects are critical to master: pollination—both self-pollination and cross-pollination—and seed storage.

It's also helpful to know that some species ripen seeds over a long period, while in others the seeds shatter, exploding the head and scattering the seeds to the wind. Either bag the seed head in the garden or bring the partially mature seed head inside and bag it before it shatters.

See the "Heirloom Gardens" chapter for a more detailed discussion of pollination, plant reproduction, and the values and advantages of seed saving.

Varieties

The term variety as used here refers to horticultural variety, also known as a clone or a cultivar. These are varieties developed in the nursery—not in the wild. They are usually choice varieties bred for special qualities and are designated by single quotation marks—for example, 'Bintje' potatoes.

Some horticultural varieties are hybrids—that is, a cross between two species or varieties or strains, or even between two plants belonging to different genera. Hybrids have also been bred for special desirable characteristics. For instance, 'Sweet Success' cucumbers have been bred to eliminate bitterness.

The knowledgeable gardener needs to be aware of another aspect of the horticultural variety—an unofficial, unlabeled one—a variation referred to as a strain. When you order a hot pepper called 'Jalapeño' from a seed company in Maine, say, versus a seed company in New Mexico, chances are planting both companies' seeds next to one another would reveal a number of differences in the plants. The strain from Maine might bear earlier, be shorter, and have smaller fruits, say, than the one from New Mexico. That's because over the years as the seed companies have bred the 'Jalapeño' pepper, each breeder has emphasized different characteristics. Some horticultural varieties are very stable, such as 'Sugar Snap' peas and most hybrids, because most of the breeding is done by only a few breeders, and in some cases just one. But many of the old varieties, even though they have the same name, can be quite different strains.

What this means to the home gardener is, get to know your seed companies. Where possible, if you are purchasing nonhybrid seeds, it's best to order from companies specializing in seeds for a particular climate similar to your own.

Most of the varieties listed have been selected because they are recognized to have some superior value, such as outstanding flavor, particularly attractive or unusual visual appeal, climate adaptability, or disease resistance. I have tried to give particular attention to varieties unusual in flavor or appearance, since relatively little attention has been paid to these qualities in recent years. Both open-pollinated and hybrid varieties are included.

The open-pollinated varieties give us a broader range of flavors, colors, and sizes than the more standardized hybrids, but both have their advantages. The open-pollinated varieties give us the opportunity to save some of our own seeds, help maintain a genetic resource, and give us a huge range of unusual produce to experiment with. On the other hand, the hybrids often produce more heavily, some species are more disease resistant, and the performance of the plants and the harvest are more consistent and predictable. For me, both are wonderful and have their place. It would be a shame not to have open-pollinated 'Moon and Stars' watermelons and 'Brandywine' tomatoes, or hybrid 'Ambrosia' cantaloupes and 'Better Boy' tomatoes.

Whenever the information was available, I have given the number of days to harvest at the beginning of each variety description. This number usually refers to the number of days from planting to harvest, but this is a very rough estimate, as the days will differ greatly from one climate to another and from year to year. To further confuse the issue, some seed companies list the number of days from planting the seeds, others from when the transplants are put out in the garden, so it is best to use these numbers just as relative figures.

At the end of each variety description, seed sources are listed. A complete list of nurseries and seed companies, with addresses and descriptions, can be found in Appendix C, "Suppliers."

Preserving

Methods of preservation, such as canning, freezing, drying, and root cellaring, are recommended whenever the particular vegetables lend themselves to these processes.

Purchasing

Time, space, and a good many other factors make it difficult, if not impossible, to grow all the produce and herbs you might like to have when preparing family meals or triumphant celebrations. Therefore I've provided hints on how to select the highest-quality, freshest produce when you purchase it from the supermarket or produce stand, including comments on most desirable size, color, and weight.

ARTICHOKES (GLOBE)
Cynara Scolymus

Effort Scale
NO. 3
Plants need renewing every 3 to 4 years
Spent fronds need cutting
Must be kept constantly moist
Mulching and fertilizing needed
Occasional pests
Winter protection required in some areas

Thumbnail Sketch
Herbaceous perennials sometimes planted as annuals
3 to 5 feet tall
Propagated from seeds, offshoots, or divisions
Germination takes 12 to 15 days at 70° F
Need full sun; will tolerate partial shade in hot climates
Leaves gray-green fronds, 4 feet long
Blooming time varies, usually spring
Flowers lavender thistles, 4 to 6 inches across
Flower buds edible; harvest season variable
Used in vegetable gardens, herbaceous borders, as
    interest plants, in containers

The artichoke is a giant thistle whose flower buds, when cooked, are deliciously—and expensively, for those who must buy them—edible. The bud is served whole as a vegetable or, with the choke removed, as an edible container for seafood and chicken. When eating a whole artichoke, pull off the outside leaves and use your teeth to scrape the flesh from the bottom of the leaf. Tender young hearts of artichokes are canned, marinated or not, and also frozen. The hearts are used as an hors d'oeuvre or as an addition to salads or casseroles.

The artichoke has a dramatic, sculptured look when placed in the back of an herbaceous border. It is fountain shaped, and under average conditions it grows to about 4 feet and spreads as wide. Six to eight plants should be ample for the average family and will still allow you to let some of the buds flower. When not picked for eating, they develop into massive blue-purple thistles that are extremely showy and fragrant. They make spectacular dried flowers.

Artichokes are rich and sweet flavored with an ever so delicate undercurrent reminiscent of tender grass. Their texture is meaty and dense, and the flavors seem to stimulate salivation, making the artichoke a particularly good candidate for a meal's first course as it seems to wake up the taste buds and prepare them for what is to come.

How to Grow
Artichoke plants prefer cool, moist summers and mild winters but will grow well in summer heat if the soil is kept continually moist. In cold winters (below 28° F) they need protection. An overturned basket filled with leaves or straw and placed above the roots is one way to provide it. In coldest-winter areas artichokes are usually not successful unless the roots are brought inside during winter and kept moist and cool. In hot, early summers the artichoke buds open too soon and are tough. Artichokes prefer full sun in cool-summer areas and partial shade in hot-summer climates.

They need to be dug up and thinned out every 3 or 4 years or they slowly decline from overcrowding. Artichokes require rich, constantly moist, but well-drained soil with plenty of organic matter. They respond well to deep mulches. Compost and manure are beneficial. Extra nitrogen should be added halfway through the growing season and after harvest.

Pests and Diseases
Aphids, earwigs, and snails are sometimes a problem. Knock aphids off with a strong jet of water. Wash earwigs out with the hose, or after the buds are harvested, soak them in a bucket. Hand pick snails. In commercial artichoke-growing areas the biggest pest is the plume moth. Control it with *Bacillus thuringiensis*.

Botrytis, a fungus disease, is serious but not common. It forms gray mold on leaves in warm, muggy summers. Since there is no known cure, affected plants must be destroyed. Send them to the dump or burn them.

Containers
Artichokes grow well in large containers if they are always well watered and fertilized. Because the plants die back in hot-summer areas, containers that can be moved out of sight temporarily are ideal. The need for protection in cold-winter areas also makes movable-container planting useful.

Harvesting
Pick young artichoke buds before they start to open. The younger the bud, the more tender it is and the more of it is edible.

Seed Saving
Artichokes are not often planted from seed in the home garden. One of the reasons for this is that only a half to two-thirds grow true to seed so an inordinate number need to be planted and raised before the gardener can determine the result.

Seeds are not difficult to collect or save if you can get them before the birds do. Let the flower dry out and cut it off when completely dry. Dig the seeds out from the head and store in a dry place. If birds threaten, cover the drying flowers with small paper bags until the drying is complete.

Varieties
Only one variety of artichoke, 'Green Globe', is readily available. If you search around a bit, however, it is now possible to find a few others. Purple and/or Italian varieties

are now available from Fratelli Ingegnoli, Le Marché, Redwood City Seed, and Shepherd's. When dealing with Italian varieties, it is interesting to know that it is common for cities and towns to have their own varieties, which differ more or less slightly one from another.

Preserving

Freeze or pickle artichoke hearts, or pickle whole small artichokes less than 3 inches in diameter.

Purchasing

In the market, select artichokes with flat, tightly closed leaves, and bright-green coloring. For sweetness, select the small (baby) buds. If you prefer the larger buds, make sure the lower leaves break off with a snap. An unseasonable frost can brown the outer leaves but actually improves the flavor.

ASPARAGUS

Asparagus officinalis

Effort Scale

NO. 3
Initial soil preparation is heavy work
Weeding necessary
Constant mulching needed
Vulnerable to some pests

Thumbnail Sketch

Herbaceous perennial; dormant in winter
3 to 5 feet tall
Propagated from crowns and seeds
Germination takes 14 to 21 days at 75° F
Needs full sun
Leaves tiny and fernlike
Blooms in summer
Flowers white to green, insignificant
Female plant has red berries
Young shoots edible; harvested in spring
Used in vegetable gardens, as background for an
     herbaceous border, or to line a walk

Asparagus means spring to most of us. Despite the cost, those first bunches in the market are irresistible to asparagus lovers. Think of the pleasures you could have every spring from a bed of your own. Young, tender shoots are delicious raw in salads or served with flavorful dips. Most aficionados favor the simple approach to cooking asparagus; they like the stalks steamed or boiled just until tender and served with salt, pepper, and a touch of butter. Left-

overs can be served vinaigrette the next day or put in an omelette for breakfast. Asparagus can be frozen or pressure canned successfully. These processes alter the taste of the vegetable, but they do bring green to the winter table.

When I eat asparagus I know I'm eating a green plant; it just tastes like one. It has an almost grassy taste. Other words to describe the taste of asparagus might be rich, sweet, intense, and sharp. The texture can be silky, stringy, crisp, tough, woody, or tender.

Asparagus is an herbaceous perennial, dormant in winter, whose edible spears show themselves early, heralding an end to winter. The shoots that are not cut for eating develop into airy, ferny foliage plants 3 to 5 feet high that can line a walkway or a split-rail fence, or serve as a billowy background in a flower bed.

How to Grow

Asparagus grows in most areas of the United States except for the very coldest sections and, according to some authorities, the very warm, humid areas.

Asparagus plants need full sun. Start them from seed, seedlings, or year-old rooted crowns (the base of the plant). The average family will need about thirty to forty plants.

Because asparagus plants remain in one place for many years, the soil must be prepared very well. You will need about 200 square feet for two rows 20 feet long and 4 to 6 feet apart. Spade the soil and turn it over. In this spaded area dig two trenches 8 to 10 inches deep, 12 inches wide, and 20 feet long; amend the soil in the trenches with compost or aged manure. Then place the crowns in the bottom, about 12 inches apart, with their roots well spread out. Cover with 3 to 4 inches of soil. As the shoots emerge, continue to fill the trench with soil. The trench dimensions above are for the back of a flower border. Vary the length of the trenches according to your design.

Asparagus needs a deep organic soil with good drainage. The pH of the soil should be 6 to 8. Use organic mulches 4 to 6 inches deep to provide nutrients and to help control weeds. Supplement with a balanced fertilizer in the spring.

Only moderate amounts of water are needed during the growing season. In the arid Southwest, to encourage dormacy do not irrigate in winter. In fall, when the foliage dies back, remove it and fertilize before next year's new shoots appear.

See the discussion on blanching vegetables in the "French Gardens" chapter for information on white asparagus.

Pests and Diseases

Asparagus beetles are generally the most serious pest. Fall cleanup helps remove some of the breeding adults. Keeping all the spears cut in the spring for a few weeks seems to help also.

The chalcid wasp is the asparagus beetle's natural predator. If you see the wasps around and do not find beetles in great numbers, do nothing. If the beetles are taking over, knock them off into a bucket of soapy water. Spray the larvae with pyrethrum.

Snails and a fungus disease called asparagus rust are occasional problems. The latter is associated with very damp weather. Plant resistant varieties, such as 'Waltham Washington', where asparagus rust might be a problem.

Where gophers are numerous they can be a serious problem. Plant the crowns in wire baskets to protect them.

Containers
Because of its deep and heavy root system, asparagus is not a good subject for container culture.

Prolonging the Season
Asparagus can be harvested from spring into fall in most parts of the country. The plant must be allowed to leaf out fully to produce and store the sugars and starches for next year's crop. But you can alter the timing of that growth period with no adverse effects, thereby lengthening the harvest season. Allow one portion of your bed (Bed A) to go to leaf without harvesting any of the spears. When the harvest from the other area (Bed B) is just about to end, cut the ferns in Bed A back to the ground. In a few weeks, new spears will emerge in Bed A while Bed B goes to leaf. This procedure can be repeated year after year. However, you might want to consider doubling your proposed number of plants to have plenty for serving when only half the plot is available for harvest at one time. The beds should be fertilized more frequently as well for they are working overtime.

Harvesting
Do not harvest until the second year, and then only very lightly. In subsequent years, harvest until the spears begin to thin to less than ½ inch in diameter. Cut the stems about 2 inches below the surface of the soil. This should be done carefully to avoid injuring the crowns. An asparagus knife is available just for this purpose.

In mild climates cut down plants when they turn brown; in cold climates wait until spring.

Seed Saving
Asparagus plants cross-pollinate, resulting in small red berries borne on the female plants. In fact, the berries are really seed pods, each containing several seeds.

Cut ferns while the berries are still red but the foliage has begun to droop and bend. After hanging the ferns to dry, soften berries in water so the seeds can be separated from the pulp. Air drying for several weeks should be followed by storage in airtight containers.

Growing asparagus from seed lengthens, by 1 year, the amount of time you must wait before harvesting in your yard. Only you can decide whether that extra year is worth it.

Varieties
Asparagus is purchased as seeds or 1-year-old rooted crowns. The plants are readily available bare root in early spring and occasionally through early summer in containers from local nurseries or mail-order firms. Local nurseries generally carry varieties that are national standards or that are particularly well suited to the area.

All-male plants of several new varieties are becoming available commercially. This is a decided advantage for the asparagus lover since male plants are considerably more productive than female plants.

'BROCK IMPERIAL 84' hybrid, vigorous productive plants. (Field's, Gurney)

'HOWARD GREEN HYBRID' much heavier and fatter stalks than most. (Farmer)

'LARAC' French variety, spears thick and fat, traditionally blanched for white asparagus. (Le Marché)

'MARY WASHINGTON' fairly rust resistant. (Readily available)

'PURPLE GENOA' Italian variety. (Fr. Ingegnoli)

'WALTHAM WASHINGTON' fairly rust resistant. (Readily available)

Preserving
Asparagus may be frozen or canned.

Purchasing
Spears should be straight, compact, and have pointed tips and uniform green color. Avoid spears with more than an inch or so of white, woody tissue at the bottom—this is too tough to eat and silly to pay for.

Asparagus lovers argue as to whether thin or thick spears are the most tender and succulent. That you will have to judge for yourself.

BASIL
Ocimum Basilicum

Effort Scale
NO. 2
Must be planted annually
Pinching needed
Watering usually needed
Harvest timing not critical
Usually grows poorly in cool, damp-summer areas

Thumbnail Sketch
Perennial grown as warm-season annual
1½ to 2 feet tall
Propagated from seeds
Plant seeds ¼ inch deep
Germination takes 7 to 10 days at 70° F
Thin to 1 foot apart
Needs full sun; will tolerate some shade; tolerates no
    frost
Leaves bright green or purple, 2 to 3 inches long
Flowers white or pink
Leaves, flowers, and seeds edible; harvest in summer
Grown in herb or vegetable gardens, flower borders,
    containers, greenhouses

The aromatic leaves of basil are used fresh or dried in many dishes—soups, salads, stews, and spaghetti sauce, to name a few. To many people, basil is best known as the base for pesto, an Italian herb sauce. To others it is the "only" accompaniment to fresh, ripe tomatoes. In France it flavors the famous soup pistou. Basil vinegars and oils add their rich perfume to salads all over the Mediterranean. Hindus float the seeds on top of sweet drinks for their reputed cooling effect.

The taste of basil is somewhat reminiscent of its close cousin mint, but with an additional strong overtone of licorice and a clean, heavy flavor quality of "basilness" that it has all to itself. Someone calculated there were at least sixty different varieties of this very pungent herb. Try the lemon-, cinnamon-, and anise-flavored ones for a change. Fox Hill Farm has written a book on basil, called *The Basil Book*. This nursery specializes in herbs and carries many types of basil, even hosting an annual basil festival.

How to Grow
Basil is a bright-green herb that has white or pink flowers. Enjoy it in herb gardens, vegetable gardens, or flower borders, in containers, on a sunny windowsill, or in a greenhouse. Basil plants are particularly beautiful when combined with nasturtiums, petunias, zinnias, and dwarf marigolds. They also add solidarity to the carrot bed, and the dwarf varieties make a formal edging plant. The 'Opal' with its red foliage and pink flowers and some of the scented basils that have red-leafed flower spikes and pink flowers are colorful in amongst peppers, eggplants, and bush beans.

Choose an area of the garden that is well drained, in full sun (or with a light amount of shade), and where the soil is fairly fertile. If your family loves basil, put in four to six plants of sweet basil to give you enough for pistou and pesto, and plant at least two each of the 'Opal' and scented varieties for flavoring and coloring salads, vinegars, and oils. You will probably need three or four plants of the lemon basil for your kitchen as it is not as vigorous as the others.

There are a number of ways to start basil. You can sow seeds in the garden or start seeds inside to plant out later. The more common varieties are also available as plants in many nurseries in the spring or summer. If seeding in place, plant seeds ¼ inch deep only after the weather is getting summery and the soil is warm, and certainly when there is no danger of frost. Basil put out in the garden before the weather is really warm will just sit there and suffer. Basil seeds are slippery and can be easily washed out of the row if you don't water the seeds very gently. They will sprout in about 7 to 10 days. Thin seedlings to about 1 foot apart.

If starting your seeds inside, plant them about 4 to 5 weeks before the weather warms up. Transplant out into the garden, placing the plants about a foot apart. Keep the plants fairly moist during the growing season. If your soil is not very fertile, feed monthly with fish emulsion and liquid kelp or a commercial balanced fertilizer. Make sure they have enough nitrogen to keep the leaves quite green. If the leaves seem to pucker a lot (some is normal) and get small light-yellow splotches, treat with dolomite for a calcium deficiency.

Pests and Diseases
Basil is occasionally bothered by slugs and snails. Hand pick the pests at night, or if the infestation is severe, bait. Japanese beetles can also be a problem. Hand pick, trap in a beetle jar, or use pyrethrum. In very moist, cool-summer areas the plants will not be very vigorous.

Containers
While all basils can be grown in containers, the best varieties for this culture are dwarf varieties. Give the full-sized basils at least an 8-inch-diameter pot, and make sure that the soil for all your container-grown basils is kept moist.

Prolonging the Season
If you sow your seeds thickly you can harvest the thinnings early in the season. Pinching off flower stalks as they develop prolongs the growing season and keeps the plants bushy. Pinch back to the third node, or to where the main stalk seems to branch into two or three small branches. My experience with 'Spicy Globe' and 'Piccolo', is that an occasional harvesting is all the cutting back that's needed. To further extend the season, bring in container-grown basil well before the first frost, or take sprigs off some of your garden plants and root them in water to keep them growing for a few months on a sunny windowsill. To keep them vigorous, occasionally add fertilizer to the water.

Harvesting
You will be able to harvest your first leaves about 80 days from sowing, and usually you can continue until frost. Leaves may be picked or cut.

Seed Saving

At the end of the season, as the plants go to seed, save some seed from the healthiest plants for next year's planting.

Basil is pollinated by bees, and crossing of varieties occurs readily. If saving seed from several varieties, separate the seed plants as much as possible.

Varieties

Basil is a member of the mint family and has some of the same aromatic characteristics. The different types of basil are flavored with some familiar flavors: cinnamon, anise, and lemon. Try them all. Many basils also have different growth habits. There seems to be confusion as to the names of some of them, and a number have two or three names. Seed companies that carry a large selection of different basils, including the varieties listed below, are Nichols, Richter's, Seeds Blum, Shepherd's, and Taylor's. Fox Hill Farm carries eighteen different kinds of basil.

ANISE BASIL   large plant with purple-tinged, slightly serrated foliage; strong aniselike aroma.

CINNAMON BASIL   perfumed cinnamon taste; decorative; green, shiny foliage; pink stems and flower stalks.

'DARK OPAL'   ornamental purple foliage and pink flowers; great for coloring basil vinegar pink but makes dreadful-looking brown pesto.

DWARF BASILS ('FINO VERDE', 'PICCOLO', 'SPICY GLOBE')   very compact and tasty green basils, great for borders and containers.

LEMON BASIL   wonderful citrus flavor, smaller leaves and plants than standard basils, one of the best tasting; seems to be more difficult to grow; when using in a recipe that calls for basil, use more, as it is mild.

'PURPLE RUFFLES'   dark-purple foliage, dwarf habit.

SWEET BASIL   most commonly grown basil, great taste, green foliage.

Preserving

To preserve the fresh flavor as much as possible, make pesto and freeze it. You can then use it a spoonful at a time through the winter. You can also freeze the leaves in plastic wrap, or put them in oil or vinegar. Basil can be dried the same way most herbs are, but it does not dry as well and much of the flavor is lost.

Purchasing

Fresh basil is sometimes offered in the summer in specialty grocery stores. It usually comes in large bunches, enough to make a recipe of pesto. Look for freshness, and avoid wilted and bruised foliage. Put the bunch in water in a not-too-cold refrigerator, or on a sunny windowsill, and it will keep for days; sometimes it will even root.

BEANS

BUSH BEANS   *Phaseolus vulgaris*
POLE BEANS   *P. lunatus, P. vulgaris*
RUNNER BEANS   *P. coccineus*

Effort Scale

NO. 3
Must be planted annually
Watering and light fertilizing needed
Vulnerable to some pests
Harvesting is time consuming

Thumbnail Sketch

Annuals, or perennials treated as annuals
Vines, 6 to 8 feet long; bushes, to 2 feet tall
Propagated from seeds
Germination takes 6 to 14 days, depending on variety, at 70° F
Need full sun
Bloom in summer
Flowers white, purple, or red
Seeds, pods, and flowers of some varieties edible; harvested in summer and fall
Bush types used in vegetable gardens, flower beds, raised beds, containers; vine types used in vegetable gardens, and to decorate arbors, trellises, fences

Green beans, cooked until they are just tender, are one of life's better gustatory experiences. All they need is a little salt and pepper and a dab of butter; a touch of grated fresh ginger is nice. Marinated whole beans are an attractive addition to a relish tray. Beans can be dressed up with water chestnuts or cheese sauce for gala occasions. There are purple beans that lend color to a salad when added raw but that turn green when they are cooked.

There is a huge range of tastes and uses for the great number of different kinds of beans. There are the *haricots verts,* long and succulent, thin string beans, and the famous horticultural beans for fresh shelling, both preferred in France; or try the meaty Italian 'Romano' beans or tender wax beans. See the "French Gardens" and "Italian Gardens" chapters for more information on these. Other snap/string beans are 'Royalty' and 'Royal Burgundy', deep-purple beans that turn green when they are cooked. Children call them magic beans.

Then there are all the different types of dried beans. Some, like kidney and pinto, are quite familiar, but there are numerous heirloom varieties such as 'Jacob's Cattle' and 'Lazy Wife' that are sensational in soups and baked beans. See the "Baked Bean Gardens" chapter for many more ideas about dried beans.

Whether bush or pole, beans are grown as annuals. Well-grown plants have attractive leaves and handsome long pods. Most varieties of beans do not have showy flowers. If you want color, try combining the bush types with nasturtiums or petunias. The brilliant and delicious red flowers of the scarlet runner bean, the large and also edible flowers of white runner varieties, and the purple flowers of 'Royal Burgundy' all look decorative on a trellis, arbor, or fence.

Snap bean flavors are described as meaty, beany, or bland. Their texture can be described as tender, melting, spongy, tough, dry, even squeaky. Shelling bean flavors are sometimes called delicate, nutty, sweet, beany, or starchy. The texture can be moist, creamy, mealy, hard, or dry. See the "Baked Bean Gardens" chapter for more information on the tastes of dried beans.

How to Grow
Beans grow in most areas of the country. They are planted after all danger of frost is past; the purple and wax varieties can tolerate colder soil than the standard green snap bean. All beans need full sun and a good, loose garden loam with plenty of added humus. If your soil is fairly fertile, no extra fertilizing is usually needed. If beans look pale midseason, fertilize with fish emulsion. They are best watered deeply and infrequently at the base of the plants to prevent mildew from getting a start.

Sow seeds of bush beans 1 inch deep in rows 18 inches apart. Thin seedlings to 2 inches apart. Pole beans need a fairly strong trellis or teepee to climb on. Plant the seeds 1 inch deep with the plants 6 inches apart. On poles, plant seeds in a circle surrounding the pole and 6 inches away from the pole.

Pests and Diseases
In some parts of the country bean beetles can be a very serious pest and can get out of hand in numerical terms very quickly. In early summer watch for their yellow egg clusters on the undersides of leaves and rub them off. If the numbers multiply quickly, spray or dust the undersides of the leaves with rotenone or malathion.

Beans have their share of other pests, including beanloopers, whiteflies, aphids, and cucumber beetles. Small numbers of these organisms are no problem. For large numbers, use water sprays to remove. Treat beanloopers with *Bacillus thuringiensis*. See Appendix B, "Pests and Diseases," for a discussion of whiteflies, aphids, and beetles.

Containers
Most varieties grow well in containers, providing the container is large enough—at least 8 inches deep. Bush varieties are the most successful.

Prolonging the Season
The most important way to prolong the season for fresh string beans is to make sure you pick all the young beans as they come along. If you leave any beans to mature, the plant says to itself, "OK, now I've accomplished my job of reproducing and I'm done." If you want a long season of beans, plant bush beans first as they produce in the least amount of time. 'Royal Burgundy' can be planted 1 or 2 weeks sooner than other bean varieties as it does better in cool soil. About 2 to 3 weeks later, plant another bush variety, and then plant a pole variety 2 to 3 weeks later. If you aren't sick of beans at that point, plant more bush beans. If you are growing in a very short-summer climate, ask neighboring gardeners about their harvest schedule.

According to John Withee, expert bean grower and collector, there is another trick for extending the bush bean season. After some of the bush beans "have gotten too beany (large) for snap, you go over the row and pick off *every* pod, tiny and large, including flowers. Scratch in some booster fertilizer, and you have grown plants anxious to reproduce."

Harvesting
Immature beans, whether you call them snap, green, or string, are most delicious when the seeds are still very small.

Seed Saving
See the "Heirloom Gardens" chapter for information on seed saving.

Varieties
Beans are grown from seeds, most of which are readily available in local nurseries and from mail-order sources. Most of the specific varieties mentioned below are usually available only by mail order. Vermont Bean Seed Company specializes in beans and peas and has a large selection of both.

'BLUE LAKE' POLE   55 days, heavy producer of fine-quality beans, famous for canning and freezing; many strains available, including bush variety. (Readily available)

'FRENCH HORTICULTURAL'   64 days, bush form, 6- to 8-inch red-and-white pods, shelled beans good eaten green or dried. (Harris, Stokes, Vermont Bean)

'HAMMOND SCARLET RUNNER BUSH'   55 days, 18-inch-high plant, handsome flowers. (Thompson & Morgan, Vermont Bean)

'HENDERSON BUSH LIMA'   65 days, very prolific producer of 3-inch dark-green pods, creamy seeds, good for freezing and canning, good in all climates. (Readily available)

'KENTUCKY WONDER'   60 days, pole, most popular bean grown in the U.S., producing many 9-inch stringless pods, rust resistant, good also as shelling bean; many strains available, including bush form. (Readily available)

'KING OF THE ROAD' 88 days, pole lima, very large pods and seeds, excellent quality. (Readily available)

'ROMANO' 60 days, bush and pole varieties, broad flat bean with distinctive flavor, good for freezing. (Readily available) Yellow varieties available from Fr. Ingegnoli, Le Marché, and Shepherd's.

'ROYAL BURGUNDY' bush, purple flowers and pods, tolerates fairly cold soil; an improved 'Royalty'. (Readily available)

RUNNER BEANS both white and scarlet flowering vine, green pods; perennials, live through winter in mild-winter areas, strong growers; attract hummingbirds; pods and seeds delicious, sweet; pest and disease resistant. (Readily available) Selected superior strains carried by Shepherd's, Sutton, and Vermont Bean.

'WREN'S EGG' 65 days, pole, large shelling beans of high quality. (Good, Seeds Blum, Vermont Bean)

Preserving

Snap beans can be frozen whole or pureed, dried in a food dryer, pressure canned, or pickled.

Shelled beans can be blanched for 2 minutes and frozen or blanched for 5 minutes (to prevent insect damage during storage) and dried. Store dried beans in airtight containers. See the "Baked Bean Gardens" chapter for more information on drying beans.

Purchasing

When choosing snap beans at the market, look for velvety textured, brightly colored, firm pods with no shriveled ends and no lumps that indicate mature beans inside.

BEETS
Beta vulgaris

Effort Scale
NO. 2
Must be planted annually
Thinning usually needed
Watering, mulching, and fertilizing needed
Some weeding necessary

Thumbnail Sketch
Annuals, or biennials planted as annuals
6 to 18 inches tall
Propagated from seeds
Plant seeds ¼ to ½ inch deep
Germination takes 6 to 10 days at 70° F
Germination best if seeds soaked in water 24 hours before planting
Thin to 3 inches apart

Need full sun; prefer partial shade in hot weather
Leaves green, or green with red veins
Flowers not usually seen
Roots and leaves edible
Used in vegetable gardens, flower borders, raised beds, containers

Beets are one of my favorite vegetables. I try to keep them coming along in the garden most of the year. I particularly enjoy the yellow and white varieties because they allow me to use the sweetness of beets in many dishes in which red beets would bleed and turn everything red.

There are many wonderful ways to cook beets. Simply boil or steam them and serve with butter, particularly the young beet-thinnings. If you love the beet flavor as much as I do, try baking them unpeeled at a very low temperature—300°—for about an hour, in a covered casserole with no water. I first learned of this method when I met Marian Morash, the author of *The Victory Garden Cookbook*. I asked her what her favorite recipe in the entire book was, and she replied without hesitation, "Baked beets!" Cold beets are great, too. Use them in salads and as pickled beets with onions. (I remember being severely scolded as a child because my cousin and I, try as we might, couldn't stop eating the pickled beets my aunt had made. They were like potato chips. We ate the whole batch that she was preparing for a party that night.) Beet greens are some of the most tender and tasty of greens. Gently steam, add a little butter, and you have a meltingly smooth vegetable.

I describe the primary taste of beets as earthy, with an overtone of sweet corn. The flavors of the flesh can be densely rich, sweet, or bland. The skin can be sweet or slightly sour. The texture can be dense, firm, juicy, tender, succulent, or woody.

How to Grow
Grow beets in full sun, or in light shade in warm weather. Sow beet seeds directly in rich, well-drained soil in early spring or in the fall. Make sure the soil is not too acidic—a pH of 6 to 8 seems best. Many gardeners are convinced that beets are sweeter if they have some chilling as they mature. They can take some frost. Plant the seeds ¼ inch deep in wide rows or broadcast over a 2- or 3-foot-wide bed. (I mix the seeds of three or four different kinds of beets—say, a red variety, a yellow one, and a white one—for planting at one time. Then I have all types to choose from for different recipes, or I can cook beets of all colors—separately, so the colors do not run—and serve them cold on a salad plate together.) Beet seeds are actually a cluster of seeds; therefore, thinning is essential to prevent crowding. Thin to 3 inches apart and harvest the thinnings. They are great as very tender cooked greens. Fertilize midseason with a balanced fertilizer if plants are growing slowly or look pale. Probably the most important element in the

successful culture of succulent beets is even watering. Do not let them dry out!

Sugar beets can be sown somewhat earlier than normal beets, although you must wait until the worst frost has passed. Then the seeds should be planted about 1 to 1½ inches deep and 6 inches apart, with a little less than a foot between rows. In the late fall the roots are at their best and can be harvested and stored and cooked in the same way as regular beets and turnips in stews and even for certain dessert dishes.

Pests and Diseases

Beets have very few pest and disease problems. Occasionally they are bothered by whiteflies or leaf miners that tunnel through the leaves but do not burrow into the beet root. Leaf miners are the larvae of a small fly that can be controlled somewhat by using insecticidal soap. An infrequent disease is a virus that is spread by leaf hoppers and flea beetles. The insects are controlled by rotenone. More common is Cercospora, a fungus that grows best in wet and humid conditions and makes orange spots on the foliage. To control Cercospora, clean up the old foliage when you harvest and destroy it. A rust fungus can also be a problem. Use drip irrigation to help keep the leaves dry, and rotate your beet crops with other vegetables.

Containers

Beets grow well in containers, as long as you can give them plenty of depth, constant moisture, and fertilizer.

Prolonging the Season

As beets can take quite low temperatures, they can be started early in peat pots in greenhouses in cold climates. In mild climates beets can be grown most of the year.

Harvesting

Harvest most varieties when 2 to 3 inches across. Most varieties are ready in 50 to 60 days. Baby beets can be ready in 6 weeks. The large winter keepers can grow as big as a baseball and still be sweet and tender. The greens, too, are tasty and full of vitamins unless the weather has been hot or the beets are quite large, in which event the greens will be tough.

Seed Saving

Beets are biennials and need two seasons to produce seeds. Their windblown pollen travels readily, and they will cross with swiss chard and sugar beets if the blooming plants are not isolated. In mild climates, sow beet seeds in fall and let the beets bloom and ripen seeds in the spring. In cold climates, lift the roots of six or seven of your best beets, cut off the tops, and store them in a cool basement

or root cellar. Plant them out again in the spring. According to Nancy Bubel in *The New Seed Starter's Handbook,* the roots need some chilling before they will bloom.

Varieties

When choosing varieties of beets, try to look for a number of different qualities. The essence of "beet" seems to have a complex, earthy taste. Many beet varieties have sweetness and an even, tight texture, but a few are one-dimensional in taste and almost watery in consistency. The sweetness of beets in my garden seems related to the weather. If it has been cold they seem to develop more sugars. If you want to pickle beets, consider the cyclindrical varieties as they will give you even slices.

'ALBINO WHITE BEET'   50 days, white all the way through, not as beety tasting as some red varieties; quite sweet, will not bleed into your other food. (Field's, Seeds Blum, Stokes)

'BURPEE'S GOLDEN'   55 days, great sweet yellow beet, cooked greens particularly good; does not germinate as successfully as red ones; plant more seed than usual. (Readily available)

'CHIOGGIA'   sweet Italian beet, cherry-red on outside, white inside with red rings like bull's eyes. (Le Marché, Seeds Blum, Shepherd's)

'CYLINDRA'   60 days, up to 8 inches long, cylindrical, deep red, convenient for even slicing; must be grown in deep, soft soil so roots will not be deformed; good for canning. (Readily available)

'DETROIT DARK RED'   60 days, standard beet of commerce, one of the most popular red varieties for the home gardener, uniform in color and shape, reliable producer, high-quality beet. (Readily available)

'FORMANOVA'   60 days, outstanding flavor, 8-inch-long cylindrical shape good for slicing. (Johnny's)

'LUTZ GREEN LEAF' ('LONG SEASON', 'WINTER KEEPER')   80 days, old variety with many names; great tasting, irregular in shape but worth growing; sweet and tender no matter how large. (Good, Le Marché)

Preserving

Cooked beets can be pressure canned and pickled. Because successful freezing requires the absence of as much air in the freezer container as possible, the rounded beet shape does not naturally lend itself to tight packing. Cooked beets do freeze quite well, however, when sliced for compact packaging or pureed in advance.

Purchasing

Select beets that are not too large and that don't have corky-looking shoulders. The greens should look fresh and bright green and red. Some specialty markets carry baby beets.

BROCCOLI AND CAULIFLOWER

BROCCOLI   *Brassica oleracea,* Botrytis Group
CAULIFLOWER   *B. oleracea,* Botrytis Group

Effort Scale

NO. 3
Must be planted annually
Constant moisture and fertilizing needed
Susceptible to many pests and diseases

Thumbnail Sketch

Annuals, or biennials planted as annuals
24 to 30 inches tall
Propagated from seeds
Plant seeds ¼ inch deep
Germination takes 5 to 10 days at 70° F
Need full sun; prefer light shade in hot climates
Leaves bright green to blue-green
Flowers edible, usually not seen
Unopened flower buds, young leaves, and broccoli stems
    edible
Used in vegetable gardens, herbaceous borders,
    containers

Broccoli and cauliflower have always seemed a bit more regal than their close relatives—rather like king and queen of the cabbages. Broccoli's posture is upright and erect and considerably more statuesque than its funny-looking cousin the Brussels sprout. Cauliflower plants hide their treasured heads among the leaves to protect them from sunburn.

Both broccoli and cauliflower are clusters of flower buds. Broccoli is usually green, but some varieties have purple, white, or chartreuse buds. The tastes of broccoli and cauliflower are somewhat similar and can be defined as sweet, peppery, rich, "cabbagy," or metallic and tasting of sulfur. Their textures can be smooth and melting to stringy, tough, or grainy. Generally the cauliflowers are richer in taste and more tender in texture than the broccolis.

How to Grow

Broccoli and cauliflower culture is much the same as for their relatives the cabbages. See "Cabbage and Brussels Sprouts" for more specific information. The major difference is that broccoli and cauliflower are a bit fussier about soil, temperature, and water requirements, particularly cauliflower, and will grow poorly if these needs are not met. Broccoli and cauliflower are very heavy feeders, and it is important for uninterrupted growth that they have a consistent supply of water and nutrients, especially nitrogen. Work compost and blood meal or 5-10-10 fertilizer into the soil before planting and again 3 or 4 weeks after planting.

Broccoli is an annual and is preferably planted in very early spring for summer bearing, or in summer or fall for winter bearing. Plants should be spaced 1½ to 2 feet apart, or 3 feet for the Romanesco varieties. In mild climates, overwintering varieties can be planted.

Cauliflower is a biennial treated as an annual. It is generally slower growing than broccoli and in cool-season areas should be started indoors in early spring for summer harvest. (Transplant at about 4 weeks as cauliflower will not tolerate a longer stay in flats.) In warmer climates, start plants in summer in flats or in the ground for winter or spring harvest. Plant or thin cauliflower to grow about 2 feet apart.

Pests and Diseases

See "Cabbage and Brussels Sprouts."

Containers

Both broccoli and cauliflower grow very nicely in containers if provided with continued nutrients and moisture and if the containers are large enough and deep enough to accommodate their tap roots.

Prolonging the Season

Prolong the season for both broccoli and cauliflower by planting both spring and fall crops and by choosing varieties carefully. Further extension of the broccoli season can be achieved by harvesting the side shoots often.

Harvesting

Broccoli must be harvested when the buds swell but before they start to open and loosen. The heads will flower very quickly if left on the plant too long. (If allowed to open, broccoli flowers are still a delightful addition to salads and soups.) Cut the stem about 6 inches below the head. In many varieties, smaller side heads will develop; these should be harvested as soon as they are mature.

In order to preserve cauliflower's creamy white "curds" and mild flavor the heads must be protected from the sun as they mature. Tie the outer leaves over the heads, or choose a self-blanching variety. Be sure to check the heads every day or two for pests and maturity. Cut the heads from the base when very full but before the curds have begun to separate.

Both broccoli and cauliflower need a brief soaking in salt water to rout insects.

Seed Saving

To save broccoli seed, select an early-bearing variety and start seeds indoors. Transplant into the garden at the appropriate time. Do not harvest buds but allow them to flower. Broccoli is cross-pollinated by insects, so have at least two flowering plants of the same variety in close proximity. When the seed pods have dried, cut down the entire plant and allow it to dry further in a dry and well-ventilated place. Collect seeds and store in an airtight container.

Saving seeds for cauliflower is considerably trickier. It is a biennial and needs a period of cold to flower and set seed but will not overwinter in cold-winter areas and is most difficult to store in a root cellar for spring replanting. It too is insect pollinated and will cross easily with cabbage, broccoli, Brussels sprouts, kale, and kohlrabi. If you should want to take on this challenge, more information can be found in *Growing Garden Seeds*.

Varieties

Broccoli
'DECICCO' 65 days, long cutting season with many small heads; leaves used like collards after plant is well established. (DeGeorgi, Johnny's, Le Marché, Southern Exposure)

'GREEN GOLIATH' 55 days, heads mature early but over a period of several weeks; many side heads, freezes well. (Burpee)

ITALIAN SPROUTING see the "Italian Gardens" chapter.

ORIENTAL see the "Oriental Gardens" chapter.

'PREMIUM CROP' 60 days, hybrid, rich and sweet, main head up to 10 inches across, side heads fewer than many varieties, heat resistant, especially good for spring planting. (Readily available)

ROMANESCO conical, chartreuse broccolis; quite different from usual green American varieties; see the "Italian Gardens" chapter for more information. 'Romanesco' slow grower but worth the time; most attractive conical whorl of mild, sweet chartreuse florets; large plant, needs extra fertilizer. (Cook's, Le Marché, Seeds Blum, Shepherd's)

Cauliflower
'SNOW CROWN' 54 days, hybrid, large heads mature a week before other snowball types. (Readily available)

'VIOLET QUEEN' 65 days, hybrid, early, easy to grow; purple heads colorful raw in salads, turn green when cooked; intermediate between cauliflower and broccoli, grown more like the latter. (Johnny's, Shepherd's)

'WHITE SAILS' 68 days, hybrid, outstanding, high yield, high heat tolerance, self-wrapping leaves. (Southern Exposure, Stokes)

Preserving
Both broccoli and cauliflower freeze very well. Cauliflower can also be pickled with cucumbers and other vegetables.

Purchasing
The freshest broccoli can be identified by its tight heads of blue-green florets. They should be so tight as to show no yellow hints of opening buds, and the stalks should be upright, solid, and firm.

When buying cauliflower, look for tight white heads. Brownish or rust-colored patches or a strong smell indicates age, as do florets that crumble when touched.

Cabbage and Brussels Sprouts
CABBAGE *Brassica oleracea*, Capitata Group
CHINESE CABBAGE *B. Rapa*, Pekinensis Group
BRUSSELS SPROUTS *B. oleracea*, Gemmifera Group

Effort Scale
NO. 4
Must be planted annually
Constant moisture and fertilizing needed
Susceptible to many pests and diseases

Thumbnail Sketch

Cabbage
Annual, or biennial planted as annual
12 to 36 inches tall
Propagated from seeds
Plant seeds ¼ inch deep
Germination takes 5 to 10 days at 70° F
Needs full sun; prefers light shade in hot climates
Leaves ornamental, curled, ruffled, green, blue-green, red, purple, or blue
Blooms in warm weather of second season
Flowers yellow, edible but usually not seen
Leaves edible; harvested throughout the year
Used in vegetable gardens, herbaceous borders, flower beds, containers

Brussels Sprouts
Biennial planted as annual
To 3 feet tall
Propagated from seeds
Plant seeds ¼ inch deep
Germination takes 8 to 10 days at 70° F
Need full sun; prefer light shade in hot climates
Bloom in warm weather of second season
Flowers yellow, usually not seen
Buds edible; harvested in fall and winter
Plant appearance more novel than attractive

I find the cabbages to be quite splendid in all their variety. The puckery Savoy types with their handsome crinkled leaves and rich texture are real eye-catchers, as are the red and purple ball-like heads, as vibrant as any color in the garden. The flowering, or ornamental, cabbages, which look like giant reclining peonies, are spectacular in raised beds, containers, and flower borders. Their foliage is fringed or crinkled and comes in shades of pink, coral, lavender, purple, blue, white, or marbled cream. Together all varieties form a kaleidoscope of color and texture.

Cabbage is a succulent vegetable used in salads, soups, and such main dishes as New England boiled dinner, corned beef and cabbage, and stuffed cabbage. It is a great favorite served pickled, as sauerkraut or kimchee (Korean pickled cabbage). In fact, nearly every country in the temperate zone has a favorite cabbage recipe. Red cabbage and flowering cabbage are colorful and tasty in salads. All types are very low in calories and high in fiber as well as nutritive value. The cabbage is a truly versatile vegetable.

The early green heading cabbages are generally round, although some are conical or dome shaped, and are most often used for boiling greens and slaws. Red heading cabbages are also outstanding for slaws and favored for pickling. The late dense-headed varieties, some as large as a drum, are best for sauerkraut. The Savoy types are particularly attractive as well as some of the most flavorful cabbages, according to many. The Chinese types, which develop much more quickly, are more tender than the European types and are used extensively in stir-fry dishes and other treatments where their succulence is advantageous. Developed from cabbage, Brussels sprouts are essentially tiny cabbages that pop out along the length of the plant stem and are harvested one by one from the bottom upward. While the plant is not nearly as attractive as the cabbages, its delicious sweet flavor, hardiness, and extremely high nutritive value make it a vegetable crop well worth growing.

The tastes of all the types of cabbages are closely related. They all have a mustardy quality to them. Some can have a sweetness or a musky taste, others have a pungent bite, and most have overtones of sulphur. They can be juicy, dense, tender, crisp, and succulent, or dry and tough, with almost a squeaky quality. The Chinese and the young Savoy cabbages are among the mildest flavored of the group.

How to Grow

Juggling varieties and harvest times based on climate is a complicated business. For an overall discussion of the complexities of growing cabbage family members, see the "How to Grow" section of the "German Gardens" chapter.

Although both are biennials, cabbage and Brussels sprouts are best grown as cool-season annuals; they will bolt and go to seed in extremely hot weather. In cold climates cabbage is started in early spring or early summer, depending on variety. In the South and warm-winter parts of the West, it is started in late winter or midsummer. The colorful flowering cabbages prefer a frost or cool nights to turn their deepest red or purple so are best planted in summer for fall display. Brussels sprouts take longer to mature than most of the other members of the cabbage family and are really only successful as a fall or winter harvest when their flavor improves with frost. All cabbages and Brussels sprouts need full sun, although they prefer light shade in hot climates.

Cabbage seed does not germinate well in cold temperatures even though it is a cool-season vegetable. Buy small plants at a local nursery, or plant seeds indoors for transplanting out into the garden about the last average frost date for your area. Seeds or plants can also be planted in midsummer for a fall crop. Brussels sprouts seeds or small plants should be planted in midsummer to mature in the fall, but gardeners in the Southeast can often sneak in an earlier spring crop by planting as for cabbage. Plant each 12 to 24 inches apart in rows spaced no closer than 2½ feet. When transplanting cabbage and Brussels sprouts, place them lower in the soil than you would most transplants—up to their first set of true leaves (the first leaves after the seed leaves). As these plants tend to be top-heavy, planting them too high results in plants that are not sturdy enough to support their interior weight as they develop. Chinese cabbages do not transplant well, tending to bolt if disturbed. It is probably best to start them from seeds planted directly in the garden in midsummer so they can mature in the cool weather without having to be moved.

Both cabbage and Brussels sprouts are heavy feeders and grow best in soil that contains a good deal of organic matter; add bloodmeal and manure, or a 10-10-10 fertilizer, at planting time. Cabbage and Brussels sprouts also need regular and even watering. They seem to grow best where the soil has the capacity to hold onto the large amounts of moisture they require for the development of firm heads and sprouts. Mulching also helps retain this necessary moisture. Both these plants benefit from high-nitrogen fertilizer added every 3 or 4 weeks throughout the growing season.

Brussels sprouts need particular attention paid to the later stages of their culture. Toward the end of their development, it is useful to cut off the growing tip of each plant. This diverts the remaining plant energy into development of the sprouts rather than into more leaf growth.

Pests and Diseases

The biggest problem in growing cabbage and Brussels sprouts is keeping ahead of the pests. The white cabbage butterfly, which is a threat to all members of the cabbage family, has flitted her way across the entire country, and her caterpillar offspring happily chew on cabbage and Brussels sprouts all season long. I have never grown a cabbage without this pest. If you get a severe infestation, the pesticide *Bacillus thuringiensis* controls the caterpillars very effectively at very little cost to the environment. I usually pick the eggs off the undersides of the foliage where the butterfly deposits them every few days. These eggs are cream colored and about the size of a large pinhead.

Cabbage root fly is another troublesome pest. You can

prevent the larvae (a maggot) from entering the soil by placing a 12-inch square of tar paper or black plastic directly over the roots of the plant. To do this, cut a slit about 6 inches long from one edge directly to the middle of the square and slip it around the plant. Cutworms often attack young cabbage plants. A good preventive measure is to place a collar of cardboard around each seedling (see Appendix B, "Pests and Diseases"). Aphids sometimes are a problem too. Try a heavy spray of water or consult Appendix B.

Clubroot is a serious fungus disease of the cabbage family, as are black rot and yellows. Good garden hygiene is your best preventive here. Buy disease-free plants and do not accept plants from friends who have had the problem. Rotate members of the cabbage family with other vegetable families so that they do not grow in the same area for more than 1 year. And pull up all cabbage family weeds: mustard and shepherd's purse are the most common.

Containers

All the cabbages grow beautifully in containers, and if the plants are not too chewed, many are decorative enough to warrant a place of honor. Brussels sprouts, however, are not very attractive plants, so choose a container that can be moved when the plant begins to look its worst. Both plants require large containers and particularly close attention to their fertilizer and water needs.

Prolonging the Season

The cabbage season can be prolonged by planting a selection of different varieties that will mature at different times. Marian Morash in *The Victory Garden Cookbook* describes a method of root pruning in which the roots along one side of the maturing cabbage are severed to stop growth; the cabbage will then stay fresh in the ground longer without splitting or getting overly large and tough.

The Brussels sprouts season can also be lengthened by manipulating culture. The sprouts mature along the central stem from the bottom up. By removing the leaves growing between the sprouts as they develop up the stem, growth energy is diverted to the buds and the plant is able to mature more sprouts up the length of the stem. If the plants are kept well mulched with straw (sometimes even covered in very cold climates), sprouts will often develop and mature well into the winter.

Harvesting

Harvest head cabbages anytime after they have started to head up well and before they become so large they split. Mature cabbages can take temperatures as low as 20° F, so do not rush to harvest all of them before a frost. The Savoy types are the most hardy. If a hard freeze is expected, harvest all the cabbages and store them in a cool place, stacking them in straw if possible. Most cabbages will yield about 3 pounds per 1½ feet of row.

Brussels sprouts mature up the stem from the bottom to the top so are harvested a few at a time in that direction. They have a richer flavor when touched by frost, so try not to pick them all too early. They should be harvested when small—no larger than 1 inch in diameter.

Seed Saving

Cabbages and Brussels sprouts are biennials and produce seeds in their second growing season. Cabbage plants grown to mature in the fall should be dug up, root and all, and stored either in a cold and humid root cellar or in an outdoor trench well covered with soil. In early spring, return the cabbages to the garden. Cut an opening—¾ to 1 inch deep—in the top of the head. A seed stalk will grow up from this gash. In warm-winter areas, cabbages started in the fall and left in the ground all winter will set seeds in early spring. (To guarantee seed stalk production, make a gash in the head in early spring when cabbages are fully mature.) Pick seed pods as they ripen and turn brown. Do not wait to gather until all the pods are dry as they have a tendency to shatter and throw their seeds to the winds.

While more difficult to do, the same procedure is used for the saving of Brussels sprouts seeds.

All members of the cabbage family are cross-pollinated, usually by bees, and will cross easily. This causes no problems with the current crop but will produce impure seed for the next year. If you intend to gather seeds, place different cabbage family members at least 1 mile apart. More practically for the home gardener, you can cover the plants with a polyester row cover and hand pollinate. See the "Chili Gardens" chapter for a discussion of hand pollination. Be sure to also keep your garden and surrounding areas free of cabbage family weeds, such as mustard and shepherd's purse, as they will also cross with your edible crops.

Varieties

There are many different types of cabbages: red-leaved ones, Savoy types with their crinkly leaves, miniature ones for small areas, Chinese cabbages, and the multicolored flowering cabbages. Some types are better for winter storage; some grow better in different times of the year; others are resistant to some of the cabbage diseases. Consult seed catalogs and packages to choose the varieties best suited to your needs and conditions. Cabbage seeds are readily available from local nurseries and mail-order sources. Companies with a large selection are Johnny's, Stokes, and Territorial. Many flowering cabbages are available from Nichols. Consult the "German Gardens" chapter for European varieties. A good selection of Chinese cabbage is available from Johnny's. See also the "Sources" section in the "Oriental Gardens" chapter.

The following varieties seem particularly worthy of note.

Cabbage

'EARLY JERSEY WAKEFIELD' 63 days, green heading type with pointed head, longtime favorite, yellows resistant, fine flavor. (Readily available)

'EMERALD CROSS' 63 days, hybrid, round head up to 9 inches across, fine flavor, excellent for home garden. (Burpee)

'GRENADIER' 63 days, medium green, solid heads, slow bursting. (Stokes)

'JOI CHOY' 45 days, hybrid, vigorous, long standing pac choi; heavy yielder of crisp and tender white stalks with deep-green leaves. (Park, Stokes)

'MARKET PRIZE' 76 days, vigorous and uniform, wide cultural adaptability, resistant to yellows, stores extremely well. (Harris)

'NAGODA' 50 days, hybrid, tolerant of spring cold and summer heat, Chinese type common in produce markets. (Johnny's)

'RUBY BALL' 68 days, hybrid, bright red-purple color, 3 to 4 pounds, holds up well in hot weather. (Readily available)

'SAVOY ACE' 75 days, hybrid, good quality, almost round, up to 4½ pounds, highly resistant to yellows and insect damage. (Burpee, Harris, Park)

'SAVOY KING' 85 days, hybrid, deep-green color, fine flavor, superior for slaw, highly resistant to yellows and insect damage. (Readily available)

'STONEHEAD' 70 days, hybrid, compact head 6 inches in diameter, requires less garden space, highly resistant to yellows, stores well. (Burpee, Nichols, Park, Stokes)

'W R GREEN 60' 65 days, lovely plant; bred for resistance to mosaic virus, soft rot, and mildew. (Johnny's)

Brussels Sprouts

'JADE CROSS' 90 days, hybrid, heavy producer, tolerates more heat than most. (Readily available)

'LONG ISLAND IMPROVED' 97 days, yield somewhat smaller than hybrids but good, old favorite. (Readily available)

'ORMAVON' 117 days, hybrid cabbage-sprout, grows sprouts up stem with small cabbage on top, novelty space-saver. (Thompson & Morgan)

'PEER GYNT' Excellent quality sprout on dwarf plant. (Thompson & Morgan)

'PRINCE MARVEL' 90 days, hybrid, heavy producer of highest-quality sprouts. (Readily available)

'VALIANT' 110 days, hybrid, heavy yielder of exceptionally tender sprouts, rot and burst resistant. (Shepherd's)

Preserving

Cabbages with solid cores can be stored in their fresh form for several weeks in the vegetable bin of your refrigerator or for up to 4 to 5 months in a dark, humid, cool place such as a basement or garage. The temperature should be above 32° but not higher than 40° F. Separate the heads from each other so air circulates around them. Savoy and loose-leafed cabbages do not preserve as well and should probably not be saved in this manner. Perhaps the best way to preserve large amounts of cabbage is to make sauerkraut.

Brussels sprouts generally ripen over a fairly long period of time. They are not damaged by moderate cold but actually improve in flavor with mild frost, so there is usually no need to harvest and preserve them in large quantities. If preserving is necessary, it is best done by blanching and freezing.

Purchasing

When picking out cabbages at the market, look for brightly colored firm leaves that show no signs of yellowing or wilt. Heading cabbage should feel heavy, so pick up several and compare. Brussels sprouts should have tight green heads with no hint of yellowing foliage or drooping leaves around the base. Select small sprouts of uniform size that will make for ease in cooking.

CARROTS
Daucus Carota var. *sativus*

Effort Scale
NO. 2
Must be planted annually
Thinning needed
Watering, mulching, and fertilizing needed
Some weeding necessary

Thumbnail Sketch
Biennials planted as annuals
4 inches to 2 feet tall
Propagated from seeds
Germination takes 7 to 10 days at 65° F
Need full sun, partial shade in hot weather
Leaves ferny, green
Flowers not usually seen
Roots and young foliage edible
Used in vegetable gardens, flower borders, raised beds, containers

One of the most outstanding soups I have ever eaten was a cream of carrot and almond soup at Chez Panisse restaurant in Berkeley, California. It was the essence of carrots, with the subtle overtones you taste when a vegetable is so very fresh. Your tongue explores a little earthiness, some sweetness, some sharpness, maybe—the tastes have so many dimensions. Of course, an experience like that can be frustrating, too, because now I measure every carrot soup against that one!

When you taste carrots, think about some of the adjectives the professionals use to describe them: metallic, rich, soapy, herby (as in parsley and celery), even popsicle-like. For texture, think about fine-grain, tough, stringy, rubbery, tender, and dense.

Well-grown carrots straight from the garden bear absolutely no relationship to those dreadful orange cubes I have pushed aside in many restaurants. Only the color is the same. Grow your own, as Chez Panisse does, and harvest little ones for hors d'oeuvres or steaming. Use larger ones in stir-fries or in grated or molded carrot salads, or bake them in the drippings of a roast. The large keeper carrots, those that have been raised to be stored and used slowly over time, are wonderful used grated, baked, or cut up for soups and stews. See the "Heirloom Gardens" chapter for more ideas.

Grow carrots in a vegetable garden, in a flower border, or in containers. In a flower border they are striking with apricot violas or dwarf nasturtiums, both of which have edible flowers. Carrots grow under similar circumstances and with the same limitations as beets.

How to Grow

Carrots are generally considered to have the best flavor and are easiest to grow when raised in the cool part of the year, but acceptable carrots can be grown through most of the summer and fall, even in the winter in mild climates. You can plant carrots in early spring, as soon as your soil has warmed, or you can plant them as a fall crop. In cool-summer areas you can plant them in the summer, and in mild-winter areas they can be grown as a winter crop.

Sow carrot seeds directly in rich, well-drained soil in early spring. Seeds germinate best at 70° to 85° F and poorly under 50° F or over 95° F. Cultivate and loosen the soil down to at least 6 inches to give the thick roots a place to spread. Carrots do best in light organic or sandy soils, so if you have heavy clay soil, mix in lots of organic matter and select some of the short, stubby varieties. The best soil amendment for carrots is well-aged compost (do not, however, use fresh manure as it causes the carrots to fork). Cover the seeds with a very light dressing of soil and keep the seed bed evenly moist. *It must never dry out.* In warm weather it helps to cover the seed bed with burlap or an old sheet to keep the moisture in, but be sure to remove the cloth the instant the seedlings appear. Thin to 1½ to 2 inches apart. Carrots transplant very poorly. You can use the thinnings as baby carrots if you wait until they are of good size to thin. In most parts of the country, once sprouted, carrots are easy to grow. When the plants are about 3 inches tall, mulch with compost or manure or side dress with fish emulsion. They do take time to develop well, however, and need 3 months from seed to table. For the best germination use fresh seeds, as carrot seeds are very short lived.

Pests and Diseases

Once the seedlings are up, protect from snails, slugs, and sometimes even birds. One pest, the carrot fly, makes it difficult to grow carrots in some parts of the country. The maggots of this fly will infest the carrots, making them nearly inedible. Some control is gained with wood ashes and crop rotation. Two diseases that can also be a problem are alternaria blight and cercospora blight. Crop rotate and choose resistant varieties if available.

Containers

The short and round varieties of carrots are best suited to container growing. Make sure they never dry out.

Prolonging the Season

Before the weather warms in the spring, start carrots out in the ground in tunnels made of plastic sheeting stretched over arcs of PCV pipe stuck into the ground. See the variety list below for suitable types. To prolong the fall harvest, mulch plants well with a foot of dry straw and cover with plastic weighted down with something heavy so the wind won't blow it off. The mulch is to prevent the ground around the carrots, and the carrots themselves, from freezing. Carrots protected this way can often make it through the winter. Just spread the snow and mulch aside to harvest your carrots. In mild-winter areas, carrots can be grown all winter long.

Harvesting

Most carrot varieties are ready for harvesting in 70 to 90 days. Harvest when they are ½ inch across or greater and have started to color. These guidelines are appropriate be it spring, summer, or fall.

Carrots are at their optimum for harvesting for only about 3 to 4 weeks after they mature, less in very warm weather. Do not let them get too big or they will be woody and tough. After a month in the ground during the growing season, some will split. For the highest quality, sow seeds every few weeks to stagger your harvest.

Harvest when the soil is moist to reduce the chance the carrot will break off in the ground and to avoid disturbing its neighbors.

Seed Saving

As biennials, carrots produce seeds during their second year. In mild-winter areas, leave carrots in the ground until seed heads form. In moderately cold areas, mulch the carrots to get them through the winter. In coldest areas, dig roots before heavy ground-freezing frost. Store carrots in sawdust or sand in a humid, cold place—32° F is ideal—and replant them in the spring. Nancy Bubel in *The New Seed Starter's Handbook* recommends gathering seed heads when the second set has ripened. Should you wait until the third or fourth set, early heads will have shattered.

Carrots are easily cross-pollinated by insects. You can expect some crossing between blooming varieties if they are closer than 150 to 200 feet. Carrots also cross freely with that much-loved wildflower Queen Anne's lace, to which they are related. Keep any nearby flowers removed when your carrots are blooming.

When you save seeds from your carrots, grow a few extra seed plants so you will have extra flowers. Carrot flowers are great for cutting, and the stunning blossoms, looking like extra-fluffy Queen Anne's lace, will last inside for a week to 10 days. Try combining them with sweet peas for an old-fashioned bouquet.

Varieties

Carrots can be orange, scarlet, or white. There are even old Afghanistan varieties that are purple with yellow flesh inside. Carrots are usually long and pointed, but there are blunted and round varieties as well. In my experience, regardless of variety, the sweetest carrots are grown in fairly cold weather. Some carrot varieties have a stronger carrot flavor than others (the white ones seem to be the strongest).

Different types of carrots have different uses in the kitchen. The very tender carrots are used for eating fresh. Some varieties are so tender they sometimes break when you pull them out of the ground. These are seldom sold commercially because the machines break them when they are harvested. Tender varieties of garden carrots are great for nibbling, but they turn to mush when you cook them. For cooking, dense, rich carrots, like some of the keepers, are best. Still other very dense and juicy types are used for juicing. Analyze the taste you like in your carrots and choose the ones that taste best to you and those best for how they are to be prepared. Try many different varieties to see which ones you prefer and which perform best in your climate.

A current favorite with some cooks is baby carrots, which seem like naturals for the home gardener. Baby carrots are not just the young of all varieties; most are specific varieties that mature when still small. If you harvest some varieties when they are very small they will have little taste, nutrition, or color. If you want the best baby carrots, try European varieties bred for that purpose: 'Amstel' (Herb Gathering), 'Dutch Minicor' (Le Marché), 'Planet' (Shepherd's), and 'Round Paris Market' (Le Marché), to name a few. If you want to grow carrots for juicing, try 'Nantes Tip Top' (Shepherd's), 'Red Muscade' (Le Marché), and 'Touchon' (Cook's, Farmer, Le Marché, Stokes). Carrot varieties for a cool greenhouse (freezing to 60° F) are 'Caramba' (Shepherd's), 'Minicor' (Cook's, Le Marché, Stokes), and 'Clarion', 'Kinko', and 'Parmex' (all from Johnny's).

'AMSTEL' 62 days, very tender sweet carrot, stubby to about 5 inches, particularly good for baby carrots. (Herb Gathering, Park)
'DUTCH EARLY SCARLET HORN' old variety good for heavy soils, can be harvested young, slow to bolt in warm weather. (Le Marché)

'KURODA CHANTENAY' 70 days, fall variety, good eating quality, some resistance to alternaria blight, will bolt if planted before mid-June. (Johnny's)
'MOKUM' fine-textured carrot, recommended by Cook's for early cropping under poly tunnels. (Cook's)
'NANTES FANCY' excellent-quality open-pollinated carrot, holds well in the field, adapted to wide range of soils, great for storing. (Johnny's)
'PLANET' 65 days, small round carrot, good for baby carrots, grows well in shallow soils and cold frames. (Cook's, Seeds Blum, Shepherd's, Stokes) Johnny's carries what they call an improved 'Planet', named 'Parmex'.
'ROYAL CHANTENAY' 70 days, old reliable carrot, broad and blocky, good for average to heavy garden soils. (Readily available)
'WHITE BELGIUM' truly white carrot, often mistaken for parsnip; in my garden the taste got too strong in summer, but was great in cool spring weather. (Seeds Blum)

Preserving

Store your keeper carrots in a place that is as close to freezing as possible. For detailed information on preserving, as well as recommended varieties that are good keepers, consult *Root Cellaring*, by Mike and Nancy Bubel. Carrots can also be frozen (though they lose a lot of flavor and become mushy) or dried. The best way to preserve good taste and texture is to root cellar or, in all but the most severe areas, leave them in the ground mulched with a heavy layer of straw to keep the ground from freezing.

Purchasing

Produce departments and farmer's markets often sell carrots both in bunches with their greens still attached and without greens (clipped). Those with the greens are new or young carrots and should be firm and light orange to golden in color. Select bunches that are undamaged by insects or disease and uniform in color. Clipped carrots are modern-day keepers and are sold singly. They are sold year round and should also look fresh, uniform in color, and free of insect damage and forked roots.

CELERY, CELERIAC, AND SEASONING CELERY

CELERY *Apium graveolens* var. *dulce*
CELERIAC *A. graveolens* var. *rapaceum*
SEASONING CELERY (wild celery, cutting celery, leaf celery, soup celery, smallage) *A. graveolens*

Effort Scale

Celery and Celeriac
NO. 3
Must be planted annually

Thinning usually needed
Constant watering, fertilizing, and mulching needed
Particular about soil and climate

Seasoning Celery
NO. 2
Must be planted annually
Watering and fertilizer needed

Thumbnail Sketch

Celery and Celeriac
Biennials grown as annuals
Propagated from seeds
Plant seeds ⅛ inch deep
Germination takes 10 to 20 days at 65° F
Need full sun, tolerate partial shade in hot climates
Leaves light green, deeply lobed, edible
Celery stalks to 18 inches long, edible
Celeriac root to 5 inches across, edible
Celery leaves and seeds edible
Flowers usually not seen
Generally planted in vegetable gardens or flower borders

Seasoning Celery
Biennial grown as annual
Propagated from seeds
Needs full sun; tolerates partial shade in hot climates
Leaves dark green, deeply lobed, edible
Narrow stalks to 18 inches long, edible
Flowers usually not seen
Used in flower borders, vegetable and kitchen gardens,
    containers

Celery is an aromatic vegetable often called on to lend its flavors to other ingredients. Famous, of course, in Thanksgiving turkey stuffing, chicken and tuna salads, and soups and stews, celery can also be braised or made into an elegant cream soup. Its close cousin seasoning celery is stronger in flavor, has much smaller stems, and is best used as a flavoring herb. Celeriac is a bulbous celery vegetable that tastes quite similar to celery, but because it has a dense texture it is often used in salads, braised and served with a cream sauce, or mixed with pureed potatoes.

The taste of these celery vegetables can be described as sweet, aromatic, grassy, parsleylike, salty, bitter, biting, and watery. The texture of stalk-celery can be crisp, succulent, and juicy, or flabby, stringy, watery, and tough. The texture of celeriac can be dense, crisp, fibrous, woody, or dry.

How to Grow
Celery is a little tricky to grow, but it's worth a try if you live in a climate suited to its demands. As a cool-season vegetable, it grows best as a winter crop in warm-winter areas of the South, or as a summer crop in coastal areas or near large rivers and lakes where moderate temperatures are likely. Celery needs a highly organic or mucky soil that retains moisture well but drains quickly. It is a heavy feeder and requires a continuous supply of both fertilizer and water.

Celery takes 3 to 4 months to mature and is generally started indoors in pots or flats 10 to 12 weeks before planting outdoors. Celery seeds stay viable for shorter periods than most vegetables, so be sure they are fresh. You can speed up germination considerably by soaking the seeds in warm water for 24 hours before planting. Otherwise, you can expect germination to take from 15 to 20 days. Sometimes nurseries carry plants.

After the weather has warmed to degrees in the upper 50s (at temperatures lower than 55° F, plants may bolt to seed), move seedlings into the garden and place 8 to 10 inches apart in all directions. Give them supplemental fertilizer applications throughout the season and make sure they are continually moist. Mulching is very helpful.

Although new self-blanching celery varieties have been developed, some gardeners still elect to blanch their celery. This produces white stalks of more delicate flavor but with fewer nutrients. See the "French Gardens" chapter for information on blanching techniques.

Celeriac is grown under the same conditions as celery. While it takes longer to mature—up to 5 months—it is less demanding. It is rarely available in the seedling stage. Celeriac is not blanched.

Seasoning celery, on the other hand, is easy to grow. Its climate and soil requirements are not rigid, it is less susceptible to pests and diseases, requires less nitrogen, and its harvest period is much longer. The directions for the culture of seasoning celery are much the same as those for celery and celeriac, but the watering and feeding requirements are much less critical. Like celeriac, seasoning celery is not blanched and is rarely available as seedlings. Similar in appearance to Italian parsley, it makes an attractive border.

Pests and Diseases
Celery worms, vegetable weevils, and wireworms can all attack celery and celeriac, with celeriac somewhat less susceptible.

In warm climates, celery is occasionally afflicted with early blight fungus, which causes yellow spots on the foliage and stalks. Late blight, another fungus, grows and spreads in cool, damp weather. It appears on older leaves, and the yellow spots that accompany it eventually become speckled with tiny black dots. Yellows is another disease of celery. It is spread by leafhoppers. For control, rid the garden of all diseased plant residue over the winter. For yellows, control leafhoppers with insecticidal soap.

Containers
Both celery and celeriac are difficult to grow in containers. The more attractive seasoning celery is less fussy so is a good candidate for container growing.

Prolonging the Season
Probably the best way to prolong the celery season is to harvest one or two stalks at a time. Celeriac can be used over a long period of time if left in the garden or root cellared over the winter.

Seasoning celery can be harvested continually from spring to hard freeze. Cut off all flowers as they appear. Seasoning celery will not provide those large, crunchy stalks that are so nice for fresh-vegetable trays, but it does make available the flavorful leaves so useful in soups and stews.

Seed Saving
As biennials, celery and celeriac set seeds the second season, but in severe-winter areas they will not overwinter. In such areas, carefully dig your best plants and store them in moist sand in a cool place. In spring plant them out, and seed stalks will develop. The seeds from both plants shatter easily so must be collected frequently.

While I have no personal experience with saving seed from seasoning celery plants, I would assume the above procedures are appropriate.

Celery, celeriac, and seasoning celery are all cross-pollinated and, for seed purity, need to be separated from plants of their own species as well as from each other. Separation distance should be in excess of 200 feet, and considerably more if purity is required.

Harvesting
Celery can be harvested as soon as the stalks are large enough to pull off. New stalks will continue to form from the plant center, and thus harvesting can be continuous. Alternatively, harvest the whole head by cutting the plant off at the ground with a sharp knife.

Celeriac should be harvested when the roots are 2 to 4 inches across—larger than that they tend to become fibrous and tough. They can be left in the ground until the first few frosts have arrived (many feel they are sweeter after the frost), but lift and store inside once heavy frosting occurs.

Seasoning celery can be harvested a few leaves or one or two stems at a picking, from the time it has eight to ten stems or enough to renew itself. Flowers should be removed as they develop unless seed is to be saved.

Varieties

Celery
'GIANT PINK CELERY' stalks pink to red depending upon degree of cold; in hot areas, plant in fall for spring crop. (Le Marché)

'GOLDEN SELF-BLANCHING' 115 days, open-pollinated, popular variety of pale color. (Readily available)

'TENDERCRISP' 105 days, open-pollinated, heavy producer of long, straight stalks. (Gurney, Lockhart)

'VENTURA' 100 days, early producer of long, crisp stalks; some resistance to yellows. (Johnny's, Stokes)

Celeriac
'ALABASTER' 120 days, large roots average 4 inches; does not discolor when cut, good keeper. (Burpee, Seeds Blum)

'LARGE SMOOTH PRAGUE' 110 days, fine flavor and texture. (Burpee, Jung, Lockhart, Park)

Seasoning Celery
Seasoning celeries of different names and varieties but all quite similar are available from Le Marché, Seeds Blum, and Shepherd's.

Preserving
Neither celery nor celeriac freezes or cans well. Bring inside and store as directed under "Harvesting," above. Celery leaves can be dried like herbs. Celery seeds can be preserved by collecting seed pods before they have fully dried on the plant. Allow them to dry further before collecting seed and storing it in airtight containers.

Seasoning celery leaves can be frozen or dried in a very cool oven. They are then crushed and stored in an airtight container.

Purchasing
When purchasing celery, look for tight, compact heads with fresh, upright leaves. Avoid cracked, browning, or limp stalks.

Select celeriac roots from 2 to 4 inches in diameter that are firm with no signs of external harvesting or shipping damage.

Seasoning celery is generally unavailable commercially—an excellent reason to grow it yourself.

CORN
DENT CORN *Zea Mays* var. *indentata*
FLINT CORN *Z. M.* var. *indurata*
POPCORN *Z. M.* var. *everta*
SOFT CORN *Z. M.* var. *amylacea*
STARCHY SWEET CORN *Z. M.* var. *amylea-saccharata*
SWEET CORN *Z. M.* var. *saccharata*

Effort Scale
NO. 2
Successive plantings of sweet corn suggested
Some weeding, watering, and fertilizing needed
Some pest control needed

Thumbnail Sketch

Annual

Normally 6 to 8 feet tall, some to 15 feet

Medium-green, broad-leafed grass

Propagated by seeds

Plant seeds 1 inch deep

Germination takes 6 to 10 days at 70° F

Needs full sun

Seeds and young cobs edible

Used in vegetable gardens

Next to the tomato, sweet corn is undoubtedly the most popular vegetable in the United States. It is boiled, roasted, and cooked over campfires. Otherwise very nice people have been known to become sneaky and underhanded all in the name of a really fresh ear of corn. My friend and design partner Jane was roundly scolded by her mother one year when she discovered that her darling Jane was being so selfish as to give her three- and six-year-old daughters second-rate supermarket corn while saving the home-grown 'Silver Queen' for the adult members of the family. What kind of a mother is that!

While sweet corn stands right up there with hamburgers and apple pie as a food typically associated with the United States, corn is grown and eaten in this country in more ways than most of us are aware—corn syrup, tortillas, cornbread, hominy, and popcorn, to name just a few. And different types of corn are used in different ways. In simplistic terms, sweet corn is the type that bears those long, luscious ears we smother with butter; dent, flint, and soft corns are used primarily for their grinding properties; dent and starchy-sweet varieties are used as roasting ears; and popcorn's name describes its special function. For an in-depth look at what might be called the alternative corns, see the "Native American Gardens" chapter. We will consider only sweet corn and popcorn in this section.

The flavors of corn can be described as "corny," sweet, starchy, floury, rich, and juicy, and young ears have what I can only describe as a fresh green-pea taste. The texture of the kernels can be tender, succulent, and juicy, or pasty and tough. The preferred taste of sweet corn seems to be more personal than with many vegetables. Some people like the ears when young and sweet; others prefer their ears more mature and with more "corn" flavor. Some like the more delicate taste of the white corns, others the heartiness of the yellow varieties. All agree the fresher the better.

How to Grow

Corn is generally planted from seeds directly into the garden. Unless you have serious germination or pest problems, buying already-started seedlings is a waste of money since corn seed is easy to handle, germinates quickly, and direct-seeded plants seem healthier. Birds can be a real nuisance, though, because they steal the seeds out of the ground. If birds are a problem, plant the seeds a bit deeper than usual and cover the seedlings with bird netting as soon as they emerge. For early corn, start seeds indoors in paper milk cartons, six to eight plants per carton, 6 weeks before the last frost date in your area. To stagger your crop of sweet corn, sow more seeds directly into the garden at the same time you move the seedlings into their permanent homes. Seeds should be planted 1 to 1½ inches deep (2 inches in dry climates) and spaced six to eight to a foot of row, with 2 to 3 feet between rows in rich soil. Thin seedlings later to stand 1 foot apart along the row. Space transplants about 1 foot apart. By planting in this manner you already have two crops and can add more by succession planting throughout the season. If you are growing corn in raised beds or in a soil rich in organic matter, put stakes in the ground at the corners of the bed and connect them with twine about 3 feet off the ground. This is to prevent the stalks from falling over.

Corn seeds are often treated with a fungicide to prevent them from rotting before they germinate and to repel some insect pests that overwinter in the soil. However, most gardeners find they do fine with untreated seeds.

Corn pollen is transferred by the wind, when pollen from the male flower (the tassel) falls onto the female flower (the silk). If planted in long single rows, the silks might not be well pollinated if the wind direction is unfavorable at pollen time. It is much more effective to plant in a block formation of shorter multiple rows, a minimum of four being ideal.

Corn is a heavy feeder and requires high levels of nutrients, particularly nitrogen, throughout the season. It also requires water as it develops, especially at tasseling time, or your harvest will be small and ears poorly filled out. Mulching will help conserve moisture. (Grain corns, particularly the Native American varieties, are lighter feeders and usually more drought tolerant.)

A warm-season vegetable, corn requires both heat and full sun to develop properly. It is particularly important that the soil be warm and the weather settled before planting extra-sweet varieties. The seeds tend to rot before germination otherwise. Your corn-planting area should be north of the rest of the garden so as not to shade other sun lovers as it matures. The range of days needed to maturity varies considerably from variety to variety. Some are ready for harvest in less than 60 days, while others take over 110 days to mature. Take this into account, particularly in short-summer areas.

Pests and Diseases

The most common diseases of corn are Stewart's bacterial wilt, root rot, corn smut (see the "Native American Gardens" chapter for an edible approach to this disease), and southern corn leaf blight. Resistant varieties, crop rotation, and good garden hygiene at the end of the season are your best preventative.

The corn earworm is the most common pest, but it is

primarily an annoyance. The worms nibble at the kernels after having fed on the silk and are often smothered by a bit of mineral oil squirted into the ear just as the silk is beginning to dry, or by the application of *Bacillus thuringiensis* to the plant and silk. Plants are most likely to be affected late in the season, so planting early-maturing varieties helps.

Other insect pests you might encounter are corn borers; southern corn rootworms; corn flea beetles, which transmit Stewart's bacterial wilt; and seed corn maggots.

Containers
Corn is difficult to grow in containers.

Prolonging the Season
Early, intermediate, and late-season varieties can be planted all at once and then at 2-week intervals to provide a succession of sweet corn throughout the summer and fall.

Harvesting
Sweet corn is ready to eat when the silks have dried out and turned to brown and the ears are well filled out. The kernels themselves can be tested for ripeness by puncturing one or two with a fingernail. Ripe corn kernels will squirt a milky liquid when squeezed (the "milk" stage), whereas underripe kernels will release an almost-clear watery liquid. Corn that is overripe will have tough exterior skins covering the kernels and will release little if any liquid.

Since sweet corn begins to lose its sweetness as soon as it is picked, it is best not to harvest it until as close to cooking time as possible. If cooking must be delayed, refrigerate the ears while still in their husks. New types have been developed that retain their sweetness longer after harvest (see "Varieties," below).

See the "Native American Gardens" chapter for information on harvesting grinding corns.

Seed Saving
Most sweet-corn varieties available today are hybrids and should not be saved for seed purposes. There are a few open-pollinated sweet corns, however, such as 'Golden Bantam', 'Aunt Mary's', and 'Stowell's Evergreen'. These, added to the flour corns and popcorns, most of which are open-pollinated, make the saving of seed corn a worthwhile endeavor. Because corn is wind pollinated, at least 300 feet must separate different varieties tasseling at the same time. Varieties with tassel times that are 2 weeks apart may be planted somewhat closer. Even at 300 feet, some crossing will occur. At least 1000 feet of separation is needed for absolute purity. You need also to take into consideration what corn your neighbor is growing. Unfortunately the wind has no respect for property lines.

Corn should be ready for seed harvest about 6 weeks later than for eating as fresh sweet corn. Preselect several of the earliest and fullest ears, mark them with a piece of

ribbon, and allow them to dry in place until they are ripe for seed harvest. Since incompletely dried corn will germinate poorly, peel back the husks, hang the ears in an airy place, and allow the kernels to continue to dry on the cob until they can be twisted loose with relative ease. Store in an airtight container.

Varieties
Sweet corns are commonly described in categories based on their genetic makeup. Hybrid sweet corn is characterized by varying sugar content, dependent upon variety, and by a tendency for the sugars to convert to starches very rapidly after picking. Most of the corn available today is in this category, which is sometimes called "normal" corn.

Everlasting Heritage corn (or EH) contains a gene that modifies hybrid sweet-corn genes so the kernels are somewhat sweeter and more tender. They also do not convert their sugars to starches as quickly as do the "normal" varieties. They are sometimes referred to as "sugary enhanced" (or SE) corns.

The third group is called Shrunken (or SH2). The dry kernels of these corns appear very shriveled, hence the name, and their genetic makeup produces an even sweeter kernel that does not convert to starches after harvest for an even longer period of time. They are also identified by the names "super sweet" and "extra sweet." You should probably taste them before you plant any for two reasons: many people do not like their heightened sweetness, which tends to obscure the corn flavor, and they must be isolated so as not to cross-pollinate with normal or SE corns or there will be tough, starchy kernels on both types.

Next, there are the old-fashioned open-pollinated varieties that are treasured for their deep corn flavor, their genetic continuity, and their historical significance. And finally, there are numerous varieties of popcorn with their shiny hard kernels.

Hybrid Sweet Corn
'BURGUNDY DELIGHT' 84 days, stays sweet and tender long past its prime, purple stalks and tassels. (Johnny's, Stokes)

'HONEY AND CREAM' 78 days, bicolor, 5- to 6-foot stalks; tight husk discourages earworms. (Burpee, Gurney)

'POLAR VEE' 53 days, yellow, 6-inch ears, popular in northern gardens. (Field's, Gurney, Stokes)

'SILVER QUEEN' 94 days, generally considered the best of the whites, 8-inch ears, needs warm soil to germinate, resistant to wilt and drought. (Readily available)

'SUGAR DOTS' 80 days, bicolor, 6- to 7-foot stalks, two fully packed ears of equal size; excellent germination in cool, damp soil. (Hastings, Nichols, Territorial)

Everlasting Heritage (EH or SE)
'EARLY GLOW' 74 days, yellow, 8-inch ears on 7-foot stalks. (Field's, Gurney)

'KANDY KORN'   89 days, yellow, ears to 8 inches, purplish stalks and husks, stays sweet well after picking, one of the best of the SE series. (Readily available)

'MIRACLE'   82 days, white, exceptionally tender, stays sweet well past maturity, excellent for freezing as well as eating on the cob. (Burpee, Le Marché, Nichols)

Shrunken (SH2)

'EARLY XTRA SWEET'   71 days, yellow, 2 weeks earlier than 'Illini Xtra Sweet', All-America winner. (Burpee, Hastings, Twilley)

'HOW SWEET IT IS'   85 days, yellow, one of the best of its type, twice as sweet as SEs at harvest, freezes well. (Readily available)

'ILLINI XTRA SWEET'   85 days, yellow, one of the best of the shrunkens, twice as sweet as the SEs at harvest, good for freezing. (Burpee, Gurney, Hastings)

Open-Pollinated

'AUNT MARY'S'   see the "Heirloom Gardens" chapter for extensive information on this variety. (Seeds Blum)

'COUNTRY GENTLEMAN' ('SHOEPEG CORN')   92 days, white, old favorite, kernels unevenly distributed on ear, excellent both fresh and canned, resistant to wilt. (Readily available)

'GOLDEN BANTAM 8 ROW'   75 days, yellow, small ears on 5- to 6-foot stalks. (Bountiful, Gurney, Le Marché, Redwood, Territorial)

'STOWELL'S EVERGREEN'   100 days, silvery white, large ears on 8- to 10-foot stalks, introduced in 1848. (Good, Gurney, Le Marché, Redwood, Seeds Blum)

Popcorn

'STRAWBERRY'   105 days, open-pollinated, pops white from deep-red kernels, several ears on short stalks, small kernels. (Readily available)

'TOM THUMB'   85 days, open-pollinated, early yellow kernels on dwarf plants, can plant very close together. (Johnny's)

'WHITE CLOUD'   95 days, hybrid, larger kernels than most, virtually hull-less. (Pinetree, Stokes, Vermont)

Although most corn can be harvested when immature and used as baby corn, there are varieties bred particularly for use as tiny ears. One of these is 'Baby Asian', a hybrid available from Le Marché. Plant seeds and thin to 1 foot apart. Keep well watered. For baby corn, harvest the ears when the silks first appear.

For grinding corn varieties, see the "Native American Gardens" chapter.

Preserving

Sweet corn can be frozen on or off the cob, or creamed. Kernels can also be successfully canned with or without creaming. Sweet corn can also be dried, preserved in brine, or used to make relishes. See the "Native American Gardens" chapter for information on the many techniques used to preserve grinding corn and popcorn.

Purchasing

Always try to purchase the freshest-possible sweet corn. The stem of the ear should be pale green and slightly damp. Older ears will be opaque passing to brown as aging continues.

Where to purchase grinding corn is a bigger problem than what to look for when you've found it. The largest selection of corn for grinding (or already ground) will probably be found in a good-size natural foods store or a Mexican market.

CUCUMBERS
Cucumis sativus

Effort Scale
NO. 3
Must be planted annually
Training of vining type necessary
Frequent watering needed
Fertilizing and mulching necessary
Some weeding needed
Vulnerable to some pests

Thumbnail Sketch
Annuals
Bush types, 2 to 3 feet tall; vining types, to 6 feet long
Propagated from seeds
Plant seeds 1 inch deep
Germination takes 6 to 10 days at 70° F
Need full sun
Leaves light to dark green, large, vary with species
Flowers bright yellow, 1 to 2 inches across
Fruits and flowers edible; harvested in summer and fall
Used in vegetable gardens, herbaceous borders, raised beds, containers

I can think of no vegetable that lulls me more into a cool, comfortable attitude toward summer heat than the cucumber—its taste, its look, even the sound of its name. Cucumbers, along with squashes and melons, are members of the Cucurbitaceae family and are sometimes referred to as the cucurbits. These succulent fruits are associated with meals on warm summer days. Crispy cucumbers served with yogurt dressing are cooling and delicious, as are cold cucumber soup, sliced cucumbers in summer salads, and even classic dill pickles.

Cucumbers have rough, hairy, ivy-shaped leaves and lemon-yellow, cup-shaped flowers that stand out in contrast to their green leaves. The bush types are useful in herbaceous beds near a patio or walk and do well in large containers on balconies, porches, or patios. The vining types can be used on low trellises, fences, over embankments, or spilling over the sides of large hanging baskets.

When evaluating the taste of cucumbers, taste for flavors that can be described as delicate, green-leafish, herblike, sweet, icy, crystalline, or bitter. The textures of cucumbers can be crisp, tender, juicy, soft, mushy, slippery, or dry.

How to Grow

Cucumbers are warm-season annuals. In short-summer areas, seeds may be started indoors. They should be planted in peat pots to avoid excessive root disturbance when moved into their permanent location. (Jan Blum feels planting indoors is usually not necessary, however. She feels that direct-seeded plants do better all season long.) Cucumbers are usually grown in hills with two or three plants per hill. They can also be planted 8 to 10 inches apart in rows 5 to 6 feet apart. If direct seeding, plant the seeds about 1 inch deep, five to six seeds to a hill, or 6 inches apart in rows, and thin later to two plants per hill or 1½ to 2 feet apart. Vining varieties grow better with support, and trellises or other supports should be put into place at the time of planting so as not to damage the plants at a later stage. Trellised cucumbers grow straighter and take up less space.

Cucumbers need rich, humus-filled soil and ample water during the growing season. Without the latter, some tend to get bitter, so do not let the plants dry out. Keep young plants well weeded. Mature plants can usually crowd any weeds out. High-phosphorus fertilizers are best, but cucumbers are sensitive to fertilizer overdoses; so if using commercial fertilizers, cut the dose recommended on the fertilizer package in half. Pick cucumbers often or fruit production will slow dramatically.

Pests and Diseases

Young plants are susceptible to cutworms and snails. For cutworms, apply protective cardboard collars around the main stems. For snails, hand pick, use traps, or bait.

Striped or spotted cucumber beetles are sometimes a problem. Their larvae attack the roots of corn, and the adults attack cucumber vines. As yet there are no biological controls for large numbers of cucumber beetles. See Appendix B, "Pests and Diseases," for other control suggestions.

Mildew is sometimes a problem on members of this family, particularly late in the season. Choose mildew-resistant varieties if mildew is a problem in your area. I find that the mildew begins to show up just as the plants have almost finished producing, so I just pull the plants out.

Other diseases affect cucumbers, the most serious of which are mosaic virus, scab, and anthracnose. The symptoms of mosaic disease are a mottling or shriveling of the leaves. Scab attacks the fruits and is characterized by dry,

corky patches dappled with a velvety olive-green growth. Anthracnose symptoms show up as moldy fruit and brown patches on the leaves. Pull up affected plants as no cure is known for any of these conditions. If they are a problem, plant resistant varieties and rotate your crops.

Containers

Standard vining varieties are attractive in large hanging baskets or tall planter boxes if provided with support. The smaller bush varieties also look handsome in containers. Plant either variety singly in containers, and make sure the containers are large and kept moist.

Prolonging the Season

Start cucumber seeds indoors and move them out when the weather warms to give these heat lovers a head start. Succession planting in areas where the weather stays warm long enough will provide cucumbers even into the fall.

Keep plants harvested and picked of all overripe or damaged fruits as well to encourage maximum production.

Growing cucumbers in greenhouses, particularly in northern short-season areas, has become increasingly popular. Be sure to plant self-fertile varieties, listed as such in seed catalogs, as you'll get no cooperation from pollen-transporting insects indoors.

Harvesting

Cucumbers are generally ready for picking from 50 to 60 days after seeding, and you might expect a 6-week harvest period. Harvest cucumbers regularly every other day during this time. They are ready when they are young and firm but filled out. Remove any overripe or damaged fruits to encourage the plant to continue production. Small bush cucumbers yield about three or four cucumbers per plant, while the larger vining types can be expected to produce ten to fifteen fruits per plant unless you pick them small for pickling. In that case, you can expect a much larger crop.

Seed Saving

There is probably less reason to save a cucumber seed today than there is to save seeds from many of the other vegetables discussed in this book. Because the need to solve major disease problems has led to the development of numerous disease-resistant hybrids, the seeds from older cucumber varieties unprotected from these afflictions are less and less sought after. (See the Pliny Freeman garden in the "Heirloom Gardens" chapter.) On the other hand, if you are interested, it is suspected that there are some old, undiscovered varieties that have good resistance to disease. Much more research must be done to fill in the informational gaps and to find sources of disease-resistant varieties of old cucumbers. The more people try the old varieties and keep track of the consequences, the more quickly we will have this information.

Cucumbers as a group contain both self- and cross-pollinated varieties. While cross-pollinated varieties will not cross with other members of the curcurbit family (squashes, melons, and gourds), they can cross among themselves, and up to ¼ mile of separation distance is probably necessary to ensure seed purity.

Collect seed from fruits that are fully mature—cucumbers that have remained on the vine until yellow and fat. Cut the fruit lengthwise and scoop the seedy pulp out of the center with a spoon. Separate the seed from the pulp as thoroughly as you can, wash, rinse, and allow to dry.

Varieties

Cucumbers are generally classified or arranged in one of two ways: by primary method of use (slicing or pickling) or by reproductive type. When reading catalogs it is useful to know a bit more about cucumber reproduction. The most popular cucumbers today, for either slicing or pickling, are probably the self-fertile hybrid cucumbers. They are particularly popular due to their disease resistance. The fact that they do not need to rely on insect pollination also makes them more reliable producers where inclement weather keeps bees from making their rounds. Because they are self-pollinating, these cucumbers are called "parthenocarpic" and often labeled with a *P* in print.

Two other types of cucumber are also available—both needing insect pollination. The first is called "monoecious" and is labeled as such (or with an *M*) in seed catalogs or on nursery stakes. These cucumbers produce both male and female flowers and are pollinated by bees. The second type is called "gynoecious" (*G*)—these are hybrids that produce only female flowers but still need pollination from bees. Seed packagers usually add a few seeds of the monoecious type to make pollination possible. This type of cucumber is often labeled High Female. Its advantage is an earlier harvest because the female, fruit-bearing flowers do not have to wait for the male flowers to reach maturity before them, as is usually the case with the monoecious types. Varieties with no description are monoecious.

I recommend the following varieties.

'ARMENIAN' ('YARD LONG')   65 days, long slender fruits, mild flavor, excellent for slicing; related to the muskmelon, with which it will cross. (Readily available)

'BUSH CHAMPION'   M, 55 days, bush type, short, compact, very productive vines, 9- to 11-inch fruits. (Burpee, Nichols)

'GOURMET #2'   G, 60 days, hybrid, greenhouse-forcing type, sweet crisp fruit, 14 to 16 inches long, resistant to scab and leaf spot. (Nichols)

'JORDAN'   50 days, crisp and burpless, developed for Mideast, ripens quickly; good for home gardener, many

fruits borne on few vines, resistant to cucumber mosaic. (Le Marché)

'LEMON'   60 days, lemon-shaped, chartreuse-colored fruits, very mild and pleasant flavor; should be picked when small and before fruits turn yellow. (Readily available)

'LIBERTY'   M, 54 days, hybrid; excellent for pickles, either whole or sliced; very productive, high resistance to cucumber diseases. (Readily available)

'MARKETMORE 80'   M, 61 days, slicing type, 8- to 9-inch dark-green fruits, earlier and less bitter taste than 'Marketmore 76'; less susceptible than most to cucumber beetles but more vulnerable to spider mites; good disease resistance. (Johnny's)

'POT LUCK'   45 days, hybrid, bush variety, good for containers, tolerant to mosaic. (Readily available)

'ROLLINSON'S TELEGRAPH'   60 days, 15- to 18-inch fruits with smooth skin, burpless, delicate flavor. (Shepherd's)

'SWEET SUCCESS'   P, 58 days, hybrid, 12- to 14-inch fruits, excellent sweet flavor, good disease resistance, can be grown outside or in greenhouse. (Readily available)

'WEST INDIAN GHERKIN'   60 days, heavy producer of 2- to 3-inch fruits for pickling, superb flavor, not useful as slicing cucumber; heirloom variety. (Readily available)

'WHITE WONDER'   heavy yielder of crisp, white slicing cucumbers; heirloom variety with strong resistance to fusarium wilt. (Seeds Blum)

Preserving

Pickling is the most widely used method of preserving cucumbers. Typically pickling cucumbers are used, but slicing cucumbers can be made into pickles nicely as well.

Uncooked cucumbers do not dry or freeze well. They can be cooked into soups, however, and frozen in that form.

Purchasing

At their prime, cucumbers will be deep green in color and firm—almost hard—to the touch. Those with hints of yellow on the peel are older than desirable, as are fruits with soft spots or a pitted exterior. The latter also suggests exposure to excess cold, either in the field or in a refrigerator truck.

Unless you can find a local roadside stand or farmer's market, you will probably be able to purchase only cucumbers that have been sprayed with wax or oil to prevent dehydration and thereby lengthen shelf life. If only waxed fruits are available, peel them before use.

EGGPLANT
Solanum Melongena var. *esculentum*

Effort Scale
NO. 2
Must be planted annually

Watering and fertilizing needed

Vulnerable to numerous pests and diseases

Thumbnail Sketch

Herbaceous perennial grown as annual

2 to 3 feet tall

Propagated from seeds

Plant seeds indoors, or outdoors only after soil is thoroughly warm

Germination takes about 7 days at 80° F

Thin to 2 feet apart

Needs full sun

Leaves green or gray-green and velvety, 4 to 5 inches long

Blooms in summer

Flowers pink or purple with yellow stamens, 1 to 2 inches across

Fruits dark purple, lavender, pink, green, or white; edible; harvested in summer

Used in vegetable gardens, flower beds, herb gardens, raised beds, containers

Ratatouille, moussaka, parmigiana—the names of eggplant dishes indicate the area of origin of this versatile plant. Although eggplant, a member of the potato family, is often used in combination with meats or other vegetables, it has a distinct life of its own when flavored with olive oil and garlic, soy sauce, or mixed herbs and broiled. A favorite Oriental dish is eggplant with garlic sauce.

Eggplant is a tender, herbaceous perennial that is usually grown as an annual. Grow it in full sun in rich soil. It does well in a standard vegetable garden. Because healthy eggplants are beautiful in all phases of their growth, they are an addition to any part of the garden as well as usable in a border or alone in a decorative container. Eggplants show off best up close with their pink or purple flowers. But if flea beetles, verticillium wilt, or heavy rains break off the branches or disfigure eggplants in your climate, grow them in a vegetable garden.

The taste of eggplant can be described as mild, bitter, or metallic. The texture can be creamy, stringy, slimy, rubbery, dry, or seedy. Some of the differences are due to varieties and others to how mature the fruit is. Overripe eggplants sometimes get seedy and bitter. Some of the small white varieties can be tough and dry, and 'Rosa Bianca' I describe as creamy. All in all, eggplant is not a strong-flavored vegetable, and its virtue is often the fact that it gives richness to a dish and absorbs flavors like garlic, basil, and oregano.

How to Grow

The eggplant's climate requirements are similar to those of its relative the tomato. The plant is highly susceptible to frost, so if you start your own from seeds, do not put the seedlings into the ground until all frost danger is past and the ground is warm. Eggplants grow best in a well-drained garden loam that is fertilized with blood meal and manure or fish emulsion about three times during the growing season. An alternative is a pound and a half of 5-10-5 fertilizer for 50 square feet. When the soil has warmed, mulch with organic matter to retain both heat and moisture. If you are growing eggplants in a cool climate, cover the soil with black plastic to retain heat. Eggplants need moderate watering and should never be allowed to dry out.

Eggplants are so susceptible to freezing that it is probably best to start seeds indoors 6 to 8 weeks before the average date of your last frost. The seeds germinate best at 80° F. Plant the seeds ¼ inch deep, in flats or peat pots. Eggplants take about a week to germinate in a warm room. When summer is here and the soil has warmed up, place the plants 18 to 24 inches apart and water well. To increase yield and to keep the plants healthy, feed them throughout the growing season with fish emulsion and liquid kelp. In areas of the country with a long, warm growing season, they will need even more room to spread. In fact, in winter areas with no frost they will continue to grow for a number of years, and will spread to 2 or 3 feet across and need staking.

Pests and Diseases

Flea beetles, spider mites, and whiteflies can be a problem. Flea beetles seem to be the most common. They appear early in the season, right after transplanting. Some gardeners report that planting radishes when transplanting eggplants attracts the beetles to the radishes and away from the eggplants. If flea beetles become a severe problem, cover plants with a polyester row cover or treat with diazinon. Spider mites can be a nuisance in hot or dry weather. Washing down the foliage every few days should help. Nematodes are sometimes a problem in the South. Sterilize the soil (see Appendix B, "Pests and Diseases") or plant in containers.

Verticillium wilt and phomopsis blight are common problems in humid climates. Verticillium wilt can sometimes be beaten by feeding and watering the plant so much that it outgrows the disease. Crop rotation, good garden hygiene, and the use of tolerant varieties, such as 'Agora' (fusarium resistant), 'Florida Market' (phomopsis resistant), and 'Midnight' (verticillium resistant), are also recommended.

Containers

Eggplants grow well and look absolutely smashing in containers.The dwarf and compact-growing varieties are the most successful.

Prolonging the Season

There are a few early varieties that will bear slightly sooner than average. Try 'Agora', 'Dusky', and 'Early Beauty Hybrid'.

Harvesting

The fruit is ready to pick when it is full-colored but has not yet begun to lose any of its sheen. Marian Morash in *The Victory Garden Cookbook* suggests the following test for ripeness: Press down on the eggplant with your thumb. If the flesh presses in but bounces back out, it is ripe. If it does not give under pressure, it is not yet ripe. If it gives to pressure but does not bounce back out, it is overripe. This is a useful test and can keep you from harvesting (or purchasing) those overripe fruits that have such a bitter taste. To help prevent fruits from deteriorating, they should be cut rather than pulled from the plant. Plants will produce more if fruits are picked regularly. Average annual yields are six to eight fruits per plant, though many varieties and warm-summer areas will produce more.

Seed Saving

Select slightly overripe fruits from open-pollinated varieties. They should have lost their sheen and look a bit shriveled and, depending on the variety, either brownish or yellowish. Scrape out the interior pulp and separate and rinse the seed. Dry it thoroughly before storing in airtight containers.

Varieties

Eggplants can be white, yellow, green, red, orange, lavender, or the more familiar deep purple. They can be a solid color, striped, or mottled. They can be round, oblong, or cylindrical, large or small, or even scalloped like some of the Oriental varieties.

'BLACK BEAUTY'   73 days, most common standard-size-fruit variety; produces large, good-quality, purple fruits. (Readily available)

'BURPEE HYBRID'   70 days, quite resistant to drought and disease. (Burpee)

'DUSKY'   60 days, good choice for northern gardens, produces medium-size purple fruits early in season. (Readily available) 'Agora' (Shepherd's) is an improved selection of 'Dusky'.

'FLORIDA MARKET'   85 days, phomopsis resistant, open-pollinated, good in lower South. (Hastings, Seeds Blum)

'ICHIBAN'   61 days, Japanese type, long, slender, purple, good in cooler climates. (Herb Gathering, Lockhart)

'LISTADA DE GANDIA'   a lavender-and-white-striped oblong fruit of very good quality. (Seeds Blum)

'RONDE DE VALENCE'   round-fruited eggplant from France, productive and beautiful, open-pollinated. (Le Marché)

'ROSA BLANCA'   my favorite eggplant, spectacular, bright, lavender-fruited, vigorous, productive; decorative, with creamy, mild-flavored, high-quality fruits; open-pollinated. (Le Marché, Seeds Blum)

'VIOLETTE DE FIRENZE"   spectacular lavender eggplant from Italy, large fruits sometimes with wide white stripes. (Cook's, Fr. Ingegnoli)

'WHITE BEAUTY'   unusual and decorative white-skinned fruit, open-pollinated. (Seeds Blum)

Preserving

Except when prepared as a luxury item, such as pickled baby eggplant, this vegetable is used fresh.

Purchasing

The most important part of selecting a good eggplant in the market is getting it fresh and not too mature. Look for very shiny skin and a fresh green cap, or calyx. Make sure the fruit is firm—not soft to the touch. See "Harvesting," above, for additional suggestions for determining ripeness. Some specialty markets carry lavender and white varieties. Oriental markets often have the long, thin Japanese varieties.

GREENS

COLLARDS   *Brassica oleracea*, Acephala Group
CORN SALAD (fetticus, lamb's lettuce, mâche)   *Valerianella Locusta*
CURLY ENDIVE and ESCAROLE   *Cichorium Endivia*
DANDELION, COMMON   *Taraxacum officinale*
KALE and FLOWERING KALE   *B. oleracea*, Acephala Group
MUSTARD (India mustard) and SPINACH MUSTARD   *B. juncea*
NEW ZEALAND SPINACH   *Tetragonia tetragonioides*
SORREL   *Rumex Acetosa;* French sorrel   *R. scutatus*
SPINACH   *Spinacia oleracea*
SWISS CHARD   *Beta vulgaris* var. *cicla*

Effort Scale

NO. 2
Must be planted seasonally
Watering, mulching, and fertilizing usually needed
Some weeding necessary

Thumbnail Sketch

Annuals, biennials, or perennials planted as annuals
4 to 24 inches tall
Propagated from seeds; sorrel from divisions also
Need full sun; partial shade in hot weather
Leaves vary with species
Flowers usually not seen
Leaves edible; most harvested in cool part of year
Used in vegetable gardens, flower borders, herb gardens, raised beds, containers

What would we do without greens? Not only are they lovely to look at, they are delicious in all their variety, and healthful, while low in calories to boot. Collards, dandelions, mustard, kale, and chard are good steamed, and a pot of fresh greens flavored with butter, olive oil, or pork drippings is a springtime delight. Spinach and sorrel make savory cream soups. Spinach soufflé, spinach omelette, and my favorite, spinach or chard feta strudel, make rich entrees. All of the greens named here add variety to a tossed green salad, while a spinach salad with raw mushrooms and artichoke hearts is nearly a meal in itself.

The flavors of greens range from the acidic bite of sorrel to the mild nutty flavor of corn salad, the slightly metallic taste of spinach, and the spicy bite of mustard. Some greens, like New Zealand spinach, have a somewhat fleshy leaf, the escaroles a chewy one, and sorrel a smooth tender leaf.

Information on other greens, including arugula, cress, and purslane, is included in appropriate places throughout the book. Check the index for exact location.

Designing the garden with the varied textures, forms, and colors this plant group offers can be great fun. All shades of green are represented, from the yellow-green of endive to the deep green of spinach. Leaf shapes range from curly to smooth. The possibilities for planting and creating your own patterns—geometric or free form—are endless.

How to Grow

Chard, dandelion, endive, kale, corn salad, mustard, and spinach are all cool-season crops. Collards and New Zealand spinach prefer cool weather but do quite well in the hot summer. Endive and escarole have a tendency to become slightly bitter tasting and strong in flavor if the weather is too warm, so harvest your spring crop before hot weather. During warm weather, these leafy vegetables need partial shade. The greens should be started from seed in early spring and should be planted in rich, fertile loam and be kept fairly moist. Sorrel can be started by seed, or divisions can be taken from a large plant and planted.

To become tender and succulent, greens should grow quickly and vigorously. To encourage such growth, give supplemental organic matter and an extra source of nitrogen during the growing season to most. Corn salad, New Zealand spinach, and sorrel are exceptions.

Pests and Diseases

With the exception of collards, kale, and the mustards, the greens mentioned here are vulnerable to very few pests or diseases, though aphids, flea beetles, slugs, and snails are occasional problems. Collards, kale, and the mustards are members of the cabbage family and are often plagued by the pests that bother cabbage. See "Cabbage and Brussels Sprouts" for information on these.

Containers

The relatively small size and attractive foliage of most greens make them suitable for container planting. Containers also offer the option of moving the plants into the shade if the weather becomes too warm or the sun too intense.

Prolonging the Season

Start harvesting the thinnings a few weeks after sowing. For more information, see "Harvesting," below.

Harvesting

All greens can be harvested a few leaves at a time as they are needed, although corn salad and spinach are usually harvested in their entirety because of their small leaf size. Wash greens well to remove dirt, grit, and an occasional slug before using.

Seed Saving

For saving collard, kale, and mustard seeds, see "Cabbage and Brussels Sprouts." See "Beets" for saving the seeds of Swiss chard as they are saved in the same manner.

Corn salad produces seeds easily in the garden. Typically, the seeds are left where they fall, and in time they produce next year's crop.

Endive and escarole are both biennials and produce seeds their second season. Self-pollinated, they have no need for separation unless seed purity is required, and then a separation of several yards is adequate. Mulch plants over the winter and harvest seeds in the late spring. See "Lettuce" for collection details.

Spinach is an annual and goes to seed in the summer when the weather is warm. Plants produce either male or female flowers, or occasionally both. The female flowers are wind pollinated over long distances. If seed purity is required, plant only one variety per season. To select for slow-bolting progeny, save seeds from the plants that are last to ripen. Allow seeds to remain in their pods until dry and brown, then remove from pods and store in airtight containers.

Dandelion, sorrel, and New Zealand spinach all seed easily in the garden. Sorrel will cross with wild sorrel; New Zealand spinach is related to ice plant and may cross with it.

Varieties

Collards

Collards are large-leafed greens with a soft, smooth, cabbage flavor. They are often cooked in soup stock, either alone or mixed with other greens. If harvested a few leaves at a time, collards will produce over a long period. They are valuable as a fall crop as their flavor sweetens with frost.

'GEORGIA'   60 days; tall, upright plant produces sweet leaves even in poor soil and hot weather. (Burpee, Hastings, Park, Seeds Blum, Wyatt)
'HICROP'   75 days, hybrid; mild, sweet flavor even in hot weather, slow to bolt. (Park)

Corn Salad

Corn salad, also called mâche, is a low little plant whose leaves grow from a central rosette and produce soft and tender spoon-shaped greens with a delicate nutty flavor. It is an easily grown annual that needs cool weather. Plant seeds ½ inch deep. Depending upon the variety, start seeds inside in late winter and transplant into the garden in early spring, spacing plants 4 to 6 inches apart in rows or wide beds. You may also direct seed in late summer for fall harvest, or in fall for spring harvest. For winter use, direct seed in cold frames in fall. Corn salad seeds germinate poorly in hot weather, so shade the seed bed until they germinate. The seeds germinate unevenly and grow slowly but steadily. Harvest starts in 40 to 70 days, depending on the variety and season. Pick individual leaves or the whole head, either when tiny (six to eight leaves) for baby corn salad or when mature. If corn salad is allowed to go to seed, most gardeners find it will come up by itself every spring. Though the flavor is not too variable, some varieties grow better in one season than another. Seed companies list this green under corn salad or mâche.

'GROTE NORDHOLLANDSE' ('GROSSE GRAINE')   70 days, large-seeded, tender variety for fall harvest, not hardy. (Herb Gathering, Le Marché, Nichols, Shepherd's)

'VERTE DE CAMBRAI'   75 days, fine-textured little plant with flat leaves and exceptional tenderness, hardy variety for fall or overwintering. (Burpee, Herb Gathering, Johnny's, Le Marché, Shepherd's)

Curly Endive and Escarole

Endive is the name given to a group of plants that fall into two primary categories most commonly referred to as curly endive (also known as frisées) and escarole. Both groups are popular in fresh salads or cooked as greens. (Do not confuse curly endive with Belgian or French endive, known as Witloof chicory, which is actually the blanched sprouts of another species, *Cichorium Intybus*.)

Curly endive has narrow, finely cut, curled and twisted leaves. The outer leaves are usually dark green fading to a paler color toward the center of the head. The plant is rather shaggy and low growing. Escarole is a larger, more upright plant with longer and broader leaves, also twisted at the base, and a less-pronounced pale interior.

Unless young, endive and escarole become tough and bitter and often go to seed in hot weather, so to appreciate them, plant in early spring or late summer. Some varieties are best if blanched (see the "French Gardens" chapter). Many modern varieties need not be blanched.

'CUORE PIENO'   a broad-leaved escarole that has golden inner leaves and is popular among Italian market growers. (Le Marché)

'ELODIE'   50 days, very finely cut curly endive from France, excellent in salads, milder than most varieties, good flavor either as baby or mature head. (Shepherd's)

'FINE MARAICHERE'   very finely cut leaved endive, elegant small plant, good for individual servings; use young for mesclun. (Le Marché)

'NUVOL'   50 days, self-blanching escarole with sweet and tender heart, slow to bolt. (Johnny's)

'PANCALIER'   very attractive pink-ribbed endive, tender plant. (Seeds Blum)

'SALAD KING'   45 days, curly endive with curled and toothed leaves, heavy producer, early, slow to bolt. (Johnny's)

Dandelion

Dandelions prefer acidic soil and require a year of growth before harvest, so pick a permanent spot with these requirements in mind. Sow the seeds directly in the soil in spring or fall. For the most delicate flavor, plant named varieties and blanch the leaves by tying them up at the top. Harvest only the youngest leaves. Do not let dandelions go to seed or they will become a pest. They can be cooked alone or with other greens in water or, better yet, bouillon.

'THICK-LEAVED'   95 days, large leaves good as potherb, blanched leaves good in salads. (Burpee)

'VERT DE MONTMAGNY'   long green notched leaves may be blanched or not. (Le Marché)

Kale and Flowering Kale

Curly, blue-green kale is beautiful as well as tasty, but its show-off cousin, flowering or ornamental kale, while not as flavorful, puts most flowers to shame. Both can be enjoyed in the early spring or fall, and neither does well in warm weather. Flowering kale will not produce its brilliant red or purple foliage without some cold, and the flavor of both plants is improved by frost.

Kale is very nutritious and contains large quantities of calcium, iron, and potassium. It is usually eaten cooked, but the tender new growth is also good raw in salads. Unlike endive, kale is never bitter. The ornamental types add color to a green salad in winter. Both Park and Nichols seed companies have a good selection of the ornamental varieties. Yellow kale flowers are tasty and colorful in a salad or as a garnish.

'DWARF BLUE CURLED VATES'   55 days, very hardy. (Readily available)

'RAGGED JACK'   heirloom kale with frilly red-veined leaf, stays very tasty through summer heat. (Seeds Blum)

'VERDURA'   60 days, dark blue-green leaves, productive, winter-hardy variety from Holland, very sweet flavor. (Shepherd's)

Mustard (India Mustard) and Spinach Mustard

These stout-hearted members of the cabbage family are spicy and crisp when eaten raw and superb when cooked with salt pork. All mustards need sufficient moisture while growing or they will become too hot to eat. The younger the leaf, the less bite it has. Mustard flowers are edible well after the leaves are too strong to eat. Use them in salads and on cream soups.

The mustard used as a condiment comes from the ground-up seeds of plants in this family. The best condiment mustards are made from white mustard, *Brassica alba* (obtainable from Richters), or black mustard, *B. nigra*. The young leaves of these plants can be used as potherbs. To make condiment mustard, allow these plants to go to seed and harvest when the pods turn yellow. Put the seeds in a blender with wine vinegar, black pepper, allspice, salt, and water if needed. See the "Gourmet Salad Gardens" chapter for more information.

Some Oriental varieties of mustard have a rich mustard flavor, and others are peppery and have bronze foliage. See the "Oriental Gardens" chapter for more information.

'FORDHOOK FANCY'　lovely leaves with frilly edges and mild flavor. (Burpee, Seeds Blum)

'GREEN WAVE'　American mustard with hot mustardy flavor; good with smoked meats and sausage or, in small amounts, in salads; slow to bolt. (Harris, Johnny's)

'TENDERGREEN' (MUSTARD SPINACH)　smooth-leaved, easier to clean, taste less hot than others. (Burpee, Hastings, Park, Seeds Blum, Wyatt)

New Zealand Spinach
New Zealand spinach is a trailing annual with succulent, triangular leaves. It is not related to spinach but tastes somewhat similar to it. Although tougher and stronger in flavor, New Zealand spinach is sometimes used as a substitute in recipes calling for spinach, either raw or cooked. Standard spinach will go to seed quickly after a few days of warm weather, but New Zealand spinach can tolerate much heat. It tastes better in cool weather but if shaded in summer will bear the whole summer. Keep harvesting the new growth to stimulate new young shoots. Old or drought-stricken leaves are tough and bitter. New Zealand spinach has few pest or disease problems.

Seeds are readily available, but named varieties are not sold commercially in this country.

Sorrel
Sorrel is a perennial with light-green, spade-shaped leaves emerging from a rosette. It stands about 18 inches tall and is quite attractive. Soup lovers claim that cream of sorrel soup is without peer. The slightly lemony taste of the leaves in combination with chicken broth, cream, and eggs is delicious and satisfying. A few leaves added to any bland salad will really perk up the flavor.

Garden sorrel seed is readily available. Le Marché seed company also carries two French varieties. 'Sorrel de Belleville' is a small productive plant with 3-inch leaves that are ready for harvest about 10 weeks from planting. 'Blonde de Lyon', named for the city of Lyon, has large, thick leaves and is the variety grown in warmer regions.

Spinach
Just think of spinach soup or spinach soufflé to measure the value of this noble vegetable. If the weather is cool and the soil rich and filled with humus, spinach is easy to grow. It has few pests and diseases.

'BLOOMSDALE'　48 days, heavy yielding, slow to go to seed. (Readily available)

'MELODY'　42 days, hybrid, large adaptable plants resistant to downy mildew and mosaic virus. (Readily available)

'TYEE'　42 days, dark-green wrinkled leaves, upright vigorous growth, very slow to bolt, tolerant of mildew; good for spring, summer, and fall crops, overwinters well. (Johnny's)

'WOLTER'　45 days, rapid growing, tender, smooth-leaved, developed by Dutch breeders, resistant to mildew. (Shepherd's)

Swiss Chard
Chard grows upright and straight. Its strong supporting midribs are either white, pink, or cherry red, and its deep-green leaves are usually ruffled and rich looking. The red chards, often called rhubarb or ruby chards, look handsome when planted with the other greens.

'FORDHOOK'　60 days, large and crinkled, dark-green leaves. (Burpee)

'LARGE WHITE RIB'　60 days; smooth, large green leaves with white ribs. (Harris)

'PAROS'　58 days, tall French chard with mild, sweet leaves; good spinach substitute. (Shepherd's)

'RUBY'　excellent flavor, formerly known as rhubarb chard. (Readily available)

'VULCAN'　60 days, bright-red stems contrast with dark-green ruffled leaves, exceptionally sweet. (Park)

Preserving
While some greens are frozen and occasionally even canned, they lose most of their charm in the translation and are best eaten fresh.

Purchasing
Look for greens that are crisp and green without signs of yellowing or otherwise discolored leaves.

LETTUCE (HEAD, ROMAINE, AND LEAF)
Lactuca sativa

Effort Scale
NO. 2
Continuous planting needed
Some weeding, watering, and fertilizing required

Thumbnail Sketch
Annual
6 to 12 inches tall
Propagated by seeds

Barely cover seeds with soil
Germination takes 5 to 10 days at 55° to 65° F
Thin to 4 to 12 inches apart, depending on variety
Needs sun or partial shade
Leaves light to medium green or red, 4 to 12 inches long
Flowers not seen
Leaves edible; harvest season varies
Used in vegetable gardens, flower beds, herbaceous
    borders, raised beds, containers

Americans are most familiar with iceberg types of lettuce. They are available in the supermarket year round, sometimes looking full, crisp, and appealing, but more often looking pale. Home gardeners are seldom happy growing only iceberg when there is such a fabulous array of other forms, colors, and textures to choose from. The choices for the table and garden are exciting: frilly red lettuces, silky-smooth green rosettes, and varieties with exaggerated, undulated leaf shapes. Some lettuce varieties, namely iceberg and romaine (cos), are crisp; others, like 'Bibb', are soft and buttery. Lettuce can even be cooked! The French sometimes braise it with peas.

These decorative edibles can grace both the flower border and the buffet table. They can be planted near herb gardens and are effective in dappled shade mixed with impatiens. For a rich blend of colors, try them in hanging baskets with lobelia. A mixture of red and green lettuces, or ones with different textures, can make a garden by themselves. Lettuces are particularly suited for winter and greenhouse growing; cold frames and special so-called forcing types are available for such use.

When I think of the taste and texture of lettuce I think of grassy, sweet, sour, bitter, and waxy, succulent, crisp, soft, buttery, papery, and tough. Generally the less stressful the growing conditions and the faster the lettuce grows, the sweeter and more succulent it will be.

How to Grow

Lettuces can be categorized in different ways—by the form of the plant, say, or by the season, or even the way they are grown. While all lettuces grow best in cool weather, some will tolerate no hot weather and are referred to as spring lettuces. Other more tolerant ones are called summer lettuces.

Lettuce is a cool-season annual crop that can be grown in most areas of the country. Most varieties will go to seed or become bitter rapidly when hot weather comes, although leaf lettuces will take more heat than the heading types. In warm weather lettuce will grow in considerable shade, and in mild-winter areas it can be grown at all but the hottest times of year. In cold-winter areas you can grow forcing types of lettuces in a greenhouse or a cold frame (see "Forcing Lettuces" under "Varieties," below), or seed hardy overwintering types in the fall and harvest them in early spring.

Most lettuce is easy to grow when its requirements are met. It prefers a slightly alkaline loam, rich with added humus. It needs regular moisture and profits from light feedings of a fish emulsion type of fertilizer to keep it growing vigorously. Sow seeds in early spring, either in flats or directly in the ground. Lettuce seeds will germinate at quite low temperatures, but most varieties will not germinate if the soil temperature is above 68° F. Some of the crisp heading types are exceptions, with varieties that will germinate when soil temperatures are above 80° F.

Few vegetable crops benefit as much from succession planting as does lettuce. Every 10 to 14 days sow new seeds to keep your next crop coming along. Establish a planting and harvest schedule that works for you. Growing transplants is easiest to do inside on a sunny windowsill in small containers so you can keep an eye on them.

You can start lettuce outside in place or in flats 3 to 4 weeks before setting it out. Barely cover the seeds with fine soil. Too much covering screens the seeds from light, which they need to germinate. Black-seeded varieties need even more light than others so should be pressed into the soil but left uncovered. Keep seed beds uniformly moist until seedlings appear. Lettuce seeds planted indoors in flats or containers usually germinate within 1 week. Outdoors, if the soil is cold, germination can take 2 weeks. When seedlings have their first set of true leaves (after their initial seed leaves), space them 2 inches apart in larger flats. When transplanting them outdoors, space them about 18 inches apart.

If you have direct seeded, thin the seedlings to between 4 and 12 inches apart, depending on the variety and size you prefer for harvesting. Failure to do this can result in disease problems and small, stunted plants. Use the thinnings in your salads.

Seeds for all kinds of lettuce are readily available, and nurseries offer seedlings. Seedlings can be transplanted into empty spaces left by harvested plants. One advantage of leaf lettuce is that the outer leaves can be picked as needed, rather than having to harvest the entire plant. As a result, harvesting does not leave gaps in your garden.

See the "Gourmet Salad Gardens" chapter for scissor-cutting methods of harvesting lettuces, special seeding techniques, and other specialized information on lettuce growing.

Pests and Diseases

Succulent young lettuce leaves are ambrosia to slugs, snails, aphids, and cutworms, so protect your seedlings until they get fairly good sized. Under cool, humid conditions, Botrytis, a gray mold fungus disease, can cause the plants to rot off at the base. Downy mildew, another fungus, will cause older leaves to get whitish patches that eventually die. In both cases, practicing good hygiene is the best medicine. Rotate your lettuce plantings with other vegetables and keep the plants spaced well apart for good air circulation.

Water in the morning, wetting the soil but not the leaves, and try not to handle the plants when they are wet.

Containers

All lettuces do very well in containers. Try the miniature varieties like 'Tom Thumb' or 'Little Gem' in small decorative pots. The larger varieties are also beautiful in larger containers at least 6 inches across.

Prolonging the Season

In most regions you can have lettuce almost all year long. This abundance will be in question only under the hottest conditions in the South and in Hawaii. In very cold areas you can grow lettuce in a greenhouse or cold frame. Staggering the crop during the growing season is the tricky part of having a constant supply. It will take you a few years to get the timing down for your climate and your family's consumption. The secret is to keep small amounts of lettuce coming all the time. Sow a few seeds every 10 to 14 days.

Harvesting

Lettuce can be harvested as soon as it has a few true leaves, though most people prefer to wait until the plants are more mature and develop more flavor. Leaf lettuces can be harvested one leaf at a time. Head lettuces are harvested a full head at a time by cutting off the head at the soil line. Harvest during the cool of the day.

Seed Saving

Leaf lettuces provide some of the easiest annual seeds to save. When the yellow flowers have dried to feathery white seed heads, remove the seeds by shaking them into an open container where they can continue to dry indoors for about a week. Lettuce seeds shatter from the pods very easily. When selecting the plants from which to save seeds, select those that are the slowest to bolt.

Saving seeds from head lettuces sometimes requires an additional step. Select the most uniform and vigorous heads for parentage. If the seed stalk appears to be having difficulty unfurling, cut a 1-inch-deep cross (+) in the top of the head to make it easier for the seed head to emerge. Follow the same directions as for saving leaf lettuce seeds. After complete drying, store the seeds in airtight containers.

Lettuces are mostly self-pollinated, so you can grow several varieties for seed saving, but some crossing does occur, both from one variety to another and with wild lettuce, sometimes known as prickly lettuce. Seed purity requires careful planting and attention to surrounding weeds.

Varieties

See the "Gourmet Salad Gardens" chapter for information on lettuce varieties.

Spring Lettuce

When the ground can be prepared—usually February or March in mild climates, late May in the coldest climates—you'll be ready to plant spring lettuces. However, most varieties (with the exception of overwintering types) do well with early spring planting.

'BIBB' ('LIMESTONE')   57 days, bolts readily in hot weather. (Lockhart, Nichols, Park)

'BLACK-SEEDED SIMPSON'   42 days, matures in 45 days under good conditions; light green, delicious, one of the earliest lettuces. (Readily available)

'DEER TONGUE'   heirloom green lettuce with unusual spear-shaped leaf, texture similar to spinach. (Good)

'ERTHEL' ('CRISP MINT')   5 days to baby stage, 80 days to maturity; large upright leaves sweet and crisp; mildew and mosaic tolerant, extremely slow to bolt. (Thompson & Morgan)

'GREEN ICE'   45 days, recently developed; dark green and crisp, holds well in the garden. (Burpee, Park)

'ICE QUEEN' ('REINE DES GLACES')   62 days, beautiful frosty-green head of deeply notched leaves; early plantings yield best results. (Cook's, Seeds Blum)

'LOLLO ROSSA'   56 days, mild-flavored loose-leaf; beautiful and distinctive, a real eye-catcher; frilly leaves and red margins fading to pale green at the heart. (Cook's, Le Marché, Shepherd's)

'MARVEL OF FOUR SEASONS'   60 days, known in France as 'Merveille de Quatres Saisons'; striking, with bright-red outer leaves, pale pink and cream interior; tender yet crisp. (Cook's, Good, Le Jardin, Le Marché, Shepherd's)

'RED SAILS'   45 days, fast growing, heat tolerant, slow to bolt, won 1985 All America Trials; deepens in color as it matures. (Readily available)

'RUBY'   47 days, ruby red traditional plant with excellent reputation. (Burpee, Nichols, Park, Stokes, Twilley)

'TOM THUMB'   65 days, solid butterheads about the size of tennis balls; can be served whole as individual salads; ideal for containers or other small spaces. (Readily available)

Summer Lettuces

Summer lettuces can tolerate a little more heat than most but should still be planted soon after the last frost to get them well on their way before the hot weather sets in. Seed every week or so for continuous harvesting at all stages. Water lavishly during hot months.

'BUTTERCRUNCH'   60 days, deep-green compact head, crisp and juicy; tolerates heat better and larger than 'Bibb'. (Readily available)

'CONTINUITY'   70 days, similar to 'Marvel of Four Seasons' but deeper in color and longer standing during dry summer weather. (Bountiful, Cook's, Nichols)

'CRAQUERELLE DU MIDI' ('CRAQUANTE D'AVIGNON') open-hearted cos type, well suited for warm climates, similar to 'Buttercrunch'. (Cook's, Le Marché)

'LITTLE GEM' ('SUGAR COS') 60 days to baby lettuce, 80 days to maturity; delicious, trouble free; small, deep-green cos-type head, with very few outside leaves; moderately frost tolerant, slow to bolt in hot weather. (Cook's, Good, Shepherd's, Thompson & Morgan)

Fall/Winter Lettuces

For a fall harvest, plant after the heat of summer. However, when shortened days bring temperatures down to the 40s or below, most lettuces will deteriorate. To flourish in these conditions, special varieties have been bred. They should be sown from about Labor Day until the first frost. If you plant them earlier they may bolt prematurely.

'BRUNE D'HIVER' 56 days, French heirloom variety, between a romaine and bibb in form; bronzy-red-edged leaves tapering to green at the centers; one of hardiest varieties. (Cook's, Le Marché, Shepherd's)

'ROUGE D'HIVER' 60 days, another French heirloom; romaine, deep-red leaves, resistant to heat and cold; lovely in the garden and the kitchen. (Cook's, Shepherd's)

'WINTER DENSITY' 60 days, hardy green variety, semi-cos type, resembles a tall buttercrunch; can be grown nearly year round in mild climates. (Cook's, Johnny's, Seeds Blum)

'WINTER MARVEL' 68 days; if planted in fall, produces large, pale-green head in early spring; very hardy. (Cook's, Herb Gathering)

Forcing Lettuces

These pale-green butterheads have been bred for growing in greenhouses, tunnels, or cold frames and can survive colder temperatures than many varieties. Forcing lettuces should be planted in flats about a month before you plan to transplant them.

'CAPITANE' 62 days, large Boston type, superb quality. (Shepherd's, Stokes)

'MAGNET' pale green and tender, produces large head, withstands early summer heat quite well. (Cook's)

Cutting Lettuces

These are vigorous, loose-leaf lettuces. While they can be grown and harvested in the normal manner, if you sow the seeds continuously and thickly, you can have a continuous crop of baby lettuce leaves. Harvest by scissor cutting when the lettuces are 4 to 6 inches high. See the "Gourmet Salad Gardens" chapter for information on this technique.

'RED SALAD BOWL' 50 days, pale-red color increases to deep red with maturity, withstands heat well. (Readily available)

'ROYAL OAK LEAF' 50 days, large deep-green rosettes with oak-leaf shaped leaves, holds well in the garden; a beautiful complement to any salad. (Burpee, Cook's)

'SALAD BOWL' 45 days, lime-green, deeply lobed, fairly heat resistant, easy to grow; great mixed with 'Red Salad Bowl'. (Bountiful, Johnny's, Nichols, Park)

Preserving

Lettuce cannot be preserved.

Purchasing

When purchasing lettuce from the produce market, look for crisp leaves of bright color. Avoid those that are wilted or that show signs of rust or brown spotting. The largest selection of best-quality lettuces is in spring and fall.

Be on the alert for the epicurean leaf lettuces as the season is fleeting. The finest leaf-lettuces are very fragile, and some of the most conscientious growers offer individual plants with the roots still attached to assure freshness. In very select markets, baby lettuce leaves are packaged and ready for eating the same day they are picked.

MELONS

CANTALOUPE *Cucumis Melo,* Reticulatus Group
HONEYDEW *C. Melo,* Inodorus Group
WATERMELON *Citrullus lanatus*

Effort Scale

NO. 3
Must be planted annually
Training of vining type necessary
Occasional watering necessary
Fertilizing and mulching needed
Vulnerable to some pests and diseases

Thumbnail Sketch

Annuals
Bush types, 1 foot tall; vining types, to 6 feet long
Propagated from seeds
Plant seeds ½ to 1 inch deep
Germination takes 5 to 10 days at 75° F
Need full sun
Leaves light to dark green, large, vary with species
Flowers bright yellow, 1 to 2 inches across
Fruits edible; harvested in summer and fall
Used in vegetable gardens, herbaceous borders, raised beds, containers

The melons are here—it must be summer! Members of the Cucurbitaceae family along with cucumbers and squash, melons certainly do their share to announce the arrival of summer, at long last. Honeydew served with ham slices, cantaloupe filled with cottage cheese, and a mix of melons served in fruit salad are all great treats that aren't even fattening! And what image recalls a Fourth of July family picnic more vividly than a child eating watermelon out of hand, pink juice dripping from her chin.

Melon vines have lemon-yellow, cup-shaped flowers nestled in between deep-green, ivy-shaped leaves. Bush-type melons fit nicely into containers. The vining types can be used on low trellises, fences, or spilling over embankments.

The taste of cantaloupe is complex and can be described variously as musky, earthy, sweet, aromatic, floral, spicy, berryish, and cucumber-like, or fermented, flat, tasteless, sour, and watery. The textures can be evaluated as crisp, succulent, and juicy, or stringy, rubbery, and mushy. The taste of watermelon is fruity, sometimes with overtones of strawberry and sometimes of cucumber. The texture is crisp, almost like a popsicle. The flavor of honeydew can be described as sweet, rich, aromatic, floral, or cardboard-like and watery. The texture can be juicy and melting or stringy and tough.

How to Grow

Melons, like other members of the cucurbit clan, are warm-season annuals. In short-summer areas, seeds should be started indoors and moved into the garden after the soil has warmed and the weather has settled.

Melons are usually grown in hills spaced 6 to 8 feet apart, with two or three plants 6 inches apart in a hill. They can also be planted in rows with 10 to 14 inches between plants and the rows 6 to 8 feet apart. If space is at a premium, melons can be grown against a fence or trellis, but you must be sure to provide slings (these can be made from netting or old stockings) or wooden supports for the fruits as they develop.

These plants need full-sun locations, rich humus soil, and ample water during the growing season. Do not let them dry out. Prepare the soil by adding much organic matter and half a cup of bone meal for each hill. Side dress with fish emulsion when fruits are starting to set. Keep young plants well weeded. Mature plants can usually crowd weeds out, but a black-plastic mulch assures a weed-free area. In addition, black plastic around these heat-loving plants raises the soil temperature, keeps it warmer longer, and reduces moisture evaporation at the same time. See the mulching information in Appendix A, "Planting and Maintenance."

Reduce watering toward harvest time. Too much water then results in insipid fruits, and uneven watering can actually split the melons.

Pests and Diseases
See "Cucumbers."

Containers
Small bush-type melons can be grown in large containers, one plant per container. Larger, vining melons need strong support or trellising as well. One advantage of container culture is that it allows roots to absorb extra heat.

Prolonging the Season
See "Cucumbers."

Harvesting
Allow fruits of all types of melons to remain on the vine until they are fully ripe, as a melon's full sugar content is not reached until the last few days of growth. Cantaloupe is ready to harvest when its netting has turned from green to tan, when it smells rich and fragrant, and when a crack has formed on the stem right near the area where it attaches to the melon. At this stage of maturity, called the "slip stage," most cantaloupe should detach or "slip" from the stem with little pressure. In fact, if it takes too much effort to detach the melon, it is almost certainly not ripe.

Color is the best indicator of honeydew ripeness. The melons are ready for harvest when their icy-green color shows hints of yellow.

Watermelon is ripe when the fruit's surface skin is dull, tough, and difficult to puncture with your fingernail; when the bottom of the melon has passed through green to yellow; and when the tendrils on the stem near the fruit are shriveled and brown.

Seed Saving
Melons are monoecious (having both male and female flowers on the same plant) and cross-pollinated, usually by honey bees. They will cross with other melons but not with other members of the cucurbit family. See "Seed Saving" under "Cucumbers" and "Squash" for more detail.

Collect watermelon seeds from mature fruits as they are prepared for kitchen use. Wash the seeds and allow them to dry for several days before storing in an airtight container.

Most other melon seeds need to be separated from the fruit's pulp before washing and storing. Remove seed-containing pulp from mature fruits. Soak the seedy pulp in water, at room temperature, stirring once or twice a day. In a few days the pulp will have dissolved, and the heavy, viable seed will have sunk to the bottom. Collect seeds, wash with clear water, and dry thoroughly before storing in airtight containers.

Varieties
Botanically speaking, most of the melons that we commonly refer to as cantaloupe are really another species of melon called muskmelon. For simplicity's sake, I will refer to this species here as "cantaloupe," as I have in the rest of the entry.

Only cantaloupe, honeydew, and watermelon varieties are listed below. There are many other melons, including Persian, crenshaw, and casaba, to name but a few. Generally they need a longer and warmer growing season than the more common melons. These melon varieties are available from Le Marché, Redwood City Seed, and Seeds Blum.

Cantaloupe and Honeydew

'AMBROSIA'   86 days, hybrid, standard-size fruit, one of the best eating cantaloupes, long vines, mildew resistant. (Readily available)

'CHACA HYBRID'   68 days, French charentais-type melon, large vines, 3-pound sweet salmon-colored fruits, resistant to fusarium wilt and powdery mildew. (Nichols)

'HONEYLOUPE'   75 days, honeydew and cantaloupe cross, delicious white-skinned melon with orange flesh, verticillium resistant. (Stokes)

'LIMELIGHT HYBRID'   96 days, early-maturing honeydew. (Burpee)

'MINNESOTA MIDGET'   75 days, small sweet cantaloupe, good in short-season areas, 3-foot vines, good for small planting space. (Burpee, Gurney, Park, Seeds Blum)

'OLD TIME TENNESSEE'   90 days, old-time favorite, salmon-colored cantaloupe, outstanding flavor if picked at the peak of ripeness; fragile, so should be eaten quickly after harvest. (Le Marché, Southern Exposure)

Watermelon

'CHARLESTON GRAY'   85 days; fruits average 10 inches across, 24 inches long, and 30 to 35 pounds; sweet juicy flavor makes it one of the most popular varieties of all time. (Field's, Gurney, Stokes, Twilley, Vermont Bean)

'CRIMSON SWEET'   80 days, deep-red flesh in blocky 20- to 25-pound melon; juicy and sweet with few seeds, resistant to fusarium and anthracnose. (Field's, Gurney, Harris, Southern Exposure, Twilley)

'MOON AND STARS'   20 to 25 pounds with fine flavor, rind dark green with golden splotch (moon) and gold speckles (stars). (Seeds Blum)

'SUGAR BABY'   75 days, probably the easiest and sweetest watermelon grown in the family garden; small fruits, 8 inches across. (Readily available)

'YELLOW BABY HYBRID'   70 days, fruits oval to round, 7 inches across, sweet juicy yellow flesh. (Burpee, Harris, Le Marché, Park)

Preserving

Melons can be frozen as melon balls packed in a sugar syrup or in orange juice. Watermelon rinds can be made into pickles and relishes.

Purchasing

Cantaloupe and many similar melons can be judged ripe as much by a full-body fragrance as anything else. Additionally, the melon surface should be firm but also give to moderate pressure applied at the stem end. I test honeydews by shaking them—if the seeds rattle, the melon is ripe. Melons that are soft or blemished or surrounded by fruit flies should be avoided. Identifying a ripe watermelon is difficult and takes experience. Look for dull melons with a yellow underside and an exaggerated sense of weight—the heavier feeling the better.

OKRA   (GUMBO)
Abelmoschus esculentus (Hibiscus esculentus)

Effort Scale
NO. 2
Must be planted annually
Vulnerable to a few minor pests
Harvest every 2 days to prolong crop

Thumbnail Sketch
Herbaceous annual
Standard, 4 to 6 feet tall; dwarf variety, 2 to 4 feet tall
Propagated from seeds
Plant seeds indoors, or outdoors only after soil is thoroughly warm
Plant seeds ½ to 1 inch deep
Germination takes 10 to 14 days at 70° F
Germination best when seeds soaked overnight in tepid water
Thin to 1 to 2 feet apart
Needs fun sun
Leaves lobed, 6 to 10 inches across
Blooms in summer
Flowers hibiscus-like, yellow or red and yellow, 2 to 3 inches across
Seed pods edible; harvested in summer and fall
Used in vegetable gardens, in back of flower beds, and in containers
Some older varieties bear spines that are irritating to skin

Okra, like the olive, is usually an acquired taste. Its best-known use is in seafood or chicken soup or stews, commonly called gumbo. In addition to its flavor, it is valued there for its thickening properties. The pods are also served as a hot boiled vegetable or chilled and served vinaigrette as a salad. Okra can also be fried and is often used in lamb dishes. Cajun and Creole cooking glorify it. See the "Cajun Gardens" chapter for more information.

Okra has a rich vegetable taste, sometimes with sweet or acidic overtones. Others describe the flavor as almost like a snap bean. The texture of okra is generally its most controversial characteristic. Some describe it as slimy, others as slippery. If you object to the slippery quality, see the "Cajun Gardens" chapter for detailed information on cooking okra to eliminate the slipperiness. I am told that straight from the garden and eaten raw, okra is quite sweet, but I have not tried it personally.

How to Grow

Okra needs plenty of heat and summer sun. Plant it in a vegetable garden, or because it is beautiful, use it in the back of a large flower bed. The flowers are creamy-yellow blossoms that usually have red throats, and the large leaves are handsome. Some varieties will grow to 6 feet, so give them plenty of room. One variety, 'Red Okra', has deep-red stems, yellow-and-red flowers, and red pods—a real eye-catcher. Try combining it with peppers and large red salvia. Dwarf varieties grow nicely in large containers.

Okra must have heat and will not tolerate cloudy, cool summers. However, because it matures relatively quickly (50 to 60 days), with patience and careful planning it can be raised anywhere that corn grows well. Besides heat, it requires well-drained soil that includes plenty of humus. Too much nitrogen fertilizer will make it go to leaf instead of producing pods, so keep the applications light. Side dress with manure or a 10-10-10 fertilizer after you have thinned the plants, again after the pods are beginning to set, and once more midway through the season. Okra requires about an inch of water a week. Mulch well to conserve moisture. In cool-summer areas, mulch with black plastic for extra warmth.

Pests and Diseases

Okra has a few pest problems, but they usually are not serious. Ants are sometimes attracted to the flowers, and if caterpillars show up, hand picking is often sufficient since you probably will not be growing very many okra plants (a dozen are usually enough for all but the most ardent okra lovers). *Bacillus thuringiensis* can be used for a serious caterpillar infestation. Stinkbugs can also be controlled with hand picking. Nematodes can be a problem. See Appendix B, "Pests and Diseases." Okra is sometimes prone to verticillium wilt and fusarium wilt. Crop rotate to control these.

Containers

Dwarf okra varieties grow nicely in large containers.

Prolonging the Season

Start your okra seedlings indoors 3 to 4 weeks before the last frost date. To make sure you have a long harvest season, keep the pods picked off regularly or the plants will stop production.

Harvesting

When the plants are about 60 days old they will start producing. Okra pods are best picked before they are 3 inches long. If they are allowed to mature much beyond that, they will probably be woody and the plant will stop pod production. Use a knife or clippers to cut the pod off at its base.

Seed Saving

Okra is usually self-pollinated. Allow pods to ripen completely on the plant before collecting. Cull by hand and allow to dry (about a week) before storing. Because okra ripens seeds one pod at a time over a period of weeks, and is a seed shatterer as well (see "Cabbage and Brussels Sprouts"), if you cannot collect regularly, tie small paper bags over developing heads to catch the seeds.

Varieties

The biggest difference between varieties is in the height of the plant and the color of the pods. Most varieties taste very similar.

'ANNIE OAKLEY' hybrid, 50 days, pods green, spineless, very productive, matures early; plant grows 3 to 4 feet tall. (Gurney, Harris, Hastings)

'CLEMSON SPINELESS' pods green, good for thickening soup; plant grows 4 to 4½ feet tall. (Readily available)

'DWARF GREEN LONG POD' pods green and ribbed, bears early (55 days); plant grows 2½ to 3½ feet tall. (Hastings, Seeds Blum)

'EMERALD' green medium pods, leaves somewhat grayish, plant tall, 6 to 9 feet. (Harris, Lockhart)

'PARK'S CANDELABRA BRANCHING' green thick pods, bears 4 to 6 branches per plant, high yield. (Park)

'RED OKRA' 60 days; red, tender, tasty pods; ornamental plant, tall, to 5 feet, with red stems and leaf veins, flowers yellow with red. (Gurney, Park, Seeds Blum, Southern Exposure)

'WHITE VELVET' large, light-green, tender pods; plant grows to 3½ feet. (Hastings, Seeds Blum)

Preserving

Okra can be pressure canned, frozen, or dried.

Purchasing

If you purchase okra in the market, look for those that are bright green and velvety looking. Small ones are generally the most tender.

ONIONS

BULBING ONIONS *Allium Cepa*
CHIVES *A. Schoenoprasum*

EGYPTIAN ONIONS (tree onions, catawissa onions)   *A. Cepa*, Proliferum Group

GARLIC   *A. sativum*

GARLIC CHIVES (Oriental garlic, Chinese chives)   *A. tuberosum*

LEEKS   *A. Ampeloprasum,* Porrum Group

POTATO ONIONS (multiplier onions)   *A. Cepa,* Aggregatum Group

ROCAMBOLE (serpent garlic, Italian garlic)   *A. sativum* var. *Ophioscorodon*

SHALLOTS   *A. Cepa,* Aggregatum Group

WELCH ONIONS (multiplier onions, ciboule)   *A. fistulosum*

Effort Scale

NO. 2
Some must be planted annually
Thinning or transplanting usually needed
Watering, mulching, and fertilizing needed
Some weeding necessary

Thumbnail Sketch

Annuals, biennials planted as annuals, or perennials
4 inches to 3 feet tall
Propagated from seeds, divisions, sets (bulbs)
Most need full sun; some need partial shade in hot weather
Bladelike leaves vary with species
Flowers usually not seen
Stems, bulbs, young leaves, and in most species flowers edible
Used in flower and vegetable gardens, borders, raised beds, containers

The onion is surely the queen of the kitchen and her various relatives as interesting, useful, and perhaps as eccentric as the assorted members of many royal families. Chives, scallions, leeks, shallots, onions, and garlic make unequaled flavoring additions to many dishes that would be bland and uninspired without them. Onions, in particular, can also stand on their own, baked, boiled, braised, and stuffed. They make you cry because peeling disrupts their volatile compounds, one of which dissolves in your eye fluids, making sulfuric acid.

The several varieties of onions, along with garlic, are members of the same clan, the genus *Allium.* As a group, they all prefer cool weather, particularly in their juvenile stages, and thrive on soil rich in organic matter and phosphorous. They are heavy feeders and should be fertilized, as well as watered, throughout the growing season.

A good deal of confusion and overlap exist among onion types and named categories. This is a particular nuisance when discussing scallions, green onions, and bunching onions. In common usage, scallion is just another name for a green onion. Further, a green onion is really nothing more than the immature shoot of any onion. However, there are varieties of onions that produce particularly fine immature shoots, and they are bred and sold as "green onions" or "scallions." To further confuse the issue there are green onions and scallions banded together and sold as a bunch in grocery stores, and these are sometimes called "bunching onions." Yet some green onions renew themselves from seed, whereas others form bunches underground that may be harvested over a long period and divided and transplanted. The latter are called "multiplier," "Welch," or sometimes "bunching" onions. And "multiplier" is sometimes a name given to potato onions.

The onion clan has flavors and aromas all its own, each a little different from the other but very characteristic of the group as a whole. The tastes and smells can be described as mild and sweet, or strong, hot, biting, odoriferous, or sulfurlike. Onions, in particular, will vary in taste, and one variety will be much hotter in one part of the country than another, or when grown in different soils. Most modern onion breeding has been for sweet onions, but the sharp, less-sweet varieties are better for some dishes.

As there is a good deal of variety amongst the group members, the information below will apply mainly to bulbing onions and leeks. More specific information on the characteristics and culture of each of the other members is discussed under "Varieties."

How to Grow

Bulbing onions are grown from seeds or from young bulbs, called sets. As biennials, onions bulb up the first year when grown from seed and will flower the second if replanted. When planted from sets, they will usually both bulb and flower the first year.

It is important to select the right variety for your climate and time of year because the bulbs are formed according to day length. There are short-day, mid-day, and long-day onion varieties. Short-day onions will bulb when they get about 12 hours of light per day. This makes them most successful when spring-planted in southern regions of the country. Long-day onions require 15 to 16 hours of sunlight each day to bulb up, which makes them ideal for northern areas with their long summer days. Mid-day-onion light requirements fall somewhere in between. Check catalogs for the right variety for your garden, and season as well if you live in a mild-winter area. The wrong variety is most apt to go to flower before it bulbs up.

Sow seeds ¼ inch deep in spring or put out sets; seeds or sets may be started in fall or winter in mild climates. Make sure that the soil is rich and well drained and keep the soil moisture even during the growing season. Fertilize with a balanced fertilizer when plants are about 4 to 6 inches tall and beginning to bulb. Grow onions scattered in wide rows, in single rows, or interplanted in groups or in a border. Depending upon variety, they should be thinned to give each adequate room for unhampered development. Use the thinnings as scallions.

Leeks may be started from seeds directly in the garden in spring or late summer, or they may be started in flats indoors and transplanted. Sow seeds ¼ inch deep in soil rich in organic matter and phosphorous. Seeds and plants are best planted in trenches, about 8 inches deep. As the leeks begin to grow, mound soil up around their stem bases to blanch them as they develop. If sown in place, the plants should be thinned to stand 2½ inches apart. Provide with continued moisture and fertilizer. The thinnings can be used as scallions. Leeks can tolerate more shade than many vegetables, but they will grow slowly without full sun. To grow full-size leeks, plan on 4 to 5 months.

Pests and Diseases
The most common pests attacking onions are onion maggots and thrips. Pyrethrum might be needed to control thrips, and crop rotation and mixing your planting among other plants help control the onion maggot.

Containers
All members of the onion clan grow nicely in containers as long as they are deep enough to allow for adequate moisture and nutrients.

Prolonging the Season
The bulbing onion season can be prolonged by planting seeds indoors 6 to 8 weeks earlier than you could safely plant them outdoors. Transplanted into the garden when small, plants will give you a healthy jump on the new season.

The leek season can be prolonged on the other end by leaving leeks in the ground until freezing weather arrives. They are quite cold tolerant.

The easiest way to have early scallions is to plant some of the perennial multiplier types that come up early in the spring.

Harvesting
Do not harvest bulbing onions for storage until their tops die down. You can hasten this process by bending the tops over. Then dig up the onions and let them stay on top of the soil to dry out for at least a day. The bulbs must be protected from sunburn, which you can do easily by covering them with their tops. Most varieties are ready for harvest in 90 to 110 days. Place them on a screen or hang them where there is good air circulation to "cure" (allow the skins to dry) for several additional weeks before their final storage.

Leeks are generally harvested as they are needed and used right away. They are lifted when 1 to 3 inches in diameter.

Seed Saving
Onion and leek plants used to produce seeds should be lifted from the ground in the late fall and planted out to bloom in the early spring. In warm-winter areas, they can be left to overwinter in place. Seeds should be collected promptly and gently as they shatter easily. Cut off seed heads, place on cloth to dry, and collect seeds over the cloth.

All onions are pollinated by insects and will cross within their own species (leeks with leeks and onions with onions) but not outside it. For this reason, it is best to plant only one variety of whatever type you will save seed from in any given year.

Varieties
Bulbing Onions
'BARLETTA' 70 days; baby onions used for stews, soups, and boiling; 1½ inches ideal size. (Le Marché, Shepherd's, Stokes)

'FIESTA' 110 days, hybrid, long-day; yellow, sweet Spanish type; good storage qualities, very productive. (Lockhart, Park, Shepherd's, Stokes)

'FRESNO WHITE' medium-day; large, pungent white onion; holds zesty flavor when cooked. (Lockhart)

'GRANEX' ('VIDALIA') 80 days, hybrid, short-day; large and exceptionally sweet when grown in South; seldom as sweet when grown away from its preferred home in Georgia or Texas. (Readily available)

'RED HAMBURGER' 95 days, medium-day, extra sweet, mild, deep-red skin, white flesh. (Readily available)

'SWEET SPANISH' 110 days, hybrid, long-day, large storage onion with mild flesh. (Burpee, Gurney, Johnny's, Stokes)

'WALLA WALLA SWEET' 125 days if spring seeded, 300 days if sown in late summer and left to overwinter; long-day, large Spanish type, known for sweet and juicy flesh; best if seeded in late summer and left to overwinter. (Readily available)

Chives
Chives are generally propagated from divisions or seeds, or purchased in pots. These miniature onions can sit on a sunny windowsill for a couple of months or be planted close to the kitchen door for easy access. Chives are small, tufted plants with bright-green, upright tubular leaves and small lavender flowers. They do not have swollen bulbs, but their mildly onion flavored leaves are cut from the plant as needed and used fresh. The plant goes dormant during winter months.

Chives are not usually sold by variety, but seeds and container plants are readily available.

Egyptian Onions
This onion, also called tree or catawissa onion, is a perennial and probably the hardiest and easiest to care for of

them all. It is also, perhaps, the strangest in behavior and appearance. Unlike bulbing onions, Egyptian onions do not have a swollen base but rather a more rounded base that splits into several sections and sends out slender green shoots that can be used as green onions. After these shoots have flowered, little bulbs, called "bulbils," form at the end of each shoot. If they are not harvested, when their weight is too great to be supported by the hollow stems, they fall over and take root, and the next generation is begun.

When ordering Egyptian onions you will receive bulbils in cluster form. If the bulbils are as large as the end of your little finger, plant them singly. If they are smaller, plant the whole cluster. They should be planted in trenches about 6 inches deep and 1 foot apart. As their green shoots begin to emerge, fill in the trench with soil a bit at a time. This will produce long, white, blanched stalks.

While all parts of Egyptian onions are edible, most popular are their young stalks, which are tender in the spring and used much like green onions, and their bulbils, which although quite small are used much like cloves of garlic. Egyptian onions are readily available from mail-order sources but are not sold by named variety.

Garlic

Garlic plants are grown from cloves of garlic that can be purchased in heads from nurseries or food markets. Although easily grown, garlic performs best in milder, dry climates. It should be planted in the fall or early spring for best development before the summer harvest season. Ample and consistent water is needed for the first 4 or 5 months of development, as well as full sun. Garlic is hardy to all but the most severe cold and virtually free of pests and diseases.

Divide heads into individual cloves and plant about 1 inch deep and 4 inches apart. Garlic does best in soil with a good deal of added organic matter. In areas of severely cold winters, mulch with straw to protect fall-started plants.

Garlic is ready for harvest when the plant tops turn brown and die back. Dig the heads carefully and allow them to dry on a screen in the shade, protected from sunburn, as with onions. To prevent rotting and to allow you to braid them, several inches of dried stalk should be retained on each head. Store them in a cool, dry area with good air circulation.

Garlic is available through catalogs or from nurseries and food markets. Occasionally unique varieties appear, such as a pink-skinned type. Elephant garlic, larger and more mildly flavored, is readily available. It is not a true garlic and stores poorly. Overall, smaller types are considered to have the best flavor.

When purchasing garlic in produce departments, either for the table or for garden planting, look for well-filled-out heads ("buxom" seems a good description) that are very firm to the touch. Soft cloves are beginning to deteriorate, so avoid them.

Garlic Chives

The leaves of this small, tufted plant—also known as Oriental garlic or Chinese chives—are flat and bladelike and in Western kitchens are used like chives to add a garlic flavor to salads, soups, and eggs. In the Orient, they are treated as a vegetable and are considered a delicacy. The plants are grown like regular chives and are started from slow-germinating seeds or divisions and produce white flowers. See "Chives" above and the "Oriental Gardens" chapter. (Readily available)

Leeks

There are a great number of leek varieties, but the following are of particular interest.

'BLUE SOLAISE'   exceptionally attractive heirloom variety, cold tolerant, turns almost violet with cool fall weather. (Cook's, Le Marché)

'BROAD LONDON' ('LARGE AMERICAN FLAG')   130 days, hybrid, thick stems, mild onion flavor, good overwintering variety. (Burpee, Lockhart, Park)

'DE CARENTAN'   early variety for spring planting and late-summer harvest; mild enough for salads, productive, good keeper in the ground. (Shepherd's)

'TITAN'   110 days, stalks extra long and thicker than most. (Burpee, Seeds Blum)

Potato Onions

Potato onions, also called "multiplier onions," derive their common names from their method of reproduction and its similarity to that of potatoes. Potato onions are perennials that generally do not produce seeds but rather reproduce by dividing underground to produce clusters of new 2- to 4-inch bulbs. A large potato onion bulb should be planted in early fall or early spring, and after the top dies down, a cluster of small bulbs will be found at its base. These are harvested and thoroughly cured. The clusters are then broken apart, generally with some being used for eating and others reserved for next year's crop. The small bulbs will produce single large onions, and the large ones produce clusters. If you plant a variety of bulb sizes you will not only have both sizes for eating but also keep a variety of sizes coming along all the time. They are a marvelous way to have onions in the garden most of the year without continual replanting.

Potato onions are very hardy, highly productive, resistant to most pests and diseases, and easy to grow, particularly in soils with a high clay content, in which onion culture can be difficult.

As is true with any continued inbreeding, there is a greater chance of continuing diseases from year to year with potato onions, so be sure to get your first set of bulbs from a reputable dealer. It is also wise to rotate your onion bed every few years.

Potato onions are available from Southern Exposure and Seeds Blum.

Rocambole

Rocambole, also known as Italian or serpent garlic—the latter for the shape of its stem—is a top-setting garlic forming bulbils at the top of the stem. Either these or the cloves formed underground may be used in the kitchen or planted to continue the crop. Rocambole is available from DeGiorgi and Seeds Blum.

Shallots

Shallots are a form of multiplier onion that develops an elongated bulb. They are very mild in flavor and are prized for kitchen use, particularly in French cuisine. As is the case with potato onions, they are planted from sets (small bulbs) in spring or fall and are very hardy. Each small bulb divides during the growing season to form a cluster of six or more new bulbs. The 'French Shallot', the traditional reddish-pink bulb, is available from Gurney, Johnny's, Le Marché, and Southern Exposure. The latter also carries several other varieties.

Welch Onions

Welch onions, sometimes called "multiplier onions" or ciboule, do not develop bulbs but rather slightly swollen, elongated roots with hollow stems and leaves. They are planted from seeds, and while they do flower and set seeds, most varieties also multiply at the base, much like potato onions and shallots. They are used in salads, soups, and stir-fries and are among several types commonly known as "green onions" or "scallions."

If you enjoy having scallions available for much of the spring and summer and are pressed for time, Welch onions are the best way to keep a constant, effortless supply as they don't need replanting each spring. They are a wonderful example of the many options available to the home gardener that have been discarded over the years in the push for "progress" (agriculture finds it easier to replant a harvest by machine). Why is it we have all been led to plant scallion seeds every spring when they will come up by themselves if we choose a multiplying type?

Plant Welch onions from seed in loose garden loam in the spring. They should reach a good size the first year, with some division at the base. If you prefer long, white blanched stems, when growth begins the second year, dig the onions up and replant them in 6-inch-deep trenches lined with compost or manure. As the plants grow, gradually fill in the trench. See "Leeks" above. Harvest as needed. Seed stalks will form at the end of the second season. When young they may be harvested as well and can be used like chives.

'BELTSVILLE BUNCHING' 65 days, crisp mild flavor that stands up under dry summer heat, perhaps best variety for August harvest. (Seeds Blum, Stokes)
'EVERGREEN HARDY WHITE' 65 days, most cold hardy of the bunching onions. (Readily available)

'HE-SHI-KO' 80 days, light green, early maturing; clusters of two to three stalks 12 to 14 inches long; Welch onion formerly known as 'Prolific White Bunching'. (Gurney, Nichols)
'RED BEARD' 60 days, vigorous, harvested late summer and early fall, shaft turns red in cool fall temperatures; lovely to look at, crisp and mild to the taste; not a true "multiplier" onion. (Shepherd's)

Preserving

Store cured bulbing onions in a cool, dry place with about 2 inches of their tops left in place. Hang them by the tops, preferably in a place where they do not have to touch one another.

Although freezing changes their flavor slightly, bulbing onions can also be cut into small pieces and frozen in plastic freezer bags until needed for seasoning.

In all but the coldest climates, leeks can be stored in the ground if well mulched. If harvesting is necessary, they can be frozen.

Purchasing

When purchasing bulbing onions, look for globes that are totally dry to the touch and that have no onion odor. Either moisture or smell suggests an internal bruising.

Leeks are best selected on the basis of size desired and freshness. Generally leeks larger than 2 inches in diameter become tough and exaggerated in flavor. Europeans prefer young, ½-inch-wide leeks. You might want to try yours at this stage too.

PARSNIPS, RUTABAGAS, AND TURNIPS

PARSNIPS *Pastinaca sativa*
RUTABAGAS *Brassica Napus*, Napobrassica Group
TURNIPS *B. Rapa*, Rapifera Group

Effort Scale

NO. 2
Must be planted annually
Thinning usually needed
Watering needed
Some weeding necessary

Thumbnail Sketch

Annuals, or biennials planted as annuals
6 inches to 3 feet tall
Propagated from seeds
Plant seeds ¼ to ½ inch deep
Germination time dependent on vegetable
Most need full sun; some need partial shade in hot weather

Leaves vary with species
Flowers not usually seen
Roots edible; some have edible leaves
Used in vegetable gardens, raised beds, containers

These wonderful, hearty vegetables bring to mind cold winter days with a steaming bowl of soup or stew filled with rutabagas and parsnips, or a savory pork roast served with mashed turnips. In the Orient young turnips are enjoyed raw or lightly sautéed in oil. The rutabagas and parsnips represent security to many who enjoy living off the land as they are easily grown and will store reliably through the winter.

The tastes can be strong, aromatic, metallic, sweet, bitter, hot, or even mustardy. Generally the taste of these vegetables improves with a light frost, and they are at their best in late fall or winter. The textures can be crisp, dense, fibrous, smooth, or mushy.

How to Grow
These vegetables prefer cool weather and need well-drained, loose soil that will not impede their growth or contort their shape. They need little fertilizing if planted in good soil.

The most important elements in successful parsnip culture are good soil and timely seed sowing. Parsnips need a deeply prepared bed free of rocks and obstacles in order to develop straight, smooth roots.

Parsnips are best sown in place. They are slow to germinate (2 to 3 weeks) but will sprout faster if seeds are soaked in warm water for 24 hours before planting. Use fresh seeds and plant ¼ inch deep in rows 12 to 18 inches apart, or broadcast in wide rows. Keep damp until the seedlings emerge. Thin to 4 to 5 inches apart. Water evenly.

Parsnips take from 100 to 130 days to mature. Since their starches are converted to sugars at temperatures approaching freezing, it is best to time their planting so the roots may be touched by frost but harvested before the ground is likely to freeze. In mild-winter areas, seeds can be sown in the late summer as well for late winter harvest.

Turnips and their close relatives rutabagas should also be planted in place. Their seeds germinate much more quickly than parsnip seeds—in 5 to 10 days. Plant turnip and rutabaga seeds about ½ inch deep in rows or wide beds. If turnips are being grown for greens, do not thin. If growing for roots, thin to 3 to 4 inches apart when plants are about 4 inches tall. Thin rutabagas as you would for turnip roots. Use thinnings cooked or in salads. Both need about 1 inch of water per week. Underwatered turnips and rutabagas are bitter tasting.

Turnips mature in 1 to 2 months. Many people prefer young, tender "baby" turnips. These can be planted in early spring for harvest before warm weather but are best planted in late summer for harvest in the fall when they are much sweeter. Rutabagas take about 3 months to mature, so it is more difficult to get in a spring crop before warm

weather sets in. Summer or early fall planting of rutabagas is preferred as frost improves both their flavor and texture and they store well.

Pests and Diseases
Parsnips are virtually free of pests and diseases, being bothered only occasionally by canker. Turnips and rutabagas are sometimes bothered by flea beetles, cabbage root maggots, and cabbage caterpillars.

Containers
Parsnips, rutabagas, and turnips can be grown in containers if they are large enough and deep enough to allow the roots to develop unimpeded.

Prolonging the Season
The thinnings of all three vegetables can be eaten early in the season. The mature roots keep for some time in the ground in fall and winter, and the parsnips and rutabagas can be stored in the refrigerator or root cellar for months.

Harvesting
Harvest parsnips after a few frosty nights have started to change stored starches into sugars. In cold-winter areas, parsnips may be left in the ground all winter if mulched. In mild-winter areas, they can be allowed to remain in the ground, to be harvested as needed. Overwintered parsnips must be harvested before they begin to grow again in the spring, or their texture will become woody and tough.

Turnip greens should be used when they are young and tender. Pick a few leaves from each plant as soon as the leaves are large enough to handle. Keep doing this until the greens get tough or bitter. Special varieties have been developed for their superior greens; see "Varieties," below, for information on these. The particular variety determines the harvest time for turnip and rutabaga roots. Generally speaking, the standard varieties are best when harvested about the size of a tennis ball, while the hybrid whites are better at half that size.

Rutabagas may be harvested at about the same size as turnips or larger. They remain of high quality when left in the ground to be harvested as needed.

Seed Saving
As a biennial, the parsnip sets seed during its second growing season. Because parsnips overwinter even in areas with very cold winters, the plants can be left in the ground and will develop seed heads in late spring or early summer. The seed shatters, so gather seed pods as they turn brown. Parsnips are cross-pollinated, usually by bees.

Rutabagas are also biennials. In cold-winter areas, remove the leafy tops from firm, healthy roots at the fall harvest. Store the roots in a cool, humid place until spring. Replant roots in spring and collect seed pods as they dry but before they shatter. In mild-winter areas, roots can be mulched and left in the garden until spring. Rutabagas are also cross-pollinated by insects.

Turnips are annuals and will produce seed the same season if planted early in the year. In mild-winter areas, if planted in the fall, they will overwinter in the ground and set seed the following spring. Where winters are severe, they need to be lifted in the late fall. Though they are more perishable, they are generally stored as with rutabagas and replanted in the spring. They are cross-pollinated and must be separated from other turnip varieties as well as from mustard and Chinese cabbage, with which they will also cross.

Varieties

Parsnips
'COBHAM IMPROVED MARROW' 120 days; half-long, tapered white root with extremely high sugar content; resistant to canker. (Johnny's)
'HARRIS MODEL' 120 days, 10- to 12-inch white root, fine texture and flavor, very few side roots. (Readily available)
'HOLLOW CROWN' 105 days, 12-inch tapered root, relatively free of side roots, fine-grained flesh. (Readily available)

Rutabagas
'AMERICAN PURPLE TOP' 90 days, pale-yellow flesh with purple shoulders, sweet and fine grained, stores well. (Readily available)
'CANADIAN GEM' extremely hardy, good choice for northern gardens. (Seeds Blum)
'LAURENTIAN' 95 days, fast becoming the most popular variety in North America, good keeper with uniform roots, cooks orange. (Johnny's, Jung, Seeds Blum, Stokes)

Turnips
'DE MILAN' 35 days, very fast flat-shaped spring variety, white bottoms with rosy red shoulders, pick when small. (Le Marché, Shepherd's)
'JUST RIGHT' 40 days, hybrid, good-quality greens and roots, good keeper. (Harris, Park, Twilley)
'PURPLE TOP WHITE GLOBE' 55 days, most popular variety for home gardens, grown for both greens and roots, globes with white bottoms and purple shoulders. (Readily available)
'TOKYO CROSS' 35 days, hybrid, grown for both greens and roots, pure white and smooth, stays nonwoody even when left in ground past maturity, disease resistant. (Readily available)

Preserving
Parsnips and rutabagas can be harvested and preserved in a cool, damp, dark place for many months. They can also be left in the ground. Parsnips, rutabagas, and turnips can be frozen using standard freezing techniques.

Purchasing
When shopping for parsnips, look for plump roots that are smooth and free of pits or cuts. They should be firm with no sign of shriveling.

Rutabagas and turnips should also be smooth and unshriveled. In the market, the rutabaga that feels heavy is preferable to a lightweight one. Rutabagas are very susceptible to drying out and are often sprayed with a waxy coating to prevent dehydration. Turnips should be about the size of tennis balls—you will know the roots are fresh if the greens are still attached. Turnips are more fragile than rutabagas and will last only a week in the refrigerator. Rutabagas will store there for over a month.

PEAS
SHELLING PEAS (garden peas, English peas, green peas) *Pisum sativum*
EDIBLE-PODDED PEAS (Chinese pea pods, snow peas, sugar snap peas) *P. sativum* var. *macrocarpon*

Effort Scale
NO. 3
Must be planted annually
Trellising needed with tall varieties, recommended with dwarfs
Watering and fertilizing necessary
Some weeding needed
Pests occasionally a problem
Harvesting is time consuming

Thumbnail Sketch
Herbaceous annual vines
2 to 6 feet tall
Propagated from seeds
Plant seeds 1 to 2 inches deep
Germination takes 6 to 15 days at 60° F
Need full sun; will tolerate some shade in warm climates
Leaves blue-green, oval, 1 to 2 inches long
Bloom in spring, fall, or winter
Flowers leguminous, white or purple, grow in clusters
Seeds, pods, shoots, and flowers edible; harvested in spring or fall
Used in vegetable gardens, raised beds, containers

Few garden vegetables are as succulent or sweet as fresh garden peas. Steamed shelled peas are a luxury to be savored one spoonful at a time, or if the harvest is generous, to be squandered in soups, salads, and stews.

Used fresh, the sweet, crunchy, succulent pods of the edible-podded pea, frequently referred to as the Chinese or snow pea, dress up a salad or add sophistication to a raw-vegetable platter. The pods can be steamed briefly and served as a cooked vegetable and are often used in stir-fried Oriental dishes. Snow peas are extremely expensive in the market, adding to the pleasure of growing your own.

Sugar snap peas, close cousins of snow peas, are also edible podded. Their pods are thicker and more succulent than snow or Chinese pea pods, and their peas are larger and sweeter. It is not necessary to shell them, but they sometimes need stringing. Sugar snap peas have become very popular in the last few years, and many gardeners will no longer grow any other type.

The pea plant's full range of edible parts and the interesting options in pea varieties are generally underutilized. The young shoots are considered a great delicacy in the Orient and taste much like the peas themselves. They can be enjoyed steamed and served with butter or included in a stir-fry. The blossoms too are edible and are elegant used to decorate canapés, cream soups, salads, or even a spring wedding cake. Consider broadening your use of peas and grow some of the varieties selected for drying or making fresh pea soup. These peas contain more starch, which makes them store better dry and gives a special creaminess to the soup. To determine which peas are best for soups and drying, look at the pea seed. As with corn seeds, the smoother the pea seed is, the more starch it usually contains; the more wrinkled, the more sugar.

Pea plants are either short bushes or long climbing vines from 5 to 6 feet tall. They have bluish-green leaves 1 to 2 inches long, white or lavender legume-type flowers, and some tendrils. Most varieties of both shelling and edible-podded peas have attractive foliage and can be grown on a trellis or fence combined with a flowering vine such as nasturtium.

The flavors of fresh peas seem elusive, yet so distinctive. They can be sweet, rich, aromatic, grasslike, astringent, or starchy. Their texture can be succulent, creamy, tough, or pasty. The pods can be tender, succulent, crunchy, stringy, or tough.

Caution: Do not confuse shelling or edible-podded peas with sweet peas, or grow them together. Sweet peas are poisonous.

How to Grow

Peas are annuals requiring well-prepared, humus-rich soil, full sun, high humidity, and cool weather. They can tolerate some frost but do poorly in hot weather. They are grown in the spring in cold climates; in the spring, fall, and winter in mild-winter areas; and in summer in locations where temperatures at that time of year are cool.

The soil should be nonacidic and well drained. Pea seeds should be planted directly into the garden in early spring. Plant seeds 1 to 2 inches deep and 3 to 6 inches apart in double rows. Peas do not suffer from crowding, so 2-inch spacing between rows is sufficient. Sets of double rows can be planted 24 to 30 inches apart, which allows path space for future care and harvesting.

Peas, like other legumes, have the ability to take nitrogen from the air and, with the help of soil bacteria, put it to use in their own growth cycle, then leave it behind in nodules on their roots. This process takes place efficiently only in the presence of the bacteria specific to the crop being planted. Powdered inoculants containing the specific bacteria can be used to treat the seed prior to planting, and I recommend their use. Many seed companies carry them, as do well-stocked local nurseries. There are different types of inoculant, so make sure to get the one for peas. Inoculants are inexpensive, easy to use, and absolutely harmless.

Most pea varieties profit from trellising or some other form of support. Even the dwarf varieties look and produce better if given something to lean on. Trellising allows the pods to hang down straight, which makes for better-shaped pods and ease of picking. Supports should be placed in the ground at the time of planting. Peas need only a light fertilizing when about 6 inches tall but profit from regular and deep watering—1 inch per week is ideal. They also respond well to organic mulches.

Pests and Diseases

Peas are in the most danger from pests as seedlings. At this stage, they are most attractive to slugs, snails, and birds. Cover the seedlings until they are 6 inches high. Another pest, the pea weevil, is not usually a serious problem, but large numbers should be controlled. To deter, try lightly dusting wet or dew-covered foliage with lime. Pea moths can be controlled with *Bacillus thuringiensis*. For pea thrips, try a hard spray of water with a nozzle, or sponge foliage with a mild soap solution. To prevent mildew, do not water plants from above and avoid afternoon watering so that plant foliage is not damp when darkness falls. Plant varieties resistant to sometimes troublesome diseases such as fusarium wilt, downy mildew, leaf curl virus, and in the Northwest, enation virus.

Containers

Dwarf varieties are attractive in large containers, either alone or mixed with other colorful annuals, if never allowed to dry out.

Prolonging the Season

The pea season is short—generally no longer than 4 to 6 weeks. While there is little that can be done to lengthen this time period, you can get the most out of those productive weeks by being careful to pick all peas as soon as they are fully ripe.

Harvesting

Ideally, peas should be harvested every day during the mature-pod stage. If left past maturity, they begin to lose their sweetness and become tough. The plants also will cut back on production. To avoid damaging the plants, peas should be picked carefully, and with two hands—one to hold the stem and the other to pluck or cut off the ripe pod.

Shelling peas are ripe when the pods are filled out but before they begin to lose their glossy green color and start to harden. Pick Chinese or snow peas when the pods are still soft and pliable and the seeds inside are still small. Sugar snap peas should be harvested looking as filled out as shelling peas, even though they will be eaten pod and all. They tend to get sweeter and sweeter as they get larger and larger inside their pods.

Seed Saving

According to Jan Blum of Seeds Blum, although peas are self-pollinating, they have an unexpectedly high incidence of crossing resulting from the wanderings of insects. She recommends that different varieties be separated by at least 150 feet. Pods should be left on the vine until thoroughly dry. In wet climates, harvest the plants and put in a cool, dry place. Less than fully dry peas will result in inferior seeds next season. When fully dry, pods should be pulled from the vines and left to dry for another week or two, just to be sure they are truly dry. Collect seeds from dry pods and store in airtight containers.

Varieties

Shelling Peas

'ALASKA' 55 days, earliest of all the peas, low sugar content, dries very well as split peas; vines 30 to 36 inches tall. (Burpee, Park, Seeds Blum, Vermont Bean)

'ALDERMAN' ('TALL TELEPHONE') 68 days, high quality and production; large vine, to 6 feet. (Readily available)

'CORVALLIS' 65 days, 2- to 3-foot semi-bush type; does well in cool, damp areas; highly resistant to mosaic virus and pea enation. (Nichols, Territorial)

'GREEN ARROW' 70 days, very sweet peas, high-yielding vines of exceptional production, 24 to 28 inches tall; resistant to downy mildew and fusarium wilt. (Readily available)

'LITTLE MARVEL' 63 days, early and heavy producer; small vines, to 2 feet; peas freeze well. (Burpee, Park, Seeds Blum, Stokes, Vermont Bean)

'NOVELLA' 57 days, semi-leafless variety, pronounced flowers and pods; fiberless shoots taste like broccoli; neat and uniform bushy plants, 18 to 24 inches high; a similar variety is 'Bikini'. (Nichols, Park, Seeds Blum, Stokes, Thompson & Morgan)

'WANDO' 68 days, very productive 30-inch vines, good in warm-weather areas. (Readily available)

'WAVEREX' 65 days, petit pois type, very tiny and tasty, intense pea flavor; 15-inch semi-bush plants, require staking. (Bountiful, Le Marché, Thompson & Morgan)

Edible-Podded Peas

'DWARF GRAY SUGAR' 65 days, snow pea type, prolific producer, good cold and heat tolerance; semi-bush, 2 to 2½ feet tall, reddish-purple flowers. (Readily available)

'OREGON SUGAR POD II' 64 days, snow pea type, very hardy and prolific, vines to 4 feet; exceptional resistance to heat, cold, and pea enation; perhaps most popular of this type. (Readily available)

'SUGAR MEL' 68 days, sugar snap type, short bush variety with vigorous 3-foot vines, very large sweet pods, very high resistance to heat and powdery mildew. (Park, Shepherd's)

'SUGAR SNAP' 62 days, delicious, very prolific; frost, heat, and wilt resistant; vines to 6 feet; many gardeners swear they will never grow another variety. (Readily available)

See the "French Gardens" and "Heirloom Gardens" chapters for additional varieties.

Preserving

Garden peas are best preserved by freezing, and the starchy varieties can be dried. Canning is tricky and does not produce a quality result, so is not recommended.

Snow peas may also be preserved by freezing, though they lose some of their crunch, but do not dry or can well.

Purchasing

Peas are high in natural sugar. As is the case with corn, the sugar begins to turn to starch as soon as the pods are picked. Secure the freshest-possible peas when buying them at the market. Look for pods that are bright in color and snap, rather than bend, when pressure is applied to them. Old peas are generally obvious—they look a little withered and are dull in color.

PEPPERS
Capsicum spp.

Effort Scale

NO. 3
Must be planted annually
Some watering, fertilizing, and weeding necessary
Easy only within a fairly narrow temperature range

Thumbnail Sketch

Herbaceous perennials usually treated as annuals; occasionally grown as perennials in frost-free climates
1½ to 3 feet tall
Propagated from seeds
Plant seeds ¼ inch deep
Germination takes 10 to 15 days at 70° F

Need full sun; will tolerate some shade
Leaves deep green, 2 to 4 inches long
Bloom in summer
Flowers small, white
Fruits edible; harvested in summer
Used in vegetable gardens, flower borders, raised beds,
    herb gardens, containers

Peppers are far and away my favorite garden vegetable. Some, like the sweet bell, are elegantly beautiful with their glossy green color and soft curves. Others are like sassy children, peeking out jauntily from the plants in a variety of shapes, sizes, and colors. Their garden and kitchen uses are probably more numerous and varied than those of any other vegetable. And their caloric content is very low (22 calories per medium-size bell), while their nutritive value is exceedingly high. Even the leaves of some species are eaten in some cultures.

Pepper plants are so decorative, with their handsome, bushy, dark-green foliage, that they are welcome in the flower border, where they might be combined with dwarf salvia, verbena, and dwarf marigold ('Lemon Gem' or 'Tangerine Gem', perhaps).

Some varieties display their yellow or red fruits upright at the top of the plant. If you plant this kind, be sure to provide some afternoon shade to protect them from sunburn.

There are many adjectives to describe the flavors of peppers. When you are tasting a pepper and judging its qualities, and which variety might appeal to you, think about these characteristics: fragrant, sweet, sour, grassy, lively, fruity, rich, full-bodied, earthy, nutty, applelike, bitter, metallic, and even an alum aftertaste. And of course there is a fiery hotness in the chili peppers. The textures of peppers can be described as juicy, crisp, tender, tough, dry, or even papery.

How to Grow

Peppers are a warm-weather crop. They cannot tolerate frost and won't set fruit unless the weather is at least 65° F but does not exceed 80° F. They also need a long growing season—120 days from seed to maturity—so it is most useful to start them indoors and move them out into the garden, but only after the weather has warmed. Start them in flats or peat pots 8 to 10 weeks before the average last frost date for your area.

After they are 3 to 4 inches tall and all danger of frost is past, transplant them into the garden. Do not move them out too early as too cool weather at transplant time will result in poor growth all season. It is best to wait until night temperatures are above 55° F and the air and soil are warm and settled.

Plants should be placed at least 18 inches apart in full sun or partial shade. They require deep, rich soil and regular watering and fertilizing. The fertilizer used should not be too high in nitrogen as that element encourages leaf development at the expense of fruit development. Peppers are heavy feeders and respond well to regular applications of manure, fish emulsion, and kelp. According to Craig Drummond of the Redwood City Seed Company, who has done extensive research on the growing of peppers, in many soils they frequently suffer from calcium deficiency, the symptoms of which look a good deal like nitrogen deficiency. Should these symptoms occur (paler than normal and curling leaves), try adding calcium in the form of dolomite.

Pests and Diseases

Tender pepper plants are popular with snails, slugs, aphids, and cutworms. Otherwise, the plants are relatively pest free. They are occasionally prone to the same diseases that afflict tomatoes. Keep plants mulched and weeds under control.

Containers

Most pepper plants are striking in containers. They look especially nice in large, old-fashioned clay pots. The colors seem meant for each other.

Prolonging the Season

Peppers will continue to produce fruits until the weather cools, so Mother Nature has the most influence on the length of the harvest at the end of the season. However, because peppers require such a long growing season, in many cooler areas the season can be lengthened by starting seeds indoors, and by covering the plants at night in the fall.

Harvesting

Sweet peppers can develop and ripen through a wide range of colors, depending upon the variety. Many are green through most of their development but turn red as they reach full maturity. Others go through a series of color changes—from green to purple to red; from green to yellow to red; from green to black to red; from green to brown; and any number of other variations on the same range of colors.

Once sweet peppers get near full size they can be picked at their green, red, purple, brown, or yellow stages. If you wait for them to color up (change from green to whatever color comes next for that variety), they will have more flavor and nutrition. They produce from 1 to 2 pounds per plant.

Hot peppers can also be picked at any color stage, but most are hotter if allowed to ripen fully. For more information on the maturing of hot peppers, see the "Chili Gardens" chapter. Hot peppers also produce from 1 to 2 pounds per plant.

Seed Saving

Peppers, like cucumbers and tomatoes, carry their seeds within edible flesh. To gather seeds, harvest the fruits when they are just slightly overripe and beginning to look a little bit withered. Select those peppers that are just past the point you'd want to eat them. The fruits, however, must not be rotting. Generally speaking, ripe peppers are red in color. There are numerous exceptions, however. See above for more information on the color progression of various varieties.

To collect the seeds, you can spoon them out or cut the stem end of the pepper off and tap the seeds free. Dry seeds for about 2 weeks, then store for next year.

If you have had problems with seed-borne bacterial diseases, you may want to soak your seeds for 20 to 25 minutes. Remove seeds from peppers, soak in warm water (122° F), rinse in cool water, and dry well.

In those areas where a short growing season prevents peppers from ever ripening to the fully mature, seed-saving stage, slightly underripe peppers can be harvested and brought inside to mature on a sunny windowsill, or the whole plant may be pulled up and hung in a shed or garage.

While peppers are usually self-pollinated, insects sometimes transfer pollen from one type and variety to another. Hot peppers cross much more readily than sweet, and they will cross with sweet as well. In this case the fruits can become as hot as the dominant gene in the hot variety. (See the "Chili Gardens" chapter for specific information on pollination of chili peppers.) If you are concerned about cross-pollination, grow only one variety or cover the plants with one of the new row covers, like Reemay, to restrict insect activity. In this event, you should hand pollinate the hot peppers for the best fruit set. See the "Chili Gardens" chapter for more information on hand pollination of peppers.

Varieties

Sweet Peppers

'ACE'   50 days, hybrid, exceptionally early crop of green bells; very prolific, even in areas where peppers are problematic. (Burpee, Johnny's)

'BLOCKY BELL'   70 days, hybrid, very large crunchy green bells, good resistance to tobacco mosaic virus. (Park, Vermont Bean)

'EARLY PIMENTO'   75 days, medium-size plant; delicious red, heart-shaped fruit, thick walled, sweet. (Burpee)

'GOLDEN BELL'   70 days, hybrid, compact plant; large, sweet fruits; first green, then turning to yellow. (Lockhart, Park, Twilley, Vermont Bean)

'GYPSY'   65 days, hybrid; fruits medium size, wedge shaped, yellow, thin walled, tender and crunchy; plants 12 to 20 inches tall; more reliable producer in cool climates than most. (Readily available)

'PURPLE BELL'   72 days, hybrid; fruits color from green to purple to red as they mature; excellent flavor and unique color when fresh, turn green when cooked. (Burpee, Park, Stokes)

Hot Peppers

'LARGE RED CHERRY'   77 days, bright-red hot pepper, round, thick walled, good for pickling. (Harris, Nichols, Seeds Blum, Twilley)

'PAPRIKA'   85 days, quite mild; flattened, four-lobed fruits 2 inches long, 4 inches in diameter; dried and ground to make paprika. (Le Marché, Nichols, Seeds Blum)

'PEPPERONCINI'   65 days, slightly hot green pepper, often pickled for antipasto; shrubby 3-foot plant. (Le Marché, Nichols, Seeds Blum, Stokes)

'THAI HOT CHILI'   very hot, 1- to 1½-inch-long peppers grow upright, turn red when mature; can be used fresh or dried; exceptionally attractive plant. (Le Marché, Park)

See the "Chili Gardens" chapter for additional varieties.

Plants and seeds for peppers are available from local nurseries, but for a wide selection of varieties you will need to contact a mail-order firm. For a large selection of European varieties contact Le Marché and Shepherd's; for a good selection of particularly ornamental varieties such as 'Park's Pot', 'Tequila Sunrise', and 'Thai Hot' contact Park; and for a good selection of heirloom varieties contact Redwood City Seed and Seeds Blum. Two seed companies that specialize in peppers are The Pepper Gal, Dorothy Van Vleck, 10536 119th Avenue N, Largo, FL 33543, and Horticultural Enterprises.

Preserving

Both sweet and hot peppers can be frozen or dried. Thin-walled peppers are best for drying, thick-walled ones for freezing. Freezing will soften peppers, but the flavor is still excellent. Both types of pepper are used in the preparation of pepper jelly, a wonderful condiment for use with meat and delicious with cream cheese on crackers as an hors d'oeuvre. Peppers can also be pickled.

To freeze, wash and cut into small pieces. (I use my food processor for large batches.) Pack in thin layers in freezer bags for use throughout the year. Just break off the amount you need and return the rest to the freezer. Or brush split fruits or strips with a little olive oil, put them on a cookie sheet, and roast them at 400° until they are just starting to brown. Keep turning them every few minutes once they start to sizzle. Take out and cool, then put in containers and freeze. See *The Victory Garden Cookbook* for much more information on preserving peppers.

For information on hang drying hot peppers, see the "Chili Gardens" chapter.

Purchasing

When shopping for either sweet or hot peppers, look for fruits that are bright in color and firm to the touch. Sallow, anemic-looking fruits are probably underripe, while fruits that appear withered or wrinkled are past their prime. Fancy bell peppers are sometimes waxed, and some of the waxes contain fungicides. Before using, wash with water and a bit of detergent and rinse.

POTATOES
Solanum tuberosum

Effort Scale
NO. 2
Must be planted annually
Water, mulching, and fertilizing needed
Some weeding necessary

Thumbnail Sketch
Annuals
To 2 feet tall
Propagated from tubers, less often from seeds
Germination takes 5 to 10 days at 70° F
Need full sun
Leaves deep green, heavy textured, poisonous
Flowers white or lavender; some varieties showy
Tubers edible
Used in vegetable gardens, in back of flower borders, and in large containers

Potatoes, comforting potatoes. When life is pressing in, I love to make myself a baked or boiled potato. I dress it with a little butter, some salt and pepper, put it in a bowl, and savor each mouthful—somehow the balance returns. Beside being comforting, potatoes are nutritious, full of vitamins, minerals, and even limited amounts of protein. They are also filled with slow-burning fuel and fiber and are low in sodium. But most of all they taste great. Fried, scalloped, and mashed potatoes, shepherd's pie, hashbrowns, potato pancakes, vichyssoise, deep-fried potato skins, beef stew, potato bread, and potato salad—the potato is the Houdini of vegetables, showing up in many guises.

There are different tastes in potatoes. Some are earthy, some almost sweet; others have an astringent bite you can feel on the top of your mouth. When boiled, the skins can have almost a sour taste. All have a starchy quality. Potatoes are not always known for their individual flavor, but often for the fact that they absorb other flavors well. Combine them with meat or onions, say, or leeks, garlic, or butter, and it is hard to determine where one flavor begins and the other starts. Texture is very important, too, when evaluating a potato. A potato can be fine-grained, mealy, waxy, light, heavy, gluey, fluffy, creamy, floury, or granular. Color is important too. While usually we think of potatoes as white, in fact they come in many colors: purple, red, and yellow. The purple ones are fun, but some people don't like them; they think purple/blue food unnatural. As my son says, they "gross him out." Yet others just smile when I serve them lavender mashed potatoes. The all-red ones are fun, too—how about pink mashed potatoes? The yellow varieties are wonderful; they almost seem to be richer. Jan Blum says her yellow-fleshed fingerling potatoes seem like they are magically buttered from the inside. Potatoes are much more than the modest brown lumps that most appear; they are truly soul food.

How to Grow

Potatoes prefer cool weather. You can plant them as soon as your soil has warmed in the spring, or late in the summer for a fall crop if your growing season is long enough. In cool-summer areas, they can be grown in the summer as well.

Potatoes are generally started by planting seed potatoes—pieces of the tuber that contain at least one "eye," but preferably two or three. The eye is the little indentation from which the foliage will sprout. Potatoes should be set out as soon as the ground can be worked in the spring, if you can protect the young plants from hard frosts. They are best grown in well-drained, fertile, organic soils. For an easy and large harvest, plant seed potatoes in a trench 6 inches wide by 6 inches deep. They should be spaced about 12 inches apart and covered with 3 to 4 inches of soil. As they begin to sprout and develop sturdy foliage, fill in the trench with more soil until it is level with the existing bed or higher. Some gardeners mound potatoes with straw or even black plastic to allow them to inspect and harvest without damaging the tubers. For highest production, keep the plants moist. If planted with plenty of organic matter, in the form of compost or green manure—not animal manure, they generally require little fertilizer. Add organic matter early in the season, not just prior to planting, as fresh organic matter, particularly manure, can cause disease problems.

Care should be used when selecting the seed potatoes to be planted in your yard. Potatoes are susceptible to a large number of diseases that can be easily spread if infected tubers are planted. When buying seed potatoes, be sure to purchase only those inspected and certified as coming from disease-free stock. Don't waste time trying to make commercial potatoes into seed potatoes. Most of them will not grow as they have been treated with hormones to keep them from sprouting in grocery store bins.

Potatoes can be grown from seeds rather than tuber pieces, and that may be necessary if you cannot locate seed potatoes. Should you choose to try this method, start seeds indoors 6 to 8 weeks before the last average frost date for your area. When the weather warms, move the plants into the garden and grow as you would for seed potatoes.

Pests and Diseases

Potatoes are bothered by a number of pests and diseases. Colorado potato beetles, flea beetles, and aphids can attack the foliage, and wireworms and white grubs can damage tubers. The foliage pests can be fairly well controlled with insecticidal soap or pyrethrum, and the tuber pests are best controlled by crop rotation. If your soil is highly alkaline, your potatoes may develop a disease called scab; make the soil more acidic (ideal is a pH below 5.5) to correct this condition, or plant resistant varieties.

Containers

Growing potatoes in containers can be attractive, productive, and fun. The dark-green, coarse-looking foliage is pleasant looking and will cascade softly over the edges of a barrel or other large container. Small children love to mine for potatoes, and they can take special care of their crop if it is in containers. Containers must be large enough, at least 18 inches deep, to permit free tuber growth, and should have loose, well-drained soil.

Prolonging the Season

Potatoes take in the neighborhood of 100 days to develop sizable tubers. They are generally harvested when the tops have died back, but you can prolong the season by harvesting smaller tubers earlier in the season. These are delicious boiled and served very simply—a treat too few people have experienced.

Harvesting

Of all the fruits and vegetables I have grown, the potato is my favorite to harvest. Digging potatoes is like a birthday party where all your presents are hidden in a grab bag. As the caretaker of these plants for now nearly 100 days, you know that there are edible treasures beneath their wilted foliage, but you can only guess as to the number and size. Exploring the "grab bag" is one of my greatest garden pleasures.

When foliage has wilted and died back, dig or lift tubers from one plant to check the crop for tuber size. When ready to harvest, dig others carefully and at some distance from the crown of the plant to avoid damaging underlying tubers by putting your fork or shovel through them.

Seed Saving

Potatoes are most often started from tubers called "seed potatoes." The real seeds, which are formed in round seed balls, right where the flowers appear, are generally ignored. While the true seeds can be collected and planted in the spring to grow small tubers by fall, these tubers must then be dug and stored for the winter, to be used as seed potatoes the following spring. Unless you are trying to develop new and better potato varieties, why go to all this bother when perfectly grand varieties are already available as seed potatoes.

To save tubers for use as seed potatoes next year, select tubers from your best plants or simply save the small tubers that were harvested this year. While there is no advantage to saving particularly large tubers for seed purposes (and a good many reasons to use them in the kitchen instead), tubers smaller than a medium-size egg are too small. Allow collected tubers to dry in the sun for a week or two to cure. They may turn green during this period but are not dangerous as they will be planted rather than eaten. The ideal storage temperature is 35° F. If the tubers sprout before you're ready, rub off the sprouts and pop the potatoes into the refrigerator.

If you are serious about saving potato varieties, you might want to know a technique used by professional breeders. When it gets time to plant, precut each seed potato into seed-size pieces, but don't sever the pieces; leave them barely attached. When you plant the potatoes, put a small marker in the soil, break off the pieces, and plant all of them from a single tuber in a row; then put in another marker. By this method, all the seed pieces from a single tuber are grown together. This becomes important when a plant is affected by some disease, because now you know which other plants come from the original seed piece. Harvest and eat the ones that are from the same potato as the one that is affected and don't save any seed from these as they are probably quite disease prone.

Varieties

Two major types of potatoes—baking and boiling—are grown in this country today. The average local nursery will generally carry only one of each type even though over four hundred potato varieties are grown. There are a number of different varieties available from seed companies and specialty houses. Be aware, however, that while many of the unusual varieties are extremely tasty as well as fun to use (think of blue fried potatoes), most of the old potato varieties are not as vigorous, disease resistant, or high yielding as some of the newer hybrids. The following varieties are recommended:

'ALL BLUE'   purple flesh all the way through, some strains more gray and muddy-colored than others; Seeds Blum's is a clear vibrant blue; combined with 'All Red' and your favorite white variety, it makes a fun and festive patriotic potato salad. (Gurney, Seeds Blum)

'ALL RED'   red flesh all the way through, very light producer, difficult to locate; try seed exchanges. (Seed Savers)

'BINTJE'   yellow-skinned, yellow-fleshed baking potato, outstanding in physical appearance and flavor, high yield of large to medium-large tubers, quite disease free. (Seeds Blum)

'BUTTE'   large baking potato of high quality, excellent dis-ease resistance, high nutritional value; developed at University of Idaho. (Gurney)

'KENNEBEC'   excellent-quality all-purpose potato, heavy yield, midseason, resistant to blight and mosaic. (Readily available)

'LADY FINGER'   brown skin and yellow flesh, small and slender, 4 to 5 inches long by 1 inch in diameter, good for baking, outstanding for boiling or frying; a type of German fingerling. (Gurney)

'LEVITT'S PINK POTATO'   all-pink flesh, light producer. (Gurney)

'NORLAND'   red skin with white flesh, heavy producer of early tubers, highly resistant to scab. (Readily available)

'RED PONTIAC'   early to midseason, excellent for boiling but poor for baking, good choice for heavy soil, good keeper. (Readily available)

'RUBY CRESENT'   pink fingerling with yellow flesh, out-standing flavor baked or steamed. (Seeds Blum)

'URGENTA'   red skinned, yellow fleshed, smaller than 'Bintje' but of equal quality, often sold as new potato in specialty markets. (Seeds Blum)

'WHITE COBBLER'   early season, excellent flavor, most popular of white potatoes, good for baking, does not store well. (Burpee)

'YELLOW FINN'   delightful yellow-fleshed tuber, now available to gardeners as well as specialty market shoppers. (Seeds Blum)

If you are interested in growing some of the more unusual varieties, contact Becker's Seed Potatoes, R.R. 1, Trout Creek, Ontario, Canada POH 2LO. They ship potatoes in the spring only. Another source is Tater Mater Seeds, R.R. 2, Wathena, KS 66090.

Caution: Potato foliage, sprouts, and green tubers contain toxins that make them more or less poisonous. With modern varieties, it is generally sufficient to remove the green portion of the tuber. With the older heirloom varieties, however, whether such removal is enough to pre-vent toxicity is questionable. To be safe, dispose of all por-tions of a tuber showing any green coloration.

Preserving

Many white potatoes store very well. Check particular varieties for storage suitability. Brush the potatoes free of soil and place in containers (bushel baskets, wooden car-tons, crates, or cardboard boxes). It is wise to separate each potato from the others by wrapping or layering them between paper so that if one spoils, they will not all be affected.

Keep the potatoes in a dark, humid place at 50° to 60° F for 2 weeks to cure. Move to a dark, dry area for more prolonged storage at 35° F, or as close to that as possible. If stored at freezing or below, potatoes will become sweet and probably rot, and above 50° F they are in danger of

sprouting. Do not store them alongside apples, as the eth-ylene gas apples give off will hasten the sprouting process.

I do not recommend other methods of preserving potatoes.

Purchasing

When purchasing potatoes in the produce market, look for ones that are firm and unblemished and that feel heavy. Avoid those that are mottled in color or have green areas or that show signs of sprouting. The latter have probably been sitting around for longer than they should.

The consumer generally has little choice of potato varieties when buying in the market or at the produce stand. The potatoes offered for sale are usually labeled only by locale from which they came—Idaho, Long Island, Maine—but rarely by type and virtually never by variety. For more specificity you'll probably have to grow your own.

RADISHES
Raphanus sativus

Effort Scale
NO. 2
Must be planted annually
Thinning usually needed
Require light soil
Watering and mulching needed
Some weeding necessary

Thumbnail Sketch
Most annual, some Oriental varieties biennial
4 inches to 3 feet tall
Propagated from seeds
Plant seeds ½ inch deep
Germination takes 4 to 6 days at 60° F
Need full sun; will tolerate partial shade in hot climates
Leaves lobed, slightly hairy
Flowers usually not seen
Roots, leaves, seed pods edible; harvest season varies
     with variety
Short-season radishes used in vegetable gardens,
     containers; long-season varieties in flower borders
     as well

To many gardeners, the first radish picking of the year is the happy signal that spring has sprung and the new sea-son's fresh vegetables can't be far behind. Fast to sprout and mature, radishes are the first of spring's vegetable offerings and carry the promise that peas, lettuce, and other fast-developing home-grown foods will soon be available in the kitchen and at the table.

The taste of radishes is most often described as hot or pungent, though some can be quite mild. But they also can have a slightly sweet taste, as well as overtones of sulfur or a mustardy flavor like other members of the cabbage family. The textures range from dense, tender, crisp, and succulent to dry, pithy, woody, or rubbery.

There are two types of radishes. The type that grows and matures quickly—sometimes as fast as 3 weeks from seed to table—is what I will refer to as short-season radishes (often called spring radishes). They are generally planted in the spring or, even better, in the fall so that they may mature during cool weather, which they prefer. They need plenty of water, and are best when harvested young. Short-season radishes are crisp, have varying degrees of hotness to their taste, depending upon variety, and do not preserve or store well. They grow hotter when planted in heavy soil, when deprived of constant moisture, or when grown in hot weather. If not harvested promptly but left in the garden too long, they loose their crisp texture and turn fibrous and pithy.

The second type I call long-season radishes. They are also referred to as daikon, Oriental, or winter radishes. These are most often planted in the late summer or fall as they prefer to germinate in warmth and grow in cool weather. They are much larger than short-season radishes—sometimes several pounds and up to 2 feet in diameter—and take anywhere from 60 to 90 days to mature. They are most often used in Oriental cooking and store reasonably well.

Short-season radishes are small enough to be tucked here and there in the garden without much concern as to their visual impact—unless flea beetles disfigure them, and then they belong out of sight. The placement of long-season radishes is less flexible because of their size and length of time in the ground. They are such lovely plants, however, that they are well worth the effort required to find them an appropriate home. Their foliage grows from 8 to 18 inches in height and is at once dramatic and ruffled. They look handsome in front of tall flowers and behind lower annuals such as pansies and calendulas.

How to Grow

Radish seeds are quick to sprout and are generally one of the easiest and most rewarding vegetables for children to grow. Sow seeds directly in the garden after the last frost, or sow them in fall in mild-winter areas. Like most of the root vegetables, radishes prefer cool weather but can be grown in the summer in cool-summer areas. Plant seeds ½ inch deep, and thin to 2 inches apart, or more for large-rooted varieties. They can be planted in rows or blocks, or interplanted with slower plants that will be just coming into their own when the faster radishes are harvested. Radishes can also be planted in configurations that will help identify areas where slow-to-germinate seeds have been planted. The soil should be light and well drained. Generous amounts of compost will produce better radishes as it improves the texture of the soil. Radishes are light feed-

ers, however, so need little if any fertilizer. It is critically important to keep the young radishes constantly moist to avoid cracking and a bitter, too-hot taste. Most varieties are ready in 20 to 30 days, but some of the long-season types take 60 days or more.

Pests and Diseases

In some areas of the country radishes are bothered by root maggots. These pests are best controlled by crop rotation. It is particularly important not to plant radishes where cabbages or other cole crops have been grown recently. It is also helpful to plant radishes in small clusters throughout the garden rather than in large concentrations or long rows, where they become targets one after another. Wood ashes mixed into the soil are said to give some measure of control.

Flea beetles can also cause a considerable problem. They chew tiny holes in the foliage and can so severely stress young plants that they are unable to survive. A dusting of wood ashes can be helpful as can good garden hygiene, particularly in the fall when debris left lying around encourages the overwintering of pests.

Containers

Most short-season radishes are small enough to grow easily in containers.

Prolonging the Season

Seeds can be sown progressively from several weeks before the last average frost date until fall, depending upon variety and climate.

Harvesting

Variety determines time, size, and appearance of radishes at just the right time for harvest. Generally speaking, short-season round radishes should be harvested when they are about the size of cherries—¾ inch in diameter—or 1 inch across for the long, narrow type. If they are left in the ground too much longer they have a tendency to get hotter and more fibrous in texture. Exceptions are some of the large black and golden varieties, which will reach 2 inches across, and the very large long-season radishes, which can grow to 2 feet long and sometimes weigh 4 to 5 pounds.

Seed Saving

Allow short-season radishes to go to seed in place. Harvest the entire plant after the seed pods have turned yellow. Hang the plants upside down in a dry place for several weeks. Remove seeds from pods and store in an airtight container. You can also plant seeds in the fall and allow the plants to overwinter in place, mulching to protect them in areas where the ground freezes.

Long-season radishes are biennials and ripen seed the second year. After the first growing season, lift the roots and remove the tops, leaving 1 inch of green leaf growth.

Store them in sawdust or sand in a cold, humid place over the winter and plant them out again in the spring. When the plants go to seed, collect seeds as above.

Radishes are cross-pollinated, primarily by bees. Most crossing can be eliminated by separating varieties grown for seed by 200 feet, but over 1000 feet is needed if absolute seed purity is desired.

Varieties

Short-Season Radishes

'BURPEE WHITE'   25 days, all white, mild, ¾-inch diameter. (Readily available)

'CHAMPION'   28 days, red skinned, size of golf ball. (Readily available)

'CHERRY BELLE'   22 days, bright-red skin, white flesh, mild, ¾-inch diameter. (Readily available)

'D'AVIGNON'   25 days, long, slender, red skin with white tip. (Johnny's)

'EASTER EGG'   25 days; multicolored, including pastels; mildly tangy, crisp white flesh, 1 to 1½ inches in diameter. (Readily available)

'FRENCH BREAKFAST'   24 days, red-and-white skin, mild, 1-inch diameter, long and narrow. (Readily available)

'INCA'   22 days, scarlet skin, white interior, 2-inch roots, more resistant to heat than most so can be grown in summer in most areas. (Johnny's, Park)

Long-Season Radishes

'APRIL CROSS HYBRID'   60 days, white flesh, root up to 18 inches long and 3 inches in diameter, crisp, mild, slightly sweet, holds well in the ground. (Park)

'CHINA ROSE'   55 days, pink skin with white flesh, 5- to 6-inch root, mild flavored and crisp, keeps well. (Gurney, Seeds Blum, Stokes)

'ROUND BLACK SPANISH'   60 days, black skin with pure white flesh, keeps well. (Readily available)

WHITE CHINESE   60 days, all white, medium to hot, mildest of the winter radishes, 24 inches long. (Burpee, Stokes)

See the "Heirloom Gardens," "Rainbow Gardens," and "Oriental Gardens" chapters for additional varieties.

Preserving

Short-season radishes do not preserve well and should be eaten fresh. They can be kept crisp and fresh in cold water in the refrigerator for up to a week. Long-season radishes can be stored, either mulched in the ground over the winter or layered in sand.

Purchasing

Buy radishes in the market when they are small to medium in size, firm, and crisp. Avoid overlarge radishes as they are likely to be pithy or hollow, and put aside any that are soft or blemished.

SQUASH

SUMMER SQUASH   *Cucurbita Pepo* var. *melopepo*
WINTER SQUASH and PUMPKINS   *C. maxima,*
    C. moschata, C. Pepo

Effort Scale

NO. 2
Must be planted annually
Training of vining type needed
Occasional watering necessary
Fertilizing and mulching needed
Some weeding necessary
Vulnerable to some pests
Summer types need constant harvesting
Winter types need less attention

Thumbnail Sketch

Annuals
Bush types, 2 to 3 feet tall; vining types, 6 to 10 feet long
Propagated from seeds
Plant seeds 1 inch deep
Germination takes 6 to 12 days at 70° F
Need full sun
Leaves light to dark green, large, vary with species
Flowers bright yellow, 1 to 4 inches across
Fruits, flowers, young shoots of most species edible; harvested in summer and fall
Bush summer types used in vegetable gardens, herbaceous borders, raised beds, containers

Summer squash, along with their close relatives the cucumbers and melons, are associated with meals on warm summer days. Lightly steamed pattypan and zucchini sautéed with garlic, basil, onions, and green pepper are summer staples, as are books and articles promising to provide one hundred completely new ways to use zucchini. Keeping up with the harvest can take a good deal of ingenuity, but summer wouldn't be summer without the "squash shuffle," as my children named the yearly job of sharing the harvest with neighbors and friends.

Winter squash are less in need of population control than their summer cousins. Although referred to as winter squash (or hard-shelled squash), like summer squash they grow in warm weather. Traditionally they were grown to be stored and eaten in winter, but we have a hard time staying away from them until winter. While most varieties hold their own in flavor, and some even get sweeter, keep an eye on them in storage as some varieties, or those held at too warm a temperature, will have their flavor deteriorate somewhat during storage.

Pumpkin is the common name we use in this country to designate those squashes used primarily for pies, animal feed, and jack-o'-lanterns. They are usually orange skinned with paler flesh and commonly less sweet than those fruits we call winter squash. As they are essentially winter squash, their culture is the same, and only their size, taste, and varietal names are of sufficient difference to merit separate discussion.

The tastes of summer squash can be described as sweet, nutlike, cucumberish, meaty, delicate, or bitter. The textures can be dense, tender, melting, grainy, creamy, floury, custardlike, or rubbery. Summer squash do not have strong flavors and are at their best absorbing other flavors, like those of onions, garlic, tomato, and many herbs. The most often used words to describe the tastes of winter squash are rich and sweet. They can also be aromatic and chestnutlike. The winter squash textures can range from dry, flaky, floury, tender, and melting to stringy or rubbery. As compared to winter squash, pumpkins tend to have less flesh, which is somewhat more watery and stringy and less sweet.

Squash, like other members of the cucurbit family, have large, hairy, rough, ivy-shaped leaves. Some are 2 to 3 inches across and light green; others, like the zucchini, have 2-foot-wide dark-green leaves that can be variegated and deeply lobed. Their cup-shaped yellow flowers are large, showy, and edible. The bush types are useful in herbaceous beds near a patio or walk. They all do well in large containers on balconies, porches, or patios. The vining types can be used on low trellises, fences, and spilling over embankments.

How to Grow
All the squash, be they classified as summer or winter, are warm-season annuals. In short-summer areas, seeds must be started indoors. The plants are usually grown in hills, with two or three plants to a hill. Space hills 5 to 6 feet apart for summer squash and 7 to 10 feet apart for winter squash and pumpkins. Squash can also be planted in rows, with 2 to 3 feet between plants and the rows spaced as for hills. If direct seeding, plant seed somewhat more thickly and later thin to the above distances. In containers, squash are planted singly.

This group of plants needs rich humus soil and ample water during the growing season. They also benefit from regular applications of fish emulsion or a commercial fertilizer, as long as it is not too high in nitrogen. Do not let the plants dry out. Keep young plants well weeded. Mature plants can usually crowd out any weeds.

Pests and Diseases
Squash are afflicted with many of the same diseases and pests as cucumbers. See "Cucumbers" for more detail.

Squash vine borers are worms that hatch at the base of the vines and eat their way up the inside of the vine, causing wilt. It is sometimes possible to dig them out with a small screwdriver, nail, or bent paperclip, but you may have to resort to rotenone applications.

Containers
The small bush squash are most attractive in containers, with their deep-green leaves and handsome and interesting fruits. Choose from a large selection of zucchini, yellow summer squash, and pattypan types. All are bush-type squashes.

Prolonging the Season
See "Cucumbers."

A second sowing of squash seeds in all but short-summer areas can also extend the summer squash season.

Harvesting
Most people prefer summer squash when they are young and tender. My assistant Wendy Krupnick prefers squash in their "adolescent" stage and likes to pick them when the blossoms have just withered, indicating that the squash is still tender but has developed its flavor. Sometimes the squash are 6 inches long, sometimes 9 inches before this happens. It depends on the variety, the climate, and how vigorously the plant is growing. If you want "baby" squash, pick them more immature, in the early morning, just as the blossoms are in full bloom. Do this carefully as the babies are easily bruised. To keep them fresh, refrigerate the squash immediately and use them the same day because they are very perishable. If you want the blossoms to stay open for an hors d'oeuvre tray or for stuffing, place the squashes, with the fully open flowers still attached, cut end down in cold water in the refrigerator. Use the blossoms the same day they are harvested.

You can also choose to harvest summer squash when they are quite a bit more mature. Large but still tender squash are great for stuffing. Scoop out the seeds, peel the skin, and prepare the flesh in many ways. The English enjoy their "marrow" squash, as they call their zucchini-type summer squash, when they have developed to 18 inches to 2 feet. In Cajun cooking, too, squash are often allowed to get quite large. The key is to choose varieties that do not get woody and tasteless. See the "Varieties" list below.

Anyone who has grown summer squash probably has at one time or another had too many squash. It is, however, important to keep this excess picked as otherwise the plant will drastically slow its production. Zealous producers, many zucchini varieties can supply about two or three fruits a day. A pattypan will produce in flushes of two or three a day and then cut back to one a day. The yellow crooknecks are not so ambitious and often will only produce a squash every day or two.

Unlike summer varieties, winter squash are almost always picked when fully mature, though most of the varieties produce very flavorful immature fruits, which are eaten much like summer squash. As there is sometimes the need to thin a portion of the crop so as not to overtax the plant, the sacrificed thinnings can be used in the kitchen.

Generally, however, we use the winter squash at its mature stage for its wonderful deep flavor and texture. Be careful not to harvest this fruit before it is fully mature as it will not have had time to develop its full sugar content and is likely to taste a bit like watery cardboard. The rinds should be too hard to be punctured with your fingernail. Leave about 2 inches of stem attached or the squash is likely to rot.

See the "Italian Gardens," "Native American Gardens," and "Edible Flower Gardens" chapters for information on harvesting squash blossoms.

Seed Saving

Squash are monoecious (both male and female flowers on the same plant) and cross-pollinated, primarily by bees. They will not cross with other members of the cucurbit family—cucumbers and melons—but will cross with other members of their own species. For example, zucchini (*Cucurbita Pepo* var. *melopepo*) will not cross with cucumbers (*Cucumis sativus*) but will cross with pattypan squash (*Cucurbita Pepo* var. *melopepo*). This will have no effect on the taste or any of the other characteristics of the fruits during the first season. It is of concern if you are saving seed, however, as the seed will reflect the cross, and next year's fruits will demonstrate it. If saving seed, allow approximately ½ mile between plants of the same species to ensure seed purity, or hand pollinate and cover the flower with a bag and tie it closed.

Collect seed from summer squash that have been allowed to become fully mature. The squash will be large and hard and at the appropriate age about 2 months after the stage at which they would have been edible. Scoop out the seeds and allow them to stand in water for several days to separate from the pulp, stirring a time or two each day. Most of the heavy, viable seed will fall to the bottom for easy collection. Wash in fresh water, dry thoroughly, and store in airtight containers.

Collect seeds from winter squash and pumpkins as they are being prepared for kitchen use. Wash, dry, and store.

Varieties

When considering which summer squash to plant, it is probably wise to plant only half of the plants you are tempted to put in. The average family needs only one or two. When you can get the mailman to pick up and deliver your excess all over town, you can safely consider more.

Summer Squash

'ARISTOCRAT'   53 days, hybrid, widely adapted dark-green zucchini type. (Readily available)

'ARLESA'   48 days, hybrid, zucchini variety, strong producer over long season, attractive fruits held high on plant. (Shepherd's)

'COCOZELLE' ('ITALIAN MARROW')   50 days, versatile fruit, can be harvested small or large. (Good, Nichols, Plants of Southwest)

'GOLD RUSH'   50 days, hybrid, yellow zucchini, early, very prolific. (Readily available)

'GOURMET GLOBE'   50 days; sometimes referred to as zucchini, sometimes as apple squash; round green fruit. (Readily available)

'SUNBURST'   50 days, hybrid, mild buttery flavor, yellow scalloped type with green ends, highly ornamental. (Readily available)

'SUNDANCE'   55 days, strong-growing yellow crookneck, nutty taste. (Stokes)

Winter Squash

Most families cannot fit in as many winter squash as they might like because of the garden space these squashes require. Therefore it is useful to know which type has the characteristics you are seeking, either for cooking or storage purposes. In general the acorn type (*Cucurbita Pepo*) is relatively small, is outstanding for baking, but does not store as well as the others. The butternut type (*C. moschata*) is the best of the keepers. When stored properly, it can be held all winter and gradually sweetens over time, which neither the acorn or buttercup squash does. The buttercup type (*C. maxima*) is known for its sweet, starchy flesh, which is dry and stringless. While its storage potential lies somewhere between the acorns and the butternuts, it is so full-flavored and sweet it is the perfect candidate for pies, cakes, and breads, in addition to baking.

In "Cooks' Guide to Winter Squash" (*National Gardening,* November 1986), Judy Chaves describes the following method for distinguishing the winter squashes by group: acorn types have five-sided stems that gradually increase in diameter as they approach the fruit; butternut stems are five-sided, narrow, and woody, and they expand right at the fruit; buttercup stems are cylindrical, smooth, and do not expand at the fruit. These visual tools can be very useful in the produce market when neither you nor the produce person can identify a particular squash.

'BUTTERCUP'   105 days, turban shaped, 4 to 5 pounds, exceptional flavor, keeps well. (Readily available)

'DELICATA'   100 days, acorn type, dark green with vertical stripes; sweet 8-inch fruits similar in flavor and texture to sweet potatoes; heavy yield, stores well. (Gurney, Johnny's, Nichols, Seeds Blum)

'GOLD NUGGET'   85 days, bush buttercup type, orange skin and flesh, stores well; early, good for short-summer areas. (Gurney, Johnny's, Seeds Blum)

'GREEN HOKKAIDO'   98 days, buttercup type, slate green, 3 to 5 pounds, rich and flaky, not a heavy yielder. (Johnny's)

'HONEY DELIGHT'   95 days, hybrid, buttercup type, 2 to 4 pounds, flattened globe, excellent new variety. (Johnny's)

'JERSEY GOLDEN ACORN'   80 days (also eaten as summer squash at 50 days), light orange, less fiber than green acorns. (Readily available)

'ORANGETTI'   50 days, hybrid, spaghetti squash with orange skin and flesh; see 'Vegetable Spaghetti' below for general description. (Nichols, Twilley)

'RED KURI' ('ORANGE HOKKAIDO', 'BABY RED HUBBARD')   92 days, hybrid, buttercup type, 5 to 8 pounds, bright red flesh, very flaky and sweet, nutty flavor, select Japanese variety. (Johnny's, Seeds Blum)

'SWEET DUMPLING'   very similar in flavor to 'Delicata' (Le Marché, Shepherd's, Vermont Bean)

'SWEET MAMA'   85 days, hybrid, buttercup type, 2½ to 4 pounds; sweet, mild flavor, heavy yield. (Readily available)

'VEGETABLE SPAGHETTI'   100 days, acorn type, very stringy, used as substitute for pasta, stores well. (Readily available)

'WALTHAM BUTTERNUT'   85 days, large fruits, pest and disease resistant, heavy yield. (Readily available)

Pumpkins

Pumpkins vary considerably in their characteristics. Some are planted for their future culinary use as pies, winter vegetables, or even for their superior seeds. Others are selected as good candidates for the family jack-o'-lantern. And others are so decorative that they scarcely need a utilitarian purpose for being.

'AUTUMN GOLD'   90 days, hybrid; colors to yellow when still immature so can be harvested early; good in short-season areas, similar to 'Spooky'. (Readily available)

'BIG MAX'   120 days, great for pumpkin contests, sometimes grows to over 100 pounds, pinkish-orange flesh, rough skin. (Readily available)

'JACK BE LITTLE'   tiny miniature fruits, only 3 inches across. (Johnny's, Le Marché, Seeds Blum, Twilley)

'LADY GODIVA'   110 days, grown for hull-less seeds that need no shelling. (Park) .

'MUSQUÉE DE PROVENCE'   small, flattened shape with deep ribs, very decorative, used in France as winter squash. (Le Marché)

'SMALL SUGAR'   100 days, sweet, fine-grained flesh just right for pies, keeps well. (Readily available)

'SPOOKY'   90 days, cross between pie and jack-o'-lantern pumpkin, uniform globe with flat ends, 8-inch diameter. (Harris, Shepherd's, Stokes)

'TRIPLE TREAT'   110 days, good for pies, carving, and hull-less seeds; sweet flesh, 7- and 9-inch diameter, uniformly round fruit, 6 to 8 pounds. (Burpee, Farmer, Seeds Blum)

'WHITE CHEESEQUAKE' ('WHITE CHEESE PUMPKIN')   flattened-shape white pumpkin, orange meat, delicious flavor, old variety. (Le Marché)

Preserving

Summer squash can be pickled, made into relish, or dried. While the texture deteriorates when fresh frozen, summer squash can be made into soups and ratatouille, both of which freeze well.

Winter squash can also be cooked and frozen but is traditionally bred and grown for dry storage in winter. It stores best in a dark, well-ventilated place where, ideally, the air should be a humid 50° F.

Purchasing

Summer squash should be small and firm to the touch. The zucchinis should have a shiny exterior surface, and the pattypans should be light green—when their color has progressed to white they are too old. The oldtime fingernail test is useful here. If the skin is easily pierced by a fingernail, the summer squash is still young and tender.

Winter squash, on the other hand, should be large, with hard exterior skin, and heavy. Hoist a few in the market and avoid the lightest, which are probably somewhat dehydrated. The surface should be smooth and the exterior color highly saturated.

STRAWBERRIES

ALPINE STRAWBERRIES   *Fragaria vesca (F. alpina semperflorens)*

GARDEN STRAWBERRIES   *F. × Ananassa*

Effort Scale

Alpine Strawberries
NO. 2
Perennials
Replanting necessary every 2 to 3 years
Watering necessary in most areas
Fertilizing and weeding needed
Winter protection needed in many areas
Picking fruits is time consuming

Garden Strawberries
NO. 4
Perennials
Replanting necessary every 2 to 3 years
Runners must be controlled
Watering and fertilizing necessary
Weeding necessary
Susceptible to some pests and diseases, including birds
Winter protection needed in many areas
Harvesting the large, perishable yield is time consuming

Thumbnail Sketch

Herbaceous perennials
6 to 12 inches tall
Alpine strawberries propagated from seeds
Garden strawberries propagated from runners
Alpine seed germination takes 14 to 21 days at 70° F
Garden needs full sun; Alpine prefers partial shade
Leaves compound; garden species, deep green; Alpine
    species, medium green
Bloom in spring, summer
Flowers white, small, edible
Fruits edible; harvested in spring and summer
Used in vegetable gardens, flower beds, raised beds, rock
    gardens, hanging baskets, containers, to line a
    woodland path, and as ground covers

That first luscious, juicy strawberry shortcake is for many the culinary signal that spring is nearly past and summer is now on its heels. A bowl of garden strawberries served with a little powdered sugar and cream is my idea of the perfect dessert. Close behind are strawberry pie—whether plain, chiffon, or cream—strawberry Bavarian cream, strawberry soufflé, and meringues filled with strawberries, all of which dress up these lovely red fruits without spoiling their flavor. Scandinavians use the berries in a wonderful pudding and soup, and Australians often top their meringuelike cake Pavlova with fresh berries. Strawberry jam is such an American tradition it hardly needs mentioning. What a pleasure jam is when it brings the taste and smell of summer to our winter breakfast table!

If you like garden strawberries, you will love Alpine strawberries. They are strawberries with the flavor volume turned up. I remember paying eight dollars for a bowl of small, fragrant Alpine berries in France; you can enjoy this delicacy for very little if you choose to grow them yourself.

The taste of strawberries can be defined as sweet, fragrant, fruity, spicy, floral, rich, full bodied, sour, tasteless, metallic, moldy, vinegary, or fermented. The texture ranges from melting, juicy, and smooth to dry, watery, mushy, seedy, or hard. The taste of strawberries seems to differ with the variety and, in my experience, the temperature. When my strawberries first appear in spring they can be pretty tasteless, but as the temperature warms up they get flavorful.

How to Grow

A good strawberry variety exists for nearly every area of the United States and Canada. Strawberries are not the easiest plants to grow, and their fruit is not always predictable in terms of sweetness and texture, but with the correct variety anyone should be able to produce luscious berries with not too much effort. To my mind, it is well worth it as nothing is sweeter than a home-grown strawberry picked at the height of maturity.

Garden strawberries prefer full sun, moderately cool temperatures, and a light, fast-draining soil slightly on the acid side. Alpine strawberries should be planted where they will receive morning sun or filtered shade from a high-branching tree. Avoid, if possible, planting them in full sun or in hot, afternoon sun in warm-summer areas. At the other end of the temperature scale, garden strawberries are very cold tolerant and can be grown in very low temperatures if properly mulched. Alpines are also quite hardy and can be grown well in areas where winter temperatures fall to as low as −20° F. In areas with coldest winters, mulching with straw is necessary. In fact, in cold climates all types of strawberries should be covered with a heavy mulch, preferably straw, when heavy frosts are expected, and the mulch should not be removed until hard freezes are over. Mulching prevents the alternate freezing and thawing of the soil that can heave the plants out of the ground.

Strawberries can also be grown in desert climates and regions that receive over 300 frost-free days. In these areas, garden strawberries are usually treated as a winter annual. See "Varieties," below, for ones adapted to this method of growing.

Garden strawberries are generally planted in spring or fall. In warm-winter areas, fall planting is preferred. In areas with cold winters, it is best to plant in spring as soon as the soil can be worked.

Buy garden strawberries bare root in early spring from local nurseries or mail-order sources, or in containers through the fall season. Alpine strawberries are planted in spring. They are usually started from seeds, which are available from mail-order firms and, occasionally, from local nurseries.

Both types need fairly rich, well-drained soil that is high in organic matter. They prefer a slightly acidic soil with a pH of 5.8 to 6.8. Plant bare roots or seedlings in beds that have been well prepared with humus. The plants should be spaced about a foot apart in rows, with the rows several feet apart to allow for ease of maintenance. When good drainage cannot be assured, strawberries are often planted in hills. It is very important to plant the crowns of the plants at ground level. Strawberry plants that are planted too deep will rot; if they are planted too high they will dry out. Alpine strawberries are usually started from seeds. Follow package directions.

Both types of strawberries should be kept well mulched with manure, compost, or straw. Side dress strawberry plants in the spring with blood and kelp meal or a 5-10-10 commercial fertilizer. Apply small amounts of fish emulsion two to three times over the spring and early summer. Do not fertilize with large amounts of nitrogen, but watch for symptoms of nitrogen starvation—foliage turning light green or yellowish—and treat by applying small amounts of nitrogen.

Strawberry plants need to be kept moist. They have a low tolerance for salt, and in areas with high water salinity, as in some high-desert areas, strawberries are difficult to grow.

For spring-bearing varieties of garden strawberries, prune off flowers the first year after planting to encourage strong growth. This means you will have no strawberries the first year from these plants. Prune off the spring flowers on everbearing varieties but allow fall flowers to fruit the first year.

Garden strawberry plants send out runners as they grow. These runners develop small plantlets that will eventually take root and form new permanent plants if left undisturbed. The "mother plant" may produce six or eight or more runners during the season, and obviously something must be done to keep the strawberry bed from becoming a tangled thicket, with so many plants that none develop properly. There are a number of ways to thin and organize this growing "family," but I prefer to remove all runners as they develop and concentrate my efforts and nature's resources on a few select plants that will produce considerably more and larger berries with minimal competition. You might want to keep some of the runners intact to provide replacements for the older plants as they decline, but these runners should be moved to the site of a new strawberry bed. The potential of all strawberries for disease problems makes it wise to change growing areas every 2 to 3 years. Since berry number and size of garden strawberries begin to decline rapidly after several seasons, I find it easier not to cultivate baby plants and to start over entirely with new plants in a new location every 2 or 3 years. Alpine strawberries need no pruning.

About two dozen garden strawberry plants will supply a family of four with plenty of berries for eating fresh each season. Alpine strawberries are less prolific and have smaller berries, so plan to raise a minimum of five or six dozen for a similar-size family.

Pests and Diseases
A number of pests bother strawberries, but usually chemical controls are unnecessary. Snail and slug problems are an exception. Hand picking helps, but there are so many places for these pests to hide in a lush patch that snail bait is usually necessary. Use it before the fruits form. Japanese beetles are sometimes a problem. To control these pests, hand pick and use milky spore disease. A preventive planning measure is to keep strawberry patches away from lawns, where the grubs overwinter and to cover the rows with a polyester row cover. Where weevils are a problem, use spring-bearing berries. Pull up the plants after the second spring and plant something else in their place for the next few years to prevent the weevil population from building up. Aphids, another potential problem, can usually be controlled with a sharp blast of water from the hose nozzle or

a soap-based pesticide. Nematodes and mites can be a problem in the Southeast. To control the former, use the soil solarization method discussed in Appendix B, "Pests and Diseases," before planting or plant in containers; mites usually require chemical control.

The diseases that affect strawberries—verticillium wilt and red stele (root rot)—can be serious but are not common with homegrown plants if they have been purchased from a nursery that carries certified disease-free plants. The most important control is crop rotation. Once plants have become diseased, remove them and do not plant strawberries again in the same bed for 3 to 4 years. Even if diseases have not affected your fruit, you should alternate strawberries with other plants in succession in the same garden spot. Fungicides are sometimes needed to control leaf spot.

Containers
If kept well watered, both garden and Alpine varieties make ideal container plants.

Prolonging the Season
Garden strawberries are classified as either spring-bearing or everbearing. Spring-bearing varieties set their flowers in response to long winter nights and produce one good-size crop that is ready for picking in late spring or early summer. Everbearing varieties are not dependent on day or night length and produce flowers and fruits in smaller crop numbers but over a considerably longer period of time.

The strawberry season can be lengthened by planting everbearing varieties solely or, if you have room for several varieties, both everbearing and spring-bearing varieties.

Seed Saving
Garden strawberries are generally grown from transplants, so seed is not saved. Alpine strawberries reseed themselves easily. Crop continuity is assured by these volunteers, and seed is rarely saved.

Harvesting
In the second season, when the first crop of garden berries should be harvested, berries will be ripe about 4 weeks after the plants flower. Pick strawberries the day they become ripe—when they are fully colored and slightly soft. Pull garden strawberries off carefully with the stem and cap still attached. This is most easily done by grasping the stem between your thumb and forefinger just above the berry. While pulling slightly, sever stem with your fingernails. Alpine strawberries will easily fall off in your hand. Check the vines daily, and with garden strawberries remove both ripe berries and any that are damaged, bruised, or deteriorating as they will get moldy. Unpicked Alpine strawberries just dry up and fall off. Refrigerate all the strawberries

immediately, but use them quickly as the quality declines rapidly. This is most critical with Alpine strawberries as they seldom keep for more than 8 or 10 hours.

A mature garden strawberry plant should produce about one pint of berries each season. Alpine strawberries produce a much lighter harvest.

Varieties

Alpine Strawberries

Alpine strawberries are sold as seeds. Some local nurseries also sell plants. A number of varieties of Alpine strawberries exist, all quite similar to each other in fruit quality and growth habits. The varieties sold commercially are runnerless, though they are descendents of running, wild ancestors.

'ALEXANDRIA'   medium-size red fruit; good flavor. (Burpee, Harris, Le Marché, Thompson & Morgan)

'BARON SOLEMACHER'   old-favorite variety. (Bountiful, Johnny's, Nichols)

'RUGEN IMPROVED'   dark-red berry, improved quality. (Burpee, Le Marché, Nichols)

'YELLOW FRUITED'   small yellow fruits, sweet. (Le Marché, Thompson & Morgan)

Garden Strawberries

It is very important to choose strawberry varieties appropriate for your climate. Local nurseries or your university agricultural extension service will be able to tell you most about which varieties are superior in your area. The following varieties are disease resistant. Look for them in your local nursery or from mail-order sources.

'FT. LARAMIE'   everbearing, large, aromatic berries; extremely hardy, good for Midwest as well as southern states; nice for hanging baskets. (Field's, Jung)

'GUARDIAN'   midseason crop, fruits good for fresh eating or freezing, resistant to many diseases; for Southeast. (Readily available)

'MIDWAY'   midseason, exceptional yield and flavor; resistant to red stele; good for northern and north central gardens. (Gurney, Rayner, Stark)

'OZARK BEAUTY'   everbearing, large berries, very hardy, adaptable to many climates. (Readily available)

'SEQUOIA'   early, one of the best-tasting strawberries; resistant to many diseases, somewhat tolerant of soil alkalinity; for West Coast and southern gardens. (Hastings)

'SUNRISE'   early, good flavor; resistant to red stele, mildew, and verticillium wilt; for Southeast. (Rayner, Stark)

'SURECROP'   early, good-quality fruits, resistant to most major strawberry diseases and drought; excellent for freezing; for East Coast. (Readily available)

'TENNESSEE BEAUTY'   late, good-quality berries, resistant to a number of diseases; for South and central states. (Hastings, Rayner)

Preserving

Garden strawberries can be made into jelly, jam, syrup, fruit leather, and wine. They can be frozen whole with sugar or as an ingredient in ice cream. Alpine strawberries are best eaten fresh or combined with garden strawberries in jam.

Purchasing

Strawberries should be purchased as soon as possible after harvest as they deteriorate very rapidly. Try to do so from a local grower. They should be vivid and evenly red. Pale berries and ones with pale areas or green tips are not ripe and will not be as sweet as fully mature fruits. Berries should be firm and red with as little yellow or green as possible.

SWEET POTATOES
Ipomoea Batatas

Effort Scale
NO. 4
Must be started from slips
Specific soil requirements
Vulnerable to many pests and diseases

Thumbnail Sketch
Perennial roots planted as annuals
Trailing vines, usually kept to 1½ to 4 feet
Propagated from shoots or cuttings
Need full sun
Leaves vary from oval to lobed, 4 to 6 inches long
Flowers sparse, rose to pale pink, 2 inches across
Tubers edible; harvested in fall
Used in vegetable gardens, herbaceous borders, containers, and spilling over retaining walls

Sweet potatoes make most people think of holiday meals. Serving bowls filled with this sweet yellow or reddish-orange root seem to go naturally with ham or turkey on festively set tables surrounded by smiling people of many generations.

It was not until relatively recently that I began to serve sweet potatoes more often and in a wider variety of ways. They are delicious boiled, fried, or baked. They make a pleasant change from the more routinely served white potatoes. They are good both plain and as ingredients in casseroles and pies. A southern favorite, "candied sweets," is a method of cooking boiled sweet potatoes with a sauce of brown sugar and orange juice; it is delicious.

Sweet potatoes are generally divided into two groups, moist and dry, referring to their texture. The moist sweet potato converts most of its starches to sugar during cooking, resulting in a soft, sweet flesh. It is often referred to and labeled as a yam, which, technically, it is not, and most often has rust-colored skin with orange flesh. It is the sweet potato generally associated with the South. The dry sweet potato, traditionally preferred by the northern cook, converts fewer starches to sugars in preparation so is less sweet and has more the texture of a regular potato. Its skin is more likely to be a soft, fawn-colored brown and its interior flesh a pale yellow.

The primary flavor of sweet potatoes is, of course, their sweetness. They can be described as mellow, rich, and starchy. The texture can be creamy, dry, dense, woody, or stringy.

The sweet potato vine produces lovely, 2- to 3-inch lobed leaves that cascade gracefully over the sides of planters and retaining walls. On rare occasions, a pink morning-glory-type flower nestles among the leaves. Sweet potato vines are perennials but are used as annuals in most areas. Try them as a ground cover in front of a flower bed combined with low-growing, pink zinnias, or around a patio planted with pink petunias.

How to Grow

Sweet potatoes are the most heat-tolerant vegetable grown in the United States. In fact, they not only tolerate heat but must have a good deal of it—at least 140 to 150 days—to produce a good crop.

Sweet potatoes are planted out in spring by slips, which are sprouts produced by the roots. To start your own slips, place roots in a hotbed (a wooden tray with heating coils in the bottom and filled with sand) about 6 to 8 weeks before the weather warms up. Cover the potatoes with damp sand and maintain a hotbed temperature of 75° to 85° F. Pull, do not cut, the shoots off; they and their roots will pull off easily.

Another way to grow slips is to partially submerge a sweet potato in a jar of water, using toothpicks stuck into the flesh on either side and balanced on the top of the jar to suspend it partially out of the water. Leafy shoots will appear within a few weeks, and these shoots will sprout their own roots shortly thereafter.

You can also order slips from mail-order companies. If they look a bit bedraggled when they arrive, do not be concerned as they are pretty tough little plants and should perk up quickly.

Sweet potatoes are customarily grown on raised mounds. Dig and loosen the planting area well and form mounds 6 to 10 inches high and about 4 feet apart. The soil should be sandy loam, not clay. Sweet potatoes grown in heavy clay become gnarled and stringy. In planter boxes and containers, use a rich, light soil mix. At planting time,

use a generous amount of a fertilizer high in potassium and phosphorus. Mix in well. Bury bottoms of slips 4 inches deep and 1 foot apart. Keep the vines fairly moist until they are well established. The plants require less moisture after they are growing vigorously. When transplants are about 3 to 4 weeks old, side dress with a 5-10-10 fertilizer or its organic equivalent.

Pests and Diseases

A number of pests and diseases affect sweet potatoes. Check with your local university agricultural extension service, since problems differ with region. Choose sweet potato varieties that are resistant to the diseases in your area.

Containers

Sweet potatoes are generally too large for containers, but the smaller, more compact bush varieties can be grown successfully in large containers. Container growing provides the advantage of mobility should a sudden frost threaten.

Prolonging the Season

The sweet potato season is almost totally determined by the warmth of the weather. As it takes a full season of hot weather (140 to 150 days, typically) for the roots to mature, and because the crop must be harvested before the first frost to avoid fruit deterioration, this is not a season that can be prolonged in the usual ways.

Harvesting

Harvest sweet potatoes in late fall, or roughly 140 to 150 days after planting the slips. Exposure to temperatures under 50° F causes the roots to deteriorate in flavor and texture, so be sure to get them out of the ground before frost. They should also not be kept in the refrigerator unless they have been cooked, in which case they keep quite well. Sweet potatoes bruise easily when handled, so dig and sort the roots carefully. Blemished or damaged roots should be used quickly, but undamaged sweet potatoes can be cured and stored for 4 to 6 months.

Seed Saving

Sweet potato seeds, carried on top of the plant after the flowers have come and gone, are of little interest to most gardeners. Sweet potato plants are started from roots rather than seeds, so it is this year's roots you want to save for next year's crop.

To collect roots, harvest as you would for eating, being careful not to damage those you will save for next year. These should be from the best plants you have raised but do not need to be the largest tubers—small ones are fine as long as they are not damaged when harvesting. Cure and store as for eating. See "Preserving," below, for more information on the curing and storing of sweet potatoes.

Varieties

Because sweet potatoes are susceptible to many diseases, it is important to choose varieties that are resistant to diseases that affect your area. Local nurseries or your university agricultural extension service can advise you. Varieties available are:

'ALLGOLD'   moist type; resists viral disease, internal cork, and stem rot; stores well, good in Midwest. (Hastings)

'BUNCH PORTO RICO' ('BUSH PORTO RICO')   moist type, compact vines, grows to 18 inches; good for smaller areas, greenhouses, and containers. (Fred's, Hastings)

'CENTENNIAL'   moist type, highly resistant to wilt, very popular in South but good in northern climates as well. (Burpee, Fred's, Hastings)

'NANCY HALL'   dry type, ready in 110 days, resistant to soft rot. (Hastings)

'PURPLE'   deep-purple-fleshed variety that stays purple even when cooked; heirloom variety with sweet, moist flesh. (Seeds Blum)

'RED JEWEL'   moist type; easy to grow, good for home garden. (Fred's, Hastings)

Slips are available in spring from some local nurseries and mail-order houses. Two mail-order nurseries, Fred's Plant Farm, Dresden, TN 38225, and Steele Plant Farm, Box 807, Gleason, TN 38229, offer a large selection of varieties in spring.

Due to local agricultural restrictions, sweet potato slips cannot be shipped into California and Arizona. As these restrictions sometimes vary, based on current agricultural circumstances, it would be wise to check with your local university agricultural extension service before placing sweet potato orders from other states.

Preserving

Before you can store sweet potatoes, they must first be cured. To cure, place the roots indoors, out of direct sunlight, in a humid, 70° to 80° F location for about 10 days. This exposure toughens the outside skins and helps heal blemishes that would rot if left untended. Roots should then be wrapped individually and stored at a humid 55° F, but never lower than 50° F, as they are exceedingly susceptible to cold damage. Properly cured and stored, they should store nicely for 5 to 6 months.

Sweet potatoes can also be çanned or frozen.

Purchasing

When selecting sweet potatoes on the commercial market, look for those with tapered ends, smooth skins, and no blemishes. Unlike many other vegetables, size should be of no particular concern as they do not toughen or lose sweetness as they get larger. Choose the size that best suits your culinary purpose.

TOMATOES

Lycopersicon Lycopersicum   (L. esculentum)

Effort Scale

NO. 2
Must be planted annually
Tying and staking usually needed
Moderate amounts of watering, fertilizing, and mulching needed
Vulnerable to some pests
Harvest continual

Thumbnail Sketch

Perennials treated as annuals
18 inches to 8 feet tall
Propagated from seeds
Plant seeds ¼ inch deep
Germination takes 6 to 14 days at 70° F
Need full sun
Leaves compound, medium green
Bloom in summer
Flowers yellow, not showy, small
Fruits edible; red, yellow, white; harvested in summer or fall
Used in vegetable gardens, on fences, and in hanging baskets, flower borders, containers

Tomatoes need no introduction. Have you ever tried one ripe from the vine with the heat of the sun still upon it? If you have, you will know why the tomato is the most commonly grown vegetable in the United States. Whether you grow 'Tiny Tim' or 'Big Boy' does not matter. Once you have tried a fully vine ripened tomato, ones from the store will seem a travesty. Enjoy them from your yard all through the season—sliced, quartered, or stuffed. Their flavor and color can enhance all summer meals.

Home-canned and home-frozen tomatoes add interest to winter meals in stews, soups, casseroles, and spaghetti sauce. It's hard to imagine meals without chili sauce, salsa, tomato paste, and tomato puree. And dried tomatoes marinated in olive oil and garlic make a wonderful sauce for fresh pasta.

When the tomato was first introduced to European gardens from the New World it was thought to be poisonous. Since the plant belongs to the nightshade family, the fruits were suspect, so tomatoes were used only as showy ornamentals. Now the reverse is true; the tomato has been relegated to the vegetable garden. How fickle we are! The bright-green, lobed, hairy leaves and cascading red or yellow fruits of the tomato plant are indeed ornamental, and the large vining types can be trained to cover a fence.

The taste of a specific tomato variety seems to differ from garden to garden, season to season, and even plant to plant in the same garden, which complicates trying to choose a variety. Tomato tastes range from sweet to acidic, and the preferred balance between these two flavors seems to be a personal matter that determines which variety someone chooses. Other taste subtleties can be described as fruity, spicy, aromatic, earthy, or fermented. The textures can be juicy, tender, uniform, or seedy, dry, mushy, grainy, and tough skinned.

How to Grow

Tomatoes are heat-loving plants. They grow best in warm-summer areas and can tolerate no frost. Though perennials, they are grown as warm-weather annuals. Buy tomato seedlings from your local nursery in spring, or for a larger selection of varieties, less expense, and more fun, start your own.

About 6 to 8 weeks before your last frost, plant tomato seeds ¼ inch deep in flats or milk cartons filled with good potting soil. Keep the plants in a very sunny place near a window or under grow lights. When all danger of frost is over and the plants are 4 to 6 inches in height, transplant them out into the garden. They should be planted several feet apart, in full sun and in well-drained soil amended with a good amount of organic matter. Plant the transplants deeper than you would most—the soil should come up to the first set of new leaves. Most gardeners prefer to stake or trellis tomatoes. It takes up less room and keeps the fruit from spoiling on the ground.

In addition to a lot of organic matter, fertilize with fish emulsion, chicken manure, or a balanced fertilizer at transplant time, again when the fruits have begun to set, and every 3 weeks after that. A form of calcium is often needed to prevent blossom-end rot. Liming may be needed every few years if you live in an acid-soil area. Tomatoes prefer a soil pH between 6 and 7.

Keep your tomato plants evenly watered. Deep, fairly infrequent waterings are best. Mulching is usually beneficial to help retain moisture, but it should not be done until the soil has warmed thoroughly. In California and Mediterranean gardens, even though there is no summer rain, often some varieties are grown with heavy mulches and only a biweekly or triweekly watering. This cuts down on production and causes some blossom-end rot but results in tomatoes with a more intense flavor. You might want to experiment with restricted watering in your garden and see what results you get.

A good resource for more information on growing tomatoes and the varieties available is *All About Tomatoes*, by the publishers of Ortho Books.

Pests and Diseases

A few major pests afflict tomatoes, including tomato hornworms, cutworms, tobacco budworms, nematodes, and whiteflies. The first three are easily controlled by hand picking or *Bacillus thuringiensis*. See Appendix B, "Pests and Diseases," for more information. A number of diseases are fairly common to tomatoes, including fusarium and verticillium wilt, alternaria, and tobacco mosaic. Control them by crop rotation, planting resistant varieties, and by good garden hygiene. See the "Varieties" section of this entry for more information on resistant varieties.

Containers

Small fruiting varieties are both lovely and productive in hanging baskets and decorative containers. 'Tiny Tim', 'Patio', 'Pixie', 'Small Fry', and 'Toy Boy' do well in containers, and 'Red Pear', 'Yellow Pear', 'Red Cherry', and 'Yellow Cherry' are good varieties for large hanging baskets.

Prolonging the Season

Planting early varieties of tomatoes inside in late winter is probably the best way to extend your tomato season. In addition, while the fruits will not be as tasty as your vine-ripened summer ones, tomatoes can be enjoyed for 4 to 8 weeks past the season by harvesting the vines before fruit is fully ripe and then hanging the vines—fruit and all—from the rafters of a cool garage or shed.

Harvesting

Pick tomatoes as they ripen. Color and a slight give to the fruit are the best guides to ripeness. Remove fruits from the plant with care to not break stems bearing fruits that will develop later. Harvesting is best done with a slight twist of the wrist if hand picking, or with scissors or shears.

Seed Saving

Tomatoes are susceptible to numerous soil-borne diseases. Collecting viable seed and taking precautions against the spread of these diseases can be accomplished at the same time.

Your seed sources should be the finest fruits from the best plants of your favorite nonhybrid varieties. Pick these fruits just a day or two past fully ripe. Place mashed tomato pulp and seeds together in a glass jar with ¼ to ½ cup of water. Allow the mixture to ferment at room temperature for 3 to 4 days or until obviously moldy. Letting it stand longer than necessary is not good for the seed. Stir the mixture on days 1 and 3 and skim off floating pulp and seeds on days 2 and 4. Retain the seeds that have sunk to the bottom of the brew. Rinse with clear water, spread on paper toweling and dry for 5 to 6 days. Place in airtight containers for winter storage.

Varieties

Tomatoes grow in a surprisingly wide variety of colors and shapes. See the "Rainbow Gardens" chapter for more information on unusual-colored tomatoes. Tomatoes are also used in an assortment of ways far broader than as salad ingredients or sandwich fillers. Some varieties are bred with less juice and more pulp particularly for sauces, paste, and general cooking. See the "Italian Gardens" chapter for more information on these varieties. Even stuffing tomatoes, with extra-firm walls and meaty flesh that hold filling well, are available.

Disease resistance is a most important quality in tomato varieties as it is sometimes the only way to avoid destructive diseases, particularly if your garden is too small for crop rotation. Many varieties are actually named to include an indication of their disease resistance, and the capital-letter disease abbreviation included in the name gives you this information. For example, a standard name followed by the letters VF or VFF indicates that the variety is resistant to some strains of verticillium and fusarium wilt. Other initials are N, for nematodes; T, for tobacco mosaic; and A, for alternaria.

Tomato varieties are either "determinate" or "indeterminate." For practical purposes, determinate plants are those in which the vines grow little or not at all once the fruit is set. They can usually be grown with little or no support, and you can expect the fruit to ripen within a short period of time. These varieties are valuable for short-summer areas and for container growing or borders. Indeterminate plant vines continue to grow after the first fruit is set and continue to set new fruit all throughout the season. They need staking or other support, and their fruit ripens over a long period of time.

There are hundreds of varieties of tomatoes to choose from. Tomato plants are generally planted from seedlings purchased at local nurseries, which tend to carry varieties that are most popular and appropriate to the climate and disease conditions in that area. For more unusual varieties or for heirloom or foreign varieties, you will probably have to order seed and start your own plants. See the "Italian Gardens" and "Burpee All-Time-Favorites Gardens" chapters for more variety information.

The mail-order seed company with perhaps the largest selection of varieties for containers is Park. For unusual varieties try Gleckler's and Seeds Blum. European varieties are carried by Le Marché and Shepherd's, and Hastings has a large number of varieties for southern gardens. Heirloom varieties are available from Abundant Life, Redwood City Seed, and Seeds Blum. The seed company with the largest selection of tomato varieties is Tomato Growers Supply, P.O. Box 2237, Fort Myers, FL 33902. It carries over one hundred varieties.

Large Red Tomatoes

'ACE 55 VF'   80 days, determinate, low-acid tomato with meaty walls and bright-red exterior, heavy bearer; widely adapted but especially good in hot, dry areas of the West. (Burpee, Tomato Growers)

'BEEFMASTER VFN HYBRID'   80 days, indeterminate, tasty giant tomatoes up to 2 pounds, needs staking. (Park, Vermont Bean)

'BETTER BOY VFN HYBRID'   72 days, indeterminate, long and heavily productive vines; large, bright-red fruits; firm, good for slicing. (Readily available)

'BONNY BEST'   76 days, indeterminate, heirloom variety well loved for its tasty fruits; early producer, well adapted to northern gardens. (Good, Nichols, Seeds Blum, Tomato Growers)

'EARLY GIRL'   54 days, hybrid, indeterminate, produces heavy crop earlier than most and extending longer than most. (Burpee, Nichols, Tomato Growers, Vermont Bean)

'QUICK PICK VFFNT'   68 days, indeterminate, long season, medium-size fruits, excellent flavor and texture. (Tomato Growers)

'RUTGERS VF IMPROVED'   80 days, determinate, bright-red thick-walled fruit, compact vines; more disease resistance and bigger, earlier harvests than original 'Rutgers'. (Readily available)

'STRIPED CAVERN'   70 days, indeterminate, good flavor; very large vertically striped tomato shaped like a pepper; handsome appearance, excellent for stuffing. (Seeds Blum, Thompson & Morgan)

Large Yellow

'LEMON BOY'   VFN, 72 days, hybrid, indeterminate, lemon-yellow in color, very mild in flavor, low in acid, widely adapted. (Readily available)

'MANDARIN CROSS YELLOW'   90 days, hybrid, determinate, deep-golden fruit, excellent flavor and vigor, grows to about 3 feet. (Le Marché)

Cherry Tomatoes

'SWEET 100 HYBRID'   65 days, indeterminate, very sweet, low in acid; large yield of 1-inch fruits; plants tall and good for trellising, need staking. (Burpee, Le Marché, Shepherd's, Twilley, Vermont Bean)

'YELLOW PEAR'   78 days, indeterminate, heirloom variety; bite-size yellow tomatoes shaped like small pears, low in acid; plants rangy, need staking. (Readily available)

Sauce Tomatoes

'ROMA VF'   80 days, determinate, improved cultivar of old 'Roma' with considerably more disease resistance; large harvests of thick-walled fruits ideal for sauces, paste, and canning. (Readily available)

'SAN MARZANO'   80 days, indeterminate, probably most popular of paste tomatoes, bright red, mild flavor, meaty texture; outstanding for paste, sauce, and canning. (Readily available)

'SUPER ITALIAN PASTE'   exceptionally large meaty paste tomato, makes handling easy and quantity processing fast and easy; ripens midseason. (Seeds Blum)

Preserving

To preserve tomatoes, freeze or can them as catsup, sauce, paste, puree, juice, or stewed tomatoes. They are also often kept in the form of soups, relishes, and jams and marmalades. When canning tomatoes make sure you are using acidic varieties to prevent botulism.

Green (unripe) tomatoes can be pickled or made into chutney.

Purchasing

Except for the rural roadside stand or the occasional farmer's market, commercial sources for vine-ripened tomatoes are next to impossible to find these days. But when you do shop for tomatoes, try to find ones that are bright in color, firm without being rock hard, and that feel heavy. The latter qualification is subjective, to be sure, but an apt description of a ripe tomato. Pass over tomatoes with a pinkish color in favor of those with a slightly more orangish cast. Bert Greene in *Greene on Greens* describes good tomato color as the shade of red that lies between a fire engine and a field of poppies. It is true that some of the German heirloom varieties and increasingly popular Japanese types are meant to be pink skinned, but these are the exception. In general, Bert Greene's description is most accurate.

PART
FIVE

RESOURCES
AND
REFERENCES

APPENDIX A:
PLANTING AND MAINTENANCE

Covered in this section are the basics of soil preparation, starting seeds, transplanting, fertilizing, composting, staking, mulching, watering, and maintaining vegetables and herbs. For more detailed information on this vast subject I recommend *Gardening: The Complete Guide to Growing America's Favorite Fruits and Vegetables,* put out by the National Gardening Association; *The Why and How of Home Horticulture;* and the many other garden books listed in the bibliography.

Seeding and Planting

The first step in planning your garden is choosing a suitable site. Most chefs recommend locating the vegetable and herb garden as close to the kitchen as possible, and I heartily agree. Then it's an easy trip out to get a few handfuls of salad greens or a few sprigs of mint. Another consideration is that the majority of edible plants need at least six hours of sun, fairly rich organic soil, and good drainage to thrive. These plants can be in a bed by themselves in a classical vegetable garden, interplanted in a flower bed, or set out in large planter boxes. Vegetable gardens are best for large harvests, or for plants that need special care, and are sometimes easier to maintain, but as I have stressed throughout the book, most edible plants are attractive enough to be used in any ornamental border.

Once you've decided on a planting area, it's time to choose your varieties. Your major consideration will be, of course, what you like to eat. With this in mind, look for varieties that will grow well in your climate—and in your particular garden's microclimate—and those that will be as disease resistant as possible.

After you've chosen your varieties and sent for the seeds, it's time to think about the soil. If you can start your garden in the fall, prepare the soil as described below and seed it with a cover crop of clover or winter rye to grow through the winter. Spade the cover crop under a month or so before you want to start planting in the spring.

PREPARING THE SOIL

To prepare the soil well for a new garden, first remove large rocks and weeds. Then, where large, established, deep-rooted trees and shrubs are growing near a planting bed, prune off some of the large roots that intrude into the area; usually such shrubs and trees can tolerate the removal with no ill effects. Next, spade the area over and, if you have not already done so, supplement your soil with organic matter and a source of nitrogen, as most soils are deficient in these materials. After the area has been spaded up, cover it with four or five inches of compost and an inch or two of well-aged manure. Add lime if your soil is acidic. Distribute the supplements evenly and incorporate them thoroughly by turning the soil over with a spade or tiller. If you can do these steps a few weeks before you plant, so much the better.

Finally, grade and rake the area. You are now ready to form beds and paths, seed, and dig planting holes. The most convenient bed size is one not more than five feet wide so you can easily reach in to weed or harvest. Some sort of mulch on the paths is usually needed so your feet won't get wet and muddy.

STARTING FROM SEEDS

You can grow most vegetables and herbs from seeds, though many varieties are also available as young plants at the nursery. Seeds can be started indoors in flats or other well-drained containers, outdoors in a cold frame, or directly in the garden. Consider starting seeds inside when you are concerned about giving your seedlings an early or safe start, since most young plants, especially warm-weather annuals, are susceptible to frost damage. Other reasons for starting plants indoors are to extend the growing season, to protect plants from pests, or to start vegetable and fruit production as soon as possible. When all danger of frost is past, the seedlings can be planted into the garden.

When starting from seeds, you may want to consider using cold frames (essentially, minigreenhouses) to extend the length of the growing season. Cold frames provide extra warmth early in the year, so you can get a head start on your spring planting. These minigreenhouses can also be used to grow lettuces and other cool-season greens throughout the winter in many parts of the country. Cold frames can be purchased from mail-order firms or local nurseries, but you can also fashion your own by placing an old storm door or window over a sunken planting bed.

As cold frames are usually best located on the south side of a building or in full sun, good air circulation and temperature control must be provided so that tiny plants do not fry on a sunny day. A simple propping or shading device can help avoid that problem.

Propagation from seeds is a complex subject because the cultural needs of seeds vary widely among species. Still, some basic rules apply to most seeding procedures. First, whether starting seeds in the ground or in a container, make sure you have a loose, water-retentive soil that drains well. Good drainage is important because seeds can get waterlogged and too much water can lead to "damping off," a fungal disease that kills seedlings at the soil line.

Smooth the soil surface and plant the seeds according to the directions on the package; additional planting information may be found in Part Four, "An Encyclopedia of Superior Vegetables," and in *Plant Propagation—Principles and Practices* (see bibliography). Pat down the seeds, and water carefully to make the seed bed moist but not soggy.

While gardeners traditionally plant most kinds of seeds in parallel rows, some kinds of edibles lend themselves to what is called the wide-row method. Wide-row beds have the seeds scattered a uniform number of inches apart to completely cover the bed. Vegetables well suited to this technique are lettuce, carrots, beets, scallions, salad greens, and radishes. The advantages to this method are higher production and a living mulch formed when the plants grow together.

If you have started your seedlings in containers, do not transplant them until they have their second set of true leaves (the first leaves that sprout from a seed are called seed leaves and usually look different from the later true leaves) and, if the seedlings are tender, until all danger of frost is past. In fact, don't put heat-loving vegetables out until the weather has thoroughly warmed up and is stable. Young plants started indoors or in a greenhouse should be hardened off before planting in the garden; that is, they should be put outside in a sheltered place for a few days in their containers to let them get used to the differences in temperature, humidity, and air movement.

If your garden is small, or if you are planting in containers only, buying a whole packet of some types of seeds is often a waste. When you intend to grow only a few tomato, cabbage, or squash plants, for example, it is less work and cheaper to buy young plants from a reputable nursery. However, root crops such as carrots, beets, or parsnips and unusual varieties such as yellow tomatoes or red okra are not generally sold as transplants and must be bought as seeds.

TRANSPLANTING
When setting out transplants, whether your own seedlings or ones from the nursery, if a mat of roots has formed at the bottom of the root ball, it is important to remove it or open it up so the roots won't continue to grow in a tangled mass. In most cases, set the plant in the ground at the same height as it was in the container. Pat it in place with gentle hand pressure and water it well. Tomatoes and members of the cabbage family should be planted deeper in the ground, as they tend to be top-heavy and need the extra soil support. If the plants are large or vining and are going to need staking, put the stakes in place at planting time, on the north side of the plant to avoid shading it. In most cases, transplanted seedlings should be shaded by wooden shingles, polyester row covers, or other protective devices for a day or two.

Polyester row covers look a little like cheesecloth. They are gently laid over the planting bed and anchored with soil piled over the borders or with large wire fasteners stuck into the ground. These row covers are sometimes called floating row covers, since if they are not put on too tightly they can easily be pushed up by the growing plants and can be kept on throughout the entire growing season as protection from insects or to give extra shading in summer. Row covers are particularly valuable to protect members of the cabbage family from cabbage worms, lettuce from slugs, eggplants and radishes from flea beetles, and onions from root maggots. The polyester fabrics, the best known of which is Reemay, appear to have the advantage of keeping plants both warmer in winter and cooler in summer. When used over bee-pollinated plants, the fabric is removed when the plants begin to flower. Conversely, if you plan to save seeds from your vegetables, row covers can prevent cross-pollination in insect-pollinated varieties. In this case you would pollinate your flowers by hand with a cotton swab. When row covers are kept in place throughout the growing season, the material is usually stretched over wire supports to create tunnels, thus providing better air circulation. The supports are commercially available, but you can also make your own out of PVC pipe or other flexible tubing. Fasten the material to the tubing with large clips available from plumbing supply houses.

Maintaining the Edible Garden
The backbone of appropriate maintenance is a knowledge of your soil and weather, an ability to recognize basic water and nutrient deficiency symptoms, and a familiarity with the plants you grow. Be aware, though, that you'll never know all about growing vegetables, as it's not like learning to ride a bike or memorizing your ABCs. Growing vegetables is an art as well as a science, and part of the enjoyment is the continual challenge.

Annual vegetables and herbs are growing machines. As a rule they need to grow rapidly and with little interruption so they will produce succulent leaves and fruits and will grow with few pest problems. By far the most important step in growing vegetables is good soil preparation. But once the plants are in the ground, continual monitoring for nutrient deficiencies or drought can head off other problems. In addition, to maintain plants, you must have basic information on fertilizing, composting, staking, mulching, and watering.

PLANT NUTRIENTS

Plant nutrition is a complex subject, and to maintain their gardens well, serious gardeners need to understand basic soil chemistry as well as basic botany. The goal of fertilizing is to provide your plants with the nutrients that they might not be getting naturally, when they need them, and in appropriate quantities. You must therefore be familiar with your plants' nutritional needs and with your soil's composition. If possible, get your soil tested for primary nutrients and pH. Some university extension offices will do this at no charge. Soil kits are also available for a rough home testing.

To live and be healthy, all garden plants need a number of nutrients. The three major nutrients and their chemical symbols are nitrogen (N), phosphorus (P), and potassium (K), often referred to as potash. In addition, ten minor nutrients are necessary for plant growth. Each of these nutrients is discussed in turn below, and further information on the sources of these nutrients is given in the following section, "Fertilizing."

Nitrogen

Nitrogen stimulates shoot and leaf growth, and it is important to supply the correct amount. A nitrogen deficiency is usually signaled by pale-green or yellowish leaves. This symptom first appears on the lower or older leaves, which might start to drop. Too much nitrogen can be as harmful as too little. Excess nitrogen can cause the leaves to become too succulent, thus more prone to disease and frost damage, and sometimes stimulates leaf growth at the expense of fruit production. As a rule, many of the new hybrid vegetables need more nitrogen than some of the open-pollinated varieties. Most perennial herbs usually need no extra nitrogen, except on sandy soils.

Nitrogen renewal in the soil is accomplished via the decomposition of animal and plant wastes, the deposition of ammonium and nitrate salts from rainwater, the action of nitrogen-fixing bacteria that live on the roots of some plants, and the application of organic or synthetic fertilizers that contain nitrogen.

Nitrogen from organic sources is made available to plants slowly, by means of bacterial action. That action is further slowed by cold, very acid, or poorly drained soils. Organic fertilizers are made from animal or plant residues, and most are quite low in nitrogen. While organic sources of nitrogen are extremely variable, some approximate percentages can be given: blood meal, 10 to 14 percent nitrogen; fish meal, 8 percent; cottonseed meal, 7 percent; and

castor pomace, 4 percent. The rest of the organic fertilizers—such as most manures, bone meal, leaf mold, pine needles, seaweed, and most compost—are quite low in nitrogen, containing only 3 percent at most.

Inorganic or synthesized organic sources of nitrogen—fertilizers such as sulfate and calcium nitrate—make high amounts of nitrogen readily available to plants. Many of these fertilizers contain as much as 30 percent nitrogen. Synthetic nitrogen is available in fast-acting forms, usually labeled nitrate or nitric, or in slow-release forms, labeled ammonic or slow release. The fast-acting forms are directly available to plants and do not depend on bacterial action to make the nitrogen available.

Phosphorus

Phosphorus contributes to root growth, fruit development, and disease resistance. It is present in soil solutions (the microscopic film around the soil particles) in different forms, most of which are not available to plants. Microorganisms present in soils with sufficient organic matter help make phosphorus available to plants. Very acidic soils tie up phosphorus in a form unusable to plants.

A symptom of phosphorus deficiency in some plants—such as corn, tomatoes, and cabbage (except red cabbage)—is a red-purple discoloration of the stems, leaf veins, and leaves.

Natural sources of phosphorus are finely ground phosphate rock, bone meal, and fish meal. Small amounts of phosphorus can be found in cottonseed meal, blood meal, hard wood ash, and most manures. The most commonly used synthetic forms of phosphorus are superphosphate and ammonium phosphate. If you are growing high-yield vegetable or fruit crops, in addition to manure or compost you should add some form of supplemental phosphorus to the soil every year or two. Because phosphorus moves very little in the soil, it should be worked well into the soil to make it available to the roots or applied to the bottom of planting holes.

Potassium

Potassium, or potash, is the third major plant nutrient. Sufficient amounts of potash promote resistance to disease, cold, and drought. Potash deficiencies result in poor crop yields, uneven ripening, poor root systems, leaves streaked or spotted with yellow, and dried or burned leaf edges. Potash deficiency is usually hard to diagnose, and potassium is usually added for safety because deficiencies often show up too late to be rectified.

More potash is available to plants in arid climates than in other climates. Natural sources are manures, compost, plant residues, granite dust, and green sand. Commercial sources are muriate of potash and sulfate of potash. In eastern sections of the country it is customary to add some form of potash in the spring.

The Minor Nutrients

Certain micronutrients are necessary in varying amounts for healthy plant growth. These are calcium, magnesium, sulfur, and the trace elements zinc, manganese, iron, boron, chlorine, copper, molybdenum, and for some plants, cobalt. Most soils containing sufficient organic matter can supply enough micronutrients. The major exceptions are acid soils with calcium deficiencies and alkaline soils with iron deficiencies. Regular applications of some form of lime to renew calcium are necessary in acid-soil areas. Iron can be supplied by applications of chelated iron. Other micronutrients are sometimes lacking in a few areas of the country. If you notice discoloration, stunted growth, chlorosis (a yellowing of the leaves while the veins remain green), or a dieback of the leaves and branches in your plants, it would be wise to have your soil tested for nutrient levels and pH. Local authorities can alert you to nutrient deficiencies prevalent in your area.

FERTILIZING

Fertilizers are available in many forms. So-called organic types may be powders, liquids, or fibrous materials such as manures. Synthetic fertilizers can be liquids, granules, or powder. Some are combination formulas and others contain only a single nutrient.

By law, synthetic fertilizers must be labeled to indicate the percentage of each of the three major nutrients they contain. The percentages are always designated in the following order: nitrogen, phosphorus, and potassium (N, P, and K). Thus the labeled formulation might read 16-20-0, meaning that the product contains 16 percent nitrogen, 20 percent phosphorus, and 0 percent potassium. In actual use, not all of the phosphorus and potassium are available to the plant. The formulation, therefore, is chiefly a statement of the relative amounts of the nutrients. The remaining material is filler. Labeling also includes information about the sources of these primary nutrients and the presence of other micronutrients in the product. The nitrogen may be in the form of ammonium sulfate or urea, for instance, and the product may also contain other nutrients, such as iron or zinc.

The contents of organic fertilizers often are not labeled in the same manner because it is too difficult to determine and standardize the exact amounts of nutrients in most of these materials.

In the last few years, much has been written about organic, or natural, fertilizers versus synthetic fertilizers. There are advantages and disadvantages to each. The advantages of organic fertilizers—such as manures, bone meal, blood meal, fish meal, and fish emulsion—include the following:

1. Many improve the structure of the soil and provide optimum conditions for soil microbes.
2. They recycle valuable materials.
3. They release their nutrients slowly and evenly.
4. Their nitrogen content is less likely to be leached from the soil (thereby wasting the nutrient and possibly polluting water sources).
5. They usually contain fewer soil contaminants.
6. Most are less likely to burn or overfertilize plants.
7. Some forms can be very inexpensive or free.

The disadvantages of organic fertilizers include:

1. Bulk and weight make some hard to store, handle, and apply.
2. Many are expensive and limited in quantity.
3. They are variable in nutrient content.
4. Most are slow to act.
5. Some of the nutrients are unavailable when the soil temperature is under 50 degrees Fahrenheit.
6. Some forms of manures are contaminated with weed seeds.

The advantages of synthetic fertilizers are:

1. Most are less bulky and easier to apply and store.
2. They are often less expensive.
3. The amounts of nutrients are quantifiable.
4. They are generally fast acting.
5. Some can be used effectively under cool soil conditions.

The disadvantages of synthetic fertilizers include:

1. In general, more petroleum is used in their manufacture than for organic types.
2. Many of the nitrate forms leach from the soil relatively quickly.
3. Some contain soil contaminants, and many are high in salt.
4. They provide little or no benefit to soil structure, microbes, or earthworms; some may be detrimental to soil inhabitants.

Organic Fertilizers

BLOOD MEAL
Blood meal is a powdered substance made from slaughterhouse blood. It is high in nitrogen (10 to 14 percent) and can burn plants if applied too heavily. It is expensive.

BONE MEAL
Bone meal is made from steamed and ground-up slaughterhouse bones. It is high in phosphorus (15 to 25 percent), contains some nitrogen (2 to 4 percent), and releases its nutrients slowly. Bone meal is useful in reducing soil acidity and is expensive.

COTTONSEED MEAL
Cottonseed meal is made from ground-up cottonseed. It is 6 to 7 percent nitrogen, 2 to 3 percent phosphorus, and has an acidifying function. It is expensive.

FISH MEAL AND FISH EMULSION

Fish meal and fish emulsion are made from ground-up fish by-products. They are fairly high in nitrogen and phosphorus, have an intense odor, and are expensive.

GREEN MANURES

Green manures are growing plants, usually legumes, planted as cover crops and then tilled back into the soil to increase the amount of nutrients and organic matter. Plants generally used as green manures are rye grass (not a legume), clover, vetch, wheat, and alfalfa.

MANURES

Manures are animal excrement. Nutrient content varies from batch to batch; approximate percentages are given. Poultry manure: N, 2 to 4½ percent; P, 4 to 6 percent; K, 1 to 2½ percent. Steer manure: N, 1 to 2½ percent; P, 1 to 1½ percent; K, 2 to 3½ percent. Manures are generally inexpensive or free and are valuable as soil conditioners as well as for the nutrients they contain. They should be weed free and generally should not be used fresh. Some forms, such as steer manure, are high in salts and should not be used often.

PHOSPHATE ROCK

Phosphate rock is finely ground rock high in phosphorus as well as many micronutrients. It is nearly insoluble in water and is made available by microbial action. The nutrient release is slow and steady. To encourage microbial action, phosphate rock must be applied in conjunction with an organic substance, such as manure. Incorporate the manure a few months before applying the phosphate rock.

SEWER SLUDGE

Sewer sludge is granulated or fibrous waste from municipal sewage treatment plants. It comes in two forms, activated and composted. The activated form has a higher nutrient content: N, 5 to 6 percent; P, 3 percent; K, 5 percent. Sewer sludge is potentially a valuable fertilizer, but contaminants, such as industrial wastes and pesticides, currently make it unsafe for use on edible plants.

Synthetic Fertilizers

AMMONIUM-BASED FERTILIZERS

Ammonium-based fertilizers, such as ammonium sulfate and urea, are high-nitrogen fertilizers that are fairly stable in the soil and not as prone to leaching as the nitrate forms of nitrogen. These fertilizers have an acidifying effect on the soil and leave salt residues.

MURIATE OF POTASH (POTASSIUM CHLORIDE)

Muriate of potash, or potassium chloride, leaves a fair amount of salt in the soil but produces no soil pH reaction. It is easily dissolved in water and has a high percentage of potassium.

NITRATES

Nitrates—ammonium nitrate, calcium nitrate, and potassium nitrate—are fast-acting nitrogen fertilizers that work in cold or sterile soils. Except for these conditions, nitrates should generally be avoided because they are easily leached by rainwater or irrigation.

SLOW-RELEASE NITROGEN FERTILIZERS

Slow-release nitrogen fertilizers have special formulations or coatings designed to release fast-acting forms of nitrogen in a more controlled way. They include solid granules as well as some wax- or paraffin-covered pellets. These fertilizers are quite expensive initially, but less fertilizer is wasted and the dosages are more even. They are particularly valuable for containerized plants.

SUPERPHOSPHATE

Superphosphate is a rock phosphate treated with sulfuric acid to make the phosphorus more quickly available to the plants. It also provides sulfur and calcium.

Fertilizer Needs of Annual Fruits and Vegetables

Annual fruits and vegetables have high nutrient needs. In vegetable gardens, green manures such as winter wheat, rye, and clover are a valuable source of nutrients. In areas where cover cropping is not feasible, supplement the soil with large amounts of organic matter. In either case, incorporate phosphorus into the root zone. Supplemental nitrogen is usually needed, particularly for leafy vegetables. Tomatoes often need extra phosphorus, and root and tuber vegetables often need extra potassium.

COMPOSTING

Compost is the humus-rich result of the decomposition of organic matter, such as kitchen wastes, leaves, and lawn clippings. Organic materials will decompose whether or not they are in a compost pile—the breakdown of organic material takes place continually under every tree, shrub, and flower growing on the earth. The objective in maintaining a composting system is to speed up decomposition and centralize the material so you can gather it up and spread it where it will do the most good.

There need be no great mystique about composting. Basically, microbial action converts a pile of organic matter into the most beneficial soil amendment you can find. This section covers two different systems of composting: a very simple, cool, low-production method for dry wastes such as lawn clippings, leaves, and corn husks; and a more sophisticated high-production system for processing most kitchen wastes.

Low-Production Systems

I have in my yard a very serviceable example of a low-production method that is simplicity itself. The materials it uses are dry and do not attract pests. All disease-free garden clippings are piled in a screened-off part of the yard. Excluded are weeds that have gone to seed, ivy clippings, and Bermuda grass clippings because they do not always completely decompose and can lead to the growth of weeds, ivy, and Bermuda grass in the garden. Dry kitchen wastes such as pea pods, egg shells, carrot tops, and apple peels go in when I have them.

This system is a cool, slow-acting means of recycling needed organic matter; in its own small way it also helps alleviate the pressure on our already full dumps. Because I do not often turn or water the pile, microbial action is slow and does not produce enough heat to kill weed seeds or diseased material. Also, many of the nutrients are leached out by rain before they reach the garden. But much organic matter that would have ended up wasted at the dump ends up in my yard instead, in the form of soil-building humus.

If you choose a low-production compost system and you feel ambitious, you can speed production by occasionally turning the pile, adding some form of nitrogen, and, in arid climates, watering it once in a while. The point to remember is that composting does not have to be a big production. Every yard should incorporate some method of developing this valuable material.

High-Production Systems

A well-designed high-production compost heap creates an environment in which decay-causing bacteria can live and reproduce at the highest possible rate. There are three requirements for this kind of environment: keeping a suitable amount of air in the pile; keeping the pile moist but not wringing wet; and maintaining a good balance of compatible material so that the microbes have sufficient nourishment. Much technical information has been circulated among experts regarding the optimum ratio between available carbon and nitrogen. It is usually sufficient to know that if you build the pile with layers of fresh green material, alternating with layers of dried material and thin layers of soil, and occasionally add nitrogen in some form, you will have a successful compost pile. In warm weather the composting action will be much faster than in the winter. Omit or cut up large pieces of compost material, because they decompose very slowly. Corn stalks and husks, woody branches over a half inch in diameter, and other such large items may take two or three years to break down and should be put in a pile by themselves or sent to the dump.

Once the organic matter is composted, apply it to the garden or cover the compost pile with a tarp to prevent valuable nutrients being leached out by rainwater.

Use whatever method you want, but do compost. It's the best possible thing you can do for the health of your plants. For further composting information, see some of the general books on organic gardening listed in the bibliography.

STAKING

Many annual vegetables benefit from being given some support as they develop. While there are bush bean and bush pea varieties, many of the most popular varieties require trellising or some other form of support for the best development. Cucumbers produce considerably greater harvests when staked, and most gardeners stake large varieties of tomatoes to save space and to keep the fruits from rotting on the ground. Vertically supporting plants is also a simple way to increase the entire harvest of a given space as it effectively adds another dimension of square footage: up in this case, rather than out.

While there are probably hundreds of ways to stake or trellis plants, try wooden or metal stakes, twine nailed on a fence, or for peas, prunings from shrubs. To make a narrow planting in a small area, use a square wooden frame of two by twos, at least five feet high by five feet or six feet wide. Space nails at two-inch intervals across the top and bottom stringers and weave strong twine up and down the height of the trellis. Indeterminate tomatoes, vining cucumbers, and pole beans and peas can be trained on the twine. You can create a tomato tower by making a large tube of concrete reinforcing wire; just be sure the openings in the wire are large enough to allow you to withdraw your hand once it has a tomato in it. Stakes of all sizes and materials are now available in local nurseries, as are towers and trellises.

MULCHING

A mulch is any material laid on the soil to reduce moisture evaporation and control weeds. Besides these primary functions, mulching can have a number of secondary roles in garden maintenance. Mulch helps keep soil from becoming packed down by foot traffic and rain. A mulch at least three to four inches deep helps smother many weed seeds. Mulch acts as insulation and helps keep weather extremes from affecting plants. The soil stays cooler in summer and warmer in winter. Usually, mulching material is organic in nature and will improve soil structure and fertility while performing its other functions, but nonorganic materials are also used for their water-retentive properties or their ability to absorb and retain heat. Clearly, mulching is an important part of garden maintenance.

Mulching Materials

Mulches can be made from organic materials, such as compost, pine needles, or grass clippings, or from other substances, such as sheet plastic, rock, or gravel.

COMPOST

Well-aged compost, screened and spread around landscape areas, is both pleasing to the eye and of great value as a soil conditioner. The major problem is production. Most families do not produce enough compost to fill all their mulching needs, so I strongly suggest that you give priority to your vegetables when applying this valuable material.

PINE NEEDLES

Pine needles are attractive and lightweight and add acidity to the soil. Use them for acid-loving plants, but do not use them if you have excessively acid soil. They work well on strawberry plants to keep the berries from rotting on the ground.

PLASTIC SHEETING

Sheet plastic is available both clear and black in color. Black plastic, in particular, is very popular as a mulch around heat-loving plants such as tomatoes, melons, squash, eggplant, and peppers. It absorbs heat from the sun and makes the soil around the plants warmer. At the same time, it is an effective agent for controlling weeds and reducing evaporation. Plastic does have its drawbacks, however. If applied to the soil too early in the spring, it keeps the soil winter-cold longer than it would be if left uncovered. On the other hand, if left on the soil in the fall, it keeps it warm longer. Another drawback is that plastic is not water-permeable, so care must be taken to ensure that water being delivered to the plants does not run off to waste, leaving the plants dry. While plastic is not a problem-free mulching material, on balance I recommend it, especially for use around the heat lovers. Four mil is the minimum thickness I would recommend, and expect to replace it every second or third season.

SAWDUST

Sawdust can be used raw, well aged, or treated. When treated, it is often called soil conditioner. If you use raw, fresh sawdust, treat it with ammonium sulfate or an organic nitrogen-rich fertilizer, such as blood meal or cottonseed meal. The decomposition of the sawdust by soil microbes takes available nitrogen from the soil that has to be replaced. (This aspect is valuable if you want to prevent plant growth; raw sawdust spread three or four inches deep on garden paths is a valuable weed deterrent.) Well-rotted or treated soil conditioner can be used without supplemental nitrogen.

WEED CLOTH

A fabriclike material named Weed Cloth has recently become available as a mulching agent. While it does not absorb heat in the same intensity as black plastic, this material is water-permeable, easier to handle, and more attractive than the former.

WATERING

While we usually associate garden watering problems with arid climates, most garden experts recommend supplemental watering in the vegetable garden at specific times during the growing season. For instance, watering is needed for all seed beds and young transplants, corn when it's tasseling, and salad greens in warm weather. Rain seldom can be relied on at these times. Therefore most gardeners need some sort of supplemental watering system and a knowledge of water management.

No easy formula exists for the correct amount or frequency of watering. Proper watering takes experience and observation. In addition to the specific watering times noted above, the water needs of a particular plant will depend on soil type, wind conditions, air temperature, and the kind of plant it is. To water properly you must learn how to recognize water stress symptoms (often a dulling of foliage color as well as the better-known symptoms of drooping leaves and wilting); how much to water (too much is as bad as too little); and how to water. Some general rules are:

1. Water deeply. Except for seed beds, most plants need infrequent deep watering rather than frequent light sprinkling.
2. To ensure proper absorption, apply water at a rate slow enough to prevent runoff.
3. Do not use overhead watering systems when the wind is blowing.
4. Try to water early in the morning so that foliage will have time to dry out before nightfall, thus preventing some disease problems. In addition, because of the cooler temperature, less water is lost to evaporation.
5. Test your watering system occasionally to make sure it is covering the area evenly.
6. Use methods and tools that conserve water. When using a hose, a pistol-grip nozzle will shut the water off while you move from one container or planting bed to another. Canvas soaker hoses and other drip irrigation systems apply water slowly to shrub borders and vegetable gardens.

Drip Irrigation Systems

Drip, or trickle, irrigation systems are advisable wherever feasible, and many vegetable gardens are well suited to them. Drip systems deliver water a drop at a time through spaghetti-like emitter tubes or plastic pipe with nozzles that drip water right onto the root zone of the plant. Drip irrigation is one of the few watering systems devised for containerized plants. Another similar system, called a porous-wall or ooze system, delivers water through porous plastic hoses along the whole length of a garden row. These drip systems do have the disadvantage of letting the foliage get dusty in arid climates. This sometimes encourages spider mites, so an occasional overhead watering is in order. Seed beds will also need overhead watering.

Yet another variation of these systems is the Microjet system, in which the spray heads are on little risers and emit a mist rather than a trickle. Spider mites and seed beds are not a problem with this system, but it encourages fungal problems in some disease-prone crops. See "The Golden Door Garden" in the "Spa Gardens" chapter for more information on this system.

Other problems with drip systems are that tubes and emitters clog easily. Without a good filter system, often every emitter must be checked each time the system is used, especially if the water source has occasional grit in it. Obviously, this can be a chore in a system with twenty or thirty emitters and makes it worth getting a good filtering system. The porous-wall or ooze system, while not as versatile, has fewer clogging problems and is ideal for vegetable gardens. All these systems are, however, vulnerable to vandalism.

Problems aside, all forms of drip irrigation are more efficient than furrow or standard overhead watering in delivering water to its precise destination. They deliver water slowly so it doesn't run off, and they also water deeply, which encourages deep rooting.

GROWING SEASON MAINTENANCE

Maintaining vegetables and herbs through the growing season can range from effortless to effortful, depending on what you have chosen to plant. With easily grown vegetables—such as carrots, radishes, grinding corns, garlic, sunflowers, wheat, and potatoes—it can simply mean occasionally checking if the plants are vigorous; making sure they get enough water in dry weather; seeing that no pest populations are growing to large numbers; and pulling an occasional weed. These vegetables are simple to maintain, usually need no supplemental fertilizing, get few pest problems, and are not harvested over a long growing season. They are perfect for the busy gardener and the beginner.

Other vegetables and herbs may need a little more supervision because of pest problems: dry beans sometimes get bean beetles or Japanese beetles; onions sometimes get root maggots; and mints occasionally get whiteflies. Some vegetables and herbs are easy to grow but usually need supplemental fertilizing: peppers, sweet corn, beets, basil, lettuce, spinach, pumpkins, winter squash, and most of the leafy greens need fairly frequent applications of nitrogen. Other easily grown vegetables need supervision because they have a long and continual harvest: bush snap beans, zucchini, okra, summer squash, Alpine strawberries, and cherry tomatoes all produce for weeks at a time and need to be picked continually.

There are, of course, edibles that need supervision on a number of fronts, such as vining cucumbers, large tomatoes, and pole beans and peas. Vines need tying up and pruning, continual supervision for pests and diseases, and continual harvesting. Many cabbages, Brussels sprouts, cauliflower, and broccoli need staking so they won't fall over, and garden strawberries need continual pruning. And in all these edibles there are consistent pest problems that need monitoring.

You can see there is great variability in the effort required to grow different vegetables. Before making your choices, consult the effort scale rating given under each vegetable in Part Four, "An Encyclopedia of Superior Vegetables." If you are a beginning or busy gardener, try not to choose too many that are given threes and fours on the scale.

APPENDIX B:
PESTS AND DISEASES

Your garden may appear to be a quiet place, but in reality it is an arena where hundreds of life-and-death dramas are played out every day. Birth and death, killing and nurturing, even intrigue and cunning are all part of the complex community of life waiting to be discovered—and sometimes struggled with—in your garden.

This hidden world can add a new dimension to your gardening pleasure. For example, on an April day, I can turn flowerpots over to find startled earwig mothers waving their pincers at me, protecting their broods. And every June the baby katydids hatch and start chewing on the new leaves of my grapevine. Within a week, three different species of spiders have divided up the territory around the grapes, and all day long they stalk the katydids. While not all pest problems are so easily solved, there are many ways in which you can use predator-prey relationships in garden maintenance. Knowledge of how plants and animals interact in the garden is at the heart of organic, or natural, gardening, and your chief tool for pest control is your power of observation of this miniworld around you.

Potential garden problems come in many forms: weeds, fungi, snails, slugs, insects, diseases, and even such wildlife as rabbits, deer, and birds. The list may seem overwhelming at first, but most gardeners are actually faced with only a few pests. Everyone has to contend with weeds, however, so we'll consider weed control first.

Weed Control

A weed is any plant that is growing in the wrong place. Weeding is one task few gardeners can avoid, and over the years numerous manufacturers have come out with various weed control products. Having seen many plants damaged by improper, or sometimes even proper, use of herbicides, and being leery of the effects of herbicides on the human body, I never recommend using them around edible plants.

There are a number of ways to control weeds without herbicides. My favorite is four or five inches of organic mulch. Then I not only have weed control, but I also add organic matter to the soil. Don't put the mulch on until the soil has warmed up in the spring, though, unless you are trying to keep the soil cool.

Weeds can, of course be pulled out by hand, and this works best if the soil is moist but not wet. Long-handled weeding hoes can do wonders on cutting down on the stooping and reaching. A particularly effective hoe is the scuffle hoe; its flat, sharp blade is parallel to the soil and moves back and forth, cutting most weeds off at the soil line. The most important aspect of weed control is not letting weeds get out of hand. It's similar to washing the dishes when they are first dirty, before the food hardens. Weeds that are large, particularly perennial ones with long taproots, are hard to pull and often come back up. The biggest problem, however, is when you let the seed heads develop. Then you are in for the long haul. Even if you do not let seed heads develop, if you leave fairly mature pulled weeds lying around the garden, often they will still develop seeds. Always throw them out unless you have a very hot compost pile.

Pest Control

Though a few insects and mites, sowbugs, snails, and slugs are potential garden pests, most insects are either neutral or are beneficial to your purposes. Given the chance, the beneficials will do most of your pest control for you. The insect world is a miniature version of the animal world. Instead of predatory lions stalking zebra, predatory ladybugs or lacewing larvae hunt and eat aphids. Many gardeners are not aware of predator-prey relationships and are not able to recognize beneficial insects. The following sections will help you identify both helpful organisms and those that may give you problems. A more detailed aid in identifying both predatory as well as pest insects is *Rodale's Color Handbook of Garden Insects,* by Anna Carr. It contains full-color pictures of the insects, both predator and prey, in all stages of development.

PREDATORS AND PARASITOIDS

Insects that feed on other insects are divided into two types, the predators and the parasitoids. Predators are mobile. They stalk the plants looking for such plant feeders as aphids, mites, and caterpillars. Many predators—the praying mantis, for example—consume any smaller insect they find. Others, such as ladybugs, consume aphids or mealybugs only.

Though predators are valuable insect enemies, they are usually less effective than parasitoids, which are insects that develop in the bodies of other host insects. Most parasitoids are minute wasps or flies whose larvae (young stages) eat other insects from within. Some of these wasps are small enough to live within an aphid or an insect egg. Or one parasitoid egg can divide into thousands of identical cells, which in turn develop into thousands of identical miniwasps, which then can consume an entire caterpillar. Most of the fly parasitoids are larger; a single bombex-fly maggot grows up within one caterpillar. In any case, the parasitoids are the most specific and effective means of insect control.

It should be obvious that indiscriminate use of broad-spectrum pesticides to kill pest insects will usually kill the beneficial parasitoids as well. In my opinion, many so-called organic gardeners who use organic broad-spectrum insecticides have missed this point. While using an "organic" pesticide, they may actually be eliminating a truly organic means of pest control.

My garden contains a perfect example of such predator pest control. Every spring, like clockwork, aphids appear on the growing tips of my ivy. Soon I begin to see syrphid flies (flowerflies), whose larvae eat aphids, hovering around the ivy. They've come to lay eggs. Within a month there is none but an occasional aphid around. The hatched syrphid maggots have eaten most of them. In a case like this, patience is the key to pest control. If I had sprayed with a broad-spectrum insecticide to kill the aphids, I would have killed the syrphid flies as well. The aphid population would have built up again, more quickly than the syrphid fly population, and I would have had to spray again. This is often referred to as the pesticide merry-go-round.

The point is, you don't have to purchase a ticket for the pesticide merry-go-round to begin with. In my example, nature has the system arranged so that the hatching time for syrphid flies, and for most other predators, does not occur until a steady food supply is available. Furthermore, more prey organisms are provided than the predator can eat; thus, in this case, some aphids survive the predation of the flies. The system has to stay in balance, and the predator would not survive if all the prey were destroyed. Therefore, if you are committed to the idea of nonchemical pest control, you must be prepared to tolerate some insects on your plants.

Sometimes the natural system breaks down. For example, a number of imported pests have taken hold in this country. Unfortunately, when such organisms were brought here, their natural predators did not accompany them. Two notorious examples are the European brown snail and the Japanese beetle; neither organism has natural

enemies in this country that provide sufficient controls. Where such organisms occur, it is sometimes necessary to use selective pesticides that kill only the problem insect and do not upset the balance of the other insects in a yard.

Another problem is that sometimes predator-prey relationships become extremely unbalanced. When this happens, you may want to spray with a selective insecticide or, in rare cases, purchase live predators from insectaries.

Following are a few of the predatory and parasitic insects helpful in the garden. Their preservation and protection should be a major goal of your pest control strategy.

Ground Beetles
Ground beetles are all predators. Most are fairly large black beetles that scurry away when you uncover them. Their favorite foods are soft-bodied larvae and slugs and snails.

Lacewings
Lacewings are one of the most effective insect predators in the home garden. They are small green or brown gossamer-winged insects that in their adult stage eat nectar and pollen as well as aphids and mealybugs. In the larval stage they are fierce predators of aphids, mealybugs, and moth eggs and larvae.

Ladybugs
Ladybugs are the best known of the beneficial garden insects. They include about four hundred species besides the familiar red one with black spots. Ladybugs and their fierce-looking larvae eat aphids, mealybugs, and other small insects. I do not recommend buying ladybugs for garden pest control, because most studies have shown that they usually fly away, often before eating any pests.

Spiders
Spiders are close relatives of insects. There are hundreds of species, and they are some of the most effective controllers of pest insects.

Syrphid Flies
Syrphid flies (also called flowerflies or hover flies) look like small bees hovering over flowers, but they have only two wings. Most have yellow and black stripes on the body. Their larvae are small green maggots that live on leaves, eating aphids, mealybugs, other small insects, and mites.

Wasps
Wasps are a large family of insects with transparent wings. Unfortunately, the few that sting have given wasps a bad name. In fact, all wasps are either insect predators or parasitoids. The parasitoid adult female lays her eggs in such insects as aphids and caterpillars, and the developing larvae devour the host. The predatory wasps feed on caterpillars, crickets, flies, and leafhoppers, among others.

Other Beneficial Insects

Tiger, soldier, and rove beetles; big-eyed and minute pirate bugs; snipe and robber flies; and assassin, damsel, and ambush bugs: all these predators help control plant-eating pests.

No conversation on beneficial insects would be complete without mentioning bees. Although bees are not directly involved in pest control, as the major pollinators of fruits and vegetables they are probably the most valuable insect in the edible garden. Without them, our nation's food production would be severely affected. Attract bees to your garden by planting flowering plants, avoid spraying broad-spectrum insecticides at blooming time, and never use insecticides, such as Sevin, that are lethal to bees.

PESTS

The following insects and the like are sometimes a problem in the vegetable garden.

Aphids

Aphids are soft-bodied, small, green, black, pink, or gray insects that can produce many generations in one season. They suck plant juices and exude honeydew. Sometimes leaves under the aphids turn black from a secondary mold growing on the nutrient-rich honeydew. This unsightly mold will not directly harm the plant, though it does block sunlight coming to the leaves. The mold can be removed with a soapy spray (two tablespoons of dishwashing liquid per gallon of water).

Aphids are a major food source for syrphid flies, ladybugs, lacewings, and wasp parasitoids. Among mammals, mice are analogous since they are a fast-reproducing food source for coyotes, owls, hawks, and the like. An aphid population can increase rapidly. If this happens, look for aphid mummies and other natural enemies mentioned above. Mummies are swollen brown or metallic-looking aphids. They are valuable, so keep them. Inside the mummy a larval wasp parasitoid is growing.

If natural enemies are not present, or if the growth of the plant is impaired or the leaf tips are curling, you may need to intervene. Since aphids suck plant juices, large numbers of them can weaken a plant. In addition, some aphids spread viral or fungus diseases to vulnerable plants.

To control, wash the affected plant with a strong stream of water. Some kinds of aphids will leave the plant under these conditions. If the aphids stick tightly, apply the soapy spray described above. The surfactant in the soap dehydrates aphids. Be sure to spray thoroughly the top and bottom of all leaves as well as the growing tips. Especially waxy aphids may need to be treated twice at twenty-four-hour intervals. Wash the plant with clean water twenty-four hours after any of the soap applications. Usually, if the above steps are carefully followed, conventional pesticides are not needed for aphid control. When all else fails, use malathion.

Beetles

While many beetles are beneficial insects, a number are garden pests, including asparagus, bean, cucumber, potato, flea, and Japanese beetles. Asparagus beetles look like elongated red ladybugs with a black-and-cream-colored cross on their back. Bean beetles look like brown to orange ladybugs with oval black spots. Cucumber beetles are elongated ladybuglike beetles with chartreuse wings and either black stripes or black spots. Colorado potato beetles are larger and rounder than ladybugs and have red-brown heads and black-and-yellow-striped backs. Flea beetles are miniscule black-and-white-striped beetles hardly big enough to be seen. Japanese beetles are fairly large and metallic blue or green with coppery wings.

The larger beetles, if not in great numbers, can be controlled by hand picking whenever you see one. Larger populations need more control, however. Try a spray of some of the insecticidal soaps first; if not successful, use rotenone or pyrethrum. Polyester row covers securely fastened to the ground will provide some control if the population is not large. Obviously, row covers are of no use if the beetles are well established, as you will just keep them in and protect them from predators. This technique works best in the spring before the insects appear.

Japanese beetles were accidentally introduced into the United States early in this century and are now a serious problem in the eastern part of the country. The larval stage lives on the roots of grasses, and the adult beetle chews its way through leaves and flowers. In Japan, milky-spore, a naturally occurring soil-borne disease, controls the beetles in the larval stage. Milky-spore can be purchased at nurseries here under the trade name Doom. The disease is slow to cut down the population, often taking three or four years to take hold. If serious infestations are a problem and you can't wait that long, hand pick the beetles, knock them off into soapy water, or buy Japanese beetle bug traps from nurseries or seed companies. The traps contain a pheromone (insect hormone) that attracts the beetles. They seem to be most effective when located at some distance from the plant to be protected, thus drawing the beetles away from the area.

Borers

Borers are the larval stage of a number of different insects. The larvae damage plants by boring through the stems, often killing the plant. The first sign of damage is usually wilted foliage. Squash family vegetables are the most susceptible. Control borers by cutting off damaged stems or leaves and by locating and squishing the borer.

Cutworms

Cutworms are small chewing insects of the caterpillar family. They are usually found in the soil and will curl up into a ball when disturbed. Cutworms are a particular problem on annual vegetables when the seedlings first appear or when young transplants are set out. The cutworm often chews the stem off right at the soil line, killing the plant. Control cutworms by using cardboard collars or bottomless tin cans around the plant stem; be sure to sink these collars one inch into the ground. Severe infestations can be controlled with *Bacillus thuringiensis*. Trichogramma miniwasps and black ground beetles are among cutworms' natural enemies.

Earwigs

Earwigs are fierce-looking brown insects with large pincers in the back. Earwigs are sometimes your ally and prey on many bothersome pests, but they are occasionally a problem on young vegetable seedlings. They tend to eat out of the middle of leaves, leaving roundish holes. Observe them at night with a flashlight. If you find they are eating your vegetables, trap them by laying rolled-up newspaper, bales of bamboo stakes, or corrugated cardboard around the garden. Earwigs will hide in these materials, and you can destroy the insects in the daytime by shaking the collectors over soapy water. If you are getting very large numbers, you may need to use specific earwig bait. Use this bait well away from the vegetable garden.

Grasshoppers

Grasshoppers are occasionally a garden problem, particularly in grassland areas in dry years. Try controlling them with a bait containing a grasshopper disease, *Nosema locustae*. It is available from Reuter Laboratories, 2400 James Madison Highway, Haymarket, VA 22069.

Mites

Mites are among the few arachnids (spiders and their kin) that pose a problem in the garden. Mites are so small that a hand lens is usually needed to see them. They become a problem when they reproduce in great numbers and suck on the leaves of such plants as beans, eggplants, and strawberries. The symptoms of serious mite damage can be dried-looking silvery or yellow leaves, sometimes accompanied by tiny webs. The major natural predators of mites are predatory mites. Mite-eating thrips and minute syrphids also help in mite control.

Mites are most likely to thrive on dusty leaves and in dry, warm weather. A routine foliage wash and misting of sensitive plants helps mite control. Mites are seldom a serious problem, because large quantities of vegetables can still be harvested.

Nematodes

Nematodes are microscopic worms, sometimes called threadworms or eelworms. They inhabit the soil in most of the United States, particularly in the Southeast. Most nematode species live on decaying matter or are predatory on other nematodes, algae, and bacteria. A few types are parasitic, attaching themselves to the roots of plants. Edible plants particularly susceptible to nematode damage include beans, cantaloupe, eggplant, lettuce, okra, pepper, squash, tomatoes, watermelon, and some of the perennial herbs. The symptoms of nematode damage are stunted-looking plants and small swellings or lesions on the roots.

Rotate annual vegetables with less susceptible varieties; keep your soil high in organic matter (this encourages fungi and predatory nematodes, both of which act as biological controls); and before planting, try the soil solarization procedure outlined later. If all else fails, grow edibles in containers with sterilized soil.

Snails and Slugs

Snails and slugs are not insects, of course, but mollusks. They eat most commonly grown vegetables. They feed at night and can go dormant for months in times of drought or low food supply.

In the absence of effective natural enemies (a few snail eggs are consumed by predatory beetles and earwigs), several snail control strategies can be recommended. Since snails and slugs are most active after rain or irrigation, go out and destroy them on such nights. It is obviously impossible to find and collect all of them, particularly the slugs, and only repeated forays will provide adequate control.

Most people do not have time for such sustained collection and therefore may occasionally need to use some form of metaldehyde bait as well. For best effect and safety, put the bait between shingles or other scrap lumber. Place these traps on dampened soil near young seedlings or near the creatures' favorite hiding spots. Never apply bait on a regular schedule, such as weekly or even monthly. This practice has in some areas resulted in new generations of metaldehyde-resistant snails and slugs. A good time to bait is in the early spring, when snails and slugs are most active, and again in early summer when the majority of young hatch.

Sowbugs

Sowbugs (pillbugs) are not insects but crustaceans. They often roll up into a ball when they are disturbed. They prefer to eat decaying material, and if you mulch your garden you may see thousands. Unfortunately sowbugs often eat young seedling vegetables or strawberry fruits. Sufficient dry mulch under vulnerable strawberries sometimes helps prevent damage. If the problem is severe in the spring, you might have to bait around the perimeter of the vegetable garden with a sowbug bait.

Whiteflies

Whiteflies are sometimes a problem in mild-winter areas of the country, as well as in greenhouses nationwide. In the garden, encarsia wasps and other parasitoids usually provide adequate whitefly control. Occasionally, especially in cool weather or in greenhouses, whitefly populations may begin to cause serious plant damage (wilting and slowing of growth, flowering, or fruiting). Look under the leaves to determine whether the scalelike, immobile larvae and pupae are present in large numbers. Adults can be trapped by the following method: Apply Stickem or Tanglefoot to a mustard-yellow file folder. (No one knows why this color attracts whiteflies, but it does.) Hold the folder open near the affected plant and give the plant an occasional shake. The adult whiteflies will fly to the folder and adhere to the sticky surface. Commercial insecticidal soap sprays can be quite effective as well.

PESTICIDES AND HOW TO USE THEM

Weather, good cultural techniques, and natural enemies are the most important elements in controlling pests. As you gradually learn how these natural controls operate, you will find that chemicals are seldom required. If additional help is needed, try a nonchemical control method such as water, soapy water sprays, or traps. If all these attempts fail and pests are doing substantial damage, you may have to resort to a chemical pesticide.

Recommended Insecticides

No pesticide can be recommended unequivocally. Environmental effects and eventual toxicity sometimes take years to surface. The following substances have the least potential for harm as of this writing. Your best defense is to stay informed.

If a pesticide is called for, your first choice should be a selective pesticide, since these do not directly kill beneficial insects. Of the available materials, the most selective are not chemicals but microorganisms. *Bacillus thuringiensis* (BT) contains bacterial particles that cause a caterpillar disease. It kills no other group of insects. BT is sold under the trade names Dipel, Thuricide, and Orcon Caterpillar Control. Milky-spore disease *(Bacillus popilliae)* is a soilborne bacterial disease that helps control Japanese beetle grubs. And grasshoppers are being controlled by a bait containing a grasshopper disease called *Nosema locustae.* Currently no other insect diseases are available for home garden use. Remember that even these very selective disease-causing materials should be used sparingly. It has been experimentally demonstrated that repeated use can disrupt garden ecology by destroying the prey (food source) of beneficial insects and causing them to starve. Still worse, there is now documentation that some of the pests are getting resistant to their control diseases. So again, use them only as a last resort, and never routinely.

Spraying in the evening allows you to use some broad-spectrum insecticides (those that biodegrade rapidly) while still protecting some beneficial insects. Resmethrin, a synthetic pyrethroid, disappears in a few hours, leaving day-active beneficials such as bees, wasps, and parasitic flies unaffected; other beneficial insects will come back rapidly. Naturally, this technique should be used sparingly. Malathion, too, is less damaging (especially at low concentrations) when used this way, though its residues may still kill for about two days.

A broad-spectrum pesticide can become selective when it is formulated to attract the pest. For example, the short-lived organophosphate metaldehyde is marketed in a bran bait that attracts snails and slugs. These baits should be used with care, however, since they can kill animals or children that eat them (see "Snails and Slugs," above, for application directions).

Soap solutions are valuable in insect control because they remove some of the insect's waxy coating, causing dehydration and death, or they break the surface tension of water so that insects drown. Hold a jar of soapy water (one tablespoon dishwashing liquid per quart of water) under plants laden with plant-feeding beetles or bugs, flip them into the solution, and they drown immediately. This is a good technique to control earwigs, adult cucumber beetles, Japanese beetles, asparagus and harlequin bugs, and other hard-to-control mobile pests.

Two widely available insecticides that should be avoided are carbaryl and nicotine. Carbaryl (Sevin) is relatively persistent, extremely toxic to bees and wasps, and can sometimes lead to aphid and mite outbreaks. Nicotine is a broad-spectrum contact insecticide and is extremely toxic to humans.

Disease Control

Plant diseases are potentially far more damaging to your crops than are most insects. Diseases are also more difficult to control because they usually grow inside the plant, and plants do not respond with immune mechanisms comparable to those that protect animals. Consequently, most plant disease control strategies feature prevention rather than control.

PLANT RESISTANCE

Research on plant diseases that have plagued commercial agriculture has resulted in the widespread availability of disease-resistant cultivars of several important vegetables. Certain varieties of wilt-resistant tomatoes are examples of plants that resist diseases by genetic means. If a disease is a problem in your garden, choose disease-resistant varieties when they are available.

In other instances—potatoes are an example—strict inspection and quarantine help to ensure that most commercially available plants are disease free. You should avail yourself of these products whenever possible. In addition, it is advisable to plant two or three different varieties of a particular vegetable in your garden to help prevent total crop wipeout from an invading disease.

CULTURAL TECHNIQUES

Changing the location in your garden of some disease-prone plants on a regular basis is helpful, as pests and diseases often build up in the soil. This is called crop rotation. Light, exposure, temperature, fertilizing, and moisture are also important factors in disease control. The entries for individual plants in Part Four, "An Encyclopedia of Superior Vegetables," give specific cultural information.

Diseased plants should be discarded, not composted.

SOIL SOLARIZATION

It has recently been discovered that a variety of soil-borne fungi, nematodes, and weeds can be controlled by a plastic-mulch technique called soil solarization, which uses heat to sterilize the soil. If you have problems with any of the serious soil-borne plant diseases, such as verticillium or fusarium wilt, or if you have a serious nematode infestation, soil solarization is appropriate. (A significant reduction in weed growth can also be expected.) This technique should not be used frivolously, however, as it is a nonspecific treatment and a good many beneficial life forms are killed along with the pathogens and harmful life forms.

The steps of soil solarization are outlined below. The complete process takes one month during the warmest season of the year.

1. Obtain sufficient clear polyethylene plastic film (four-mil thickness) to cover the treatment area.
2. Irrigate the plot one week before laying down the plastic tarping.
3. After one week, cultivate and level the treatment area. Install drip emitters or ditches on three-foot centers for irrigation during treatment.
4. Place plastic film tightly over treatment area. Do not leave air spaces. Weight edges of plastic with soil.
5. Thoroughly irrigate area under plastic once a week.
6. One month later, remove plastic and plant as desired.

PLANT DISEASES

The most common diseases of edible plants are described below. Conditions related to deficiencies and their symptoms are covered in Appendix A under "Plant Nutrients." Symptoms and cures, if any, are suggested.

Damping Off

Damping off is caused by a parasitic fungus that lives near the soil surface and attacks new plants in their early seedling stage. It causes them to wilt and fall over just where they emerge from the soil. This fungus thrives under dark, humid conditions, so it can often be thwarted by keeping the seedlings in a bright, well-ventilated place in fast-draining soil.

Fusarium Wilt

Fusarium wilt is a soil-borne fungus. It causes an overall wilting of the plant visible as the yellowing and dying of leaves from the base of the plant upward. While a serious problem in some areas, this disease can be totally controlled by planting only resistant varieties. Crop rotation and soil solarization are also helpful.

Mildews

Mildews are fungus diseases that affect some plants, particularly peas and squash, under certain conditions. There are two types of mildews: powdery and downy. Powdery mildew appears as a white powdery dust; downy mildew makes a velvety or fuzzy patch. Both affect leaves, buds, and tender stems. The poorer the air circulation and the more humid the weather, the more apt your plants are to have mildew. Make sure the plants have plenty of sun and are not crowded by other vegetation. If you must use overhead watering, do it in the morning so the water will evaporate by nighttime.

Viruses

A number of viruses attack plants. Symptoms are stunted growth and deformed or mottled leaves. The mosaic viruses destroy chlorophyll in the leaves, causing them to become yellow and blotched in a mosaic pattern. There is no cure for viral conditions, so affected plants must be destroyed. Tomatoes, strawberries, cucumbers, and beans are particularly susceptible. Virus diseases can be transmitted by seeds, so seed savers should be extra careful to learn the symptoms in individual plant species. Some gardening books recommend using tobacco or cigarette extracts as a source of nicotine for use in controlling insects. This is a poor idea, since tobacco itself is susceptible to many viral diseases that will readily spread to such plants as peppers, tomatoes, and potatoes.

Verticillium Wilt

Verticillium wilt is a soil-borne fungus that is destructive in many parts of the country. The symptom of this disease is a sudden wilting of one part of the plant, the whole plant, or more than one plant. If you continually lose tomatoes or eggplants, this or one of the other wilts could be your problem. There is no cure, but soil solarization should help prevent it. Plant resistant species or varieties if this disease is in your soil.

Wildlife Problems

Rabbits and mice can cause problems for gardeners. If you suspect these animals of disturbing your garden, use fine-weave fencing around the vegetable garden. Gophers and moles can also wreak havoc in some areas. Plant large vegetable plants such as artichokes, peppers, tomatoes, and squash in chicken wire baskets. Make sure the wire sticks out of the ground at least a foot to keep the critters from reaching over the wire. For lettuces and root crops, if the population is severe, you might have to line the whole bed with chicken wire. Trapping for gophers usually is needed as well. Trapping for moles is less successful, as they seldom return to the same place in the garden on a regular basis. Cats help with all the rodent problems but seldom provide adequate control.

In rural areas, deer can cause such severe problems that edible plants cannot be grown without nine-foot fences or a dog.

Songbirds, starlings, and crows can be major pests of young seedlings, particularly lettuce, corn, and peas. Cover the emerging plants with bird netting and firmly anchor it to the ground so birds can't get under it and feast. Corn cobs, grains drying in the field, and strawberry fruits sometimes need protection as well.

This section, by necessity, has covered a large number of pests, diseases, and other garden problems. An individual gardener, however, will encounter few such problems in a lifetime of gardening. Good garden planning, good hygiene, and an awareness of major symptoms will keep problems to a minimum and give you many hours to enjoy your garden and feast on its bounty.

APPENDIX C: SUPPLIERS

Nurseries and Seed Companies

Abundant Life Seed Foundation
P.O. Box 772
Port Townsend, WA 98368
> This organization, dedicated to preserving heirloom vegetables and self-sufficient living, specializes in plants for the Northwest. Membership: $6.00 to $10.00, depending on ability to pay.

Bountiful Gardens
Ecology Action
5798 Ridgewood Road
Willits, CA 95490
> This seed company specializes in open-pollinated vegetables and supplies for organic gardeners. In addition to a large selection of vegetables, it carries seeds for herbs, grains, and cover crops.

W. Atlee Burpee Company
Warminster, PA 18991
> Burpee is the largest seed company devoted to the home gardener.

The Cook's Garden
P.O. Box 65
Londonderry, VT 05148
> This seed company carries numerous superior varieties of vegetables, many of which are European. The catalog lists twenty-two varieties of lettuce.

The Country Garden
Box 455A
Route 2
Crivitz, WI 54114
> Country Garden specializes in cutting flowers, many of which are edible. Catalog: $2.00.

DeGiorgi Company, Inc.
P.O. Box 413
Council Bluffs, IA 51502
> DeGiorgi carries many Italian varieties of vegetables and ones of unusual color.

Farmer Seed & Nursery
Faribault, MN 55021
> Farmer has a large general seed selection.

Henry Field's Seed & Nursery Company
Shenandoah, IA 51602
> Field's has an extensive general seed selection.

Fox Hill Farm
444 West Michigan Avenue
Box 7
Parma, MI 49269
> This nursery carries one of the nation's largest selections of herb plants—for example, thirty-two types of thyme, eleven kinds of rosemary, and seventeen varieties of mint.

Fratelli Ingegnoli
Corso Buenos Aires, 54
Milano, Italy
> Ingegnoli is an Italian seed company that carries numerous vegetable varieties unfamiliar to American gardeners. Catalog: $10.00 in lire. See the "Italian Gardens" chapter for more ordering information.

Gleckler's Seedmen
Metamora, OH 43540
> Gleckler's carries standard vegetable seeds and many unusual varieties.

Good Seed
P.O. Box 702
Tonasket, WA 98855
> Good specializes in open-pollinated varieties of vegetables and carries an unusually large list of beans, amaranth, cabbages, and corn.

Gurney Seed & Nursery Company
Yankton, SD 57079
> Gurney has a large general selection of flower and vegetable seeds.

Halcyon Gardens Herbs
P.O. Box 124-M
Gibsonia, PA 15044
> Halcyon carries a large selection of herb seeds.

Harris Seeds
Moreton Farm
3670 Buffalo Road
Rochester, NY 14624
 Harris has a large selection of standard vegetable varieties and some herbs.

Hastings
434 Marietta Street NW
P.O. Box 4274
Atlanta, GA 30302
 Hastings specializes in vegetable varieties for the South.

Heirloom Gardens
P.O. Box 138
Guerneville, CA 95446
 Heirloom Gardens carries a large number of open-pollinated varieties of vegetables as well as many herbs.

Herb Gathering, Inc.
5742 Kenwood
Kansas City, MO 64110
 Herb Gathering is an importer of French seed, including French varieties of sorrel, chamomile, Alpine strawberries, dwarf basil, and other herbs.

Horticultural Enterprises
P.O. Box 810082
Dallas, TX 75381
 A specialist in peppers, this nursery carries thirty varieties of sweet and hot peppers, as well as tomatillos, jicama, and epazote.

J. L. Hudson, Seedsman
P.O. Box 1058
Redwood City, CA 94064
 Hudson carries a wide selection of different types of vegetables. Catalog: $1.00.

Johnny's Selected Seeds
Foss Hill Road
Albion, ME 04910
 Johnny's is a large company that specializes in vegetable seeds for northern climates and carries many Oriental varieties as well.

J. W. Jung Seed Company
Randolph, WI 53957
 Jung's large general seed catalog has sixteen pages on vegetables.

Kitazawa Seed Company
1748 Laine Avenue
Santa Clara, CA 95051
 Kitazawa specializes in seed for Oriental vegetables, including bitter melon, spinach mustard, and edible chrysanthemums.

Le Jardin du Gourmet
West Danville, VT 05873
 Le Jardin carries a large selection of French vegetables plus seeds for herbs. Catalog: $.50.

Le Marché
Seeds International
P.O. Box 190
Dixon, CA 95620
 Le Marché specializes in superior vegetables. Many of the varieties come from Europe or Japan and are well worth trying. Catalog: $2.00.

Lockhart Seeds, Inc.
P.O. Box 1361
3 North Wilson Way
Stockton, CA 95205
 Lockhart carries a comprehensive list of vegetable seeds, including a great number of onion varieties.

Logee's Greenhouses
55 North Street
Danielson, CT 06239
 Logee's specializes in ornamentals and house plants.

Long Island Seed and Plant
P.O. Box 1285
Riverhead, NY 11901
 This organization is interested in seed saving, heirloom vegetables, and self-sufficient living.

Earl May Seed & Nursery Company
Shenandoah, IA 51603
 May has a large general seed catalog.

Meredith Seeds
16545 Northwest Germantown Road
Portland, OR 97231
 Meredith carries compact and dwarf varieties of vegetables for small gardens, patios, and indoor gardens.

Native Seeds Search
3950 West New York Drive
Tucson, AZ 85745
 This organization carries a large number of Southwest native vegetables and varieties grown by Native Americans. Membership: $10.00. Price list for nonmembers: $1.00.

Nichols Garden Nursery
1190 North Pacific Highway
Albany, OR 97321
 Nichols has an extensive list of herbs (plants as well as seeds) and unusual vegetables, including miniature flowering kale.

Park Seed Company
Cokesbury Road
Greenwood, SC 29647

Park is one of the major suppliers of vegetable and flower seeds in the United States. Its large selection of vegetable seeds includes many varieties for small gardens.

Pepper Gal
10536 119th Avenue N
Largo, FL 33543

Pepper Gal carries only hot and sweet peppers.

Pinetree Garden Seeds
New Gloucester, ME 04260

Pinetree has a broad selection of vegetable seeds sold in inexpensive small packets, as well as garden supplies and books.

Plants of the Southwest
1812 Second Street
Santa Fe, NM 87501

This company carries a good selection of southwestern native plants, plus vegetable varieties for the cool growing seasons of the high plains of the West. Catalog: $1.00.

Rayner Bros., Inc.
P.O. Box 1617
Salisbury, MD 21801

This nursery, while carrying some fruit and nut trees, specializes in berries.

Redwood City Seed Company
P.O. Box 361
Redwood City, CA 94064

This company carries seeds of many of the unusual plants mentioned in this book. It specializes in vegetable and herb seeds from Europe, Mexico, and the Orient. Catalog: $1.00.

Richters
Goodwood, Ontario
Canada L0C 1A0

Richters is an herb seed specialist carrying many unusual varieties. Catalog: $2.50.

Roses of Yesterday and Today
802 Brown's Valley Road
Watsonville, CA 95076

This nursery specializes in old rose varieties. Catalog: $2.00.

Seed Savers Exchange
Kent Whealy, Director
P.O. Box 70
Decorah, IA 52101

This organization is devoted to saving heirloom varieties of vegetables. An annual membership fee entitles you to its large quarterly newsletter and list of seeds available for trade among members. Membership: $12.00.

Seeds Blum
Idaho City Stage
Boise, ID 83706

Seeds Blum carries seeds of ornamental, heirloom, and open-pollinated vegetables. Its catalog offers great information on seed saving, edible flowers, and landscaping with ornamental vegetables. Catalog: $2.00.

Shepherd's Garden Seeds
7389 West Zayante Road
Felton, CA 95018

Shepherd's specializes in seeds of superior European vegetables and herbs selected for vigor and flavor. It carries many varieties unavailable through other seed companies. Catalog: $1.00.

Southern Exposure Seed Exchange
P.O. Box 158
North Garden, VA 22959

Southern Exposure is interested in family heirlooms, popular hybrids, and varieties best suited to the Mid-Atlantic region. Catalog $3.00.

Stark Bro's
Nurseries and Orchards Company
Louisiana, MO 63353

Stark Bro's is one of the nation's largest fruit and nut tree suppliers.

Stokes Seeds, Inc.
P.O. Box 548
Buffalo, NY 14240

One of the country's largest seed companies, Stokes carries a vast collection of vegetable and flower varieties, with particular emphasis on northern gardens.

Sunrise Enterprises
P.O. Box 10058
Elmwood, CN 06110

Sunrise specializes in Oriental vegetables and herbs. In addition to vegetable seeds, it carries ginger and taro tubers and Chinese chive plants.

Tater Mater Seeds
R.R. 2
Wathena, KA 66090

Tater Mater carries an unusual selection of seeds, including Native American corns and uncommon tomato varieties of the company's own breeding.

Taylor's Herb Gardens, Inc.
1535 Lone Oak Road
Vista, CA 92084

Taylor's carries a very large selection of herb plants, including many unusual varieties. Catalog: $1.00.

Territorial Seed Company
P.O. Box 27
Lorane, OR 97451
  Territorial is a regional seed company specializing in vegetable varieties for the maritime Northwest.

Thompson & Morgan, Inc.
P.O. Box 1308
Jackson, NJ 08527
  Thompson & Morgan is an English seed company specializing in unusual vegetables and flowers. The seed is expensive.

Tomato Growers Supply Company
P.O. Box 2237
Fort Meyers, FL 33902
  This seed company carries over one hundred varieties of tomatoes, plus supplies for tomato growers.

Tsang & Ma International
P.O. Box 294
Belmont, CA 94002
  Tsang & Ma carries a large selection of Chinese vegetable seeds, including Chinese chives, bitter melon, and Chinese parsley.

Twilley Seed Company
P.O. Box 65
Trevose, PA 19047
  Twilley is a major seed company carrying many vegetable varieties for the home gardener.

Vermont Bean Seed Company
Garden Lane
Fair Haven, VT 05743
  This company, while specializing in beans, carries seeds of most other vegetables, including a collection of Oriental greens.

Wyatt-Quarles
Box 739
Garner, NC 27529
  Wyatt-Quarles carries vegetable varieties particularly suited to the South.

Dr. Yoo Farm
P.O. Box 290
College Park, MD 20740
  This seed company specializes in Oriental varieties.

Mail-Order Gardening and Cooking Suppliers

Aphrodisia
282 Bleeker Street
New York, NY 10014
  This mail-order firm carries rose and orange water; dried petals of hibiscus, orange blossoms, peonies, primroses, red clovers, and rosebuds; and hundreds of dried herbs.

Balducci's
Mail Order Division
334 East Eleventh Street
New York, NY 10003
  While specialists in Italian foods, Balducci's carries many French specialty ingredients, particularly those of Provence.

Casa Moneo
210 West Fourteenth Street
New York, NY 10011
  Case Moneo carries dried peppers and spices for Mexican cooking.

Dean & Deluca
Mail Order Division
110 Greene Street
Suite 304
New York, NY 10012
  This mail-order firm carries an extensive selection of international cooking ingredients and gourmet cookware.

Gardener's Eden
P.O. Box 7307
San Francisco, CA 94120
  Gardener's Eden is the garden-supply catalog from Williams-Sonoma. It carries a large selection of both basic tools and gifts for gardeners.

Gardener's Supply
128 Intervale Road
Burlington, VT 05401
  This large mail-order firm carries a vast selection of tools and supplies for gardeners, including some children's garden tools.

Kam Man Food Products, Inc.
200 Canal Street
New York, NY 10013
  This company carries a large selection of Oriental cooking ingredients but has no catalog. To order, request specific items.

Oriental Food Market & Cooking School
2801 West Howard
Chicago, IL 60645
  The school carries a full selection of nonperishable foodstuffs and basic equipment. A catalog is available but does not give brands.

Orient Delight Market
865 East El Camino Real
Mountain View, CA 94040
  Orient Delight offers a good supply of specialty items, including meats, teas, tools, and nonperishable food-

stuffs. Catalog available. Address inquiries to Robert Yin.

Santa Cruz Chili and Spice Company
P.O. Box 177
Tumacacori, AZ 65640
This company is a source for chili powders, pastes, and salsas.

Sears and Roebuck Farm Catalog
Sears' mail-order farm catalog carries tools for harvesting and grinding grains. The catalog is available from local Sears stores.

Smith & Hawken
25 Corte Madera
Mill Valley, CA 94941
Smith & Hawken carries a very large selection of basic high-quality tools and numerous other supplies for gardeners, including some children's garden tools.

Whole Earth Access Catalog
2950 Seventh Street
Berkeley, CA 94710
The Whole Earth Access catalog lists some basic grain milling equipment, Römertopfs, pizza oven bricks, nonstick cookware, Oriental cooking utensils, mortars and pestles, salad spinners, tortilla presses, and other cooking equipment at reasonable prices. The catalog costs seven dollars, but five dollars are refunded when you make a purchase.

Williams-Sonoma
Mail Order Department
P.O. Box 7456
San Francisco, CA 94120
Williams-Sonoma stocks a large selection of sophisticated cooking equipment and ingredients for European cooking.

ANNOTATED BIBLIOGRAPHY

General Information

Bienz, Darrel R. *The Why and How of Home Horticulture.* San Francisco: W. H. Freeman, 1980.
   An excellent book covering basic botany, plant propagation, growing techniques, landscape planning, and how to preserve harvests.

Brody, Jane E. *Jane Brody's Nutrition Book.* New York: Bantam Books, 1987.
   The updated version of one of the best basic books on nutrition available to the public.

Bubel, Nancy. *The New Seed Starter's Handbook.* Emmaus, Pa.: Rodale Press, 1988.
   Informative text on how to start most plants from seed, including saving your own seed.

Carr, Anna. *Rodale's Color Handbook of Garden Insects.* Emmaus, Pa.: Rodale Press, 1983.
   Three hundred color closeups of insects useful for identification.

Creekmore, Hubert. *Daffodils Are Dangerous.* New York: Walker, 1966.
   Detailed information on many poisonous garden plants.

Crockett, James. *Crockett's Tool Shed.* Boston: Little, Brown, 1979.
   A comprehensive book on garden tools.

Diamond, Denise. *Living with the Flowers: A Guide to Bringing Flowers into Your Daily Life.* New York: Quill, 1982.
   A complete look at the use of flowers in garden aesthetics, table decoration, potpourris, and edible flowers.

Duhon, David. *One Circle.* Willits, Calif.: Ecology Action, 1985.
   How to grow a complete diet in less than a thousand square feet.

Hartmann, Hudson T., and Dale E. Kester. *Plant Propagation: Principles and Practices.* 3d ed. Englewood Cliffs, N.J.: Prentice-Hall, 1975.
   Basic detailed information on propagation of edible plants.

Hobhouse, Penelope. *Color in Your Garden.* Boston: Little, Brown, 1985.
   A magnificent book giving detailed information on designing your garden with flowering plants.

Humphrey, Richard V. *Corn: The American Grain.* Kingston, Mass.: Teaparty Books, 1985.
   A booklet in an antique eating series with much information on corn.

Jabs, Carolyn. *The Heirloom Gardener.* San Francisco: Sierra Club Books, 1984.
   The definitive book on heirloom gardening.

Jeavons, John, and Robin Leler. *The Seed Finder.* Berkeley: Ten Speed Press, 1983.
   A detailed guide on locating open-pollinated vegetable varieties.

Johnston, Robert, Jr. *Growing Garden Seeds.* Albion, Maine: Johnny's Selected Seeds, 1978.
   A primer on seed saving from Johnny's Selected Seeds.

Kourik, Robert. *Designing and Maintaining Your Edible Landscape Naturally.* Santa Rosa, Calif.: Metamorphic Press, 1986.
   A basic text covering mulching, drip irrigation, planting techniques, double-dug beds, and much more.

Lawrence, James, ed. *The Harrowsmith Reader,* vol. 2. Camden East, Ontario: Camden House Publishing, 1980.
   An anthology of country living and basic self-sufficiency. Includes information on grain mills.

McGee, Harold J. *On Food and Cooking: The Science and Lore of the Kitchen.* New York: Scribner's, 1984.
   A resource book for cooks with detailed information on the chemistry of food.

MacNeil, Karen. *The Book of Whole Foods: Nutrition and Cuisine.* New York: Random House, Vintage Books, 1981.
   Covers detailed basic nutrition with information on many health issues.

Martinez, Maximino. *Catalogue of Common and Scientific Names of Mexican Plants.* Republica del Salvador, Mexico: Imprenta Mexicana, 1937.

A book valuable to scholars who need the correct Latin and Spanish names for plants used in Mexico.

Mooney, Pat Roy. *Seeds of the Earth: A Private or Public Resource?* Ottawa: Inter Pares, 1979.
A global view on the shrinking gene pool of edible plants.

Parker, Arthur C. *Iroquois Uses of Maize and Other Food Plants.* In *Parker on the Iroquois,* edited by William N. Fenton. Syracuse: Syracuse University Press, 1968.
A new edition of a 1910 book on Iroquois cooking.

Pavel, Margaret Brandstrom. *Gardening with Color: Ideas for Planning and Planting with Annuals, Perennials, and Bulbs.* San Francisco: Ortho Books, 1977.
A discussion on the use of color in the garden.

Schmutz, Ervin M. *Plants That Poison: An Illustrated Guide.* Flagstaff: Northland, 1986.
A comprehensive list of poisonous plants.

The Second Graham Center. *Seed and Nursery Directory.* Pittsboro, N.C.: The Second Graham Center, n.d.
A valuable catalog of seed companies that carry open-pollinated varieties of seed. Catalog: $2.00. c/o Rural Advancement Fund, P.O. Box 1029, Pittsboro, NC.

Skelsey, Alice, and Gloria Huckaby. *Growing Up Green.* New York: Workman, 1973.
A must for parents who want to help their children enjoy the garden.

Sunset Books and *Sunset* magazine editors. *Sunset New Western Garden Book.* 4th ed. Menlo Park, Calif.: Lane Publishing, 1979.
A comprehensive western plant encyclopedia.

Taylor, Norman. *Taylor's Guide to Annuals.* Rev. ed. Edited by Gordon P. DeWolf, Jr. Boston: Houghton Mifflin, 1986.
A handbook of annual plants with rudimentary growing information and detailed photos for identification.

Von Welanetz, Diana, and Paul Von Welanetz. *The Von Welanetz Guide to Ethnic Ingredients.* Los Angeles: Warner Books, 1987.
A must for every adventurous cook's library.

Whealy, Kent. *The Garden Seed Inventory.* Decorah, Iowa: Seed Saver Publications, 1986.
A basic text for all gardeners interested in seed saving. A computer inventory of all the known nonhybrid vegetable seeds now being offered by seed companies.

Yeatman, Christopher W., David Kafton, and Garrison Wilkes, eds. *Plant Genetic Resources: A Conservation Imperative.* Boulder, Colo.: Westview, 1985.
A text for people deeply involved with the subject of corn and genetic diversity.

Information on Edible Plants

Andrews, Jean. *Peppers: The Domesticated Capsicums.* Austin: University of Texas Press, 1984.
A most complete and beautiful book on the subject of peppers.

Bennett, Jennifer. *The Harrowsmith Northern Gardener.* Camden East, Ontario: Camden House, 1982.
A very fine basic book for growing edible plants in a cold climate.

Bianchini, Francesco, Francesco Corbetta, and Marilena Pistoia. *The Complete Book of Fruits and Vegetables.* New York: Crown, 1975.
A small amount of text accompanying masterful paintings of Italian vegetables and herbs.

Boxer, Arabella, and Philippa Back. *The Herb Book.* London: Octopus Books, 1980.
A comprehensive and delicious look at the world of herb growing and cooking.

Brooklyn Botanic Garden Handbooks. *Handbook of Herbs* (no. 27). *The Home Vegetable Garden* (no. 69). *Japanese Herbs and Their Uses* (no. 57). Brooklyn, N.Y.: Brooklyn Botanic Garden.
Thorough discussions on single subjects. Available for a charge from Brooklyn Botanic Garden, 1000 Washington Avenue, Brooklyn, NY 11225.

Bubel, Mike and Nancy. *Root Cellaring: The Simple No-Processing Way to Store Fruits and Vegetables.* Emmaus, Pa.: Rodale Press, 1979.
A complete guide to root cellaring, including techniques and suitable vegetables.

Chan, Peter. *Better Vegetable Gardens the Chinese Way: Peter Chan's Raised Bed System.* Rev. ed. Pownal, Vt.: Garden Way, 1985.
A detailed text outlining Peter Chan's productive and soil-enriching garden techniques.

Creasy, Rosalind. *The Complete Book of Edible Landscaping.* San Francisco: Sierra Club Books, 1982.
A basic text on landscaping with edible plants.

DeWolf, Gordon P., Jr., ed. *Taylor's Guide to Vegetables and Herbs.* Boston: Houghton Mifflin, 1987.
A pocket guide with basic growing information and numerous color pictures.

Doty, Walter L. *All About Vegetables.* Rev. ed. San Francisco: Ortho Books, 1980.
Excellent book on vegetable garden basics.

Esplan, Ceres. *Herbal Teas, Tisanes and Lotions.* Wellingborough, Northamptonshire: Thorsons, 1981.
A guide to growing, preparing, and using herbs for making infusions and refreshing drinks.

Fell, Derek. *Vegetables: How to Select, Grow, and Enjoy.* Tucson: HP Books, 1982.
> A basic book on vegetable growing with many basic how-tos and extensive variety information.

Fitz, Franklin Herm. *A Gardener's Guide to Propagating Food Plants.* New York: Scribner's, 1983.
> A handy little guide for propagating popular edible plants.

Garland, Sarah. *The Herb Garden.* New York: Penguin Books, 1985.
> A complete guide to growing scented and culinary herbs.

Gessert, Kate Rogers. *The Beautiful Food Garden: Creative Landscaping with Vegetables, Fruits, and Herbs.* Charlotte, Vt.: Garden Way, 1987.
> How to use beautiful food plants in the landscape. Contains a wealth of information on varieties for the Northwest.

Harrington, Geri. *Grow Your Own Chinese Vegetables.* Pownal, Vt.: Garden Way, 1984.
> Extensive information on thirty-eight Oriental vegetables.

Herklots, G. A. C. *Vegetables in South-East Asia.* London: George Allen & Unwin Ltd., 1972.
> A valuable compendium of vegetables grown in the Orient.

Jeavons, John. *How to Grow More Vegetables Than You Ever Thought Possible on Less Land Than You Can Imagine.* Berkeley: Ten Speed Press, 1982.
> The basic primer on the Biodynamic/French Intensive Method. Covers soil preparation and double digging in detail.

Larkcom, Joy. *The Salad Garden.* New York: Viking, 1984.
> For the salad gardener and cook. Includes color photos of many unusual salad greens.

Lathrop, Norma Jean. *Herbs: How to Select, Grow and Enjoy.* Tucson: HP Books, 1981.
> A basic text covering the use and growing of herbs.

Logsdon, Gene. *Small-Scale Grain Raising.* Emmaus, Pa.: Rodale Press, 1977.
> The definitive book on grain.

Maxwell, Lewis S. *Florida Vegetables.* Tampa: Lewis S. Maxwell, 1974.
> Valuable book for Deep South vegetable gardeners.

National Gardening Association. *Gardening: The Complete Guide to Growing America's Favorite Fruits and Vegetables.* Reading, Mass.: Addison-Wesley, 1986.
> A comprehensive guide for growing edible plants, with basic growing information on individual vegetables and fruits and many how-tos. A must for the vegetable gardener's library.

Organic Gardening magazine editors. *Gourmet Gardening.* Edited by Anne Moyer Halpin. Emmaus, Pa.: Rodale Press, 1981.
> How to grow and where to obtain forty-eight unusual vegetables.

Pitzer, Sara. *Whole Grains: Grow, Harvest, and Cook Your Own.* Charlotte, Vt.: Garden Way, 1981.
> Covers large-scale grain growing in detail.

Proulx, E. Annie. *The Fine Art of Salad Gardening.* Edited by Anne Moyer Halpin. Emmaus, Pa.: Rodale Press, 1985.
> Much in-depth information about salad greens and how to grow and prepare them.

Reilly, Ann. *Park's Success with Seeds.* Greenwood, S.C.: Park Seed Co., 1978.
> A valuable aid for starting most plants from seeds.

Rodale Press editors. *Amaranth Round-up.* Emmaus, Pa.: Rodale Press, 1977.
> A valuable booklet for those interested in growing and cooking with amaranth.

Seymour, John. *The Self-Sufficient Gardener: A Complete Guide to Growing and Preserving All Your Own Food.* Garden City, N.Y.: Doubleday, Dolphin Books, 1979.
> Emphasis on deep-bed method of growing more food in less space.

Simmons, Adelma Grenier. *Herb Gardening in Five Seasons.* New York: Dutton, 1977.
> Extensive information on growing and harvesting herbs.

Solomon, Steve. *Growing Organic Vegetables West of the Cascades.* 2d rev. ed. Seattle: Pacific Search Press, 1985.
> Detailed information on growing edibles in the Pacific Northwest.

Southern Living magazine staff. *Southern Living: Growing Vegetables and Herbs.* Birmingham, Ala.: Oxmoor House, 1984.
> A comprehensive look at growing vegetables in the South.

Sunset Books and *Sunset* magazine editors. *Sunset Vegetable Gardening Illustrated.* Menlo Park, Calif.: Lane Publishing, 1987.
> An excellent basic growing text for beginning vegetable gardeners.

Tolley, Emelie, and Chris Mead. *Herbs: Gardens, Decorations, and Recipes.* New York: Clarkson N. Potter, 1985.
> Magnificently illustrated book on herbs.

Vilmorin-Andrieux, M. *The Vegetable Garden*. Berkeley: Ten Speed Press, 1981.
   Reprint of a classic vegetable book from 1885.

Recipes and Food Preserving

Anderson, Jean, and Yeffe Kimball. *The Art of American Indian Cooking*. New York: Simon & Schuster, 1986.
   A large sampling of Native American recipes.

Andoh, Elizabeth. *At Home with Japanese Cooking*. New York: Knopf, 1980.
   A classic text on Japanese food preparation.

Angers, Trent, and Sue McDonough, eds. *Acadiana Profile's Cajun Cooking*. Lafayette, La.: Angers Publishing, 1980.
   A recipe collection from the cooks of southern Louisiana, the heart of Cajun country.

Beard, James. *The New James Beard*. New York: Knopf, 1981.
   One thousand recipes from an American cooking legend.

Brennan, Georgeanne, Isaac Cronin, and Charlotte Glenn. *The New American Vegetable Cookbook*. Berkeley, Calif.: Aris Books, 1985.
   A charming, up-to-date book on cooking with vegetables.

Brennan, Georgeanne, and Charlotte Glenn. *Hot and Chili*. Berkeley: Aris Books, 1986.
   An instructional manual for cooking with chilies.

Brown, Edward Espe. *The Tassajara Bread Book*. Rev. ed. Boston: Shambhala, 1986.
   A classic covering whole-wheat bread and pastry cooking from the ground up.

Brown, Edward Espe. *The Tassajara Recipe Book: Favorites of the Guest Season*. Boston: Shambhala, 1985.
   A compendium of recipes from the Tassajara Zen monastery.

Bugialli, Giuliano. *Giuliano Bugialli's Foods of Italy*. New York: Stewart, Tabori & Chang, 1984.
   A celebration of Italian cooking.

Burpee, Lois. *Lois Burpee's Gardener's Companion and Cookbook*. New York: Harper & Row, 1983.
   Lois Burpee's favorite recipes from the garden.

Child, Julia, Louisette Bertholle, and Simone Beck. *Mastering the Art of French Cooking*. 2d ed. New York: Knopf, 1985.
   The basic text for French cooking. A must in everyone's library.

Chu, Lawrence C. *Chef Chu's Distinctive Cuisine of China*. New York: Harper & Row, 1983.
   A comprehensive book on Chinese cooking, including many photos and recipes.

Clifton, Claire. *Edible Flowers*. New York: McGraw-Hill, 1984.
   A charming little book filled with many delightful edible-flower recipes.

Crowhurst, Adrienne. *The Flower Cookbook*. New York: Lancer Books, 1973.
   An interesting collection of flower recipes.

Dahlen, Martha, and Karen Phillipps. *A Popular Guide to Chinese Vegetables*. New York: Crown, 1983.
   Watercolor drawings of Oriental vegetables for identification.

Dille, Carolyn, and Susan Belsinger. *New Southwestern Cooking*. New York: Macmillan, 1986.
   An innovative and up-to-date book on Southwestern cooking.

Dragonwagon, Crescent. *The Bean Book*. New York: Workman, 1972.
   A small collection of recipes for dry beans.

Eckhardt, Linda West. *The Only Texas Cookbook*. New York: Bantam Books, 1986.
   A classic Texas cookbook.

Fisher, M. F. K., and the editors of Time-Life Books. *The Cooking of Provincial France*. New York: Time-Life Books, 1968.
   A classic text on French cooking, containing cultural background on the cuisine, as well as many basic recipes.

Greene, Bert. *Greene on Greens*. New York: Workman, 1984.
   Another one of those basic cookbooks that belong in the kitchen library.

Greer, Anne Lindsay. *Cuisine of the American Southwest*. New York: Harper & Row, 1983.
   A comprehensive collection of modern recipes using southwestern ingredients.

Guérard, Michel. *Michel Guérard's Cuisine Minceur: Original Low-Calorie Recipes*. New York: Wm. Morrow, 1976.
   Covers classic French cooking with alternative methods and ingredients for fewer calories.

Hahn, Emily, and the editors of Time-Life Books. *The Cooking of China*. New York: Time-Life Books, 1968.
   One of the Time-Life classic cookbooks.

Hanle, Zack. *Cooking with Flowers: Wherein an Age-old Art Is Revived*. Los Angeles: Price/Stern/Sloan, 1972.
   A small book with a nice collection of flower recipes.

Hawkes, Alex D. *A World of Vegetable Cookery*. Rev. ed. New York: Simon & Schuster, 1984.
  A very rich selection of 188 usual and unusual vegetables.

Hazelton, Nika. *Nika Hazelton's Way with Vegetables: The Unabridged Vegetable Cookbook*. New York: M. Evans, 1986.
  A wonderful collection of vegetable recipes. Covers a vast selection of unusual varieties.

Hazelton, Nika, and the editors of Time-Life Books. *The Cooking of Germany*. New York: Time-Life Books, 1969.
  A classic that gives not only recipes but also cultural background for German cooking.

Health and Travel International. *Spa Dining*. New York: St. Martin's Press, 1979.
  A rich and varied collection of low-calorie recipes.

Hewitt, Jean. *The New York Times New Natural Foods Cookbook*. Rev. ed. New York: Avon Books, 1986.
  A compilation of recipes calling for fresh, unrefined, and not highly processed foods.

Hom, Ken. *Ken Hom's Chinese Cookery*. New York: Harper & Row, 1986.
  A wonderful collection of basic Chinese recipes with clear instructions on how to prepare them.

Hom, Ken, and Harvey Steiman. *Chinese Technique: An Illustrated Guide to the Fundamental Techniques of Chinese Cooking*. New York: Simon & Schuster, 1981.
  A valuable photo how-to for most of the common Oriental cooking techniques.

Hsiung, Deh-ta. *Chinese Vegetarian Cooking*. Secaucus, N.J.: Chartwell, 1985.
  A good selection of basic cooking techniques and a large array of very fine recipes.

Hughes, Mike. *The Broken Arrow Ranch Cookbook*. Austin: University of Texas Press, 1985.
  Includes a number of basic chili recipes, particularly those made with wild game.

Jaffrey, Madhur. *A Taste of India*. New York: Atheneum, 1986.
  A book with both the cooking and cultural aspects of India.

Katzen, Mollie. *The Enchanted Broccoli Forest: And Other Timeless Delicacies*. Berkeley: Ten Speed Press, 1982.
  A collection of vegetarian recipes reflecting many different ethnic styles. A continuation of the classic *Moosewood Cookbook*.

Katzen, Mollie. *The Moosewood Cookbook*. Rev. ed. Berkeley: Ten Speed Press, 1977.
  A real classic. One of the first, and best, books on vegetarian cooking.

Kavasch, Barrie. *Native Harvests: Recipes and Botanicals of the American Indian*. New York: Random House, Vintage Books, 1979.
  Probably the most complete book on Native American cooking.

Kavena, Juanita Tiger. *Hopi Cookery*. Tucson: University of Arizona Press, 1980.
  A cookbook packed full of native recipes.

Kennedy, Diana. *The Cuisines of Mexico*. Rev. ed. New York: Harper & Row, 1986.
  The definitive cookbook on Mexican cooking.

Kennedy, Diana. *Mexican Regional Cooking*. New York: Harper & Row, 1984.
  Expands upon the basic information in Kennedy's *The Cuisines of Mexico*.

Lo, Kenneth. *The Complete Encyclopedia of Chinese Cooking*. New York: Crown, Crescent Books, 1979.
  A compendium of basic Oriental cooking.

McLaughlin, Michael. *The Manhattan Chili Company Southwest-American Cookbook: A Spicy Pot of Chilis, Fixin's, and Other Regional Favorites with 65 Recipes and Other Essentials*. New York: Crown, 1986.
  The best book available on how to make all different kinds of chili.

MacNicol, Mary. *Flower Cookery: The Art of Cooking with Flowers*. New York: Fleet Press, 1967.
  One of the most complete books on the subject of cooking with flowers.

Madison, Deborah, with Edward Espe Brown. *The Greens Cook Book: Extraordinary Vegetarian Cuisine from the Celebrated Restaurant*. New York: Bantam Books, 1987.
  A collection of sophisticated vegetarian recipes, sure to be a classic in its field.

Meyer-Berkhout, Eda. *German Cooking*. Tucson: HP Books, 1984.
  A vast selection of German recipes.

Moore, Isabel, and Jonnie Godfrey, eds. *Foods of the Orient: India*. London: Marshall Cavendish, 1978.
  A book with many traditional Indian recipes.

Morash, Marian. *The Victory Garden Cookbook*. New York: Knopf, 1982.
  A must if you have a garden. Tells in the greatest detail how to prepare vegetables and gives numerous recipes for all the basic ones.

Niethammer, Carolyn. *American Indian Food and Lore*. New York: Macmillan, Collier Books, 1974.
  A comprehensive study of Native American foods, including 150 recipes.

Nix, Janeth Johnson. *Adventures in Oriental Cooking*. San Francisco: Ortho Books, 1976.
A fine how-to book for beginners and experienced cooks using Oriental vegetables.

Ortho Books editorial staff. *Adventures in Mexican Cooking*. San Francisco: Ortho Books, 1978.
A comprehensive book on Mexican cooking helpful in explaining how ingredients from the garden are used.

Pappas, Lou Seibert, and Jane Horn. *The New Harvest: A Cook's Guide to Exotic Fruits and Unusual Vegetables*. San Francisco: 101 Productions, 1986.
How to select and cook with many unusual fruits and vegetables.

Pepin, Jacques. *La Technique*. New York: Pocket Books, 1978.
A valuable how-to text with detailed photo directions on how to make many classic French dishes.

Phillips, Roger. *Wild Food*. Boston: Little, Brown, 1986.
A beautifully illustrated cookbook on wild foods.

Prudhomme, Paul. *Chef Paul Prudhomme's Louisiana Kitchen*. New York: Wm. Morrow, 1984.
One of the most comprehensive and enjoyable books on the subject of Southern cooking.

Puck, Wolfgang. *Wolfgang Puck's Modern French Cooking*. Boston: Houghton Mifflin, 1986.
Includes a number of sophisticated French recipes.

Renggli, Seppi. *The Four Seasons Spa Cuisine*. New York: Simon & Schuster, 1986.
A wonderful adventure in delicious but healthful cooking.

Robertson, Laurel, Carol Flinders, and Bronwen Godfrey. *The Laurel's Kitchen Bread Book: A Guide to Whole-Grain Breadmaking*. New York: Random House, 1984.
An extensive book covering just about everything that can be made with whole wheat and other grains.

Robertson, Laurel, Carol Flinders, and Bronwen Godfrey. *The New Laurel's Kitchen*. 2d ed. Berkeley: Ten Speed Press, 1986.
Probably the best book available on cooking with healthful ingredients.

Rohde, Eleanour Sinclair. *Rose Recipes from Olden Times*. New York: Dover, 1973.
A little book packed full of recipes using roses.

Rombauer, Irma S., and Marion Rombauer Becker. *Joy of Cooking*. Rev. ed. Indianapolis: Bobbs-Merrill, 1975.
If you have only one cookbook in your kitchen, this has to be it. It covers just about every aspect of basic cooking you can imagine.

Rosso, Julee, and Sheila Lukins, with Sarah Leah Chase. *The Silver Palate Good Times Cookbook*. New York: Workman, 1985.
A further look at imaginative cooking and entertaining by the authors of *The Silver Palate Cookbook*.

Rosso, Julee, and Sheila Lukins, with Michael McLaughlin. *The Silver Palate Cookbook*. New York: Workman, 1982.
An upscale, imaginative cookbook using a great variety of ingredients.

Safdie, Edward J., and Judy Knipe. *Spa Food: Menus and Recipes from the Sonoma Mission Inn*. New York: Clarkson N. Potter, 1985.
A beautiful book filled with imaginative, healthful recipes.

Scaravelli, Paola, and Jon Cohen. *Cooking from an Italian Garden: Classic Meatless Recipes from Antipasti to Dessert*. New York: Holt, Rinehart & Winston, 1984.
The best book on how to cook Italian vegetables. A must for your cookbook library.

Schmaeling, Tony. *German Traditional Cooking*. Secaucus, N.J.: Chartwell, 1984.
One of the most authentic German cookbooks available in English.

Shepherd, Renee. *Recipes from a Kitchen Garden*. Felton, Calif.: Shepherd's Garden Publishing, 1987.
A lovely little book filled with recipes created directly from the garden.

Shere, Lindsey R. *Chez Panisse Desserts*. New York: Random House, 1985.
A wonderful dessert cookbook with a large selection of recipes using the garden harvest.

Sloan, Sarah. *A Treasury of Mexican Cuisine: Original Recipes from the Chefs of the Camino Real Hotels, Mexico*. Chicago: Contemporary Books, 1986.
An elegant collection of Mexican recipes.

Smith, Jeff. *The Frugal Gourmet*. New York: Wm. Morrow, 1984.
A rich assortment of recipes from international cuisines using basic ingredients familiar to most cooks.

Smith, Leona Woodring. *The Forgotten Art of Flower Cookery*. Gretna, La.: Pelican, 1985.
A compact book filled with interesting flower recipes.

Sunset Books and *Sunset* magazine editors. *The Best of Sunset*. Menlo Park, Calif.: Lane Publishing, 1987.
A fabulous collection of imaginative and fun recipes.

Szekely, Deborah, and Chef Michael Stroot. *Golden Door Cookbook: The Greening of American Cuisine*. Escondido, Calif.: Golden Door, 1982.
A basic cookbook for those interested in cutting calories and adding healthful foods to their diet.

Thompson, Terry. *Cajun-Creole Cooking*. Tucson: HP Books, 1986.

A colorful book on Creole and Cajun cooking, with many wonderful recipes.

Tropp, Barbara. *The Modern Art of Chinese Cooking*. New York: Wm. Morrow, 1982.

A compendium of Chinese food information. A real help to American cooks.

Turvey, Valerie. *Bean Feast*. San Francisco: 101 Productions, 1979.

A compendium of international bean recipes. Contains a few baked bean recipes plus lots of other great recipes for dry beans.

Waters, Alice. *The Chez Panisse Menu Cookbook*. New York: Random House, 1982.

A fine cookbook that has had great influence on modern cooking.

Waters, Alice, and Patricia Curtan, Martine Labro. *Chez Panisse Pasta, Pizza, and Calzone*. New York: Random House, 1984.

A great collection of imaginative Italian specialties.

Willan, Anne. *Basic French Cookery*. Tucson: HP Books, 1980.

A good how-to book for basic French cooking.

Withee, John E. *Growing and Cooking Beans*. Dublin, N.H.: Yankee, 1980.

The definitive book on growing and cooking beans. Covers dry beans and how to bake them in great detail.

PHOTO CREDITS

INDEX